The Gospel Train.

The gos-pel train is coming, I hear it just at hand,

I hear the car-wheels moving, And rumbling thro' the land.

Chorus

Get on board, children, Get on board, children. Get on

board, children, For there's room for many a more. more.

I hear the bell and whistle,
  The coming round the curve;
She's playing all her steam and power,
  And straining every nerve.
    Get on board, children, &c.

No signal from another train
  To follow on the line,
O, sinner, you're for ever lost,
  If once you're left behind.
    Get on board, children, &c.

She's nearing now the station,
  O, sinner, don't be vain,
But come and get your ticket,
  And be ready for the train.
    Get on board, children, &c.

The fare is cheap and all can go,
  The rich and poor are there,
No second-class on board the train,
  No difference in the fare.
    Get on board, children, &c.

This is the Christian banner,
  The motto's new and old,
Salvation and Repentance
  Are burnished there in gold.
    Get on board, children, &c.

DARK
MIDNIGHT
WHEN I RISE

BOOKS BY ANDREW WARD

Fits & Starts: The Premature Memoirs of Andrew Ward

The Blood Seed: A Novel of India

A Cry of Absence

Out Here: A Newcomer's Notes from the Great Northwest

Our Bones Are Scattered:
The Cawnpore Massacres in the Indian Mutiny of 1857

DARK
MIDNIGHT
WHEN I RISE

THE STORY OF THE JUBILEE SINGERS
WHO INTRODUCED THE WORLD TO
THE MUSIC OF BLACK AMERICA

ANDREW WARD

FARRAR, STRAUS AND GIROUX

NEW YORK

Farrar, Straus and Giroux
19 Union Square West, New York 10003

Library of Congress Cataloging-in-Publication Data
Ward, Andrew, 1946–
    Dark midnight when I rise : the story of the Jubilee Singers, who introduced the world
to the music of Black America / by Andrew Ward.—1st ed.
        p.   cm.
Includes bibliographical references and index.
ISBN 0-374-18771-1 (alk. paper)
1. Jubilee Singers. 2. Afro-American musicians—Biography. I. Title.

ML421.J77 W37 2000
782.42162′96073′00922—dc21
[B]

99-086036

Grateful acknowledgment is made to the following sources for permission to reprint images from
their collections: photograph of John King by courtesy of the Trustees of the Boston Public Library;
photographs of the elder Thomas Rutling and Susan Gilbert White and woodcut of Dwight Lyman
Moody by courtesy of the author; painting of Queen Victoria and the Jubilees by courtesy of the Fisk
University Galleries, Nashville, Tennessee. All remaining images by courtesy of Fisk University Library's Special Collections.

This Book Is Dedicated to the Memory

of

Charles H. Williams

1846–1933

Master Tinsmith

Teacher

African Methodist Episcopal Minister

and

Member of the Fisk School's First Singing Troupe

Whose Path Led Me to the Story

of the

Jubilee Singers

CONTENTS

PART TWO

For ye shall go out with joy, and be led forth with peace; the mountains and the hills shall break forth before you into singing, and all the trees of the field shall clap their hands.

Isaiah 55:12

PREFACE

In October 1871, a troupe of young former slaves and freedmen set out from Nashville, Tennessee, under the direction of a white Northern missionary named George Leonard White. Their purpose was to raise enough money to rescue their school, Fisk University, from bankruptcy. For months, they journeyed through Ohio and Pennsylvania and into New York, singing the secret soul music of their ancestors. Expelled from hotels, their clothes running to rags, they struggled in obscurity, performing at small-town churches, halls, street corners, and train stations. But as word of their extraordinary artistry spread, they began one of the most remarkable trajectories in American history: from whipping post and auction block to concert hall and throne room.

For most white Americans, the music of the Jubilee Singers was their first lesson in African American culture, the promise of emancipation, and the meaning of the Civil War. The Jubilees introduced vast white audiences to slave hymns: the first authentic African American music most whites had ever heard. In a tradition that continues to this day, they established the spiritual as a permanent part of the universal liturgy, a staple of religious expression. In their wake has rolled wave after wave of African American song.

Over the years, however, many came to regard the Jubilee Singers as accommodationists: the meek and pious agents of Northern white mission-aries. But what astonished me as I read through their letters and diaries and clippings were their militancy and fierce autonomy. After writing this book, I have come to believe that they deserve to be included with Dou-glass and Du Bois and Martin Luther King, Jr., in the pantheon of great African American champions of civil rights; that the impression they made, their uncompromising artistry and faith, the dignity and outspoken courage they showed as representatives of American freedmen were like a constella-tion in the dark midnight from which they rose.

Many would dismiss spirituals as mere white crowd pleasers, anthems of helplessness and resignation, vestiges of bondage whose authenticity was muddled by the intercessions of white arrangers and composers. But writ-ing this book forced me to listen to them in the context of their times. "Gospel Train," for instance, which I remember innocuously singing as a schoolboy, took on a new meaning when I discovered that at the dismal dawn of Jim Crow's reign—when "uppity" blacks were being lynched and their schools and churches burned to the ground—the Jubilees rose up be-fore the first integrated audience ever to share Louisville, Kentucky's Li-brary Hall (they refused to sing for segregated audiences) and protested the segregation of Southern railway lines. By the time they were done singing "No second-class on board the train, / No difference in the fare," the city's blacks and whites, unionists and secessionists alike, had risen to their feet and cheered, creating such a furor that George Pullman himself rolled in one of his parlor cars to carry the Jubilees to Nashville, announcing that from that day forward his trains would be integrated.

By then, the Jubilee Singers had attained almost unprecedented fame throughout America, Britain, and Europe, performing in churches and cathe-drals and palaces for such luminaries as Ulysses S. Grant, Queen Victo-ria, William Gladstone, and the emperor of Germany. But fame did not make them cautious. In fact, it emboldened them. With increasing vehe-mence and eloquence, they denounced racism wherever they encountered it.

Though I have studied American folk songs and sung in choruses and choirs that dipped their pallid toes into the Jubilee Singers' repertoire, I am not a musician nor a musicologist. My interest is in the story of the Jubilee Singers' remarkable trajectory from slavery to celebrity, from entertainers to champions of the rights of their people, and the effect they and their music had on a world that had yet to acknowledge even the existence of African American culture.

I do not share the religious faith that motivated and sustained so many of the characters in this book. Nothing has made me consider that faith with greater awe and admiration—even envy—than the Jubilees and their music. But descending in more ways than one from ministers and missionaries, I may betray in these pages an unseemly fascination with the foibles of the virtuous men and women who went south after the Civil War. After all, they did a great deal more good than I will ever do, and at a far greater cost than most people are prepared to pay. I hope that in this story the courage, decency, and extraordinary sacrifices of men like George Leonard White, Adam Knight Spence, and Erastus Milo Cravath will win out over their occasional sins of pride, pettiness, and paternalism, for they helped accomplish a great thing against terrible odds.

On the other hand, it does not profit a historian to be pious about anyone, least of all people who were often so pious about themselves. With the possible exception of Ella Sheppard, there are no saints in this story but something infinitely more interesting: human beings. The task I set myself was to try to understand the Jubilee Singers and their managers not as archetypes but as people, to observe them as they converged from such disparate worlds on a mission that changed the hearts of their countrymen.

This is a book of voices. As much as possible, I have tried to let the characters tell this story in their own words, especially the Jubilees themselves. Fortunately, they left a rich record, and against my ignorant expectation that newly emancipated young men and women must have been at best semiliterate, I quickly discovered that they had acquired an impressive degree—in some cases, the highest degree—of literacy in a matter of only a few years. A reader who might share my initial misapprehension may suspect that I have cleaned up and corrected the hundreds of quotations from the singers' diaries, interviews, speeches, and letters. For clarity's sake, I have indeed replaced the feverish dashes of their mentor, George White. But, except for the occasional addition of a comma or insertion in brackets of a missing word, I have tried not to change a single word of the sharp-eyed observations of Ella Sheppard, America W. Robinson, Maggie Porter, Mabel Lewis, Georgia Gordon, Frederick J. Loudin, and Benjamin M. Holmes—all of whom provide a century-old vision of literally the entire globe that is at once unique and transformative.

Andrew Ward
Seattle, Washington

THE FISK JUBILEE SINGERS

Parentheses indicate performers who participated only a few months in a particular tour.

First Tour October 1871 to March 1872	Second Tour May 1872 to May 1874	Third Tour January 1875 to July 1878	Voice and/or Instrument
—	—	Hinton Alexander	tenor
(Phebe Anderson)	—	—	contralto
—	—	(Minnie Butler)	unknown
—	—	Maggie Carnes	soprano
Isaac Dickerson	Isaac Dickerson	—	bass
Greene Evans	(Greene Evans)	—	bass
—	Georgia Gordon	Georgia Gordon	soprano
—	—	(Ella Hildridge)	soprano
Benjamin Holmes	Benjamin Holmes	—	tenor
Jennie Jackson	Jennie Jackson	Jennie Jackson	soprano
—	Julia Jackson	Julia Jackson	contralto
—	Mabel Lewis	Mabel Lewis	contralto
—	—	Frederick Loudin	bass
—	—	(Patti Malone)	mezzo-soprano
—	(Josephine Moore)	—	piano
—	(Henry Morgan)	—	tenor
—	—	(Gabriel Ousley)	bass
Maggie Porter	Maggie Porter	Maggie Porter	soprano
—	—	America Robinson	contralto
Thomas Rutling	Thomas Rutling	Thomas Rutling	tenor
Ella Sheppard	Ella Sheppard	Ella Sheppard	soprano, piano, organ, and guitar
Minnie Tate	Minnie Tate	—	contralto
—	—	Benjamin W. Thomas	bass
—	—	(Lucinda Vance)	contralto
Eliza Walker	—	—	contralto
—	Edmund Watkins	Edmund Watkins	bass
(George Wells)	—	—	performer

PART ONE

GOD'S OWN TIME

ELLA SHEPPARD

1851–1865

In the late 1860s, students excavating the grounds of a Nashville freedmen's school called Fisk University made a gruesome discovery. Digging just beneath the surface of the earth, they came upon heaps of chains and manacles from Porter's Slave Yard, where, up to the time of Yankee occupation, enslaved men, women, and children had been bought and sold. They did not let these rusted relics of their bondage lie buried. They gathered them together instead and sold them for scrap iron and, with the proceeds, bought Bibles and spellers, turning the instruments of their enslavement into the agencies of their liberation.

The Jubilee Singers would use the same alchemy to champion the freedmen and rescue their school from oblivion. Impoverished, bedraggled, half starved, they took the secret, sacred hymns of their bondage and not only "sang up the walls of a great university" but taught the nation and the world an enduring lesson about the dignity and educability of black Americans.

The matriarch of the Jubilees was a frail, tenacious former slave named Samuella Sheppard. She was quintessentially American: her ancestors were Indian, African, and white. Her maternal great-grandmother, Rosa, was the free, full-blooded daughter of a Cherokee chief. But in order to remain with her enslaved African husband, himself the son of a chief, she lived as a slave of the Donelsons, one of the founding families of Nashville and the in-laws of General Andrew Jackson.[1] Whenever the Donelsons gave her trou-ble, Rosa would return to her tribe, threatening vengeance on anyone who might try to mistreat her enslaved children in her absence. Rosa had four-teen children and lived to the age of 109. Among her daughters was Ella Sheppard's grandmother, Rebecca, who married a fellow Donelson slave and gave birth to twelve children, including Ella's mother, Sarah Hannah Sheppard.[2]

Ella Sheppard's paternal grandfather was James Glover Sheppard, a white planter who had moved from North Carolina to Hernando, Missis-sippi, in the early 1800s. Glover Sheppard sired at least one black child by his female slaves: a bright, enterprising boy named Simon. When Glover's white son, Benjamin Harper Sheppard, married Andrew Jackson's grand-niece, Phereby Donelson, the slaves of both families were combined into one household and lived on Phereby's father's Nashville estate about a mile from the Cumberland River.

Sarah was a slave playmate of Phereby's children and grew into a volu-ble but pious and capable domestic servant. Though marriages between slaves were not legally binding, in about 1844, seventeen-year-old Sarah was wedded to Harper Sheppard's slave half brother, Simon, who worked for the family as a coachman. Having risen to the position of the white Sheppards' head nurse and housekeeper, Sarah gave birth, in February 1851, to a frail, skinny baby daughter she named Samuella, or Ella for short.[3]

When Ella Sheppard was about three years old, Sarah discovered that her mistress had trained the child to spy on her. This was common enough in slaveholders' households. With buttered biscuits and sweet cakes, own-ers bribed black children to inform on parents suspected of shirking, sabo-tage, plotting escapes or insurrections; there are even stories of owners posting parrots in their fields and cookhouses to act—or so they told their slaves—as spies.[4]

"I had made my first report, which the mistress had magnified, and threatened mother," Ella recalled.

> Stung by this revelation and realizing that it would lead eventually to the alienation of our affection and teach me to lie and deceive, in agony of soul and despair she caught me up in her arms, and while

rushing to the river to end it all, was overtaken by Mammy Viney, who cried out, "Don't you do it, Honey. Don't you take that that you cannot give back." She raised her eyes to Heaven and said, "Look, Honey, don't you see the clouds of the Lord as they pass by? The Lord has got need of this child."

In another version, the old slave's name was Aunt Cherry, and her prophecy was even more explicit: "God's got great work for this baby to do," she is supposed to have said. "She's going to stand before kings and queens."[5]

Whatever it was Sarah was told, she hugged "her helpless baby to her breast" and walked "back into slavery to await God's own time."

Major Harper allowed his half brother, Simon, to hire himself out. For several years, Simon worked as a liveryman at the Hermitage with an industrious freedman named William Napier, the father of James Carroll Napier, the "Frederick Douglass of the South," and with "Uncle Alfred" Jackson, Old Hickory's head coachman.[6] Simon eventually bought his own freedom for eighteen hundred dollars and began saving another thirteen hundred dollars toward purchasing Sarah's liberty as well.

In 1854, Harper Sheppard and his family moved out of their Nashville home and lingered briefly at the Hermitage in preparation for their move to a plantation in Okolona, Mississippi. Up to then, Phereby Sheppard seemed resigned to Simon's purchasing and manumitting her head housekeeper. But one night, Sarah overheard Phereby tearfully confess to her husband that she had simply pretended to agree to sell Sarah to Simon in order not to prolong Sarah's grief at their separation. The major implored her to let Simon buy her freedom, but Phereby was adamant.

"Sarah shall *never* belong to Simon," she declared. "She is *mine* and she shall *die* mine. Let Simon get another wife."

In her despair, Sarah again considered drowning herself and her daughter, but by the next morning she had decided to seek out her mistress instead. She told her that if Phereby allowed Simon to purchase Ella, Sarah would remain her faithful slave. But if she refused to let Ella go, she would kill herself and her daughter.

"My baby," she told her mistress simply, "will never be a slave."[7]

Phereby knew this was no idle threat. In a recent—but by no means unique—case in Nashville, a mother who had been sold and separated from her three small daughters had gathered them together, slit their throats, laid them out side by side, and killed herself.[8]

Phereby gave in. The next day, Simon was allowed to purchase his daughter for $350 and keep her with him in Nashville. Jimmie Sheppard, Sarah's father, promised his desolate daughter "that she would be free and that she would yet join her daughter, and spend her last days under her own vine and fig tree." But, as Major Sheppard's caravan rumbled southward, that day seemed far away.

Ella's father, Simon, eventually acquired a livery stable, four carriages, and eight horses and lived among the barbers, grocers, ministers, hack drivers, and tradesmen that constituted the upper echelon of Nashville's freedmen community. Recognizing that the Sheppards would never release Sarah to him, Simon borrowed enough money to purchase a new wife, Cornelia Rohelia, for thirteen hundred dollars, and to send little Ella to school.

Nashville's "educational facilities &c." were so impressive that the city dubbed itself the "Athens of the South." "We have one of the most flourishing Medical Colleges in the Union," raved a booster, "and another being established. Our Female Academy and female Schools are unsurpassed. Our high school is a fixed fact, and is doing as much good for Nashville as any one thing among the many good things we have here."[9] But black schools were not among them. Before the war, the city council tabled or voted down resolutions to permit schools for freedmen, and black schools had to operate in secret. But no matter how circuitous the route children took every morning, nor how staggered the nocturnal shifts in which they arrived and departed, it was impossible to run such a school undetected. A few slave owners allowed their slave children to attend, but not one white Nashvillian donated so much as a dime, nor did any intervene to protect teachers and students from attack.

Black schools were few in the North, scarcer still in the antebellum South. The first recorded African American school in Nashville had been opened in 1833 by a black barber named Alonso M. Sumner. But within two months, Sumner had been accused of forging passes and corresponding with fugitive slaves. Whipped almost to death by a white mob, he was "compelled to leave the state, never to return." In 1841, Sumner's assistant barber, a Disciples of Christ preacher named Daniel Wadkins, resolved to continue his exiled mentor's work. He hired a white teacher, who taught about thirty black pupils for a few months before moving on to less hazardous pastures. A year later, Wadkins himself defiantly and heroically stepped up to the chalkboard. Though forced to move from place to place to avoid detection, he somehow sustained his little academy for fourteen years, teaching both free and enslaved black children on the sly; it was in one of his schools that James Carroll Napier first learned his alphabet.[10]

At the time Ella Sheppard entered his school, Wadkins was an old man. "He was a typical 'John Bull' in appearance and an 'Uncle Sam' in vivacity," she remembered.

> He used the old Webster blue back spelling book. Each class stood up against the wall, head erect, hands down, toes straight. I recall only three classes: the Eb, Ib, Ob class; the Baker, Maker, Taker class; and the Republication, Replication class. They spelled in unison in a musical intonation, swaying their bodies from side to side, with perfect rhythmical precision on each syllable, which we thought grand. Mr. [Wadkins] gave out each word with such an explosive jerk of the head and spring around the body, that it commanded our profound respect. His eyes seemed to see every one in the room, and woe be to the one who giggled or was inattentive, whether pupil or visitor, for such a one constantly felt a whack from his long rattan. We little visitors soon learned to spell many of the words of each class and sang them at our homes.[11]

In the middle of the John Brown insurrection scare of 1859, a gang of whites warned Wadkins that if he did not close his school he had better "watch out for the consequences." Before he found out what they might be, the city council officially closed him down and a year later also shut down William Napier's humble academy for free black children.[12] When Wadkins reopened his school, the police abruptly shut him down again, citing evidence that his students "contemplated a general insurrection." At the beginning of the Civil War, there were apparently no black schools operating in Nashville.[13]

Ella Sheppard would see her natural mother, Sarah, only once before the outbreak of the Civil War. When Sarah had reached Okolona, Mississippi, conditions among the plantation's slaves proved so hideous that the mere sight of the field hands and their families standing in rags along the route to the mansion house had reduced her and her mistress to tears and prayer.

For three years, they had labored to improve the condition of the major's field hands and convert them to Christianity. When Ella was about six years old, Major Harper Sheppard brought Sarah with him on a visit to Nashville and arranged for Sarah to see her daughter. "But when she came to leave me," Ella recalled, "she found it so hard, and screamed so loud, that they said she never should see me again."

Ella's stepmother, Cornelia, did everything for Ella "that [my] own mother could." But her status as the slave wife of a freedman was perilous. Though self-sustaining African Americans like Simon Sheppard were more secure in Tennessee than in Mississippi, some lived in a kind of twilight: neither slave nor free. The barber James Thomas, for instance, was a biracial slave but lived as a freedman, thanks to a benignly neglectful master and the protection of influential patrons like Andrew Jackson. But after his former master and half brother moved to Mississippi, Simon Sheppard enjoyed no such protection, and when, six months before the outbreak of the Civil War, he fell into debt, he suddenly found the freedom of his wife and daughter in jeopardy.[14] He had neglected to take out manumission papers on either of them, and though he was free, his wife and daughter could now be claimed by his creditors to settle his debts. Tipped off that they intended to do just that, a penniless Simon Sheppard fled with his family 270 miles north to Cincinnati, in the free state of Ohio.

> *You want to know where we is from?*
> *It sure will make you shiver.*
> *We's from that there old Ragtown*
> *On the old Cincinnati River.*

The sixth-largest city in the nation, Cincinnati was laid out on the Philadelphia model, amid hills overlooking a broad expanse of the Ohio River and the slave state of Kentucky beyond. During a visit in 1842, the usually disapproving Charles Dickens wrote that he had rarely "seen a place that commends itself so favorably and pleasantly to a stranger at the first glance as [Cincinnati] does; with its clean houses of red and white, its well paved roads, and footways of bright tile."[15]

For up to ten weeks of the year, the river was choked with ice, across which one of Cincinnati's most distinguished residents, Harriet Beecher Stowe, had imagined a runaway slave girl and her baby trying to flee to freedom. Cincinnati had inspired another mythologizer of the American

South, Stephen Foster. Arriving as a nineteen-year-old clerk in 1846, he was drawn to the riverfront, where he listened to the roustabouts singing. He soon began to compose "Ethiopian" songs for the minstrel troupes at Cincinnati's National and Melodeon Theaters and, strolling among the mansions of the city's gentry, wrote such popular ditties as "Open Thy Lattice, Love," and "Stay, Summer Breath."

In February 1861, newly elected president Abraham Lincoln paused here on his "long, ominous journey to Washington." Until then, Cincinnati had owed its prosperity to its trade with the South. The city packaged the South's hams, shipped its tobacco, milled its cotton. Though the Queen City was a notorious port of entry for fugitive slaves, its movers and shakers tried not to give off even a whiff of abolitionist sentiment to their Southern customers. They did not interfere when a pro-slavery mob destroyed an abolitionist press and chased its editor out of town, and the mayor forbade the police from interfering when Southern sympathizers drove the antislavery orator Wendell Phillips from the stage of the Pike Theater and threatened to lynch him.

In 1829, there had been more than two thousand blacks in Cincinnati. But the growth of their numbers had so alarmed local whites that they invoked Ohio's "black laws" and demanded that all black residents show security or get out of town. During a three-day riot, a mob burned down the printing press of the same Alonso Summer who had been chased out of Nashville for teaching school. More than a thousand African Americans left the city.

Local whites were divided, though by no means equally, among three groups: proponents of slavery, abolitionists, and advocates of colonization. Bridging the gap between the latter two was the nationally prominent theologian Lyman Beecher, who arrived in 1832 to run the fledgling Lane Theological Seminary. It was commonly said at the time that America had two great assets: the flag and the Beecher family. So driven that he used to shovel heaps of sand from one corner of his basement to the other just for the exercise, Lyman Beecher raised seven sons into manhood, every one of whom became a minister, including the leading American divine of his day, and one of the most ardent champions of the Jubilee Singers, Henry Ward Beecher. Lyman's daughters were no less impressive: some would credit— or blame—Harriet's *Uncle Tom's Cabin* for precipitating the Civil War; Catherine became a champion of women's education and, with Harriet, a founder of the field of home economics.

Lyman Beecher tried to reconcile Cincinnati's abolitionists with the colonizationists. But his students would have none of it. In 1834, they renounced all schemes to return blacks to Africa and, declaring themselves staunch abolitionists, set out to evangelize among the impoverished African American residents of Ragtown. When Lane's tremulous trustees ordered the students to cease their agitation, a brilliant senior named Theodore Weld persuaded fifty-three students to leave Lane and eventually proceed—most of them—to abolitionist Oberlin College, which would become the principal training ground for Fisk University's missionary faculty.

As Cincinnati became a major stopover on the Underground Railway, members of the Beecher family had helped hide runaway slaves. In fact, Harriet would base some of her characters on the fugitive slaves she and her husband sheltered in their Cincinnati home. When a pro-slavery mob menaced the black community, Henry Ward Beecher strapped on a pistol and rose to its defense. Catherine Beecher worked to provide schools for African American children. But from the wreckage of his seminary, Lyman Beecher denounced the excesses of the proponents of slavery and abolition alike, whose "infatuation," he had concluded, must have been "permitted by Heaven for purposes of national retribution."[16]

Despite the city fathers' staunch pro-slavery line, when the Confederates bombarded Fort Sumter on April 12, 1861, Cincinnati turned against its Southern customers. Within a week, in every public park, regiments of Irish and German recruits stumbled through the Union army's drills and exercises. Some ten thousand Cincinnatians volunteered for Union regiments and Home Guard companies, one of them named Storer's Rifles after a bombastic local judge and consisting of "old, mostly wealthy, gray-headed men, some of them very obese, with aldermanic protuberances."

Of all the Union's major cities, prosperous, bustling Cincinnati was the most vulnerable to Southern attack. After Confederates chased a large Union force out of Richmond, Kentucky, in August 1862, the vaunting rebel general Kirby Smith advanced on Cincinnati. On September 4, Union general Lew Wallace, the future author of *Ben Hur*, rushed to the city's rescue, suspending all commerce, declaring martial law, and fortifying the city's defenses with every resource at his disposal.

Until General Wallace's arrival, Cincinnati's pro-slavery mayor had ignored the pleas of the city's black men to serve the Union cause. But now Irish police rounded them up from Ragtown and the waterfront and drove them into guarded pens to create a captive pool of laborers for the city's barricades. "Often bare-headed and in shirtsleeves," they were marched out to the southern approaches to the city, where they eventually dug three miles of entrenchments.

Ella's father, Simon, could not have escaped the labor dragnet. A white observer described the workers on their daily marches to the city's outskirts:

> Starting back on the honest, substantial, coal-black foundation, all shades of color were exhibited, degenerating out through successive gradations to an ashy white, the index of Anglo-Saxon fatherhood of the chivalrous American type. Arrayed for dirt-work in their oldest clothes, apparently the fags of every conceivable kind of cast-off, kicked-about, and faded-out garments; crownless and lop-eared hats, diverse boots; with shouldered pick, shovel, and hoe; this merry, chattering, piebald, grotesque body, shuffled along amid grins and jeers.

Despite the grins and jeers, they saved Cincinnati. Peering at her defenses through his telescope, Kirby Smith wisely abandoned his designs on the Queen City and in the midst of a thunderstorm beat a "ruinous" retreat. "When the history of Cincinnati during the past two weeks comes to be written," said Wallace in his farewell address, "it will be said that it was the spades and not the guns that saved the city."[17]

Without the protection of his white Sheppard patrons, Ella Sheppard's bankrupt father did not prosper in Cincinnati. "We had literally nothing to start with," Ella recalled, "but collected household furniture piece by piece." Her stepmother took in washing and ironing and eventually opened a small boardinghouse.

Up to the age of twelve, Sheppard attended the Seventh Street school, a holdover from the days of the Lane Theological Seminary disruption, where she proved bright and almost agonizingly conscientious. But Ella was a tense rail of a girl and so frail that she had to drop out for long periods. Amid the damps and drafts and stinking open drains of Ragtown, she was prone to respiratory and ear infections that rendered her a semi-invalid for two entire years of her early adolescence.

She had large gray eyes and a thin upper lip and usually wore her hair in a small, tight bun that accentuated the elongated oval of her face. In her heyday as a Jubilee Singer, portraitists had a difficult time capturing her. When a German artist found her face and mouth particularly "difficult to get," her mentor, George White, joked that it was "because there is no expression to catch."[18] But there was an innate dignity about her, a gravitas in her slender frame, that made her stand out among the free blacks of Cincinnati.

She possessed a true if not robust soprano voice and an aptitude for music that induced a local German lady to tutor her. Despite her ill health, Ella continued her lessons for a year and a half and, with her long, slender fingers and delicate sensibility, developed into an accomplished pianist. Her father purchased an old piano for her on which she practiced constantly. But in 1865, when she was fourteen years old, the desperately pestilential conditions in Ragtown caught up with the Sheppards and brought Ella's childhood to an end.

FROM EVERY
GRAVEYARD

SLAVERY

1860–1865

As Simon Sheppard and his fellow freedmen dug Cincinnati's entrenchments, "thousands upon thousands" of white Ohioans and Hoosiers had
rushed to the city's defense. Known as the Squirrel Hunters, companies of
them arrived at Cincinnati's station "in all kinds of costumes, and armed
with all kinds of firearms, but chiefly the deadly rifle, which they knew so
well to use."

Among them was Ella Sheppard's future mentor and impresario, the pious, restless, and enterprising George Leonard White. With his long rifle,
black schoolmaster's clothes, and ever-present Bible, he must have seemed
an unlikely warrior among his buckskinned comrades. He was born in
1838 in the Cattaraugus County town of Franklinville, New York, about
forty miles south of Buffalo. He had attended school until the age of fourteen, then abandoned his consumptive father's blacksmithing trade and set
out for Ohio to become a schoolteacher. He stood almost six feet five
inches—a little taller than Lincoln—with thick, coarse hair, a full beard, a
broad, tempestuous brow, and commanding gray-blue eyes that could
pacify a tumultuous country schoolroom with a single glance.

On first meeting, White seemed blunt almost to the point of crudeness,
but his religious faith, combined with an innate empathy for the downtrod-

den, usually kept his delicate temperament under precarious control. He preferred to communicate with God without the intercessions of preachers, deacons, or anyone else. He spoke directly to his Maker, and as far as he was concerned, his Maker spoke directly back to him.

Though White lacked any formal musical training, he played the fiddle and had a passion for vocal music that, combined with an exquisite ear and a totalitarian temperament, made him a born choirmaster. Long before he would take the Jubilee Singers on the road, he was well known in southeastern Ohio for his ability to exact "from his scholars just the tones and harmonies that captivated the people."

White was an abolitionist by instinct and, despite threats from local whites, organized a black Sunday school "in the woods, using rails for seats." He saw the Union cause as a holy crusade against the wickedness of Southern slaveholding and may have volunteered to defend Cincinnati to prevent Confederate general Kirby Smith and his men from enslaving the freed black children White taught in the woods.

When he saw he would not be needed in Cincinnati, White immediately proceeded to Chillicothe, Ohio, and on September 29, 1862, enlisted in the Union army for three years, joining Company H of the Seventy-third Ohio Volunteer Infantry in Fairfax, Virginia. Within a month, he had been promoted to second sergeant. From January 19 to 24, his regiment took part in General Burnside's futile and career-destroying "mud march," trying and failing in the midst of severe winter storms to cross the Rappahannock. Though he recovered enough to continue serving, White blamed a lifetime of semi-invalidism on the slush and ruts and torrential streams of Virginia.

The Seventy-third Ohio was one of the hardest fighting regiments in the Civil War. By the time White joined up, it had already distinguished itself at Manassas. At Chancellorsville, White and his comrades turned the flank of Lee's Army of Virginia and, after finally fording the Rappahannock, were spared the carnage of the rout of the Union's Eleventh Corps. At Gettysburg, the regiment lost almost half its troops holding Cemetery Hill against rebel attack. In September, the Seventy-third accompanied its corps to Tennessee, where a few weeks after, in the midnight battle of Wauhatchie, it stormed a strong rebel position in a charge that General Grant deemed "one of the most daring feats of arms of the war."

During the Chattanooga campaign in the fall of 1863, White's Seventy-third took part in a grueling and courageous charge up the steep slopes and rocky precipices of Lookout Mountain, which wore White down to near immobility. As the sick and wounded were being carted back to Chattanooga, White tried to follow the overcrowded ambulances on foot for four miles but "broke down completely. . . . I was compelled to lie down by the road side, in front of Lookout Mountain," and "lay there several hours unable to go on. I was finally recognized by a driver in the wagon train from my company; he gave me water and stimulant, lifted me to his wagon seat and took me as near the Hospital as the train went."[1]

White remained in the hospital through May and June, hoping "to get well enough to rejoin my company, but symptoms of incipient consumption increased and were complicated by heart trouble." By this time, the army had recognized White's musical ability and made him first sergeant in the regimental band. But when his musical duties proved too taxing, he was assigned as a clerk to General "Fighting Joe" Hooker's headquarters in Chattanooga. Even this proved too much. By July, coughing and night sweats had reduced the weight of his six-foot-five-inch frame to a mere 140 pounds. His doctor assured him "that the only chance of saving my life was to send me home at once." White was at last discharged on July 6, 1864, and returned home to Ohio a skeletal vestige of the vigorous and conspicuous young schoolteacher who had punctuated the buckskinned ranks of Cincinnati's Squirrel Hunters less than two years before.[2] He would never entirely recover his health.

The war the slaves experienced was a grotesque escalation of the violence they had come to expect of white people. Slavery was predicated on violence and the threat of violence. Slaves had learned what whites were capable of doing to blacks, but even that paled next to what they now saw whites doing to each other.[3] "There was killing going on so terrible like people was dogs," recalled Cato Carter, "and some of the old ones said it was near to the end of time 'cause of folks being so wicked."[4]

Nothing could drive home the sheer horror of war like serving on a burial detail. "They make us pick up all the dead and burn them," recalled a slave named Jack Harrison. "Master, he examine white soldiers that was not dead. If he thought there wasn't a chance for him to get well, he take his knife and cut white soldier throat. But sometimes he would shoot him, so we could pile him on fire or dig great long ditch and pile them in it. That was terrible time," Harrison sadly recalled. "All that killing for nothing."[5] Standing amid the horrors of a Yankee hospital, William M. Thomas wondered why whites "couldn't settle their disputes without killing."[6]

Some slaves professed themselves ignorant of the causes of the conflagration—many of them called it "Abe Lincoln's War"—that was turning their world upside down.[7] "Somebody from across the water sent a shipload of money to us colored folks" was Anderson Brown's best guess, "and somebody stole it; and now they gwine fight it out."[8] Charles Davenport believed that "Lincoln was a fighting man, and he come down here and tried to run other folks' plantations. That made Marse Davis so all fired mad that he spit hard twixt his teeth and say, 'I'll whip the socks off them damn Yankees.'"[9] Hearing federal gunboats booming from the Rappahannock, one elderly Virginia slave who had lived through the War of 1812 exclaimed, "Well, I declare before God, there's the damn Britishers again."

Considering the measures masters took to keep their slaves ignorant of the war, however, what is more remarkable is the number of slaves—probably the vast majority—who knew exactly what the war was about. Slave owners had always been alarmed and astonished by the rapidity with which news traveled through the slave quarters, and this was even truer during the war. From snatches of overheard dinner-table conversation, from passersby on the roads and river paths, from the few literate slaves who managed to get a peek at letters and papers, slaves were sometimes the first to know when a battle was fought, a fort had fallen, or Yankee troops were approaching. Sometimes they communicated in code: when a Virginia slave told another he was "looking greasy," it meant he had war news to pass on, and slaves in at least one locality referred to Lincoln as "Old Ride-Up."

Most tried to disguise their knowledge. After the war, the white citizens of one Southern town passed a resolution thanking their former slaves for their fidelity. But they "needn't have," a former slave remarked dryly, "for every now and then we were falling behind a stump or into a corner of the fence and praying for the Union soldiers." It was hard, however, to hide which side most of them were rooting for. An editor in Chattanooga, Tennessee, noticed how slaves' spirits fell and rose "with the ebb and flow of this tide of blue devils, and when they are glad as larks, the whites are depressed and go about the streets like mourners."

In some prayer meetings, blacks obliquely hinted at the hopelessness of the Southern cause. "Lord," an elderly slave prayed before a wartime congregation of whites and blacks, "be pleased to blow with Thy breath and sink the ships of the wicked enemy. Our boys, good Master, will drive them from the land, but Thou alone can reach the gunboats." When a black preacher was asked by a fellow slave after a service why he had noisily prayed for the rebels, he replied, "Don't worry, children; the Lord knew what I was talking about." In the fervor of her slaves' worship, an Alabama mistress saw "the mantle of our lost cause descending."[10] A semiliterate slave preacher in Wilson County, Tennessee, led his fellow bondsmen in prayers whenever he heard of a Yankee defeat. "By and by the rebels kept getting beaten, and then it was sing, sing, all through the slave quarters. Old missus asked what they were singing for, but they would only say, because we feel so happy."[11]

Sometimes they could not contain themselves. During the battle of Manassas, an old slave woman greeted every roar of Yankee cannon with "Ride on, Master Jesus."[12] The black cowboy Nat Love, who grew up outside Nashville, recalled that he and his fellow slave children always played at Civil War, but since none of them was willing to play a Yankee, they all pretended to be Union men and made war on nests of yellow jackets and bumblebees.[13] As his master's son rode off in his new uniform to fight for the Confederacy, a slave named Leonard exclaimed within his master's hearing, "Look at that God damn soldier. He fighting to keep us niggers from being free." His master leveled a gun at his breast and demanded that Leonard open his shirt. The slave "opened his shirt and stood there big as a black giant, sneering at Ole Marse." Despite his wife's pleas, his master shot him, and Leonard died where he lay with "that sneer on his black mouth."[14]

Slaves relayed information to Union soldiers and helped Yankee prisoners escape north. But short of running off to the federal lines, slaves were too pragmatic to risk rising up against their owners, especially when they knew the Union would eventually prevail and abolish slavery. "Deliverance from slavery was not a surprise to them," observed a Yankee soldier, "they had been hoping and praying for it for years with perfect faith that their prayers would be answered. It seemed that they had always expected it to come from some outside source, and had never entertained a thought of taking a part themselves in their deliverance."[15]

He was forgetting the tens of thousands of slaves who escaped their masters to fight in the Union army. In September 1861, for instance, a former slave of Colonel William O. Brown's apparently was "tickled to death" to shoot his former master in the Battle of Boonville.[16] And thousands of others worked against their masters' cause in other ways. But many did believe that if whites wanted to kill themselves over slavery that was their business; God would free them in His own good time.

In the short run, the prospect of emancipation put some slaves in greater peril than before because masters infuriated by Confederate defeats were likelier to injure or even kill their slaves if they knew they were about to lose them anyway. When one slave owner received news that one of his sons had been killed in the war, he

> jumps up and starts cussing the war and him picks up the hot poker and say, "Free the nigger, will they? I free the nigger." He hit my mammy on the neck, and she starts moaning and crying and drops to the floor. . . . Him takes the gun off the rack and starts for the field, where the niggers am working. My sister and I sees that, and we starts running and screaming 'cause we has brothers and sisters in the field. But the good Lord took a hand in that mess, and the master ain't gone far in the field when him drops all of a sudden.

He died the next day.[17] Katie Rowe of Arkansas recalled how her master, a remote man who left his slaves entirely in the care of his overseer, galloped up to them in the fields one day and gave a speech:

> You niggers been seeing the Confederate soldiers coming by here looking pretty raggedy and hurt and wore out, but that no sign they licked! Them Yankees ain't gwine get this far, but if they do, you all ain't gwine to get free by them, because I gwine free you before that. When they get here they gwine find you already free, because I gwine line you up on the bank of the Bois d'Arc Creek and free you with my shotgun![18]

"Of late the accusations of masters shooting their slaves are more frequent," wrote an abolitionist paper, "indicating . . . that the desperation of the rebels increases."[19] During the war, a Nashville slave remembered, "they used to stand slaves backwards to the river and shoot them off into the river."[20]

Slaves who might previously have been whipped for running away were now more likely to be treated as outright traitors and insurrectionists. Two Memphis slaves who attempted to run to the Union lines were hanged and their fellow slaves forced "to go and see them where they hung," recalled

Louis Hughes. "The bodies hung at the roadside, where the execution took place, until the blue flies literally swarmed around them, and the stench was fearful."[21] Archy Vaughn of Memphis was captured trying to flee to Union lines and returned to his master, who "took me down to the woods, and tied my hands, and pulled them over my knees and put a stick through under my knees, and then took his knife and castrated me and then cut off the lop of my left ear."[22]

Some rebel units were notorious for shooting the slaves they came upon on their marches. Sarah Debro told a North Carolinian interviewer:

> I remember when ["Fightin' Joe"] Wheeler's Cavalry come through. They was 'federates, but they was mean as the Yankees. They stole everything they could find and killed a pile of niggers. They come around checking. They ask the niggers if they wanted to be free. If they say yes, then they shot them down, but if they say no, they let them alone. They took three of my uncles out in the woods and shot they faces off.[23]

Sometimes soldiers kidnapped stray slaves and sold them elsewhere.[24] Working together, the city police of Nashville and the sheriff of Davidson County made a lot of money recapturing slaves and transporting them to the markets of the Deep South.[25]

Some slaves grew insolent and indolent during the war. A Tennessee mistress reported that in January 1863 overseers were "doing very little good, and they complain of the negroes getting so free and idle," but she thought it was "because most everyone is afraid to correct them." "The negroes care no more for me," wrote one Texas mistress during the Civil War, "than if I was an old free darkey and I get so mad sometimes that I think I don't care sometimes if Myers [her brutal and troublesome overseer] beats the last one to death. I can't stay with them another year alone."[26] After the Yankees occupied Williamson County, south of Nashville, an old slaveholder attempted to whip an adolescent for laxity. The boy shoved his owner to the ground, picked up an ax, and walked away.[27] While serving as a Yankee soldier, another Williamson County slave marched past his former owner's home and encountered his mistress. "She came to me and said, 'Don't you remember how I nursed you when you were sick? And now you are fighting against me!' I said, 'No, ma'am, I am not fighting against you. I am fighting for my freedom.'"[28]

Despite the depredations of Union foragers, the proximity of Yankee troops proved a blessing to some slaves. Harriet Robinson's mistress used to beat her slaves during the war. "[Your] master's out fighting and losing blood trying to save you from them Yankees," she used to tell them, "so you can get your'n here." Once she ordered her brother to beat Harriet, but when her husband got home, he exploded. "You infernal sons o' bitches," he said, "don't you know there is three hundred Yankees camped out here and iffen they knowed you whipped this nigger the way you done done, they'd all kill us? Iffen they find out, I'll kill all of you."[29] The morning the Yankees came to Nashville, a master hit his slave. "He didn't know the Yankees were in town," recalled a former slave, and when he found out, "he come back beggin' me to stay with him, and said he was sorry."[30]

Some slaves stuck by their masters and their families. One saved his master's silver by hiding it in his boots, pretending to greet the Yankees, and ingratiating himself with them by slapping one of his master's children; after the soldiers left, he "cried like a child."[31] Southerners consoled themselves with tales of trusted slaves who diverted Yankee patrols, hid valuables, saved livestock, protected women and children.

"There are, at the present time, thousands of plantations where the only whites are women and children," wrote a visiting Irish journalist named Ross Fitzgerald, "and if the negroes were as wicked as many good people wish they were, nothing could prevent them from murdering their mistresses and the children, and escaping in bodies wherever and whenever they choose. But not a single instance of this kind has ever occurred."[32]

An eager apologist for the Southern cause, Fitzgerald was mistaken. In October 1862, the slaves on one Louisiana plantation drove off the overseer and "destroyed everything they could get hold of. Pictures, Portraits and Furniture were all smashed up with Crockery and everything else in the house. Other slaves erected a gallows in order to hang their master and marched around with drums and flags, shouting, 'Abe Lincoln and Freedom.' "[33] Such uprisings were as dangerous as they were isolated. In Amite County, Mississippi, in September 1864, a band of slaves armed themselves with their masters' guns and rode off toward the river cheering and shouting until overtaken by Confederate scouts, who killed most of them.[34]

Slaves who remained with their masters began to see them in a whole new light. Some slaveholders rode off to war like the chivalrous gentlemen they made themselves out to be, but slaves were quick to recognize they were fighting for a lost cause. One master bragged that he was going to "eat breakfast at home, go and whup the North, and be back for dinner. He went away, and it was four long years before he come back to dinner. The table was sure set a long time for him."[35]

Other masters behaved less nobly.

Old Major had both a Rebel and a Union suit, and he wore whichever seemed to be most fitting at the time. Sometimes a spy would come along in advance of an army and I'd call to Old Major, who was sitting on the porch, "Major, here comes a spy." And Old Major, he'd start up from his chair and bawl, "Who-o-w-a-at?" If I said, "It's Johnny," and he was in a Rebel suit, he's throw out his chest and prepare to greet them. But if I said, "Union," he'd sneak to his room, change into the blue uniform with its red-lined cape, and come back out on the porch. As he sat down, he'd throw back the corner of his blue cape to show its red lining.[36]

Some slaves were ashamed of their masters' cowardice. Lee Guidon of South Carolina recalled how his master's son used to "lay out in the woods" to avoid Confederate recruiters. "He say no need in him getting shot up and killed. He say let the slaves be free. Mr. Jim say all they fighting about was jealousy." The son of a slave owner named Hawkens returned on furlough from service in the Confederate army and spent the rest of the war living in a cavern like a runaway slave.

Slaves sometimes saved their masters from humiliation, or even death, at Yankee hands. A group of Union soldiers arrived at John Williams's plantation in Louisiana and

just laughed and talked with him, but he didn't take the jokes any too good. Then they asked him could he dance and he said, "No," and they told him to dance or make us dance. There he stood inside a big ring of them mens in blue clothes, with they brass buttons shining in the light . . . and he just stood and said nothing, and it look like he wasn't wanting to tell us to dance. So some of us young bucks just step up and say we was good dancers, and we start shuffling while the rest of the niggers [stood] pat.

As Union troops approached his gate, an elderly Texas slave owner ran for his gun. "When he come hustling down off the gallery," recalled Liza Jones, "my daddy come running. He seed old Massa too mad to know what he do-ing, so quicker than a chicken could fly he grab that gun and wrastle it out of old Massa's hands. Then he push old Massa in the smokehouse and lock the door. He ain't do that to be mean, but he want to keep old Massa out of trouble."[37]

Slaves did all this for masters who in many cases "had shown them no mercy and had given the Negroes good reasons for retaliating," the Nashville barber James Thomas would write many years later.

> It would be useless to say they knew no better. The Negroes knew as well what was going on as other people did. . . . At this late day he is spoken of by the coarse and profane class as the "dam Nigger," with no right to standing room on God's blessed foot stool. [But] while the Negroes' superiors were trying to break up the best government on earth, The Negro was caring for the defenseless.[38]

Even slaves who ran to the Yankees did not always entirely sever their ties with their masters. Some Tennessee slaves paid their owners whatever they earned from serving federal officers.[39] Others returned occasionally to visit their masters. Some owners, many of them convinced that their blameless slaves had been corrupted by Yankee propaganda, sent their runaways affectionate notes and gifts.[40]

The slaves who would later join the Jubilee Singers—Greene Evans, Ben-jamin Holmes, Isaac Dickerson, America Robinson, Thomas Rutling—ex-perienced the Civil War in sundry ways.

Born in 1848, Greene Evans was one of over fifty slaves of the richest man in Fayette County, Tennessee. From March 1862 almost to the end of the war, his master was in full flight from the Yankees and eventually be-came separated from his slaves. Lost in the countryside around Selma, Al-abama, Evans and his brother stumbled upon a battalion of Yankee soldiers whose commander hired Evans as his body servant and eventually em-ployed him at his hotel in Indianapolis.

A thin, enterprising man with a sharp, triangular nose and imploded cheekbones, Benjamin M. Holmes was born around 1846 in Charleston, South Carolina, and bound as an apprentice to a black tailor. As Yankee troops approached Charleston, his white owners sold him to a trader, who fed him on "cow's head, boiled grits, and rice." While imprisoned in a slave pen, Holmes somehow managed to get hold of a copy of Lincoln's Emancipation Proclamation and read it aloud. "Such rejoicing as there was then!" he recalled. "One old man held a prayer meeting right there in the mart."

Holmes was eventually bought by a man named Kaylor and taken to Chattanooga, where he was first hired out to a hotel and then employed by his owner as a clerk. In 1863, his owner and the rest of the staff were conscripted, and Holmes was left minding the store. In September, Rosecrans's Union forces were defeated at Chickamauga and retreated to Chattanooga, where Holmes volunteered his services as a valet to Jefferson Davis: not the president of the Confederacy but General Jefferson Columbus Davis, the thin-skinned Yankee commander of the Army of the Cumberland's First Division who started his war on the wrong foot by killing his commanding officer in a duel. Holmes remained with Davis until the end of the war, dusting the general's epaulets and bearing his tantrums from Atlanta to the Carolinas.[41]

Isaac Dickerson was born in Wytheville, Virginia, in 1852 and orphaned by the age of five. His earliest memory was his father's sale to a slave trader in Richmond, Virginia. Young Isaac was treated kindly by his master, J. F. Kent, who, at the beginning of the war, became a colonel of Confederate Home Guards. Kent never strayed very far from Wytheville, but, on his constricted rounds, Dickerson accompanied him as a camp servant. When Yankee troops captured Wytheville in December 1864, Colonel Kent escaped on horseback. But Dickerson was captured, marched seventy-five miles, and paroled. He promised to serve as valet to a Yankee officer, but when he saw his master's Home Guard straggle by, he ran after them and eventually rejoined Colonel Kent. Two weeks after the close of the war, Kent released him, and Dickerson eventually worked in Chattanooga for a Jewish shopkeeper, whose son taught him how to read and write.

Around New Year's, 1863, an eight-year-old slave girl named America Robinson watched Union and Confederate soldiers fighting through the streets of Murfreesboro.[42] Minié balls whistled into her master's yard, cavalrymen tumbled from their bloody saddles in the street, and through the doorway of her owner's parlor she observed the wounded and dying of both armies screaming and writhing. When Union troops finally evacuated the town, America and her father hid themselves in an army wagon and escaped into Nashville's Union lines.

Thomas Rutling's mother spent so much time hiding from her master in the wilds of Wilson County, Tennessee, that he often wondered if he had been born in the woods. She was always found and dragged back and savagely whipped, but she kept running off anyway, and eventually her owners decided to sell her south. His earliest memory was the selling of his mother in 1856. "I must have been about two years old then. . . . I can just remember how the steps looked to our sitting room door, where I was when she kissed me and bade me good by, and how she cried when they led her away." In middle age, Rutling would recall the feel of the lash licking his infant arm as they struck her for clinging to him.

After Rutling's mother had been handcuffed, tied behind her new owner's buggy, and driven away, his master's daughter found him weeping in his cabin. She "took me in her arms and carried me into master's house and made me look at myself in a mirror. The sight of my face in the glass stopped all tears, because such an object I had never seen before." The last Rutling ever heard about his mother was that she had been taken south and whipped nearly to death.

When Rutling's master died, his daughter traded two of her slaves for Rutling and brought him with her to her elderly husband's plantation, where, toting water, fetching kindling, playing with her children, and singing and dancing for his mistress's "own amusement," he evolved into a full-fledged house slave.

As a young table servant, Rutling often overheard his owners conversing about the war. "Now, Tom, you mustn't repeat a word of this," his mistress would admonish him. "I would look mighty obedient," Rutling remembered, "but—well—in less than half an hour, some way, every slave on the plantation would know what had been said up at Massa's house."

In the closing days of the Civil War, Confederate guerrillas paused by Rutling's master's house with a Yankee soldier they had captured. Rutling approached the prisoner to see for himself whether, as his master had warned him, the frightened, angry Yankee had horns. It was common practice for masters to try to keep their slaves terrified of Yankees.[43] Some slaves apparently equated the Yankees and "Lincolnites" with boogeymen and banshees.

When the captive Yankee "saw that I was a black boy, his eyes changed to the softness of those of a dove, and, with his head, he beckoned me," Rutling remembered.

He said, "Untie my hands," and, as I stooped to comply, one of the
guerrillas came round the corner of the house and . . . kicked him
and slapped his face. . . . As the sun went down, the "Bushwhackers"
rode into the forest with their prisoner and before the last rays of
the sun disappeared from the sky a sharp crack of rifles was heard
and a fine young man fell.[44]

The guerrillas left the soldier to bleed to death, but late that night a party
of slaves found him in the woods, fashioned a litter, and spirited him to the
nearest Union camp. A few days later, a column of Yankee troops marched
through, announcing that from now on Rutling and his fellow slaves could
consider themselves emancipated.

"Tom, we are free!" exclaimed Rutling's older brother. "Now we'll have
horses and carriages like master."

But the horses and carriages did not materialize, and Rutling and his
brother fled to Nashville.

3

BY THE THUNDER

NASHVILLE

1860–1865

In 1860, Nashville's State House was like an extravagant signature on a promissory note. Designed by William Strickland and constructed by convicts and slaves, the vast Grecian building with its cupolaed spire was the grandest capitol outside of Washington.[1] But as the Civil War approached, work on its grounds had to be put off. In 1861, it stood forlornly among the blackberries on Nashville's highest heap, frowning down upon a slip-slapped Southern town of seventeen thousand souls.

Nashville's ambitious reach extended beyond its two- and three-story houses and shops to include a state penitentiary, the campus of the University of Nashville, a rail yard, a market square, a tannery, slave pens, and stolid houses of worship. A half hour's carriage ride in almost any direction brought you through "broadly undulating" corn and tobacco fields and "tufts of poplar and magnolia" to a diadem of feudal estates, including Andrew Jackson's Hermitage, the vast stud farm and deer park at Belle Meade, and the Acklin family's preposterous complex at Belmont, which had a zoo, a bowling alley, the South's largest private art gallery, a three-hundred-foot-long hothouse, and so many statues of "Negros dancing" that it reminded one visitor of a "first-class cemetery."[2]

Hanging down like a bauble from the bent wrist of the Cumberland, Nashville had started out as a river port. But in 1860, it was not the Cumberland but a convergence of railroads that promised to turn it into a major metropolis. In 1858, Nashvillians could send their slaves to the station to pick up goods from Europe and New York via rail links to the Great Lakes and the Eastern Seaboard.[3] "The rapid growth of Nashville," boasted an ad in the *Republican Banner*, ". . . is conclusive proof that when all our railroads are completed, the wildest dreamer can scarcely imagine what Nashville will be."[4]

Nor could the wildest dreamer have imagined that within three years Nashville would become the primary western camp of the Union Army of the Cumberland, a bristling, bustling supply depot for the Northern conquest of the middle South. When Tennessee's legislature voted to secede from the Union in May 1861, white Nashvillians had thrown themselves into the rebel war effort. By New Year's Day, 1862, everything from gunboats and cannon to percussion caps and trousers was rolling from the city's factories down to its riverfront and railroad terminus and out to the Confederacy's far-flung armies, while secessionist vigilantes galloped around Davidson County, running off unionists and forcing their more ambivalent neighbors to sign loyalty oaths.

On the evening of Saturday, February 15, 1862, a great crowd gathered at Market Square for a torchlight rally honoring the twenty thousand Confederate soldiers at nearby Fort Donelson fighting to block Grant's advance along the Cumberland and the Tennessee. There were speeches, "flags, emblems, and transparencies." As ranks of boys and old men marched about, "bearing aloft huge, rough iron pikes," the upper-class women of the city collected a steamboat's worth of bedding and carpets to protect their soldiers from the cold.[5] But midway through the next day's Sabbath, the governor himself rode through the streets to sound the alarm: Fort Donelson had fallen to the Yankees.

White Nashville flew out of its churches and into a panic. A mob broke into the Confederate storehouses. Despite frigid blasts of water from the fire brigade, "women and children, even, were seen scudding through the streets under loads of greasy pork."[6] As retreating rebels limped four abreast through the trampled slush of the city streets, somebody blew up a powder magazine; others set riverboats ablaze and destroyed the railroad bridge across the Cumberland. Convinced that Union gunboats would raze the city as an object lesson to the South, people threw their most precious belongings into buggies and wagons and, in their thousands, choked the southern pikes.[7]

Some Nashville slaves were terrified to see their masters in such a state, but others were amused and delighted and sang mocking songs about their owners' unmasterful panic:

> He look up the river,
> And he see that smoke
> Where the Lincoln gunboats lay.
> He big enough, and he old enough,
> And he ought to know better,
> But he gone and run away.[8]

Only an exalted few Nashville whites had owned more than a dozen human beings. Middle-class slave owners tended to own two or three, and Nashville had proportionately the largest middle class of any city in the South.[9] Those who were too poor to own slaves were mostly Irish laborers and their families, who "camped out" in the Sixth Ward on a filthy tract of land called the Broad Street Bottoms that the Cumberland regularly turned to bog.[10]

Much of Nashville's slaveholding upper crust had been the "old Virginia set," whose birth and education had distinguished them from the river-borne entrepreneurs who had to scrabble up from the bottom rungs. But the city's most august resident was the lowborn son of humble Scotch-Irish immigrants, former president Andrew Jackson, whose Hermitage lay just outside town and who, until his death in 1845, often came into the city to confer with his cronies and get his hair cut.

At one time, Jackson owned more slaves—some 150—than anyone in the Nashville area. But the Jacksons had no children, and by the late 1850s so many of his wife's relatives—the Donelsons and Sheppards—had dispersed that the plantation was reduced to a ghostly crew of freed hangers-on like Simon Sheppard, William Napier, and Uncle Alfred Jackson.

Jackson's almost-lifelong body servant was George Jackson, who, after Old Hickory's death, left the Hermitage and went to Memphis to be near his enslaved wife, Amanthus.[11] Among their grandchildren was one of the stars of the Jubilee Singers, the charismatic Jennie Jackson. Her mother had been born a slave, and Jennie's father, George's son, had died before Jennie was born. But because her mother was the beneficiary of another slaveholder's deathbed manumission, Jennie was born free. The status of Nashville's freedmen was always precarious, however. When the trustee appointed by her mother's late mistress tried to destroy the family's "free papers" so he could re-enslave them, Jennie's destitute mother fled into the city with her three-year-old daughter.[12]

Slaves lived throughout Nashville in quarters of one kind or another, along alleyways or in their owners' yards, stables, and houses. But free blacks lived mostly in the Fourth Ward, an aggregation of shanties, tenements, and bawdy houses popularly known as Smoky Row.[13] There Jennie grew into a sturdy and resourceful young woman. Years of laboring with her mother over a washboard scrubbing the clothes of local whites and Northern officers had given her powerful hands and shoulders. "My mornings were spent at the wash-tub," she remembered, "and the afternoons in learning my letters."

Other Jubilee Singers would claim that it was the novelty of Jackson's almost-jet-black complexion that made her so popular with audiences in the Northeast, Britain, and Europe. But it was just as likely her beauty. With her soft, buoyant features, sweetly forthright gaze, and clear, powerful soprano, she had all the makings of a star. Her mother was so protective of Jennie's soprano that she refused even to let her sing in choirs. "Save your voice," she told Jennie, "and you may have a chance to do some good with it some day."[14]

The loss of Fort Donelson in February 1862 forced the Confederacy to give up not only its foothold in Kentucky but a large part of Tennessee as well. Nevertheless, the residents of Nashville need not have panicked. The Yankees did not reach the city until a week later and had no intention of destroying their prize. Nashville, after all, was the first rebel capital they had captured. Eventually outnumbering the city's civilian inhabitants three to two, Union soldiers began to settle into the sullen, half-abandoned city and run their fortifications through its elegant, outlying estates and regal manors.[15]

Among these last was the home of a wealthy planter from Lebanon,

Tennessee, named Henry Frazier, who, at the outbreak of the Civil War, had taken refuge in Nashville with his family and house slaves, among them a Mrs. Porter, his chief domestic servant, her husband, and three daughters, including her little girl Maggie. When the Yankees reached the outskirts of the city, Frazier left the household in Mrs. Porter's care, taking her husband and two of her daughters with him, possibly as insurance against her absconding with Maggie. But when the Yankees proved less fearsome than the Visigoths Nashville's secessionists had expected, Frazier returned and meekly freed the Porters upon the publication of Lincoln's Emancipation Proclamation. They agreed to remain in his service. But Mrs. Porter had the temerity to demand wages, and when Frazier refused, she promptly hired herself out to another family.

As the city's residents adjusted to the new order, the Yankees converted churches, warehouses, livery stables into barracks and hospitals. The view from the commandeered statehouse became a vast sprawl of tents and vertical-sided barracks. The Yankees erected a field hospital of more than twenty-three hundred beds in framed, floored tents and housed Confederate prisoners of war in the penitentiary.[16] They reserved Tennessee's entire railway network for their exclusive use, and, under Yankee stewardship, it would enter a period of phenomenal expansion.

To accomplish all this, the Union army needed laborers. For a time, it seemed that the stream of fugitive slaves who now poured into the city would provide an inexhaustible supply. But the Yankees did not pay them regularly nor adequately clothe and shelter them. Some of them began to melt away with their picks and shovels and crowd the contraband camp that emerged along Smoky Row. Union army press-gangs chased after them, raiding black churches and barbershops, rampaging through the cellars and attics of slaveholders' homes, sweeping through black Fourth of July celebrations, carting off the entire staff of the Commercial Hotel one morning, until they had collected a crew of two thousand.[17]

A slave from a neighboring county recalled reaching Nashville "just as the Yankees were taking the Negroes out to work. There must have been about a thousand slaves," he remembered, "and they all had axes, going out to cut wood." As much to keep the workers from running away as to protect them from rebel bushwhackers, "one troop of cavalry went in front and another behind."[18]

White troops were removed from work details and returned to the field as quickly as black replacements could be found. Soon there were no black males "about the camps or in the army who were unemployed," an officer reported.

> Indeed the great trouble is to get as many as can be profitably used—They are generally industrious and faithful. The prejudice in the army against them is fast giving away—The majority of the troops in this Dept strongly endorse the policy of the administration including the [Emancipation] proclamation. . . . I have yet to see one [slave] that wishes to return or does not prefer even the very imperfect freedom they enjoy with the army to slavery.[19]

Not every Union soldier rejoiced in the liberation of Tennessee's slaves. Army commanders constantly feared that the swarm of contrabands would mean disease and deprivation for their troops. "Men paused in bewilderment and panic, foreseeing the demoralization and infection of the Union soldiers and the downfall of the Union cause."[20] Yankee soldiers were not always friendly. A chaplain remarked that contrabands often "met prejudice against their color" in the Union lines that was "more bitter than that they left behind."[21] Union soldiers sometimes went out of their way to confirm fugitive slaves' worst fears about the Yankees. Shortly after making his way into the Union lines, George L. Knox, whose master "had been telling us all the time that the Yankees wanted to get us and sell us in Cuba as slaves," overheard a Yankee remark that he could get two thousand dollars for one of Knox's fellow contrabands. Even more disconcerting was the Yankee soldier who watched over a gang of contraband laborers with a "great long wagon whip, striking [it] as though he would strike at some one." Knox remembered muttering to one of his fellows that it seemed "that our master's words are about to come true," but he "afterwards found out that the whip was all for mischief."[22] Some Yankees were worse than mischievous: they raped black women and lured them into prostitution, robbed and beat runaway slaves, tricked and intimidated black families into handing over their possessions.

By 1863, a "homeless, friendless, pitiable throng" of about seven thousand freedmen had surged into Nashville.[23] "Long trains of fugitives might be seen coming in with barely enough of covering to serve the purposes of decency," one observer reported, "the stronger before, carrying infants and little bundles, the feebler and little children dragging away behind, with naked feet and legs, plunging through mud and snow, and at night camping on the wet and frozen ground with no roof but clouds."[24]

"Imagine if you will," proposed John Eaton, the Union army's superintendent of contrabands, "a slave population, springing from antecedent bondage, forsaking its local traditions and all the associations of the old plantation life, coming garbed in rags or in silks, with feet shod or bleeding, individually or in families and large groups—an army of slaves and fugitives, pushing its way irresistibly toward an army of fighting men, perpetually on the defensive and perpetually ready to attack." He continued,

> The arrival among us of these hordes was like the oncoming of cities. There was no plan in this exodus, no Moses to lead it. . . . A blind terror stung them, an equally blind hope allured them, and to us they came. There were men, women and children in every stage of disease or decrepitude, often nearly naked, with flesh torn by the terrible experiences of their escapes. Sometimes they were intelligent and eager to help themselves; often they were bewildered or stupid or possessed by the wildest notions of what liberty might mean—expecting to exchange labor, and obedience to the will of another, for idleness and freedom from restraint. . . . A few had profited by the misfortunes of their master and were jubilant in their unwonted ease and luxury, but these stood in lurid contrast to the grimmer aspects of the tragedy—the women in travail, the helplessness of childhood and old age, the horrors of sickness and of frequent death.[25]

Nashville would provide many abolitionist Northern whites with their first flesh-and-blood encounters with slavery. Just as they had known slavery only as an abstract evil, they had regarded emancipation as an abstract good. But here were thousands of human beings of every shade crowding in their rags into tents and hovels, a teeming, lousy mass of virtues and vices.[26] Many missionaries had never seen conditions like this before. The camps were almost indescribable.

"This is hell, isn't it?" the fugitive slave George L. Knox remembered saying to his brother as they sought shelter in Nashville's camp. His brother agreed but determined that "if we made our bed hard, we would lay on it, and never go back until we were taken or times were better."[27] But times never did get better for Knox's brother. He died a few weeks later.[28]

4

CAN'T YOU READ?

JOSEPH GILLESPIE MCKEE

1862-1865

I dream not now as formerly
Of the dear in distant lands;
But sadly ponder what to do
With these crowding contrabands.
Joseph Gillespie McKee

In 1862, the general assembly of the United Presbyterian Church had heard "the providence of God" calling on it "to enter upon the fields of missionary labor . . . in places where the power of slavery, which once drove us away from the South, is now broken." The assembly was determined that "anti-slavery churches" should establish themselves in the South "as a means of securing freedom of speech and promoting the interests of truth and righteousness in those parts of our country." The "altered circumstances" of the contrabands "were so sudden and unexpected that the church had neither time nor opportunity for consulting and moving as a whole, so the work began in a fragmentary way and in different localities." The board sent "bands of laborers," each consisting of "an ordained minister, a male assistant, and four or five female teachers," to contraband camps in Louisiana, Mississippi, and Tennessee.[1]

Their man in Nashville was tubercular, tenacious Joseph Gillespie McKee. He was a small, chin-whiskered Irishman with a stub nose, a bulbous brow, and brooding eyes that made him look like a dour leprechaun. He had immigrated to America from County Down, Ireland, when he was fourteen years old and attended Westminster College in New Wilmington, Pennsylvania. His first mission was in the American West, where he "traveled thousands of miles over the prairie, much of this distance on foot." McKee was inspired by the martyrdom of American Presbyterian missionaries during the Indian mutiny of 1857, and when the Second United Presbyterian Synod of the West approached him about a posting to Nashville, he was considering joining his toiling brother James in Burma. But the plight of the impoverished freedman immediately displaced the idolatrous Hindu in his moral imagination. As he admonished his brother in 1863:

> Tell me not of Burmah's heathen
> Far away o'er ocean's foam.
> Teach them, teach them
> Who can reach them,
> We have heathen nearer home.[2]

Arriving ahead of his team on the brink of one of the bitterest winters in Nashville's history, a newly ordained Joseph McKee stepped off the train into the grinding clamor of Yankee occupation.[3] He must have cut a drab and negligible figure toting his satchel from the railway station and into the rutted street, ducking out of the way of horsemen, infantrymen, and the thousands of groaning government teams that nearly monopolized the muddy city.[4] Hurrying past stinking, makeshift, open-air latrines, McKee made his way into the contraband camp, a vast ramshackle of discarded Union Silbey tents and improvised shacks and lean-tos teeming with "a homeless, friendless, pitiable throng" of starved and ragged former slaves.

McKee tried to find shelter for himself, but at first no one would take him in. Whites dubbed him "the nigger preacher" and refused to rent him a room. The army did not welcome troublemaking self-styled champions of the contrabands it was ruthlessly pressing into service, and the established freedmen of the city were either too suspicious or too hard-pressed them-

selves to offer him lodgings. Some freedmen regarded white charitable efforts with suspicion. "I ought to tell you frankly," Frederick Douglass
warned the head of the American Freedmen's Aid Society, "that I have my
doubts about these Freedmen's Societies. They may be the necessity of the
hour . . . but I fear everything looking to their permanence. The negro
needs justice more than pity, liberty more than old clothes." He feared that
white charitable efforts on behalf of blacks would only "furnish an apology
for excluding us." He believed that if anything should help the freedmen besides the freedmen themselves, it should be the government.[5]

During McKee's first nights in the city, the consumptive little preacher
had to sleep outdoors on the limestone steps of the capitol, his coughing
fits ruffling the artillery crews who dozed and loafed by the idle muzzles of
Yankee cannon on the terrace above. It took McKee almost a week to find
"shelter from the rude blasts of Autumn" in a tenement on McLemore
Street, to whose "bare walls . . . he would return in the evening to rest his
weary limbs."[6] But even this was more than most contrabands could boast.
Everywhere he went, McKee found fugitive slaves "seeking shelter in sheds,
cellars, and stables, even camping in fence corners."[7]

McKee applied to Tennessee governor Andrew Johnson for surplus tents
for the contrabands, but the future president refused. As he saw it, "anything that will tend to promote [the contrabands'] comfort will only increase the number flocking in and exasperate still more their haters and
persecutors, thus increasing their misery." McKee defied Johnson's logic,
however, and applied for help to the presbyteries of Ohio.[8] Within a few
weeks, money, food, "tons of clothing, books and other accessories" began
to pour into his mission, transported on Union trains and at federal expense.

With his assistant M. M. Brown, McKee established four preaching
stations that doubled as distribution centers. He and Brown held street
services, arranged prayer meetings, opened a Sabbath school. But most of
McKee's time was spent touring the camps to hand out food, clothing, and
fuel to the thousands who flocked to his mission. His labors were grueling,
heartbreaking. One winter morning, McKee found a family lying freezing
on the floor; they had burned their bedstead the day before and eaten their
last morsel of food.[9] The luckier families received two rations a day, but
"the meat was so old," recalled one fugitive, "that when thrown against a
wall it would splatter like mud."[10] There were occasional windfalls. A slave
from Williamson County recalled that the contrabands ate convulsively:

some days they had nothing to eat at all, other times the army allowed them to slaughter a captured cow and cut it into big chunks.

> Then we would put our meat on a long, forked pole, one end buried in the ground and the other slanting up and pointing toward the fire. . . . When the meat was done, such eating and smoking you never heard. It used to make me awful sick at times, and I would throw up a lot. But I was hungry, and kept trying until I made it stick in my stomach.[11]

Cholera and tuberculosis were epidemic.[12] Smallpox killed one of McKee's assistants and would have carried off another, but for "a kind Negro woman" who nursed her back to health.[13]

Perhaps McKee's most arduous task was finding night shelter for the lines of refugees that kept streaming into town. Most lodgings were out of reach of the contrabands; rent for "a poor, leaky room" was an unheard-of five to ten dollars a month. "Often have we labored until late at night," McKee reported, "to get them crowded into quarters, and have been compelled to leave some of them on the street unprovided for, and returning in the morning, have found them beyond the power of cold and hunger."[14] For all his efforts that first winter, exposure, starvation, and disease would wipe out more than a thousand men, women, and children.

The number and destitution of the contrabands threatened to overwhelm not just McKee, the army, and Nashville's municipal authority but the community of freedmen as well. Until the Civil War, the division between freedmen and slaves had been enforced by anti-insurrectionist statutes prohibiting the two groups from associating. But the division went deeper. A high proportion of the freedmen were the light-skinned children of their masters or their masters' sons or, like Uncle Alfred Jackson, the emancipated favorites of their owners' families. The majority of the contrabands, like the majority of slaves, were darker-skinned laborers and field hands, many of them as neglected as the ragged Mississippi laborers whose misery had reduced Sarah Sheppard and her mistress to tears. Divided by race and class, many members of each group looked on members of the other with distrust, even disgust.

Old Daniel Wadkins, Ella Sheppard's first teacher, hoped to bridge the gap by extending his freedmen's school to the contrabands. For two decades, Wadkins had battled at great personal risk for the education of Nashville's African American children. Not until the Union army set aside the municipal ban on black schools in 1862 had he been able to reopen his academy, this time in the basement of the First Baptist Church's Colored Mission.[15] Until then, most of his students had been free blacks like Ella Sheppard. Now a missionary for the Disciples of Christ, Wadkins applied to the army to help him establish schools for the contrabands. But the army doubted the grizzled old freedman was up to the task. Anticipating the arrival of white Northern missionaries like McKee, the military authorities turned Wadkins down. To make ends meet and impress upon his people the value of an education, Wadkins began to charge his students a nominal fee for books and slates: sometimes as little as a few pennies.

> *When I done been redeemed and done been tried*
> *I'll sit down beside the lamb.*
> > *Can't you read?*
> > *Can't you read?*
> *When I done been to heaven then,*
> *I can read my title clean.*
> *When I done been to heaven,*
> *I's going to get my lesson,*
> > *I's going to read,*
> > *I's going to read my title clean.*[16]

For as long as it was forbidden them, slaves had dreamed of being able to read and write. Literacy seemed to some slaves the key to white hegemony, a kind of magic that kept whites in power. In fact, it was even more magical than some slaves imagined. "For a long time," wrote John Sella Martin, "I could not get it out of my head that the readers were talking to the paper, rather than the paper talking to them."[17]

Some masters allowed or even encouraged their slaves to learn to read. It was convenient to have a cook who could read recipes, for instance, or slave foremen and artisans who could read directions and keep track of accounts. Charlie Davenport recalled that in his master's household, "they learned the house servants to read."[18] But even this education had its limitations. "Mighty few niggers learned to read and write," said a former Nashville slave. "They thought niggers only needed to know enough reading or writing to know how to count rails or stock or something like that."[19] It was a shame, remarked an ex-slave named Allen, "that a man couldn't read like he wanted to, cheap as paper is."[20]

Even if masters were inclined to "improve" their slaves, in most states they were forbidden by law from teaching them to read. Kentucky and Tennessee were two of only three states that allowed slaves to be taught to read and write, but local statutes, prejudices, and practices made it risky. Literacy was so rare among Bluegrass slaves that, in all his twenty years as a Kentucky slave, Lewis Clarke met only three or four slaves who could read and only one who could write.[21]

"If Marse catch a paper in your hand, he sure whip you," said Ellen Butts.

> He don't allow no bright niggers around. He sell them quick. He always say, "Book learning don't raise no good sugar cane." The only learning he allow was when they learn the colored children the Methodist catechism. The only writing a nigger ever get am when he get born or marry or die, then Marse put the name in the big book.[22]

"A literary Negro was disgusting," Martha Browne recalled her mistress telling her, and "not to be tolerated." "Just to be caught looking at a clean sheet of paper," recalled Maggie Matthews, "was enough to get a scolding, but to look at a piece of paper that had writing on it, and if we made like we knowed what was wrote on it, we sure got a whooping for it."[23] If a slave picked up even a little piece of paper, said Millie Simpkins of Nashville, "they would yell, 'Put that down, you. You want to get in our business.' "[24] The ban on literacy extended even to arithmetic. Once Edward Walker worked out a complicated mathematical problem in his head. His masters tried to check his answer but "got stuck" and claimed "it didn't amount to anything." When Walker showed them how he did it, they told him "it was a good piece of figuring," then warned each other that Walker was "a long-headed nigger and needed watching."[25]

Some white children took it upon themselves to try to "civilize" their slave playmates. "The little white children would learn us our speeches," recalled Maggie Matthews, "and then we'd say them to one another."[26] A mistress named Mrs. James had two little girls, recalled Emma Knight of Missouri: "One of them learned me not to be such a tomboy and not to be so rough. I was a bad girl when I was young—I could climb every tree on the master's farm, and my clothes were always in worse rags from being so rough. . . . The master's girls taught us to read and write, but they weren't supposed to."[27]

"The time was," sighed a white Nashville woman during the war, "when the niggers carried the white children's books and dinner and waited outside to bring them home."[28] Slaves picked up a little learning just hanging around outside schoolhouses or listening to their masters' children reciting their lessons. Even as a boy, John Sella Martin knew that the "hobgoblin" laws against slave literacy could tear him away from his comparatively lenient master:

> But though the white boys would not teach me to read, they could not control or prevent the acquisition of a quick and retentive memory with which I was blessed, and by their bantering one another at spelling, and betting each on his proficiency over the other, I learned to spell by sound before I knew by sight a single letter in the alphabet.[29]

Slave children were watched carefully for signs of literacy. "One day old Mistress saw us with a book," John Crawford remembered. "She come outside with a stick of candy [and] held out her hand, and she say, 'I give you all of this you want if you tell me where you got that book and learned your letters.' I spoke up smart as you please and told her. They was about six of us little niggers, and she took us in the house, and she held our heads between her legs, and she whipped our back ends with a wooden paddle. Then she stuck us up the chimney where it was dark and kept us there forty minutes."[30] Some slaveholders bribed slave children out of learning to read. One day, Levi Pollard's otherwise parsimonious Virginian mistress unaccountably distributed frosted biscuits to her child slaves. After the children gobbled them down, she offered them another round in exchange for the primers they had been secretly studying. The children gave up their primers.[31]

Some slave owners regarded literacy as a dangerous contagion and rid themselves of any slave they caught reading or writing. After repeatedly warning Charles Alexander, a slave boy, not to play schoolmaster to her white child, Alexander's mistress sold him.[32] Other literate slaves were simply killed. "Back then," recalled Joseph Farley, "even if they thought

once that you wanted an education they would kill you." When insurrection panics set in among whites, literate blacks were the first to suffer.
Around 1861, a woman named Fredonia Gallatin announced that Tennessee's slaves were about to rise. Recalling the uprising of the literate Nat
Turner, frightened whites thereupon sought out all the slaves they could
find who could read and whipped them to death.[33]

Slaves were further handicapped by the contempt in which whites held
black intelligence. Mattie Hardman's master was a doctor and "very fractious and exact. He didn't allow the slaves to claim they forgot to do thus
and so, nor did he allow them to make the expression, 'I thought so and so.'
He would say to them if they did, 'Who told you you could think!' "[34] John
McAdams's owners said that they "could come just as near learning their
horses how to read as they could us."[35]

A slave named Sol proved such a prodigious reader that his master
called in a phrenologist, who fingered Sol's skull for a while and pro-
nounced him "an uncommonly smart man."[36] Some literate slaves were
placed in positions of responsibility. Sarah Berliner, the white daughter of a
slaveholder, recalled a slave named Jim, who "was taught to read and write
before father bought him, somewhere in Alabama. His ability to read and
write cost father quite a bit extra, but it was worth it since he was able to
put Jim in charge of the commissary."[37] But it could be dangerous to be
known as a smart slave. "The brighter a slave is," wrote Lewis Clarke, "the
more he has to lie; for the more the master is jealous of what's working in
his mind, and the harder he has to try to hide it."[38] Lunsford Lane made
sure he "never appeared to be even so intelligent as I really was. This all colored people at the South, free and slaves, find it peculiarly necessary for
their own comfort and safety to observe."[39] Slaves had to be careful how
they expressed themselves. One slave "unconsciously partook more or less
of the forms of life, language, traits and habits of the white folks, even to
the extent that suddenly his mistress discovered that he was adopting their
language entirely, which she solemnly forbade. While giving ready promise
to resume the plantation patois, he found it impossible."[40] A slave might be
sold for answering "I presume" to a master's question. "Cause[?]" asked
James Thomas. "Nigger too smart."[41]

Within the slave communities, the ability to read and write bestowed
power and status. When John Sella Martin's fellow slaves found out he
could read, they would take him aside "that I might read some book or
newspaper which they had filched from their masters' libraries."[42] Other

slaves asked the literate Stephen Jordan to forge passes for them "so they could go and see their wives that lived off the place."[43] Elijah Marrs was taught to read by his white playmates, who "did not know that it was dangerous for a slave to read and write." Eventually he became so accomplished that he could read the envelopes and newspapers he delivered as a mail boy. At night, he learned how to write in a secret school but gave himself away by writing his name on the fence posts. By the time of the war, he had become known as "the Shelby County negro clerk," and his master warned him not to instruct others or receive letters lest the rebels catch wind of it.[44]

The Bible was a special inspiration to literacy. "I do wish I could read," sighed Charlotte Brooks. "I long to read the Bible and the hymn-book."[45] A former Nashville slave testified that he was "no mathematician, neither grammarian, but when it comes to handling the Bible I knocks down verbs, break up prepositions and jumps over adjectives. I tell you, I am a God-sent man!"

Some slaves resigned themselves to illiteracy. The hoe "was my fountain pen and pencil," recalled a former Nashville slave, "and my slate was the ground."[46] But many persisted. Louvinia Young Pleasant never went to school but remembered that during slavery, "when I was a little child, I'd see some letters and words on pieces of old paper. I'd go outside and trace them letters in the sand with my finger. That is the way I tried to learn my A-B-C's."[47]

So it was with at least two of the Jubilee Singers. While toting bundles around town for his master, Benjamin Holmes used to study the letters on signs and doors and his boss's measuring books and by 1860 had taught himself how to read and write. Georgia Gordon was so impressed when she heard a preacher quoting the first verse of the Gospel of St. John—"In the beginning was the Word, and the Word was with God, and the Word was God"—that she memorized it. When she got home, she asked someone who could read to point out the verse in the Bible. She learned to recognize the words one by one and searched through the Bible for others like them until, little by little, she could read.[48]

The contrabands' desire for education astonished and moved Joseph McKee and his assistants. He quickly recognized that their hunger for literacy was a match even for their hunger for food and immediately set about opening a school. In October 1863, Nelson Merry, the African American minister of the First Colored Baptist Church who had housed Wadkins's school in his basement, now offered to share it with McKee. But McKee did not charge for books or tuition, and little by little Wadkins's most promising students began to melt away from the new school he had established behind his house on High Street, among them the twelve-year-old future prima donna of the Jubilee Singers, Maggie Porter. The exodus so outraged Wadkins that he got into a fistfight with the Reverend Merry. To make peace in their own congregation, Merry's deacons expelled McKee.[49]

McKee pressed on, however, and soon reestablished his school in a large storeroom over a shop that manufactured boilers. The constant "tap tap" of hammers was "never ceasing," and railway workers attacked and stoned his five hundred students as they came and went.[50] Laboring "in the face of the bitterest and most fiendish opposition and hate," McKee himself was pelted occasionally, and rocks crashed through the windows of his school so frequently that after a while they hardly interrupted his pupils' recitations.[51] In the meantime, several more pay schools sprang up, one in the basement of Capers African Methodist Episcopal (A.M.E.) Chapel, whose managers asked McKee to take charge and enroll their teacher as one of his students.

McKee's labors took a terrible toll on his minute, consumptive frame, and within less than a year of his arrival, he was compelled to flee to Europe to recuperate. Besieged by the smallpox that was raging through the city, his staff floundered without him. When the school closed for vacation in June, McKee's students feared they would see their teachers' "faces no more."[52] The mission was not revived until the Reverend A. S. Montgomery arrived in September, determined to reestablish his school in the basement of the Capers A.M.E. Church. But a young firebrand named Napoleon Merry took the pulpit to fulminate against the invasion of Northern whites. If his congregation let them take over their schools, the community would merely exchange one set of white masters for another. Like many another A.M.E. minister, Merry entertained few illusions about white liberalism and unilaterally forbade Montgomery from using his church.

Merry's parishioners were not so sure, however. Whatever the trade-off might be, time was wasting, and no one in the black community, not even their beloved Daniel Wadkins, had the resources to address the needs of the thousands of freedmen cramming every interstice of the Fourth Ward. These pious Northerners might, as Merry suspected, be in it for themselves, might even be the flip side of the same old oppressive coin, but poor shivering, tubercular McKee did not seem to have profited materially from his mission; nor was he showing signs of accommodating to local whites. In fact, local whites despised and abused him. If McKee and his fellow white missionaries departed, it would fall entirely to the freedmen to care for the refugees, something they did not have the means to do. So Merry's deacons overruled their new pastor and voted to permit the McKee School to hold its classes in their church. Whatever McKee's game might be, they figured they could play it.

As 1864 drew to a close, it seemed that McKee's band of missionaries had won. But before the new year, they were to labor "not merely in the midst of hostile passions, and prejudices, but under the cannon's mouth and amid the rattle of musketry."[53]

5

WE'LL OVERTAKE
THE ARMY

NASHVILLE

1864–1866

I've 'listed and I mean to fight
Yes, my Lord,
Till every foe is put to flight . . .
The God I serve is a man of War.
Yes, my Lord.
He fights and conquers evermore.
Yes, my Lord.

By December 1864, wartime Nashville was no longer the "Athens of the South." Entrenchments scarred "many a smiling yard and fruitful garden," and "the marring hoof of war" had left its mark in every street.[1] Nashville had become, for all intents and purposes, a Yankee town. But even though the Union fortifications were formidable—half a dozen commanding forts linked by twenty miles of entrenchments and breastworks—they were not necessarily invulnerable. All through the first year of Union occupation, Nashville was under a remote and sputtering rebel siege, which, as Andrew Johnson observed, had "a great tendency to keep the rebellious spirit alive."[2] As Nathan Bedford Forrest, John Hunt Morgan, and Joseph

Wheeler attacked federal forts and supply lines throughout middle Tennessee, many local whites continued to taunt and hector Union troops in the street out of a faith that someday a sizable body of rebel soldiers would yet rid their city of the Yankees.

In the ice and snow of December 1864, the blue-eyed and delusional Confederate general John Bell Hood apparently decided to reward this belief. He led an army of about fifteen thousand rebels to within sight of Nashville's statehouse and, with characteristic recklessness, deployed them on frozen ground along a broken three-mile front. With one arm maimed at Gettysburg and one leg amputated at Chickamauga, Hood had to be hoisted into his saddle and strapped in. His ragged, barefoot Army of Tennessee was almost as crippled, having just engaged the Yankees at nearby Franklin with a loss of five generals and more than six thousand men: two and a half times more than the Yankees' casualties.

A few days before what became known as the Battle of Nashville, an army chaplain

> met an old negro out near the picket line. He was bent with age and rheumatism, and his short hair was as white as a snow ball. He seemed to be out for a [reconnaissance] for his own benefit. I said to him:
>
> "Well, what do you think? Will General Hood take Nashville?"
>
> "That's just it. That's what I was studying on myself. And I reckon General Hood won't come to Nashville."
>
> "Why not?" I asked.
>
> "Because he couldn't do justice to hisself in here."[3]

The old man was right. Hood had set a trap for himself, committing his troops to an attack that could never succeed from a position he could neither defend nor abandon.

In the days before the battle, hundreds more contrabands had swarmed into the city, many of them refugees from a Pulaski camp that had been overrun by the rebels. A Franklin slave recalled that the capitol "was just packed with women and children, both white and colored. We were all huddled there together, slept together and ate together, and there was no distinction either in the food we received or the care we got. We all had to stay inside until the fighting was over."[4] The contrabands mixed uneasily with an almost equal number of poor white refugees "in a more hopeless &

helpless condition than the Freedmen," wrote a Northern observer, "for the mass of them are just as poor & ignorant & degraded, as the slaves themselves, & twice *as mean*, and they don't seem to have energy enough to *die decently*."[5]

Just before one o'clock in the afternoon of December 15, a vastly superior Union force under General George Henry Thomas marched forward to sweep Hood's shivering army from the field. For Nashville's contrabands, the Battle of Nashville would be not just another lesson in the horrors of war but a crucial test. Until then, General Thomas, a Virginian, had deprecated the fighting spirit of black men, convinced that they would be useless in open combat. Contrabands had applied to Thomas for weapons, but Thomas gave them spades and shovels instead, rounding up a thousand "loafing or unemployed negroes or white men" to reinforce the city's defenses. Nevertheless, by 1864 the Union army was actively recruiting black soldiers in middle Tennessee, and as Thomas's troops advanced on Hood, eight black regiments took the field.[6]

A former slave named John Finnely recalled:

> There am no fighting at first, but before long they starts the battle. The noise was awful, just one steady roar of the guns and the cannons. The window glass in Nashville . . . all shook out from the shakement of the cannons. There am dead mens all over the ground and lots of wounded, and some cussing, and some praying. Some am moaning, and this and that one cry for the water, and, God almighty, I don't want any such again. There am men carrying the dead off the field, but they can't keep up with the cannons.[7]

"It sounded like the cannons would tear the world to pieces," recalled a Nashville contraband. "I could hear the big shells humming as they came. They cut off treetops just like a man cutting off weeds with a scythe. Big shells and little ones. Some were chained together and what not. You could hear them hit the ground and then burst."[8]

Outnumbered, outgunned, and outmaneuvered in one of the most decisive battles of the war, Hood's army was decimated. Between his defeat and Sherman's devastating march through Georgia, the Confederacy would be reduced thereafter to defending "Richmond and its dependencies."[9] The Union action was so decisive, and the rebel flight so complete, that there were relatively few casualties. But on the federal side of the equation, black regiments sustained some of the heaviest losses: 630 out of a Union total of 3,057 men.[10] A Yankee chaplain recalled coming upon "the ranks of colored soldiers, filling a long trench dug on the hill side in front of our earthwork where the fiercest fighting occurred."[11] Touring the smoking battlefield, his horse stepping among the intermingled bodies of black and white troops, General Thomas himself turned to his officers and declared, "Gentlemen, the matter is settled; Negroes will fight."

Thomas's victory put to rest any local white hopes and black fears that Nashville would ever again come under the rebel banner. But for the contrabands crowded even more densely into their freezing Nashville camp, the battle meant disruptions and suffering. During the battle itself, "the sounds and scenes of a near warfare was a constant strain," and though most continued to attend religious services and Sabbath schools, many withdrew from their classes.[12] The fighting destroyed scores of nearby farms, and Hood's retreating foragers stripped the countryside of supplies. In the cold, harsh weeks after Hood's defeat, about one out of every six contrabands died.[13]

In late December, a somewhat recuperated Joseph McKee returned to Nashville, determined to construct his own facility. The contrabands themselves contributed $150.70 to his building fund, "bringing their offerings gladly, and telling with shining eyes how the pennies had been saved."[14] He rented property on Ewing Street and ordered a modular building kit from Cincinnati that was almost lost in a steamboat wreck. But at last, a month after the close of the Civil War, the timbers were raised for the McKee School.

McKee believed he had won his race with consumption to secure an enduring legacy at Nashville. General Clinton Bowen Fisk of the Freedmen's Bureau congratulated him for the "perseverance and patient faith with which you have steadily through the storm and sunshine persecuted your labor of love among the freedmen of Nashville. . . . You may be assured of my most hearty cooperation. Command me at any time, for any aid, within my power to bestow."[15]

Clinton Bowen Fisk was born in 1828 on the western frontier of New York State. When Fisk was two years old, his father moved the family to Michigan and promptly died, leaving his wife and children in poverty. The man after whom Fisk University would be named received a truncated education in fits and starts but succeeded as a small-town banker in Coldwater, Michigan, and played the tuba in the village band. The panic of 1857 nearly ruined him, and three years later he migrated with his wife to St. Louis, Missouri, where he got involved in politics and not only made the acquaintance of Abraham Lincoln but got to know a hapless, hardscrabble farmer and firewood dealer named Ulysses S. Grant. (Though Grant's wife unapologetically owned slaves, Grant had upset white locals by freeing the one slave he personally owned, paying freedmen white men's wages, and intervening to stop the whipping of a neighbor's slave.[16])

At the outbreak of the war, Fisk joined the unionist Home Guards and took part in the seizure of Camp Jackson from the supporters of Missouri's secessionist governor while Grant, now an Illinois mustering officer, looked on admiringly. As commander of the Thirty-third Missouri Volunteers, Fisk fought all over Arkansas and Missouri and took part in the vain pursuit of Confederate general Sterling "Pap" Price. By the time Fisk was mustered out, he was a brevet major general. With a round tuba player's face, an equally genial gaze, and a full beard that only underscored the brilliantine sheen of his comb-over, Fisk was a popular man and very good company. But he was first and foremost a teetotaler and, two years before his death in 1890, would receive a quarter of a million votes as the Prohibitionist Party's presidential candidate.

After the war, Fisk was detailed as assistant commissioner of the Tennessee and Kentucky department of the newly formed Freedmen's Bureau, or, as it was known officially, the Bureau of Refugees, Freedmen, and Abandoned Lands. "Fisk ain't a fool," President Andrew Johnson is supposed to have said. "He won't hang everybody." The Freedmen's Bureau was established by Congress in March 1865 to provide food, clothing, and fuel to the destitute and to redistribute abandoned lands among the freedmen. But after Lincoln's assassination, the latter initiative collided with President Andrew Johnson's intention to restore property to pardoned rebels. Pulling back from its redistribution program, the bureau concentrated its efforts on education, relief, and legal protection.

Fisk saw in the plight of the freedmen an opportunity to put his ardent Methodism into practice. In October 1865, at a freedmen's barbecue presided over by Daniel Wadkins, Fisk took it upon himself to deliver a long bootstrap peroration on the value of work to a people who had been worked almost to death.[17] Like his friend Grant, he urged the freedmen to remain in the countryside with their former masters and to avoid the cities. But to his credit, he did not turn his back on those who wisely disregarded his advice. Imbued with the spirit of the time, Fisk championed black education and welcomed, encouraged, and supported the missionaries who came to minister to the freedmen.

On his rounds evangelizing for black schools, Fisk once rode out to meet former Confederate general and Union prisoner William G. Harding, the owner of one of Davidson County's largest plantations. Harding declared that a colored school was something he would "never have on his plantation." But Fisk managed to persuade him to put it to a vote of his former slaves. "There sat the ex-rebel planter and general," wrote the *American Missionary*, "and before him a congregation of ex-slaves, whose dusky faces, when they heard of the school, were lighted up with a joy better imagined than described. One old man broke out—'Bless the Lord, Massa General, that is just what we want, exactly!'" Seeing his workers' enthusiasm, "Harding gracefully surrendered one of the most wicked prejudices of the south, and agreed that a school should be opened on his plantation," to which he would give every possible encouragement.[18] "I can't tell you how eager these colored people are to learn," Fisk declared, "—how they are hungry and thirsty for knowledge, how marvelously they have progressed in their educational efforts. You must come among them to see it."[19]

General Fisk could not but admire McKee's heroic pioneering work among the contrabands, but as assistant commissioner in a besieged bureau, he could not afford to be partial. McKee was not the only Northern missionary in Nashville.[20] In early 1865, a Methodist missionary named Gee set up his own school in the much-contested basement of the First Colored Baptist Church and began sowing the seeds for Fisk University's eventual rival, Central Tennessee College. Nor was McKee the most politic. In fact, he sometimes seemed to go out of his way to alienate people. Restless, consumptive, expressing his heavy pieties in a heavier Irish brogue, McKee could be tiresome and discomfiting. No longer dependent on local freedmen for space, McKee and his missionaries openly criticized them for failing to come to the assistance of the contrabands. One of McKee's teachers, Aggie Walker Simpson, accused them of forgetting "the Giver in the gifts" and withholding the "cup of water" from their enslaved brethren.[21] By naming his school after himself, McKee had opened himself to the charge of empire building.

Among those in the Freedmen's Bureau who dismissed McKee as a romantic improviser was the methodical and pragmatic professor John Ogden, a former normal-school principal from Wisconsin who, while serving under General Rosecrans as a lieutenant of cavalry, had been captured after his commander's abrupt departure from Chickamauga and incarcerated in various Confederate prisons of which he had "bitter recollections."[22] As an agent of the Western Freedmen's Aid Commission, Ogden had been appointed superintendent of education for the Freedmen's Bureau in Tennessee. With Fisk's encouragement, he was determined to turn Nashville into a model of educational reform.

Ogden found allies in a pair of ordained ministers who had been sent to Nashville by the American Missionary Association (A.M.A.). The A.M.A. had its roots in the alliance of New England abolitionists who had championed Cinque and his fellow Africans in the *Amistad* case of 1839. Founded in 1846, the A.M.A. refused to accept donations from slaveholders, thereby freeing itself to oppose slavery without inhibition or reservation. It claimed to be nonsectarian but limited its membership to people "of evangelical sentiments," and most of its members were Congregationalists. The A.M.A. was dedicated to the eradication of a whole range of sins, but it was principally a creature of two silk merchants and unshakable abolitionists, Lewis and Arthur Tappan, and widely regarded as an emancipationist enterprise.

Until 1866, Lewis Tappan had been the A.M.A.'s guiding light. Shrewd, stubborn, materialistic, Tappan was an operator. But he had an empathy for black people that was as unusual for its time as it was remote and abstract. He was absolutely fearless, sticking to his guns even after a white mob vandalized his house and burned his belongings in a bonfire. A ferocious champion of the men and women he sent out to the field, Tappan was a scourge of the home-office bureaucrats who were sometimes too overwhelmed and disorganized to keep up.

With the end of the war, Tappan's right-hand man, George Whipple, switched the A.M.A.'s gears to address the needs of the men, women, and children its members had expended so much time, energy, and money to free. One of its first causes was the mistreatment of contrabands by the Union army, which often pressed large numbers of them into work gangs and failed not only to pay them wages but to provide them with food and shelter. A.M.A. agents hounded Lincoln with reports of Union soldiers raping, whipping, and robbing refugee slaves.[23] But the association's great mission was the conversion and education of the freedmen. It opened a Middle Western field office in Cincinnati with the thirty-seven-year-old Reverend Edward Parmelee Smith at the helm. Courtly, soft-spoken, Smith was a Yale man who had taught briefly in Alabama before the war, spending his off-hours preaching to black children. After two years at the Union Theological Seminary, he took part in a movement that shipped "destitute and vagrant children" out West to be adopted by farmers. During the war, he volunteered for the Christian Commission, providing aid to Union soldiers in Nashville and Chattanooga.[24] In the summer of 1865, Smith took the train to Nashville to scout a likely site for an elementary school with one of the association's field agents: a tall, sonorous New York abolitionist named Erastus Milo Cravath.

Fisk and Ogden understood and admired men like Smith and Cravath. Like the general and his subordinate, they were war veterans who combined the requisite abolitionist and academic credentials with a strong entrepreneurial streak. Fisk and Ogden embraced the A.M.A.'s mission with such ardor that it made McKee fear for his own survival. But Ogden assured him he had nothing to worry about. Their intention was merely "to open a school for poor whites and classes not otherwise provided for." Even if, in the end, they did establish another freedmen's school, they promised to locate it well beyond McKee's hard-won sphere of influence.[25]

They may have meant it at first, but they had no more luck finding a site for their school than McKee had. "I have been 'prospecting' for houses in Nashville for the last four days with no success whatever," Smith wrote in October 1865. "No rent *at all* suitable can be had of an ordinary dwelling fitted for a teachers home short of $1,000 per year. School Rooms can not be had at *any price*, & yet there (are) from two to three thousand children here that could be gathered into schools." Even General Fisk had to live in his own headquarters. "There is nothing now to be had from *the Gen* by way of facilities," and "from the *citizens*," Ogden added, "the less you expect the lighter will be your disappointment. They will not countenance negro teaching in their present temper. They will not rent for negro schools if they know it. They will not fancy a home for teachers of Colored Schools."

Then on October 9, while ambling west of the Chattanooga Depot, Smith and Cravath "struck a lead": an abandoned complex of twenty yellowish Union hospital barracks that had been "very carefully built with reference to the comfort & health of hospital patients & can be adapted to *Home*, School, & Church purposes . . . [in] the center of the thickest negro population."[26] Fisk persuaded General Thomas to let the A.M.A. have the buildings for nothing, but the land itself—more than three hundred square feet—was going to cost it sixteen thousand dollars.

"The grounds . . . are plentifully supplied with good water," Ogden would write, "and are handsomely ornamented with shade and fruit trees, grape arbors, flowers, shrubbery, green sward and graveled walks."[27] But it was not the healthiest site in the city. It lay on low ground, subject to damps and pestilences. As Fisk's legend would have it, the school would grow where once the groaning wounded of the Union army suffered from the wounds they acquired fighting to free the slaves. But a high proportion of those patients, possibly even a majority, had been victims not of gunfire but of venereal disease picked up from the hundreds of prostitutes who plied Smoky Row, an area one soldier described as "a foul breathing hole of hell . . . belching forth its pestilential breath."[28]

The barracks themselves were "arranged for rows of cots each side of a center aisle," but they could be readily adapted for classroom purposes.[29] The board of the A.M.A. deemed the price extravagant, however, and Ogden was finding it "next thing to impossible . . . to arouse" the established freedmen community "to liberal contributions here when they say they already pay taxes and have for years for the education of white children."[30]

But no one could deny the refugees' own hunger for education. "Few people who were not right in the midst of the scenes," wrote Booker T. Washington, "can form any exact idea of the intense desire which the people of my race showed for an education. . . . It was a whole race trying to go to school."[31]

"Brighter, keener, more studious or loving children," wrote a Northern missionary, "never rejoiced a teacher's heart, . . . nor droller, or more vexatious, or stupid ones . . . but each day [I] commit them all to God."[32] Freedmen believed that "better days were coming and education held the key." "We are climbing, Jacob's ladder," they used to sing in class. "Every rung goes higher, higher."[33]

Inspired by the eager promise of the refugees who clamored for an education at Nashville, Ogden, Cravath, and Smith pledged their own personal notes to raise the four-thousand-dollar down payment.

In September 1865, McKee, like Wadkins before him, began to charge tuition. With a student body of more than six hundred and a paid faculty of three, the school needed money. "Any person disposed to 'lend to the Lord' the means of increasing our efficiency," ran his ad in the *Colored Tennessean*, "is hereby solicited in the name of God's poor ones, to send by mail or Adam's Express, money, clothing material, or books and papers suitable for Sabbath School." But by now McKee had learned, as Wadkins had tried to instruct him years before, that unless his students had a material stake in the school they would not take their studies seriously.[34]

Besieged by local whites, alienated from the established freedmen community, McKee counted more and more on General Fisk's support. But as Ogden, Smith, and Cravath busily made their rounds and the full dimension of their mission slowly unfolded, the general's reassurances had a hollow ring. He had denied McKee's requests for housing, because "it was useless to open more colored schools and we would probably have to hunt up some new funding in order to get the families out of the city." The A.M.A. itself had favorably reviewed McKee's efforts in Nashville. "It is truly encouraging," wrote one of its agents, "to see the progress made especially among the young where they are regularly taught by faithfull teachers who are earnest and devoted to their work."[35] But now such praise seemed to McKee like a subterfuge, an attempt to keep him off guard as Ogden and the A.M.A. plotted to displace him. Perhaps it was symptomatic of McKee's deteriorating health that he would later claim not to have suspected what Ogden and his allies were up to, until the new school's opening day.

Ogden, Smith, and Cravath did not make McKee's mistake of naming their school after themselves. They knew that Clinton Bowen Fisk was the key to their success and no more immune to flattery than any other general. His name prominently displayed on the school's banner and shingle and stationery would give their institution immediate credibility with ex-slaves, who were increasingly turning to the general and his bureau for protection. Fisk was warned that if he permitted Smith and Cravath to name their school after him, ex-slaves would think it was the general's own official academy, and "the wholesale depletion of other schools will lead to mischief in which the Bureau will be involved."[36] But Fisk, whose own education had been piecemeal, rather liked having a school named after him, and on January 9, 1866, he rode with pride to the dedication of the Fisk Free Colored School.[37]

Fisk's opening was "celebrated first by a street parade," recalled alumna Lula Crosthwaite, who was five years old at the time:

> The parade was headed by a band of colored men, some dressed in soldiers' clothes. Most of them were from the army, but they all looked like soldiers to me. Some had on uniform caps and some had on hats. Their musical instruments were mostly brass horns. I stood on the corner of Church and Summer Streets holding my grandmother's hand. There were open carriages . . . filled with citizens both white and colored . . . followed by men, women and children on foot going out to become students of Fisk. . . . There were some women dressed in cotton dresses and handkerchiefs on their heads taking with them their grandchildren by the hand.[38]

Under a flapping banner of stars and stripes, McKee sat miserably as General Fisk exchanged pleasantries with Smith and Ogden and Tennessee's newly elected Reconstructionist governor William Gannaway "Parson" Brownlow, the denunciatory scourge of secessionism, bombilated about the necessity of freedmen working and studying to make themselves productive citizens (though not exactly full-fledged: the governor would not favor black suffrage until his second term, when he needed black votes to hold back the rising Democratic tide of reenfranchised former rebels). It was characteristic of the advice whites tended to give black people in that era that just as General Fisk, himself a refugee from rural life, had urged ex-slaves to return to the countryside, the legendarily precipitous and intemperate Brownlow advised the faculty to be "prudent and cautious" and the freedmen "mild and temperate" to avoid antagonizing local whites.[39]

General Fisk held himself up as an example of what a man of humble origins could accomplish with the benefit of an education. He recalled his own boyhood, when his mother had bound him out to a farmer, "how the farmer sat in his mother's cabin, and how the contract was written by which he was bound out; how he was to be clothed and sent to school; how his bundle was tied up, and how he was put up on the horse, behind the farmer, with his mother's blessing and tears." Only a few months ago, said Fisk, a citizen of Central Tennessee was tied up to a stake and whipped with forty stripes, and "for what? Because he had taught a class of eight colored boys to read the spelling book." He rejoiced that "the times are not now as they used to be. Why a little time ago," he said, gesturing toward the phalanx of black army musicians arrayed behind him, "those boys up there who have been discoursing such sweet music, were listening to the notes of the horn of the overseer. Today, thank God, they blow their own horn."[40]

McKee did not comprehend the full dimension of Fisk's betrayal until the cultured, towering Erastus Milo Cravath stood up to explain his mission. Speaking in a thunderous voice, Cravath not only offered to the thousands of freedmen in attendance a tuition-free education and "the inducement of help in books and clothing" but actually had the audacity to proclaim his school "the first fair chance of education ever enjoyed in this locality."

A devastated Joseph McKee sat through the rest of the festivities like a gloomy troll. "Your declared design," he later wrote the general, "of discountenancing commitments of one association on the field of another . . . wholly blinded me as to the aim of the Fisk School till the inauguration, & first week's practice forced upon me the following conclusions[:] . . . 1st That I am not *needed* . . . 2d that I am not *wanted*."

McKee tried to stick to a tuition system that Fisk School had deemed "oppressive" and "belittling," but now his students and their parents began to bargain with him. "Those hitherto quite able and willing to pay the small rates imposed for books, clothing, fuel, now, all at once, profess the most abject poverty," he reported. "Foolishly supposing that, to compete with the new school, we will do anything, many shrewdly hint that in consideration of such and such favors, they & their children will continue at our school."

Cravath, however, was defiant. He conceded that the school "*is* near that owned by [McKee's] Mission, being by the street two squares distant," but he

did not hesitate to take the property notwithstanding the one objection to it. These [freedmen] are ignorant and impulsive, and we cannot help it if in some instances they act foolishly and show fondness for novelty. We cannot prevent [McKee's] children from leaving his schools, or threatening to come over if disciplined. We cannot prevent the people fleeing poverty or sinking to sell their children to the school for favors. We experience no such difficulty.

McKee had been "laboring to build up a self sustaining denominational school and he thinks our enterprise interferes with that." But "as a mission work," he insisted, "there is more than we both can do."[41]

Alarmed by the controversy, General Fisk proposed that Cravath and company meet with McKee. But the little Irishman had had enough. He accused Ogden and the other founders of having established their school "in violation of the plainest principles of comity, and in the exercise of what seems so much worldly *strategy*," an accusation that would be leveled at Fisk's founders for the rest of the century.

Thus, just as McKee had undercut Daniel Wadkins by not charging tuition, Fisk had now undercut McKee. Young Maggie Porter, who had abandoned Wadkins for McKee, recalled standing in the playground at the McKee School when a friend rushed up and "said there was a school out on Cedar where they will give you books, and you don't have to pay a dollar a month, and your mother can keep the dollar. Everybody went. They didn't say anything—just grabbed up their things and left. It was the beginning of Fisk."[42]

6

THE ANGELS
CHANGED MY NAME

FISK

1866–1868

Oh, in Dixie's land they've took to education
And joined the whole universal Yankee nation,
Look away, look away, look away, Dixie Land.
Fisk student song

Among the crowd of ex-slaves who jostled with Maggie Porter for a place
at Fisk that opening day were at least four other future Jubilee Singers: Jennie Jackson, to whom more and more of her ailing mother's laundering
work had fallen; America Robinson, whose father had smuggled her into
the city on an army wagon after the Battle of Murfreesboro; Eliza Walker,
the nine-year-old daughter of a manumitted slave woman and her husband,
an emancipated slave who kept an icehouse in the city.

The fourth was Thomas Rutling. With his older brother, Rutling had fled
his former master's farm to Nashville and lived with his sister, who taught
him some rudiments of reading and figuring. He had grown into a strong,
round-faced man with soft, almost feminine features. He "worked at level-
ing breastworks for a while," he recalled, driving a cart for a few cents a
day, and "made the acquaintance of some soldiers, thinking I might get a

chance to beat the drum, which had long been the height of my ambition."[1] The soldiers dubbed him "Rollicking Tom" for his high jinks, a nickname that would eventually follow him onto the stage.[2]

Once the breastworks were demolished, the only work Rutling could find was shining boots.

> Among my customers was an army surgeon, who seemed to have a liking for me, so, one morning, as I blacked his boots, he asked, "Would you like to be my Buttons?"
>
> Although I did not know what he meant, I said, "Yes, sir."
>
> . . . A few hours later I was walking up and down the hall of the doctor's house, counting my brass buttons and believing I was the most important boy on earth. The doctor's wife was very kind to me and taught me the alphabet and how to spell "Tom," and many other monosyllable words.

Before the Yankee surgeon left the service, he recommended Rutling to Mrs. Cravath at the Fisk Free Colored School, where he would remain for the next five years, waiting tables and "working and studying as I could."[3]

The Fisk Free Colored School recruited teachers of an evangelical bent, drawing many of them from Cravath's alma mater, Oberlin College. It was not work for just anybody. If there were "any poor broken down teachers in the North," Ogden asserted, "let them stay there, but let the good ones be sent here where they are most needed."[4] A Memphis missionary made a special plea for female teachers, for each "sensible, educated, good woman," he said, "is a fountain of immeasurable good."[5]

Edward Parmelee Smith warned that Nashville's whites did not support schools, "countenance negro teaching," or rent rooms to teachers.[6] The school provided horsehair mattresses and carpeted the creaking floors of the barracks with cocoa matting, but recruits were advised to bring bedding ("i.e. tick for straw & hay pillow, sheets, blankets, muskito bat [netting]"), towels, dishes, knife and fork, teacup and saucer, plate, washbasin (preferably tin), and "whatever stores they can bring . . . as eatables are high."[7] A teacher named Helen Clarissa Morgan was distressed to find on her arrival nothing provided but a hospital cot, a washstand, a table, a crude wardrobe, and a small "very unmanageable" stove.[8] Female teachers were obliged to split kindling, haul coal, and build fires in the public sitting rooms, which were the only heated spaces in the school.[9]

Their pay was poor—the board proposed paying one of its missionaries (a family man) a hundred dollars a year—and seldom on time.[10] Another Fisk teacher was offered fifteen dollars a month. The food was even worse, and sickness dogged them all year long. The first teachers were "heartily abused, . . . accused of the greatest immoralities, insulted on the public streets, socially ostracized by the respectable portion of the community, and of those who professed to be followers of Him who went about doing good, 'passed by on the other side.' "[11] Northerners who sacrificed "home, and the comforts of refined life, to discharge their duty to the poor and the needy," wrote one of Tennessee's Methodist missionaries, "have been insulted, treated with contempt and indignity, if not with personal violence."[12]

"The first and greatest thing now is to secure regularity and punctuality in attendance," wrote a Memphis missionary, "and in order to do this I find it necessary to know the pupils at home as well as at school. . . . The tendency of the majority, I think, is to rove around or lie down in idleness when left entirely to themselves, but there are noble exceptions."[13] Some rules struck former slaves as gratuitous. Yankee schoolmasters enjoined their students, many of whom had little clothing at all, not to bring silk, satin, or velvet gowns and thereby "prevent extravagance and check the spirit of rivalry in costly and gaudy dresses."[14]

Teachers found some of their pupils impeded by their humility. "They were afraid to talk lest they not give back what the book said; afraid to write lest they spoil the fine white paper."[15] The severe corporal punishment of slavery's regime led some parents to expect and in some cases even demand that teachers whip their children. One of McKee's pupils used to spring to her feet and strike her disruptive sister on the head or shake her by the shoulders, thinking she was doing the teacher a service.[16] "I was never able to please parents about discipline," wrote a later A.M.A. missionary. "They said I was too easy." "Why didn't you strop her, Ma'am?" a former slave asked about his granddaughter after she had defied her teacher. "I'm her grandfather and I put her into your hands. If she don't learn, Ma'am, use your strap." "Please, Ma'am, whip Isaiah," begged another mother. "I pays for him to learn." "Whipping would go on in the homes," black teachers predicted, "until slavery's generation was gone."[17]

Some slave children were so starved for affection that the slightest kindness transformed them. The black educator and preacher Henry Hugh Proctor of Fisk recalled an incident "that vitally affected my life." On his way to a mission school, he met his teacher, who simply put his hand upon his head:

> I am sure he was not conscious of the impression he was making. But that touch awakened in me sensations that have not yet died away. My teacher loved me. Although that occurred many years ago, I could take one to within ten feet of the exact spot where it occurred. It was the place of the touch of life.[18]

For many former slaves, however, Northern teachers took some getting used to. One recalled that she had been scared of her teacher "because he was a white man," and up to that point, her interactions with white men had been terrifying.[19] But even after they had adjusted to the color of their teachers' skins, black Southerners could still find even the best-intentioned white Northerner almost as confounding as white Southerners did.

Wayman Williams of Texas recalled his first impression of his Northern teachers:

> They did not talk like the folks here, and they did not know how to talk to us. They could not understand our language. They did not know what we meant when we said "titty" for "sister" and "budder" for "brother" and "nanny" for "mammy." They had to learn how we talk. Just for fun we would call ourselves big names to the teacher. Some be the name General Lee and Stonewall Jackson. We be name one name one day and another name the next. Until the teacher got to know us she could not tell the difference, for we looked alike to her.[20]

Names were a serious matter among former slaves struggling to establish their own identity.[21] Booker T. Washington remembered of his first day at school:

> I noticed that all of the children had at least two names, and some of them indulged in what seemed to me the extravagance of having three. I was in deep perplexity, because I knew that the teacher would demand of me at least two names, and I had only one. By the

time the occasion came for the enrolling of my name, an idea occurred to me which I thought would make me equal to the situation; and so, when the teacher asked me what my full name was, I
calmly told him "Booker Washington," as if I had been called by that
name all my life; and by that name I have since been known.[22]

Martin Jackson recalled that emancipated slaves usually adopted their
former masters' names "because it was the logical thing to do and the easi-
est way to be identified than it was through affection for the master. Also,
the government seemed to be in a almighty hurry to have us get names. We
had to register as someone, so we could be citizens."[23] But many freed
slaves discarded the names their masters gave them: names like Donkey,
Coffee, Quaminy that were tortured anglicizations of the African names of
their ancestors—Dongko, Kofi, Kwame.[24]

One Northern teacher recounted how her former slave pupils responded when she called the roll. "No one answered, and I was obliged to
go round again and make out a new list." At first she could not distinguish
one from another, nor even their sexes, but "in time I began to get acquainted with some of their faces. I could remember that 'Cornhouse' yesterday was 'Primus' to-day." A boy who had called himself "Quash" was
now "Brian" and ready to "mash" the mouth of anyone who called him
"Quash."[25]

"Among the first questions Northern teachers asked blacks was, 'Were
you a slave? Where did [you] live &c,' " recalled James Thomas.

If the fellow said he lived in Arkansaw, he was corrected and told
that Arkansaw was not correct, that the proper name was
[Arkansas]. If the fellow said he lived near Helena, he was told that
was wrong. You must say Helleena. About that time the Negro
would scratch his bald head. Then [the Yankee] would express his
surprise and say that he "never knew colored people got bald."

"They were a little tiresome," Thomas concluded, "but as their mission was
to instruct, we had to make the most of our lessons."[26]

They did. A Fisk teacher and Oberlinian named Elizabeth Easter was assigned the task of writing dispatches back to the A.M.A. for publication in
its journal. ("We must have things spicy and good," advised an A.M.A. func-

tionary.) Easter reported her astonishment at the rapid progress the children made, and, over the years, many white teachers would assert that black students memorized faster than white children, possibly due to a centuries-old oral tradition.[27] But Easter was perhaps most moved by the elderly former slaves who attended night school poring over their McGuffey's *Readers*.[28] "An old lady by the name of Lizzie Wilson was a slave for over 50 years & has made such progress in reading as would surprise one unaccustomed to the zeal of these poor people," wrote Easter.

> Beginning with the alphabet she has mastered words of two sylla-ble[s] in less than twice that number of weeks.
>
> On inquiry I found the key to her success. She said—"I have been praying for this very time for near 50 years and now that I is here I must work with all my heart. Yes miss, my whole heart is set on learning to read five chapters in the Bible before I die. Then I will be ready to go."
>
> Could she study all day like some others she might soon do so, but all day she toils for bread and nights are given to study.[29]

"Most of those who attend the night school are adults," added Easter's colleague Catherine Crosby.[30]

Their teachers learned that "an idea was clearer to them than the printed page. As one old woman read, 'A soft answer turneth away wrath, but grievous words stir up a fuss.' "[31] At night school, the Bible lessons were "most attractive of all to the older ones. Their own questions and remarks are very interesting and instructive. . . . When a new truth, either in science or religion, draws upon their minds, their whole face is radiant with surprise and gratitude."[32]

A white minister once asked an ancient former slave why she was carrying around a schoolbook. " 'Well,' she said, 'I has got so old I can't learn the letters' ":

> I am three or four hundred years old. I tries to learn the letters, but I forgets them as fast as I learns them. I was only looking to see how they looks, for when I dies and goes home to heaven, I hopes to be able to learn to read the blessed Bible, and I thought I might remember how it looked to me here.[33]

Within a month of Fisk's opening, the school's enrollment soared from 200 to 600 students, a hundred of whom studied in night class. By May, there were 788, by June, almost 900, and still enrollment grew, until it averaged the school's self-declared maximum of 1,000.[34]

"I clap and sing / Like anything," a young Nashville freedman named Benny Bilboe used to versify on his way to Fisk:

> And when I grow some bigger
> I'll read and spell
> So very well
> You'll never call me nigger.[35]

Local whites, especially the idle and impoverished Irish boys from the Broad Street Bottoms to whom no education was offered, deeply resented the sight of blacks marching to school with their books and slates. Fisk was periodically damaged by vandals, "and our pupils are almost daily assailed on their way to and from School, and frequently are cut and bruised to an alarming extent." Black children did not take this treatment lying down, however. Ogden complained of "the disgraceful mobs of boys, white and black, that throng the alleys and byways, west of the Chattanooga Depot, throwing stones and other missiles at each other."[36]

Things could have been worse. They were far worse in Memphis, where the Reverend E. O. Tade of the American Missionary Association had established a mission called Lincoln Chapel that included a freedmen's school similar to Fisk. Near a Union bastion called Fort Pickering, a community of ex-slaves had gathered under the protection of an artillery regiment of black troops, one of several that had been assigned the task of enforcing martial law in the city. The local Irish police bitterly resented their patrols, and when the black troops were mustered out and disarmed, the police sought them in the saloons of the black district and began to make arrests, beating several soldiers severely with their nightsticks.

No one knows exactly what ensued. The Southern press claimed that on May 21, 1866, a large body of blacks, incited to riot by "the teachings of Northern 'school marm's' in the nigger schools," turned on the police, killing one of them.[37] But a congressional inquiry would find that black troops had merely protested the brutal treatment of their comrades. In any case, somebody fired a gun, whereupon a white mob armed with knives and revolvers began to rampage through the black neighborhood. "Robbery, burning & murder continued all night in every part of the city," Tade reported. The next day, black men, women, and children were shot in broad daylight "as if they were mad dogs. . . . The sick were murdered in their beds—a young lady of rare promise as a teacher, & who had worked hard to get an education, undertook to flee [but] was met in her doorway, shot down—pushed back into the house & the house set on fire."

For the next two nights, Memphis was "brilliantly illuminated" by the flames from four black churches, twelve schools, and ninety houses. Tade's mission lost $2,000 worth of property; the black community, $110,000. On Thursday, May 24, men, women, and children gathered in the rubble of Lincoln Chapel. "In silence they pressed our hands, and tears redeemed the ashes at our feet." Some asked if they would ever have a school again. "Be of good courage," Tade replied. "There are ashes enough to build two Lincoln Chapels."[38]

"This nation has set the black man free with the bayonet," a Freedmen's Bureau agent wrote General Fisk, "then let the nation if needs be protect his life with the same weapon."[39] Fisk took his advice to heart. There were cases of arson in Nashville; a black church and school were burned down twice in September 1866; five schools were destroyed in 1868, when the Ku Klux Klan openly paraded in the city streets.[40] The vigilance of Fisk and his successors, the presence of armed black troops, and a sizable armed freedmen community prevented anything approaching the riot's horrors in Nashville, but it represented a horrifying potentiality that haunted the city for decades to come.[41]

However secure Nashville's black community may have felt under Fisk's regime, conditions remained desperate. A local reporter wrote:

> Right here in Nashville, we already have examples of sloth and filthiness that can hardly be surpassed in any other city. The lower class of Negroes inhabit what were once stables, old rickety out-houses, small unventilated cabins and hovels. . . . Now in all these places . . . from three to ten Negroes live crowded up together like so many pigs, breathing over and over again their poisonous breath, until diseases seize them and they die. The black hole of Calcutta was a little more severe, but not more sure of death than in these over-crowded hovels.[42]

The grace in suffering of some ex-slaves astonished missionaries like Elizabeth Easter. "I wish I had a thousand dollars," one old lady told her. "I would give it all to you teachers that come to teach us poor black people."[43] But the marks of slavery were a daily horror. "Another of this number died a few days ago," wrote Miss M. A. Parker. "Her every appearance was that of abuse and trembling servitude." When asked about the scars on her face, she replied, "Oh, that's where my mistress pushed me into the fire." But what made her so lame? "My master kicked my knee and knocked the bone off."

"When I expressed sympathy and interest in her, tears of gratitude flowed down her wrinkled face which was itself a picture of wonder and affliction." "O, Missus," she said. "I thank you for talking so pretty to me."[44] From the refugees themselves, wrote Easter, "we have many testimonies of their appreciation of our work. It was but yesterday that the members of the 13th Col^d regiment voted unanimously to present to the Fisk Col^d school . . . their fine melodion."[45]

Not every encounter was inspiring. For all the progress at Fisk School, Ogden warned about raising expectations too high:

> Few people who talk about the Negro character seem to understand it. It is a most lamentable fact that as a race they are exceeding low both in morals and intellect. And how could they be otherwise? They have endured enough to spoil an angelic nature. . . . I never realized the deep and *damning* effects of human slavery until I was brought in close and daily contact with these people. Their depravity is frightful, and their ignorance mournful. Years and years & *years* of patient and persistent labor must ensue in order to remove these obstacles. Yet there is much, very much, that is promising.

Exaggerating black progress, Ogden warned, "injures the Negroes themselves, by encouraging arrogance and pride which with their necessary ignorance is truly pitiable. And then it leads the people of the North to expect more than can be realized." He feared that "much harm" was being done by the sentimentalized, "whitewashed accounts" of the freedmen he read in Northern papers and missionary literature. "The fact is simply this—these people are not extraordinary in any of their peculiarities. I believe almost any race of people submitted to similar treatment and influences, would present similar characteristics both in vice and virtue."[46]

An Oberlinian reported "that among the undesirable traits of character that meet our view is an intense selfishness. One negro is with difficulty brought to aid another, however great the distress, unless he is a member of the same family. In our camp, orphan children have been left nearly to perish, and but for our interference, evils of this nature would be constant."[47] And yet, after the war, missionaries would marvel at the acts of generosity they routinely witnessed in the midst of the greatest deprivation. "Families are sadly broken & many many orphan children are in our midst," wrote Catherine Crosby, "yet we find a kind & benevolent spirit among many of this people and some who are sometimes obliged to beg their own bread are willing to share their last crust with the poor houseless wanderers."[48]

Missionaries were especially troubled by what they saw as rampant infidelity as, in the blast of emancipation, some slave marriages fell apart. "An unusual number of family quarrels and dissentions has come to my notice during the few weeks past," wrote Parker. "Wives have been shamefully abused and in sickness have been left without the least provision for their comfort. I found one young woman entirely alone and very sick. The night before her husband left her without light or fuel and unable to rise from her bed." When Parker asked her if she had been alone all night, she replied "with a subdued but pleasant smile and said, 'Yes, God & I.' She also said that words could not describe her sufferings, either mental or physical, during the time of her husband's abuse and desertion."[49]

Some missionaries were horrified by the amount of theft they witnessed in the camps. But others marveled that there was not more. Mrs. Crosby came upon three children "out gathering rags, old iron, coal—anything that can be *eaten, burned* or *sold.* Can we wonder that they should covet and steal?"[50] That some were lazy "we would not deny," she conceded. "Yet it is often difficult to judge of real worth in the midst of *real* and almost *hopeless want.* . . . Alas, how little we can realize the sad reality of their lives."[51]

Perhaps it was too much to ask of sheltered young Northern whites to judge former slaves fairly. But for some slaves, lectures from whites, be they Southern or Northern, on such virtues as honesty, hard work, chastity, and fidelity were intolerable. Stealing was a case in point. For many slaves, theft had been a necessity. Some of the masters who stole their labor, their families, even their identities encouraged their slaves to steal from neighboring farms. Even foraging federal troops employed former slaves to steal on their behalf on their marches through the South.

Had the missionaries understood the conditions under which many slaves were wedded before the war, they would have marveled at the devotion of free black fathers and mothers, husbands and wives. Many slave marriages were arranged by masters purely on the basis of what they deemed the principles of sound breeding. Masters routinely bought slaves and assigned them to mates in order to improve the quality of what they called their "stock." Eliza Elsey's Texas master took "the strongest men and women, put them together in a cabin so's they raise him some more husky children."[52] If a slave woman proved fertile, her masters "were proud of her. . . . I was stout and they were saving me for a breeding woman. . . . I'd hear them saying, 'She's got a fine shape; she'll make a good breeder.' "[53] A Mississippi slave owner named William B. Trotter exulted that it was "remarkable the number of slaves which may be raised from one woman in the course of forty or fifty years with the proper kind of attention."[54] Masters took great pride in the young their slaves produced and exhibited them like prize calves and ewes.[55]

If couples failed to produce a lot of children, they were often separated. "If the woman didn't have any childrens," recalled Sylvia Watkins of Nashville, "she was put on the block and sold and another woman bought. You see they raised the childrens to make money on, just like we raise pigs to sell."[56] Lulu Wilson's mother said that

> she took with my paw, and I's born, but a long time passed and didn't no more young ones come. So they say my paw am too old and wore out for breeding, and they want her to take with this here young buck. So the Hodges sent the nigger hounds on my paw and run him away from the place, and maw always say he went to the free states. So she took up with my step-paw, and they must have pleased the white folks what wanted niggers to breed like livestock, because she birthed nineteen children.

Some slave marriages did not survive emancipation. "When we was freed," recalled Primous Magee, "the slaves that was married all had to get license and be married over again. My pa quit my ma when he found this out, and wouldn't marry her over again. A heap of them quit that way. I reckon they felt free sure enough, as they was freed from slavery and from marriage."[57] Forced to breed together, Mollie Dawson's "mother and father never did loves each other likes they ought to, so they separated as soon as they was free."[58]

General Fisk insisted that most slave couples were faithful and understood "what marriage is among the whites."[59] During the war, McKee's missionaries conducted mass weddings of as many as seventy-five couples, many of whom were already living together; it was a law of the camp that men and women could not live together unless united in marriage. The chaplain made them promise to avoid "improper intimacy with any other till God shall separate you by death." Afterward, the brides and grooms who were students "begged the chaplain and others who went around to see their tablets to take some of the wedding cake for themselves and friends." They were each presented with a wedding certificate "bearing a picture of the 'old flag.' "[60] Albert Todd remembered laughing "when a black man and his wife has already been married for fifty years and has to go out and get a license and get married again."[61]

A Union officer maintained that "the Negro has domestic relations in as strong a degree as a white man, and however far south his master may drive him he will sooner or later return to his family."[62] So it proved among many former slaves after the war. Lulu Wilson did not get along with her slave stepfather but admired him for being "a fool for his own young'uns, 'cause at the end of the wars when they set the niggers free, he tramped over half the country, gathering up them young'uns they done sold away."[63]

Nashville's *Colored Tennessean* ran scores of "Information Wanted" ads asking the whereabouts of long-lost kin. A single issue contained twelve seeking the whereabouts of twenty-five relations. Despite their poverty, Benjamin and Flora East offered two hundred dollars for the return of their children, Polly and George Washington, who were taken from them in 1849 and removed to Texas. Augustus Bryant and his wife, Lutitia, sought their five children, ages eight to twenty, whom they had not seen in five years. Eliza Van Ratlie sought her two sons, who had been sold in Nashville to a trader and taken to Virginia.[64]

"Most of them never got together again even after they [were] set free because they don't know where one or the other is." The practice of freed slaves to rename themselves, illiteracy, the hostility of past owners and local officials, the absence of public records—the federal census had listed slaves only by age, sex, and color under their owners' names—made the

odds of finding a long-lost relative daunting. "After freedom a heap of people say they was going to name themselves over," recalled Lee Guidon.
"They named theirselves big names, then went roaming around like wild,
hunting cities. They changed up so [that] it was hard to tell who or where
anybody was. Heap of them died, and you didn't know when you hear
about it if he was your folks hardly."[65]

Thomas Rutling of the Jubilees never found the mother who had been
sold away from him when he was two years old, but the soprano Maggie
Porter had a fitful reunion with her older sister, who had been sent to another plantation during the war. Ever since emancipation, Porter's mother
had hoped she might appear someday "in the tide of homeless freedmen
that in those days ebbed and flowed through every Southern city." On her
way to and from Fisk School, Porter used to pass the Chattanooga Depot
and scan the passengers for someone who looked like her sister. One day
when she was alone in the house that her mother kept for a local white
family, a woman appeared at the door asking for her mother. Instructed
never to admit a stranger into the house, Porter refused to let her in. The
woman protested that she was her long-lost sister, but Porter refused to believe her. In tears, her sister returned to Mississippi, "and it was some time
before she could get over the chill of this reception sufficiently to come
make her home with her mother."[66]

The effect of such reunions on former slaves was profound. A slave
named Diana Wagner was separated on the auction block from her son
"when he was a nursing baby," but he was told her name and after emancipation he eventually found her. "She said she was willing to die that the
Lord let her live to see her baby again and had taken care of him through all
these years."[67] When Louis Hughes was reunited with his brother William,
whom he had not seen since early childhood, "it seemed, and indeed was,
wonderful that we should have met again after so long a separation. . . . As
I looked into the faces of his wife and children, I seemed to have entered a
new and broader life, and one in which the joys of social intercourse had
marvelously expanded."[68]

GIDEON'S BAND

COUNTRY SCHOOLS

1867–1870

In 1865, at the age of fourteen, Ella Sheppard left her father's home in Cincinnati to visit her long-lost mother, Sarah, in Nashville. Sarah Hannah Sheppard had remained with her master's family in Okolona, Mississippi, where she had given birth to a second daughter, Rosa, apparently by a white man.[1] But after the war, she sent word to Ella that she had returned with them to Nashville to live with the Donelson family. When Sheppard saw her mother, "I did not even know her face." Their visit lasted three months, during which Sarah told her daughter the story of her Cherokee great-grandmother, Rosa, of Mammy Viney's prophecy by the Cumberland River, of the bargain Sarah struck with her mistress to free little Samuella from bondage. "My back was never struck," she told her daughter, "but my heart is like a checkerboard with its stripes of sorrow."[2]

By now, Ella's father, Simon, seemed to be prospering again and could afford to send his family to Xenia, Ohio, to spend the summer with the freedmen community that lived around the once-moribund Wilberforce University. Recently reopened as a freedmen's college under the sponsorship of the African Methodist Episcopal Church, Wilberforce was under siege. A few months before, on the very night of Lincoln's assassination, white arsonists had burned down the university's main building, and it is

possible that Ella and her stepmother traveled to Xenia to assist in rebuild-
ing the campus at Tawawa Springs. But soon after they arrived, word
reached Sheppard that her father, Simon, had died in one of the cholera
epidemics that periodically swept through Cincinnati's Ragtown.[3]

Sheppard and her stepmother hurried home to find creditors and
lawyers teeming over her father's hard-won property. When they withdrew, the family was destitute. "Everything went," she wrote, "even my own
private piano." Sheppard sought work as a seamstress, nurse, maid, laun-
dress: whatever she could find. A free black photographer named James
Presley Ball took an interest in her and bought her vocal lessons from
Madame Caroline Revé, who agreed to take a black student only on condition that Sheppard not endanger Revé's position in the music department
of the exclusive Glendale Female College by disclosing to anyone who her
teacher was.[4] "More than all that," Sheppard recalled, she was required to
enter through "the back way, and received my lessons in a back room up
stairs, from nine to quarter of ten at night."

After only a few lessons, Ball withdrew his patronage, and necessity
compelled Ella Sheppard to accept an unlikely assignment as the teacher of
a black subscription school in Gallatin, Tennessee, about twenty-five miles
northeast of Nashville, which had been built under Ogden's supervision
with donations from local blacks totaling four hundred dollars.[5] All
through the South, blacks had begun to establish small country schools to
teach themselves and their children the rudiments of reading and writing.
The schools were often no more than shacks set off in the woods. It is hard
to conceive of the dangers and hardships this slender, sickly, and solitary
fifteen-year-old faced as she trudged up to her school yard. Such schools
were a favorite target of white arsonists; only recently, a similar academy in
Brentwood, south of Nashville, had been burned to the ground.[6] At Trenton, in western Tennessee, local whites refused construction funds from the
Freedmen's Bureau for a proposed church and school on the grounds that
"the Bureau might want to control it and would furnish a yankee teacher
who would teach incendiary doctrines to the colored people 'and . . . they
did not want [to expose] their nigger subject[s] to any such influences.' "[7] A
Northern missionary in Somerville, Tennessee, reported that he labored "at
the risk of my life every day. The spirit of hell and damnation is rife here &
it would take but a spark more to cause it to boil over and manifest itself in
the most diabolical outrages."[8] Another teacher in rural Tennessee reported
how " 'Fellows of the basest sort' broke up his benches, broke down his

door, and gave him such broad hints of visiting him with their wrath, that he shook off the dust of his feet against them and left."[9]

The danger varied from place to place. In nearby Franklin, returning rebels threatened to destroy a school for freedmen and told blacks they would not be employed if they supported such schools. But nobody interfered with the school for the first seven months of its existence. A visit converted an ex–rebel colonel to the cause of black education. From what he saw, he said, "he could not doubt that their capacities for learning were equal to those of any other race." He told the teacher "he would do all he could to protect the school." A local lawyer warned that "it is not safe, now that slavery is destroyed, to have the freedmen uneducated amongst us, and that the prosperity of this place as well as the entire South demands the educated laborer." Some whites were also grateful to the mission's Sabbath school for occupying the black children who had formerly spent their time "in all sort of amusements—to the annoyance of the white citizens and . . . the peace and quiet of the place."[10]

In 1865, two Gallatin schools had been burned to the ground; however, it was not the threats of local whites that chased off Ella Sheppard but her inability to earn a living.[11] Though thirty-five students crowded into her makeshift schoolhouse, most of them "did not pay, and from the first term's work I was able to save but *six dollars*." Cutting her losses, she made her way down to Nashville, where Ogden allowed her to enroll at Fisk on condition that she find work. A friend sent her a music student, "and in a few weeks I had two others." Though often too ill to attend classes, and able to support herself only from "the sewing I did at odd moments" in her sickbed, her musical talents soon came to the attention of Fisk's self-proclaimed maestro, George White. "If she is the right sort of stuff," White wrote his brother-in-law, "I shall hope to raise money by a concert or two after a while."[12]

First Sergeant George Leonard White of the Seventy-third Ohio Volunteer Infantry had been medically discharged at Chattanooga in July 1864 and "was sent North on the Hospital train." After regaining a little of his weight and strength back home in Chillicothe, Ohio, he decided to return to Tennessee and dedicate himself to the uplift of the freedmen. Employing what skills he had picked up clerking for General Joseph Hooker, White went to work in the quartermaster's department at Nashville in 1865, and then became assistant to John Ogden in the newly established Freedmen's Bureau, where he was able, "with some ups and downs, to do fairly regular work."[13]

He volunteered for a while at the McKee School but saw in McKee's nemesis, Erastus Milo Cravath, a man of vision. As soon as Fisk opened, White began to dedicate his off-hours to the school, teaching music and penmanship. By June 1866, he had become such a fixture at the Fisk Free Colored School that he was included in the back row of its first faculty portrait, towering over his colleagues like a gaunt, Lincolnesque ghost.

White's attachment to Fisk was romantic as well as messianic. In the portrait, he stands next to the first female teacher at Fisk, Cravath's younger sister Laura. Laura Amelia Cravath was a handsome, somber young woman who had attended the Ladies' Department of Oberlin College with another of Fisk's first teachers, Elizabeth Easter. Like Easter and so many of the women who taught at Fisk, Laura Cravath's health was poor. (Two years after submitting her eloquent reports on the freedmen to the A.M.A., Easter would die of illness contracted at Fisk.[14]) Laura was plagued with migraines and neuralgia that knocked her out of commission for weeks at a time. Nevertheless, she and the consumptive White reached an understanding that in due time, God prosper Fisk School and the freedmen, they would be married.

In March 1867, the state of Tennessee passed a bill that provided free education for blacks and whites alike. This was a blow to Fisk's primary-school department, many of whose paying students would drift away to free public schools in September. Ogden believed that the state program had been designed in part to flush out Northern teachers like himself and put the education of black children into the hands of their former masters. "We cannot retire from the field at present," he insisted.

> Should we leave now it is not certain that these incipient efforts of the state and some of the cities would be continued. The progress of the ten thousand beginning to learn must not be arrested—others of the ninety-thousand of school age must be gathered in. . . . We implore the christian public to continue its contribution until this crisis is past.[15]

Ogden's competitive, entrepreneurial streak came out in a letter to Edward Parmelee Smith. "A working school—poor at that—will not flourish in the woods. . . . What we want in this state . . . is a thorough, well organized system of Normal training for colored teachers. . . . I regard Nashville as one of the best points in the state," he said. Fisk was already "looked upon as the pioneer in the work. It has the inside track. It may just as well be first as second or third. My great anxiety is that it may be *ready* and *free* to accept of any help that may turn up for us."[16]

Though the vast majority of its students were black and most of its staff Congregational, Fisk held that it offered an education "without regard to race or sex" and "entirely free from any denominational biases."[17] Only a few whites availed themselves of the school, including a German boy, "who is now teaching with marked success." Though local whites still maintained that "these niggers can't learn," Ogden predicted that "*their children*, if taught at all, will be taught by colored teachers before ten years." But if Fisk was to become the "leading state Normal University," it had to remain fastidiously "clean of any ecclesiastical complications." An 1868 report that the school's new Howard Chapel was Congregational would bring howls of outrage from the staff, who signed a petition of protest and sent it to the home office.[18] Ogden constantly had to reassure the ministers of various black congregations that their parishioners could regard Fisk as neutral ground.

Within a few weeks of opening ceremonies, the Fisk Free Colored School had already begun to change names in its inexorable march to full university status. Over the following months, it changed from the Fisk Free Colored School to Fisk Academy,[19] then to Fisk School, Fisk High School, and, eventually, Fisk University: apparently only "Fisk" was non-negotiable.[20]

By the fall of 1867, Ogden had established his Normal Department to train the black teachers the state would require to staff its far-flung schools. He rejected proposals to include agricultural and industrial training at Fisk; what the South needed, he insisted, was teachers.[21] One of Ogden's goals was to demonstrate "in practice, what most educators are willing to admit in *theory*, that conversion is the proper door into the kingdom of science, as well as into the kingdom of heaven; . . . that religion can be taught without teaching sectarianism; that science and religion were meant to go hand in hand; that the two joined are the Heaven-appointed means of lighting humanity to its proper standing and true dignity."[22]

Tennessee's public education program also gave an indirect boost to Erastus Milo Cravath's long-derided dream of turning Fisk into a full-fledged university.[23] Cravath believed that black Americans would need a highly educated elite to lead them to true equality and prosperity. Thomas Jefferson had doubted if he could find a single black "capable of tracing and comprehending the investigations of Euclid." Not that he had looked terribly hard, but Jefferson claimed never to have found a single Negro who "had uttered a thought above the level of plain narration" nor "seen the elementary trait of painting or sculpture."[24] John C. Calhoun once mockingly suggested that "if a Negro could be found who could parse Greek or explain Euclid, I should be constrained to admit that he had human possibilities."[25] Cravath was determined to elicit just such an admission from Jefferson's and Calhoun's descendants.

Erastus Milo Cravath grew up in an atmosphere of temperance, piety, and abolitionism. His father, Oren, was an emancipationist farmer from Homer, New York, who used to shelter fugitive slaves. His son never forgot the sight of the runaways huddled in his root cellar: their feet were "swollen, shapeless masses from sleeping in the woods in the dead of a northern winter, when to have kindled a fire would have brought upon them the slave hunter and the blood hounds."

Egged on by Erastus's mother, Oren Cravath braved ruinous fines of a thousand dollars a fugitive to take them in his sleigh to a local black stationmaster for the journey to Canada. Oren also established a Congregational church in Homer, but when a gang of local men disrupted an appearance by Frederick Douglass, his wife persuaded him to resign his deaconship. In 1851, Oren sought refuge among like minds in the abolitionist haven of Oberlin, Ohio. By this time, his son Erastus had grown into a tall, formidable eighteen-year-old. He attended an abolitionist school called New York Central College, studying among black students as well as white and under a black professor of oratory, in whom Cravath first saw "what the colored youth of the land might aspire to."

After a year at New York Central, Erastus and his sister Laura followed their father to Oberlin and enrolled in the Middle Preparatory class. Fortified in its abolitionist zeal by the influx of refugees from Cincinnati's Lane Theological Seminary, Oberlin admitted black students (though not very many: only 3 percent of the eight thousand students who graduated in the decade preceding the end of the war). An earnest student, Cravath helped pay his way by teaching Greek and mathematics and eventually majored in theology under the spellbinding theologian Charles Grandison Finney, who preached that salvation was not limited to some "Elect" but could be attained by "all who ask it."[26]

As one wag described it, the country around Oberlin was "so flat that there is no outlook save heavenward."[27] It was not exactly a party school: social gatherings were condemned as "a grand device of the devil" that led to "vain conversation" and "nameless fooleries" that distracted students from their prayerful pursuit of "perfectionism." At Oberlin, said an alumnus, "one breathed the atmosphere of perpetual revival."[28] Students addressed each other as "Brother" and "Sister" and called revered teachers "Father." The college was a main station on the Underground Railway and a hotbed of radical abolitionism. Fearing they would bring their politics to the pulpit, many congregations would not hire Oberlin graduates, which may partly explain why thirty-eight of Fisk University's faculty would be former Oberlinians and fully a third of the faculty who taught the black student body at nearby Wilberforce University would be Oberlin alumni.

In 1860, Cravath married a Quaker student named Ruth Anna Jackson. Ordained as a minister in nearby Berlin Heights, in December 1863 he accepted an appointment as chaplain of the 101st Ohio Volunteers and served until he was mustered out in June 1865. He was present at the battles of Franklin and Nashville and, well before he was commissioned by the American Missionary Association, had decided to make the education of African Americans his life's work.

He served as the A.M.A.'s field secretary first in Cincinnati and later in New York, where he was put in charge of the association's educational missions in the South. He surveyed them like a military commander. "We hold five vital points," he wrote to his board in 1866: "Nashville and Memphis, Tenn.; Atlanta and Macon, Ga.; and Lexington, Ky." Fisk he touted as "one of the most thoroughly furnished of all the schools in the South." Cravath toured constantly, delegating "but little" as he personally oversaw the construction of buildings, the wording of contracts, the purchasing of supplies. He believed that "thoroughness is the first requirement in all these schools" and recruited as competent a corps of teachers and administrators as he could find.[29]

In the summer of 1867, Laura Cravath married George White while he was still working for the Freedmen's Bureau and volunteering at Fisk.[30] A few months later, to John Ogden's everlasting regret, Cravath appointed White treasurer of Fisk University. It was an odd choice, and some suspected Cravath of nepotism in hiring his brother-in-law. There was no questioning White's ferocious dedication, and he had acquired some bookkeeping skills during the war. But he was mercurial, tactless, grandiose, and disorganized: more temperamental artist than methodical clerk.

Nor would he shrink from using his leverage as keeper of accounts to get his way. Almost immediately, sparks began to fly between White and Ogden. Ogden saw White as a dangerous visionary who might recklessly impede Fisk's progress toward the kind of solid respectability after which the former normal-school principal hankered. White saw Ogden as an embittered, small-minded bureaucrat incapable of leading Fisk to the heights White and his brother-in-law envisioned. Another faculty member suggested that Ogden might be guilty of some irregularities. "Is it right," wrote one, "for a Supt. to *chuck* young ladies under the chin—and especially for a man who wooed and won his present wife while a school girl. . . . What can the religious influence of such a man be?"[31] It did not help Ogden that his young wife was proving a haughty and incompetent, albeit unpaid, matron. Little by little, in his councils with the staff and his letters to his brother-in-law, White chipped away at the school's confidence in its co-founder.

By the summer of 1867, just as Wadkins and McKee might have predicted, the Fisk Free Colored School was free no longer. To support an extended family of twenty teachers, matrons, missionaries, and administrators, the school inevitably began to charge tuition.[32] It plainly needed the money but couched its new policy in the same terms Wadkins and McKee had employed: students had to pay eventually for their education, whether directly or through service, in order to "afford them motives for self reliance and manly independence afterwards."[33] Fisk's retreat from its initial offer of a free education did more than remove "Free" from its name and provide an ailing Joseph McKee with a certain dismal satisfaction. It hastened the exodus of many of its elementary students to the state's new public schools.

In August 1867, Fisk University was formally incorporated, and in September, its Normal Department opened for business with twelve students.[34] By January, a second class had enrolled, and Ogden had established a model program for sixty primary-school pupils. His normal-school program progressed as well as any Ogden had ever seen. An inspector for the Peabody Fund was so impressed by their progress that he gave Fisk an eight-hundred-dollar grant to aid its best students. Two years later, the fund would deem Fisk the best teachers' training school in the entire South.[35]

It was not, however, the most prosperous. "The school was very poor and the food was scarce," recalled Ella Sheppard.

> So many of us shivered through . . . winter with not an inch of flannel upon our bodies. . . . The wind whistled around and groaned so fearfully that we trembled in horror in our beds, thinking the sounds were the cries of lost spirits of the soldiers who had died in them. Our privations and limited food began to tell on the vitality of the students, and some of our best pupils were sacrificed. There was no money even for food, much less for repairs. Many a time a special prayer was offered for the next meal.[36]

Nothing went to waste. Teachers put up hundreds of jars of preserves to keep the students fed. It was during this period that a group of Fisk students dug up the heap of rusty manacles and chains from Porter's slave pen and exchanged them for Bibles and spellers.[37]

When Tennessee introduced universal public education in September 1867, scores of literate and semiliterate African Americans stepped forward to earn their livings teaching in country schools. "I know I can't do much," one young freedman wrote his teacher, "but when I see how ignorant my people are, and how much there is to be done, I want to do my share."[38] Even the wariest of them could not have anticipated what awaited them in the countryside. The prospect of literate blacks voting and competing for jobs horrified whites, many of whom were barely eking out a living in the ravaged South as it was. There was little impetus in Tennessee to educate poor whites, all but a few of whom refused to attend school with blacks. Nor would upper-class Southerners have anything to do with Northern missionaries and their black disciples. "Now look," one merchant fumed, "them blue bellied scoundrels went to Africa, stole the niggers, brought them here, sold them to us, then stole them from us, starved them and otherwise mistreated them, [and] now they . . . want to tell us what to do with the balance of them."[39] To whites "born and raised in the South, accustomed to keeping the Sons of Ham in their proper place," a Tennessee planter remarked, "the impudence of these Negroes is hard to endure. They are entirely corrupted."[40]

White groups like the Knights of the White Camelia, the Order of Pale Faces, and the Order of Zoroaster terrorized freedmen in the postwar South, but in middle Tennessee the hardiest of the brotherhoods was the Ku Klux Klan. Founded in Pulaski by former Confederate officers to oppose black suffrage, disarm black militias, chase out Northerners and intimidate their Southern allies, the Klan patrolled its Invisible Empire with whip, gun, and torch, meting out punishment to its enemies, including two Fisk students in Dresden, Tennessee, whom Klansmen dragged out of their school with ropes around their necks and "cruelly lacerated" with whips.[41]

Among the Klan's enemies was the future Jubilee Singer Benjamin Holmes. After leaving the employ of the high-strung General Jefferson Davis of the Union army, Holmes had proceeded to Nashville to clerk for a black barber. "I had learned how to make change," he recalled, "though hardly know how the knowledge had come." He had grown into a gawky, earnest, pockmarked young man with a gaze at once alert and askew. When the barber died, his estate went to Holmes, making him the first black estate administrator in Tennessee. But the estate proved insolvent, and for his pains Holmes ended up three hundred dollars in debt. In 1868, he enrolled at Fisk, by which time he had already taught himself enough reading and math to advance to the high school department in a mere two months. To earn his tuition, he taught a Davidson County school of sixty-eight pupils for "the promise of thirty dollars a month." At a second school farther out in the countryside, his class was smaller but the conditions more perilous. "Here, a shot came into the room one day, while I was hearing a class, but the source was never ascertained." He returned to Fisk, studied "history, Latin, practice of teaching, and analysis," and became a deacon at Howard Chapel. "I usually walked home on Friday evening to attend the literary society connected with the University, worked at my tailor's trade on Saturday, making from one to three dollars a day, and returned on Saturday night or Sabbath morning, in season to conduct my Sunday school; and felt that I lacked neither work nor 'exercise.'"

Holmes's fellow Jubilee Isaac Dickerson, who had been taught to read and write by the son of a Jewish shopkeeper in Chattanooga, was among the students burned out of the Reverend Tade's school in the Memphis riot of 1866. Before coming to Fisk, he taught for a time in Wauhatchie, Tennessee, where he was greeted many mornings by racist slogans and threats of violence daubed on the trees in his school yard. Promised twenty-five dollars a month, he was never paid, and proceeded, like Holmes, to Fisk. He proved an ardent student of the Bible with an extraordinary gift for extemporaneous speaking.

Like Dickerson, Greene Evans, another Jubilee, had attended night school at Tade's academy in Memphis and left his job as a porter to proceed to Fisk, where, working as a groundskeeper, he paid his way through school. Decorous, fastidious, and enterprising, Evans taught in the summer near the Mississippi border. Scrounging timber from the surrounding woods, he built his own desks, benches, and a schoolhouse, which "did not lack for ventilation, for a bird could fly through anywhere."[42]

Among the first Fisk students to obey the call to teach in the state's public schools was fifteen-year-old Maggie Porter. The state board of commissioners gave the future Jubilee a second-grade certificate and appointed her to a school in Bellevue, Tennessee, where she taught for thirty-five dollars a month. Nevertheless, her family insisted that she return to Nashville for Christmas, which was a time of "excess" in the postwar South, celebrated with fireworks and drink. When she returned on the first Monday of the New Year, she found that her schoolhouse had burned to the ground. "No definite clew to the incendiaries could ever be obtained, but probably the house was burned by the Ku-Klux, as the surest way of ridding themselves of a colored school." The school was moved, but Porter did not follow it, choosing instead a second country school elsewhere, "a rough log building, having a rock chimney and broad fireplace; one long window without any sash, but with a board blind; and benches that were simply logs split open and supported by sticks."[43] Here the indomitable Maggie Porter taught until the county's treasury ran out of funds to pay her, whereupon she taught in yet a third school, in Murfreesboro, all while still in her teens.[44]

8

HARD TRIALS

FISK UNIVERSITY

1867-1870

Back in Nashville, Fisk was crumbling. Designed as temporary shelter on a damp and pestilential site, its barracks were rotting out, while the school's support from the American Missionary Association was rapidly drying up.[1] The grim task of keeping the school solvent fell more and more on George White's shoulders.

White spared himself no pains. He fended off creditors and even dug into his own savings to keep the school from sinking. His treasurer's desk was littered with letters from parents pleading for time, charity, special "arrangements."[2] Many faithfully kept up their payments, even when they were unable to attend. "Some, who have paid their dollar for tuition," wrote Catherine Crosby, "have been obliged to stay at home because it was too cold to come to school *bare*footed."[3] A. J. Barker promised White that, even though he was removing his child because of ill health, "you must not think that I wont pay if she comes home, I will pay you just as well as if she was there & want to do what is right."[4] But many others were not regular in their payments. Malnida Stone begged the school's indulgence; she sent in twenty dollars but could not afford to pay her daughter Mary's "full account" because she had been "disappointed in getting some money that is due me."[5] Rachel Ferguson asked White to forgive her tardiness in paying her daughter Ellen's tuition bill, but "the times is so hard that I had to use it at home. . . . Here is six dollars that is all i have at Present give my love to ellen and tell her to be a good girl."[6]

White pleaded, scolded. "We spare no pains or expense in the education of the people," he reminded Alfred Ernest Anderson, the courageous, pioneering Methodist minister and father of a future Jubilee Singer named Phebe. But from the beginning, Anderson had argued that as a minister he deserved special consideration. He was "getting a very poor salary," he pleaded, and had "a delicate wife to support, consequently I ask you for whatever favor you can give."[7] But White was desperate. "We give you these advantages *on credit for less than they cost us in money*. I write thus plainly and earnestly—yet kindly—because a great and good enterprise is in danger of being crippled by this lack of prompt fulfillment of your obligations."[8]

Fisk's board tried to find a healthier site, but local whites refused to sell them land. Teachers went unpaid for months at a time, and many of them sickened in the pestilences that still infested the city. The school pleaded for funds, but the A.M.A. was heavily committed to hardier freedmen's schools elsewhere in the South and seemed to be preparing to wash its hands of its failing experiment in Nashville.

Amid the destitution of his crumbling dream, George White consoled himself and his students with the group sings he conducted in his apartments each evening, drawing on his makeshift training as a choir director and military bandleader. Shortly before his wedding in the summer of 1867, White organized a troupe of his best singers to perform at a fundraising concert in Nashville. It consisted of such contemporary numbers as "National Song and Chorus" and "The Sultan's Polka," abolitionist hymns like "No Slave beneath the Starry Flag," and the Scottish "Are Ye Sleeping, Maggie?" There were gymnastics, recitations, piano duets, and tableaux titled "Sleeping Beauty," "Emancipation," "Home of Slavery," and "Home of Freedom." Performed before an audience composed largely of freedmen, the concert raised four hundred dollars for Fisk.

By 1868, White had grown more ambitious. Since few members of his choir could afford to buy their own songbooks, he begged for donations of secondhand books like *Some Anthems* and *Bradbury's Anthems Book*. As it was, he said, "we have to manage to keep some of the *best* in school at all, so poor are they." His aim in developing a choir was to build up "a good congregation—which we have never had heretofore."[9] His students performed as part of a "Grand Musical and Literary Entertainment" that included debates, declamations, and "an original legendary drama" titled *Nicodemus*, after the slave "who died years ago, very old," exemplifying "Valor, Industry, Temperance, Faith, Hope, Love, Justice, Wisdom, &c., &c., &c."[10]

In these very first performances, White began to see the promise of Fisk's salvation.

In 1870, John Ogden finally had enough of the criticism, privation, and ostracism. "Being despised," wrote Ella Sheppard, the white teachers "were shut in to us and shut out from all intercourse among the whites."[11] Ogden removed himself and his family from Nashville to become principal of the Ohio State Normal School. With his departure, Cravath saw his chance to emphasize the university aspect of Fisk by hiring a fellow Oberlinian as Ogden's replacement: a respectable, if somewhat hapless, academic named Adam Knight Spence.

Some of Spence's students at Michigan had gone on to work among the freedmen. "I have often thought of you since I landed here," one of them wrote, "and also when I traveled through Virginia. I thought that a man of your stamp could do so much good. The great field of labor is indescribable."[12] Spence was tempted. "If ever I am a missionary," he wrote his mother, "it will be in the South or among the colored people. We need not look away off for souls to save. They are here perishing . . . all around."[13] In 1866, Spence had visited Fisk while searching for the lost slave relatives of a member of the black Sabbath school he conducted in Ann Arbor.[14] During his brief stay, he had delighted in this "community of abolitionists. How hard it would be for some to think any good thing of some others," Spence exclaimed to his wife, Catherine.

> What a pity it is we know so little of the good there is in the world and how fortunate that we know so little of the evil. After tea and some conversations I went into the evening school where the teachers with loving patience taught classes of men and women who after a hard day's work spent an hour in learning to read, the hour beginning with religious exercises.[15]
>
> . . . You know from your experience in teaching how slow a matter it is to accomplish this with white children and you could not expect it to be other with the colored children, and adults in school. It seemed to me that their progress is good.[16]

Adam Knight Spence was born in 1831 in the little Aberdeenshire town of Rhyme in Scotland. His father was a failed mill manager who took his family to America in 1833 and became prominent on the outskirts of Detroit's abolitionist and prohibitionist circles. But the senior Spence "was not really well suited to farming," wrote his son, "either by his physical frame or . . . previous experience," so he worked mostly as a doctor and was paid by his neighbors in produce and labor.

His son was a small-boned, hesitant child, who spent his days in the majestic woods of Washtenaw County, tending his father's livestock and keeping forest creatures as pets. At the age of about seven, Adam was "filled with the happiness of God," and after his father's death, his pious, exacting, and indomitable mother, Elizabeth, became his guiding light. Confirmed in his abolitionism by the murder of the emancipationist publisher Elijah Lovejoy, Spence worked as a farm laborer to pay his way through Oberlin, where, like his friend and classmate Cravath, he fell under the influence of Charles Grandison Finney.[17]

After three years, Adam Spence transferred to the University of Michigan, where he established the collegiate unit of the Young Men's Christian Association and not only performed temperance work among imprisoned drunks but stood their bail when they regressed. He assisted in the classics department, evangelized among Ann Arbor's freedmen, and sheltered runaway slaves in his house. "When his [Sabbath school] pupils went astray, he sought to reclaim them, and was often near them when they were called before the courts." He became a professor of languages at the university but was never entirely comfortable with its "hard skeptical spirit in general, especially among the medical students."[18]

At the time Spence was offered the post at Fisk, his infant daughter had just died; another daughter was so feeble that she was rarely out of her mother's arms. He had been shoved aside by the head of the languages department at Ann Arbor and spent a dispiriting few months in Canada trying to hone his French.[19] His brothers tried to talk him out of going to Fisk:

We feel that if you can possably secure a position in some established educational institution in the north east or west it would *be better* than going south to undertake the education of the colored people & we think you ought to at once make inquiry accordingly. . . . I don't agree with you that the Heathen come *first* with *anybody*. A man's *first* duty is to provide for himself and his family.[20]

Spence's brother-in-law, Frederick Chase, who himself would come to Fisk, also tried to dissuade him:

Do not throw yourself away on the freedmen. The great show hold of Satan is in the intellectual classes. Stay and fight before the walls of his citadel. It seems to me very clear that there is a most urgent demand for christian men in the ranks of literary and professional men.[21]

Spence tried to find the best of both worlds: an endowed chair at a well-established freedmen's college like Howard, perhaps. But there was no such thing. In August 1870, Spence wrote to the Freedmen's Bureau for advice. An agent recommended "the whole South" to him:

From all points of that section the freedmen are asking instruction, and are availing themselves of every opportunity for the acquisition of knowledge. *There* you cannot go amiss; it is a *grand* field for the honest, zealous worker, but one requiring much sacrifice. The freed people of the south are poor, and, as yet, unable to pay proper salaries to their teachers, and the bureau is not now employing teachers. Mr. Cravath . . . will no doubt be able to give you more definite information.[22]

"O my weak heart," Spence grieved, "how weak it is. I shall be stronger by and by no doubt. Things must generally turn out better than I expect."[23] In early September, he accepted Fisk's offer and stopped in Cincinnati en route to Nashville to meet with a grateful Cravath, who sent Spence south with a letter of introduction to his fearsome brother-in-law. "I have assured him that you will give all needed information [in] relation to school," he instructed White, "and most hearty cooperation in making the school a greater success than ever before."[24]

Spence arrived in Nashville on September 9, 1870. He described the city to his wife as

most charmingly situated, but most wretchedly kept. Hogs & dogs and mule teams and broken pavements and filthy children black &

white and lazy, lounging, worthless looking people of all shades of color impede your progress, offend your eyes & nose and sicken your heart. I suppose Nashville is an entirely changed city since the war.[25]

Fisk itself, however, looked

a good deal better than I expected as far as general comfort is concerned. The locality is more inviting, buildings not so dilapidated. The grounds are quite nicely kept and clean. No bad smells. Then they are not built in all around as I feared they might be in a city. Across the street in front is a fine residence with extensive grounds finely laid out. . . . They live here rather more genteely than I had expected. The teachers are really refined and intelligent people. . . . Family prayers *delightful*. I thought how Mother would enjoy them.

As Spence wrote home amid a swarm of mosquitoes, Ella Sheppard was "playing the piano quite well in the ladies hall. A good deal of attention is paid to music, vocal and instrumental."

"It seems my past life was a myth or my present one a dream," he wrote after his first day at Fisk.

Two parts of the same life so different. Think of me if you can in my new situation: hunting up my number on a long line of doors and half of the time stumbling or just about to stumble into somebody else's room. Then in the dining hall there stands a motley group of 50 or 60 or more (from the blackest to the whitest, teachers, scholars) they are all wating the ring of my bell, each standing behind his chair. The bell rings, a blessing is asked, we sit down. The tables run crosswise of the room, twelve at each and so arranged for the most part that a gentleman and lady teacher sit opposite each other at the center of the table.

His second day ended disastrously when Spence placed his pocketbook on the piano during an evening sing and somebody stole it. "The teachers looked sad enough at this my first welcome to Fisk University," he wrote. "And so did the students who knew." As he went to bed, he wondered if he had "dropped down among thieves" whom he was expected "to eat with and treat as my equals." He continued:

I told them if one of the houses had burned down it would not have hurt the school so much. . . . The eye of God was on the one who had done the deed & he would know no happiness or peace with the money. . . . Finally I said that if the one who had done it would restore the stolen property it should be forgiven.

Sure enough, the next morning,

two young men [possibly Dickerson and Rutling] came running almost breathless & said *the book had been found.* One great tall fellow hurried me off, his arm around my shoulder, to the spot. There was a crowd around and on the ground untouched lay the book. *And such joy. There it was.* I found it and not a cent out of it. I bore it off in triumph, opened a general shout. Some one whose conscience or fear had panicked him had slyly dropped the book there to get rid of it. . . . I had not been at that place at all since the loss.

Perhaps it was likelier that the "great tall fellow" had convinced whoever stole it to return it, but at least Spence's pocketbook was safe. Though he felt "on the whole a good influence may be got out of the affair," he promised never to "lay such temptation in the way of the work again."

Spence agonized over his decision to come to Fisk. "Just what our future in connection with the work will be we cannot now know." But by fits and starts the place and the mission grew on him. "In some respects," he said, "I have been the happiest here in my life and then again my heart has gone down within me like lead."

George White proposed that Spence's family and his eventually occupy adjoining suites and share a dining room. Spence warned his wife that Ogden's old rooms were dark and "very public," and "I fear you may find the self denial too great," he wrote. "Then my health may fail or the funds of the A.M.A. may give out." The job was obviously going to prove a bumpy ride.

A multitude of questions of all kinds keeps coming up: punishment, grading, methods of teaching, clashing of hours and schools and interests, boarders and day scholars, conduct in rooms, every where relations of boys to girls, love notes and love engagements, fusses, criminations, reports, falsehoods, bad language, violation of study

hours, irregularities of the bell from half past four in the morning
till ten at night.

"The weight of the race is upon us," he wrote. "We are enveloped in its
darkness and have joined ourselves to its destinies if the Lord will."[26]

Starting with the bishop of the African Methodist Episcopal Church,
Spence set out to improve relations with local black congregations. The
meeting was cordial.

> [It] encouraged us as one of our great difficulties is more or less of
> opposition and jealousy in the part of the colored people. This de-
> nomination for example has given us heretofore the cold shoulder as
> being congregational. They are working for their own school . . . ,
> Wilberforce University. Then we are called aristocratic and educat-
> ing our students away from the masses. Then we have this disadvan-
> tage: we are white. Some want the colored man to have the control
> of every thing pertaining to their affairs. This I think is especially so
> with the African [Methodist Episcopal Church]. They exclude the
> whites. Some of them think the school a money making thing and
> that we are all getting rich off of them.

But there were others in the black community "who just worship us," he assured his wife, "and our scholars are just as pleasant as can be. They are really interesting and promising young people. I do think some of them will
be heard from in the future. We seek to cultivate them in all respects."[27]

Hoping to encourage his best students to become missionaries, Spence
led delegations out into the community to hold prayer meetings, "drawing
people to them by singing slave hymns and then launching into sermons."
One Sunday about three hundred people gathered, white and black, and
"who will say that much good has not been done . . . ?"[28] Spence was
touched by the scenes he witnessed: "I noticed a little girl go into a house &
saw it was one of our *bible readers* I had stumbled upon." He followed her inside and found her "sitting in a chair, one woman was ironing, another had
left her work and was leaning against the side of a door, a third was sitting
down on the door sill at Sallie's foot and looking up into her face while she
read the 55th chap. of Isaiah":[29] "For ye shall go out with joy, and be led
forth with peace; the mountains and the hills shall break forth before you
into singing, and all the trees of the field shall clap their hands."[30]

In the spring of 1870, Fisk's self-appointed choirmaster, George White, mounted a concert in Memphis at Greenlaw Opera House.[31] In December, he launched a new project with his ever-changing band of singers: a performance of a contemporary cantata called *Esther, the Beautiful Queen*. For the title role, he chose Maggie Porter, the strongest and best trained of Fisk's student voices, and invited her to leave her school in Murfreesboro and spend Christmas with his family. She had to decline because "the sabeth school I have been attending have made me promise to stay to their christmas tree which is to be Tuesday— . . . and I have a great many presents promised me if I will stay." But she had read through the music White had sent her "and like my parts very much. I see they require a great deal of hard work to sing them well. . . . I shall do my best toward doing both the school and myself credit," even though her rehearsals at the piano discomfited her white neighbors. "The[y] think it very strange for a nigger to Play," she explained. "This is a real reble town."[32]

As a small girl in Nashville, Maggie Porter used to linger outside churches, listening to the music. "I began sitting on the curb to listen to the choir with my feet in the gutter. Finally I got courage enough to sit on the last step and listen to the music, and the leader asked me if I wanted to go up and hear the music." Ever since then she had worked to cultivate her powerful soprano. Apparently inspired by stories of the Swedish Nightingale, Jenny Lind, Porter's "greatest ambition . . . was to get the people to cry." When White chose Porter to sing Esther over lighter-skinned candidates, "it raised cain!" Porter recalled. "Some of the members didn't like it a bit. One girl said she had never heard of a black queen before, but he kept the black queen just the same."[33]

The cast included most of the singers who would go on to form the Jubilee Singers, including Thomas Rutling, Benjamin Holmes, Greene Evans, Isaac Dickerson, Jennie Jackson, and a seventeen-year-old contralto named Phebe Anderson, the daughter of the Reverend Alfred Ernest Anderson of Knoxville, who had "determined to give [Fisk] my patronage by sending my only child."[34] (Anderson, a confidant of Governor Brownlow, was a vigilant father, however.[35] He complained about the lack of heat in his daughter's room and urged that she pursue "all the studeys that is necessary for a female" and be prevented from receiving love letters, because "when marering gets in the head thair is no studying."[36])

The youngest featured singer in the cast was a thirteen-year-old contralto named Minnie Tate, whose lower register was astonishingly rich and
pure.[37] Ever since her maternal grandmother's manumission, her people
had been freedmen. Early in the 1800s, they left their native Mississippi for
the free state of Ohio, paying their way with hard labor, but when they
reached a German settlement in Tennessee, the locals treated them so kindly
that they decided to remain. Minnie's mother, Adella, attended school with
white children and, by the time of Minnie's birth, had moved with her husband, Andrew, a steamboat steward and barber, to Nashville. Small, pale,
with a sweet, heart-shaped face, Minnie was the baby of the family and, before entering Fisk, had learned her three Rs from her mother.[38]

Another future Jubilee in the cast was a brilliant fifteen-year-old literary department student named Georgia Gordon. Her antecedents were extraordinary. Her maternal grandmother was a Scotch-Irish woman named
Nancy Duke from the wealthy tobacco family of North Carolina who had
been disowned for eloping with her own slave, a fiddler named Bill. Though
never legally married, she bravely lived with him as his wife in Sumner
County, Tennessee. Nancy's daughter, Mercy, had a child by a white Nashville doctor named Warner but eventually married a slave named George
Gordon, after whom their freeborn daughter was named. As a small girl,
Georgia "did not realize that life was for anything but fun and play, and I
had my share of it. I saw very little of the trials of slavery. Sometimes I used
to hear that the slaves were badly treated yet I did not realize the wretched
condition of my race." Nevertheless, this "petite, magnolia-skinned woman
. . . felt the indignities and humiliation of growing up as a mulatto—
shunned by the white society and unaccepted by black folks."[39]

Some mulattoes even had a hard time being accepted as ex-slaves by
Freedmen's Bureau agents. J. W. Stinnett recalled:

> Mother was awfully light. She had gray eyes and straight hair and
> when she got to the bureau man he said, "What are you coming here
> for, you ain't no nigger. You are a darned Secesh white, and I ain't got
> time to fool with you." Mother done everything she could to con-
> vince him that she was a colored woman, but she couldn't do it.[40]

On the other hand, a light skin brought many former slaves to the special
attention of Northern missionaries, who were shocked by evidence of miscegenation. "The evils of slavery become more and more apparent to a

truly loyal mind every day," wrote an A.M.A. agent from Nashville. "There are a great many colored people in the rebellious city, & I presume you could not find a genuine black among them all under ten or twelve years of age."[41] Some Northern whites could not help but be particularly moved by the plight of people who looked so much like themselves.[42] Abolitionists had found that *cartes des visites* of light-skinned slaves were more effective in stirring their Northern white constituents than pictures of their darker fellow sufferers. So it was that coffee-colored orphans with blond hair and blue eyes who spoke the slave patois were likelier to be scooped up by missionaries and brought under the wing of institutions like Fisk, even if, in the end, a majority of A.M.A. teachers would observe that they were no brighter than blacks, and some teachers would assert that "true Africans" were smarter.[43]

The proportion of mixed-race students was further increased by the fact that some house slaves had been biracial and had enjoyed special privileges, including opportunities to learn, whereas less privileged field hands tended to be darker. White masters were likelier to keep their slave children out of the fields and provide them with better food and clothing and even, as in Simon Sheppard's case, eventually free them and even educate them,[44] prospects that induced some slave women to submit to their masters.[45]

If they derived any benefits from these submissions, however, the cost was sometimes universal ostracism.[46] Many mulatto children were singled out for abuse and ridicule by disgraced mothers and shamed slave stepfathers, guilty white fathers,[47] and outraged mistresses.[48] Slaves who believed themselves to be descended solely from Africans could be hard on slaves of mixed race. "The old time blacks," wrote James Thomas, "never used to take much stock in the 'Yaller' Nigger. They called him 'No Nation,' 'a Mule,' 'yaller hammer.' "[49] Robert J. Cheatham told an interviewer that he believed "the negro a unique race and is glad his tribe has been all black. He says it is proof of the honor of his and his forefathers' masters that their blood was never mingled together to produce a mixed race."[50] Sarah Fitzpatrick maintained that "the 'Lamp Black Nigger' is the most dependable, 'cause he is 'honest got,' " though even she had to concede that judging from appearances was confounding.

> Some folks say that when a "Nigger" is so black he just naturally mean. I tell them he may be so black till he's slick and shines, but he

can be honest. Sometimes "Jet Black Niggers" is shamed of they self, especially when they gets with white folks and yellow "Niggers." That ain't no use 'cause he is just as good as any of the rest of them.[51]

Lewis Clarke recalled:

The slaves used to debate together sometimes . . . the reason that the yellow folks couldn't be trusted like the dark ones could. As a general rule they seem to be dissipated, devil-may-care fellows; and . . . we concluded it was because they was the sons of their masters, and took after their fathers. . . . I have heard them talk on about it, and bring up this here one, and that 'ere one, that was the son of a dissipated master, till I felt ashamed of the white blood in me.[52]

Some mixed-race freedmen renounced their white ancestry. "Any [black] man of the South who is a descendant of a slave holder who upheld the system of American slavery, ought to blush with shame for his degraded origin," wrote Isaac Johnson. A former slave named Harding recalled riding on a Nashville streetcar long after emancipation and passing the cemetery where his white father was buried. Suddenly he "started cussing—'Let me off this damn car and go see where my God damn father is buried,'" he recalled, "'so I can spit on his grave, the God damn son of a bitch.' I got no mercy on nobody who bring up their children like dogs. How could any father treat their child like that? Bring them up to be ignorant like they did us? If I had my way with them, all I would like to have is a chopping block and chop every one of their heads off."[53]

Some biracial African Americans chose to distance themselves from their white forebears by ascribing their lighter skins to Native American antecedents, "another proud race exploited by the white man."[54] But others took a kind of pride in their mixed ancestry and ascribed their special progress to white genes. "You can't scare me," a schoolteacher once overheard a ten-year-old declare to a school-yard bully. "I've got white blood in me." "'The talented tenth,'" wrote Lura Beam, "was, at birth, farther along than the others. It was lighter in color and had inherited land or education or money from white or free ancestors. It had the first higher education and produced most of the early professional men."[55]

The preponderance of biracial students among Fisk's elite was so marked that the university's Howard Chapel came to be known as the "blue-veined church" in that its congregation tended to be sufficiently light for their veins to show through the skin of their wrists. Along with denominational rivalries, class divisions, regional roots, caste distinctions between emancipated slaves and prewar freedmen, color would complicate not only the relation of lighter-skinned students like Georgia Gordon and America Robinson to darker-skinned classmates like Jennie Jackson but Fisk's own relation to the rest of Nashville's black community.[56]

9

GETTING READY TO DIE

THE MISSION

1870–1871

In December 1870, Catherine Spence arrived with her children to find her husband, Adam, "sadly in need of me. His bed was actually sticky with dampness and so cold it gave me a chill to stay in his room. Many nites he said he had lain cold for hours. . . . I wonder he was not sick." Nevertheless, "in position and influence, in power," her husband stood "higher than he did [at the University of Michigan]. . . . I never saw him so happy nor so well satisfied with his work," she reported to his mother. "I hope he will keep well and be able to spend a long life here." But immediately she saw that the greatest threat to that hope was lack of funds. "An institution that absolutely does not have *one dollar* to expend, must have very soon, . . . 50,000 or a 100 thousand [dollars], or it will die. . . . The way to get it in my opinion is prayer, and the right rise of means."[1] Spence was considering raising funds on a speaking tour in Britain, where such men as the Reverend Newman Hall, the evangelist Charles Haddon Spurgeon, the novelist George MacDonald (a friend of Spence's mother),[2] "and scores of such men would be accessible." But Cravath ordered him to remain at his post for now.

In the meantime, Spence had "one thing more" in his favor. "He just carries the colored people," Catherine reported, "and that means students. . . .

The students all love him so." Some mothers complained because their daughters "never wrote anything about themselves, it was all Professor Spence."[3] To prevent Christmas celebrations from getting out of hand that year, Spence tried to keep his students constantly busy through the holiday season with receptions, socials, promenades, prayer meetings, Sunday school festivals, and exhibitions. At one social, Spence served "apples, nuts & candies" to a "very fine company mostly of colored people," he said.

> Quite a select affair, ladies and gentlemen in gloves &c. I don't see but they know just as well how to act in such a place as any body. When you come to conversation of course you find their lack of early culture. . . . I gave the students the privilege of looking at my stereoscopic views all the week and I had readings with a select few.

After two young men declared themselves Christians, Spence was jubilant about the New Year. "I never began one so happily," he told his mother. "The school never was so peaceful," wrote Catherine, "never was so smooth."

And never so poor. The school was deeply in debt to local merchants, some of whom refused to provide Fisk with further supplies until its accounts were settled. The barracks remained damp, cold, drafty. The food was execrable. "The beef was so tough," Ella Sheppard recalled, that "the boys called it 'Old Ben,' and declared that every time they met a cow they felt like apologizing."[4] Beef was so constant a staple that when a bunch of boys were asked why they were in such a commotion they replied that they had just encountered a cow on Seventeenth Avenue "and they had so much beef with them they were afraid to face her."[5]

Catherine Spence blamed the bad food on the "economies" of George White, to whom she took an immediate dislike. She wrote:

> Adam has trials here of many kinds, [but] perhaps the greatest is Mr. White, a very valuable man but a perfect autocrat. The man really does not know how to be polite. He will stride past me day after day without so much as a look, to say nothing of a bow. I never saw him lift his hat in all the time I have been here. Adam treats the meanest person on the place with more politeness than he does Adam. Then he holds the finances in his thumb, and spends where *he* thinks best, often Adam thinks very unadvisedly, and leaves things undone.

"All must be changed," she ominously concluded,[6] but her decent, fretful, fastidious husband, with his pale, balding pate and "light" voice, would prove no match for George White.[7]

White continued freely to take full advantage of his control of the university's treasury and his fraternal relationship with Cravath to get his way. In February 1871, White reported to his brother-in-law that Fisk had twenty-nine female and fifty male students and a staff of twenty-three, including twelve teachers and a matron. He believed they had room for perhaps twenty-one more students. "Financially we struggle along," he reported to Cravath.

> I have not collected quite so much from the students as I had hoped—and it is costing more to live this term—yet I am gaining slowly on my indebtedness. I shall do my best to make both ends meet—at the close of the year I hope to nearly do so. I expect to come out as well or a little better than I did last year.

A local doctor recommended that the teachers eat at least one meal away from the students on the theory that their illnesses resulted from "disordered stomachs resulting from eating with present care and anxiety on the mind which he claims is in itself dyspepsia." White himself believed that "half our quarrels and troubles arise from sour stomachs." He thought the food was better, and yet, he said, alluding indirectly to the Spences, "we have *never* had half the complaint & fault finding which we have had this year."

By now Erastus Cravath, touring the South as an A.M.A. field secretary, was so alarmed by conditions at Fisk that he commanded his brother-in-law to stop wasting time and energy on his music classes and concentrate, instead, on his stewardship of the university's dwindling finances. But Cravath had no more control over White than Spence did. "Contrary to your direction," White defiantly replied, "but by request of the faculty, my singing class is kept up, meeting the first half hour after school."[8]

Among the missionaries who joined the faculty in the fall of 1870 was yet another Oberlinian named Henrietta Matson, perhaps the most fervid evangelical in the history of Fisk. She had been forced by a malarial delirium to withdraw from her first posting to Africa and proceeded to Tade's

Lincoln Chapel in Memphis before replacing Mrs. Ogden as matron at Fisk.[9] Perhaps her ague (or Mrs. Ogden's gardening) accounted for the nostomania with which she would look back on her first sight of Fisk:

> The old barrack buildings . . . seemed then, and in memory still, a beautiful spot. Those long verandahs, shaded with the rich glossy leaves of the Madeira vine, the Cypress, whose foliage was like delicate tracery, out of which peeped crimson blossoms, and the rich variety of Couralvuli in their "morning glory," displaying every color to gladden the eye. How lovely it was on that spring morning when I first arrived in Nashville![10]

Matson shed "buckets of tears" when she first arrived, but quickly established herself as a mainstay and one of Spence's most loyal allies.[11] She was in some ways a caricature of the "old maid" that the A.M.A.'s missionaries patronized and ridiculed.[12] "Imagine if you can," Spence wrote of her, "the shortest, dumpiest, chubbiest person and face set off with the plainest attire and eyes so asquint you can never see but one of them and an Irish looking head of hair sprinkled in its thick mattedness with a little frost of gray. God bless her," Spence exclaimed, "he doubtless had a mission for her or he never would have made her so. . . . But goodness and good sense and divine charity carry the day and this same dumpy little woman is growing good to see as she steps in or out followed by her girls."[13]

Fisk's staff posted rules and regulations all over the school prescribing obedience, cheerfulness, punctuality, neatness, soft-spokenness, piety, courtesy, and decorous language. They forbade students from visiting each other's rooms during hours of study (5:30 to 8:30 a.m., 1:00 to 4:00 p.m., and 6:30 p.m. on). Men and women were not to visit each other "under any circumstances" unless in the presence of a teacher. There were to be no games of chance, of course, and no liquor or tobacco. All students were required to deposit all of their money with the treasurer "and to draw upon him as they may need."[14]

"It would be difficult to find any school in the country," Fisk boasted to the Peabody Fund, "which has excelled this school in a careful observance of all the proprieties of social life."[15] An alumnus was especially proud of the proprieties of coeducational life at Fisk. "During all the years of their residence with these young colored men I never heard the least complaint

by these women concerning any ungentlemanly conduct by a single student."[16]

Such extraordinary constraints had some unfortunate roots, however, it
being "old Southern doctrine that any unobserved Negro, man or boy, will
commit rape at the slightest opportunity," wrote MacKinley Helm, Roland
Hayes's biographer.

> It was therefore a rule at Fisk that students should be under constant
> surveillance. There was a definite schedule of hours for calling on
> girls who lived in the women's dormitory. A boy was expected to ask
> permission to make an engagement with his girl, and when he called
> to keep it, he was met by a chaperon who sat in plain sight through-
> out the evening. Girls were only rarely permitted to go out after
> dark, and then they went in squads, led by lady sergeant-majors.

Boys and girls were not permitted "to stop and pass the time of day together on the campus."[17] But that did not prevent them from trying to
communicate, which was how Isaac Dickerson and Thomas Rutling ran
afoul of Fisk's regime.

By 1870, Rutling had become a favorite of the Cravaths and the Whites.
Cravath's son Paul, who grew up to become one of America's most powerful corporate attorneys and a champion of trusts, recalled trying to imitate
everything Rutling did.[18] "Miss Laura I hope you are well," Rutling wrote
the Whites during a summer break:

> If you aint I hope you are well enough [to] start here soon. So that
> you will be able to come back shortly. Kiss your little Baby for me
> and tell him to grow fast. Mr. White you must excuse my bad writ-
> ing for you know I can't write anyway. I wrote this in a hurry but
> did the best I could. I commenced at half past & now it is ten min-
> utes after 10 o'clock. . . . P.S. Have you gone a fishing yet and how
> many fish did you catch and how long did you stay out on the lake.[19]

But the warmth of Rutling's relationship with Cravath and White did
not immunize him from their wrath. Caught passing a note to a female student, Rutling was required to write a letter of contrition before the managers would readmit him:

I have wrote to young ladies which I knew would bring me to a deep solom hearts pledge. I hereby make a full and frank confession to my Friend who are trying to make a man of me and adding that by the help of GOD and the aid of man I never will be guilty of such a thing again.

He threw himself on the mercy of his friends and agreed to suffer "any punishment they may inflict upon me."[20]

Caught in the same net, his friend Isaac Dickerson also begged the administration's forgiveness. "I hope that you will be willing to try me again. And if I fail to do what I say, then I am willing that you should not try me again. I want to make a man of my self," he pleaded. "And I know that what you say is for my own good."[21]

Underpinning Fisk's regime was the knowledge that even a hint of scandal could ruin it, destroying not only the grudging acceptance and even respect it had begun to earn from middle-class merchants and upper-class whites but the faith of the freedmen families who entrusted their children to its care.

At Fisk, conversion and education vied for primacy. Education was seen as a means to the sacred end of bringing every emancipated slave to Jesus. "The religious feature of the institution is very prominent," wrote Spence, "and is to me most delightful. Many have made a profession of religion but what is better, the young people go forth as missionaries in the city doing such work as they are able to do, holding conversation & prayer, reading the bible, giving tracts, holding meetings, teaching in the Sunday school, getting scholars into it &c &c."[22]

Fearing that freed slaves might revert to the animism of their African forebears or, perhaps worse, turn to "the Papal Church with its pictures and dresses and music and gaudy trappings and showy ceremonies," Cravath and White, Spence and Matson were determined to turn them into Protestants of the Northern stripe. The managers kept a monthly scorecard of conversions and reported them home to the A.M.A.[23]

Henrietta Matson was largely responsible for the revivalist fever that swept through the school in 1870.[24] "I remember the first Wednesday evening prayer meeting of the term," she wrote, "held in a recitation room, most quietly conducted, with considerable formality at the opening on the part of some who had joined the Exercises. But the spirit of God breathed upon us, and sinners began to cry out for mercy. Sobs, groans and tears were on every side." The commotion alarmed even young Henry Bennett, the school's informal and cheerful young chaplain.[25] Because Bennett did not know how to proceed,

> Prof Spence advised dismissing the students to their rooms, where they could pray in quietness. They did so, and never throughout Eternity shall I forget the scenes in the Dormitory. We went from room to room, and in little groups prayed around the mourning ones, till one by one, many accepted Christ—and then the peace of God so rested down upon them, that the stillness and awe of Heaven pervaded the rooms and hushed the tumult of every heart.[26]

Many of Matson's charges, of course, had been Christians long before the A.M.A. entered the Southern field. But considering the few narrow and self-serving Bible passages to which masters exposed their slaves, it is a wonder that Christianity took such hardy root. "He that knoweth his master's will and doeth it not, shall be beaten with many stripes!" was the text William Wells Brown recalled hearing repeatedly when he was a slave.[27] Another quotation cited to slaves was "Brethren, let every man wherein he is called abide therein with God." "If ye be willing and obedient, ye shall eat the good of the land," white preachers read from Isaiah. "But if ye refuse and rebel, ye shall be devoured with the sword: for the mouth of the Lord hath spoken it."[28] But perhaps the most explicit biblical defense of slavery was in Leviticus:

> Both thy bondmen, and thy bondmaids, which thou shalt have, shall be of the heathen that are round about you; of them shall ye buy bondmen and bondmaids. Moreover of the children of the strangers that do sojourn among you, of them shall ye buy, and of their families that are with you, which they begat in your land; and they shall be your possession. And ye shall take them as an inheritance for your children after you, to inherit them for a possession; they shall be your bondmen forever.[29]

Solomon Northrup's cruelest master was "an impressive commentator on the New Testament" who always emphasized Luke 12:47: "And that ser-

vant, which knew his lord's *will*, and *prepared* not himself, neither did
according to his will, shall be beaten with many stripes." The master's interpretation: "That nigger that don't take care—that don't obey his lord—
that's his master—d'ye see?—that 'ere nigger shall be beaten with many
stripes. Now, 'many' signified a *great* many—forty, a hundred, a hundred
and fifty lashes," he told his slaves. "*That's* scripter!"[30]

Slaves were generally unimpressed by Southern white ministers. "Why
the man that baptized me had a colored woman tied up in his yard to whip
when he got home, that very Sunday, and her mother belonged to that same
church," said C. H. Hall.

> We had to sit & hear him preach, and her mother was in church
> hearing him preach. The daughter was as pretty a young woman as
> you would ever find in a day's run. He only hired her. She had a light
> skin, & her hair just hung down on her shoulders. And he had her
> tied up & whipped. That was our preacher![31]

"The white preachers . . . would only preach to the niggers about being
good, obedient and work good and hard for their master," Robert Burns
remembered:

> He would preach and tell the niggers that they didn't have any souls,
> and that niggers didn't go to heaven. Only white people had souls
> and went to heaven. He told them that niggers had no more souls
> than dogs, and they couldn't go to heaven any more than could a
> dog.[32]

Frederick Douglass used to delight his abolitionist audiences by mimick-
ing the white Southern preachers he had heard as a slave. "Oh, consider the
wonderful goodness of God!" he exhorted his listeners. "Look at your hard,
horny hands, your strong muscular frames, and see how mercifully he has
adapted you to the duties you are to fulfill," for the masters had "slender
frames and delicate fingers" and "brilliant intellects, that they may do the
thinking while you do the working."[33]

Occasionally, a white minister would preach something subversive to
slaveholding, but he would not last long. One white preacher named
Dickey began to preach to his Georgian congregation about the evils of
slavery:

He preached for freedom for the niggers and say that all should be
set free and given a home and a mule. . . . Right away Reverend
Dickey done such preaching they fired him from the church and
abused him, and some of them say they gwine hang him to a limb or
. . . ride him on a rail out of the county.[34]

The Gospel had become "so mixed with slavery," Peter Randolph recalled, "that the people could see no beauty in it, and feel no reverence for
it."[35] Some slaves suspected that if there was a true Bible somewhere, "it
was not the master's."[36] But the New Testament burst with verses inconve-
nient to slaveholding, and it took constant monitoring of slaves and their
preachers to keep them under wraps.

After years of hearing white ministers preach exclusively about obedience, many emancipated slaves were astonished to find how much else the
Bible contained. When James Curry began to read the Bible, he "learned
that it was contrary to the revealed will of God, that one should hold another as a slave." He had always heard the slaves say that their ancestors had
been "stolen from Africa, where they were free men and free women."
Now he read that "God hath made of one blood all nations of men to dwell
on all the face of the earth."[37]

Slaves heard the echoes of their own plight in the stories of Abraham
and Moses, Joseph and his brothers, and the children of Israel. In Jesus they
found a fellow sufferer who had not only endured the same kind of
grotesque tortures to which they had been subjected but ultimately prevailed. Whatever their own tribulations in this world, Christianity offered
slaves the promise of salvation—home, rest, reunion, and justice—in the
world to come.[38]

In the late 1860s, Fisk was surrounded by African American churches. "The
baptists are perhaps the strongest in numbers & influence," wrote a visiting
white Congregationalist, "& certain it is that they are so in that spirit of sec-
tarian bitterness which has no word of consolation or even the shadow of
hope for any but the duck family." There were two Baptist churches in the
neighborhood, a Presbyterian church (though "these are not numerous &
so far as I have seen are friendly"), and two African Methodist Episcopal
churches, one so near the school "that we can stand on our chapel steps
& hear the minister preach, the people pray & the choir sing. . . . I con-

fess that I often feel that Nashville is already sufficiently stalked with churches."[39]

Many newly arrived missionaries had never considered that there might be such a thing as a Southern black religious culture. They believed that slavery must have been so destructive of any kind of human expression and aspiration that the freedmen would present a tabula rasa on which they could create a Northern utopian vision of the South: a black outpost of Yankee Protestantism. Instead they found a well-established network of black churches with their own rituals, liturgies, and interpretations of scripture.

"It don't seem as if we poor ignorant Africans can come to the Savior as you educated folks do," explained a former slave. "We have to worry it out." But for Northerners accustomed to the most constrained and formal observances, the improvisational ardor of black worship was alarming. In their view, slave doctrine lacked the necessary ethical imperatives.[40] "The rags of their heathenism are neither worn nor thrown away," warned a white Presbyterian minister:

> Superstition permeates their whole society, and manifests itself as an atmosphere about the world of piety they inhabit. Visions, revelations, and rhapsodies sweep through their confused ideas of worship until their religion becomes an inebriation. Their songs of praise are too often an exemplification of the vain "repetitions," used as artificial stimulants to secure soul intoxication and to shut out sober thought, and destroy the power of truth.[41]

Another was discouraged to find that the black families he visited seemed satisfied with "the old time religion" and "their ignorant blaster in the pulpit & wild frenzy in the pews."[42] The A.M.A. tried to establish Congregational churches for the freedmen, in part to please its Congregational contributors, but they mostly failed. Freedmen wanted their own ministers, their own autonomous churches. The best the A.M.A. could hope for was to train a new generation of black ministers.[43]

Not all whites despaired of black religion. Joel Grant of Oberlin was encouraged to find that "the African nature" was "eminently religious. Almost every one of them is easily affected in this direction and with a fair religious education and an open Bible I think they would realize sooner than any other people the promise, 'All shall know me from the least to the greatest.' "[44] Black religion was "very demonstrative and, at times, reaches absurdity," conceded Charles A. Crosby of Fisk, but "some are beginning to see the absurdity of the *excessive* physical demonstrations of their worship. We heard this expression from one of their pulpits a short time ago. 'I entreat you to be calm. The religion of Jesus Christ never takes away our senses.' " There was "often such depth of feeling and richness of experience and withall such originality of expression," he declared, "that almost any christian heart might achieve a blessing from communion with them. There is such an appreciation of the sacred truths of the Bible which they have hitherto been unable to read, that it is indeed a delightful service to read it to them."[45]

An editorial in the A.M.A.'s journal went so far as to suggest that a little exposure to black religion might do whites good. "One of the beautiful and blessed effects of a real Christian culture for the negro would be the reflex influence of his emotive religion upon the unimaginative and unemotional white people who are now benefiting him."[46] Edward Parmelee Smith warned that the African Methodist Episcopals were "going to swamp the field. . . . The strong preacher who promises perfect independence from White control and direction carries the cold heart at once. Our preachers must be wide awake men who will not only allow *fervor* of worship in both expression and form, but will heartily enjoy it."[47]

Ogden believed that education was the solution to what he regarded as the dangerous emotionalism of African American worship. "We wonder at and condemn the frenzy of these ignorant religionists," he said. But "give these poor narrow minded people our education, and they will not only contain more, without running over, but they will control themselves and their religion too. The reason their religion is all impulse and animal excitement, is because there is nothing but impulse and animal there for it to operate upon. What else could we expect? But better this than nothing."[48]

Many missionaries were nonetheless inspired and sustained by the deep religious faith of many of the former slaves they encountered. Henry Bennett of Fisk conceded that

> in their meetings there is a great deal of wildfire, and . . . the excellence of a sermon is measured by the amount of noise in it, and the ability of the preacher to make his hearers shout. Yet, after having made this admission, I am free to affirm that the more I have seen of their religion and of the power it has over their lives, the more re-

spect I have felt for it . . . Amid all the trials through which they have passed since the war—poverty, outrage, abuse, and contempt—they have faced the pitiless storm without retaliation or retort. They have a moral and religious character which is as clear, and as positive, and I might say as unique as that of any people in the world.[49]

Henrietta Matson used to visit an ex-slave in Memphis who was known to the missionaries as "Happy Mary," for her joy at her conversion. She used to sit by her fire, "thinking how good the Lord is."

"A breath of praise goes through my soul," she said, "and I have to say, 'Praise Jesus, praise Jesus.'"

When Matson read to her about Judgment Day, she scooted close to her seatmate, declaring that on that day "I would get up *so* by Jesus, and then I should not be afraid."[50]

"I have patriarchs and prophets, saints and seers," Crosby reported. "Abram, Isaac and Jacob are seated side by side, and I sometimes think they are *almost* as good, as their long ago predecessors."[51] Crosby met an old man bent over because he had been shot a year before by a white man, about whom "he manifested a most cheerful and forgiving spirit. He said, 'If I should *wish* to raise my hand to hurt one hair of his head, I should be deep in the mud as he is in the mire. Oh no, if God can forgive him, I am sure I can.'"[52]

PART TWO

LISTEN TO THE ANGELS

NASHVILLE

1866–1871

Nothing so touched and astonished Northern missionaries as the secret and sacred music they sometimes chanced to overhear as they made their rounds through the refugee camps. Henrietta Matson once heard a cook named Queen Victoria ("not her Royal Highness but her namesake") singing "one of the wildest of plantation melodies. It ran thus":

> Remember Daniel . . . in the Lion's den
> Dear Hebrew children too
> Cast in the burning fiery furnace.
> Thou [didst] deliver them.
> O! Lord, deliver me.
> Thou didst deliver them.
> Why not deliver me?

"*There* is argument and pleading," declared Matson, "such as only goes up from hearts shut up to God for help."[1]

Such songs were a revelation. Missionaries struggled to find a name that would adequately describe their mysterious power. Before they came to be called "Negro spirituals" or "songs of Jubilee," they were known as "plantation melodies," "slave hymns" and "cabin songs," "plantation songs," "sorrow songs." It was difficult sometimes for Northern missionaries to persuade freedmen to sing them for them. "The slave songs were never used by us then in public," wrote Ella Sheppard. "They were associated with slavery and the dark past, and represented the things to be forgotten. Then, too, they were sacred to our parents, who used them in their religious worship and shouted over them."[2]

"In the Summer of 1871," wrote Adam Knight Spence, "when Fisk University was still in the old hospital buildings, one day there came into my room a few students with some air of mystery. The door was shut and locked, the window curtains were drawn, and, as if a thing they were ashamed of, they sang some of the old time religious slave songs now long since known as Jubilee songs."[3] Sheppard recalled "sitting upon the floor (there were but few chairs)" and practicing "softly, learning from each other the songs of our fathers. We did not dream of ever using them in public."[4]

George White began to collect the secret hymns he heard former slaves singing in schools and camps. Ella Sheppard brought him "Before I'd Be a Slave" and "Swing Low, Sweet Chariot," songs her mother, Sarah, had taught her and later claimed to have composed.[5] Jennie Jackson apparently introduced him to "I'll Hear the Trumpet Sound," which she had learned from "a very elderly slave."[6] Matson may well have brought him "Didn't My Lord Deliver Daniel?"[7] Ella Sheppard transcribed these and a host of other slave hymns on sheet after sheet of music paper: by 1881, they would collect well over a hundred.[8]

Sometime before the outbreak of the Civil War, a Connecticut man found himself waiting for a train at City Point, Virginia, when he first heard slaves singing. "About daybreak, the 'hands' on an adjoining plantation passed on their way to the tobacco field to begin their hopeless and to them profitless toil," he recalled.

> They were singing; not in joy, for the song was too sadly plaintive for that; not in despair for the hopeless do not sing. What the words were I could not tell, nor did I care to know; but wave on wave of wild, weird melody, that told what no language can tell, came

rolling over us, as the ghostly shadows of the night . . . were flying before the beautiful morning. The captives had not hung their harps upon the willows, nor did they refuse to sing to those who had wasted them. Their song was at once a burden of woe and a glad prophecy. Wrongs which another race would have avenged with bloody knife and flaming torch uttered themselves in plaintive murmur.[9]

It was the Civil War that introduced many Northerners to the spiritual. A Union officer named Thomas Wentworth Higginson made a study of the songs he heard sung in camp by the black troops under his command. He took to writing down their lyrics and eventually published them in the *Atlantic Monthly*. One of them was "Many Thousands Go," as he transcribed the title: a slow, plaintive song that he guessed had been composed by slaves not long before the outbreak of the Civil War and sung, understandably, in secret:

> *No more driver's lash for me,*
> *No more, no more.*
> *No more driver's lash for me,*
> *Many thousands gone.*
>
> *No more mistress' call for me*
> *No more, no more.*
> *No more mistress' call for me,*
> *Many thousands gone . . .*

Higginson wondered whether such spirituals

had always a conscious and definite origin in some leading mind, or whether they grew by gradual accretion in an almost unconscious way. On this point, I could get no information, though I asked many questions, until at last, one day when I was being rowed across from Beaufort to Ladies' Island, I found myself, with delight, on the actual trail of a song. One of the oarsmen, a brisk young fellow, not a soldier, on being asked for his theory of the matter, dropped out a coy confession. "Some good spirituals," he said, "are start just out of curiosity."

Whereupon he sang a song of his own composition while some of Higginson's men gathered around and began to pick up the chorus "as if it were an old acquaintance."[10]

It may well have been, for Higginson's boatman only begged the question musicologists have been asking ever since. The origin of individual spirituals remains almost impossible to pin down. Slave populations were not static, and their songs circulated widely. When individual freedmen claimed authorship of certain slave hymns, they may have meant it in the same sense a Nolensville, Tennessee, farmer claimed authorship of a song he sang for a television production crew about Noah and the Flood, elements of which came from a host of old spirituals on the subject that he had amplified and altered and made his own. In a sense, he was right—it was his song now, just as it would become someone else's song when he or she was done working it.

The near impossibility of saying anything definitive about the origin of spirituals has made their study one of the most contentious of all musicological endeavors. Some prefer to think spirituals emerged full-blown from individuals, others that they were the result of the folk process: the aggregate expression of an entire people. Certainly they must have originated with individuals in some form, but determining which individual, and in what form, has proven one of the casualties of the enforced obscurity and illiteracy of slavery.

The usual musical form of the spiritual—alternating verses and choruses, call and response—extends back to the work songs and ritual shouts and circle dances of Africa. Many tribes sang in harmony, but it may be that the sturdy harmonies of Southern blacks around the time of the Civil War derived also from the influence of the Protestant choirs many of them heard and sang along with while seated in the slave sections of their masters' churches. European folk songs and ballads exerted their influence, as did the cross-pollination of the camp meetings of the American frontier, where blacks and whites sang and prayed together, though many African Americans were neither impressed nor satisfied with white religious music.

Nothing influenced the form and content of the spiritual more than the sheer experience of bondage. Born in the slow, counterclockwise circle dances that characterized many slave prayer meetings, spirituals pulsed with the rhythm of labor: hoeing, chopping, toting, shucking. A leader in a corn row might sing the first line of a couplet—"These shoes I wear are

Gospel shoes"—and the rest would respond—"Oh, my Lord," or "Zion, Zion," or "Send them angels down"—and then the leader would follow with the second line—"And you can wear them if you choose"—whereupon everyone would repeat the refrain.

These couplets were repeated in song after song: "When I set out, I was but young / But now my race is almost run," "If you get there before I do / Tell all my friends I'm coming too," "When I get to heaven, I'll walk about / There's nobody there to turn me out." There might be a chorus to follow that everyone sang together, but call and response was the soul of the spiritual.

Spirituals fell into two broad categories: sorrow songs like "Go Down, Moses" or "Swing Low, Sweet Chariot"; and jubilees like "Gospel Train" and "This Little Light of Mine." They not only declared faith but carried news, raised protests, expressed grief, asked questions, made jokes, lubricated a slave's never ending toil. "You start singing a song, and when you're singing it first, according to the slaves, you're just singing the words," explains Horace Clarence Boyer.

> But after a while, it's almost like *therapy*. It begins to take the frown out of the face. The shoulders begin to come back to their natural position. What's happening is, you're going through a cleansing process. You're coming back to where you wanted to be. Things are not quite as bad as you think they are. And the more you sing it, the more you find relief, the more you believe that there is a way out of this.[11]

"There is no parallel instance," wrote Higginson, "of an oppressed race thus sustained by the religious sentiment alone. These songs are but the vocal expression of the simplicity of their faith and the sublimity of their long resignation."[12] But in the African tradition of hitting "a straight lick with a crooked stick," spirituals conveyed many meanings simultaneously. "Paradise," "Canaan," "the Promised Land" could stand for heaven, the North, Canada, or emancipation. "Freedom" could mean release from the grief and toil of this life, or it could mean independence, autonomy, escape from slavery. Frederick Douglass found his inspiration to run away from his master in the lyrics of a spiritual,[13] and Booker T. Washington observed that with the approach of emancipation, slaves "threw off the mask; and were not afraid to let it be known that the 'freedom' in their songs meant freedom of the body in this world."[14] But first and foremost their songs were *spirituals*, sung in voices raised up to God.

In more than half the songs the Jubilees collected, the melodies were written in the same pentatonic scale in which Gaelic and even ancient Greek songs were written, with the fourth and seventh left out.[15] "The tunes was brung from Africa by our granddaddies," a Kentucky slave recalled. "They was just familiar songs."[16] But in performance, these distilled and resonant melodies were mere skeletons to which slaves applied their own improvisational genius. Whites had a hard time representing them on paper, for there was no notation that could adequately convey the "blue" notes, syncopations, swoops, whoops, slides, and hollers that made them so distinctive.

African Americans had experienced an uprooting so total and an oppression so fundamental that the songs they raised in yearning and protest struck a universal chord. "These songs came from the heart, and they go to the heart," wrote Henry Proctor of Fisk.

> They have the very tone of the gospel in them. They breathe the odor of spiritual sacrifice. As the bruised flower yields the sweet perfume, and the crushed grape the blood-red wine, so the hearts of these people, bruised by oppression and crushed by adversity's iron heel, poured forth the sweetness and purity of the gospel in song.[17]

Moved by the mysterious force of the songs his students brought him, White began to rehearse them with the same exactitude he brought to their official repertoire of cantatas and hymns and popular songs. George White's transcriptions were no doubt crude, and his arrangements formalized the tunes and lyrics his singers brought to him so that they could be repeated with some consistency in performance. But his transcriptions were not his primary source. The true sound of the spirituals he could summon from the singers themselves. Their performances remained resonant with their ancestors' sorrow, resignation, stubborn hope of redemption—and justice, for there was little doubt who the sinners were whom they consigned to hellfire in their songs.

His singers came to believe that White's ability to elicit the most polished performances from their otherwise untrained voices was God-given, a mystery of his birth. "He was wonderful in the interpretation of those old Negro melodies," Georgia Gordon recalled. "He would keep us singing them all day until he was satisfied that we had every soft or loud passage to suit his fastidious taste. We sometimes thought him too exacting, but . . . our success was through the rigid training received at his hand."[18]

Conducting his rehearsals while standing some distance from his singers or pacing with his fiddle at the ready to check for pitch, White would try "plan after plan, covering days, perhaps weeks, before the results satisfied him. . . . He insisted they use the same naturalness of expression they would use if they were speaking to the audience."[19] White believed that if singers made "the vowels plain, . . . the word would be understood." "Pronounce it," he used to tell them. "That is enough."[20] He had a horror of harsh tones: everything was softened; in fact, esses were not just softened but sometimes omitted.[21] They were to sing with their mouths open wide enough to fit a finger between their teeth.[22] The singers had to blend with each other, listen to the entire ensemble; no voice except a soloist's was to be heard above another.

Because they were reluctant to expose their songs to white ears, and because they would so often have to rehearse their pieces in hotel rooms, their pianissimi would become a kind of signature of the Jubilee sound.[23] White used to "tell the singers to put into the tone the intensity that they would give to the most forcible one that they could sing, and yet to make it as soft as they possibly could." "If a tiger should step behind you," he told them, "you would not hear the fall of his foot, yet all the strength of the tiger would be in that tread."

The result was a sweet, coherent, monolithic sound that rose and soared and faded like a passing breeze. "Mr. White drilled incessantly," wrote Spence's daughter Mary, drawing on Ella Sheppard's memories. "His ear was exquisite. . . . The minutest thing was of importance to him. . . . In rehearsals his indomitable will never rested until the effect he wished was produced."[24] A later member said they sang with "so much feeling in every syllable" because "Mr. White drilled that into us."[25] Once, when his singers' attention seemed to drift, he suddenly thundered, "in tones which almost frightened them," *Do you believe that?*[26] Their tempo was "rather slow just according to our feeling. In fact, in old times the people sang as they felt."[27] The spiritual represented not the salvation but "the Christian life of the Negro," Maggie Porter recalled as an old lady. White's troupe "didn't sing in the Negro dialect; always in good English." Nevertheless, she said, "just coming out from slavery, having been free just a little while," they had not been schooled "long enough to shake off the old pronunciations," though she did not think "we used very bad English."[28]

The idea of taking a choir of his best singers on the road began to seem the only hope for Fisk, and a natural consequence of White's immersion in both music and the school's all but empty treasury. Cravath was still supportive, but the board of the A.M.A. was not. Seventy-eight thousand dollars in debt, it was hard-pressed to support the archipelago of schools—some twenty-one schools employing 110 teachers—it had established throughout the South. The board insisted that Fisk be self-supporting.[29] But how? There was as yet no economic base upon which to build; even those students who found work as teachers in the state were often never paid by the bankrupt school boards that hired them.[30] White could not cut down any more on expenses: teachers and students were already falling by the wayside from disease and malnourishment. The entire complex of barracks was on the verge of rotting away, and the city was threatening to run an alley through them. Rival schools like Central Tennessee College, with its emphasis on training freedmen in crafts and trades, were beginning to make a dent in Fisk's enrollment.[31]

Then there was the problem of the Spences. "They call for this change & that change in food—as in other things," White complained to his brother-in-law, and "in my despair I have bought & bought & bought."[32] For her part, Catherine Spence had the feeling "that Mr. White does not like me." Though she tried, she said, to be perfectly polite, she thought it "hardly in human nature to feel quite pleasantly" while White and Fisk's cook were "starving my husband to death."[33]

"Money we must have," wrote a despondent Adam Spence. "When is it to be got? Will it come to us without going for it or must we go for it? If so, who must go and when? . . . We need a permanent site and permanent buildings. We need an endowment. We need everything."

Despairing of Fisk's future, Spence pondered looking for work elsewhere. "Kate thinks I could do more good in a first position having a better opportunity to impress my ideas on others, especially my religious ideas." But he could not bring himself to part with the students who attended his Tuesday and Friday reading circles. "I do enjoy it so much," he wrote his mother. "I have faces from the blackest to the whitest and some of the blackest are the most interesting."[34] Repeating his old dedicatory falsehood that Fisk "was the first institution of the kind in the south after the close of the war," Cravath urged Spence to stick to his post. "We are . . . in condition to do the work that is vital to our success, while we are securing the grounds & erecting the buildings for our enlarged work," he wrote.

> It is very important for us to see the difficulties and comprehend the greatness of the work we have undertaken if we are thereby quietened and strengthened instead of being cast down & disheartened. . . . We have of course to raise money & will have to for fifty years to come. If the right man for AMA agent could be found it would be well to have him in the field but the . . . men who are in the field for other institutions [make] it very hard raising money this year.[35]

"We are considering now the question of using a company of our singers in the North under the direction of Mr. White," Spence reported in late March, "to get up an interest in our school."[36] By now White had completed rehearsals for *Esther, the Beautiful Queen*, which he intended to perform on March 9 at Nashville's Masonic Hall, with half the proceeds going "to the managers of the Colored peoples Fair Grounds. We concluded that it would win their regard—& aid them in a very good work—and that we should realize as much in giving them half as we should in keeping the whole & 'going it alone.' We hope to make *something*."[37]

The cast included most of the singers who would form the Jubilees, including Ella Sheppard on the organ, plus James and John Burrus, two of Spence's most promising students.[38] "I will be glad when the concert is over," sniffed Catherine Spence. "It has taken so much."[39] But her husband deemed it a success. "The singers looked splendid in oriental costume and their varied colors added to the effect," Spence reported. A predominantly African American audience with a smattering of radical whites raised a gate of more than three hundred dollars. "Of the balance one half went to pay for a fair ground just bought by the colored people for $10,000, the other half was for the benefit of the musical department of our school." But White had persuaded Spence that the money was not the point.

> The influence was the main thing. A fine concert given entirely by colored people is a new thing. It encourages the colored people themselves and tends to lift them into respect with others. Examina-

tions in Greek, Latin & the like cannot be appreciated. A concert can. We must do something to keep before the people. This I think was a good way to take to accomplish that. Still it took a world of labor and interrupted studies somewhat. And I think it drew our minds somewhat from religious things.[40]

When General Fisk heard about the Nashville concert, he was "greatly rejoiced," he wrote White. "That *was* a triumph worth recording."[41] The praise was not wasted on White. Though he portrayed himself to his brother-in-law as a reluctant maestro whom others were urging to tour the North, in fact he was obsessed with the idea.[42]

Convinced that he and his singers were Fisk's last hope, he promised his brother-in-law "to do what seems to be best for the School & Association."[43] He kept his singers in the public eye as much as possible. At the May 30, 1871, dedicatory exercises at Nashville's National Cemetery, they performed a special ode composed for the occasion called "The Tombs of the Brave":

> *Sleep, comrades, thy battles and warfares are o'er,*
> *Ne'er trumpet nor drum shall rouse the brave more;*
> *Let cannon boom forth and banners all wave,*
> *While we mingle our tears o'er the tombs of our brave.*[44]

In June, the troupe traveled by train to Memphis to perform *Esther, the Beautiful Queen*. Despite the heat, White deemed the "prospects good."[45] But the crowd at the Greenlaw Opera House was disappointingly small. During the intermission, Spence took the stage to explain to the audience that the troupe had come not to make money but "to become better acquainted with our colored population."[46]

On the journey home, however, White and his singers succeeded in becoming perilously acquainted with the white population. The troupe got stranded between trains at a small-town hotel, where a crowd of drunkenly electioneering Democrats began to menace them, deriding White as a "Yankee nigger school teacher." White and his troupe retreated to the train station to pray and sing. White interposed himself between the crowd and his frightened troupe and directed them in some hymns. Gradually, recalled

Ella Sheppard, one by one the riotous crowd left off their jeering and swearing and slunk back, until only the leader stood near White, and he finally took off his hat. "Our hearts were fearful and tender and darkness was falling. We were softly finishing the last verse of 'Beyond the smiling and the weeping I shall be soon—' ":

> Beyond the farewell and the greeting,
> Beyond the pulse's fever beating,
> I shall be soon.
> Love, rest and home,
> Lord, tarry not but come[47]

"—when we saw the bull's eye of the coming engine and knew that we were saved. The leader begged us with tears falling to sing the hymn again, which we did. As the train passed slowly by I heard him repeating, 'Love, rest and home, sweet, sweet home.' "[48]

Seeing the extraordinary effect his singers could have on so hostile an audience in the South, White was more determined than ever to take them North. In August, the choir sang a series of concerts, culminating in a mid-September appearance in Atlanta.[49] "Those were the days of the Ku Klux Klan and the Civil Rights Bill," Ella Sheppard recalled. "Our trips often led into many hardships and dangers. Sometimes after a concert we received private notice of such a nature that we wisely took the first train away."[50]

"Mr. White does not give up the concerting scheme yet," Spence wrote. "He is very persistent you know. He will try as far as Louisville and Cincinnati and places near. . . . Mr. White says in any event he will be 'no longer steward' as he will not spend his time on such little matters."[51]

Spence's minister brother, Edwin, urged him to support White's tour, if only to give his nemesis enough rope to hang himself. "If you and Mr. White are not agreeing well, it might be well to get him embarked in this enterprise at least for a trial," he argued.

> If he has undue conceits I think he would be apt to have them taken out of him in the matter of securing an endowment. If he can succeed, all right, and you would all succeed with him. If it is thought best for anyone to go to Scotland, you would be the one to go, but it would be hard for you to then fail in your object. Your forte seems

to me to be other than financial matters & I don't want you to risk too much. That is in Mr. [White's] line. Let him make an effort first.[52]

But the long-suffering Spence was reaching the end of his rope. White was "a schemer, ambitious for himself and the institution," he told his mother. "He has his favorites whom he delights to honor and others he treats coldly or with open disrespect. He is a man of no education obtained from books, . . . gruff and often impolite."[53]

White had given up on Spence as well, dismissing him as a weakling. "We have a *very superior* working force, I think," he wrote Cravath on September 21, "but we *shall be weak* for want of a *head with brains, ideas, & force.* We are weak now for the want and shall grow weaker. I have less courage than I have ever had before in regard to our future. Time will show." White expected to start on September 22 "to make the preliminary arrangements for our trial concerts. I *hope* to succeed tho' I am not confident as I have now so much to contend with. I have done the best I could."[54]

Arguing that his troupe consisted of an extraordinary collection of voices he could never again hope to find, he appealed for support from the A.M.A.[55] A local Fisk trustee probably did not advance his cause when, in recommending the idea to the A.M.A.'s secretaries, he "seriously" described White's troupe as "a pioneer band of genuine Ethiopian Minstrels without the burnt cork."[56] That was exactly what they were afraid of. The closest thing to African American performers the secretaries had heard of were the blackface minstrels they deplored, and they were not about to associate themselves with such vulgarity.

The association had been burned before sending African Americans on fund-raising missions. In 1862, it had sent an ex-slave named William C. Davis on a lecture tour, but he was so badly received that it proved an absolute detriment to the A.M.A.[57] Besides, the association was grossly overextended trying to keep not only Fisk afloat but Berea College, Hampton Institute, Atlanta University, Talladega College, Tougaloo College, and Straight University in New Orleans. Since there already were "many, many schools" in Nashville, Maggie Porter explained, the A.M.A. decided "there was no absolute need for Fisk and that they would drop it."[58] (Spence could not have been encouraged, for instance, when Cravath wrote to ask if Fisk had any spare desks for an A.M.A. school at Andersonville, Georgia.[59]) The last thing the association wanted was one of its own teachers embarrassing himself and his students, begging money from the association's hard-won constituency, and upsetting the balance among the fund-raising agents who were already in the field. Cravath personally put up a hundred dollars,[60] but, dismissing White's scheme as reckless and quixotic, the A.M.A.'s board also refused to endorse his tour.[61] When White tried to borrow three hundred dollars from Clinton Fisk "to take his singers north of the Ohio River," the general not only turned down the loan but urged him to give up the tour for fear "he would bring disgrace upon us all."[62]

White was outraged. Neither the good general nor the board had come up with any alternative means of raising money. Who else was going to do it? Certainly not fluttery little Adam Spence, piping his pleas on some leisurely speaking tour of Scotland.

" 'Tis time to root, hog, or die," White telegraphed the board. "I'm depending on God, not you."[63]

As a young man, Adam Spence had once harbored ambitions of becoming a violinist and gave up only when he found he had a paralyzing horror of performing. But he retained a passion for music and was as deeply moved by White's singers as anyone else. Long after his own student body had scorned it, long after White himself was dead, he would champion the Negro spiritual as an American art form.

Nevertheless, the notion of White's taking his "uncouth" students out into the world and putting them on display in hopes of raising money smacked not just of the wicked theater but even of slavery itself. Was White absolutely sure, Spence kept inquiring in his tremulous voice, that this was godly work?

"Of course it is of the Lord," White growled back. "It's as plain as day."[64]

Matson and the pastor Henry Bennett also took a dim view of the tour, but White's most formidable foe came from the academic quarter of Fisk's staff: a twenty-five-year-old Latin teacher named Helen Clarissa Morgan. Yet another of the Oberlinians who all but monopolized Fisk's faculty, Morgan had come to the school in 1869 at Cravath's invitation to help establish its college curriculum. She was so devoted to Fisk that when, in 1872, Vassar offered her a chair in Latin, she would turn it down and remain to become the first female professor in an American coeducational university.

Her students were devoted to her. "She was perfectly quiet about herself," Spence's daughter Mary recalled. "Just took up burden after burden, that excellent intellect of hers always steady, comprehensive, at the same time we loved her, just for herself, our dear Miss Morgan. She always seemed unselfconscious, just following her intellect and inner spirit." When a student's sister died, his mother recalled how Morgan entered her bedroom in silence, stroked her forehead for an hour with her "long and soft fingers," and left without saying a word. She would not retire until 1907, having taught three generations of Fisk students, including a devoted W.E.B. Du Bois.[65]

A gaunt, dignified woman with the nose of a Roman empress, she was determined to keep Fisk's academic standards irreproachably high. She bumped up against Spence as well, who worried that too much scholarship would subvert the religious mission of the school. "She is so scholarly," he fretted, "and wants to push the educational work so hard. . . . I am firm in discipline and push scholarship but must push the religious work. I shall try to be judicious about it."[66] Morgan protested White's raids on her student body and quietly backed John and James Burrus when they refused White's pleas to join the troupe, and with good reason: the bespectacled Burrus brothers, who bore an eerie resemblance to Professor Spence, made up half of her first college class.

Morgan's greatest battle with White was over the magnolia-complected Georgia Gordon, now a member of the senior college preparatory class and to Morgan's mind "the best scholar in school among the girls" and "always remarkably pleasant and exemplary." During summer rehearsals, however, Gordon apparently had a set-to with White and declared she was quitting the troupe. Not just the troupe, White fired back, but Fisk as well; she could henceforward consider herself expelled. That, she replied, was fine with her.

It was not fine with Morgan. She pleaded with Georgia to ask White's forgiveness and reapply for admission, but neither Gordon nor her mother was contrite. The proud Mercy Duke Gordon believed her daughter "had done nothing wrong, and said that [Georgia] never wished to go on the trip at all, and that she never wanted to have her go, and that she should not consent to have her join the class again." After White and his troupe had set off without Georgia, a desperate Morgan gave up on Spence standing up to his treasurer and went over his head to Cravath, gingerly suggesting that his brother-in-law might have been a tad precipitous. "I know he is sure that he is right in his course," she conceded, "but I think it is often hard for all of us or any of us to be strictly just in cases where our own personal dignity or feelings have been set at naught. . . . I know there is among many a feeling that Georgia has been unjustly dealt with."[67]

Mrs. Gordon was not the only other member of the freedmen community to have grave doubts about White's plan. Among his first troupe of singers was Charles H. Williams, a mulatto ex-slave who had been bought and sold all over Missouri, Mississippi, and Tennessee before fleeing from his slave-trading master's Davidson County farm to work with Rutling on Yankee fortifications. He had enrolled briefly at McKee's school before coming under the wing of a tinsmith named Rice Moore, whose son George would eventually marry Ella Sheppard. Moore persuaded Williams that "it would be best for me to learn the trade, 'cause I would break down in the singing troupe. . . . Dr. White didn't want to give me up, but I thought it was better, after I was a motherless boy, that I get a trade."[68]

To many parents, the tour seemed less an opportunity than a dangerous interruption of their children's progress. It is hard from more than a century's remove to gauge what White's proposal must have evoked for fathers and mothers so recently emancipated. In slavery, travel often meant permanent separation; the best hope for continuity in family life lay in riding out the changing fortunes of one's master and somehow contriving to stay put. Going south was equated with terrible hardship, obscurity, oblivion. Though going north was still associated with escaping to freedom, the cost of freedom for many runaway slaves had been never to see their families again. The parents of White's singers either knew almost nothing about the places White proposed to take their children or had learned from returning freedmen that cities like Cincinnati and Cleveland were unlikely to welcome young black men and women, no matter how cultured, courteous, or well intentioned. With the Klan abroad, their children were vulnerable enough at school; they would be doubly so on the road. Standing them up before strange white audiences was more likely to make them targets than stars. No one questioned White's zealous devotion to his mission, but as slaves, these parents had learned to be shrewd judges of white men's acumen and stability, because everything rode on one's master's prosperity. If conditions at Fisk were anything to go by, they could see that White had not demonstrated much business sense. How well would he take care of their babies when they were too far from home for their families to help them? White could not even promise them when they might return.[69]

It took White a summer of pleading with the parents of his most promising singers to persuade them to entrust these, their most prodigious offspring, to his exclusive care. Though still sickly, and despite pleas from students who did not want to lose Fisk's sole black teacher, Ella Sheppard agreed to accompany the troupe as White's assistant, perhaps, in part, to get away from the rumors that had begun to circulate through the black community that she was having an affair with the Reverend Henry Bennett.[70] In the goldfish bowl of a Southern mission, such rumors were easy to spread and hard to dispel. As a matter of common courtesy, a Northern white missionary in Alabama named John A. Bassett once shared his umbrella with a black woman as it started to rain. The next morning, the local paper ran an editorial under the headline SOCIAL EQUALITY: A WHITE MAN ESCORTING A NEGRO WOMAN and warned Yankees like Bassett "not to thrust themselves upon the white people of Eufaula." The courteous and extroverted Bennett could well have caught Ella's arm as she tripped on the chapel stairs or offered to carry her satchel in the street, behavior Nashville's black and white communities alike would have found strange and suspect.[71]

Thomas Rutling and Benjamin Holmes eagerly volunteered to be the ensemble's tenors, Isaac Dickerson and Greene Evans the basses. The four friends had been members of Fisk's Union Literary Society, honing their forensic skills in weekly debates on such issues as "Resolved: that we are under obligation to the North for our Freedom." By the time of their departure, all four, but most especially Dickerson and Holmes, had become gifted extemporaneous speakers.[72] Over the next years, they would move, amuse, and astonish white audiences with their eloquence and poise and do much toward demonstrating the intelligence and educability of freedmen.

Maggie Porter's and Jennie Jackson's mothers allowed their daughters to fill the soprano parts. Though, at the age of fourteen, the tiny contralto Minnie Tate would be the youngest singer in the troupe by far, Adella Tate permitted White to take her along. White somehow managed to persuade even the apprehensive Reverend Alfred Ernest Anderson to allow his daughter, Phebe, to sing contralto with fifteen-year-old Eliza Walker, a short, reticent ice keeper's daughter who accentuated her spherical brow with a horseshoe braid.

They granted permission on condition that White bring along a matron to look after the girls. The opposition to White's tour was such that none of Fisk's teachers would volunteer to fill the position, so he recruited a heroic young teacher from Athens, Alabama, named Mary F. Wells to act as preceptress. Wells was the principal of the Trinity School and one of the very few women the A.M.A. entrusted with a superintendency. A graduate of Mount Holyoke, which was second only to Oberlin in providing missionaries for the A.M.A., Wells was a former Civil War nurse and Michigan schoolteacher who had been disowned by her wealthy family for working among the freedmen.[73] She became a member of the black community of Athens and was almost legendarily brave. One night as she was correcting papers, Klansmen surrounded her school and, taking aim at the glow of her lamp through a tattered quilt she hung every night in her door, shot at her. But "she calmly continued her writing, [and] did not put out her lamp." For years afterward, "the colored people kept the door through which there was shooting" until the building was burned down by the Klan.[74]

Isolated, ostracized, besieged, Wells probably looked forward to a Northern jaunt. A few years later, she would confess before a visit to Boston that she was eager to be "recognized by Christians of my own race" and "feel that I am no longer a leper."[75] She arrived at Fisk with a dividend: her small, eight-year-old ward, George "Little Georgie" Wells. He had been born after the Emancipation Proclamation, but his mother never heard the news and still believed herself a slave when she died two years later. Georgie was adopted by two runaway slaves and taken to the Union lines, where he earned "an abundant supply of coffee, sugar, hardtack, &c" performing "his improvised entertainments, which consisted largely in somersaults, singing, dancing, and 'patting juba,' " an African step dance from which the Charleston would eventually derive.[76]

After the troops withdrew from Nashville, Georgie was taken on by a planter who beat him regularly and used to tie him to a gate to keep watch over his garden. Georgie eventually gnawed through the rope and ran off into the slums of Athens, Alabama, where an agent of the Freedmen's Bureau found him lying in a pile of rags by the railroad tracks, begging to be taken to the legendary Miss Wells. Wells "accepted the waif, and for a time, regarded the incident as a fearful visitation of Providence," but "in a few weeks the poor little outcast, at first so repulsive, had become the pet of the household." "Miss Wells," he used to ask her as they sat down together for their meals, "be this heaven?"[77]

On the night of October 5, 1871, White and his ten singers gathered in Fisk's chapel to pray for their mission. Resigned by now to White's plan, teachers tried to make the best of things by loaning their clothes to the bedraggled troupe. "Not one of us had an overcoat or wrap," Sheppard recalled. "Mr. White had an old gray shawl."[78]

"Every dollar was raked and scraped to go," Spence reported. "It cost about $1000 to get begun. . . . So now we have no money, no steward, no treasurer. It requires some courage to face the situation which I now have to do. . . . If money does not come in we will soon have nothing to eat," he told his mother. Though he was glad to be rid of White for a while and "glad at all events that this music is to be tested and the thing settled in one way or the other," he did not "care much which. If that is the Lord's way may it succeed, if not, may it fail. . . . Meanwhile, you see, I am left in the lurch."[79]

Standing among his students and staff, Spence gave the tour a conditional benediction. "Oh Lord," he offered, "if this thought comes from Thee, prosper the going out of these young people. Care for and protect them, and bring them back to us bearing their sheaves with them, and we shall give Thee the glory."[80]

At the Nashville station the next morning, they were met by a sobbing and wailing phalanx of mothers and fathers come to see them off.

And so, "taking every cent he had," Sheppard remembered, "all his school treasury could spare, and all he could borrow, and leaving his invalid wife and two small children in the care of a faithful colored nurse, Mr. White started, in God's strength, . . . with his little band of singers to sing the money out of the hearts and pockets of the people."[81]

"We were nothing but a bunch of kids," wrote Maggie Porter. "All we wanted was for Fisk to stand."[82]

INCHING ALONG

THE FIRST TOUR

OCTOBER–DECEMBER 1871

The North into which the Jubilee Singers now ventured had never been a congenial place for freedmen. "It seemed very strange to those colored people from the south who went north the first time," recalled James Thomas. "They were grinned at and hooted at. Some hoodlum would holler 'black cloud risin'.' Often thrown at, or jumped on and roughly handled, unless the [colored] ran for his life." Thomas had no time for impoverished white Southerners like Lincoln's family who claimed to have fled North to escape the evils of slavery. "After being at home in that new section, a negro happening among them would be held as a fugitive or hustled from their section or from their state," he maintained. "The Negro would fare better in Kentucky than in Illinois."[1]

There were pockets of Northern liberalism and, in most cities, well-established black communities where African Americans could find a measure of respect and security. But after the war, the northward migration of emancipated slaves was alarming even those Yankees who had fought to free them. To them, the legacy of the war seemed to be not Lincoln's "new birth of freedom" but an invasion of illiterate Southern blacks depressing wages and competing for jobs. Though the singers had navigated the shoals of Southern racism, nothing could prepare them for the dizzying disposition of friends and foes, hazards and havens that awaited them in the randomly segregated North.

George White's plan was to lead his singers up along the old Underground Railway, performing in the churches and homes of the former abolitionists who had helped spirit runaway slaves up to Canada. He hoped to bring the troupe through Ohio and into Pennsylvania, New Jersey, and eventually, God willing, New York.

Though White had arranged first-class tickets for his troupe, the singers were forced to travel in the caboose, "or, as one of them styled it, a 'chicken box.'" On their clackety ascent out of Tennessee and up through Kentucky, White and Sheppard must have shared with the singers their memories of wartime Cincinnati, when White marched with his musket and Ella's father, Simon, with his spade. For both White and Sheppard, it was to be a homeward journey to a city where, as White confidently declared, "the expectations of the most sanguine will be *more* than realized."[2]

They found lodgings in a black boardinghouse and proceeded to an exposition that was under way. White had Sheppard play "Annie Laurie" on a piano at a musical exhibition, and "almost at once a crowd gathered, and exclamations were heard on all sides, 'Only see! she's a nigger.' 'Do you see that?' 'Do you hear that? Why, she's a nigger.'" The exhibition's managers invited the troupe to sing, and once they launched into "The Star-Spangled Banner" and "Away to the Meadows," they began to circulate through the exposition grounds, trailing an enormous crowd.

The next day, White met with local Congregationalist ministers named Halley and Moore, who invited the troupe to their respective praise meetings to sing.[3] White then sought out an old friend of General Fisk's named Halstead, the editor of the Cincinnati *Commercial*.

"You are a friend of General Fisk," he told him, not mentioning that the general was against the tour. "I have some students of his who are going to sing Sunday morning in . . . a church. I have no money to pay for the advertisement, so will you please say in your paper that Gen. Fisk's negro minstrels from Tennessee were in the city and would sing, . . . and [advise] everybody to go?"[4]

It apparently worked. On Sunday night, they sang to full pews at Halley's Seventh Street Congregational Church, where, hoping for voluntary donations, they gave a free concert the following night.[5]

Nothing had prepared Northerners for White's young choir. What little they knew of black culture was derived from the derisive "Darktown" cartoons of Currier & Ives and the bug-eyed, burnt-cork minstrel troupes with their "Congo banjos," interlocutors, ersatz "plantation melodies," and "nigger" jokes that cavorted across the stages of the day. For many Northerners, minstrel troupes were their only African American frame of reference, and even the pious Yankees who attended White's first concerts took their seats expecting to laugh at the antics of a primitive people. Just the sight of young blacks costumed in simple suits and gowns was enough to raise a titter from the crowd.

White had intended for his singers to stick to "the more difficult and popular music of the day," wrote Gustavus Pike of the A.M.A., "composed by our best native and foreign artists."[6] Maggie Porter recalled that they had "a varied program. The idea was to see what we did do, and what we could do after Freedom."[7]

As one of White's early broadsides boasted:

> We have songs for the gay and the cheerful,
> We have songs for the rich and the poor;
> We have songs for the sad and the tearful,
> And songs for the RIGHT ever more.[8]

White did not appear on stage during the singers' performances nor conduct them from afar. He left cues and pitches to Ella Sheppard and stood like a coach on the sidelines. They opened with "Children, You'll Be Called On," "Broken-Hearted, Weep No More," and, "the masterpiece of the evening," according to the Cincinnati Gazette, "Go Down, Moses," followed by "Singing for Jesus," "Room Enough," "Washed in the Blood of the Lamb." The Gazette noted the troupe's "rich, clear voices," but its praise was somewhat backhanded. "What might be done with such voices, subjected to early, thorough and skillful culture, the singing of last night afforded a faint intimation. The unaffected, simple fervor, breathing forth the soul, were remarkable and touching qualities of the performance."[9]

They were well received by a large audience that included Spence's brother James, a Cincinnati tobacco trader, but receipts were meager and "the expectations of the most sanguine" were not, after all, realized.[10] Never mind, children, White told his disappointed troupe, they would get another chance to sing in Cincinnati and in the meantime were bound to do better in nearby Chillicothe, White's old stamping ground.

Situated at the convergence of the Scioto River and the Ohio and Erie

Canal, Chilicothe was the former capital of Ohio and now a thriving agricultural town. With his local connections from his school-teaching days, White hoped to do well here. But by the time the singers took the stage the next evening, a crisis more immediate than the plight of the freedmen had captured his audience's attention. On October 8, a great fire had begun to sweep through Chicago: the nation's largest urban fire to date. It would eventually cover three and a half square miles, killing 250 people, consuming almost 17,500 buildings, and rendering nearly 100,000 homeless. At the end of the singers' performance, there were prayers for the citizens of the Windy City, and to the approbation of their audience, White and his troupe decided to donate their earnings, which amounted to less than fifty dollars, to the relief of the victims.[11] "We had thirty dollars," as Maggie Porter recalled, "and sent every penny to Chicago and didn't have anything for ourselves."[12] White would take some comfort in a card from the mayor of Chillicothe expressing "our thanks to these young colored people for their liberality in giving the proceeds of last evening's concert to our relief fund for the Chicago sufferers."[13] But by nightfall, his feeling for his old town had waned.

It was in Chillicothe, recalled Ella Sheppard, that the singers first encountered the "caste prejudice which was to follow us, and which it was to be a part of our mission if not to remove at least to ameliorate."[14] One hotel after another refused to take them in. A third, the American Hotel, agreed only on condition that they sleep not in the guest suites but in the landlord's own back bedroom and eat not at regular mealtimes but before the other guests. As night deepened, the dejected troupe had no choice but to accept.

They returned in the rain to Cincinnati to sing at a prayer meeting at the Reverend Moore's Vine Street Church, and then perform at a concert at Mozart Hall, which White had rented for the occasion. Jennie Jackson sang "Old Folks at Home," and Isaac Dickerson first performed a medley of temperance songs, "standing out in front of the others, with a long rusty coat and mutton-legged pants, by far too short for him, and low-quartered shoes." The entire troupe trembled for him, "while his knees knocked together like chattering teeth, but, under his magnetism, the audience seemed to lose their identity, and swayed to and fro like trees in a tempest."[15]

Their receipts hardly covered their expenses, and White despaired that they were already caught in a hopeless spiral. But he was heartened by the attention the singers had begun to receive in the press. "It was probably the first concert ever given by a colored troupe in this temple, which has resounded with the notes of the best vocalists in the land," wrote one of Cincinnati's dailies after their appearance in Mozart Hall.

> The sweetness of the voices, the accuracy of the execution, and the precision of the time, carried the mind back to the early concerts of the Hutchinsons, the Gibsons, and other famous families, who years ago delighted audiences and taught them with sentiment while they pleased them with melody.

At Springfield, Ohio, where they had booked Black's Opera House, they had to cancel for lack of an audience, but a session of the Presbyterian Synod kept them singing for twice their allotted half hour, applauded them in a "decidedly unclerical manner, with hands, feet, and voices," and saw them off with a collection of $105 and an endorsement "heartily commending them to the favor of the Christian community."[16] One minister rose with tears in his eyes and recalled that, after losing two sons in the Battle of the Wilderness, he had stumbled upon a cabin where slaves were holding a prayer meeting and singing "some of their songs of faith." Their devotions had "so softened his heart," he told his brethren, that "he had from that day felt a peace and resignation that had been to him a lasting consolation."

That evening, they gave a concert to a disappointing crowd and on Sunday attended a service at a local black church to which they had been invited to sing and receive a collection. But the preacher forbade them from singing until after his service was completed and his own collection had been made, whereupon White and his singers stalked out in a huff.[17] As White traveled ahead to make arrangements for future concerts, the troupe proceeded to Yellow Springs, Ohio, where, under Sheppard's direction, they sang at a paying concert in a black Baptist church so overcrowded that Greene Evans, who stood in for White to explain the singers' mission, jokingly reproached the men and boys who avoided paying admission by climbing in through the windows.

Their next stop was Xenia, whose Presbyterians had contributed mightily to McKee's mission during the war. It was also at Xenia that Ella Sheppard had first learned of her father's death six years before. The association must have weighed on her already overburdened spirits as the troupe performed for Bishop Daniel A. Payne of the African Methodist Episcopal Church's newly resurrected Wilberforce University. Tall, humorless, almost mystical, Payne was the foremost champion of black literacy in the A.M.E. Payne did nothing by halves. When, at the age of twenty-five, he was forced by antiblack literacy laws to close his school in Charleston, South Carolina, he fled north and studied so hard at the Lutheran Seminary in Gettysburg, Pennsylvania, that he injured an eye and preached so loudly that he lost his voice for an entire year. Payne moved to Philadelphia and opened a school. He joined the A.M.E. in 1841 and from then on battled for higher educational standards with an old guard that feared that if his proposals were adopted, "discord and dissolution [would] necessarily take place in the Church between the ignorant and the intelligent portions of it." But eventually he prevailed, and in 1844, the conference adopted a resolution committing the A.M.E.'s ministers to "the diligent and indefatigable study of the following branches of useful knowledge: English grammar, Geography, Arithmetic, Rollin's Ancient History, Modern History, Ecclesiastical History, Natural and Revealed Theology."

In his dogged pursuit of theological respectability, Payne made it his mission to rid A.M.E. services of "fugue tunes" and "cornfield ditties," as he derisively called the burgeoning spirituals with which his congregations praised their Deliverer.[18] There is no record of the singers' program at Xenia; perhaps they spared the bishop their spirituals and sang the standard hymns instead. In any case, the singers were vastly relieved when, at the close of their performance, Payne gave their tour his benediction. The combined proceeds from the concerts in Yellow Springs and Xenia were eighty-four dollars.

Nevertheless, their "burdens grew," Sheppard remembered, "and our strength was failing under the ill treatment at hotels, on railroads, poorly attended concerts, and ridicule."

"There were many times," recalled Porter, "when we didn't have a place to sleep or anything to eat. Mr. White went out and brought us some sandwiches and tried to find some place to put us up."[19] The singers were often left in the railway station while White "and some other man of the troupe waded through sleet or snow or rain from hotel to hotel seeking shelter for us."[20] Alarmed by reports of the troupe's travails, a gravely ill Reverend Alfred Ernest Anderson summoned his daughter Phebe home and on his deathbed elicited a promise from her that she would never tour again.

The remainder of the troupe found a temporary haven at Worthington, where White's old nemesis, John Ogden, was now the principal of the Ohio State Normal School. Ogden was prepared to let bygones be bygones and took White and his troupe in for several days' rest, but he must have been appalled by the singers' condition. A concert at Worthington raised sixty dollars, three concerts at Wellington netted "little more than enough money to take them to Cleveland."[21] The collections were small and the concerts poorly attended, Sheppard recalled. "Many a time our audiences in large halls were discouragingly slim, except for the bootblacks and their kith, who crowded in and often joined in the chorus of 'John brown' with voices, feet and bootjacks."

Some audiences would settle for nothing but minstrel fare, and to satisfy them, Mary Wells's eight-year-old protégé, Georgie, became a feature of the troupe's appearances. Performing solo, he proved an irrepressible showboat, singing "Little Sam" ("I'm a roving little darky / All the way from Alabama / And they call me Little Sam"), reciting "Sheridan's Ride" and "The Smack in School," and performing encore impersonations of country preachers that brought down the house.[22]

White would rise at the close of the troupe's concerts and appeal for help. "If there are any of the Lord's people present with any of His treasure," he asked, "will you not help us pay our honest debts and railroad fare to our next appointment?"[23]

Their misery was not unremitting. At Delaware, Ohio, they earned more than sixty dollars and were for the first time allowed to share a hotel parlor and dining room with the other guests. The reviews were positive. "The concert is no negro minstrel affair," the Delaware *Gazette* informed its readers, "but an elevating, a refining, and remarkably delightful entertainment."[24] Back at Fisk, Spence read such "flattering accounts" at his prayer meetings. "People applauded, waved handkerchiefs, cheered & wept," he reported to his mother. "Still I don't know if it is to be a way to get money."[25]

Some of the white ministers White approached in Cleveland turned him down. Even some of the others who allowed him the use of their churches were so skittish about their congregations' reaction that they took their own seats "among the audience and near the door!"[26] The troupe sang at the First Presbyterian and Plymouth Congregational churches, and the Cleveland *Herald* declared that "no rendition we ever heard went deeper into the heart of an audience, or more perfectly conveyed the sentiments of the lines. The congregation sat as if spellbound till the last faint notes died away."[27]

Their receipts again failed to meet expenses, however. At this point, they were living hand to mouth and relying almost as much on the charity of their sponsors as on their receipts. White was reduced to scrounging money from Minnie Tate and various relatives to buy overcoats for the young men in the troupe who had been traveling without them. Wells gave Sheppard a cloak, Ogden gave a coat to one of the men, but their costume was so eccentric that Ella Sheppard was mistaken for Minnie Tate's mother, and Jennie Jackson for Eliza Walker's.

"Many times would we have given up in despair," wrote Sheppard, "had it not been for our noble friend Mr. White. He in the midst of suffering, cheered us on our mission, saying 'he had too much faith in God to fail in so great a work.'"[28] For three weeks, White had been "general manager, advance agent, musical director, ticket-seller, and porter." He often left performances and rehearsals in the hands of Ella Sheppard, and living arrangements to Mary Wells, while he moved on to the next town to arrange bookings. The obstacles seemed insurmountable, but "he depended wholly on God and trusted him literally. He used to say that if the Lord told him to jump through a wall, it was his part to jump and the Lord's to put him through."[29] As White struck off to scout out the next venue, his singers would resort to the prayerful lyrics of an old spiritual:

> *O Lord, O my Lord, O my good Lord!*
> *Keep me from sinking down.*[30]

On November 16, the singers staggered up to Oberlin College to perform before the National Congregational Council. The council's support of the A.M.A., one of three missionary societies with which it had been affiliated, was fitful; it was not until 1866 that it endorsed the A.M.A., which meant only that it would permit the association to collect funds in its churches.[31] Oberlin, until recently the hotbed of abolitionism, was itself growing more conservative. The town's once-thriving African American middle class was beginning to dwindle, displaced by an influx from the South that by 1870 had swelled the town's black population by 70 percent.[32] To host the council, the town of three thousand had to accommodate five hundred visitors, many of them distinguished clergy: at least twelve delegates were college presidents. Everywhere Oberlinians opened their doors and shut their liquor cabinets (though there were not many; the town had always been even more prohibitionist than abolitionist), and along the crisscross lanes of Tappan Square divines strolled, cajoled, debated. The singers found lodgings in the black community and on the afternoon of Thursday the sixteenth took their places in the gallery of Oberlin's First Church, which the A.M.A.'s secretary, George Whipple, had helped to build.[33]

Considering Oberlin's abolitionist roots and the number of alumni who staffed Fisk University, the troupe expected a warm welcome. But their presence was something of an embarrassment to the college. Hosting the council was part of Oberlin's bid for respectability.[34] Up to the Civil War, its seminary students had proved too extreme on the slavery question for most congregations to tolerate, which partially explained the disproportionate number who entered the missionary field. The singers were a reminder of a radical past Oberlin would never renounce but nonetheless chose to de-emphasize in order to establish itself as a respectable institution of learning among Northern whites already wearying of the freedmen's cause. The proceedings were to end with the laying of the cornerstone of a theological seminary, which the trustees apparently hoped would mark a new beginning for Oberlin College, a break with the turmoil and agitation that had kept this quiet, flat, leafy little place roiling and shuddering ever since the oncoming of Lyman Beecher's militant seminarians thirty-seven years before.

The singers sat through the council's dreary proceedings in a miasma of mildewed hymnals, musty wool, wet boots, and surreptitious doses of cough syrup. At last, the chairman called for a recess and asked the delegates milling around the aisles and pews to listen, if they would, to "the colored youngsters of Fisk University." A Dr. Wolcott introduced them, explaining, erroneously, that they were all former slaves and, again mistakenly, that they were singing in order to make enough money to put themselves through school.

After Wolcott's inauspicious introduction, the singers stood and sang "several of their religious songs in the characteristic style and weird cadence of their nation," wrote the Lorain County News, "and with remarkable effect." The milling divines hardly noticed at first; by one account, the troupe announced their presence not with a loud, ringing anthem but with the exquisitely hushed pianissimo of "Steal Away."[35]

Steal away,
Steal away,
Steal away to Jesus.

It was the most sublime anthem in their repertoire and one of the most difficult to perform. The singers had to hit the opening syllable in perfect balance, without hesitation. If one voice stuttered out of sync, the entire effect could be lost. And once their voices joined, they had to sustain that balance over the arc of the most gradual and delicate crescendo, floating their soft, round tones upon a vast, soulful sigh.

Steal away.
Steal away home.
I ain't got long to stay here.

As their blended voices gradually filled the whitewashed vault of First Church, the gossiping divines shushed each other and returned to their pews.

The singers' voices began to soar.

My Lord, He calls me.
He calls me by the thunder.
The trumpet sounds it in my soul,

By the time their voices hushed back down to the last line—

I ain't got long to stay here.

—the assembly was as rapt as any concert audience, tears rolling into their whiskers.

"The singing was really fine, and that it was much enjoyed by the audience was evinced by the hearty rounds of applause which greeted the close of each performance," wrote the *Lorain County News*.

The pieces sung were the old-fashioned religious plantation songs consisting of a one-line solo and an oft-repeated chorus, and gave the audience some idea of what would be the effect when several hundred of these sable singers join in the chorus in the hearty

"Methodist" style, for which they expressed a preference. A collection was taken up for their benefit, which resulted in a market basket-full of scrip and greenbacks.[36]

The collection garnered them $130, but there were other dividends. Among the conventioneers was one of the lesser Beechers: the Reverend Thomas K. Beecher of Elmira, New York, whose brother Henry Ward Beecher was by now perhaps the most popular preacher in America, with a bully pulpit at Brooklyn's prosperous Plymouth Church. Brother Tom was so taken with the singers that he promised White to write his brother about them and encouraged them, come what may, to persevere all the way to New York.

Due at least in part to the excitement generated by the troupe, "the American Missionary Association received as cordial a welcome to the Council, and was as fully and warmly endorsed in the series of resolutions passed, as we could ask." The council set a fund-raising goal of $400,000, "as much perhaps as we can hope to raise," wrote George Whipple, "and we greatly preferred the naming of an attainable to an unattainable amount."[37] Nevertheless, still convinced White and his troupe were headed for an ever more public disaster, the A.M.A. continued to deny White its endorsement.

Another dividend was a thirty-one-year-old Oberlin seminarian named George Stanley Pope. Pope was a man of some ability, having risen from private to first lieutenant in the Sixty-fifth Ohio Volunteer Infantry, fighting at Shiloh, Murfreesboro, and Nashville. He had graduated from Berea College in 1868 and worked as a school superintendent in Montgomery before going to Oberlin to train for the ministry.[38] His devotion to the cause of the freedmen would cost him an Oberlin degree but win him pastorates at Selma and Talladega and the presidency of Tougaloo College in Mississippi, where he would serve for ten years.[39] As the singers departed from First Church, Pope stepped forward to volunteer as White's advance man.[40]

He may well have rescued the tour. Had White continued his breakneck rounds, it might have killed him, or at the very least left him prostrate. What little remained of his strength was nearly drained away by the furor that followed an interview he and Mary Wells gave at Oberlin about the condition of the freedmen in the South.[41] Both of them tried "most scrupulously" to avoid raising "any of the questions which have caused strife in political circles," and characterized the situation in Tennessee as "hopeful" compared with the recent past. "It is the only time either of us have spoken of any thing that could even be tortured into political capital," White asserted, "and then by a reference to the past of three or four years ago." But the reporter went off and wrote an article that "made both Miss Wells and myself to say *just the opposite* of what we *did say* by condensing," and when word reached the Nashville papers, there was an outcry.

"The *Banner* made a heavy attack on Mr White and Miss Wells for remarks they made . . . on the subject of Ku Klux outrages," wrote Spence, "the article being headed, 'What the Fisk University choir went north for—Radical teachers poisoning the northern mind against the South, &c.' There was a mob-inciting ring about the whole thing," he told his mother. "But *we fear no evil*."[42]

From Oberlin the somewhat invigorated troupe returned to Cleveland to give two concerts at Case Hall, but after a Saturday concert on the eighteenth, White again had to play the humiliating role of beggar, "frankly admitting that he had barely money enough to pay for the hall, and nothing with which to meet their hotel bills over Sunday and their expenses to Columbus, where they were advertised for a concert." Members of the audience sent up checks and cash totaling $140, more even than they had collected at Oberlin, and the Cleveland *Herald* described their music as "beauty unadorned." But by now, White knew that such sums and such praise were not enough when halls rented for $75, advertising cost as much as $50, hotels another $25. Though White had believed, and reported to Spence, that their endorsement by the council would force the American Missionary Association to give its blessing as well, the board continued to keep his enterprise at arm's length.[43]

"Please do what you can to stir up a public sentiment ahead of us through the papers and Churches," White begged Cravath. "How would it do to print a *circular* setting forth the facts regarding the class—and the enterprise—with [excerpts] from papers—resolutions &c.—and distribute either through some newspaper or send direct to churches for distribution? Or both."[44] The most the A.M.A. would do was include a brief and noncommittal squib in its journal that seemed designed more to warn congregations that White had proceeded without its endorsement than urge anyone to attend.

At Columbus, the discouraged and tattered singers were met by their pastor, Henry Bennett, who prayed with them about whether to press on

or return to Fisk. "No light was found on any other course but to go forward" to New York, but White realized that without a name that would
capture public attention they would have no chance of success. To this
point, his broadsides had advertised "colored students from Fisk University,
Nashville, Tenn."[45] After their prayer meeting, White went off by himself
and prayed on the matter. The next morning, Sheppard recalled, "Mr.
White met with us with a glowing face. He had remained in prayer all night
alone with God. 'Children,' he said, 'it shall be Jubilee Singers in memory
of the Jewish year of Jubilee'."[46]

White saw his troupe "reaching back . . . in their experience and memory—into the '*old*' " but "actively identified with the work of the '*new*,' and
looking forward with hope to a future full of promise. . . . [The] 'year of Jubilee' has been talked of and sung of so much," he explained to Cravath,
"that I can think of no expression . . . that so nearly gives the idea as 'the Jubilee Singers'."[47]

Not ten verses away from the passage in Leviticus that masters used to
cite as the essential biblical defense of slavery was mention of the year of
jubilee, the ancient Jewish semicentennial celebration when all bondsmen
were set free, all debts forgiven, and all fields left fallow. By the time of the
Civil War, the ministers who admonished slaves to be loyal and truthful to
their masters and accept their bondage as the will of God must have strayed
from their text often enough for slaves to have equated jubilee with emancipation, with the freedom White's singers sought to embody. "The dignity
of the name appealed to us," wrote Sheppard. "At our usual family worship
that morning there was great rejoicing."[48]

It was short-lived. At Zanesville, another of Ohio's early capitals and
now a center of its ceramics industry, the Fisk Jubilee Singers' concert
again earned them less than it had cost them to get there, and they had to
accept a gift of twenty-seven dollars from a friend to pay for their accommodations "in a condemned room over a porch that was so rickety we had
to lean to the wall to keep from falling," Sheppard recalled. "We found the
room so well occupied" with insects "that a part of us only could sleep
while the others slew the occupants."[49]

The next morning, a local cleric asked a shivering and sleepless Sheppard to perform on the piano of the adjoining boardinghouse. It proved a
test of Sheppard's incredible composure. "The indignation of some of the
young women belonging to the house was intense, and the language Miss

Sheppard heard was mortifying, but she continued playing one piece after another, until even the woman who had been so much disgusted came and stood by her side, and desired her to play for her own entertainment."[50]

Writing from Zanesville on November 23, Benjamin Holmes reported to Spence that for all their hardships the troupe remained undaunted. Though some of the Jubilees, as they were beginning to call themselves, were

> troubled with colds, we are enjoying our privilege of traveling through the North very much and I trust in such a way that you will never regret the time we started. It is true we are not received like the Grand Duke Alexis, but then we are glad of it, for ours is an humble mission and we are sometimes willing to be ensconced in the 3rd or even 5th story of a 2nd class hotel if we can't do better. But in the whole when we allow ourselves to think seriously of our previous condition and our present acquirements we arrive at the conclusion that "We are willing to wait a little longer till the good time coming comes" when we can be received into first class hotels without damaging their business.

"Pray for us that our mission may be an entire success," he wrote, "and that we may all return home better pupils in every respect than when we left. I feel that our enterprise will, it *must* be a success, for God is with us and has given us favor in the sight of the people."[51]

A cold rain was falling on November 26 as the Jubilee Singers pulled into Mount Vernon and slogged their way to another fleabag hotel. By now, Ella Sheppard had nothing to protect her feet but a pair of cloth slippers. She had developed a case of bronchitis so severe that a local doctor told her she "could not remain in the class longer, if there was not a change soon, except I was nursed with great care. . . . If I am not stronger soon I shall be compelled to leave. Where I should go I cannot tell for I have no home in this world. Pray for me," she begged Spence, "and I am sure the Lord will do what is best."[52] After more prayer, White decided "the Lord" did not want the company "to go East without their pianist" and refused to let her return to Fisk.[53]

At Mansfield, Ohio, they sang to a large audience composed mostly of "noisy boys," and when they reached the end of the concert and checked the collection box, it was nearly empty. In desperation, White arranged a second concert for which he charged admission, but this time the audience was small, and he was again reduced to begging enough funds at the end of the performance to pay their way to Akron. They were treated to a Thanksgiving supper at a local hotel and earned about twenty dollars performing at the local Congregational church, where Rutling was so exhausted and nervous that when he attempted to accompany his solo on the piano, he ended up singing in one key and playing in another. White made him start over once, twice, until at last he got it right.[54]

After the confusion about the troupe's purpose at their Oberlin appearance, White began to couch his appeal to the public in more specific terms. In a broadside for their appearance in Akron, he promised his prospective audience that "an opportunity will be given those who desire to help lay the Corner-Stone of a permanent building for the University to express their sympathy in a substantial manner."

It was axiomatic among fund-raisers that the general public was likelier to contribute to a building fund than to an endowment. Endowments were vaporous and abstruse: difficult to explain in a brief address to a general audience as it pulled on its coats and mufflers. Even those who understood them also understood how vulnerable they were to mismanagement. But everyone understood the need for a shelter and could envision their dollars and dimes transmuted into some handsome and enduring edifice. Endowments came and went, but buildings memorialized the generosity of their benefactors.

So White began to plead not merely for enough money to continue their journey, nor for Fisk's "support," but for donations toward a permanent facility for his troubled university.[55]

His appeal must have struck some of his sparse audiences as laughable. Shivering in the Midwestern autumn air, the sickly Jubilee Singers were as bedraggled as Dickensian urchins. They seemed better cast to beg for bread than for bricks and mortar. Their concert at Akron brought in scarcely twenty dollars.

White must have looked behind him and seen his bridges burning. Poised on the Ohio border, he knew he could not turn back even if he wanted to: proceeding east, he might raise enough money from sympathetic congregations to get to New York, but he had already used up the goodwill of the people of Ohio and could not depend on them attending more of his concerts in sufficient numbers to pay for his troupe's transportation all the way home to Nashville.

Despite the rave reviews and generous endorsements from the clergy, the tour was an even greater failure than his critics had predicted. Cravath wrote White a letter apparently reproaching his brother-in-law for leaving Fisk's accounts in disarray and recklessly endangering the school's survival. White replied that though he felt "wretched" that his brother-in-law "should be so much embarrassed by my failure," he had

> no excuses to make—or apologies. I will stand all that comes. I have done my duty. It was a great mistake starting the enterprise as I did—at the west—with the few appliances I had. I have done two solid months' work—to accomplish what might have been accomplished in as many weeks. I have never experienced as much misery in the same time as the past month has brought. We have made no headway at all since leaving Cleveland until we reached this place.

But White believed that certain "influences will begin to reach out before us again." He had "shown that with proper management . . . there is even more power for good in it than I had claimed," though if Cravath's letter was "an index of the feeling of the Secretaries," White had "not the slightest hope of success."[56]

THE GOLDEN STREET

NEW YORK

DECEMBER 1871–JANUARY 1872

Six hundred miles away in Nashville, Adam Knight Spence was floundering. Determined to build Fisk into a full-fledged university, Cravath had recruited men and women for the new year whose mission was more scholarly than evangelical. "Mr Cravath put in a certain element here of an opposite kind from Miss Matson and myself and it is a great hinderance apparently. I do not know what is to come of it."[1] Due in part to the departure of such student evangelicals as Dickerson and Holmes, conversions had dwindled to a trickle. Henrietta Matson felt "awfully about the religious state of things" and was replaced as matron by a dour, imperious woman named Mary L. Santley, who was proving to be "a *Martha* much more than a *Mary*" and had begun to alienate some of her charges.[2]

Faced with the prospect of Miss Santley and another cold, miserable winter in Fisk's leaking barracks, some of Spence's female students began to desert Fisk for the LeMoyne School, a new academy the A.M.A. was sponsoring in Memphis under the directorship of a Memphis textbook dealer and Fisk trustee named J. M. Barnum, who was "extensively known" in Memphis.[3] "The house is new & attractive while our buildings are old and the students can stay at home and be at less expense."[4] (To add insult to injury, after a piano turned up unexpectedly, Cravath wrote to inform

Spence that it had been sent to Fisk by mistake and was actually intended for LeMoyne.[5])

Spence's personnel problems were compounded by his inability to confront, let alone fire, anybody. Spence had high hopes when a Reverend George W. Anderson joined the staff, for he had successfully run a school in Selma, Alabama. But he proved "a poor dyspeptic in body and in mind. A man of much power and very valuable only terribly gloomy," Anderson could not be cheered up. When he complained that he missed preaching, Spence offered to let him preach during one of Bennett's frequent absences. But Anderson refused even to attend prayer meetings and, by allying himself with the scholarly Helen Morgan, began to prove a thorn in Spence's evangelical side. "He is a man who does not know how to do any thing unless he is at the head of it and has it all in his hands," Spence concluded. "I am sorry for him. He is in a wretched state of mind."[6] Declaring poor Spence the most decent man he had ever known, Anderson mercifully resigned.[7]

In late October, Spence got a taste of what White was going through on the road. He proposed a student concert of his own at Nashville's Exposition Hall, but the managers refused to allow blacks either on its stage or in its seats. So Spence arranged for his students to sing in the First Colored Baptist Church, which had outgrown its quarters on Pearl Street and was about to move into the largest black-owned brick structure in the city.[8] The concert put "a terrific strain on my father," wrote Spence's daughter Mary, "great labor, in addition to his heavy work and responsibilities. . . . A long week every practice, controlling 500 children, damp with perspiration. . . . The singing was excellent and the audience small the first night for the weather was very bad," Spence reported. "Then too there was denominational jealousy in the matter. Some schools did not come out at all, nominally because they thought there would not be room."[9]

Occasionally Spence received gingerly invitations from some of the school's more prosperous white neighbors. At a dancing party held by a man named Gleves, he found his hostess "not attentive. The women of the South are to be the last to placate," he said, though he "tried to be affable to those who were so inclined to be" lest anyone "snide" him. But one thing was quite plain, he told his mother, "socially we must go either with the colored people or the white at least to a great extent." For the rest of his life, Spence would go with the former.[10]

Whereas White portrayed himself in his letters as heroically wrestling the devil for the destiny of Fisk and blamed all his troubles on external influences, Spence humbly deflated his reports to Cravath with self-deprecating asides, expressing his doubts and fears about Fisk's prospects and his own capacity with greater conviction than he could muster for his wan hopes and modest ambitions. His great mistake, however, was to take too many of his troubles to the A.M.A. When a conscientious teacher named Susan Wells refused to take on the extra work Spence had assigned her, he complained to Cravath, who defended Wells in a tone of exasperation. "I think you have misunderstood her in this case," he said. "I hope that a frank conference will put the whole thing right."[11]

Influenced, no doubt, by White's subversive letters to his brother-in-law, the A.M.A. was considering replacing Spence as Fisk's head. Though Spence believed that getting a firm grip on the school's finances "would do much to put it permanently in my hands,"[12] his forte, as his brother had gently pointed out, was "other than financial matters."[13] Afflicted with ague, buffaloed by White's improvisational bookkeeping, paralyzed by his own fastidiousness, temperamentally incapable of dunning parents and holding off creditors, Spence was proving a disastrous treasurer. After a series of aggravated letters from Cravath, the A.M.A. assigned a former lawyer named Hubbard to assist him, but even then it took Spence until December to send in September's accounts.[14] "I was handling money every day," Spence complained, "and might get in a muddle. . . . Pray for us in regard to money," he begged his mother. "We need $2,000 today to pay our honest debts and begin as we should."

Mary Santley did nothing to disguise her lack of confidence in the survival of Fisk. "She has been predicting the downfall of the university and it sometimes depresses us. The other day we had meal enough for dinner and I had no money. Things looked dark." So Spence went from room to room collecting tuition payments from the students and presented Santley with $10.50 to cover the next meal.

> Unless we get financial aid it *seems* as if we must go under. . . . But I am at present where the Lord has placed me. I will stay till he removes me in some way. My own feeling would be to shrink into a quiet professorship in some one of these schools down here. I abominate the country but I do want to stay in the work.

Spence and his students eagerly followed the singers' progress. "A special service was held at the Wednesday morning chapel exercises," recalled a teacher, "in behalf of the success of the Jubilee Singers; prayers were offered for them and extracts of letters from the singers were read. He believed that the success of the Jubilee Campaign depended more upon the divine guidance and blessing than any other influence."[15]

By December 3, divine guidance had brought the Jubilees across the Ohio border into the northwestern corner of Pennsylvania, where they paused to perform in Meadville, a small town of agricultural warehouses and railway shops and home of Allegheny College. They sang at a well-attended Sabbath service and again at an evening concert on the fourth that was only "moderately successful," due in part to another of the unseasonably severe snowstorms they had been encountering since Cleveland.[16] Though she had been sick for three weeks, Sheppard tried to be game about the weather. "You would have laughed to see us coming from the *hall* through the wind and snow," she wrote to Spence. "We southerners are often pinched by the northern frost and cold."[17]

They proceeded another eighty miles toward George White's birthplace, stopping a few miles shy of Cattaraugus in the city of Jamestown, New York. Though the blizzard followed them from Meadville, White was able to drum up sufficient interest among his kith and kin to hold three concerts and, "at 25¢ and 15¢ a ticket," raise the considerable sum of $250, not including several donations.[18] At one concert, an elderly man rose to say that for him the blizzard and the Jubilees evoked the night he had helped to spirit fugitive slaves into Canada. "And now he thanked God that it was not left for him to carry these Singers out of the country that night because of the crime of slavery. A day of better things had come, and it rejoiced his heart to hear such songs of Jubilee."[19]

White was encouraged that he now had the money to bring his singers to New York, but in case he failed, he was determined not to take the entire blame. In letters to Spence and Cravath, he went on record to castigate both Fisk and the A.M.A. for their lack of support. "All the young people are well and happy," he assured Spence, "notwithstanding the fearful trial through which we have passed. . . . We have been in the wilderness two long weary months and are just coming to see light ahead," he reported.

I have had to fight my way single handed—and make a public sentiment in our favor, under the most adverse and crushing circumstances. About the only help I have had from those who ought at
least to have said "God Speed" has been severe cold criticism on the
enterprise and a continual pointing to its difficulties, and the proba-
bility of a failure. The officers of the Association have not used as
much influence in our favor as the Methodists in Delaware or the
Presbyterians in Springfield.

He noted that a recent article about the singers in the A.M.A.'s journal
contained "no cordial hearty commending of the enterprise to the people,
but a mere statement that such a doubtful craft has been launched, and an
implied, 'We shall see.' "[20]

"People don't know us yet," he said. The wife of one of Jamestown's
leading citizens told him she had read about the Jubilees but "was so used to
hearing 'puffs' of everything that she could not divest herself of the idea
that it was a sort of 'Nigger Show' fixed up to work on the sympathies of
the people." "There is enough in the papers now it seems to me," he told
Cravath, "to warrant at least a public endorsement of the enterprise by the
officers of the [American Missionary] association—and a recommendation
of the troupe to the people."[21]

The singers continued to Elmira, New York, where White vainly sought
lodgings in local hotels until at last he gratefully caught up with Pope, who
had already arranged for their lodgings elsewhere.[22] On Sunday, December
10, they sang at a praise meeting at Thomas K. Beecher's First Presbyterian
Church, "to the disgust of a few of its supporters who spelled negro with
two g's and stayed away from the service, and to the great delight of all
who attended."[23] On Monday, they gave their most successful concert so far
at Elmira's Opera House and left Elmira with a letter of introduction from
Thomas K. Beecher to his brother Henry, "warmly commending them to
his attention."[24]

On December 14, ten weeks after their tearful departure from Nashville, the Jubilee Singers arrived late at night in New York City. At the Cos-
mopolitan Hotel on Chambers Street, they were given rooms "without
demur," but the next morning the management informed White that his
singers would have to eat in their rooms at double the usual fare. White appealed to the proprietor and explained the Jubilees' mission, whereupon
they were not only admitted into the dining room but provided with a dis-

count. Even at the reduced rate, however, the hotel's bill almost cleaned him out, and he appealed to the recalcitrant A.M.A. for help.

The association itself remained unwilling to endorse White's enterprise, but three of its secretaries—Cravath, George Whipple, and M. E. Strieby—provided the Jubilees with warm clothing and took them into their private residences in their Brooklyn enclave.[25] The tour had reached its breaking point. "If they make [a success] they go on, if they fail they get home if they can," Spence mused.

> Let us pray that all may be right. The Lord seems to give them favor with the people but the outgo's are great. So many people to lodge and feed at hotels and transport to say nothing of their time. Still they are doing great good and their "praise meetings" are most highly spoken of. They are attended with immense enthusiasm, tears of joy and gratitude at the sight of such a band of singers once in slavery. But unless the hearts of the benevolent and wealthy are opened to give liberally the thing as a financial scheme must fail. Let us hope they may be.[26]

No one in America had captured more of the hearts of the "benevolent and wealthy" as the man on whom the fate of White and his Jubilees now depended. Though his reputation was teetering on the brink of scandal, Henry Ward Beecher was at the height of his fame. No longer the young radical seminarian who had strapped on a revolver to patrol the menaced black community of Cincinnati's Ragtown, he had become the leading preacher of his day.

Beecher was an odd-looking man, with bullfrog jowls and heavily pleated, almost baleful eyes. He was one of the most gifted and tireless extemporaneous speakers ever to step up to a pulpit, with a supple, resonant voice, a gift for mimicry, and a shrewd knack for reading—and working— a crowd. ("If you want to make your audience cry, take a cup of tea before you speak," he once solemnly advised Susan B. Anthony. "If you want to make them laugh, take a cup of coffee." Before some appearances, he took a cup of each.[27]) In 1846, after an evangelical stint in Indiana, Beecher was called to the newly organized Plymouth Church in Brooklyn, where he would remain until his death almost forty years later. In 1863, he had sailed to England and delivered a sermon denouncing slavery and secessionism that was widely credited with turning British public opinion against the South.

Beecher's theology was emotional and improvisational, a kind of post-Calvinist feel-good doctrine of an "all-inspiring love-power" that banished hell to the historical reliquary. He always took pains to know his audience and had long ago tempered his early radicalism to avoid discomfiting one of the most powerful and prosperous congregations in the country. "No man in this country suffers from poverty," he once said, "unless it be more than his fault—unless it be his sin."[28] On the occasions when his more impulsive ejaculations did not go over well with an audience, he tended to backpedal, sometimes for considerable distances. After blurting something in support of black suffrage, he suggested that before blacks voted they should first undergo "the hardships which every uncivilized people has undergone in its upward progress": a process, he reassured his parishioners, that might take centuries.[29]

Beecher had other foibles. Out of a belief that "God has intended the great to be great and the little to be little," he was most comfortable among the rich and powerful. He was also acquisitive. He used to fiddle with gemstones in his pocket and bought so many Persian carpets that he had to stack them one on top of another in his house. Plymouth Church, which auctioned its pews every year for as much as fifty thousand dollars, paid him the extraordinary salary of twenty thousand dollars, or about a quarter of a million in today's dollars, which was doubled by his annual earnings from his books. At one point, he was so flush as to invest fifteen thousand dollars in Jay Cooke's Northern Pacific Railroad scheme.

Some regarded him as a tad worldly for a man of the cloth, but his congregation adored him and became so invested in his preeminence that when rumors began to circulate that the great man had been having "criminal commerce" with a distraught and impressionable female parishioner named Libby Tilton, they stood by him. He never publicly admitted to more than what he called a "paroxysmal kiss," but the documentary evidence demonstrates he was almost certainly guilty, and he shrewdly and shamelessly used all his powers to threaten and cajole Mrs. Tilton into retracting her story for the greater good of Christendom. A cabal of his powerful parishioners rigged Plymouth's own inquiry into the matter, saw to it that Mrs. Tilton's husband's lawsuit ended in a hung jury, and raised

$100,000 to cover Beecher's legal expenses. But a large sector of the public never believed Beecher nor forgave him, and he would become the object of countless bawdy jokes and limericks. Charles A. Dana of the New York *Sun* would denounce Beecher as "an adulterer, a perjurer, and a fraud" whose "great genius and . . . Christian pretenses only make his sins the more horrible and revolting."

All this was heaving under the upholstered surface of his ministry when the Jubilee Singers arrived in New York. Beecher was reveling in, among other honors and delights, his incumbency as the Lyman Beecher Lecturer on Preaching at Yale and looking forward to celebrating his twenty-fifth year as pastor. He declared himself favorably disposed to the Jubilees' cause, having once stated that the business of a preacher was "to educate men along [the] common line of nature and Christianity together, and lift them up from the baselier conditions and methods to the coronal heights where understanding, moral sentiment, taste, imagination and love are intermingled."[30]

New York City was an unlikely haven for the Jubilee Singers. The roots of the slave trade coiled far back into the city's history, and far forward; New York's "blackbirders," as slave traders were known, thrived well into the Civil War. From 1852 to 1862, about half a century after the banning of the importation of slaves from Africa, twenty-six of the Port of New York's schooners and brigs were charged by the federal government with slave trading. One of them sailed under the colors of the New York Yacht Club. When Senator William Seward of New York tried to crack down on the slave trade, he said his bitterest opposition "came not so much from the Slave states as from the commercial interest of New York."

At the outbreak of the Civil War, the city's merchants and financiers had invested heavily in the slave South, making New York "almost as dependent upon Southern slavery," writes Philip Foner, "as Charleston itself." As war approached, the prospect of shutting off their Southern markets terrified New York's merchants and bankers, who so tempered their moral opposition to slavery that by 1859 a mass meeting attended by the Astors, Whitneys, Phelpses, and Griswolds of the city not only denounced abolitionism but declared slavery "just, wise and beneficent."[31] New York's mayor, Fernando Wood, declared that America's "profits, luxuries, . . . necessities—nay, even . . . physical existence depend upon the products only to be obtained by continuance of slave labor and the prosperity of the slave master!" Convinced the Union was doomed, Wood actually proposed to the city council that New York City secede and refused to fly the Stars and Stripes when Lincoln was inaugurated.[32]

Events left Wood behind. Like Cincinnatians, New Yorkers saw the firing on Fort Sumter as such an act of treason and treachery that they turned against the South. Southerners accused them of betrayal and hypocrisy. "We could not have believed," cried the Richmond *Dispatch*, "nothing could have persuaded us, that the city of New York, which has been enriched by Southern trade, and had ever professed to be true to the Constitution and the South, would in one day be converted into our bitterest enemy, panting for our blood, fitting out fleets and armies, and raising millions for our destruction."[33]

Early in the war, a quarter million New Yorkers turned out for a rally in support of the Union, but after a series of Union defeats, support began to waver, and New York became the capital city of the copperheads—Northerners who favored negotiating with the Confederacy. When Lincoln called the first nationwide draft in American history, New York governor Horatio Seymour deemed it "bloody, treasonable and revolutionary" and warned that "public necessity can be proclaimed by a mob as well as by a government!" It was like pouring gasoline on smoldering coals. Unable to pay the three hundred dollars it took to buy an exemption from the draft, tens of thousands of impoverished immigrants blamed the war on blacks, from whom they had been further alienated by local employers who had used freedmen as strikebreakers. On July 13, 1863, thousands of men and women poured sullenly out of the Lower East Side and raged up and down the avenues and through the streets, halting streetcars, severing telegraph lines.

In the rioting that followed, tens of thousands of New Yorkers—as many as seventy-five thousand of them Irish Catholics—burned police stations, captured forts, seized armories, raided whorehouses, looted banks and federal vaults. In four days of rioting, they set fire to the Colored Orphan Asylum, hunted and chased down hundreds of black men and women—laundresses, students, waiters, barbers, bellboys—hanging them from lampposts and setting their bodies ablaze. More than two thousand rioters and their victims were killed, nearly as many as all the Americans who died in the War of 1812. Almost every policeman in the city was wounded or killed, and it took ten thousand troops summoned up from their victory at Gettysburg to restore order. Of the thousands upon thousands of New Yorkers who took part in the mayhem, only nineteen were ever tried and convicted. 'This is a nice town,' declared a disgusted George Templeton Strong, "to call itself the centre of civilization!"[34]

By the time of Appomattox, the city had supplied the Union with fifteen thousand soldiers and contributed vast sums to the war effort. Supplying the needs of the Union army had quickly displaced the old Southern market, and the wealthiest sector of the city prospered. Banks and markets swarmed with profiteers. Cornelius Vanderbilt made a second fortune chartering his ships to the government. The end of the war ushered in a period of "revelry and graft," embodied in outlandish caricature by William Marcy Tweed, Jr. By the time of the singers' arrival, Boss Tweed's extravagant venality had finally landed him in jail, but his arrest by no means marked the end of an era. The evidence of corruption was everywhere the Jubilees went in the bankrupt city: from rotting wharves and crumbling public buildings to streets lined with thieves, whores, starving children, filthy tenements, broken sewage lines, and mounds of uncollected garbage.

Many of the merchants and bankers who had enriched themselves during the war lived across the East River in Brooklyn Heights. A separate municipality in its own right, Brooklyn was a comparatively prosperous and well-kept city, newly illuminated by the street lamps of the Citizen's Gas Company. Here the lions of Wall Street rode in their carriages, cavorted with their cubs, and distractibly prayed to the genial, forgiving God preachers like Henry Ward Beecher dished up for them.

Before the Jubilees arrived, George Whipple of the A.M.A. had already visited Beecher. Whipple had been Lewis Tappan's right-hand man, one of the Lane Theological Seminary rebels who converged on Oberlin, where his closest friends were black. As an Oberlin College professor of mathematics, he had been an active abolitionist and lived with John Mercer Langston, one of the leading figures in the famous Wellington Raid, in which a corps of Oberlinians had created an abolitionist firestorm by forcibly freeing a fugitive slave from his captors.[35] Tireless, reticent, he worked every day "till one or two o'clock at night, then, wrapping himself in a blanket, . . . would sleep on the table till four or five o'clock in the morning, and then spring from it to resume his writing."[36] Now elderly, but still vigorous and deeply committed to the cause of African Americans, Whipple persuaded Beecher to permit the singers to perform on December 22 at his Friday prayer service.[37]

Nowhere was Beecher's cult of personality more in evidence than at his Friday meetings. They were the hallmark of his ministry. He would sit in an enormous armchair in the lecture room, sniffing adorably at a bouquet of roses or violets provided by the ladies of the church and dilating on all sorts of subjects. His devoted parishioners cheerfully cross-examined him, reveling in his "royal, lion-like, defiant presence, fresh, hearty and jovial—a sort of evangelical Bacchus."[38]

From his throne, Beecher invited his parishioners to "hear the songs that have been sung by generations of benighted souls, on the plantation, by day and by night—songs that have enabled the captive to endure his chains, the mother to hope against hope and keep her soul up when all looked black and dark; when she had parted from all she loved, and the iron had entered into her soul. . . . I hope you may be stimulated in your sympathies and gladly help them raise funds to prosecute their studies."[39]

The singers had sneaked into Plymouth's choir loft and hidden behind a curtain. Then "Mr. White, who was more than six feet tall, got down on his knees with his little whistle and crawled along on his knees to give us the key" to "Steal Away."[40]

"I often feel my heart quicken," said Maggie Porter, "when I recall myself for the first time standing before the vast audience . . . and again hear my voice tremble as I attempted to lead, 'Steal Away to Jesus.'"[41]

The startled congregation gaped upward as the curtain was drawn aside. "A motley group!" exclaimed a parishioner and A.M.A. officer named Gustavus Pike.

> The girls, dressed in water-proofs, and clothed about the neck with long woolen comforters to protect their throats, stood in a row in front. The young men occupied positions closely in the rear, the class standing solid, as they term it, in order to secure the most perfect harmony. . . . I shall never forget the rich tones of the young men as they mingled their voices in a melody so beautiful and touching I scarcely knew whether I was "in the body or out of the body."[42]

The opening pianissimo was so "exquisite in quality, full of the deepest feeling, so exceedingly soft that it could hardly be heard, yet because of its absolute purity carrying to the farthest part of any large hall, it commanded the attention of every audience.

"As the tone floated out a little louder, clearer, rose to the tremendous crescendo of 'My Lord calls me,' and diminished again into exquisite pianissimo sweetness, the most critical enemy was conquered."[43]

> Green trees are bending,
> Poor sinners stand a-trembling.
> The trumpet sounds it in my soul,
> I ain't got long to stay here.

Beecher's congregation was transfixed. For the next twenty minutes, the singers performed a few of their livelier spirituals, some of which made Beecher laugh "till the tears rolled down his cheeks." As the last tones faded off into the silence of Plymouth Church, Beecher stepped forward and opened his purse. "Do likewise," he told his congregation. "Folks can't live on air. Though they sing like nightingales, they need more to eat than nightingales do."[44]

"I think the collection was two hundred and fifty dollars," Porter remembered. "That was our start. Every church wanted the Jubilee Singers to sing for them. . . . From that time on we had success."[45]

They were a smash. Beecher had them back to perform in a paying concert, and on the twenty-ninth White was able to send six hundred dollars to an astonished Adam Spence. "Success is sure," White declared. "It is only a matter of time." Scrambling to catch up, the A.M.A. at long last gave the tour its endorsement and printed a circular "calling for $20,000 for Fisk" and the "constantly increasing number of young people of their race who are seeking the advantages of a thorough and liberal Christian education."[46]

"I trust the crisis is past with the school," White declared, "and that we shall begin to rise again. The Jubilee Singers are doing good work. It has been a terrible struggle to get to a point where we could *touch bottom*—but we have conquered—and shown that there is all in the enterprise which we have claimed and even more of a real spiritual power. . . . Pray for us—that we may be humble," he asked Spence, who hardly needed the reminder. He had been praying for White's humility ever since coming to Fisk.[47]

On Friday, December 29, the Jubilees performed at a prayer meeting for Beecher's great rival in Brooklyn, thirty-nine-year-old Thomas De Witt Tal-

mage. Though Beecher could boast a larger membership, the tall, charismatic Talmage drew bigger crowds: so big that he had to build his own
tabernacle to accommodate them. A year after the Jubilees' performance,
it would burn to the ground, as would its two successors, eventually
prompting Talmage to move to Washington, D.C. He had a knack for marrying wealthy women, and at one point, the Brooklyn Presbytery narrowly
cleared him of "falsehood and deceit, and . . . using improper methods of
preaching, which tend to bring religion into contempt." But he cut an impressive figure at his Central Presbyterian Church and regularly published
his sermons in thirty-five hundred newspapers.

It might have pleased Beecher to hear that Talmage's congregation contributed only half as much as Beecher's. On New Year's Eve, the two ministers went head-to-head, each insisting that the Jubilees perform at his
Sunday school. Beecher more or less won out, but to avoid alienating Talmage entirely, White sent his youngest singer, Minnie Tate, to Talmage's
church, where a crowd of a thousand had been kept waiting for over an
hour. "This little plainly clad colored girl, without support or any one to
give her the key-note," wrote Gustavus Pike, who accompanied her, "stood
alone upon the platform and sang, 'Flee as a Bird to Your Mountain.' "
When the others had completed their set and rushed over to Talmage's to
rescue their "little sister," as they called her, they found an adoring crowd
erupting in applause and demanding another solo.[48]

"There is an infection in the devotion of these swarthy enthusiasts that
is rarely felt amid the artistic coldness of our fashionable churches," wrote
the Brooklyn *Times*.[49] A Binghamton minister named William H. Goodrich,
the brilliant, sickly forty-seven-year-old son of the Yale lexicographer
Chauncey Allen Goodrich, was among the first to recognize the importance of the Jubilees' contribution to American culture. Their songs were
"the only style of music characteristically American," he said.

> The slaves of the South came to begin a totally new history. Their ig-
> norance, their degradation as a class, their separation in sympathy
> from the white race, above all, their wrongs and their longing fitted
> them to produce a rude, but really original, musical utterance, in
> their broken English speech. It is this flavor of absolute novelty and
> of pathos which has given to negro minstrelsy, even when it was a
> caricature and copy, an interest that has endured.

But what the Jubilee Singers were performing was something new. "We have never listened to any music which compared with this in sympathetic power," Goodrich continued.

> We have never heard voices which were blended in a harmony so absolute. With no accessory of dress, with no stage manners, or claptrap of any kind, they have simply thrilled their audiences and held them spell-bound. . . . The most remarkable part of their singing . . . is in the "Praise songs" which they bring out of their old slave life. Born of ignorant emotion, uncorrected by any reading of Scripture, they are confused in language, broken in connection, wild and odd in suggestion, but inconceivably touching, and sometimes grand. At first you smile or laugh out at the queer association of ideas, but before you know it your eyes fill and your heart is heaving with a true devotional feeling. You see clearly that these songs have been, in their untaught years, a real liturgy, a cry of the soul.[50]

Of the eminent Brooklyn divines who invited the Jubilees to perform, Theodore Ledyard Cuyler became their most ardent champion. At fifty-nine, Cuyler was the founding pastor of the Lafayette Avenue Presbyterian Church, which boasted almost as prosperous a congregation as Beecher's. Early in his life, he had determined that "the true things were not new, and the new things were not true." Loud, long-winded, Cuyler was no match as a sermonizer for either Beecher or Talmage. He called preaching "spiritual gunnery" and fired noisily at anyone who fiddled with Presbyterian doctrine. He wrote four thousand articles, mostly on temperance, but he was also a moderate abolitionist. During the war, he had accompanied Beecher on a visit to Washington, where they urged an indulgent Lincoln to emancipate the slaves: extraneously, as it turned out, for by then the president's proclamation was already in the works.

In a letter to the *Tribune*, Cuyler declared that he was fed up with white Americans' "coarse caricature in corked-faces" of black Americans and rejoiced that he could "now listen to the genuine soul music of the slave cabins before the Lord led his 'children out of the land of Egypt, out of the house of bondage.' "[51] Cuyler's endorsement was riddled with unconscious racism. He referred to the singers as "children of nature" and Jennie Jackson as "exceeding 'black yet comely,' " but his enthusiasm was unbounded:

Their wonderful skill was put to the test when they attempted "Home, Sweet Home," before auditors who had heard the same household words from the lips of Jenny Lind and Parepa. Yet these emancipated bondswomen—now that they know what the word Home signified—rendered that dear old song with a power and pathos never surpassed. . . . I never saw a cultivated Brooklyn assemblage so moved and melted under the magnetism of music before. The wild melodies of these emancipated slaves touched the fount of tears, and gray-haired men wept like little children.

Not everyone climbed on the Jubilees' bandwagon. The New York *Herald* called them "Beecher's Negro Minstrels." After their January 3 concert at Plymouth Church, another publication, *Day's Doings*, wrote a brief and patronizing review, referring to the singers as "a very entertaining band of negro minstrels" who had filled Plymouth Church only because Henry Ward Beecher had commanded his congregation to attend. "It has not yet been announced," it concluded, "whether the next performance at Mr. Beecher's theater will be comedy, opera, or melodrama." The review was accompanied by a grotesquely rendered cartoon of the troupe singing to a distracted and appalled white audience.[52]

The highbrow New York *Musical Gazette* was especially scathing:

Were it not for the fact that they are working for a noble cause, that of establishing a college for colored citizens of the South, we could not afford a word of encouragement. Their performance is a burlesque on music, and almost on religion. We do not consider it consistent with actual piety to sit and be amused at an imitation of the religious worship formerly engaged in by ignorant but Christian people; and as for calling their effort a concert, it is ridiculously absurd. We regret to see that . . . the appreciation of music is at such a low ebb that [New Yorkers] can enjoy the "singing" of these well-meaning but unmusical people.

If audiences enjoyed the concerts, it was only because their "knowledge of music is nearly as imperfect as that of the Jubilee Singers themselves, and on the same principle that an uneducated man prefers the illiterate prattle of his associates to the well-defined and scholarly utterances of a Webster or an Everett."[53]

White was learning, however, that there was no such thing as bad publicity. Even when papers ridiculed his Jubilees, it "served to spread tidings of them, without influencing good people against them."[54] In any case, the pans and gibes were the exceptions. The vast majority of their reviews were favorable, and for the month of January 1872, the singers breathlessly performed all over the region, raising thousands of dollars for Fisk.

GET ON BOARD

One after another, divines of all stripes lined up to host the singers through-out the greater metropolitan area: preachers like the monstrously prolific Richard Salter Storrs of Brooklyn's Church of the Pilgrims; the inflexibly orthodox William Ives Budington of the Clinton Avenue Congregational Church; and the unobtrusive Samuel Dickinson Burchard, remembered chiefly for having once labeled the Democrats the party of "rum, Roman-ism, and rebellion." But Beecher remained their most influential champion and, on a January speaking tour through New England, convinced James Redpath of the Lyceum Bureau to invite the Jubilees to Boston.

Beecher went to the right man. Like Spence, James Redpath had emi-grated with his father from Scotland to the wilds of Michigan. As a reporter for the New York *Tribune*, he toured the South on foot, sleeping in slave cabins and attending slave frolics and revivals. He dedicated his account to John Brown, well before his raid on Harpers Ferry, and, after Brown's cap-ture, engaged in a plot to free him. Redpath founded Haitian immigration bureaus in Boston and New York and was largely responsible for America's recognizing Haiti as an independent nation. He served under Generals Sherman and Thomas in the Civil War and after the war established black schools in South Carolina. In 1868, Redpath founded the Boston Lyceum

Bureau and Redpath's Lecture Bureau. In later life, he roused public indignation about the treatment of the victims of the Irish famine.

Redpath arranged for the singers to appear at the Second Annual Festival of the Methodist Church of Massachusetts in Boston's vast Music Hall, where they performed their spirituals for an audience of two thousand. "It was a perfect success in every point," White told Spence.

> Mr. Redpath said he had never seen a Boston [audience] more enthusiastically moved. I send you 500$. This, I trust, with the 800$ from P[eabody] Fund will enable you to settle all outstanding obligations and go through the year.[1]

By now, the proportion of spirituals to more standard contemporary fare had been reversed. Whereas the Jubilees had once performed perhaps two or three spirituals against sixteen or so classical and popular songs of the day, they now barely squeezed in any but a couple of standards like "Home, Sweet Home."

"Our sufferings," wrote Sheppard, "and the demand of the public changed this order. . . . To recall and to learn of each other the slave songs demanded much mental labor, and to prepare them for public singing required much rehearsing."[2] According to a retired missionary named Alexander Reid, White began to ask his audiences to share with him any spirituals they might know. At a concert in Newark, New Jersey, Reid kept thinking that, as good as the Jubilees were, their singing could not compare with the singing of two old slaves named Uncle Wallace and Aunt Minerva whom he had known at his Choctaw Mission in Texas. Reid later recalled:

> It at once flashed into my mind that I could furnish him with some pieces—genuine plantation songs—equal to any I had heard that night, and thus help on the good cause of education among Freedmen. Professor White . . . was delighted with the offer and appointed a day for me to meet the Jubilees, in Brooklyn. . . . At the appointed time I went . . . to Brooklyn, and began the course of musical instruction. I gave the jubilee troop six songs in writing, spent a whole day in practicing them on the tunes, until they got them perfectly. I sometimes *feel* as if I must have been *inspired* for that special occasion. Though fond of music, I don't know one note from an-

other, and never could master courage to start a tune in meeting. Yet
on that day I stood up before Professor White and his trained "Jubilees" (eleven of them) and sang my six songs over and over again
until I had anchored the tunes firmly deep down in their hearts. Professor White . . . assured me that by giving his "Jubilees" those
songs, just when I did, the very time of need, I had made the most
valuable contribution to Fisk of any one person.

Reid claimed to have taught them, among other songs, "Steal Away,"
though by the time he met with them they had already performed it at
Oberlin. It is possible that he taught them a new or amplified version based
on Uncle Wallace's rendition, which derived, he said, from the slaves on a
neighboring plantation "stealing away" across the Red River in canoes to
worship at Reid's mission.[3]

The record of who taught them spirituals and when is murky. In 1881,
Theodore Seward would recall that the Jubilees once met an elderly black
woman in St. Louis, Missouri, "who proved to be a living fountain" of spirituals. Since the entire company did not have time to learn them, White
delegated Jennie Jackson to return to St. Louis "and tap this fountain of
song, and at the same time serve as a reservoir to hold the melodies in solution till she could impart them to the rest of the company. This feat she
actually accomplished with more than thirty different songs, an effort of
memory that is truly remarkable."[4]

As the Jubilees' repertoire of spirituals blossomed, "varied and favorable criticisms filled the dailies of our ability as musicians, of the wonderful
effect of the slave songs, now called Jubilee songs," Sheppard recalled. "We
were received with the wildest enthusiasm."[5]

"Although perhaps the singers have received sufficient culture to modify
the complete abandon style of the old plantation," wrote the Boston *Journal*, "yet the natural, crystal clear melody of their voices retained sufficient
of its original characteristics to charm the audience with its novelty, while
the deep undercurrent of religious fervor was brought out so finely as to
touch the tender chords of sympathy and pathos."[6]

As Horace Clarence Boyer points out:

[The Jubilees brought] the collard greens that they ate into their
voices. They brought the pork chops. They brought the fried green
tomatoes. . . . And that folk element provided a tinge of earthiness

that had never been heard in the United States. To hear them sing "Swing low, sweet chariot" with the grit and grime and yet the passion, was absolutely unheard of.[7]

A casualty of their success was Master Georgie Wells. By this time, the troupe's managers had established a formula of appearances at prayer meetings before each paying concert. Georgie's capers were too reminiscent of the minstrel fare from which the Jubilees were trying their best to disassociate themselves. "On the whole," wrote Mary Spence, Georgie's participation "was not quite appropriate compared with the general high standard of the company's singing."[8] Nor was it appropriate for Georgie, who almost died from a throat so inflamed that it nearly shut off his breathing. In February, Mary Wells returned with him to Trinity School in Athens, Alabama, which had not been prospering in her absence.[9]

George Stanley Pope's wife, Catherine Koontz Pope, who, unlike her husband, had graduated from Oberlin, took over from Miss Wells as preceptress. By this time, White and Pope had turned more and more for advice to an A.M.A. agent named Gustavus Dorman Pike.[10] Pike was a disciple of Lewis Tappan, who saw nothing wrong with getting rich so long as wealth was shared.[11] "From my earliest manhood," Pike once wrote, "I entertained the idea that if a person would accomplish a successful life, it would be fortunate for him to possess three things: the first was a renewed heart, the second, a liberal education, and the third, wealth," for "with these attainments he would become philanthropic, and gain a useful position among men."[12] The A.M.A. gave Pike carte blanche to capitalize on the donor lists he had been cultivating for the association. His New England contacts, especially in Connecticut, were legion. Jolly, obsequious, energetic, and methodical, Pike was a born fund-raiser and, ever since their appearance at Beecher's prayer meeting, one of the Jubilees' most ardent fans. As White and Pope began to receive invitations to perform in Connecticut, Pike signed on for a two-week stint as advance agent, a stint that would extend over the next two years, during which he would manage their engagements and write several chronicles of the Jubilees and almost ruin himself financially in the process.

New England, like New York, had its own mixed heritage on the slavery front. Human bondage had once fit right into the Puritans' conception of a

"City upon a Hill."[13] John Winthrop believed in a rigid hierarchy; just as some people were born to wealth, privilege, and power, some were born to servitude. According to the Massachusetts Bay Colony's Body of Liberties, or code of law, Puritans were at liberty to enslave "lawful captives, taken in just wars, and," it went on, "such strangers as willingly sell themselves, or are sold to us," a nice distinction. At first, they tried to enslave the Indians, but the Native Americans they defeated—such as the Pequots—proved so troublesome that they shipped a lot of them to the Caribbean and traded them for Africans.

There were differences, of course, between Northern and Southern bondage. Perhaps because there were relatively few slaves in New England to police, Northern whites were more likely at least to concede the humanity of slaves. For better or worse, they strove to bring their chattel to Christ; in fact, the farther you proceeded northward from the Caribbean to New England, the more slaves were proselytized. And Puritans extended some of their Body of Liberties to slaves, including the right to sue. Nevertheless, that slavery did not fully flourish in New England was less a consequence of Puritan benevolence than an accident of climate and soil. The region experienced such low mortality rates that labor was relatively plentiful, and most families could manage their small farms without importing much labor. To Southerners, New England abolitionism was an egregious hypocrisy, for New Englanders were among the slave trade's heaviest investors and Yankees thrived on a rum business that depended for its sugar supply on the Caribbean's uniquely brutal system of bondage.[14]

Though the North did indeed rid itself of slavery some decades before the South, New England apparently did not do so all at once—certainly not as precipitously as Yankee abolitionists would later prescribe for their Southern countrymen. Connecticut initiated what it called gradual emancipation in 1784. It proved so gradual that thirteen years later Connecticut passed a law emancipating slaves only after they had reached the age of twenty-one; so gradual that in 1800 there were 950 slaves in the state,[15] and a year later Connecticut newspapers were still publishing advertisements for runaway slaves like the "Negro wench" named City, whose New London master offered a tidy sum for her return. In New England, gradual emancipation usually applied only to children born after the various state laws were enacted, and even they were not freed until after their eighteenth, twenty-first, or, in some cases, twenty-eighth birthdays. This was to insure that the value of their labor would make up for whatever their emancipation cost their owners. If they did suffer any loss, it was probably no more than 5 percent of their slaves' initial value.[16] Slaves themselves could not enjoy what passed for their liberty until they were almost past their prime. Not until 1848 was slavery formally and completely abolished in Connecticut,[17] too late for those Northern slaves whose owners found the prospect of losing their property so distressing that they simply moved to the South or unloaded their slaves in Southern markets.[18]

It took Gustavus Pike a while to settle into his role as the Jubilee Singers' impresario. At Westport, Connecticut, he made the mistake of lecturing a "rum crowd" of Democrats about the Klan. "My audience were ready to be indignant," he reported, and a "disturbance was made," with the result that "the singers became very popular and the Reverend [Pike] a little unpopular." Though he was glad he "testified," he learned his lesson and from then on toned down his remarks.[19] But he worked well with George White, whom he described to Cravath as a "noble-souled Christian."[20] "Bro. White and I get on splendidly together," he said.[21] "I am quite clear," agreed White, "that [Brother] Pike has a mission with the Singers."[22]

In Hartford, the Jubilee Singers sang at the Asylum Hill Congregational Church and at Allyn Hall, delighting not only Governor Marshall Jewell but Samuel L. Clemens and his neighbor the Reverend N. J. Burton, who made a "flaming speech" in support of the freedmen.[23] The editor of the *Courant* described the concert as "a revelation. . . . One heard in those strange and plaintive melodies the sadness and the hope of a trusting and a really joyous race."[24]

For Mark Twain, the performance marked the beginning of a lifelong romance with the Jubilee Singers and their music. It was characteristic of Twain that he understood them both from the start. He wrote to his English publisher:

> I think these gentlemen and ladies make eloquent music—and what is as much to the point, they reproduce the true melody of the plantations, and are the only persons I ever heard accomplish this on the public platform. The so-called "Negro minstrels" simply misrepresent the thing; I do not think they ever saw a plantation or ever heard a slave sing. I was reared in the South, and my father owned slaves, and I do not know when anything has so moved me as did the

plaintive melodies of the Jubilee Singers. It was the first time for twenty-five or thirty years, that I had heard such songs, or heard them sung in the genuine old way—and it is a way, I think, that white people cannot imitate—and never can, for that matter, for one must have been a slave himself in order to feel what that life was and so convey the pathos of it in the music.[25]

The Jubilees' appearance in Waterbury apparently left the impression that the singers were performing to pay for their own education. A writer wrote to correct this "erroneous" report, pointing out that many of the singers had interrupted their education in order to raise funds for their fellow freedmen's benefit. But it was clear to White that the campaign needed a hook: something with which people could identify at once. He found it in a project he called Jubilee Hall, a new facility for Fisk University to be erected by Jubilee Singers performing jubilee songs. Fisk had been considering merely replacing the barracks with sturdier wooden buildings. But now White and Pike were "convinced," wrote Pike, "that you must . . . build *Jubilee Hall*—that is our popular key note—*that* is the thing that takes—a Hall earned by the singing of ex-slaves to be a monument at Nashville—White says he will listen to nothing else. Make Jubilee Hall the grandest building south and on the enthusiasm awakened by these concerts the thing can be done."[26]

By early February, the Jubilee Singers had been giving " 'concerts' every evening," Sheppard reported, and occasionally a matinee for school children.[27] "Don't make any appointments not already made," White begged Cravath, "the Singers *must have rest*."[28] They sang at Farmington, Plainville, Rockville, New Britain, and Bristol, where a local industrialist promised to provide Fisk with a supply of the clocks he manufactured. The owners of the Meriden Britannia Company invited the troupe to its factory to scoop up as much silverware as the university might need. Bradley and Hubbard supplied gas fixtures; Parker Brothers supplied pens; at Winsted, a group of businessmen pledged a great bell inscribed with the singers' names.[29] Blacks were as inspired by the Jubilees as whites. After one of their appearances, an African American New Englander named Julia A. Johnson wrote the A.M.A. of her desire "to teach the Freedmen if their is a place vacant please send to me i belong to the same race my self and i should like to teach them."[30]

Though Ella Sheppard was "now really suffering for want of rest," she wrote Spence from Milford, Connecticut, "*success* is now at hand. I wish I could have you visit *just one* evening a city where we are to sing. It would fill your soul with such a grateful feeling as I never felt before. We never fail to call by the hundreds. Our concerts are so well attended that many are doomed to stand and many more leave for want of room.

"We are now where you and all our friends have for months prayed that we might be," she exulted.

> "How good is He the giver whose mercies fail us *never*." . . . We make from $1200 to $2000 a week now and have been for several weeks—the last week we were in New York we made $2400.00. . . . *Oh such a grand success.* . . . The people seem to be perfectly frantic about the "Jubilee Singers." . . . Our only fear is that this grand success will "turn our heads" but I hope with the help of your prayer that we may feel all the more humble to our *Leader* above for this glorious success. We are petted and loved and flattered by every one we meet. Yet I personally am the same *humble* Ella that I was when I left. In the midst of applause and flattery I often wish to be back in some little secluded spot where I can be from every eye—in the presence of my God and pour out my soul in thanksgiving.[31]

Enthusiasm "never ran so high to my knowledge as at New Haven," Pike recalled. On the evening of Sunday, February 12, the singers "were almost obliged to march on the heads of the people to reach the pulpit; and so deep was the interest, that persons who entered the church long before time for service, remained standing till the last song was sung."[32] They were so popular that they were beginning to eclipse their own patron. Beecher himself was scheduled to deliver a lecture on Thursday the fifteenth simultaneously with the Jubilees' appearance at New Haven's Music Hall. Beecher had to cancel for lack of interest and cheerfully attended the singers' performance instead, fattening the already remarkable gate of $1,209 by calling for contributions from the floor. Up fluttered a wave of donations of everything from checks to jewelry worth another five hundred dollars. It was the Jubilees' largest haul to date.

In spite of this success, hotels continued to shut their doors to them. Two of the largest in New Haven refused to admit them on account of their color, but their fame was turning such incidents into causes célèbres. Pope made sure the papers got wind of it, and at their first appearance, several prominent men rose to declare that New Haven's best families did not sympathize with the hoteliers' "foolish prejudices" and invited the singers into their homes. The same scenario would repeat itself again and again. "Hotels refused us," Sheppard remembered, "and families of the highest social prestige invited us into their homes."[33]

The most dramatic incident took place in Newark, New Jersey. The Jubilees had just performed at Norwich for Connecticut's wartime governor and current senator, William Alfred Buckingham. Lincoln's stalwart ally, Buckingham had spared his state the draft by exceeding its quota of troops by six thousand volunteers. After twenty days of concertizing in Connecticut, the weary troupe arrived in Newark on the afternoon of February 20 and proceeded to lay claim to their reserved lodgings at the Continental Hotel. The proprietor was gone when they arrived, but a clerk saw them to their rooms. As they began to unpack, the proprietor returned and, discovering that the singers "were not 'cork' minstrels," as Sheppard put it, but actual African Americans, he ordered them all to leave. White vainly remonstrated with the proprietor, citing their triumphs and pointing out that the day before they had been the guests of Senator Buckingham. The proprietor was unmoved. White begged that they at least be allowed to eat dinner first, but in the name of "his boarders and . . . the public sentiment of Newark," the proprietor refused.

So White led his humiliated Jubilees to the train station and sent some of them back to Brooklyn, intending to follow on the next train with the rest. But by now, word of their eviction had reached influential people in the city. They sought White and his party at the station and urged them to accept an invitation to lodge at a private home and give a concert. The other singers rejoined White and gave their assent. "It was a study to watch the audience," wrote the *Evening Courier*. "Some were laughing, some crying—all seemed histericy." The Jubilees "would swing from natural to minor keys and back, with strange swayings, like boughs in the wind."[34]

The audience passed a resolution condemning the Continental's proprietor and repudiating his claim that he represented the opinion of the people of Newark. The night after this "disgraceful affair," the board of education in nearby Jersey City voted to integrate its schools. "Of course," wrote a Newark paper, "public opinion is divided as to the propriety of such a step, and, of course, there is no end of debate and arguments for and against it. But . . . like all first-rate and much-needed measures, it has been forced upon the conservative body, which, before this injustice to these poor itinerant singers, had no definite idea of admitting the colored children to public schools."

"By their sweet songs and simple ways," wrote the New Jersey *Journal*, the Jubilee Singers were "moulding and manufacturing public sentiment."[35]

14

OLD SHIP OF ZION

Now that the Jubilee Singers had paid off Fisk's debt of fifteen hundred dollars, the idea of raising a permanent facility for Fisk did not, as Spence conceded, "seem so impossible after all."[1] White was now "salting down" his receipts, depositing them not with Fisk but with the A.M.A., in a building fund he hoped would eventually top twenty thousand dollars.[2] White was determined to persuade Congress to donate Fort Houston, one of Nashville's Civil War bastions, as the university's new site. "We do need one so much," Spence agreed. "Our young men have suffered much this winter from poor rooms and general discomfort and some got sick."[3] But he would soon be troubled by the scale of Jubilee Hall's design, which he came to regard as symptomatic of White's and Cravath's worldly extravagance.

"Tomorrow we leave . . . for Washington," one of the singers wrote to his friends at Fisk, "and I suppose you are all aware of our great success, since we have been in N.Y. and Conn. so I will not say any thing about it but will confine my self to a more important subject. We very often think of home, and wish we were there. and yet we feel that we must have the $20,000 before we come home. and, we by the help of God intend to have it. We leave N.Y. having raised $10,000 and by the first of May we expect to have $21,000 and then you may begin the Jubilee Hall."[4]

On March 2, 1872, the Jubilees and their entourage set forth for Washington, D.C.

Slavery had been so ingrained in the fabric of the American Republic that by the time Abraham Lincoln took office eleven out of sixteen presidents, twenty-one out of thirty-three Speakers of the House, seventeen out of twenty-eight Supreme Court justices, and fourteen out of nineteen attorneys general owned slaves.[5] But in 1872, the nation's capital was not the same provincial, slaveholding Southern town Lincoln had stolen into a dozen years before. Nor was it the wartime Washington of hospitals crammed with the wounded and the dying, of contraband camps, of sutlers' wagons and caissons rumbling up and down its boulevards, of Union Jacks and mourning crepe flapping in windows, of soldiers tromping to and fro, of press-gangs, spies, and whores. The Civil War had transformed the nation's capital into "the axis of the Union," a vast, Yankee-dominated hub of departments, agencies, and bureaus teeming with undersecretaries, commissioners, clerks, lawyers, influence peddlers, office seekers, all scrambling for power and, in too many cases, riches as well.

The Jubilees were about to undertake an inadvertent whirlwind tour of the architecture of Reconstruction. They reached Washington at ten at night and took what Ella Sheppard described as "a long, tedious drive" to the tree-lined quadrangle of Howard University, up to the imposing edifice of Miner Hall. They found everyone asleep but a woman who had been assigned to look after them. "O we were so tired," wrote Sheppard, "I almost cried, but soon found comfort and rest in a 'good old feather bed.' "[6]

The next morning was a Sunday, and the troupe joined in Howard's student prayer service and sang in the afternoon at a meeting of the local chapter of the Young Men's Christian Association that reminded Sheppard of their prayer meetings back home. Miner Hall was an impressive precursor of Fisk's own Jubilee Hall, a vast turreted brick structure overlooking McMillan Reservoir. Like Fisk, Howard University had been named after an officer of the Freedmen's Bureau, in this case its first commissioner, General Oliver Otis Howard, a pious, burly West Point mathematics instructor who had traded an arm for a Medal of Honor in the Peninsular campaign. Under his inept commissionership, corruption so riddled his besieged bureau that, even after it was scuttled, a full court of inquiry would be required to exonerate him.

Back in 1869, Howard accepted the presidency of his namesake university, which he had helped to establish two years earlier under the aegis of the capital's First Congregational Society. Founded as a training school for black teachers and preachers, in the early 1870s it boasted a broader curriculum than Fisk's, with departments of industrial arts, medicine, law, agriculture, commerce, and military studies. The school benefited from its Washington location; the general turned it into a showcase for visiting congressmen and ensured that Freedmen's Bureau funds were made available for it. In fact, he was headquartered in one of its buildings, though not for much longer: within three months of the Jubilees' visit, Congress and the president would shut the bureau down.[7] Within a year, Howard University itself would fall on hard times; building stopped, several departments closed, and it would eventually take an annual congressional subsidy to keep it afloat into the 1880s.

On Monday, March 4, John Eaton of the Freedmen's Bureau, a Fisk trustee who had attended the school's opening in 1866, took the Jubilees to the home of a fellow attendee, former Tennessee governor and now senator, William Gannaway "Parson" Brownlow. A circuit-riding Methodist minister and Knoxville newspaper editor, Brownlow was the first civilian postwar governor of Tennessee. He hated abolitionists as much as secessionists, and during the war he had signed a petition seeking to exempt his state from the Emancipation Proclamation. Though he later supported Lincoln's policy, he was animated not by the cause of the freedmen but by his vitriolic hatred of East Tennessee Democrats and rebel sympathizers.[8] He was one of the most ferociously partisan polemicists of that partisan period, declaring once that he would join forces with the Democrats only when "Queen Victoria consents to be divorced by a county court in Kansas."[9] He took office just after the state legislature had ratified the Thirteenth Amendment abolishing American slavery.[10] As governor, he recruited a militia and even declared martial law in a few counties to protect East Tennessee unionists.

Brownlow at first declined to support black suffrage. But when secessionist candidates threatened to sweep every unionist from office in 1866,[11] he realized he would need black votes to "weigh the balance against rebelism" and head off the "approach of treason."[12] Nevertheless, he refused to consider allowing blacks to run for state office and serve on juries until after they had demonstrated their gratitude by supporting him in the following election.[13] A confirmed colonizationist, he encouraged Tennessee's blacks to leave the South for the Far West: the farther west the better. As senator, he would be denounced by Tennessee's black leaders for opposing Charles Sumner's supplementary civil rights bill of 1874. Nevertheless, by the time he entered the Senate in 1869, "Parson" Brownlow had become, for better or worse, emblematic of the Southern Reconstruction governor. Whatever his motives, his regime had offered to freedmen at least a hope for justice, which his successors would eventually dash.

His connection to the Jubilees was personal. One of his old allies in Knoxville was the Reverend Alfred Ernest Anderson, who had pulled his daughter Phebe off the tour. Propped up in his bed, his jaw slack, Brownlow greeted the Jubilees weakly but warmly. Speaking in a dry husk of a voice, he requested not a spiritual but the old sentimental standby "Home, Sweet Home."

"As we sang that good old piece," Sheppard reported, "the tears rolled down his pale cheeks and he reached his hand to us, thanking us."

Seeing him so sick, the singers performed a second song, "Keep Me from Sinking Down," and quietly departed.[14]

> I look up yonder,
> And what do I see?
> Keep me from sinking down.
> I see the angels
> Beckoning me.
> Keep me from sinking down.

The Jubilees toured the White House next, hoping but failing to catch a glimpse of General Grant and his family. They then crossed Pennsylvania Avenue to the eastern corner of Lafayette Square to admire the imposing new headquarters of the Freedmen's Savings and Trust Company, in which several of the singers were depositors.

The Freedmen's Bank, as it was commonly called, was established in 1865 for anyone "heretofore held in slavery in the United States, or their descendants" and "was supposed to have government recognition and to be as solid as the government itself," recalled the black barber James Thomas.

> The people rushed to the bank with their money [and] deprived themselves of many things that they might swell their bank account. Branches were established in all cities. The brothers were pleased with the Idea. They met at the bank frequently to talk business.[15]

The *American Missionary* gave an account of an elderly freedman who asked a representative of the bank named Hewitt "what security they would have that their money would be safe."

> Mr. Hewitt told him that the company was composed of a large number of the best and wealthiest men in the United States; but, as they were not personally responsible, he could only trust to their honor and integrity of character.
> "Were there any old rebels and slave holders among them?" continued the inquirer.
> "No," said Mr. Hewitt; "they are all Northern men, and your friends."
> "Then that's all right," was the response from several.
> "But," continued the old man, "what's done with the money?"
> "That," said Mr. Hewitt, "is invested in United States stocks."
> At this reply, the old financier stood a moment, as if in profound reflection, and then said, with apparent satisfaction, "Well, then, the bank can't break without the United States breaks; and there's no danger of that, though the rebels tried mighty hard to break it," and took his seat amid a merry laugh.[16]

In time, however, "the best and wealthiest men" began to speculate with their depositors' money. The board invested in the Union Pacific Railroad and made a loan to the railroad speculator Jay Cooke, whose brother happened to sit on the board of directors. Unknown even to the board, the bank's officers made a number of other dubious loans, and, when Jay Cooke and Company failed in 1873, the directors would not know how much trouble they were in. As the bank declined, whites hastened off the board to be replaced by blacks, and to dispel the rumble of rumors about

the bank's unsoundness, the board would appoint as president the most distinguished African American it could find: the old lion of abolitionism,
Frederick Douglass.

In early 1874, a newcomer to the troupe named Mabel Lewis would
withdraw all of her savings—some six hundred dollars—from her Freedmen's Bank account and later lend it to White to help launch the singers'
third campaign. Mabel Lewis's guardians had refused White the money and
forbade her from risking her savings, but even though she was underage,
Lewis "went on my own hook and got it anyway." She was lucky she did: after the bank failed in July 1874, ruining thousands of freedmen all over the
country, White paid her back in full.[17]

For the past eighteen years, the Washington Monument had remained un-
finished at about a third of its eventual height and would not be completed
for another twelve years.[18] The troupe's pilgrimage to the incomplete marble memorial to the father of the country may have given the Jubilees some
pause, for the closest thing to Washington America had produced had been
Robert E. Lee, and many people on both sides of the Civil War suspected
that had Washington been alive he, like Lee, might well have sided with the
Confederacy.

For many abolitionists, George Washington represented little more than
the old order and the failure of the founding fathers to abolish human
bondage. Though African Americans fought for Washington, thousands of
them sided with the British, who promised them emancipation. But the
British abandoned many of them as they departed in defeat, and Continental militia ranged up and down the coast to capture and enslave them. The
rest escaped to England and Canada.

Descendants of Washington's slaves lived in Robertson County, Tennessee.[19] Their memories of the father of our country were not necessarily
rosy. Though Washington found slaveholding repugnant, and freed his own
slaves in his will, he advised his friends on how to trick runaway slaves back
into service and once sent an agent to New England to capture a runaway
slave of Martha Washington's named Staines. Mrs. Staines recalled that
"she never received the least mental or moral instruction, of any kind,
while she remained in Washington's family." According to her abolitionist
interviewer, Staines maintained "that the stories told of Washington's
piety and prayers, so far as she ever saw or heard while she was his slave,

have no foundation. Card-playing and wine-drinking were the business at his parties, and he had more of such company on Sundays than on any other day."[20]

"I don't . . . admire George Washington," sighed Doc Daniel Dowdy of Georgia. "White men from the South that will help the Negro is far and few between."[21]

Whatever the Jubilees may have made of America's first president, they were delighted to learn when they returned to Howard that they had been invited to sing the next morning for its latest, Ulysses S. Grant. "With light hearts," wrote Sheppard, "we rested the remaining hours until evening" and set off to give a concert in Lincoln Hall. It was a "dreadful, stormy night." Nevertheless, the hall was full.

The audience included ambassadors, justices, clergymen, cabinet secretaries, and the affable, teetotaling vice president Schuyler "Smiler" Colfax and his congressional cronies. A Republican antislavery newspaperman from northern Indiana, Colfax was a skilled parliamentarian. As an advocate of the telegraph and transcontinental railroads, he eventually rose to become literally the fastest-talking Speaker of the House in American history. At the time Grant chose him as vice president, Colfax was an advocate of black suffrage and would cast his vote for Charles Sumner's civil rights bill. But he proved a flawed champion. Like so many of the president's men, Colfax would eventually be caught with his hand in the cookie jar: in his case, the money pot of the Crédit Mobilier construction firm, which was filling the pockets of crooked railway speculators and greedy politicians with millions of federal dollars. In the end, a disgraced "Smiler" Colfax would be spared impeachment only because Grant declined to nominate him for a second term.[22]

The Lincoln Hall concert was another Jubilee success. "They are black, some of them jet black, the best of the female voices coming from the thickest of negro lips," wrote a local clergyman.

They sing the most touching of Christian melodies, full of Jesus, and of Heaven; the most wild of plantation melodies, full of sorrow and aspirations for freedom. . . . Their demeanor is graceful and unassuming, and, before they close, the coldest audience is in enthusiasm, and never tires of *encoring*.[23]

The next morning, "we rose full of enthusiasm and anxious for the hour to come when we should visit the *President*," wrote Sheppard.

> At 9 we went into the chapel and sang a while for the school and at 10 the carriage came for us—bringing Gen. Eaton. We went to the White House and after waiting a while was ushered into his presence. As we entered he arose, came to us and received an introduction to each one of us, shaking our hands heartily as he did so.[24]

The Jubilees were not seeing Ulysses S. Grant at his best. The Union's military savior had not grown in his presidency but shriveled. As a general, Grant had been lucid, surefooted, and merciless; as a president, he was muddled, hesitant, and fatally chummy with the rich and powerful. He had voted in only one presidential election in his life, and that had been for James Buchanan, a Democrat. Though he had served briefly as Andrew Johnson's secretary of war, Grant knew little about government and the law. As a civilian at least, he proved a terrible judge of people, appointing dim and venal relatives and army buddies instead of the abler men he dismissed because their eyes were too close together or they parted their hair in the middle.[25]

Grant embodied the country's own postwar malaise. The drama and urgency of the war and its signal achievement of freeing the slaves were being subsumed by the conundrum of reunification. The fabric of the nation was torn by those who would punish the defeated whites of the South and those who would restore them to full participation in the life of the Republic. By threatening to resign as secretary of war, Grant had prevented his predecessor, Andrew Johnson, from prosecuting former rebels and violating the terms of surrender Grant had signed at Appomattox with Robert E. Lee. Though he owed his election to the black vote, his magnanimity did not extend with much potency to freedmen, whom he advised to seek security under the care of their former masters.

The war had turned the North into a mighty economic as well as military power, and under Grant's neglectful stewardship, lucre had seeped into every interstice of government. It was a testament to the haplessness of his opponents, and to the enduring debt the nation felt it owed Grant for his ingenious and tenacious service as commander of the Union army, that he was about to be reelected president of the United States. By the time the general stepped forward to greet the Jubilee Singers, "Grantism" had become the code word for corruption in high places.

"And these are the 'Jubilee Singers' I have read so much of," Grant said as he shook their hands. "I am very much interested and hope you may have a glorious success."

He asked them to sing a piece. They chose "Go Down, Moses," in the wan hope, perhaps, that Grant might see himself as the freedmen's deliverer, though to advocates of the freedmen, Grant sometimes seemed more pharaoh than Moses.

> *Go down, Moses,*
> *Way down in Egypt land.*
> *Tell old Pharaoh*
> *To let my people go.*

Though Grant was so unmusical that he could hardly recognize, let alone carry, a tune, he seemed pleased. He told them that he had planned to attend the concert the night before but that Colfax had gone "off without him, forgetting him," Sheppard reported.

> So he was deprived of his visit to our concert and was very sorry because . . . he would have had a reception at home. He also said he was glad to see such a good account of our concert in the papers and from Colfax. Then we bid him good bye.

That afternoon, Howard gave them a reception, where Sheppard was intrigued by one of three Chinese students Howard had folded into its student body in hopes of training them as missionaries to the Chinese laboring on the Northern Pacific Railroad. "I had been told he declaimed very nicely," she wrote.

> We asked him to speak something for us. He did so and did it grandly. After he sat down he said to me, "I can't speak your words very well but try very hard." He was very sociable and shows himself to have a cultivated taste in conversation. He has been in this school two years—is much loved by all and is said to be a fine scholar.

He no longer wore a plait, Sheppard noticed, and though the other two Chinese students did, they were "not yet very bright or much thought of."[26]

The next morning, the singers paid their last Washington visit, a pilgrimage to meet the penultimate white champion of the freedman, sixty-one-year-old senator Charles Sumner. A co-founder of the Massachusetts Republican Party, Sumner was an early and unbending foe of slavery. He was elected to the Senate in 1851 and, during a floor debate on Kansas five years later, denounced a South Carolinian colleague with such vitriol that one of the Carolinian's kinsmen beat him senseless with a gutta-percha cane. The attack disabled Sumner for years, turning him into a kind of living martyr of abolitionism.

The attack did nothing to soften him up. Disciplined and incorruptible, but also bullying and tactless, Sumner became a powerhouse during the war as the chairman of the Senate Committee on Foreign Relations. He allied himself with Lincoln but moved far ahead of the president in his advocacy of racial justice, championing not only black suffrage but the acceptance of black testimony in federal cases, equal pay for black soldiers, and the desegregation of the capital's streetcars. After the war, he tried to make enfranchisement for the freedmen a precondition of the readmission of Southern states into the Union. He came to despise Andrew Johnson and his pro-white policies and was the chief architect of his impeachment. In the election of 1872, Sumner opposed Grant as well, and when the singers met him he was engaged in trying to attach a civil rights bill to the amnesty legislation Grant favored. He would die within two years, still pleading for his bill; a year later, Congress would pass it in his memory.

Sumner promised he would see what he could do about deeding Fort Houston to Fisk, after which the Jubilee Singers and their managers quietly made their way to the depot and boarded a train for the North.

I AIN'T GOT WEARY YET

HOMECOMING

MARCH–MAY 1872

On New Year's, 1872, Adam Spence and Henrietta Matson were as cheered by the convulsion of renewed religious fervor that briefly shivered through Fisk as by the Jubilees' singing the university out of debt. Once again Matson could see in Fisk a gift that "the Lord seems to have laid . . . upon me, as he has never any thing before." Some mornings this stout, feverish woman would rise from bed and exclaim, "O! that Fisk University might live before Thee!" She credited the new wave of enthusiasm to her beloved Adam Spence. "Ever since the Lord sent Prof Spence to this Institution," she wrote his mother, "I have felt that . . . his idea of what a school of this kind should be seems so truly the Gospel idea that it . . . must prosper."[1]

Spence had begun to extend his missionary perambulations beyond the freedmen's neighborhoods to the impoverished Irish ghetto of the Broad Street Bottoms on the Cumberland flats. "O what a company of the halt, the maimed, the blind (literally so)," he reported, "the diseased in body and in soul!"[2] Some saw his evangelical forays as an escape from the continuing day-to-day pressure of making the university's ends meet and the constant strife among his staff of ten teachers.[3] *Do be careful,*" Spence's voluble brother Edwin had advised. "You have *great & important* work upon your hands, and to perform it you must be just as economical of strength as possible. [Do] not work too *much* in the religious way. . . . Feel no *great* responsibility for the salvation of souls even, or you will wear out before you are half done. . . .Your work is to establish a *great christian university*."[4]

But Spence's heart was not in it. He continued to twitter about the accounts, which he never seemed to get right with Cravath, and wrung his hands over the "burden of work" that the tidal wave of donations represented.[5] Where would he put the seven hundred books that came in, or the bell, or the silverware, or the zoological and botanical specimens for Fisk's nominal science department?

What was most damaging to Spence's prospects, however, was the remarkable success of his nemesis, George White, whose mission he had long decried. From a reckless Quixote, White had emerged as the golden boy of the A.M.A. He had the ear of not just his brother-in-law but even the association's more venerable and conservative secretaries like George Whipple. By March 1872, White's insistence that the university needed someone more "forceful" had begun to have an effect. Now that White's Jubilees had insured that Fisk University would not only stand but stand out among the A.M.A.'s ranks of schools as a beacon of freedmen's education, Cravath and his fellow secretaries began to look for someone else to lead it.[6]

Like John Braden, for instance, the dynamic president of Fisk's nearest competitor, Central Tennessee College, the Methodist Episcopal Church's entry in the Nashville field. A lifelong "Professor of Moral Sciences," Braden was yet another entrepreneurial New Yorker who had built a school from a room in an abandoned chapel to an enterprise as substantial as Fisk. In 1870, his enrollment was about two hundred, and his campus included numerous buildings plus a peach orchard and a grape arbor. But he had hastily built his facility with green lumber. As the studs and beams warped and writhed, the horsehair plaster fell away from its lath. Within a year or two, the Tennessee damps had rendered the college's unpainted poplar fence "utterly toothless," and the lack of proper boarding facilities discouraged the "best class of colored people" from attending.[7]

The "best class" of students, like W.E.B. Du Bois and Henry Hugh Proctor, would find other faults with Central Tennessee College, whose curriculum was more like Tuskegee's than Fisk's. "The men who most impress the world are those who wrestle with the problems of every-day life," Braden declared. Education should be "practical," preparing students for "the farm, the workshop, the store, as well as for the school-room, the office and the pulpit." Braden thereby took sides, eventually, in the "head versus hands" debate that would pit Cravath and Du Bois of Fisk, who believed in cultivating an intellectual elite, against Booker T. Washington of Tuskegee, who would espouse industrial education as the key to black progress.[8]

In the end, Central Tennessee College would fall victim to squabbling and fiscal miscalculations.[9] But in 1873, Braden was a formidable presence in Nashville, and Spence only suffered by comparison. Spence's decency, empathy, and humility were as much to blame as his slight voice and hopelessness with finances. He was a gifted and dedicated teacher and probably would have made an adequate, if uninspiring, chaplain. But he was not cut out to raise money and build edifices and put the best face on things; he was not, in short, college presidential material. Most missionaries, wrote Gustavus Pike, were "dull preachers" who "affected a pious twang and nasal pitch, enough to curse any sermon, and especially a begging one." They "left no inspiration, imparted no blessing, and the people have caught no zeal for the work." What institutions like Fisk needed were "generals" with "all the masterly energy required in constructing a Pacific Railroad, or in arming a nation to put down a rebellion."[10]

"Have written to Mr. Cravath about next year," Spence reported to his mother. "I want to plan for the future. If I am still to have the care of the institution I want to know it soon. . . . It would be a great relief to just teach Greek or anything and have no further responsibility. But that may not be the Lord's will."[11]

Cravath gently expressed his regret that Spence had "worked beyond your strength this year." He urged Spence to remain at Fisk and promised to create a professorship for him "if our plans for the university can be carried out." But he and the secretaries had decided to seek "some man of reputation and ability as an educator in New England for whom an endowment of $25,000 can be readily raised to take the Presidency."[12]

At least Cravath's letter put to rest a recurring nightmare Spence had begun to have—that the A.M.A. would choose George Leonard White for Fisk's presidency. But Spence's wife, Catherine, was "a great deal discouraged," and Miss Matson felt "as if the evil one had triumphed," for Cravath and the A.M.A. were too "full of worldly policy" and Spence "too well educated and too pious for them to appreciate."

"Now what shall I do?" Spence wondered. "Shall I go out of the employ of the A.M.A. and this *one-man despotism*? Or shall I take a professorship?"[13]
He would take the professorship.

On March 8, 1872, the singers performed in Manhattan at Steinway Hall, where the Reverend Dr. William Adams was struck "by the peculiar propriety of their deportment, in dress and address, in voice and manner."[14] General Fisk himself attended and reminded the audience that Thomas Rutling had once been a runaway who haunted his headquarters and earned the nickname "Rollicking Tom." "His last cash evaluation was $450," Fisk continued as the audience laughed. But now "I think he would be quick to draw $500 for continued service at Steinway Hall."[15] Fisk gestured toward little Minnie Tate, "whose sweet voice has moved you to tears." She was once considered worth $350, Fisk declared, but now, as the audience itself could "most heartily testify to-night, . . . one thousand dollars would be cheap for her."[16]
It is hard to know how the Jubilees felt about the general's remarks. They tended to bear them with humor and equanimity. Nevertheless, Fisk's quip reflected an unfortunate strain that ran through the Jubilees' press. The Newark *Evening Courier*'s review was a bizarre blend of contempt and admiration. It praised Fisk and the singers but called them "picanninies" and listed them as if they were items in a slave dealer's catalogue: "Negro man, very black, six feet high, worth in old times $2,000 under the hammer—basso"; "Jennie Jackson, full-blooded brunette; very dark eyes and hair, which seem light in contrast with a brow like that in which Shakespeare's lover saw Helen's beauty"; "Young girl, with eyes and hair (and face) as black as a beaver"; Minnie Tate, "a charming little quadroon, about 15 years of age, with straight hair, falling loosely down her back"; and "Maggie Porter, a constructive blond with curly hair—soprano."
A Connecticut paper found the Jubilees' repertoire a "mixture" that "seemed at first like an odd blending of Ethiopian minstrelsy with sacred things." The New York *World*'s critic suggested that "the troupe should sing camp-meeting and nigger melodies proper than venture on opera. Your colored individual," he continued, "is not good at Ernani but when it comes to something about the golden streets or 'de heaven gate' is all at home. It was noticeable in the singers that they had the air of well-trained monkeys when put upon the scientific, but as the programme touched a wild darky air, [they] limbered out instantly and sung with mellowness and life."[17]

General Fisk promised to pressure Congress to deed Fort Houston to Fisk "at the earliest day possible." If he had "six minutes to give to this work," he told Cravath, "we would make it jingle." But the singers had restored his confidence in his namesake school. "The good Lord will keep us 'from sinking down,'" he assured Cravath, "and deliver us as he did Daniel of Old. The songs of our melodists are yet ringing in my ear—and I am grateful to God for what my eyes have seen and ears heard."[18]

One of the Jubilees' champions in New York was Thomas Frelinghuysen Seward, a cousin of Lincoln's secretary of state and editor of the *Musical Pioneer* and the *Musical Gazette*. He was an ardent proponent of a system of musical notation called tonic sol-fa that derived from the advent of British congregational singing in the first third of the nineteenth century and had since become a kind of cult. Its adherents contended that their system of alphabet symbols would eventually supplant standard notation. One of the faithful, probably Seward himself, had tried to bully Mark Twain into advocating the system. When he politely refused, "what a scorcher I got, next mail!" Twain recalled. "Such irony! Such sarcasm, such caustic praise of my super-honorable loyalty to the public! And withal, such compassion for my stupidity, too."[19]

The system never really caught on, but it proved useful as a means of teaching sight-singing. In what Seward regarded as the natural artistry and "uncultivated" minds of the freedmen, he saw an opportunity to demonstrate its utility. Over the coming months, he worked on White to introduce tonic sol-fa into Fisk's musical curriculum. White was so swept up in Seward's enthusiasm that he would eventually entrust his Jubilees to him.

Seward's initial contribution to the troupe, however, was to produce *Jubilee Songs: As Sung by the Jubilee Singers of Fisk University*, a twenty-five-cent songbook of spirituals that the Jubilees peddled at their concerts. "When Mr. White first requested me to record these melodies, I supposed it would serve no better purpose than to gratify the curiosity of some attending these concerts, who desired to see and analyze those melodies, which had affected them so strangely," Seward later confessed.

But I find that they are really and essentially beautiful, and have the right number of measures, fulfilling the law of structure; and that they also express wonderfully the words to which they are written;

and thus they have that which the highest art aims at, and which it rarely reaches; and it has seemed to me that, coming as they do from minds having no knowledge whatever of the rules of art, and without culture, they must have sprung from something that is above us, of true inspiration.[20]

Proceeds from the sale of Seward's transcriptions became a significant part of their fund-raising and proved so popular, as Sheppard recalled, that "soon the land rang with our slave songs, sung in the homes of the people."[21] According to Rutling, however, and a number of critics who followed along in their books at the Jubilees' concerts, Seward had a tin ear for the peculiar inflections of the troupe and got a lot of the spirituals wrong. It was, in part, the old problem of representing African American inflections in standard musical notation. Seward himself warned his audience that "some of the phrases and turns in the melodies are so peculiar that the listener might not unreasonably suppose them to be incapable of exact representation by ordinary musical characters."[22] Britain's *Tonic Sol-Fa Reporter* suggested that Seward's transcription of "Nobody Knows the Trouble I See" did not jibe with the way it was performed.[23] In fact, Seward "made so many errors in many of them," Rutling recalled, "that the singers did not recognize their own songs."[24]

In his introduction, Seward also claimed that he was publishing all of these songs for the first time. But a John Davidson of New York, who wrote to Cravath in March 1872, begged to differ:

> I wish to call your attention to "Room Enough" . . . , also "Turn Back Pharaoh's Army." These two songs have been sung by the Hutchinson family for two years and are published by them through W. A. Pond & Co. New York who has the songs copyrighted and publishes them under the title of "Camp Songs of the Florida Freedmen." I know it from the fact that I heard the Hutchinsons sing them, & afterwards bought the songs at Pond's Music Store. The song "Many Thousands Gone" . . . you will find [in] "Slave Songs of the United States" a work published by A. Simpson & Co. in 1867 & containing a large collection of just such style of pieces as the Jubilee Singers sing.[25]

Some of the Jubilees' songs had indeed been published before and performed by the Hutchinson Family Singers, a popular nine-man antislavery troupe from New Hampshire. But as Twain pointed out, the Jubilees performed them in "the genuine old way" that whites could never imitate, "for one must have been a slave himself in order to feel what that life was and so convey the pathos of it in the music."[26]

"As a child," Rutling wrote in his middle age, "I was lulled to sleep by the singing of these weird melodies."[27] Sheppard had been rocked in her mother's arms as Sarah sang "Swing Low, Sweet Chariot." Jennie Jackson had learned her songs at her mother's washboard. These hymns had penetrated the Jubilees to their bones, and though Sheppard and White had to some extent formalized them, and the troupe, as Maggie Porter recalled, had performed them in "proper" English, their renditions were the first to expose most white audiences to the living tradition of African American music.

Critics were so swayed by the almost languid "ease" and "naturalness" of their performances—they sang "like mockingbirds because they could not help it," one critic enthused—that they often failed to recognize that these effects resulted from extraordinary artistry and exertion. Even their champions' praise usually neglected to acknowledge the discipline and craft that went into the Jubilee performances, as if exquisite four-part harmonies and double pianissimi that carried to the back rows of enormous halls were merely the natural attributes of a "musical" people.

"We are slowly getting ahead," White reported back to Fisk, although "slowly" was false modesty. By March 25, they had deposited fourteen thousand dollars into their building fund and expected the next string of concerts to bring them to their goal of twenty thousand dollars. "All are well—tho' we are getting very tired. . . . We are in the hands of Providence—and try to follow indications—sometimes our plans fail entirely & new ways open which we know not of. So we can't tell how soon the way will open for us to return."[28] Pike believed White deserved some reward from the A.M.A., if only a new suit of clothes, for "he can't afford to dress well and we can't afford to have him dress poor—the [laborer] is worthy of his hire and it is time we in some way showed Bro. White our appreciation."[29]

The Jubilees sang their way back to Boston, into Providence, and up into Maine, New Hampshire, and Vermont. At a Boston temperance meeting in the Park Street Church, Sheppard, "with her sweet, cultivated, plaintive voice," and Minnie Tate, with her "clear, rich alto," sang "Wine Is a Mocker." The effect was "perfectly electrical," wrote Pike. "The applause was terrific."

One secret of the Jubilees' success was that by removing Master Georgie from their troupe and the more comical and purely popular pieces from their repertoire they made their performances acceptable to even the most pious and fastidious audiences, furnishing "refined and wholesome entertainment" to men and women who would otherwise never set foot in a theater or even a concert hall. The Jubilees conducted their concerts like prayer meetings or missionary lectures and considered themselves failures if they did not elicit a conversion from at least one audience member.

One of the great strains of touring was the singers' need to be models of rectitude, at least as decorous and impeccable as the ministers who invited them to church after church. The Jubilees were proscribed from attending the theater, and White made it a requirement of all of their appearances, even in private homes, that no liquor be served. Taunted, abused, humiliated by train conductors and hoteliers and restaurateurs, they had to learn right away to contain their rage, to overcome the prejudices they encountered by constantly comporting themselves as pious, scrupulous young Christian ambassadors of their race, a role that came more naturally to some than to others.

By May 1872, within six months of their departure from Nashville, the Jubilees had "not only paid the debts at home of nearly $1,500," Ella Sheppard wrote, "and furnished other money for support of Fisk; . . . we carried home $20,000, with which was purchased the present site of . . . our new school."

No amount of success could immunize them from American racism, however, not even on their triumphant journey back to Nashville. In New York, they purchased first-class tickets from the Louisville and Nashville Railroad and rode south into Kentucky. When they reached Louisville and tried to rest between trains in the first-class waiting room, a railway employee ordered the "niggers," as he called them, out onto the platform. Brandishing their first-class tickets, White refused at first, whereupon a railroad patrolman wielding a baton grabbed Jennie Jackson, the darkest of the female singers, by the arm. "Trainmen exercised a peculiar power over Negro passengers," explained Lura Beam of the A.M.A. "They acted like wardens or prison guards, or as military cliques have sometimes acted when they thought they were on top for all time. They used to throw in the word 'nigger' for free, and if some drawling passenger offered a ticket for Tupelo when he had meant to buy to Tougaloo, they showed that they were glad that he was going in the wrong direction."[30]

With threats and curses, the railroad cop began to hustle Jennie Jackson out of the waiting room. A crowd gathered, and, fearing for the troupe's safety, White gave in and led them out onto the platform "amid the jeers," Sheppard remembered, of what seemed to her to be "about two thousand roughs."[31] Pike silenced one of them by informing him that at their last concert their receipts had been one thousand dollars. On Southern "trains and in cars, especially, Negroes were generally relegated to smoking compartments where Negro women and children were exposed to the offensive conduct of men of both races."[32] But once the train had backed into the depot, an embarrassed conductor showed them to the first-class car, and they returned to Fisk, Sheppard remembered, "amid great rejoicing."[33]

"The work done by this group of singers is without a parallel," Henry Ward Beecher wrote. "It leaves the Old Testament hopelessly in the distance, for Joshua's army only sang down the walls of Jericho—while the Jubilee choir have sung up the walls of a great university."[34]

I'VE JUST COME
FROM THE FOUNTAIN

THE SECOND TOUR

MAY 1872–MARCH 1873

The Jubilee Singers were met at the Nashville station as conquering heroes and led back to their school by their families and friends in a procession of drums beating and banners flying. Though conditions at Fisk were not to improve significantly for years to come, they had saved their school from extinction and raised enough money to buy a new site.

The fate of Fort Houston remained tied up in Congress, so Cravath took aim at an eight-acre swath of Fort Gillem, one of the Union fortifications Rutling had helped to dismantle at the close of the war. He vied for the property with a neighboring freedmen's school called the Nashville Normal and Theological Institute, which had been founded in 1864 by a white Baptist minister from Massachusetts named Daniel W. Phillips. As Roger Williams University, it would eventually become, for a time, almost as formidable a presence in Nashville as Fisk University and Central Tennessee College. But in 1872, it was still struggling to raise enough money to buy Fort Gillem for seven thousand dollars. When the bidding was over, Cravath had paid eighty-one hundred dollars for the site, and an outmaneuvered Nashville Normal had to look for a new site on Hillsboro Road.[1]

In the meantime, the Jubilees were not to rest on their laurels for long. Though exhausted by the tour, White was determined to keep striking while the iron was hot. Twenty thousand dollars might be enough to purchase a site, but it was not enough to erect the large stone hall he had begun to depict on his posters and broadsides. That would take at least another forty-five thousand dollars, and White was convinced he could get it. Fisk itself must have been a little discouraging after all the pictures he had painted of its bright and shining future. "My impression," wrote Henry Bennett, "is that Mr. White did not feel altogether at home when he was here."[2]

The troupe had performed almost nonstop. Nevertheless, White had had to turn down engagements throughout New England and had not even begun to try his hand in the upper Midwest. Within a week and a half of the singers' return, White had gathered together his wife and children and taken the Jubilees back on the road, with a young A.M.A. functionary named Susan Gilbert as preceptress. Soft-spoken, cultured, Gilbert would become a mainstay of the Jubilee enterprise and Ella Sheppard's closest friend.

The troupe sang amid the half-charred ruins of Chicago and also in Detroit and Cleveland, with little stops along the way. Even Spence's mother fell under their spell at Ann Arbor, where Pike dilated on missions to the Northwest Indians, the Chinese, Africa, and the American South. "Well," Elizabeth Spence wrote her son on May 22, "the Jubilee Singers have done themselves credit and you too. Never was there any greater success . . . in the matter of making favorable impression. The ideas of many with regard to the race seem entirely revolutionized. We have not heard of a single adverse criticism, while unqualified praise comes up from every quarter." The singers praised Spence to her, "and their cultivated manners reflect honor upon your position in a way we could never have anticipated."[3]

Be that as it may, Spence must have received his mother's remarks with mixed feelings, for the real glory went to his nemeses, White and Cravath. Not long afterward, the A.M.A. finally informed Spence that its search for a president of Fisk University had found its man. Having failed to locate a New England educator "for whom an endowment of $25,000 can be readily raised," the A.M.A. had selected none other than Erastus Milo Cravath himself. But the A.M.A. would not release Cravath from his secretaryship immediately, and thus not only had the A.M.A. humiliated Spence by passing him over for the worldly Cravath, it now expected Spence to serve in the thankless role of interim president for two years. Spence sank into a depression deepened by the death of his sickly little daughter Gracie, and he and what remained of his family retreated home to Michigan for the summer.

On Pike's recommendation, White and the reorganized Jubilees proceeded east to spend the summer in the town of Acton, Massachusetts, next door to Concord. Worn out by the rigors of performing, Eliza Walker had dropped out of the troupe, and Greene Evans was wavering. There are hints in White's letters that he had problems with the formidable Evans, who would go on to serve in the Tennessee state legislature. White had little tolerance for his singers' speaking out of turn, and judging from Evans's character and background, he may have been the first, if by no means the last, of the Jubilees to fall out with their maestro.

For Pike, the key to the second troupe's success was going to have to be discipline. Now that the Jubilees were, at five hundred dollars a year, "well paid," he believed they "ought to be educated to know they are to do what is for the good of the A.M.A. whether it be working or waiting." If some Jubilees had to be let go in mid-tour, so be it. "The possible preferences of persons who are employed to do service and paid liberally is not to be the sovereign power. If I understand human nature—we shall have but little trouble on this score if the principle be once established. If we can't establish it, I can't see how we are to be very successful in this business."[4]

White expanded the troupe with six new members. He had buried the hatchet with the brilliant Georgia Gordon, and though she was still somewhat reluctant to interrupt her studies, the troupe's success had by now captured her imagination, and over her mentor Helen Morgan's objections, she signed on for their second tour.

Eliza Walker's replacement would be a tense, pious young woman named Julia Jackson, whose mother had earned enough as a hired slave to buy her daughter's freedom. She sent Julia to live with her aunt and uncle, slaves who were also hiring out their time. When her uncle threatened to run away from his employer, he and his wife were sent to a slave-trading yard. Her uncle was sold, but her aunt was kept imprisoned in the pen so she would not run away. Julia became her one hope of escape, and as the little girl brought her aunt her meals, she smuggled in the money her aunt had kept hidden and scouted out breaks in the fence where her aunt might squeeze through. When her owner announced he was taking her up-country, the aunt escaped, and to keep the slave trader from sounding the alarm, Julia kept delivering her meals, one after another, until her aunt was long gone. After the war, Julia hired herself out at five dollars a month but was "obliged to leave on account of a felon," which apparently meant that she was assaulted, possibly sexually, by her employer, for she did not work again until she had recuperated. By 1869, she had saved enough money to go to school and after only two years proceeded to teach in another of the impoverished and besieged country schools that Fisk students staffed. She built her students' benches out of planks and stones with her own hands.[5]

Twenty-two-year-old Edmund Watkins was apparently the only member of the Jubilee Singers to have experienced the lash. He had been whipped not as a slave, however, but as a freedman. Watkins was of a different class from most of the other singers. His father had been sold into Texas when Edmund was young, and his mother worked as a field hand. Mother and son picked cotton together: her daily quota was 160 pounds; his, 200. After the war, his master refused to pay him wages and continued to treat him as captive labor.

Watkins escaped to Talladega, Alabama, and nearly starved as a railroad laborer, whereupon he gravitated homeward and found work on a farm fifteen miles from his former master's plantation. He eluded the six men his master sent to catch him, but when he sneaked onto the plantation to visit his mother and sister, he was captured, taken into the woods, and lashed. Watkins agreed at last to remain with his family and labored grudgingly for a time at a little over $1.50 a month. But he proved a defiant employee, speaking out so boldly that his former master remarked that he had "more sense than he ever saw in a *little nigger* before." At last, Watkins could take it no longer and bolted back to Talladega, where he hired himself out for fifty cents a day: ten times what his former master had been paying. He learned the value of literacy the hard way when a white flimflam artist absconded with his savings. Watkins worked his way through two years at the A.M.A.'s Talladega College cooking, washing, and cutting stock in a sawmill.

Like Fisk, Talladega started out as an elementary school, established mostly through the efforts of a former slave named William Savery. Many of its students were nominated by black congregations on the basis of pedagogic promise and moral character and arrived bearing sacks of corn and bacon to sustain themselves through the year.[6] By 1870, Watkins could read in the fourth reader and had learned enough arithmetic and geography to teach school during his vacations in Clay County.[7] He was among those armed students who guarded Talladega against white arsonists and may have been one of those who turned away a body of Klansmen by threatening to burn down the entire town if his school was harmed.[8] Elegantly handsome, dark, with a kindly, forthright gaze, Watkins was self-conscious around his better-educated colleagues. He seldom spoke, but "when he did, his word was fine & well weighed before spoken."[9]

From here on, White intended to field two singing groups: a full choir, of course, but also a quartet consisting of Watkins, Thomas Rutling, Jennie Jackson, and Maggie Porter, with a fifteen-year-old newcomer named Josephine Moore to act as an accompanist.[10] Standing in for Rutling's tenor in the main choir was a Northern freedman named Henry Morgan.[11] White's plan was for the two groups to spell each other and, if need be, capitalize on local interest by performing simultaneously in different venues.

Phebe Anderson remained true to the promise she made her dying father and would not return to the troupe. But White was told of an extraordinarily powerful African American contralto named Mabel Lewis, who was studying voice in Worcester, Massachusetts, near the Jubilees' summer training ground at Acton.

Lewis's ancestry and upbringing were complicated. She was born Marie Bohom, the daughter of a Frenchman named Falcoup Bohom and a New Orleans slave woman. Her owner had been a lawyer and relative of Bohom's named Grimes, who fell into debt. When his creditors tried to lay claim to one-year-old Marie, he hid her in the home of a Catholic general named Lewis, who took her by boat to New York and enrolled her in a convent. She was the only black girl in a student body of wealthy whites. Eventually reared in Massachusetts by relatives of General Lewis's, who renamed her Mabel, she spoke French at home and was prohibited from having any interaction with black people outside the household. "I learned in later years the reason why I was kept away," she recalled. Her white godmother, Madame De Manvil Marijar, "who had always taken a deep interest in me and provided for all my wants was afraid that I might meet with some colored person" who would inform her that she was related to her godmother's family.[12]

Her childhood was difficult. Educated by nuns, she was repeatedly spanked for singing a Protestant hymn she learned from a chimney sweep. When her guardians went abroad, Lewis was left in the care of one of the family's former slaves. "She was very abusive to me," Lewis recalled, "and finally I left and went from door to door asking if they did not want a girl to wait on the table and run errands. At one place I noticed a woman sawing wood, and I thought perhaps I could do that. . . . I was not begging," she insisted. Mabel earned her way to the abolitionist whaling town of New Bedford, Massachusetts, where she was taken under the wing of the district court judge Alanson Borden.[13] Like Maggie Porter, she was inspired by the story of the Swedish Nightingale, Jenny Lind, who as a young girl was discovered by a Stockholm ballerina while singing to a cat. So Lewis used to borrow the Bordens' accordion and walk a few blocks off and sing all the songs she knew, hoping someone might take an interest in developing her talent. "How I took in the pennies!" she recalled, but what she wanted was a musical education. Eventually Judge Borden sent her to a convent school, where a group of ladies heard her sing and arranged to send her to Worcester "to have my voice cultivated."

Coming from this strangely detached and insular background, Lewis "had never heard the Jubilee songs and did not know anything about them."[14] In fact, when Lewis first met the Jubilees, it was strange just "to be with my people. All my life I had lived among white people and was punished if I were seen talking with colored people."[15] The other Jubilees might have despaired of this strange Northern addition to their number until they heard her sing, for she had "such a strong contralto voice" that she could make herself heard over the singing of "one hundred and fifty girls."

She would need it. George White had accepted an invitation to appear that summer at a gargantuan musical extravaganza in Boston called the World's Peace Jubilee, which would require as much volume as the Jubilees could muster. The troupe was to perform a portion of "The Battle Hymn of the Republic" in the enormous Boston Coliseum over an orchestra of 1,094 instruments, a chorus of 10,371 singers, and a battery of cannon, all under the baton of a popular bandmaster named Patrick Sarsfield Gilmore.[16] Gilmore had made his reputation first as leader of a crack military band in Salem, Massachusetts, and then as conductor of an immense orchestra of massed bands in federally occupied New Orleans. The World's Peace Jubilee was a leviathan successor to the National Peace Jubilee of 1869, which he had arranged to celebrate the end of the war.

The engagement was a natural for the Jubilees, of course, but the prospect of leading his tiny choir into such a vast extravaganza drove White

wild with anxiety. "Mr. White had unusual taste and gifts," Sheppard recalled. "For weeks he trained our voices to sing the Battle Hymn of the Republic. He reasoned that the . . . instruments to be used in that great
building would very likely play it in E flat, the one key in which the various
instruments could harmonize." This meant that the singers would have to
practice singing the song three half steps higher than usual. "So little by little, each day or two going a bit higher, using his violin, he trained us on
those words from C to E flat until he was satisfied" that they would be able
to "enunciate with perfect accuracy of pitch and purity of tone every word
and every part of a word."[17]

They arrived at the coliseum in the middle of June and at first appeared
briefly at some of the festival's smaller venues to sing a few of their spirituals. Their reception was mixed. The sight of them on the stage elicited
hisses and catcalls from a sector of the audience, and though a larger contingent drowned out hecklers with applause, it was an inauspicious start to
what was supposed to be the most important engagement of their careers.
The next day was the main event, and they were to share the stage with
two black women from Boston who were supposed to take the first two
verses of "The Battle Hymn." But when the time came, it was obvious that
they had not anticipated the change in key and struggled feebly through
their rendition, barely audible over the giant orchestra. After the vast choir
behind and above them took the chorus, the Jubilees braced themselves
"like spirited race horses," Sheppard recalled, and began to sing the third
verse:

> He has sounded forth the trumpet that shall never call retreat;
> He is sifting out the hearts of men before His judgment seat;
> Oh! be swift, my soul, to answer Him, be Jubilant, my feet!
> Our God is marching on.

They sang so forcefully, and so purely, and could be heard so clearly that
they reached "the utmost of the vast building," but when the chorus came
in with the orchestra and a sputtering cannonade, they were almost
drowned out by the roar of all twenty thousand celebrants.[18] "Men and
women arose in their wild cheering," Sheppard remembered, "waving and
throwing up handkerchiefs and hats," whereupon the orchestra and chorus
followed suit. "One German raised his violoncello and thwacked its back

with the bow, crying 'Bravo, bravo!'" while "the Waltz King," Johann Strauss, "waved his violin excitedly."[19]

As the coliseum "rang with cheers and shouts of 'The Jubilees! The Jubilees forever!'" Gilmore invited them up to the apex of his vast platform and had them repeat the last verse.[20] For days afterward, they sang and sang, and "the people never tired of listening."[21]

After the World's Peace Jubilee, Greene Evans returned to Tennessee, and the remaining Jubilees went back to Acton to rest and rehearse. A former Fisk teacher named Nellie M. Horton arrived to tutor the singers and help Gustavus Pike with secretarial work.[22]

At the end of the summer, the Jubilees began a second tour of New England. On their return to New Haven, they were greeted almost hysterically. "The slave songs of the South have nearly passed into history," read an advance squib in the *Daily Palladium*. "This is one of the last—*the* last and only chance to many—that will ever be afforded for hearing the quaint and wild strains in which the Southern negroes gave vent to their pent up feelings." The demand for tickets was so great that they had to be auctioned off, and a "posse of policemen" were sent to deal with "the rowdyish conduct of a number of genteel looking loafers, who were disturbing the respectable portion of the large congregation there assembled to listen to the singers."[23]

Their fame began to overcome the barriers of discrimination that they still encountered. They sang at Philadelphia's Academy of Music at the invitation of such notables as the philanthropist George Hay Stuart, a force in the American Tract Society, in whose *Freedmen's Primer* and *Freedmen's Speller* many of the Jubilees had learned to read and write; John Wanamaker, the department-store magnate and pioneer of cooperatives; and the banker Jay Cooke, whose machinations on behalf of his Northern Pacific Railroad were about to plunge the country into a deep depression. A few months earlier, the Academy of Music had refused to allow a black U.S. senator to give an address on its stage. But the distinguished signatories to the Jubilees' invitation overcame the management's misgivings, and their concerts were "thronged night after night."

Philadelphia had been a major stop on the Underground Railway, but among the disturbances that punctuated its history were a series of particularly vicious race riots. In 1838, a pro-slavery mob burned down Pennsylvania Hall and a black orphanage. In 1842, rioters destroyed an African Presbyterian Church. Only a year before the singers' visit, two blacks had been killed in election rioting.[24] Philadelphia had a black population of thirty thousand, but in the face of white opposition, only a tiny minority had been able to establish shops or enter trades.[25] None of the city's leading hotels would accommodate the Jubilees, so they had to stay in a small and out-of-the-way boardinghouse until the manager of the Continental, claiming he had been away when his clerk refused them, invited them back. "Subsequently he entertained them in the best manner, and at a generous reduction from regular rates." In exchange for his hospitality, the Jubilees asked permission to tour the underground facilities and sing for the Continental's staff. So many guests pressed in to hear them that they had to reconvene in the enormous dining room, where, at the troupe's insistence, the black cooks and scullery workers, maids, waiters, launderers, and bellboys sat in the front rows to hear them sing.[26]

Rail lines like the Vermont Central Railroad let them ride for half fare; others, like the New Haven & Hartford, let them ride first class at second-class rates.[27] But the old pattern of segregation and outraged patronage not only continued; it seemed sometimes to worsen. Hearing that a Baltimore ticket seller was refusing to sell reserved seats to blacks, one of the Jubilees decided to apply incognito, only to have "his application to hear himself sing" refused. Just before a scheduled appearance in Princeton, New Jersey, the troupe discovered that "the color line was drawn for the first and only time in our concerts," Sheppard recalled, "in that the colored people of the audience were obliged to sit by themselves" in a distant corner of the church. Even black students whose white teacher had purchased reserved seats were ordered into the "colored" section. Though invited by President James McCosh of Princeton University, the Jubilees were tempted to cancel their performance, but "so many of their friends had come a long distance to hear them" that they decided to capitulate.[28] Nevertheless, during a break in their performance, George White took the podium and bawled out McCosh, the presiding minister, and the organizers of the concert for perpetrating something so disgraceful in a house of God, reiterating the doctrine of the A.M.A. that "no racial distinctions should be made in 'churches of Christ.' "[29] Pike deemed White's address "plainer preaching on *that* subject, probably, than had ever been heard in that church before. And most of those who greeted it with their angry hisses have doubtless lived long enough to be heartily ashamed of them."[30]

The long-sequestered Mabel Lewis found American prejudice especially grotesque. "Shall I tell you," she would later ask the readers of *Fisk University News*, "about the different times when we were turned out of hotels because God took more pains with the making of our people than of others? Is it because He stopped to paint us and curl our hair," she wondered, "that we have to suffer for these extra attentions that have been bestowed upon us?"[31]

When the staff of a boardinghouse in Elizabeth, New Jersey, learned that the Jubilees were black, they walked off their jobs. "So, there was only the proprietor, his wife and sister to do the work," Lewis recalled.

> When we had nothing to do Sunday evenings we usually felt lonely or homesick, so we asked the privilege of going into the parlor and using the piano and singing. The proprietor was perfectly willing. While we were singing we heard a great scuffling over our heads.
>
> I was frightened and looked out, and there at the head of the stairs was Mr. Proprietor tying Mrs. Proprietor with a clothes line to keep her upstairs.
>
> She said, "I'm going to keep those niggers out of my house. I'm not going to have them pawing on my piano."
>
> The next morning he seemed to be ashamed about what had happened the night before and tried to fix it up in some way. As we were about to leave, he made the expression that he was very sorry for what had happened during our stay there, and whenever we came that way again we were welcome to stop at his house.[32]

White's experiment with two groups was not working out. The singers were being paid five hundred dollars each per year and trailing an expanded entourage. Their receipts per concert were barely covering their expenses. Moreover, White did not have a large enough staff of advance agents to handle and coordinate two sets of bookings.[33] So he further trimmed the troupe by sending home the two most extraneous newcomers—Henry Morgan and the backup accompanist, Josephine Moore—and consolidated the remaining eleven singers into one troupe.[34] In the wake of the Jubilees' enormous fund-raising success, he worried that their proceeds were vulnerable to embezzlement and fraud: he suspected ticket sellers and theater owners of pocketing part of the troupe's earnings and even accused an A.M.A. agent named Carter of keeping "low company" and skimming off the receipts.[35]

The Jubilees were also beginning to run into another consequence of their success: imitators. "There is a company styling themselves the *Canaan Jubilee Singers* in this region," White wrote from New York in October. "I cannot learn where they originated. They advertise that they are giving concerts in the interests [of] 'the colored brethren' & hope not only to endow colleges & universities for colored people *but for all* who are in need of education."[36] White hurried to Brockport, New York, to check out the competition and came away unimpressed. "I could not learn where the enterprise originated or who they are. . . . They had an audience of about 100 respectable people & about 30 boys" whom he recognized from the Jubilee Singers' own audiences. "There are no very good voices," White reported, and they were poorly managed. "They sing slave songs in the rough[est], the rudest & least musical I have ever heard. . . . They will not last many days," he predicted, but he realized that they were riding on the Jubilees' coattails at the Jubilees' expense. "They get what they do get because people think they are the Fisk [Jubilee Singers]," he wrote Cravath. "I have no fear of their doing much but they ought to be prevented from humbugging the people if possible."[37]

In fact, White *was* afraid, and would become more and more concerned as other troupes entered the field. As early as August, Pike had urged that "we at once, secure for the American Missionary Association the monopoly of the term 'Jubilee Singers' so it shall be a trade mark. . . . There is talk in many quarters of forming companies like ours and we must protect ourselves in every way possible."[38] Over the next decade, there would be the Hampton Singers, the Tuskegee Choir, the Knoxville Quartet, Central Tennessee College's Tennesseans, the Cotton Blossom Singers of the Piney Woods Country Life School, the Utica Jubilee Singers of Mississippi, the Dixie Spiritual Singers, the Southernaires, the Tennessee Warblers, the Tennessee Singers, the Wilmington Jubilee Singers, plus outright impersonators calling themselves the Tennessee Jubilee Singers and two separate troupes called the Original Nashville Students. Some of these groups were every bit as well intentioned and musically ambitious as Fisk's Jubilees and would make lasting contributions to the canon and tradition of the American Negro spiritual.[39] But others, like the Famous Colored Jubilee Singers, were frauds and by association would eventually make Fisk "a stench in the nostrils" of some Northern audiences.[40]

By December 1872, the competition posed two immediate problems for White: it threatened to cut the fund-raising pie into meager slivers, and it suggested to the restless young Jubilees that there might be more lucrative and less grueling alternatives to singing night and day for the A.M.A.

Within a few months, White was scanning the horizon for new fields to harvest. Among the singers' most ardent admirers was the family of the Scottish novelist George MacDonald. In January 1873, MacDonald was recovering in New York from a speaking tour. Between performances by Edwin Booth as Hamlet and concerts by Anton Rubinstein, MacDonald and his family attended a concert by the Jubilees. The "nigger singers," as his wife called them, elicited quite a range of emotions from the excitable MacDonald clan.

"I never heard anything so droll and fervid, so touching, so pathetic, so true," wrote his wife. "Papa sat with the tears rolling down his cheeks, and I was alternately and at the *same time* convulsed with laughter and choking tears—their chanting of the Lord's Prayer was equal to any cathedral music I ever heard. Yet how odd they looked!" MacDonald's son remembered that after hearing them a second time, they were visiting with the singers in the theater's anteroom when suddenly the gaslights sputtered off and one of the singers shouted into the darkness, "All one color now!"

A thoroughly charmed George MacDonald insisted that the troupe tour Britain.[41] He was not alone. Beecher adamantly believed that they would advance not only their cause but his own reputation in England, where a wave of revivalism was rolling. Mark Twain, who had just returned from a lionizing visit to Great Britain, also encouraged them to go. A Connecticut industrialist promised that a tour of Britain could garner them a million dollars. His enthusiasm was not all that far-fetched. As early as 1865, a British minister named Massie had taken an interest in the American Missionary Association's enterprise in Nashville, inspecting Fisk's future site and promising to raise funds for it in London.[42] In 1867, the British Freedmen's Missions Aid Society had sent casks of clothing to Fisk to distribute among the freedmen.[43]

With their receipts declining, Pike and White decided to chance it.

To help pay their way across the Atlantic, they arranged for a string of "farewell concerts" in Newark, New York, Brooklyn, Providence, and Boston. On March 26, almost on the eve of their departure for England, the Jubilees made a profitable appearance at the invitation of the former boot seller and now Republican governor William Claflin. Among the luminaries in attendance were Edward Everett Hale, the clergyman, author, and reformer; the serene and equable Phillips Brooks of the Episcopal Trinity Church; the agriculturist George Bailey Loring; and the great abolitionists William Lloyd Garrison and Wendell Phillips.

"The world was as unknown to these untravelled freed people," a British paper would write, "as were the countries through which the Argonauts had to pass."[44] They were about to journey into a world they had only read about and wondered at as they peered at the tinted, three-dimensional images in Professor Spence's stereograph collection. And yet "no young people," wrote Pike, "ever bid farewell to their country laden with so many attentions and good wishes as these children of recent bondage who had been so admirably illustrating the elastic energy of the black man, when afforded an equal opportunity with others in the race of life."[45]

IN BRIGHT
MANSIONS ABOVE

LONDON

APRIL–MAY 1873

Gustavus Pike sailed ahead of the Jubilees in the company of a Welsh preacher named James Powell, who had offered to guide the troupe through the maze of British protocol. On their arrival in London on April 8, 1873, Powell led Pike along a network of British contacts, flourishing letters of introduction from such stateside celebrities as Beecher and Twain.

Their first stop was the five-year-old London publishing firm of Hodder and Stoughton on Paternoster Row, where they were met by Matthew Henry Hodder, a friend of the American publishers Charles Scribner and George Putnam. A frequent visitor to the United States, where he scouted authors for his list of primarily religious works, Hodder immediately embraced the Jubilees' cause. He put Pike and Powell in touch with the Young Men's Christian Association, which in turn introduced them to fifty-five-year-old Henry Allon, the Congregational pastor of London's Union Chapel.

Pike's most impressive letters of introduction were all addressed to Allon. George MacDonald wrote him to praise the Jubilees' "inexplicably touching" singing.[1] So did Henry Ward Beecher:

I wish to commend to your active sympathy the "Jubilee Singers." You may venture upon receiving this corps with the utmost confidence. The managers are men of good sense, integrity, and of devoted piety. We are not ashamed to send this band to our British brethren, and we are sure that their music will strike a chord which will vibrate long after their songs shall cease.

If the Jubilee Singers could not strike a chord with Henry Allon, they might as well have stayed home. He was an impressive-looking man and a brilliant liberal preacher, but he was best known in the United States as a proponent of nonconformist music. For his editing of, among other collections, *The Congregational Psalmist* and, most recently, *Anthems for Congregational Use*, Yale University had presented Allon with an honorary degree just two years earlier.

Allon offered Pike not just advice but the use of his Union Chapel for the troupe's London debut. But Pike had a different kind of London debut in mind. He had been advised that to get their British tour off the ground the Jubilees would need "the patronage of pious nobility." Fortunately for Pike, he did not have to look any further than the A.M.A.'s British counterpart, the Freedmen's Missions Aid Society, and its newly elected president, Anthony Ashley Cooper, the Right Honorable Earl of Shaftesbury.

Sixty-six years had passed since Britain had peaceably abolished the slave trade, thirty-five years since it had eliminated slavery in its colonies. That only eight years had passed since America had abolished slavery, and then only at the cost of a bloody civil war, was cause in some British circles for self-congratulation. But the unprecedented prosperity of nineteenth-century Britain had been founded in large measure on the extraordinary profits the previous century's English merchants and planters had made trading in Africans and in the Caribbean sugar that slaves died in their thousands to cultivate. Slavery had stoked the boilers of the Industrial Revolution. England's manufacturers had met the slavers' need for tons of goods with which to barter—trinkets, textiles, cookware, guns—not to mention the ships, armaments, chains, and fetters that were the tools of their trade.

The first Englishman to import Africans was Captain John Lok, who in 1555 sailed home from Guinea with five men he hoped to train and return to Africa as his trading agents. They apparently came willingly, and though the "cold and moyst aire doth somewhat offend them, [they] could well agree with our meates and drinkes."[2] Successive African immigrants were less willing. "Partly by the sword and partly by other means," Captain John Hawkins initiated the English slave trade seven years later by capturing three hundred "Guineamen" and selling them to the Spanish. The trade in Guinean slaves and gold became so important to the British monarchy that a hundred years later the Royal Mint named its new gold coin after it.[3]

In the mid–seventeenth century, black slaves remained something of a curiosity in England, exotic garnishes in upper-class households. One spots them occasionally in the backgrounds of period portraits, dressed in foot-man's uniforms with little padlocks hanging from their necks. Their status was ambiguous. Partly out of a fear that they might be Spanish agents, Elizabeth I tried to expel all "Negroes and blackamoores" from her kingdom. When a man brought home a Russian slave and scourged him, one of Her Majesty's judges declared that "England was too pure an Air for slaves to breathe in." But the first Stuarts liked having Africans around. James I approved of black servants, and even as Charles I grudgingly signed off on the Petition of Rights—protecting his subjects from arbitrary taxation, imprisonment, martial law, and the billeting of soldiers—he gave his royal blessing to the slave trade. Charles II even bought a slave for himself for fifty pounds.[4]

The British trade in human beings was a spectacularly profitable and self-perpetuating cycle of slaves, molasses, rum, trinkets, and back for more slaves. British West Indian slavery was especially brutal and profitable; almost three times as many slaves were imported into the Caribbean as into North America; from 1690 to 1820, British planters imported 748,000 slaves into Jamaica alone.[5] The profits derived from their labor on British sugar and cotton plantations were so great that planters deemed it cheaper to work their slaves to death and replace them with a fresh supply from Africa than import enough women to sustain the population.

West Indian traders amassed enormous fortunes and vied for status with the nouveau riche nabobs of India, building vast estates and marrying their daughters to nobility. They not only invested their capital in British industry but introduced new "scientific" notions about the treatment and distribution of labor based on the lessons they had learned as slaveholders about the extremities of human endurance. The effect on British workers was horrendous and might have led to revolution if not, some say, for the humane intervention of the empathetic Anthony Ashley Cooper, the seventh earl of Shaftesbury.

Lord Shaftesbury looked like an unusually natty Puritan elder. His face was long and grave, with "deep, down-cut lines." His nose was like an overturned prow, and his jaw was so substantial as to render his muttonchops gratuitous. In his later years, he acquired an unnerving squint, and, even when he was a young man, "the set form of his lips" led people to think "not only that he never acts from impulse, but that he seldom, if ever, felt an impulse in his life."

Shaftesbury's mother was vain, cold, and derisive; his father, the sixth earl, was a brusque parliamentarian whose "whole pleasure" lay in "finding fault."[6] Whatever happiness their son had known as a boy, Shaftesbury attributed to a loving and pious nursemaid, whose pocket watch he would carry for the rest of his life. But for all the emotional deprivation of his youth, Cooper grew into a handsome, personable young man and thrived, eventually, at Oxford. By the age of twenty-five, he had, by his own reckoning, winnowed his vices down to two: moodiness (he may have been manic-depressive) and hypersensitivity to slights and criticism.

In 1826, Cooper successfully ran for Parliament from the borough of his maternal uncle, the duke of Marlborough. He showed promise as a public servant but was plagued by headaches, stomachaches, and doubts. Between his first muffled appearances in the House of Commons, he holed up to study mathematics, Welsh, metaphysics, Hebrew, and especially the Bible. He subscribed to the Evangelicalism of the time, especially its emphasis on benevolent acts, and began to give away a large portion of his income to charities, "for what is money?" he asked, "but a means towards worldly happiness and a ladder to eternity?" As steadfast a defender of the class system as ever breathed air, Shaftesbury was nevertheless no mere dilettante, nor were his good works just a matter of noblesse oblige. He believed in Christian stewardship, in expending whatever resources, energy, and talent he might possess for the good of man and the glory of God.

His critics deemed him a bit of a prig. He decried impure literature, urged theaters and music halls to begin their performances with prayers, deplored Prime Minister Canning's irreligion and even the duke of Wellington's membership in a gaming club. But his zeal was a balm to his self-doubt, and the worthier the course he adopted, the more vigorous, eloquent, and self-confident he became.

His first cause was the welfare of the insane, and by the end of his life he would completely reform the lunacy acts.[7] But it was the welfare of the laboring classes that received the lion's share of his attention. On his tours of mills and factories, he was greeted by rows of workers so grotesquely deformed by injury, abuse, and overwork as to form a kind of "crooked alphabet." Touring English mines, he found not only women but children as young as four toiling in the dark, hauling coal trucks in chains and girdles. He championed the then-revolutionary notion of a ten-hour workday and so horrified and embarrassed Parliament with his firsthand reports that it passed an act reforming the apprentice system and prohibiting the employment of women and children below ground.

During a respite from Parliament in the late 1840s, Shaftesbury toured the slums of London and dedicated himself not only to their physical improvement but to the education of poor children. Due in large measure to his efforts, some 300,000 children would attend "ragged schools," as they were called. He built model villages and housing projects; mustered a bootblack brigade; attacked the ill treatment of the "climbing boys" employed by chimney sweeps to scramble up flues and across rooftops; and established a Watercress and Flower Girl's Mission to tide vendors over while their wares were out of season. He advocated window gardens to stave off scurvy, tried to reform labor conditions in the maritime industry, opposed vivisection, allied himself with Florence Nightingale on the Sanitary Commission, supported missionary work throughout the Empire, championed Bible societies and the Young Men's Christian Association.

Some mocked all this feverish do-gooding, but over time, Shaftesbury became an indispensable feature of Britain's moral landscape. His influence was felt at every level of society; he once met with a syndicate of 450 London thieves and convinced half of them to give up their vocation and emigrate. In 1848, he staved off mass riots in London by touring the slums with his City Mission in tow, dispensing aid to all and sundry. Over the course of his life, he was showered with honors and gifts: from the freedom of the city of London and the ribbon of the Garter to a donkey presented to him by London's costermongers. By the time of his death in 1885, he would become a kind of Dickensian angel, a patrician saint, the "social conscience of England." Among those who would escort his casket to Westminster Abbey were representatives of over two hundred of the missions, shelters, schools, and philanthropic societies that he had founded, redirected, scolded, and invigorated.

Two of these were the Anti-Slavery Society and the Freedmen's Missions Aid Society, the British auxiliary of Fisk's sponsor, the American Missionary Association. Once, while arguing for reforms in Bombay's factories, Shaftesbury had declared that "creed and colour, latitude and longitude, make no difference in the essential nature of man."[8] He meant it. Ever since reading Harriet Beecher Stowe's *Uncle Tom's Cabin*, he had vigorously opposed American slavery and corresponded on the subject with, among other American luminaries, Stowe, her brother Henry Ward Beecher, and the bishop of Ohio. In 1853, he urged British womanhood to denounce American slavery: "to raise your voices to your fellow citizens and your prayers to God for the removal of this affliction from the Christian world."[9] Under the sponsorship of the duchess of Sutherland, they made enough noise to reach the ears of Southern journalists who wondered why this "unknown lordling" had stirred up this "passing agitation. . . . Where was he when Lord Ashley was so notably fighting for the Factory Bill and pleading the case of the British slave?" asked one confused editorialist, who had not heard of Shaftesbury's accession to his earldom. "We never even heard the name of Lord Shaftesbury *then*."[10]

Unlike many of his countrymen, Shaftesbury took no pride in the comparative speed with which Britain had abolished slavery. "We share the guilt of our brethren in America because of the past existence of that system," he once reminded his countrymen. "We forced that system upon the United States." Now, "sharing their responsibility, we must also join with them in seeking to assist the emancipated slave."[11]

At the time Pike walked into his office, Shaftesbury was seventy-three years old and grieving over the recent deaths of his wife and daughter. But he had lost little of his vitality and embraced the cause of the Jubilees with his characteristic zeal.

Pike asked if His Lordship would sponsor the singers' first concert.

"I should be most happy to do so," Shaftesbury replied, and proposed a private benefit performance for the Freedmen's Missions Aid Society in the afternoon of May 6.

Shaftesbury issued invitation cards in his own name, distributing them among the liberal aristocrats and prominent clerics who made up his army of allies and supporters, while George Dolby, the impresario who had

For trying to learn to read and write, American slaves like John King risked beatings, maimings, and worse. After the Civil War, emancipated slaves descended on schools and missions, determined to get an education

Fisk treasurer George Leonard White was one of thousands of Northern whites who went south after the Civil War to minister to the freedmen

Ella Sheppard (*left*) with her half sister Rosa, in Nashville about 1867. As George White's assistant, Sheppard became the matriarch of the Jubilee Singers

Soon to be renamed Fisk University, Fisk Free Colored School was established in abandoned Union hospital barracks. This photograph is said to be of opening day on January 9, 1866, but it may be of the first commencement

The faculty of Fisk Free Colored School in June 1866. Erastus Milo Cravath sits in the center with his son, Paul, on his lap. George White towers over the back row, with his future wife Laura Cravath to his right. A bearded John Ogden, Fisk's first principal, stands to White's distant left, behind Elizabeth A. Easter. Mr. and Mrs. Charles Crosby sit on the far left of the group. Easter's and the Crosbys' moving reports on conditions at Fisk were featured in the American Missionary Association's literature

The first troupe of Jubilee Singers, photographed in early 1872. Seated, left to right: Minnie Tate, Greene Evans, Jennie Jackson, Ella Sheppard, Benjamin Holmes, and Eliza Walker. Standing, left to right: Isaac Dickerson, Maggie Porter, and Thomas Rutling

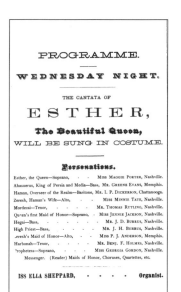

A program for a concert featuring the cantata of *Esther, the Beautiful Queen*

A derisive cartoon of a Jubilee concert at Henry Ward Beecher's Plymouth Church in Brooklyn on January 3, 1872. According to the singers, the cartoonist did not attend the concert

The tireless reformer Anthony Ashley Cooper, seventh earl of Shaftesbury, who was the Jubilees' chief patron in Britain

Below: Painting by an unknown artist of the Jubilees performing for Queen Victoria on May 7, 1873. Her Majesty was as fascinated by the troupe's color as by their music

Charles Haddon Spurgeon, the popular British Baptist evangelist who hosted the Jubilees at his vast Metropolitan Tabernacle in the summer of 1873

The American evangelist Dwight Lyman Moody, with whom the Jubilees performed on their tours of Britain

The second troupe of Fisk Jubilee Singers, painted by the English portraitist Edmund Havell. The artist had never painted black people before, and some of the singers were not pleased with their portraits. From left to right: Lewis, Tate, Holmes, Sheppard, Jennie and Julia Jackson, Dickerson, Porter, Rutling, Gordon, and Watkins

Benjamin Holmes, photographed in
Edinburgh, Scotland, in the fall of 1873.
One of the most gifted students at Fisk,
he was the Jubilees' chief spokesman
until tuberculosis prevented him from
joining the singers' third tour

Mabel Lewis, photographed in
Birmingham, England, in February
1874. The former convent student's
melancholy gaze disguised a
penetrating wit

Minnie Tate, who, at fourteen, was the youngest member of the first troupe and one of its most accomplished vocalists

A dapper Thomas Rutling posing in Manchester, England, in January 1874

Ella Sheppard in Birmingham, England, in February 1874, just as she inherited the duties of choir director from an ailing and grieving George White

Edmund Watkins in bib and tucker, posed in London. He was the only member of the Jubilees to have worked as a field slave

The aristocratic America W. Robinson, photographed in Carlisle, Scotland, in December 1876

Frederick J. Loudin, the oldest of the Jubilees. He became the third troupe's spokesman and eventually toured the world with his own troupe

Maggie Porter (*upper left*) and Isaac Dickerson (*center*), surrounded by their English fans

A grim, exhausted, and contentious third troupe of Jubilees, photographed in late 1875. Seated, left to right: B. W. Thomas, Julia Jackson, Ella Sheppard, Georgia Gordon, America Robinson, and Thomas Rutling. Standing, left to right: Maggie Porter, Frederick Loudin, Hinton Alexander, and Jennie Jackson

Susan Gilbert White, George White's second wife and the troupe's preceptress, whom Sheppard regarded as her dearest friend

Though replaced by Cravath as president of Fisk, Adam Knight Spence devoted the rest of his life to the university

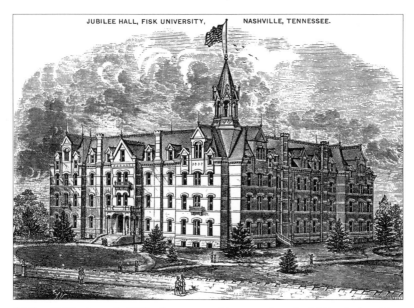

Jubilee Hall in the early 1900s. It was every bit as grand as the Jubilees' advertising promised—so grand that some Nashville blacks suspected it was intended to board white students

Fisk students in a dormitory room in Jubilee Hall in the late 1800s

Helen Clarissa Morgan, one of Fisk's most beloved figures, oversees a coeducational Latin class in the late 1800s. Morgan interceded on Georgia Gordon's behalf when White tried to bully her into joining his troupe

THE COLOUR LINE.

The "Queen's" Man.—Queen's Hotel, sir! Come right along with me, sir! Queen's Hotel, first buss—leading hotel in the city for white men—give us your checks, sir!

A cartoon printed in a Toronto newspaper in October 1881. Bearing a whip, the segregationist manager of the Queen's Hotel welcomes a disreputable white patron while the Jubilees, whom he ejected, look on

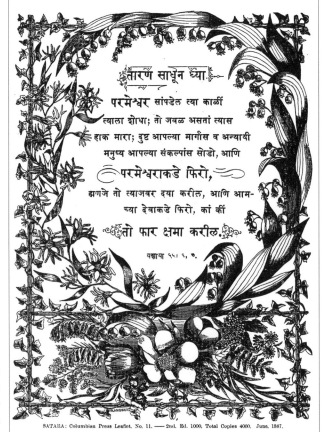

SATARA: Columbian Press Leaflet, No. 11. —— 2nd. Ed. 1000, Total Copies 4000. June, 1887.

A Maharashtran Jubilee Singers program from Loudin's 1887 tour of India

Maggie Porter Cole in the 1930s

Thomas Rutling, photographed in England in 1909. He died six years later

Ella Sheppard Moore (*center*) with her husband, George Washington Moore, and sons on the porch of the Nashville home she built with money she earned as a Jubilee. Seated far right is Ella's mother, Sarah Hannah Sheppard, who nearly drowned Ella to save her from slavery

arranged Charles Dickens's American tour, instructed Pike in "such proprieties as are acceptable to the intelligent people in England."[12]

By now, the Fisk Jubilee Singers were already steaming across the Atlantic.[13] Pike had had no luck securing cabins on any of the American
steamship lines he approached, "as the agents feared the passengers would
not like to have negroes to accompany them in the cabins." In 1845, no less
a personage than Frederick Douglass had run into the same difficulty.
Denied a cabin aboard the American sailing ship *Cambria*, Douglass had
emerged from the hold to denounce thunderously the maritime industry for its complicity in the slave trade, condemning traders and their
ships, some of which he had caulked as a slave in the shipyards of Baltimore.

Almost thirty years later, the Jubilee Singers had better luck. Working
the Boston waterfront, Pike managed to secure berths on a British Cunard
line steamer called *Batavia*. Before ascending the gangway at nine o'clock
on April 12, 1873,[14] White and Susan Gilbert read to the troupe from a
manual on shipboard decorum: "how to dress, and how not to over-eat."
After all their travails on American trains and riverboats, they were astonished to be "treated with much consideration by the officers and passengers, during the entire voyage."[15] Ella Sheppard would "never forget . . . the
kindness of the captain and crew."[16]

Maggie Porter recalled:

> I can see the young girls of the company now as they must have
> looked to our fellow passengers, each one wearing a calico wrapper
> with head bound up in long woolen scarfs, creeping cautiously to
> her deck chair, prepared to be sick. . . . Five long days I was ill. At
> last I got my sea legs, and with it a sea appetite, to which I did jus-
> tice five times a day. When I look back and recall how soundly I slept
> after eating a "welsh rarebit," a little cold chicken and a bit of cold
> ham, topped off with hot lemonade (this was my regular bill of fare,
> taken in bed . . .) I wonder that I am alive to write these lines.

Gazing out over the Atlantic, Porter kept asking herself "if it could
be true that I was really away out in that world of water, away from home
and mother, bound for England, and with the hope of seeing Queen Vic-

toria, . . . the grandest and noblest queen of them all, under whose flag . . . thousands of our race had sought and found liberty in the dark days of bondage."[17]

The worst sufferer on the voyage was Laura Cravath White. Her husband had decided to bring her along to assist him, but also in hopes that the crossing might improve her health. Instead, it was wearing her out, and over the next few months, her health would steadily decline.

The Jubilees arrived in Liverpool on the night of April 23. The English slave trade had "flooded Liverpool with wealth, . . . invigorated every industry, provided the capital for docks, enriched and employed the mills of Lancashire, and afforded the means for opening out new and ever new lines of trade."[18] Nevertheless, when the Jubilees applied for rooms at Liverpool's Northwestern Hotel, Benjamin Holmes was relieved to find they were "accommodated without previous arrangements, in the nicest manner, and as other passengers who were several shades lighter than the outside of ourselves." In the morning, they took the train to London, riding in "funny little compartment cars," as Porter described them. Holmes, who by now was something of an authority on train travel, deemed British facilities "not so good as in America, but quite convenient and comfortable." Though he had heard that "none ride the first class carriages but kings, fools and Americans," he was pleased to report that whatever your color "you can ride in any of the three [classes] that you are able to pay for."[19] As they traveled the 160 miles southeastward to London, the countryside looked to Porter like "one vast park the entire way," the grass "so green and bright," it was as if it had been "brushed and varnished."[20]

They were taken to temporary lodgings Pike had secured for them in a house on St. Aubin's Road in Upper Norwood, where they were "often stared at and followed by idle boys and girls on the streets."[21] Barely had they caught their breath when White began desperately to rehearse them for their debut twelve days later, "smoothing over the rough places in our program."[22]

White had timed the singers' arrival to coincide with the May anniversaries that drew Great Britain's aristocracy to London. Their arrival also corresponded to a renewed public outcry over reports by British explorers of the continuing slave trade in Africa's interior. Unbeknownst to the British public or anyone else but his servants, the Scottish explorer David Living-stone had miserably succumbed to dysentery in his tent by the Congo River a few days before the singers' arrival. But his letters from the interior had already rallied public opinion against the enduring vestiges of the African slave trade and in favor of a missionary effort to shine the light of Christianity upon the "Dark Continent." British missionary societies were fast establishing a network of African outposts at a cost of hundreds of thousands of pounds. When the singers arrived in London, Sir Bartle Frere was the man of the hour, having just returned from a mission to western Africa to negotiate the eradication of African slavery,[23] an institution that England and the rest of Europe may not have invented, perhaps, but had nevertheless vastly and murderously expanded in their day.

At three o'clock in the afternoon of May 6, 1873, the Jubilee Singers performed at a "favourable place for sound" called Willis's Rooms.[24] As the singers filed onto the platform and sat in a row of upholstered chairs, the duke and duchess of Argyll led an assembly of six hundred glittering aristocrats, glossy divines, and worthy reformers in a light round of applause, which one of the males—probably Holmes—rose to acknowledge with a brief bow.[25]

Shaftesbury stepped onto the stage to introduce the eleven singers. Never noted for his eloquence, he warned his audience not to expect "artistic singing." He merely promised his fellow noblemen that these "seven young women and four young men, nearly all of them emancipated slaves," would sing "the old slave songs composed by their fathers in the darkest hours of their bondage."[26]

There were uneasy titters and mutterings among the assembled guests as the singers, dressed in their comparatively shabby suits and gowns, stood and formed three small rows before an enormous grand piano last played on by the great German pianist Hans von Bülow.[27] They were "not as black as we expected," wrote one member of the audience, nor "dressed in the gay colours which are falsely supposed to distinguish the negro taste. They are simply eleven young Christian ladies and gentlemen."[28]

They stood "shoulder to shoulder, and with very close ranks, . . . with head erect and somewhat thrown back, and looking upward or with eyes nearly closed. It is evident that the audience is nothing to them; they are going to make music, and listen to one another."

The singers began with their signature piece:

Steal away,
Steal away, . . .

"The first chords came floating on our senses like gentle fairy music," wrote the *Tonic Sol-Fa Reporter*, "and they were followed by the unison of phrase, 'Steal away—to Jesus,' delivered with exquisite precision of time and accent; then came the soft chords, and bold unison again, followed by the touching, throbbing cadence, 'I hain't got long to stay here,' " like "whispering to the soul. . . . All thoughts of the grotesqueness of the language used were banished from our minds by the simple and intense sincerity of the singers."[29]

"Though the music is the offspring of wholly untutored minds, and, therefore, may grate upon the disciplined ear," sniffed the *Times*, "it possesses a peculiar charm."[30]

But after the Jubilees' rendition of "Gwine Ride up in the Chariot," many in the audience were weeping. In fact, wrote Pike, before the Jubilees' "programme was half finished they had carried their audience by storm."[31] The singers would never forget the wonderful ovation they received.[32] "We captured the hearts of the Englishmen," wrote Georgia Gordon. "We sang ourselves into their very souls. We could hear 'Bravo!' 'Hear!' 'Hear!' their way of expressing approval."[33]

The *Tonic Sol-Fa Reporter* struggled to account for the unique sensation the Jubilee Singers engendered. Ella Sheppard opened her mouth "better than any one we ever saw, except Jenny Lind. They all however open the mouth well, and this," the writer concluded, "is the secret of their wonderful speaking power. No chorus ever spoke more clearly." Their fortissimo at the conclusion of "Turn Back Pharaoh's Army" was "pure and true," not the "overstrained dissonant clattering shout, such as we have heard from choirs of no ill repute in England, Scotland and Wales." Shaftesbury had warned the audience not to expect artistic singing, but, the *Tonic Sol-Fa Reporter* wanted to know, "if the most delicate Expression, the most perfect unity of Attack, and a very beautiful Quality of voices are not artistic, what is?"[34]

After the concert, the audience closed around the singers to greet and congratulate them, some of them sporting on their bracelets, hat pins, and cuff links the Wedgwood icon of a kneeling slave titled "Am I Not a Man and a Brother?" that had been all the rage a century before. Shaftesbury was as moved and delighted as everyone else, and relieved, no doubt, that far from embarassing him in his precipitous patronage, the Jubilees had triumphed. He eagerly introduced them to his distinguished friends, including the duke and duchess of Argyll, who invited the troupe to an entertainment at their home the following afternoon.

The eighth duke of Argyll was fifty-year-old George John Douglas Campbell, who had served in the cabinets of Aberdeen and Palmerston. Despite after-dinner eloquence and a wide-ranging intellect, his most significant accomplishments were to marry his son to Queen Victoria's artistic and apparently barren daughter Louise and almost single-handedly precipitate the Second Afghan War. After falling out with his party in 1881, he would spend the remainder of his life writing indignant letters to the *Times* protesting various incursions on the rights of large landowners not unlike himself.

On the afternoon of May 7, the Jubilees and their managers arrived at Argyll Lodge, where they were shown into a large drawing room overlooking a garden sagging under a driving rain.[35] White and Pike were jittery about protocol. Pike "hoped we should be able to find consideration on the ground of our good purposes, especially if we avoided all affectation," but the stakes were high, and he feared that one belated curtsey or clumsy form of address might cost the Jubilees the patronage of the "best-appreciated families of the kingdom." Fortunately, one of the duke's guests was the famously gracious Lady Augusta Bruce Stanley, former lady-in-waiting, sister of the governor of the Prince of Wales, and wife of the dean of Westminster. She took pains to reassure Pike that all would be well.[36]

Though Argyll's ancestors had owned slaves, the duke himself was now a prominent crusader against the vestiges of African slavery.[37] He asked the Jubilees about their lives in bondage and was somewhat disappointed to learn that three of them—Jennie Jackson, Minnie Tate, and Georgia Gordon—had been born free. The singers conversed with the guests and sang a few of their songs, but a mysterious air of expectancy seemed to settle over the party.

Unbeknownst to the Jubilees, the duke was expecting as distinguished an addition to his party as the kingdom could provide. Perhaps half an hour into the visit, His Grace withdrew to greet a closed carriage, out of which, to the singers' astonishment, stepped the queen herself.

Accompanied by her youngest daughter, Princess Beatrice, Her Majesty had driven out on this "very wet" afternoon not to hear the singers but to

visit Princess Louise's in-laws; the Jubilees, she later recorded in her journal, simply "happened to be there."[38] Victoria Regina, queen of the United
Kingdom of Great Britain and Ireland and soon to be empress of India, was
fifty-four years old. She stood less than five feet, and yet "her short, stout
figure, with its folds of black velvet, its muslin streamers, its heavy pearls at
the heavy neck, assumed an almost menacing air." She had only just begun
to emerge from her seclusion after the death of Albert, her beloved prince
consort, twelve years before. Her grief was still evident in her pallor and
the deep pleats beneath her eyes, but it was "overlaid by looks of arrogance
and sharp lines of peremptory hauteur."[39]

Her marriage to Albert had been stormy. Fidgety, morbidly self-pitying,
subject to terrible mood swings during and immediately following her nine
pregnancies, she had both adored and abused her loyal husband. Nonetheless, she was the impersonatrix not simply of British power and the
continuity of European nobility but even of English domesticity and
motherhood, though she had little use for any of her children except
her first, Vicky, the future empress of Germany.

It is unlikely the queen would have liked the singers and their managers
had she gotten to know them. She took a very dim view of the piety and
evangelical fervor of the era that bore her name. Her faith was an improvised hodgepodge of disparate girlhood influences. She enjoyed wine, loved
the theater, and deplored the enforced idleness of Sabbaths. "I am not at all
an admirer or approver of our very dull Sunday," she once wrote her
daughter, "for I think the absence of innocent amusement for the poor people a misfortune and an encouragement of vice."[40] She once dismissed as
the most appalling nonsense someone's suggestion that the widowed queen
now regard Jesus as her husband. And she bristled most especially at the
heavy piety, meddlesome pedantry, and reproving frugality of her current
prime minister, William Gladstone.

Victoria was not notably philanthropic, and during the American Civil
War, she and her prince consort had supported Prime Minister Palmerston's early decision to de-emphasize Britain's opposition to slavery and
support the South in the name of protecting the cotton supply of Lancashire's textile industry. Though the queen herself was part African—her
grandmother Queen Charlotte was directly descended from a black wing
of the Portuguese royal house—the dilemma of American freedmen was
not one of Her Majesty's burning concerns.[41] But she did love oddities and

approached the Jubilee Singers' impromptu performance with the same undisguised curiosity with which she had once entertained the American midget "General" Tom Thumb.

The duke escorted Her Majesty and Princess Beatrice to an adjoining room, from which the singers were summoned into the royal presence, bowing and curtseying as best they knew how. In later life, Maggie Porter would confess she was disappointed at first with the ruler of the largest empire in the history of the world. "Poor ignorant me!" Porter exclaimed. "I received the greatest disappointment of my life. The Queen wore no crown, no robes of state. She was like many English ladies I had seen in her widow's cap and weeds. But it was the Queen in flesh and blood."[42]

Victoria sat quietly and expectantly as the singers assembled before her. "I can see her now," wrote Porter nearly seventy years later. "She had on gloves. I can see her taking off her gloves and looking at us all the time."[43]

The queen asked the duke to convey her desire that they sing "Steal Away." "Her voice was very low pitched," Porter remembered, "but we heard her."[44]

So they sang "Steal Away" in their soft voices, their eyes ceilingward, averted from Victoria's protuberant gaze.

> My Lord, He calls me.
> He calls me by the thunder.
> The trumpet sounds
> Within my soul.
> I ain't got long to stay here.

After a silent pause, they chanted the Lord's Prayer in Gregorian unison. Then Porter heard the queen's "deep, low voice saying, 'Tell them we are delighted with their songs, and that we wish them to sing 'John Brown.'" Porter "wondered why the Queen did not speak these words to us. We were within hearing and heard her words of commendation and her 'command.' But what could I know of English court etiquette?"[45] (As Georgia Gordon later explained, "Queen Victoria could only be spoken to through a royal person."[46])

According to Pike and Holmes, the song Her Majesty requested was actually "Go Down, Moses"; in any case, she listened to their rendition "with manifest pleasure," though her demeanor struck some of the singers as a little flat. Her Majesty did not applaud nor thank them directly as they filed out.[47] "When she had heard what she called for," Porter remembered, "she smiled, then she got up, and we stood still until she was out of sight."[48]

That was a mistake. They were supposed to bow and curtsey as Her Majesty stumped past. Nevertheless, the queen apparently had been pleased, though as much impressed by the color of the singers as by their music.[49] That evening, she wrote in her journal that the Jubilees were "real Negroes" and, she incorrectly noted, "have all been slaves, some having been sold several times." Reflecting perhaps on her own African ancestry, Her Majesty reported that two of the Jubilees were "quite white, others coffee coloured, & several quite black. They sing extremely well together."[50]

The Jubilees returned to the main hall to perform one more song for Argyll's guests, after which Pike and White saw the singers safely back to their temporary lodgings in Upper Norwood. Despite their exhaustion and a driving rain, Pike and White set out with hearts "joyous and light" to find the troupe a London hotel.[51]

AT THE WELCOME TABLE

LONDON

MAY–JULY 1873

Queen Victoria's blessing opened nearly every door in her kingdom, beginning with the deanery at Westminster Abbey. Dean Arthur Penrhyn Stanley was a "vivid, childlike, and infinitely lovable" man of sufficient means to carry on an "immense hospitality." Visitors like Carlyle and Disraeli "found inspiration in the width of [Stanley's] sympathies and in being brought into touch with countless people they would never otherwise have met." Introducing the singers to her guests, Lady Stanley intended to "lionize" them but faltered when various invited members of the press whipped out their notebooks and began to jot down her remarks.

Since the queen had not had a chance to converse with the Jubilees, Lady Stanley later took the liberty of informing Her Majesty that they were "most intelligent and bright, poor things," and reported that after the party they "sang one of their hymns in the Abbey, and most beautiful it was."[1] They sang "Steal Away" over the tomb of "Bloody Mary" and chanted the Lord's Prayer by the sepulchre of Mary, Queen of Scots.[2] Dean Stanley was especially taken with the grandiloquent Isaac Dickerson. Despite Dickerson's limited formal education, Stanley made a standing offer to send him to the University of Edinburgh to study for the ministry.

Invitations flooded in. Pike's companion, the Reverend James Powell, was an acquaintance of an English Quaker named Stafford Allen who had visited Fisk and donated twenty dollars. Allen had spread the gospel of the Jubilees among the English Society of Friends. Soon after the singers' visit with the Stanleys, a Quaker named Samuel Gurney invited them to his mansion in Regent Park. The Gurneys had started in the textile industry and eventually branched out into banking and philanthropy. On June 9, Gurney arranged to meet the singers in the nearby Botanical and Zoological Gardens and timed their tour so that they might reach the lions at four o'clock to watch them feed. "The keeper of the garden showed us every courtesy," wrote Benjamin Holmes, "and admitted us into places where the public was not admitted."[3] The singers were delighted, but Pike was horrified by a trained chimpanzee they encountered that opened doors for visitors and even shook their hands.

"A shudder passed over me as though the soul of man had been confined in the body of a beast. It was terribly suggestive of Darwinism," he said, "and I fled from its presence, and banished its form from my mind."[4]

The Jubilees were greeted by about sixty guests in the full spring bloom of Gurney's orchard.[5] After dining in the greenhouse, they performed in the family's somewhat austere drawing room, eliciting tears from elderly Quakers who had once profited as confectioners from the slave-based sugar plantations of the Caribbean but nevertheless contributed large portions of their fortunes to the British abolitionist movement and were all the more effective opponents of slavery for having understood its finances.[6] Though all of the guests were Quakers, Holmes reported, they had "a very nice meeting," as it seemed "the spirit made them talk." They were especially moved by the singers' rendition of "John Brown's Body," whose reception in England Holmes found "really astonishing."

"John Brown's Body" had been the most popular of all the songs in the Union army. Soldiers especially enjoyed singing "We'll hang Jeff Davis from a—" and then adding the name of whatever tree they were marching past. Soldiers wrote their own lyrics to the infectious marching tune, which was sung more rapidly than its immediate descendant, Julia Ward Howe's "Battle Hymn of the Republic," which never gained anything like the popularity of the original. Yankees who did not necessarily favor emancipation had their own versions (one began, "The bugle blasts are sounding, / 'tis time to be away"). Sometimes, instead of "John Brown's Body" lying "a-mouldering in the grave," it would be the body of a fallen Yankee hero.[7]

The Jubilees' version was purely abolitionist. "John Brown died that the slave might be free," they sang. The rebels had hanged him "for a traitor," though they themselves were "the traitor crew," but now had come "the glorious Jubilee / When all mankind is free." It may have been these last lines that reverberated in an England appalled by Livingstone's reports of African slavery.

A merchant named Heffers invited them to his home on June 17, showed them his vast gardens, and introduced them to the niceties of croquet while "the servants supplied us with tea, coffee, lemonade, cakes &c. (i.e. wines, which, of course, the 'Jubes' refused)." In the evening, Heffers took Jennie Jackson's arm and led them all to tables "groaning beneath the weight of the best the London market could produce in way of meats, vegetable, fruits, pastry, wines, etc."

Two days later, the Jubilees attended "Hospital Sunday" at St. Paul's, where the Prince and Princess of Wales presided. "It was quite an imposing sight," wrote Holmes, "to see these dignitaries in their robes of office, scepters, swords, and other ornaments glittering in the sunlight."[8]

Holmes was less approving of the shah of Persia, who arrived on June 18 for a state visit. "Millions have been spent on him," Holmes sighed, "and ere he returns to his oriental home millions more will be spent to make him welcome. If the millions . . . had been put to a practical use—namely, to spread the light of the Gospel among his benighted subjects, I even would say well done, when, as now, I can only repeat the words of the preacher: 'All is vanity'."

British reformers were at least as improvisational as their American counterparts, and few were more singular in their efforts to better their inferiors than George MacDonald and his family. Having urged the Jubilees to visit Britain in the first place, the Scottish novelist now invited them to his retreat at Hammersmith, a vast Georgian mansion on the banks of the Thames, where each spring he constructed a stage for an "elevating" family play. For an audience, the MacDonalds imported wagon loads of the poor and the lame "from some wretched street in the densely-populated metropolis." Though most of their guests were "unacquainted even with the ordinary use of the conveniences of table service," over the years Mrs. MacDonald had noted a marked improvement in their character, which she ascribed to "the kind attentions of other guests always present, and . . . the object-lessons afforded to the happy observers." Strolling amid MacDonald's fruit trees, the singers played games with the novelist's eleven children and entertained the MacDonalds' guests with a few of their songs.

On July 8, the Jubilees performed for a disappointingly small gathering of the Anti-Slavery Society at Exeter Hall, where Sir Bartle Frere gave an address on the continuing slave trade in Africa. Holmes was depressed by the small turnout and urged his African American friends "not to wink at this thing now that we are free. We should exert ourselves in breaking the chains of those who are still in bonds. . . . It is our duty to arouse those who are now liberated, to the fact that many people and especially negroes are still in bondage."[9]

Britain's prohibitionists were faring better. On a simmering day in July, the Jubilees took part in the National Temperance League's annual fete at the Crystal Palace. They performed for a cumulative audience of more than fifty-three thousand teetotalers (and, according to Holmes, one drunk, "who behaved himself as nicely as a drunken man could, and was tolerated").[10] The festivities included balloon races, boat launchings, band concerts, drills, and gymnastics; "of course the usual number of women fainted, but they were borne off by good Samaritans, who laid them in the cool and hastened back as quick as possible to finish their enjoyment." When the singers arrived, they were greeted "amid loud cheers" by the audience and a choir of five thousand voices called the Provincial Bands of Hope. In the evening, they sang temperance songs and patriotic melodies in the Crystal Palace's opera house, where the Bands of Hope joined in on the final chorus of "John Brown's Body":

> *Glory, glory, hallelujah,*
> *When all mankind is free.*

Among the Jubilees' early champions in Great Britain was the Reverend Newman Hall. A prolific Congregationalist who had firmly supported the Union during the Civil War, he was about to embark on the second of two journeys to the United States, where his books, bearing titles like *Pilgrim Songs in Cloud and Sunshine* and *Prayer: Its Reasonableness and Efficacy*, were widely circulated. Hall was a confidant of Catherine Glynne Gladstone, the wife of the prime minister, and mentioned the singers to her at breakfast one morning, whereupon Mrs. Gladstone expressed "a desire that they should come to her house."[11]

A week passed and no invitation materialized, and Pike sadly concluded that she had forgotten them. Then, in early July, the Jubilees received an invitation to perform on the fourteenth at a luncheon at Carlton House for not only the Gladstones but the Prince and Princess of Wales, Grand Duchess Marie Alexandrovna of Russia, and, as Gladstone himself put it, "all manner of notabilities."[12]

The William Ewart Gladstone who greeted them was six feet tall but had an enormous head that had the odd effect of making him appear much shorter. He had a broad beak of a nose, and restless onyx eyes that glittered beneath an animated brow. At sixty-three years of age, he was reluctantly serving out what would prove to be only the first of four prime ministerships. Brilliant, imperious, prickly, and one of the most gifted extemporaneous speakers in British history, by 1873 he had become frustrated, exhausted and discursive.

"The People's William," as Gladstone was called, was the son of a slaveholder. John Gladstone owned vast numbers of slaves on his Jamaica sugar plantations and British Guiana cotton plantations.[13] Though his son William had been "converted to God" by his pious mother, he upheld the institution of slavery as a young man.[14] Forty years before he shook hands with the Jubilee Singers, he had delighted King William IV with his maiden speech to Parliament: a filial defense of the indefensible mortality rate among his father's slaves. It was true, the twenty-three-year-old member for Newark told the Commons, that slavery was "trying," but it was hardly less healthy than, say, steel grinding.[15] Besides, slavery was sanctioned by God. Speaking out against the abolitionist machinations of the future lords Derby and Grey, he proposed emancipating only Christian, educated, and industrious slaves, and then only after their owners had been fully compensated.

Young Gladstone's glib casuistry won him many admirers. He was expressing the sentiments of a large sector of an upper class that owed its wealth to the West Indian trade, a group that included the second to last prime minister, the durable earl of Liverpool, who had himself actually traded in slaves.[16] But Gladstone's speech proved to be British slavery's swan song. Two months later, Parliament passed the gradualist Abolition of Slavery Bill, which freed all enslaved children under the age of six, held the rest as "apprentices" compelled to devote three quarters of their labors to their former masters for up to six years, and compensated British slave owners with twenty million pounds.[17] This "apprenticeship" system was so thoroughly abused, however, that in 1838 Parliament at last voted for complete and immediate emancipation.

The philanthropic spirit of the age had touched Gladstone in a peculiar fashion. So guilt ridden by his masturbatory enthusiasm for marginally pornographic literature that he regularly scourged himself with a whip, he began roaming the streets at odd hours proselytizing to prostitutes. He was as sincere as he was unsuccessful; out of the scores of whores he tried to reform, he could count exactly one whom he had actually convinced to give up her profession. Though he eventually took to further scourging himself for the "carnal" feelings the work engendered in him—feelings he called "the chief burden of my soul"—he somehow carried on his anguished crusade well into old age without leaving any indelible stain on his reputation.

In the end, politics proved a superior moral purgative to self-flagellation.[18] Gladstone was a founder of the Liberal Party and perhaps the most effective parliamentarian in British history, surpassing even his arch rival, the brilliant and mischievous Conservative Benjamin Disraeli. It was his fate to serve a sovereign who could hardly bear him, and yet he was the ultimate Victorian statesman. Gladstone's instincts were democratic; during his lifetime, the size of Britain's electorate increased tenfold, and many of the reforms he shepherded through Parliament vastly improved the living conditions of the subjects of his disapproving queen. Though Gladstone never was an outright abolitionist, it was said of him, as of Lincoln, that he spent his whole life "unlearning the prejudices in which he was educated," and by 1873 he had embraced the cause of the freedmen.

With boyish glee he now greeted the Jubilee Singers and secreted them in a dark alcove of his vast dining room, where they went unnoticed by the arriving guests until he gave a signal for them to chant the Lord's Prayer as a premeal grace. Delighting in his guests' astonishment, Gladstone immediately urged the choir to sing "John Brown's Body" as his guests tucked into their soup. Within a few months, "John Brown" would become such a favorite of the British military that the Forty-second Highlanders would sing it with dubious congruity as they vanquished the ferocious Ashanti of West Africa.[19]

Leafing through a booklet of the Jubilees' songs, the Prince of Wales next asked if they would perform "Many Thousands Gone" in honor of the grand duchess, whose father had freed the Russian serfs.[20]

"No more auction block for me," they sang as the prince nodded to the duchess, who was soon to marry his brother, the duke of Edinburgh.

No More, No More.
No more auction block for me.
Many thousands gone.

"The Princess and Cesarevna were very kind and conversable," Holmes reported. "They spoke freely to our young ladies and complimented the singing."

"I never heard anything more beautiful than 'Sweet Home,'" the princess told them.

"Yes," agreed the grand duchess, "the harmony was perfect."[21]

The other guests surrounded the singers, peppering them with questions in an atmosphere of jewels, silks, medals, hair tonic, and toilet water. The choir was dazzled by all the attention, but the honor was primarily titular; Gladstone's guests were mostly mediocrities. In addition to the eclipsed, indolent, and promiscuous crown prince and the hapless duke of Argyll, there was the good-humored but inert Earl Granville, whose father had owned slaves and whose service in the foreign office would be notable mainly for his feeble concessions to Britain's rivals and his urging General Gordon to his doom in the Sudan.[22] Though his mother had sponsored Shaftesbury's campaign against American slavery, the duke of Sutherland was an enthusiastic beneficiary of the brutal Highland Clearances that chased his clansmen off their ancestral grounds to the bleak coast of Scotland and beyond to make way for the profitable raising of sheep. His favorite pastimes were "riding on locomotive engines, and watching the fire brigade at work."

The exceptions were Gladstone, of course, and also a Mrs. Goldschmidt, the former Jenny Lind. "The Swedish Nightingale" had been the greatest opera star of her time. At the urging of Dean Stanley, she had officially retired from the stage in 1858 but still gave occasional concerts for charity. By all accounts, Lind was as magnanimous as she was gifted, the very opposite of the standard-issue prima donna. Though by the age of fifty-three she had put on weight, she retained the angelic countenance and authentic charm that, almost as much as her brilliant soprano, had spread "Jenny Lind Fever" all over Europe and the United States. Jenny Lind had been a particular inspiration to Mabel Lewis, who, as a small girl, "had heard the story of how Jenny Lind was singing and some ladies who heard her gave her an education."[23]

Another exceptional guest that afternoon was the ailing Quaker parliamentarian John Bright. A former president of the Board of Trade, Bright was sixty-two years old and serving as chancellor of the duchy of Lancaster. During the American Civil War, he had distinguished himself with a series of brilliant speeches denouncing the Confederacy and its British supporters. Bright's likeness was the only portrait a grateful Abraham Lincoln displayed in his White House office. After the war, Bright had opposed calls for the execution of rebels but proposed they be exiled instead, in order to guarantee the civil rights of their former slaves.

A few days after the Jubilees' performance for the Prince of Wales, Pike received the following letter from Gladstone himself:

> I beg you to accept the assurances of the great pleasure which the Jubilee Singers gave on Monday to our illustrious guests, and to all who heard them. I should wish to offer a little present in books in acknowledgment of their kindness, and in connection with the purposes, as they have been announced, of their visit to England. It has occurred to me that perhaps they might like to breakfast with us, my family and a very few friends, but I would not ask this unless it is thoroughly agreeable to them. With the singers, who, I believe, are eleven, we would of course hope to see you and Mr. White.[24]

For Pike, this single invitation was "worth as much to the coloured people of the world as the campaign cost us." If the prime minister of Great Britain could "ask coloured people to sit at his table," Pike mused, "can we not hope our loved country, where all men are born free and equal, where there is no aristocracy, where 'high worth is elevated place,' will sit in sack cloth for the abominations she hath done, till her wicked prejudices are taken away?"[25]

On Tuesday, July 29, Gladstone was ill with the flu but defied his physician's orders and, despite a twenty-five-mile train ride from Chiselhurst and a carriage ride from the station, greeted the singers at Carlton House Terrace with ebullience. Mrs. Gladstone and her daughters took them by the hand and led them out onto the terrace, whose door "was still covered with scarlet cloth" from the previous visit of the Prince of Wales. After all the guests had arrived, "we were invited into the spacious dining room, where two tables were very tastily arranged opposite each other, and decorated with many beautiful and fragrant little bouquets."[26] The Gladstones showed the Jubilees to their chairs, poured them tea, and "conversed with them in a manner utterly free from any approach either to pride or condescension," all in marked contrast to their reception from even their most liberal-minded American hosts.

"The guests were seated at two tables, our negro friends being equally distributed sitting between their English friends," reported Newman Hall.

> At the table where the dean and myself sat, Mrs. Gladstone, Miss Gladstone, and Mr. W. [E.] Gladstone were most assiduous in their kind attentions—not only seeing that the physical comfort of their negro guests was attended to, but conversing with them so constantly and pleasantly that they were quite at their ease. At the other table Lady Cavendish, acting for Mrs. Gladstone and seated side by side with her coloured sisters, diffused the same atmosphere of social geniality around. A number of liveried footmen ministered also to the wants of the guests, paying as much attention and deference to the coloured singers from Tennessee as to the titled ladies of the English aristocracy and to the untitled but no less noble lady whose guests we were.

Hall apologized rather fatuously to his British readers "for writing in this way." After all, the Gladstones' "trifling courtesies" toward their black guests were only to be expected of English ladies and gentlemen. But "I am told that there still exists in the United States some remnant of the old prejudice," wrote Hall, whose account would incense and shame the readers of the *New York Independent*.

> This may be found, no doubt, amongst some of the ignorant and vulgar of our own land; and so also it would not be fair to infer that such prejudice is general in America because exhibited by some low bred, unrefined, and narrow souls.
>
> I wish they had been present yesterday to see Mrs. Gladstone and her daughters, and the noble lords and ladies present, taking their negro friends by the hand, placing them chairs, sitting at their side, pouring out their tea, etc., and conversing with them in a manner utterly free from any approach either to pride or condescen-

sion; but exactly as if they had been white people in their own rank of life. And this not as an effort, nor for the show of it, but from a habit of social intercourse which would have rendered any other conduct perfectly impossible.

Gladstone lectured animatedly about his "paintings and sculptures by eminent artists, and cases filled with specimens of erratic art of all ages, . . . works by Cellini, and specimens of pottery."[27] Afterward the party retired to the drawing room, where the Jubilees sang "John Brown's Body." In the opinion of George White, the singers, their faces illuminated with "reverence and joy and gratitude to God," rewarded the prime minister and his family with their finest performance to date.

Gladstone leaned toward them as they sang, "all the intellect and soul of his great nature" playing across his features. When they were done, he kept saying, "Isn't it wonderful? I never heard anything like it!"

They sang "O Them Great Trials" next, and their rendition of "O How I Love Jesus" reduced Gladstone and his guests to tears. They all stood as the singers chanted the Lord's Prayer, and after a round of "hearty farewells," the Jubilees departed at noon, singing "Good-bye, brother, good-bye, sister," as they left Carlton House, marching past rows of astonished petitioners waiting to see the prime minister.[28]

"We do not look upon it merely as a personal favor that Mr. Gladstone invited us to breakfast," Holmes wrote home, "and invited us to breakfast with him, and invited lords and ladies to entertain us, but rather as a kind of acknowledgment of his appreciation of the effort which the negro of America is making to rise from the degradation of slavery to their place among the civilized nations of the earth. This encouragement from the Premier of England will outbalance many discouragements which low men in America put in our way."[29]

Thus ended what Gladstone referred to in his diary that evening as his "negro breakfast."[30]

Among the visitors to London that season was the Jubilees' most exalted and impassioned fan, Samuel Langhorne Clemens, who had arrived with his wife, Livy, at about the same time the singers landed. Mark Twain was at the height of his fame, and he was immediately smothered by invitations to meet fellow writers like Spencer, Turgenev, Browning, Trollope, and Lewis

Carroll, "the shyest full-grown man, except Uncle Remus," he had ever met.[31] They kept him so busy, he complained, that he did not have time enough to see the sights of London.

For the Jubilee Singers, however, Twain made time. That summer, he was in line at a London ticket booth for one of the Jubilees' concerts when the manager called out, "Don't take that money!"

"Isn't it the right amount?" Clemens wanted to know.

"Isn't this Mr. Clemens?" the manager asked. "You can't pay any money to go to this concert. Give him the best seats in the hall."

Clemens explained to his companion that he had written an article for a London paper comparing the Jubilee Singers with the claptrap impersonations of the minstrel shows. After the concert, Clemens said the audience's response was unprecedented. "Their 'John Brown's Body' took a decorous, aristocratic English audience by surprise and threw them into a volcanic eruption of applause before they knew what they were about. I never saw anything finer than their enthusiasm."[32]

Twain purchased a copy of the singers' book and later, during his lecture tour, after his wife had returned home, used to soothe his homesickness by sitting at pianos in his hotel suites and singing the Jubilees' songs.[33]

After one of the troupe's London concerts, a portraitist named Edmund Havell volunteered to paint a life-size group portrait free of charge. Though Fisk legend would identify him as the queen's portraitist, he was in fact a rather undistinguished genre painter and rates few mentions in the histories of Victorian painting. "I was the first singer to go to London," Georgia Gordon recalled, "with Miss Susan Gilbert, our preceptress, to sit for my portrait. The first evening we were there Mr. [Havell], with Miss White and a rich Jew named Bensusan, took us for a drive through Hyde Park and Rotten Row. That day we visited the Albert Memorial. . . . Every nationality of the world was represented on the four corners. Mr. Bensusan told us that he had posed as a representative of his people."[34] Havell had each one of them painted separately, Maggie Porter remembered. "I can see myself now with that waist of East Indian silk and green velvet-sleeved jacket." Havell posed her leaning on one hand and set her near the center of the group. "I forget how many days I had to pose, but he said I was a good subject and kept quiet. It was a new experience for the artist—he had never painted a colored person before."[35]

The British were fascinated by the singers' color. Here, as in the American Northeast, the variation among them astonished and titillated crowds who, entertaining visions of Africans derived from the mass of illustrated books on the market about cannibals and missionaries and explorers hacking their way to the source of the Nile, expected them all to be jet-black. That they were of many hues and shades was further evidence of miscegenation, of a heritage of African slave girls in the thrall of their Southern masters. Georgia Gordon remembered how British critics wrote that "Mabel Lewis and Georgia Gordon could pass as fair English belles in any drawing room, and Minnie Tate as coming from the south of France."

Almost thirty years earlier, Frederick Douglass, who had himself sung slave songs in the parlors of his English friends, had also observed the British enthusiasm for exotic negritude. "It is quite an advantage to be a 'nigger' here," he once reported home. "I am hardly black enough for the british taste, but by keeping my hair as woolly as possible I make out to pass for at least half a negro at any rate."[36] Sometimes the troupe detected a kind of reverse racism at work in England. "Jennie Jackson was a curiosity," Gordon recalled. "They never saw any one so black, and she was looked upon as something extraordinary."[37]

"The darker you are the better they like you, and our darker complexioned young ladies got more offers of marriage than the light ones," complained the light-skinned Mabel Lewis.

> Miss Jennie Jackson was very dark, and she had no peace. She would take her umbrella and beat her way along with it. One time a crowd was following us, and she went into a store and asked if she could go through the store and out the back door. We looked back, and there they were, all following us into the store. . . . We were great curiosities.[38]

"Our many shades of brown and black got us mixed up at times," Ella Sheppard recalled, "and then, too, their British accent was so different from ours that at first we could not easily understand each other."[39]

"Do you ever sing in Shi-ca-go?" one woman asked Mabel Lewis, who "could not think what she meant at first."

"Well," continued the woman, "I married a blackie, and he went to Shi-ca-go to live, and his name is Williams. Have you seen him?"[40]

One engulfing Englishman, who had spotted the Jubilees on the street and descended on them "to give a hearty welcome to those who fitly & fully represent that noble race—the Negro," complained that they were "very shy."[41]

Some of their fans had been so inculcated with news of Africa that they were surprised to learn that these African Americans spoke English. Mabel Lewis enjoyed playing to their ignorance:

> One time we had to wait some time at a station, and we heard someone say, "I am going to speak to some of them and see if they speak English." She came up to me and said, "Do you speak English?"
>
> "Ugh?" I said.
>
> "Do you speak English, or do you just learn the songs?"
>
> "Baca migly pan martu," I answered.
>
> And she said, "I guess they do not talk, they only sing in English."[42]

The Jubilees tended to chalk up such encounters not to racism but to well-intentioned curiosity. If such luminaries as Gladstone, Argyll, and Shaftesbury brought to their encounter with the Jubilee Singers any hint of bigotry, it was buried under so many layers of lavish courtesy that the troupe apparently never detected it. These American former slaves presented no threat to the British upper classes, who may have welcomed them in part as proof of the backwardness and enduring shame of the upstart American Republic. But mere courtesy could not account for the tears and applause and shouts of joy the choir elicited from even the most forbidding and notable countenances.

Frederick Douglass had found everything in Britain "so different . . . from what I have been accustomed to in the United States. No insults to encounter, but all is smooth—I am treated as a man and equal brother": treated so well in fact that he seriously considered living there permanently.[43] In the mid–nineteenth century, the former slave Harriet Jacobs visited England, where "for the first time in my life I was in a place where I was treated according to my deportment, without reference to my complexion," and felt as though "a great millstone had been lifted from my breast." It was her first experience "of pure, unadulterated freedom."[44]

Now to Sheppard and Rutling and the others it seemed that they had entered the "bright mansions above" that they longed for in their songs.

America's bigotry had tugged at them even as they set sail for England. Suddenly the most powerful statesmen in the world praised their accomplishments, commiserated with their former suffering, spoke to them if not as equals, at least as fellow human beings. And all in less than a decade since Edmund Watkins had been tied to a whipping post, Jennie Jackson had earned her tuition laboring at a washtub, and Ella Sheppard had been forced to sneak into her teacher's house for music lessons.

THERE'S ROOM ENOUGH

BRITAIN

JULY–DECEMBER 1873

Conducting a fund-raising concert tour in the England of the 1870s presented the Jubilee Singers' pious managers with a conundrum. British clerics urged the Jubilees to perform solely in churches and rely on collections, for it was "an established law of this country," as one cleric put it, "that all places of worship when open for religious service of any kind, are *free* to all who may come, so that we could not prevent anyone from entering without a ticket."[1] But White knew from his experience in America that depending on donations could be risky. At free concerts, the poor tended to crowd out the rich, leaving the Jubilees little to show for their efforts. On the other hand, ticketed performances in public halls and theaters risked alienating the religious community whose idea of a concert "was associated either with vulgar or debasing influences."[2] In fact, the singers themselves were prohibited from attending any theatrical productions.[3] Even when they were allowed to perform in a church, there was often such discord among the various denominations that the Jubilees risked drawing, at best, only a portion of each church's congregation.

Henry Allon arranged for them to perform at his Union Chapel in Islington in a species of private concert for which invitations were distributed that gingerly urged everyone who attended to make a donation. The concert yielded eighty pounds, and Pike thought that had the group been smaller, with more time to raise funds in Britain, Allon's model might have been the best. But by the A.M.A.'s standards, at least, sustaining the troupe was expensive. The singers had each been promised at least five hundred dollars per year, the managers and their advance men had to be paid, and if they were all to survive the grueling schedule Pike was cobbling together for them, they required clean and comfortable lodgings, first-class traveling accommodations, medical care, and decent food, all of which cost money.

Allon urged White to bring his singers to the annual meeting of the Congregational Union at the Cannon Street Terminus Hotel in London. "No company of men are more elastic, explosive, merry, and happy than a company of divines on a festive occasion," burbled Pike, and they gave the singers' performance such a warm reception that Pike feared "the brethren might think me discourteous if I should make known to the public how enthusiastic it was." In any case, they contributed generously to the Jubilees' mission. At Shaftesbury's request, the troupe performed at the annual meeting of the Freedmen's Missions Aid Society, where the Reverend John Smith Moffat, the brother of the newly widowed Mrs. David Livingstone and himself a missionary to Africa, cited the singers as examples of the results of educating Africans and converting them to Christianity.[4]

The eminently respectable Henry Allon was proving useful, but Pike found a more kindred spirit in the enterprising and aphoristic Charles Haddon Spurgeon, the British counterpart of his idol, Henry Ward Beecher. The leading British evangelist of his day, Spurgeon was a brilliant sermonizer who by 1861, at the age of only twenty-seven, had become so popular that he required and erected an enormous venue called the Metropolitan Tabernacle to accommodate his flock.

Though a strict Calvinist, Spurgeon prided himself on his informality and reproached Pike for approaching him with such trepidation. "My dear sir," he wrote, "you should have come or written to me at once, for I believe in straightforward running, and do not care for influence and persuasion and all that; you and your brother minstrels would have been welcomed as soon as you landed, and shall be welcome now." The staff of the tabernacle took over all the preparations, including the sale of tickets. After Sabbath services, the singers were persuaded to sing "Room Enough," as Spurgeon and his deacons wept.

Oh, mourners, don't stay away . . .
Oh, Sinners, don't stay away . . .
Oh, children, don't stay away . . .
For the Lord says there's room enough,
Room enough in the Heavens for you.

It was little wonder that the Jubilees chose this piece, for there was room enough in Spurgeon's Metropolitan Tabernacle for six thousand souls. That evening, he took the spiritual's lyrics for his text. Before their second appearance at his tabernacle the following week, Spurgeon invited the Jubilees to tea at his retreat at Clapham. Here they encountered his menagerie of cats and dogs and his exhausted, invalid wife. Spurgeon declared that though he was not "sufficiently acquainted with music to find fault with the songs I have heard this afternoon, and what is more, I hope I never shall be," he was "sufficiently acquainted with music to be able to say I never so enjoyed music which I have listened to in the way of performance. Our friends seem to sing from the heart; their souls are singing right cheerfully, and this gives fire to their music that cannot be in it under any other circumstances; they have touched my heart." The tabernacle had multiple offshoots—a pastors' college, a press, a tract society—and after tea, Spurgeon took the singers to his Orphan Asylum at Stockwell, which "some devoted lady" had endowed with twenty thousand pounds. Before the singers left Clapham, Mrs. Spurgeon presented them with eighteen volumes of her husband's works.

When the Jubilees arrived for their concert that evening, a huge crowd was pressed around the tabernacle's entrance. Within ten minutes of the doors opening, four thousand people had flooded in. The crowd eventually swelled to six or seven thousand, one thousand of them standing in the aisles: the largest paying audience the Jubilees had ever drawn.[5]

Spurgeon did not give up the limelight easily and remained in view, interspersing the choir's renditions with a few of his own remarks. "I do not think I ever realized the worth of Jennie Jackson," Pike proudly recalled, "as I did when I saw her stand in Mr. Spurgeon's place, and hold the attention of that vast audience as fixedly as the preacher ever had done, while she sang the gospel of, 'You may bury me in the east, / You may bury me in the west. / But I'll hear that trumpet sound / In that morning,'" after which Spurgeon stepped forward to dilate on the wasteful absurdity of consecrated burial grounds.

"Now our friends are going to Scotland," Spurgeon concluded, "and I have told them to come here, and hold their first concert when they return to London. They have come to Great Britain to raise £6,000: they will do it; and if they want £6,000 more, let them come back to this country again, and we will give it to them."

The crowd was wildly enthusiastic, and though the proceeds of £214 were small considering the size of the audience, they exceeded any the choir had yet earned in Great Britain.[6]

Before departing for Scotland in early August 1873, Pike again called upon the earl of Shaftesbury and asked for a reference in Scotland. Shaftesbury immediately wrote a letter of introduction to John Burns of the Cunard line of steamships, upon whose ship *Batavia* the Jubilees had crossed to England.

En route to Glasgow, the singers sang at private concerts in Hull, Scarborough, Newcastle, and Sunderland. Hull had been the home of William Wilberforce, the great British abolitionist. Few of the singers had ever heard of him, but, according to Pike, as they passed Wilberforce's monument and saw that it had been erected on the same day of the same month as their visit, they "felt like those who had come to an anniversary of jubilee." It was "quite strange," wrote Holmes, for they "did not take into consideration that Wilberforce lived there nor that he had slavery abolished on that day."[7] The Reverend W. C. Preston of Hull's Hope Chapel had distributed 1,650 tickets, and the concert yielded more than fifty-two pounds. Compared with British charitable fund drives, the troupe was already raising an unprecedented amount of money.[8]

Pike assured Cravath that there was almost no overhead "in this [Jubilee Singers] business. The Concerts are worked up with a thoroughness unknown to English showmen, and our profits are greater perhaps than those arising from all respectable shows in the country together, [though] business is not good in this country."[9]

The concert was such a success that Pike decided to try an experiment and held the singers over for a second concert at a venue called Hengler's Cirque, for which he intended to charge admission. That evening, as the singers sat in the Cross Keys Hotel watching the crowds of working people across the square, White proposed that they perform for the public at the base of a large equestrian statue of William III.

The Jubilees and their managers were probably unaware of the irony of the setting. In the early eighteenth century, William III had erected a statue of his own at Hampton Court: a bust of his favorite slave. Along with most of the House of Commons, half of the House of Lords, the lord chancellor, the philanthropist Thomas Guy, Alexander Pope, and the king's own mistress and bastards, His Majesty had been a stockholder in Britain's notorious South Sea Company, which in sixteen years sold some sixty-four thousand slaves.[10] At the base of William III's statue, the Jubilees conducted one of their old-time street services, with Pike delivering a brief sermon from the statue's pedestal and the Jubilees singing until "tears were trickling slowly down the cheeks of the wretched wanderers."[11] That Sunday, Dickerson preached at Hope Chapel, and the next day White took the singers to the Humber training ship for boys, which donated a copy of *Pictorial Old England* for Fisk's library. Despite a driving rain, Hengler's Cirque was packed, and the concert grossed £140.[12] "Over three thousand people were present at our last concert," wrote Holmes, "and many were refused admission because the house was filled to its utmost capacity."

Thus the Jubilee Singers began to find their formula: appearances at churches, revivals, orphanages, temperance meetings, the parlors of the rich and powerful, followed by paid concerts in the biggest venues they could locate. Rather than dilute their drawing power, the free performances for locally popular worthy causes only endeared them further to the paying public, and especially the "pious nobility" they cultivated.

In this respect, Susan Gilbert was a crucial component of the Jubilee enterprise, reassuring the British with her vigilant presence that the Jubilees, especially the young ladies, would never embarrass their patrons with unseemly behavior or disastrous affairs of the heart. English ladies fawned upon Dickerson and Rutling especially, and the sopranos and altos contended with a steady stream of calling cards and forests of bouquets from ardent young admirers. It fell to Gilbert to protect them, and the mission, from mischievous gentle ladies and stage-door johnnies.

The Jubilees were supposed to rest at Scarborough, the seaside "Queen of Watering Places," but at the insistence of a local minister named Balgarnie, they performed for the South Cliff Congregational Church. The Jubilees lodged with a prohibitionist town councilman named Whittaker and were squired around Scarborough's fashionable attractions by the ruthless Quaker chocolatier Joseph Rowntree. The children of South Cliff distributed eleven hundred tickets for the Jubilees' concert, at which Balgarnie was unable to prevent his audience from applauding. The performance netted seventy-one pounds, and when no other church would agree to host a paying concert, Pike arranged for a second concert at South Cliff, which netted another seventy-five pounds. On Sunday, August 10, White again brought his singers out for a free public performance on the green, where, despite another English downpour, they sang to a crowd of more than four thousand. When the troupe was preparing to depart Scarborough, Holmes reported, "many friends gathered at the Northeastern railway station to bid us adieu, and while we waited . . . for the train to start, they spoke kind words to us, gave us little keepsakes, and some brought baskets of choice fruits to refresh us on our way. . . . When the train started someone proposed 'three cheers for America,' which were given with a will, and the remembrance of which will forever be a pleasure to the Jubilee Singers."

A minister named H. T. Robjohns agreed to arrange for the Jubilees' concerts in Newcastle upon Tyne, where the Methodists were holding their annual meeting. By the time the singers arrived in late August, Robjohns had publicized the concerts so effectively that the first one was entirely sold out. Twenty-five hundred people attended and "encored from beginning to end."[13] In Sunderland, Pike was able to line up a series of eminent sponsors, including a local member of Parliament and an interdenominational lineup of divines, who, uncomfortable with lending their names to a paying concert, urged the Jubilees to lower the price of admission from their customary twenty-four pence to three. Fearing failure, Pike reluctantly compromised at twelve pence, but the crowd at Sunderland's Victoria Hall was so vast—thousands, it was said, had to be turned away—that the concert proved to be one of their most profitable.

As the singers made their way to Scotland, African bearers were still gallantly toting the eviscerated remains of the late Scottish missionary and explorer David Livingstone from Lake Tanganyika to the coast. British revivalism, like its American counterpart, had taken root in the antislavery crusade and eventually spread outward to address the whole range of issues that engaged reformers such as the earl of Shaftesbury. But underlying British revivalism in the 1870s was an imperial anxiety, for this small island in the North Atlantic now ruled the largest empire in the history of the world. It seemed to many Britons that only God could have arranged for so diminutive a nation to rule so large a portion of the globe and that He must have done so in order that Britain might spread the Gospel of Jesus Christ.

Imperialism always had its opponents at home, but few even of these dared argue that the Gospel would not improve the heathen. So even that portion of the public which saw imperialism as greedy, bullying, and corrupting of British character sent bands of missionaries into the far reaches of their imperial possessions. Their emissaries would sometimes prove not just a bother and embarrassment to local British authorities but, as in the Indian mutiny of 1857, an actual threat to communal harmony. Nevertheless, the stories of the pertinacity, good works, and occasional martyrdom of missionaries like Livingstone soothed the growing sense of guilt and dread that was as much a part of the imperial legacy as the Kohinoor diamond in Her Majesty's crown.

Born in an overcrowded slum in Glasgow, David Livingstone had been inspired not only by British but by American theologians, among them his brother's teacher at Oberlin College the prominent free-will revivalist Charles Grandison Finney. Finney preached that salvation was not limited to some elect, but could be attained by "all who ask it."[14] By the time of his death in 1875, he had spread the good news to hundreds of thousands of theretofore hopeless sinners all over the northeastern United States and Great Britain.[15]

Finney found an especially receptive audience in Scotland. In 1843, more than a third of the ministers and parishioners of the worldly, compromised Church of Scotland had stalked out of the assembly of the established church to found the Free Church of Scotland. Under the leadership of the Scottish theologian Thomas Chalmers, they rebeled against British parliamentary control over their churches, holding that "no minister shall be intruded into any parish contrary to the will of the congregation." The austere Free Kirk took especially rapid root in the Isles and Highlands, where the established church had failed to protect clansmen when anglicized Scottish lairds like Sutherland began to run them off their ancestral lands to make room for sheep. Independent congregations chose their own elders and enforced their own codes of discipline.

In 1845, however, Chalmers had run afoul of another African American visitor to Britain, Frederick Douglass. In Scotland, Douglass had eloquently condemned Chalmers for not only including slaveholders in his utopian vision of a moral universe but accepting donations from the slaveholding

Presbyterians of the American South to support his urban missions. "Send back the money," Douglass commanded churches all over Scotland, and some of them did.

Chalmers's Free Church of Scotland embraced a more liberal, democratic doctrine than the old Calvinist line. But in one department at least, the Scots were more rigid than the English: the matter of sacred music. The closest most Free Kirk congregations came to singing was the monotonal and strictly a cappella braying of psalms.

Glasgow was the largest city in Scotland: a grimy, muscular, truculent sister to haughty Edinburgh. Here the Jubilees intended to rest a few weeks until the city's upper class returned from its watering places along the Clyde. No one needed this sojourn more than Laura White. No sooner had she accompanied the singers to Glasgow than she was ordered to bed by a local doctor, leaving the care of her three small children to her traveling companion, Addie Williams.[16]

The day after their arrival, John Burns, a co-founder of the Cunard line of steamships, hosted the singers at a gala debut at Castle Wemyss some thirty miles from the city. By 1873, Burns had become tremendously wealthy; Cunard's fleet exceeded the German navy in number and tonnage. The singers expressed their gratitude to Burns for the kindness his line showed them by giving them berths and treating them so royally when all the American lines had refused them cabins.

Among Burns's four hundred guests were many of the same dignitaries who had attended the Jubilees' London debut at Willis's Rooms, including their patron, the earl of Shaftesbury. The Jubilees' concert was an artistic failure. With their young voices and signature pianissimi, they were never at their best in the out-of-doors, and now they had to sing on "quite an unfavorable day for a garden concert." Here they had to project from a platform erected against a castle wall, along which the wind gusted so sharply that it seemed to shatter and diffuse whole verses of their songs.

It hardly mattered, however. They were among friends. The earl of Shaftesbury—Holmes had come to call him "our father"—rose afterward to extol the Jubilees' piety and explain their mission. "They cherish no feeling of revenge against their past persecutors," he shouted over the wind, "all they desire is that the coloured race may be raised to the same level as their white brethren, and that all may walk together in Christian peace and honour and usefulness." He reminded his audience of Britain's own complicity in the slave trade and urged them "to undo the heavy burdens, and to let the oppressed go free." The concert was supposed to be "a free entertainment," Holmes reported, "but after Lord Shaftesbury's address . . . many gave their mite to help us on. . . . We feel grateful to God that such a man as lord Shaftesbury should interest himself on our behalf."[17] The Jubilees closed with "God Save the Queen."

They performed next at the United Presbyterian Church in the village of Gourock, where the pastor, an admirer of the A.M.A., displayed an American flag. The familiar sight of the Stars and Stripes "revived fond memories in many a heart," Pike recalled, "and gave new strength for days to come." At Greenock on the Firth of Clyde, the town council permitted the Jubilee Singers to use their town hall free of charge. Pike and his agents worked hard to fill it to its capacity of two thousand, persuading preachers of various denominations to urge their congregations to attend. The night of the concert, the hall was filled to overflowing, and by a special act of the council, the singers were permitted to send the entire proceeds to the A.M.A.

At a second Greenock concert, Baillie Campbell, the local M.P., stood to remind anyone in the audience who might wonder why the freedmen's cause was any concern of theirs that their Scottish ancestors had taken an active and lucrative part in the slave trade. To prove his point, he withdrew an old bill of lading dated at Kessing in 1803 for 208 slaves "to be delivered in the like good order and well-conditioned . . . (the danger of the seas, mortality and insurrection only excepted)" to the West Indies. "That shows," Campbell concluded, "how much we are bound to help them."[18]

At a "welcome meeting" at the resort of Helensburgh, a dour Free Church African missionary named Kidston felt called upon to defend the singers' unorthodox music. To several "hear, hear's" from the assembled guests, he assured his friends that their music did not "partake of the nature of an oratorio conducted by mere professional singers, which I disapprove of, but, on the contrary, solemn words are uttered, I believe, from the heart of every singer. . . . I cannot help thinking that God has some purpose to serve the African race." The gate at Helensburgh was seventy-three pounds.[19]

White grew impatient waiting for the wealthiest residents of Glasgow and Edinburgh to return from their watering places and proposed they sail across the North Channel and try their luck in Ireland. The singers were opposed at first. All they knew of Ireland were American Irish immigrants. Impoverished, despised, no immigrant group had stood to lose more from the emergence of black wage earners than the laboring Irish nor struck at the freedmen with greater savagery. They had swelled the mobs that rioted in Chicago, New York, Memphis. Moreover, many of the boys who had routinely stoned Fisk's students on their way to school had been Irish lads from Nashville's Broad Street Bottoms.[20]

Flourishing Irish letters of invitation, White insisted, however, and persuaded even his ailing wife to come with them, clinging to the hope that the salt air of the North Channel might revive her. By now, Pike's friend James Powell had returned to the United States to take Pike's place as collector of contributions for the A.M.A., and J. Hamilton Halley, a young clerk on loan from Hodder and Stoughton, had joined White's entourage as advance man. As the Jubilees worked the Clyde, Pike proceeded to Protestant Belfast, armed with a letter from the Philadelphian merchant George Hay Stuart, who had endeared himself to the Irish public by sending a boatload of supplies to relieve the sufferers of the great famine. Riding "a jolting car" from magistrate's office to magistrate's office and invoking the names of John Burns and George Hay Stuart at every stop, Pike finally gathered enough sponsors for a concert at Ulster Hall.

"The audience was one of the largest and most fashionable we have seen in the hall for a considerable time," wrote a local paper, "and they had the advantage of enjoying a troupe of real negro choralists, whose appearance was as widely different from the Christy [Minstrels'] as the character of their programme, and who, without the aid of cornermen, a skedaddle breakdown, a burlesque *prima donna*, or a plantation walk-around, succeeded in delighting the enthusiastic listeners." The crowd clamored for an encore from Minnie Tate, who "responded by giving a plaintive air, which wandered away into a wild strain of music, in which the other members of the company took parts, the chorus being one of the sweetest, perhaps, given throughout the entire evening."[21] A local magistrate named McVicker admitted that he had not been prepared "for such strange, thrilling, delightful music, rendered with such ease and pathos."

In the audience was a Miss Hamilton, who had recently donated one thousand pounds to the Freedmen's Missions Aid Society and praised the singers as a vindication "of the work her money had supported." Friends of the Irish missionary Mary Kildare, who had labored for the A.M.A. in freedmen's schools in North Carolina and Virginia, also "rejoiced in [her] labours when the Jubilee Singers sang." But the most poignant response came from an Irish missionary named James McKee, the brother of Joseph McKee, the first freedmen missionary to Nashville. On leave from his post in India, James McKee recounted his brother's martyrdom. He did not mention the bitter break with Fisk's founders that may well have hastened his consumptive brother's death, but he did remind his Irish brethren that his brother had sown the seeds from which had sprung—and he ordered them deliberately—"the Baptist Theological Institute, the Central Tennessee College, and the Fisk University."[22]

After several more concerts in Belfast, the singers proceeded to Londonderry, where they were initially required by their bleakly Presbyterian hosts to discourage applause and omit "John Brown's Body," "Three Fishers," and any other secular song from their repertoire. But at the Jubilees' concert, the response was so great that the elders had to surrender on both counts. "We had always supposed that the Irish were our natural enemies, because of experiences in both North and South," wrote Ella Sheppard. "We rejoiced at the discovery of our mistake."[23]

A few days later, the Jubilees and their entourage sailed back to Scotland. At Burns's and Shaftesbury's urging, the lord provosts of Glasgow and Edinburgh voted a welcome to the Jubilee Singers and agreed to bring them before the public under their auspices. At Glasgow, Shaftesbury had enlisted the lord provost to sponsor a concert at City Hall. Singing to yet another full house, Minnie Tate was again the star of the show, and after the concert various dignitaries popped up from the audience to urge their fellow Glaswegians to "make up the amount needed for the Fisk University." The troupe headed north to Perth, Dundee, and into the granite-gray cityscape of Aberdeen, where, at a Sunday School Union gathering, Pike had to defend the propriety of the singers' "O How I Love Jesus" by asking the audience to sing along. In the event, they did not join in, but only because "it would have been a sacrilege for any other voice to have mingled in the delightful harmony." In the end, the troupe was permitted to sing "Room Enough" for the children.

In Edinburgh, Pike sought out the publishing firm of Thomas Nelson and Sons, flourishing a letter of reference from the same George Hay Stuart who had aided the Irish during the famine. Nelson himself had died in

1861, leaving the firm to his sons William and Thomas. William was a frequent visitor to the United States; in fact, on a western jaunt three years earlier, he had narrowly escaped capture by the Sioux. Unlike Hodder and Stoughton, the firm's mission was spreading not the gospel so much as knowledge. He and his brother Thomas believed that good, cheap books were the best means of educating the public, and much of his list was devoted to "moral books" for young people: the kind of works Sunday schools doled out as prizes. The firm was currently riding a wave of success with its Royal Readers, a series devised to meet the demand for textbooks in the wake of a recent series of education acts.

Thomas Nelson and Sons was the first British publishing house to establish an American branch: one of their most popular authors was Harriet Beecher Stowe. A letter from George Stuart carried unusual weight at the firm. Stalwart supporters of the Union cause, the Nelsons had been persuaded by Stuart to invest heavily in American bonds, from which the firm profited enormously after the war. Nelson immediately offered to exercise his influence on the singers' behalf and put Pike in touch with a teetotaling magistrate named Thomas Knox. Though members of the town council of Edinburgh objected that Pike's promotional materials listed President Grant before Queen Victoria, they voted to sponsor the singers' concert in the Music Hall anyway. The provost had them to dinner at his home, where the sixty-five-year-old liberal theologian William Hanna, the son-in-law and biographer of Thomas Chalmers, was about to escort one of the titled lady guests into the banquet room when he decided instead that

> it would be more becoming in me to select one of our coloured guests. Acting at once upon this prompting, I found myself seated at table betwixt two of the female band of singers, and more intelligent or better-mannered companions at table no one could desire. After such an education as they have received at Fisk University, I was prepared for the intelligence, but I own that I was not prepared for the quiet, unassuming, cultured manner.

When a toast was proposed to the Jubilees, Isaac Dickerson rose to respond. "Ten years ago," he said, "I was a slave. Today I am not only enjoying all the privileges of a free man, but find myself sitting at such a table as this, surrounded by such kind friends. Ten years ago I was subject to the auction block and the lash. Today there is no auction block and no lash in all the United States." He hoped the troupe would "prove worthy of the deep sympathy and interest that their friends had taken in their enterprise, and that the negro race might yet be a people that no nation would be ashamed to own."[24]

As far as their "cultured manner" was concerned, the transition from slave to decorous dinner guest may not have been as great a leap as their Scottish hosts thought. Nor did Fisk deserve sole credit for their comportment. The taciturn Edmund Watkins had been a field hand, but the rest came from lines of house slaves trained in the etiquette of white society. Most upper-level slaves took great pride in their manners and added to their masters' gentility the courtesy and decorum of their African forebears, including a fundamental respect for their elders. As nurses, cooks, coachmen, and butlers, they had influenced Southern manners profoundly. Even before their preceptresses began to train the Jubilees for their tour, most of them would have been undaunted by the fish forks and butter dishes that were now set before them.

While the singers had had no choice in America but to patronize the few establishments that would take them in, here they did have a choice, and sometimes, as far as British temperance leaders were concerned, the Jubilees made the wrong one. In America, it had been enough to refuse liquor at hotels, to turn their glasses down when spirits were served. But in England, they were expected to patronize only temperance hotels. "When I heard in Edinburgh," wrote the teetotaling travel agent Thomas Cook, "that you had passed by the door of the Cockburn Hotel going to a new drinking house close by I felt aggrieved," for he had seen "so many failures of professing temperance people who coming to England and the Continent get into wretched drinking habits of those countries." Nevertheless, he was "glad to hear that the party of singers have been enabled to maintain consistency of temperance . . . in the face of wine drinking at private parties and the public drinking at hotels by which such establishments are mainly supported."[25]

In November 1873, the troupe proceeded to Paisley, Kilmarnock, and Ayr, the home of Robert Burns, whose "a man is a man for a' that" was always being quoted to them by their liberal Scottish hosts. Some highbrow Scots questioned how the public could be so charmed and moved by anything as primitive as the Jubilees and their songs. But Colin Brown, a music professor at Glasgow's Andersonian University, stepped forward to defend the simplicity of their music, comparing it with the singers of Scottish ballads and Jenny Lind's Swedish folk songs:

> Surely their singing was not the less worthy of notice because they laid aside all professionalism, and sang with the most perfect naturalness the songs of their homes. So also with the Jubilee Singers; their songs are the songs of their people, for they had no homes. The melodies, in all their simplicity, are touching, effective and characteristic. Why is it that at one time they stir up their audience to enthusiasm, and then melt them into tears?

Brown thanked George White for having "shown us how to call forth the true genius and power of natural song, and made us feel how 'one touch of nature makes the world kin'."[26]

Back at the beginning of July 1873, almost two months after the Jubilees landed in Britain, a thirty-six-year-old American evangelist named Dwight Lyman Moody had arrived at York to conduct a revival. Moody had started out as a boy shoe salesman in Boston. In 1856, he moved to Chicago and made so much money peddling footwear that before he was out of his teens he could afford to establish a Sabbath school for urchins and rent four pews at Plymouth Church, filling them every Sunday with the drunks and detrimentals he gathered from the city's flophouses and street corners. In 1860, Moody gave up his shoe business and devoted himself entirely to ministering to Chicago's poor. His religious convictions prevented him from fighting in the Civil War; nevertheless, he labored on behalf of the United States Christian Commission, providing relief to Union troops. Moody built his own nondenominational church in Chicago and in 1867 and 1870 traveled to England to study the techniques of divines like Allon, Hall, and Spurgeon.

In Pike's obsequious account of the Jubilee Singers' British campaign, he credits Moody with much of the troupe's success. But Moody may have owed at least as much of his own success in Britain to them. Two months before Moody had even landed, the singers had already triumphed in London, and their music may have been the key to Moody's breaking down the Scots' resistance to sacred song.

This was as important to Moody as it was to the singers. His tour's star attraction was one of the most peculiar evangelical phenomena of the nineteenth century: a fat, unctuous, sideburned Pennsylvanian named Ira David Sankey. "Nothing in his personal appearance was of assistance to him," nor did he possess much of a voice, and yet, playing on a reed organ and singing contemporary hymns in a clear and earnest baritone, he could mesmerize people by the thousands with his renditions of "Almost Persuaded" and "Oh Prodigal, Come Home, Come Home." After Sankey's triumphant performance at a YMCA conference in 1870, Moody invited him to join his mission in Chicago. Now, like the Jubilees, Moody and Sankey were touring the United Kingdom and peddling a songbook: the newly published *Sacred Songs and Solos*. And also like the Jubilees, they were entirely sincere, dedicating all of their net proceeds to a school: Moody's own Northfield Academy.

In early November 1873, the Jubilee Singers arrived in Newcastle to find Moody and Sankey in full swing. At the time he set off for Britain, Moody already knew about Fisk and the Jubilees. Of course, almost everyone in the Northeast, and certainly everyone in the revivalist movement, knew about them, but Moody had actually met Adam Spence and several of Fisk's teachers on his visits to Oberlin.[27] So as soon as the Jubilees hit town, Moody invited them to sing "Steal Away" at one of his meetings. The singers "stole his heart," Moody told Pike, "and led him at once to appreciate the power of their music for good."[28]

Every day, the singers went out to take part in a "noonday prayer-meeting" and on November 12 appeared at an enormous revival in one of the largest churches in town. "We arrived late and had to go into the small fifth gallery," recalled Ella Sheppard.

> During a pause following an earnest appeal to sinners we softly sang, "There are angels hovering round / To carry the tidings home." The effect was wonderful. . . . Some people said they really thought for a moment that the music came from an angelic band. Mr. Moody looked as though he would not have been more surprised had his Lord appeared.[29]

Educated in a Catholic convent in Massachusetts, untouched by the revivals at Fisk, Mabel Lewis until that very moment had been the only unconverted Jubilee.[30] But as soon as she and the Jubilees began to sing for

Moody's meeting, she was overtaken, she said, by the Holy Spirit and to the troupe's rejoicing declared herself reborn. The Jubilees' practice of singing to religious gatherings endeared them as much to the British public as it had to their American fans. When in early December 1876 they agreed to sing to a Sabbath school gathering, "they were informed," wrote a minister to the *English Independent*, "that there would be no collection nor were they promised any remuneration." But they replied that their purpose was merely "to interest the Sunday-schools in their cause. . . . That they were successful in this instance, is proved by the fact that I have promises of collections, or grants of money, on their behalf from no less than six Sunday-schools which were represented at the service."[31]

The paths of Moody and the Jubilees would crisscross throughout Great Britain, and among the singers' favorite memories were the meetings they attended and inspired with song. At Christmastime, they converged on Edinburgh and attended a revival "for men only, that did not [go to] church nor believe in God. . . . Mr. Moody came in as [if] unconcerned, took off his coat and said, 'Friends, I have some good news to tell you. Do you know that Christ died for you?' "[32]

LET ME GET UP

ENGLAND TO AMERICA

DECEMBER 1873–MAY 1874

For George White, the prospect of Jubilee Hall shone like a beacon. When the pressures of the tour bore down on him, he enjoyed imagining the singers' triumphal return in time for the dedication of the grand edifice they were constructing for Fisk from their songs. "In this old country of ours," wrote a British fan, "we raise institutions with difficulty, and we almost invariably commence them under a burden of debt. You have ventured on a novel and a much more picturesque plan in creating a University by the melody of song."[1] With a showman's opportunism, White envisioned a gala event that would draw as many of the wealthy philanthropists as he could persuade to come. Throughout his travels, fans and donors had expressed a desire to visit Fisk. Why not have them all come at once?

"Can Jubilee Hall be pushed to completion by the time we get to Nashville—say latter part of May?" White asked Cravath.

It would seem possible in that month to get every influential delegation from Philadelphia, [New York] & Boston to go to the dedication. Very many have expressed a desire to be present on that occasion but would hardly venture during the hot season. . . . A very popular occasion could be made of it.

White contemplated remaining in Britain until late March and then putting on a series of concerts in the American Northeast before returning in May for the dedicatory gala in Nashville. But in December 1873, he was worried about his wife's health and his troupe's morale. Despite the best efforts of one of the city's leading physicians, Laura Cravath White seemed simply to flag in the black soot and damp chill of Glasgow with her headaches and backaches.[2]

White worried almost as much about the singers' spirits but not because they were flagging. In fact, they were soaring. White had tried to keep them "humble"; indeed, he prayed daily for their humility at rehearsals and morning meetings. But the kind of docility he had in mind was beginning to elude his young charges. "Most of the singers keep humble," he wrote his brother-in-law in December, "but a few give me *infinite trouble*."[3]

The Jubilees were no longer the frightened, awestruck Tennessee rustics who had set out from Nashville two years before. They were stars. Praised by critics, clerics, statesmen, recognized as artists in their own right, still smarting from their encounters with American racism North and South, they were maturing into substantial and ambitious young men and women who had begun to look, quite sensibly, to their futures. When the tour was over and the troupe disbanded, what, they wondered, would become of them? "I do not believe Mr. White and his singers can *come down* to any other work," Pike worried. "I really do not see what else any of them can do and keep their position and anywhere near meet the demands of the habits they have formed."[4]

Some no longer intended to return to Fisk, or even to America. At the urging of their most ardent admirers, Rutling, Dickerson, and the troupe's emerging prima donna, Maggie Porter, among others, contemplated careers as solo artists on the Continent. They were living and traveling in high style—the management of the Great Northern Railway let them ride first class on second-class tickets[5]—and received armloads of gifts from their admirers. White was paying them at least five hundred dollars a year each, far more than the A.M.A. paid its own teachers. But as their popularity rose and the money from their concerts kept pouring in, the Jubilees demanded more.

Their spokesman was the eloquent and unflappable Benjamin Holmes. White tried to persuade Holmes that if the Jubilees set aside concerts purely for their own benefit it would cast a mercenary shadow over the entire enterprise. After all, at concert after concert, they had been advertised as performing solely for the purpose of building Jubilee Hall, and the noble sacrifice of their "free will offerings" had been crucial to their success.

Unimpressed by these arguments, Holmes and his faction threatened to pull out of the tour. It was no idle threat. Buoyed by the consistent praise he received for the inspirational talks he delivered at Britain's churches and Sabbath schools, and fawned over by hosts of young English belles, Isaac Dickerson had begun to consider more seriously Dean Stanley's offer of an Edinburgh education. Basking in the glow of his reviews, his friend Rutling contemplated a solo career. British patrons had offered to assist Porter in her musical training, and Jennie Jackson, her constant companion, had entertained at least one proposal of marriage.

Ever loyal to White, Ella Sheppard apparently opposed "Bennie" Holmes's concert. Pike saw it as a breakdown in discipline. "I tell Mr White and adhere to it with a consistent conviction that the Singers in the future should be employed by you just as the teachers of Fisk or Atlanta are employed, that they should be taught they are doing missionary work the same, that their accounts should be submitted to you just as the accounts of the teachers are submitted": that, in short, White should manage the singers like a dean of faculty. Singers performing on such terms "would in the long run provide missionary work more than it can be promoted just now . . . [and] save Mr White one half the [wear] and [tear] he now suffers."[6]

White was incapable of regarding the singers as anything other than children, and as his children grew up, he intended not to adjust his regime to their newfound confidence and self-worth but simply to get rid of them. He endeavored to strengthen his hand by developing a pool of singers—scabs, in effect—with whom he could threaten to replace any troublemakers. He asked Cravath if any effort was being made at Fisk to build up a "reserve force" of vocalists, for several singers had refused to extend their contracts past May.[7] "Only last week," White reported, "Mr [Edmund] Watkins demanded his pay, eventually intending to pull out and leave us."[8]

Stung by the singers' defiance and what seemed to White their ingratitude for his having risked his health, his reputation, and his family's entire savings to benefit their people, he nevertheless grudgingly met Holmes partway. He promised that after their return to Nashville in May and before they disbanded, the singers would be allowed to give a benefit concert on the freshly quarried limestone steps of Jubilee Hall itself.

But there were no limestone steps in the offing. Jubilee Hall was just a hole in the ground. When word reached White that it would not be completed by the time of the troupe's return, that in fact the project he had confidently touted to his audiences had hardly progressed at all, he sank into a deep depression. By early December, Pike had begun to worry about White's state of mind: "Mr White's nerves are weak and sometimes he is tortured by apprehensions that are painful to him and very difficult to manage." For a while it seemed that White had been "growing more open to advice and desirous to build up Christ's kingdom in every way." Pike could only hope that White would "recover from his disappointment and find his equilibrium."[9]

The slow progress at Nashville was due in part to Adam Spence's half-hearted support of the project. He had come to think that the building was too grandiose, worried even that it was an affront to God. But the biggest obstacle was the American Missionary Association. The nationwide depression had so diverted the attention of postwar America from the plight of the freedmen that the association's coffers were drying up. Now instead of relaying the building fund to Fisk, the A.M.A. began to borrow from it to tide itself over.

White tried to reconcile himself to the necessity of the A.M.A.'s creative bookkeeping, but it troubled him deeply. He had been assuring vast audiences of supporters that their donations were being used solely to build the hall. If word got out that much of it had been diverted to other uses, supporting schools his audiences had never heard of, paying staff members at the A.M.A.'s home office in New York, it would cause a scandal. But there was nothing White could do about it but raise more money: enough, perhaps, to counterbalance the association's borrowing and finally complete Jubilee Hall.

White was not the only manager nearing the end of his rope. Susan Gilbert was forced to abandon the tour and, like Laura White, lay prostrate in Glasgow, leaving the Jubilees without the reassuring presence of a preceptress. And two years of chasing after engagements had nearly shattered Pike's nerves:

> The unending pressure of unfinished business: the bundle of letters that are almost sure to have *one* among them every day that takes your patience or rests like a cold stone on your soul, the different feeling of different people [with] whom you have to deal tax one['s] power of adaptability and patience to the extreme.[10]

. . . I have had a terribly hard run. My mind is occupied from breakfast till midnight on the course: . . . I wish I could get a month's vacation. I think it would give me new courage, but I cannot take it,
and indeed have had no time for two years.[11]

The tour had cost Pike financially as well. Consumed by Jubilee business,
he had let his commitments at home go begging, and now his once-tolerant
bank, itself buffeted by the financial crisis that had afflicted the entire country, was threatening to take his house. Pike hired another agent to assist
him: the same Mr. Robjohns who had already proved his worth at Newcastle, where he had given up "the leading [Congregational] pulpit" he had
held for twelve years. "He is . . . a *practical* business man," Pike assured Cravath, "ambitious, and full of enthusiasm for us and America generally."[12]
Robjohns would free Pike up to write a new account of the singers, which
he hoped would serve "as an advertisement" that would capitalize on the
British Africa craze by showing "the relation of [the] Freedmen of America
to the evangelizing of Africa, putting in all possible about Africa that would
interest."[13]

Leaving his ailing wife behind, White departed Glasgow for England with
the Jubilees in early January. En route, they performed at the Scottish border town of Hawick, where the local railway ran special trains to bring
people in from outlying border towns. But Pike feared that the singing had
begun to "fall below the expectations of the people, and I often feel bad
about it. The singers do not like to practice. There is nothing to 'take them
down occasionally' as there is in America," he wrote, longing, apparently,
for a dose of American racism to put them in their place. "Mr White is
bothered to do anything with some of them. And then Mr White is always
sufficiently tired to need bolstering up himself."[14]

On January 13, the Jubilees performed in Manchester's enormous Free
Trade Hall, where, over a year before, Benjamin Disraeli had revived his
flagging career with a three-and-a-quarter-hour attack on Gladstone.[15] "We
have often enough been invited to a concert given by niggers," wrote the
Courier, "but never before, I think, to a concert given by negroes. The whole
thing is unique." The Jubilees were "veritable negroes," it assured its readers. Some of the lyrics were "quaint to a degree, and sometimes most in-
congruous; indeed, to educated ears, they savour not a little of profanity,"

wrote the *Examiner*. But the *Courier's* man "saw strong men, not much given to the melting mood, weep like children under it. Let no one go who can only find amusement from banjoes and bows, absurd grimaces, and stale jokes gathered from last year's *Punch*."[16]

Minstrel troupes grew so weary of being unfavorably compared with the Jubilees that they began to burlesque them in their shows. "There was a time in London, when they impersonated each one of us at a place for minstrels," Mabel Lewis remembered. "They had 'Steal Away' and when they came to the soft parts, they just opened their mouths; you couldn't hear a sound. It was really funny."[17]

Manchester proved one of the richest fields the singers plowed. Holmes told audiences that the Jubilees "had made more money in Manchester than in any other city or town in either England or the United States." Pike reported that they had made $5,500 in ticket sales and another $525 selling their books, over five hundred dollars more than they had made during their best week in America.[18]

On January 25, Benjamin Holmes reported to his friend James Burrus:

> [Though the troupe is] troubled with colds, . . . our work is going on nobly, and we feel that the Lord has done great things for us, whereof we are glad. We have sent to America already £6000 and hope to raise £4000 more by the first of May when we hope to sail for our native land—This is Sunday, and we rest today, and naturally our thoughts are with the dear ones at home, and some of us were so disloyal as to "wish I was in Nashville," but that is no sign of dissatisfaction. Last Sunday night we held a praise meeting in this city which was very largely attended and which the people say was very enjoyable. We are quite hopeful that it will result in good for both the church and for the propagation of the Gospel among the poor people.[19]

The old specter of competing black troupes arose in January, when General Samuel Chapman Armstrong of the Hampton Institute wrote the A.M.A. for permission to send his singers on a fund-raising tour of Great Britain as well. When George Whipple sounded Pike out on the matter, Pike did what he could to prevent it. "As far as our business is concerned, we do not apprehend it would make any difference to us," he replied.

Our campaign is mostly made out & reputation established. . . . If he would come with the singers & make himself the servant of servants, & depend upon himself to interest leading citizens & get out audiences perhaps he might get half as much money as he would if he left his singers at home & came single handed & worked with equal devotion & perseverance.

"But," Pike conceded, "it is a very delicate matter for one to write him a discouraging letter about it, as it might be misunderstood."[20]

As the Jubilees proceeded from strength to strength, letters from their friends and family followed after them, reporting on the depredations of the Ku Klux Klan: teachers beaten and even killed, country schoolhouses burned to the ground, and the federal authorities in retreat from the South. But for the singers, it all seemed so far away, and Holmes's replies were sometimes lofty and remote. "I am sorry to hear of the prejudice which still exists in America," he wrote, "and hope that you young Americans who are tinted with African hue may be awakened to the injustice of it and raise your voice against it at any opportunity. We are glad to see that the schools of New England or some of them have opened their doors to the children regardless of color. . . . Accept the kind regards of the Jubes and of yours faithfully, Benjamin."[21]

Not that the same prejudice did not exist in Great Britain. It found perhaps its epitome in the acid disdain of the reviewer for the *New Norwich Argus*. Writing of the Jubilees' concert on February 20, he confessed that he had had no intention of attending their concert until a friend advised him of their "good cause."

We hinted briefly at the thing being got up by a coloured Barnum, and that the university might be a tall euphemism for a small American elementary school. . . . The performance was prefaced by a gentleman of colour giving with a very nasal twang a short history of the dark performers' lives and sufferings. One of the lot, we shuddered to hear, was born with irons, but, to do him or her justice, we are happy to state, without any apparently injurious effect. We were so satisfied with the narrator's epitome of the Jubilee Singers' miseries, the agony was so well piled up, that we refrained from purchasing an enlarged account thereof, although bound up at 3/— without and 5/— with gilt edges. . . . The singers—seven coloured ladies and four gentlemen coloured to match—now commenced. They sang well in tune, and if the *ne plus ultra* of singing consists in effective pianos our friends have reached it. But we had grown weary by the time the first hymn was finished. The only change in the next piece was that our "freed" friends made themselves quite at home and sang sitting—a relief to them, no doubt. Noting this change, on looking at the programme we quite expected that the next thing would have been gone through kneeling, to illustrate the method which slaves employ "to drive old Satan away." If kneeling had been adopted, with an occasional judicious exposure of the whites of the eyes, this hymn would have been a perfect success; but it was performed standing, and so a splendid opportunity for that effect was lost. The Railway Hymn produced a comical effect, which would have been considerably increased had the bones and banjo been introduced. From the vigorous invitation given in the refrain, to "get on bo-o-o-ard," we inferred the niggers thought old Satan was endeavouring to persuade large numbers to "Wait for the waggon." . . . A most extraordinary fact remains to be told, that, notwithstanding the quality of the entertainment, everyone remained in his seat to the end of the very last note. . . . But we imagine [the] coloured songsters promise to come again—*for their own benefit.*[22]

Another reviewer objected strenuously to the religious content of the Jubilees' repertoire and the aggressiveness of their campaign:

Any more profane and degrading performance it would be difficult to find. Some of the most sacred names and incidents in Scripture story were set and sung to Nigger Melodies of a laughable kind. . . . These degrading and disgraceful profanities deserve the severest censure. . . . How far Fisk University deserves the efforts made in its favour we have no means of knowing. . . . The books about it were pushed most persistently and impertinently into the faces of all. . . . Only Yankee niggers could accomplish such a work with such unblushing "cheek." . . . Common good taste, not to mention the higher phases of religious feeling, should protest against such desecration of sacred names, such burlesquing of Scripture story, by which the very name of religion is dragged through the mire.[23]

In February, the Jubilees proceeded to Norwich, but their path was already being dogged by alarming news from Glasgow. First came the report that the Whites' nurse was gravely ill, and then Laura Cravath White herself contracted typhoid fever.

The headache that is symptomatic of the onset of the disease must have seemed like another of the spells—probably migraines—that had afflicted Laura White for years. But fever and delirium settled in, and she began to sink. White hurried up to Glasgow, reaching the bedside of his emaciated wife late in the night of February 22. Less than two days later, at four o'clock in the afternoon, while the singers performed far away in Leicester, Laura White suddenly exclaimed, "Oh, so happy!" tried for a moment to mouth along to her husband's recitation of the Twenty-third Psalm, and died.

White was desolate. The trip that was supposed to have revived the mother of his three children had instead killed her. "Her death to him was a terrible blow," Pike recalled, "and one from which a person of his exquisitely delicate sensibilities could not easily recover."[24] Moody interrupted his work to come to Glasgow and help White arrange for Laura's remains to be interred in a vault in Glasgow until White should be able to ship them home for burial, and a Manchester supporter of the Jubilees named James Stuart invited White's children into his home. "Let not your heart be troubled," White's son told his father one morning while at prayer, "ye believe in God." But White was inconsolable. Letters poured in from Moody, Sankey, Burns, and a host of British friends.[25] In his frantic grief, George White could hardly eat or sleep and seemed almost determined to join his wife in the hereafter.

The constant winter swirl of concerts and prayer meetings continued to take its toll on the Jubilees themselves. Jennie Jackson had been too weak to sing at Leicester, Mabel Lewis was unable to perform at Bristol, and in the heavy English fogs, Benjamin Holmes could not shake his persistent cough. Nevertheless, it fell increasingly to the singers to keep the tour alive. Not only was White out of commission, but Susan Gilbert remained an invalid in Glasgow, Halley was too ill to work, and Pike, barely strong enough to rejoin the grieving troupe in Norwich, was handing more and more of the paperwork over to his wife, who had joined him, as Pike assured his sponsors, "without any relation to the work, or expense to the mission."

"With so many of the management ill and absent," Ella Sheppard recalled, "the singers, with volunteer help, carried on the work to the close of the season."[26] Isaac Dickerson stepped up his appearances at prayer meetings and Sabbath schools and thereby raised a "liberal" sum for Fisk's library. At Ipswich, Edmund Watkins collected money for Jubilee Hall's furnishings. Sheppard took entire control of the troupe's rehearsals, worked out their programs, and continued, as before, directing them during their performances: blowing her pitch pipe, giving her cues, and indicating, by the angle of her head or the almost imperceptible movement of her hand, when one voice or another might be straying from the harmonious a cappella whole.

Offstage, the Jubilees were not so easily led. By now, Holmes and his faction had learned that the Jubilee Hall they had been singing for was nowhere near completion. This meant that instead of singing for their own profit at a gala dedication ceremony, as White had proposed, they would merely perform at commencement exercises to the usual gathering of Fisk's local supporters and alumni, most of whom were too strapped by the country's financial crisis to reward the singers with a bonus sum.

The weeks of touring successfully under more or less their own steam had further bolstered the singers' confidence. Pike had promised Henry Allon that before the troupe's departure for the United States, he would host their farewell concert; in fact, their appearance had already been advertised as their last in London. But now Holmes and his faction proposed a subsequent "farewell" concert of their own, the proceeds of which were to go directly to the singers. In addition, he organized a quartet with Maggie Porter, Jennie Jackson, and either Isaac Dickerson or Edmund Watkins, with which he contemplated remaining in Britain after the rest went home. The other male singers were also considering remaining in Britain, with an eye to conducting a European tour of their own.

Pike was not sure he could or even should stop them, but

if they do remain I shall try and utilize them for A.M.A. It would be a relief to my mind to have them go, but I am not quite clear as to what may be best for them and the cause of Christ. It does not look as [though] Mr White would have further use for these singers even if he should recover, as they make him infinite trouble. I hope for the best. God governs the world.

Still grieving for his wife, White continued to deteriorate. His tubercular lungs began to hemorrhage, and he coughed up pints of blood.[27] Pike wrote that White "is in consumption," and though he is "confident of recovery . . . I do not think his hopes are shared by most who see him."[28] Throughout England and Scotland, congregations offered up prayers for White's well-publicized travails.

Ella Sheppard trembled for her mentor's life. "Mr. White is so ill," she wrote Adam Spence in late April. "He is now prostrate, if any thing worse, not able to converse with any one or even see them." But he was strong enough to use his illness to try to manipulate the rebels in his troupe into giving up their plans for a farewell concert. In effect, if they did not bend to his will, he threatened them with death: his own. "The Doctor says there is some great anxiety on his mind," Sheppard wrote home, "and until that is removed . . . there is but the slightest hope that he can get well. That hope lies with those who are planning to continue concerting on their own responsibility. If they do not change their purpose soon I fear nothing can save him."[29]

The Jubilees' authorized farewell concert at Exeter Hall was the most profitable of the entire British tour. The earl of Shaftesbury gave their tour symmetry by presiding once again, just as he had at their London debut the year before. During a break in the singers' performance, Henry Allon stepped onto the stage and reported that the troupe had earned not only £10,000 for Jubilee Hall but £400 for furnishings, £250 toward a library, donations of books from Gladstone, Spurgeon, Dean Stanley, and many others, plus oil paintings of Wilberforce, George White, David Livingstone, and the Jubilees themselves, of course. When two little girls presented the troupe with an additional £231 from the Society of Friends, it fell to Benjamin Holmes to express the troupe's thanks.

"We feel sure," he told a cheering audience, "the foundation of Jubilee Hall, which was laid last spring with American greenbacks, will be capped with British gold. We hope," he continued after the laughter and cheering died down, "in that University a noble work will be accomplished. We hope that we who live in the Southern states will be able to prove to you that we are worthy of the liberty which, through the influence of good people and by the blessing of God, we now enjoy." This was greeted by more cheers, and Holmes went on to say a few words about the promise of African Americans pursuing missionary work in Africa. "We hope," he said, "by the blessing of God to get, before many years, even Africa to praise God and serve Him as you do."

At the close of the concert, Shaftesbury himself stepped forward to express his countrymen's delight in the Jubilees and regret at having to part with them. "As you listened to the songs," Shaftesbury asked, "did you observe the high, the tender, hallowed sentiment that pervaded all that they expressed? Did you observe, in these people singing to you the songs of their captivity, that the prayer came from their hearts to God to keep them 'from sinking down'? He has not only kept them from sinking down," Shaftesbury assured his countrymen, "but raised them in His mercy; and now they stand before you fit to compete with the very best of all the human race."[30]

And compete they did. After their Exeter Hall performance, Holmes and his faction performed their own farewell concert and collected hundreds of dollars each from the proceeds. Encouraged by a Dr. Tomkins of the Freedmen's Missions Aid Society, Holmes and his faction now considered remaining in England, a plan Gustavus Pike did his best to subvert. "I saw [Tomkins] yesterday," wrote Pike, "and told him what White had done for the Singers and also explained away some of White's peculiarities which looked a little awkward. I think the Dr. will advise them to go home, especially Jennie and Maggie. If they go the concerts planned will be given up." Ultimately, a letter directly from Cravath to Maggie Porter broke them up. Somehow, perhaps by enlisting or at least invoking her mother, Cravath at last convinced her to sail home. "That relieves me from a mountain of embarrassment," wrote a grateful Pike, and "breaks the quartette up."[31] In the end, only two singers chose to stay: Edmund Watkins remained in England for the summer, and Isaac Dickerson decided to accept Dean Stanley's offer of an education at the University of Edinburgh.

On May 5, 1874, White and his children and the remaining Jubilees sailed home with Susan Gilbert and Addie Williams on the steamer *Parthia*. Still dangerously weak, grief stricken, embittered by the troupe's intransigence and the A.M.A.'s opportunistic pilfering of the proceeds of his tour, White had to be carried onto the ship on a mattress.[32]

With his tantrums and sulks, White had not endeared himself to Pike, who could only hope that his vacation might restore at least a portion of his equilibrium. Pike worried especially that the singers' strife might reach the ears of the public and destroy their reputations as selfless toilers in the freedmen's cause. "I cautioned Mr White against threatening the Singers that he would not pay them," Pike wrote home.

> I told him the public were very sensitive about their treatment and that it would not be safe. I also tried to show him that he must recognize their Civil Rights, and that it would be wise for him to close with the Singers in such a way as would lead them to esteem him as their greatest friend.

Nevertheless, Pike could not help feeling badly for George White and urged the A.M.A. to pay him a bonus. "No man out of a mad house would go [through] what he has the past year . . . for any price," Pike wrote Cravath, "and I do feel that he ought not to get to [Minnesota] penniless, while a girl like Minnie [Tate] clears $800, besides a very large number of goods."[33]

PART THREE

NO COWARDS

IN OUR BAND

NASHVILLE

SEPTEMBER 1872–JANUARY 1875

"Things are in a very pleasant state now," Adam Knight Spence reported in the summer of 1872, and certainly it was a hopeful sign that, rather than raiding his staff and facilities to supply the A.M.A.'s more promising schools, Cravath was now asking what Spence needed in the way of teachers and equipment.[1]

In October 1872, Spence decided to put on a concert of his own at Exposition Hall, but the managers again refused him the use of their auditorium. "Southerners do all they can to keep the colored man down," he complained, "and then blame the negroes for being radicals."[2] Boycotted by several black churches, the concert was a flop. "We need more spiritual power," he concluded. "I feel it in my administrative duties. I need much more moral force. . . . I am growing arbitrary and petulant." His wife felt "the afflictions of the work" so deeply that she sometimes cried, especially when he was unwell. "Of course, I cannot escape criticism," wrote Spence.

> I must err in many things. Yet decisions must be made. My own wife and sister often think differently from me and no doubt Mr Chase does although he does not say it. Education versus religion. . . . The mind pitted against the heart. Duties to self and family and loving

all and following Christ. . . . I confess to a childish want of sympathy.

He had no sympathy at all for a white female teacher from New England who almost ran off with one of her black students. It was Spence's worst nightmare. "The scandal of a sort of a love affair between a teacher and colored young man[!]" he exclaimed. "The use that might be made of it[!]" The teacher was engaged to a young Yale student, but she had been "foolish" with "a sort of ward of our Superintendent of construction, a pretty up and down sort of a man." She borrowed fifty dollars from Spence without telling him what she had in mind, which was apparently to elope with her student. "So many nervous people all up in arms," Spence reported, but he told himself that she had done no "*great* damage" and that the "little flurry among students" would soon be over.[3] He was right; it was.

The school was full—some 269 students, including 80 boarders, plus 20 teachers and their families. Among them was Spence's own sister Julia and her husband, Frederick Chase. A very grand-looking man with a chiseled, martial nose and a somewhat imperious gaze, Chase tended to live beyond his means. He was president of Lyons Collegiate Institute in what is now Clinton, Iowa, and in 1872 he began to hit Spence up for "considerable" loans to pay his debts. Only a year before he had urged Spence not to "throw yourself away on the freedmen," but now Chase declared himself eager to enter the Southern field.[4] Perhaps in part to counterbalance the cabal of the brothers-in-law Cravath and White, Spence deemed his own brother-in-law the perfect choice to head up Fisk's science department. A jack-of-all-trades, Chase was so eager to prove that his selection had been more than a product of nepotism that within a year he had exhausted himself to the point of prostration repairing walls, digging gardens, and collecting scientific specimens.

In the summer of 1873, Spence sank into another of his depressions, this time deepened by ague and his "feeble," disappointed wife's miscarriage. Fisk was still nothing like the beacon on a hill that White had been describing to his audiences. Jubilee Hall was "only a great cellar excavation," and Fisk's students and teachers were still languishing in the leaking barracks.[5] After the spring rains of 1873, a cholera epidemic spread through Nashville. To smoke out the miasma that was still commonly believed to be cholera's cause, the authorities set fire to hundreds of barrels of tar. As vast black plumes rose around the city, choking off the sunlight, one in every forty Nashvillians succumbed to the disease: about a thousand in all, most of them African Americans. Seventy-two died in one day.[6] "The city," wrote Spence, "must be fairly washed clean."[7]

In the summer of 1873, Helen Morgan resigned "upon financial grounds," demanding that her salary be raised to five hundred dollars, the same salary as the Jubilees. "I never was so tried about anything in my life," Morgan wrote from Oberlin, but her mother and sister were strongly opposed to her returning to Nashville.

> They say and probably with some truth that I am not the same person at all that I was three years ago when I went there. My mother is sure that I need an entire change of scene and climate and that I must have it unless I wish to wear myself out prematurely. . . . As far as I am concerned, I am willing . . . to be spent in the Lord's work in the South. . . . My feelings towards the work [at Fisk] and the workers at it are unchanged.[8]

In the fall, Spence raised her salary to five hundred dollars, and she returned to Fisk, where she would remain for another thirty-four years.[9] But by early 1874, the morale among the faculty had reached an all-time low. After a long row with his officers, Spence sighed, "People do so differ. What will come of things God only knows. . . . I am sorely troubled with sin," he wrote his mother. "I am not victor. This is a place of great temptation, especially to impatience. We are all overtaxed and nervous."[10]

They had a right to be nervous. Southern whites had regained the vote in 1869, and two years later the "iron clad" pledge once required of ex-Confederates had been discarded. The result in the South was a resurgence of the Democrats against the blacks, Northerners, and Southern scalawags that made up the Republican Party's constituency. A severe economic depression and Grant's bumbling administration took their toll on the party of Lincoln, and one by one, Republican state governments began to fall. In 1873, Democrats won majorities in the legislatures of Arkansas, Texas, and Virginia and in the latter two states took over the statehouses as well. On March 10, 1874, the day Charles Sumner died, the Democrats even took New Hampshire and then, a month later, Connecticut.

In the South, the Democrats painted all measures to enforce the equal-ity of blacks as partisan Republican trickery and Yankee vindictiveness. The strategy was so successful that Republicans tried to distance themselves from the cause of the freedmen. Secretary of the Treasury Benjamin H. Bristow advised blacks to "accept with gratitude the great results that have been accomplished for them . . . and to wait with patience further devel-opments."

A Republican Senate reluctantly honored the memory of the late Charles Sumner by fitfully and painfully passing a civil rights bill on May 22, 1874, that guaranteed equal access to transportation, education, accommodation, institutions, churches, cemeteries, and juries, though not saloons, barbershops, and bathhouses. Senate passage created a firestorm in the South. "Since the issue has at last been forced upon you," roared the Memphis *Appeal*, "let every true man with a white skin rally to his color." The white leagues, emboldened by Republican apathy to the plight of the freedmen, discarded the masks and robes of the Klan and attacked blacks and their Northern sympathizers with increasing impunity.

In the fall of 1874, a black candidate for the Tennessee state legislature was among several African Americans murdered that season. The congres-sional elections became a kind of referendum on Reconstruction. In a wave of Southern Democratic fraud and violence, Reconstruction, and the Re-publican Party, went down to defeat. A lame-duck Republican Congress passed a modified version of the civil rights bill, but the language and pro-visions for enforcement were so feeble that when the South regained its an-tebellum control of Congress the bill was almost a dead issue. "The whole scheme of reconstruction," wrote a Tennessean, "stands before the country today a naked, confessed, stupendous failure."[11]

Now Fisk found itself not the protected emblem of an egalitarian fu-ture for a reconstructed South but an imperiled outpost of a dream white Americans North and South were fast discarding. Mass Klan rallies in Nashville and Franklin precipitated a decline in Fisk's enrollment.[12] At commencement in 1874, "there was so much excitement about the civil rights bill," Spence reported, "that we scarcely had a friend among the people." The papers were so vociferous in their opposition that usually friendly rags like the *Bulletin* and the *Banner* refused Spence space. In Sep-tember 1874, Spence reported a "reign of terror and blood in the state" that was "sad and fearful. . . . It is no war of races but of our race against another." The murder of a black country schoolteacher named Julia Hayden, a student from Braden's Central Tennessee College, "shocked everybody," and some of Fisk's own students had been harmed. The lives of Fisk's male students were in such danger that "none of us must go out at night."[13]

The man who constructed poor Julia Hayden's coffin was an elderly carpenter and former slave named Benjamin "Pap" Singleton. From his workshop in nearby Edgefield, he had supplied so many coffins for so many black victims of Klan atrocities that he came to believe he had been chosen by God to deliver his people from their peril. Singleton put less trust in the ballot box than he did in his own divine inspiration. In the bloody turmoil of the mid-1870s, he began a movement to lead his people out of the South and settle them in Kansas. He and his supporters called themselves "Exodusters" and received a certain amount of support from whites who saw the race problem in the South as insoluble. "They said to me, 'You have tooken a great deal on to yourself,'" Singleton recalled, "'but if these negroes, instead of deceiving one another and running for office, would take the same idea that you have in your head, you will be a people.'"

Singleton established the Edgefield Real Estate Association and "jacked up" three or four hundred African American volunteers to migrate to about a thousand acres of land on a former Cherokee Indian reservation. "There are a great number of our people who don't heed to any advice of their own color," Singleton declared, "and I say that is just the reason we are in the condition that we are to-day, so let us wake up to the sense of our duty, and begin to look after our downtrodden race." He denounced the "leading men of our race," like Frederick Douglass, who scorned his movement. "Such men as this," he said, "should not be leaders of our race any longer."

In 1878, Singleton was conducting a fitful stream of black migrants to his colony in Kansas, hoping that eventually white Southerners would see what black people were capable of accomplishing and eventually beckon them back to Tennessee. "We don't want to leave the South," he told local whites, "and just as soon as we have confidence in the South I am going to be an instrument in the hands of God to persuade every man to go back, because that is the best country; that is genial to our nature, we love that country, and it is the best country in the world for us; but we are going to learn the South a lesson."[14]

Alighting from their extraordinary triumph in Great Britain, the Jubilee Singers were once again Fisk's brightest hope. The highlight of commencement was the return of George White with the first installment of his singers—Ella Sheppard, Georgia Gordon, and Minnie Tate.[15] Sheppard invested a portion of her earnings from the second tour in a new house to be built near the site of Jubilee Hall and, after making numerous visits to a local doctor to treat the wear and tear of touring, traveled down to Okolona, Mississippi, to visit her mother. Minnie Tate retired from the Jubilees with her voice in shreds and would become so disillusioned with Fisk that she would enroll at a school run by a black woman named Early.[16] White did not linger long in the rising heat of Nashville. He limped north instead with what remained of his health and his family, making for the "pure, bracing air of Minnesota."[17]

Erastus Milo Cravath had had an even more tragic time than George White. "In a year and less," reckoned Spence, "he has lost a son, a sister, his father & a brother."[18] But his own health was robust and his sense of mission undiminished. In June, he wrote to Gustavus Pike proposing a library-endowment fund drive and predicting that Jubilee Hall would not be completed and dedicated until June 1875 (if then; in fact it would not be dedicated for another six months). In 1874, the A.M.A. was sponsoring Hampton Normal and Agricultural Institute, Berea College, Fisk, Atlanta University, Talladega, Tougaloo, and Straight University in New Orleans, plus churches and grade and normal schools, with a combined student body of some fifteen thousand.[19] Pike caught a whiff of fiscal impropriety in Cravath's proposal, an opportunity for the hard-pressed A.M.A. to lay claim to a large portion of the funds the Jubilees had ostensibly raised for the construction of Jubilee Hall. The idea of an endowment fund troubled Pike. "When that sort of thing is done," he asked Cravath in a letter he urged him to burn, "is there not great temptation to neglect or defer until the object of the donors is at least partially defeated? There have been so many *investigations* of late," he reminded Cravath, that "we ought to be especially warned lest we fail to meet the rightful expectations of our friends."

The news that the hall would not be finished until 1875 "much startled"

Pike, who urged "utmost caution." In his book, Pike had promised that Fisk would dedicate its new hall in 1873, a date he had since revised in his addresses to the Jubilees' audiences to 1874. He reported that people were beginning to ask about delays in the construction of Jubilee Hall. "Time has come when we should proceed cautiously that the A.M.A. may be praised not only for its enterprise but for its wisdom, prudence & efficiency in all its branches of work," he said.

> The money for [the] Hall has been provided and a great many persons are looking for the completion of the building. Why should not the building be completed by [October]? I have said it would be, and am before the public as somewhat responsible. I do not see how I can make any apology if it is not done by that time. It must be possible to have it ready.

Though he considered himself a practical fellow, Pike was afraid that in Cravath's zeal on behalf of both Fisk and the A.M.A., he might mislead the public and demand more of the singers than they could possibly provide. "We have now come to a pause," he wrote. "If God graciously saves me from public reproach for having to do with the raising of money that has been applied in a way that violated my conscience, I will tend never to be a party to the like again."[20]

Spence complained that Cravath's worldliness was contaminating Fisk itself. "This is not my idea of a christian school managed on the principles of the gospel," he wrote his mother. "Selfishness prevails. The workers are not consecrated to God. The spirit of the world is among us!"[21] He was dubious about the rage for African missions to which the A.M.A. had begun to subscribe. After the death of David Livingstone, African missions were a surefire theme in Britain. Now the A.M.A. began to wonder whether the promise of sending its best students to Africa might not build up the association's constituency by winning over colonizationists who still believed that the solution to "the problem of the freedmen" lay in sending them back to their ancestral home.

Cravath proposed that the Jubilees set forth on another tour, this time for the building of a second facility at Fisk to be called Livingstone Missionary Hall. Incredibly, White was for it. After resting up in Minnesota, he found lodgings in the cool heights of Lookout Mountain in Tennessee, overlooking the site of his last Civil War battle, where, like a general regrouping his forces, he began to plan for a third tour. Returning to Nashville in October, he commenced a cautious dance around his singers. "I have been looking the ground over some," he reported to Cravath, but he had "done little in the way of getting an expression from the old members here as I do not wish to commit them against the movement, and I am not certain yet how they stand."

The singers circled him as well. Maggie Porter and Jennie Jackson, her inseparable "shadow," as White put it, invited him to a tea with some of the other singers and seemed to expect him to explain his plans.[22] Conditions in Nashville and indeed the entire South being what they were, he had little doubt that most of the singers would favor a return to the Northeast and Britain. But he was afraid that given enough time the Jubilees would demand exalted salaries or even strike out on their own, especially the vaunting Miss Porter, the Jubilees' prima donna.

One of his most serious threats in that regard should have been the brilliant Benjamin Holmes, whose machinations on behalf of the Jubilees' own benefit farewell concert in London had set White's teeth to gnashing. Despite Holmes's excellent tenor and his eloquence as a public speaker, White was reluctant to rehire him after his defiance in England, unless his inclusion were a precondition of the others' signing on. But it was all moot. When he returned to Nashville, Holmes was almost as feeble as White. His coughing fits were reducing him to a wheezing husk of the once vigorous and indomitable young leader who had strode through the snows of Ohio, exhorting the Jubes never to give up.[23]

White realized that "unless I can get the best of the old company, the forming of the new will be a long, tedious, expensive work." He considered raiding the ranks of Central Tennessee College's Tennesseans, who, advertising themselves as the equals of the Jubilees, were about to go on tour. White concluded that he could do nothing at all with their singers without months of drill, but he was not above trying to raid Hampton's troupe for a bass, nor too proud to coax the rebellious Edmund Watkins to return to the Jubilee fold.[24]

One of the conditions of White's agreeing to undertake a third tour was the hiring of Theodore Seward as substitute director and a man named B. C. Unseld to act as Seward's assistant in Sheppard's absence: an arrangement that encouraged White enormously. "Mr Unseld is here and is doing good work," he wrote, "taking the young men alternately all day while Mr Seward drills the girls and has charge of the practice together. I am much gratified at the progress already made. It was very noticible in the little time I was gone." White and Seward were of such like minds about the virtues of "natural" singing and pronunciation that White urged Spence to adopt the innovative tonic sol-fa system of musical notation Seward advocated in order, he hoped, to speed up the training of future Jubilees.

Among the new singers White tried to draw into the troupe was a young soprano from Memphis named Maggie Carnes, a student in Fisk's college preparatory program and one of those whose fervent conversion had so alarmed Henry Bennett during the great Fisk revival four years before.[25] Her life in slavery had been as brief and dramatic as Sheppard's. She was born in Shelby County, Tennessee, in 1854. When she was a baby, her master announced he was going to exchange her for a pair of horses, whereupon her mother ran to a well and threatened to leap into it with Maggie until her master relented. Within three years of Maggie's birth, her entire family had been liberated.[26]

The terms of her contract were mostly professional. They included assurances from the A.M.A. that it would employ her for a year beginning November 1, 1874, would pay her five hundred dollars a year in monthly or quarterly installments, would provide "comfortable and reasonable board and transportation," and would exercise "a watchful care over her interests, safety and health." It gave her two months' vacation "during the summer or its equivalent in lighter concert work, extending over three or four months," and transport back to Nashville at the end of her service.

In return, Carnes was to work faithfully and conscientiously toward the goals of the Jubilee Singers, work "cheerfully and in harmonious cooperation" with the managers, "engage heartily in the work of training and developing the voice and power of execution," and conduct herself as befitted a representative of "Christ's kingdom." If all was satisfactory after her first year, and she continued for a second, her salary was to go up. Any differences between Carnes and the managers were to be adjudicated by the officers of the A.M.A., who of course happened also to be the managers.[27]

White returned from Lookout Mountain feeling "stronger than any time since I left Minnesota."[28] Soon after his return, the Jubilees received an invitation to sing at the Nashville Exposition, an invitation White accepted only on condition that it be made known to the public that "four of the eleven singers comprising the company, including Miss Sheppard, the pianist, and the bass singer, are absent from the city," for he could only promise that the remnant could give just "an idea of the character of their concerts."[29]

They arrived in the evening of October 21 to find some eighteen thousand people waiting to hear them. The master of ceremonies asked the vast throng to be "as still as possible while the singers were singing" and even ordered the Exposition's sputtering fountains turned off, "and the hum of the audience sank into faint whispers as the 'Jubilees' arose before them." Despite the size of the venue and the absence of four key singers, the seven Jubilees performed "with considerable ease. . . . Their programme was rendered as published, and the opinions of the audience found vent in loud applause after each song. . . . The absent singers were missed in the choruses," the *Republican Banner* noticed, "but taken all in all, and governed by the general applause elicited, their singing was a decided success, more especially their rendition of a medley which concluded with 'Dixie'." Probably in defiance of Pap Singleton's Exoduster movement, the crowd "broke out in sustained applause" when the Jubilees "brought out the line, 'I'll live and die in Dixie.' "[30]

After all his troubles with White and his fears that the Jubilees' success was somehow corrupting Fisk's mission, Spence was reminded that, for all their disagreements, White was as deeply religious as he and as firmly committed to the school's Christian mission. "White has on the whole taken a good stand" and was proving an inspiration to his demoralized students, Spence reported.[31] Frederick Chase felt that when White participated in school prayers, "he seemed to be right in the presence of God, almost talking face to face with him."[32] Spence noted hopefully that "at the last prayer meeting there seemed some movement."[33] But White did not reciprocate Spence's admiration and deplored his rule by faculty consensus. "We need a head at Nashville more than any thing else," he begged his brother-in-law. "If you, or some one as capable, were to give things *shape* and *life*—it would be *money* and *students* both."[34]

Stopping over in November, Gustavus Pike was horrified by the strife at Fisk. It was "absolutely *killing*," he wrote Cravath, for the faculty "to be, from the beginning to the end of the year, in the small pettifogging and strife which have been the characteristics of the so-called 'faculty meetings.' . . . It is terrible to me to see the interests that have cost me my *heart's blood* to win, trifled with as they have been at Nashville."[35]

White, however, was no more generous to Pike, who was in the process of rewriting his popular account of the Jubilees in the form of a kind of dialogue between himself and an anonymous doctor as they ostensibly traveled around the world. White was shocked by Pike's draft of what would become *The Singing Campaign for Ten Thousand Pounds*. White promised Cravath to "try and be as mild and gentle as possible in anything I may say or do," but he felt "keenly the unfair statements & egotism of the book" and wondered why a book could not be made by combining elements of Pike's book with an earlier account. That would be better, he thought, than Pike's " 'slaughter' of the last book." He enclosed a letter from Isaac Dickerson reporting that Pike's previous book was not well regarded in Edinburgh and assured his brother-in-law that Dickerson had written entirely independently, at no prompting from him.[36] In the end, Pike made few changes, and by 1893, 193,000 Jubilee books would be sold. But White was right about Pike's book, which made the truncated and bowdlerized saga of the Jubilees subservient to the tangle of Pike's own expositions on the call of Africa, the miracle of progress, and the beneficence of wealth.[37]

White set about casting his next troupe. By this time, he had become so invested in the Jubilee enterprise that he expended little sympathy on the singers he and Pike had worn out with their relentless touring. As ruthlessly as a latter-day coach or impresario, he intended to discard and replace them at will. Mabel Lewis's enormous voice was "about gone," he said, but rather than wait for her to recover, he began searching for a substitute among Fisk's student body, with little regard for their academic ambitions. "If the *class* had only graduated last year," he wrote, meaning Fisk's first college class, "I should take America Robinson. She is a good alto, and is such a *grand girl* that she would be worth a great deal. But I suppose," he sneered, "it would be less sacrifice to break up the Jubilees than that *class*. Matters will clear up soon."[38]

America W. Robinson was the light-skinned former slave girl who had seen her master's parlor fill with wounded soldiers before her father spirited her out of war-torn Murfreesboro in a Yankee wagon. Like Julia Jackson, Rutling, and Porter, she had attended Fisk from its opening day. Her father was his owner's slave half brother, but, unlike Ella Sheppard's father, he enjoyed no special privileges. When his white relations ran into financial difficulty, they sold him to a Virginian from Murfreesboro named Elliott.[39] An accomplished carpenter, America's father married a slave woman from a neighboring household who, like himself, was half white. They produced children so pale that their mistress once considered adopting their son as her own child. America's mother was a powerful woman and so intimidating that her mistress was "thereafter obliged to content herself, when enraged at their mother, with visiting her wrath upon the children. Once she struck America a blow that made a bleeding gash quite across the face."

The scar Mrs. Elliott left behind did not deter her classmate James Burrus from falling in love with Robinson, and no wonder. Observant, trenchant, iconoclastic, with the mordant gaze of a deposed aristocrat, she was, before the wear and tear of the Jubilees' last tour, a beauty. The couple were a third of Fisk's first country teachers and half of its first college class.[40] They were scheduled to graduate in 1875, whereupon they intended to marry. Burrus was as slight and owlish as his mentor Spence, whose influence worried Robinson. "Deliver me from such as he," she begged her beau. "I do not want to be afraid to laugh."[41] Burrus and his two brothers had attended elementary school by taking turns wearing the same pair of trousers that their mother, one of Fisk's cooks, had "turned and patched."[42] Nonetheless, James had a bright future ahead of him. He would proceed to Dartmouth to become the first African American to receive a master's degree from an accredited college. After a career as a mathematics teacher, he would make a small fortune in the drug and real estate businesses.[43]

Robinson was one of Morgan's pets, and something of a religious skeptic; she used to tease Julia Jackson of the Jubilees for reading so long and hard in the Bible.[44] Having attended Fisk since 1866, she was at first loath to lose her coveted place in its first college class or endanger her engagement to Burrus. But "the teachers & trustees," White reported, "with the exception of Prof. Spence, think it is best for her to go," and even Spence was wavering. The faculty assured her that she could finish her studies in Greek, moral philosophy, and English literature on the road and read her senior paper at commencement. No doubt the gallant and dutiful James Burrus assured her that his love was immutable. In the end, America was "quite willing to do the extra work" and was "anxious to go, both to help us & to get the advantage of travel."[45] Though she would never make it to her commencement, she would become the only Jubilee Singer to receive a B.A. from Fisk University.

Other recruits were not working out quite so well. Patti Malone's voice was "very sweet" with "a mournful appeal," but she was "sickly & weak since her spell of sickness." White had "waited and hoped she would get stronger, but she does not seem to." A tenor named Grant whom White imported had a true voice but not much power behind it. A second tenor named Patrick was proving "weak chested." His voice "seems to droop under the practice."[46] Gabriel Ousley, once a slave of Jefferson Davis's family and now a favorite of Henrietta Matson, had a solid, heavy bass voice but no training.[47]

A more durable addition was a brawny, broad-browed twenty-one-year-old former Georgia slave named Hinton D. Alexander. Like so many of the Jubilees, his childhood was one of Dickensian travail and transcendence. His father and older sister were sold away from him, never to be seen again. His mother hired herself out as a washerwoman, and when her master decided to sell her and her family, she was allowed to go out and find her own buyer. She found one who bought herself and all but one of her children and persuaded a second buyer living near the first to purchase her remaining child. After the war, they moved to Chattanooga, where Alexander worked in a rolling mill. In 1871, he enrolled at Fisk with some friends but did not like its "pervasive religiosity" and would have left had he not been too embarrassed to ask White to return his tuition.

He went home for Christmas, intending never to go back, but soon found his old life at the mill no longer suited him. So he returned to Fisk. When his money ran out, a Sunday school class in Elgin, Illinois, pledged him a dollar a week, and he earned another six dollars a month ringing the bell for hourly recitations and stoking the dormitory furnace. In 1873, he began teaching in a Mississippi school for fifty dollars a month, which seemed a fortune at the time. Apparently he was never paid in full and found himself down to seventy dollars by the time he returned to Nashville, paid his tuition, and bought himself a suit of clothes.[48] White's inducements must have seemed irresistible; White, in turn, deemed Alexander's tenor "all we could wish."[49]

"We have a new song," White reported, "which applies to our enterprise."

> *Inch by inch, keep inching along.*
> *Inch by inch, Jesus will come by and by.*
> *Inch by inch, like a poor inching worm.*
> *Inch by inch, Jesus will come by and by.*[50]

On November 10, White met with the singers and presented them with contracts. "All signed except Mr. Holmes & Rutling," Sheppard recalled. "It seemed very odd that Mr. [Holmes] should assemble with us & enter so conspicuously into all the discussions & arguments—insisting on alterations in the agreements, especially in regards to the salary, when he knew that he was going to refuse to go Jubileeing again." In fact, Holmes knew he was too ill to tour. His chronic cough had lodged ever deeper into constricted lungs scarred by tuberculosis. But he was determined to see to it that his fellow singers would be adequately paid.

Thomas Rutling sent word after hearing of the "agreements & its conditions that he didn't wish to go except on other conditions which were refused by Mr. [Cravath] & others." But Sheppard and Mabel Lewis were "much surprised" to learn that the veterans' salary was "to be $800 per year instead of $500 with an additional $200 providing the net proceeds exceeds $25,000."[51]

As the departure date approached, White grew more fretful. The troupe was "so little prepared for it," he wrote in early December, "that the energy of all is taxed to the utmost. I am feeling quite poorly today, and I don't know how I am going to stand the pressure, and I see no way of getting out of it at present until the company is complete. *Oh dear,*" he exclaimed, "why can't things be done right in the first place." White protested when Cravath hired a new man to handle the troupe's arrangements. "To put a *raw hand* onto the work now means that I shall have to go right into the midst of it and work the campaign out. . . . I am certain if I go right into the work that I shall break down within six weeks." He lobbied the A.M.A. to allow Susan Gilbert to join the tour as preceptress and urged them to send her immediately so she could take care of gathering clothing for the new recruits.[52]

Patti Malone was too sickly; Grant did not "stand up to drill"; Patrick's voice was too weak; Thomas Rutling continued to refuse to commit himself to the tour; and, contract or no contract, Maggie Carnes would not join the troupe.[53] White figured he could find a replacement for Patti among the female students at Fisk, but there was so much sickness among the males at the school that he set off for Memphis to get both a tenor to replace Rutling and a bass to supplement Ousley.[54]

On December 15, White found his bass, a man every bit as formidable and substantial as Benjamin Holmes and with a voice the likes of which no one would hear again until the emergence of Roland Hayes and Paul Robeson. His name was Frederick J. Loudin. At thirty-four, he would be the oldest member of the troupe: a towering, self-assured printer and music teacher from Portage County, Ohio. Though born free, his encounters with racism had been searing. His father's farm was taxed for public education, but his children had to fight to enter school. Loudin proved a gifted scholar, but when his teacher rewarded him for his achievements, whites pulled their children out. Though his father had donated money to a nearby college, when Frederick was grown it refused to admit him on account of his race. The same held true for the local Methodist church. He tithed a ninth of the sparse wages he earned as a printer's apprentice, but the white congregation refused to permit him to sing in their choir. Once on a trip to Cleveland, he found that the only way he could secure lodgings was to pose as a slave traveling with his master. Loudin became so discouraged that he declined his parents' offer to send him to Oberlin, but once his apprenticeship was up, no one would hire him as a printer. He traveled to Philadelphia and married a mild, tenacious woman named Harriet Johnson. Fed up with Northern pretensions of liberality, Loudin went to Tennessee after the war and gained a reputation as a basso and music teacher.[55]

His debut at Fisk was a triumph. "His name should be Mr. Loudman," Sheppard enthused. "Has a wonderful voice, & seems a man of some experience. Mr. White asked him if he thought he could 'stand being flattered and praised for one year.' Mr. Loudin . . . thought seriously for a moment, then replied he did not know, but he hoped so," Sheppard reported approvingly. "Very different indeed from Jubilee Singers' replies."[56] White was so impressed with Loudin that he paid him more than any other singer.[57]

Ella Sheppard had returned from Okolona, where she had found her mother, Sarah, in poor health and unable to accompany her back to Nashville. But Ella returned to Fisk with her half sister Rosa and enrolled her at her own expense, one of several students she assisted with tuition.[58] With Sheppard back and Loudin signed on, White decided to take the troupe on the road in the middle of January, moving fast so as to neutralize all the other troupes that were now taking the field. "There is another company, the Louisianans, about," he told Cravath. "They sang in St. [Charles], and I hear of still another [company] organizing in Milwaukee. *We must have ours right* before we start."

By December 18, the new troupe had finally fallen into place, with Seward acting as director and Susan Gilbert as preceptress. Charles Fairchild, the son of the president of Berea College and its chief fund-raiser, and a timid young man named J. Hamilton Halley were appointed the troupe's advance men.[59] "*Tom* [Rutling] has finally come to his senses and signed his contract," White reported. Mabel Lewis was deemed too weak to tour as yet. Including Rutling, the troupe now numbered ten singers: Ella Sheppard and Jennie Jackson, who were both still under a doctor's care;[60] plus Maggie Porter, Georgia Gordon, Julia Jackson, Gabriel Ousley, Hinton Alexander, Edmund Watkins, and Frederick Loudin.

"The combination is now *far superior* to what it ever was before," White would exult, though he was "sorry we had to take so expensive a company."[61] Exhausted by all the shufflings and reshufflings of his troupe's cast of characters, on New Year's Day, 1875, White declared he was too ill to lead the troupe. Leaving the singers in Seward's hands, he departed Nashville for the North. As he prepared to leave, White forbade anyone to see him who did not have business to discuss, which prevented his ever-scrupulous disciple, Ella Sheppard, from bidding him farewell. "It was hard to stand aside," she pouted, "and see others bidding him good-bye. All did not go in 'on business,' either."[62]

SEND THEM ANGELS

THE THIRD TOUR

JANUARY–OCTOBER 1875

In January 1875, America was still trying to dig its way out of the trough of the nineteenth century's longest and deepest economic depression. Among the Jubilee Singers' patrons was a man many Americans blamed for their woes: a pious, pioneering banker named Jay Cooke, who tithed a tenth of the considerable fortune he had made marketing war bonds. Known as "the financier of the Civil War," Cooke later sent his agents into the South, peddling government bonds to Southerners eager to show their loyalty to the Union. Eventually, he devoted his marketing genius to raising money for the Northern Pacific Railroad, which was projected to link the Great Lakes with the Northwest. At first, investors scrambled to climb on board, but sales began to fall off as the immigration to the upper Middle West on which the scheme was predicated failed to materialize. Nevertheless, over his manager's objections, Cooke advanced his construction crews enormous sums of money. On September 18, 1873, an overextended Jay Cooke & Company suddenly shut its doors, triggering a financial panic that was compounded by a general frenzy of postwar stock speculation and a worldwide slump in prices.

By 1875, the depression had not yet run its course. Despite the Jubilees' receipts, the American Missionary Association's funding was drying up. Hard-pressed to put food on their own tables, its aging benefactors curtailed their donations and canceled their subscriptions to the A.M.A.'s journal. The travails of the freedmen were subsumed in the financial woes of the entire nation. "Times are very hard with the A.M.A.," Spence reported. "Expenditures greater than receipts and a heavy debt to carry. . . . The society may collapse before long."[1] The Jubilees' receipts exceeded the income of the entire A.M.A., whose secretaries did not resist the temptation to dip into the Jubilee Hall fund to support the association. White was reduced to borrowing six hundred dollars from Mabel Lewis to get his tour off the ground and proposed that Cravath hit up General Fisk himself, now a commissioner in the Indian Department, for enough money to complete Jubilee Hall.[2]

On January 12, 1875, Fisk's third troupe of Jubilee Singers set out from Nashville under Theodore Seward and after a long and tedious journey arrived in the snows of Richmond, Indiana. They sang the next night in a small hall only half filled with bundled Hoosiers, who called for only one encore on "Gospel Train" and hastened back to their homes. After a tour of Earlham College, the singers performed again in the same hall for an even smaller and no more enthusiastic audience. "The new singers are rather discouraged," wrote Sheppard.

Their journey was "slow & comical," Sheppard said, and ripe: at one point, their train had to follow for sixteen miles behind carloads of swine. Stalled in a tunnel en route to Harrisburg, they entertained their fellow passengers with a few pieces, a performance that was covered in local papers. But their transatlantic fame had still not immunized them from the old bigotries that had plagued their first tour. In Dayton, they found "prejudice" in the form of a hotel manager who showed them to their own "private" dining room, separate from the other guests. In Cincinnati, the new proprietors of the Grand Hotel were thrown into "confusion," as Sheppard gingerly called it, when the Jubilees applied for rooms. In Columbus on January 24, "two or three guests left the dining room on our appearance this morning" and "made some trouble." When the proprietor refused to banish the Jubilees, the indignant guests left the hotel.

By the end of the month, the troupe had worked its way to New York to perform at Steinway Hall in a concert at which General Fisk himself presided. The audience was large and enthusiastic, and for the first time,

Sheppard said, "it seemed like old times." But it seemed like "old times" in Newark too, for though the new proprietor of the Continental Hotel—"the same hotel," wrote Sheppard, "from which we were driven years ago"—accommodated them, it was only on condition that they eat in their own separate, sparsely furnished dining room.

Their occasional victories over segregated accommodations were sometimes ambiguous and brief and did not always translate into lasting gains for lesser-known African American travelers. North and South, bigotry against blacks as a downtrodden people was calcifying into a more systematic racism. For Northern hoteliers and restaurateurs, the nationwide effort to bind the wounds of the Civil War often meant accommodating to the prejudices of resurgent Southern businessmen who refused to sleep in the same bed linens or dine with the same utensils that blacks had touched.

In early February, most of the singers went to Plymouth Church in Brooklyn to hear a much-compromised Henry Ward Beecher preach from the second chapter of I Peter about building up a "spiritual house" on the rock of Christ crucified, which he extended to include Jubilee and Livingstone Missionary Halls. Now that his indiscretions were a matter of public record, Beecher was apparently a little labile. "The whole discourse was the most beautiful, sad & impressive I ever heard," Sheppard told her diary. "He wept several times, especially while praying."

After several more appearances in the New York metropolitan area, the singers proceeded to Trenton, where they sang to a meager audience, and then retreated to Philadelphia when no hotels would take them in. They had to find accommodations in a black hotel in Baltimore, and though in Washington they managed to find rooms in one of the capital's better establishments, it was only on condition that they "be seen as little as possible in the parlor. . . . It is exceedingly unpleasant to be under such a roof," Sheppard said. "The hall through which we pass to enter our room is so offensive we almost feel nauseated."

Despite these humiliations, on February 2 the singers were honored to take tea with "our noble orator," as Sheppard called him, Frederick Douglass, at his large, mansard-roofed home on A Street. Douglass was then fifty-seven years old. He had risen like a comet in the abolitionist movement, a fearless champion of his people and arguably America's greatest public speaker. From his debut at a Nantucket antislavery rally in 1841, he seemed to emerge fully formed, equipped with audacity, eloquence, a gift for mimicry that he put to brilliant satiric use, and a sonorous, supple baritone that was by all accounts one of the most extraordinary oratorical instruments ever heard.

His treatment as a slave had been riddled with ambiguities: unexpected bonds as well as separations, indulgences as well as cruelty, respect as well as indignity. But in his wildly popular accounts of his life, he willingly bore the burden of the abolitionist abstraction. He did his best to embody the redeemed and ennobled freedman of antislavery propaganda, but so effectively and so eloquently that his white sponsors had urged this most cultured of orators to sound less educated and put "a little of the plantation" into his speech in order to convince skeptical whites that he had actually been a slave.

Douglass would have none of it. No one better understood the admixture of nobility and pettiness, generosity and condescension that constituted Northern liberalism. He was ferociously autonomous, refused to trim his sails to suit the prejudices of his audiences or the whims of his supporters. He would pay no one reflexive deference and bridled when his white hosts took him out to put him or their relationship with him on display. When he broke with the apolitical moral absolutism of his mentor, William Lloyd Garrison, and refused to abandon the Constitution as an instrument of emancipation, some white abolitionists deemed him arrogant, unmanageable, and "ungrateful."

White churches had refused him their pulpits, hotels had ejected him, Northern railroads had tried to relegate him to black-only cars. In fact, his well-publicized physical battles with railroad conductors had played an important part in the eventual desegregation of some of the Northern rail lines the singers now rode with discount tickets. His right hand had been permanently damaged in his battles with pro-slavery mobs.

In 1875, Douglass was in the middle of the worst period of his life since he ran away from his Maryland master thirty-eight years before. Believing himself the leader of his people and the apotheosis of black aspiration, he hankered after high office. But no party would run him for Congress, and to ensure his support of their dubious administrations, Presidents Grant, Hayes, Garfield, and Arthur would humiliate him with demeaning and meaningless appointments as secretary to a commission on the annexation of the Dominican Republic, ceremonial marshal of the District of Columbia, recorder of deeds.

As president of the Freedmen's Bank, Douglass proved an incompetent banker, signing off on speculative loans to Washington contractors. When

the bank collapsed, he refused to lobby Congress to cover the losses of depositors, who had been led to believe, by the bank's own advertising, that
the government vouchsafed their savings. Perhaps because he equated manual labor with his own enslavement, Douglass had grown strangely alienated from the mass of black working people. He had entered the field on
the wave of a great truth, and he was personally alert to every hint of racist
condescension among even his most devoted white supporters. But his
moral certitude blinded him to the dilemma that now faced the freedmen
of the South. Like Clinton B. Fisk, he preached bootstrap sermons to his
people and begged where he had once demanded that white Southerners
treat their former slaves with fairness and decency. Not until his advanced
old age would he revive some of his old fire to do battle against lynchings
and Jim Crow.

Douglass stood well over six feet, his muscular, stevedore's frame
crowned with a salt-and-pepper mane. His gaze was wary, shrewd, alert to
slights, and unsettlingly steady under a great brow creased deeply at the
apex of his pyramidal nose. With his penetrating voice and powerful physi-
cality, he had engendered great passions among the romantic idealists who
flocked to his banner.

"On our entrance he met us so cordially," Sheppard reported, "then, after shaking each by the hand, said he thought it a great kindness in us to
grant his request to call, that he should ever remember the favor with great
pleasure. He then spoke of our work, how he had watched our course with
intense interest." The Jubilees had not intended to stay long but ended up
visiting for over an hour while the old lion of abolitionism stood singing
slave melodies for the choir in his basso profundo, as Theodore Seward jotted them down in tonic sol-fa notation.[3]

"Though the Ethiopian may not change his skin," Douglass wrote in the
Jubilees' autograph book, "noble conduct can make his manhood respected, even in the United States, where it has been most despised and oppressed, and in their good work I gladly recognize the efficiency of the
Jubilee Singers."[4]

That his words did not end on a particularly stirring note may have been
a reflection of his general ambivalence toward the Jubilees' sponsors. He
later rejoiced that the A.M.A. "had been able to do so much of the needed
work. . . . The new times require new men and new ideas. I certainly wish
you success in your humane and educational work."[5] But on July 5, to the
A.M.A.'s horror, Douglass would suddenly denounce the "swarm of white

beggars that sweep the country in the name of the colored race," which had been "more injured than benefited by the efforts of the so-called benevolent societies. . . . We now and here denounce and repudiate all such shams, and call upon the American people to do the same."

The A.M.A. was fit to be tied. African Americans were "*not* prepared to proclaim a 'Declaration of Independence' of their former friends," it insisted, nor could they "afford to cast off their friends at once." Douglass's speech threatened to "shut up many a purse against the appeals for the negro." If "eminently gifted" African Americans like Douglass intended now "to use their special gifts and eloquence in denouncing their old friends," the A.M.A. could only express its "regrets at their ingratitude and at their unwisdom for the rest of their race."[6]

As the Jubilees looped back up through Pennsylvania, Seward and Fairchild tried splitting the troupe into smaller groups to spread them out among smaller venues. But as Seward reported to Cravath, "the small places do not appreciate our concerts, while it has been proved that large cities are prepared to do so when properly worked." A concert in Easton, Pennsylvania, in late February barely covered expenses, and it made Seward "feel sad" when he considered how much the full troupe could have made in Washington or Baltimore: days ahead of their appearance in Philadelphia, their advance sales already totaled four hundred dollars.[7] Now that the singers were a well-known entity, their new agent, Fairchild, decided he could afford to dispense with Pike and White's strategy of ingratiating the singers with local churches before appearing on concert stages.

At Williamsburg, New York, Jennie Jackson delighted a transplanted Louisianan who, like Twain, had not heard authentic black music since he left Dixie. Jackson reminded him of the musical conversation of "a coarse, hard-favored field-hand" named Sally, "who, being lame, was transferred to the kitchen. . . . That voice!" he exclaimed. "It never floated to us in poetry or song—Sally never sung—it never touched any higher subject than the business of the scullery, yet for these twenty years it has remained with us as the standard tone of music, our highest conception of melody." As the Jubilees sang, he heard the same voice again. "Not Sally's," he wrote, "—she, poor girl, in the great jostle of the races, has long ago probably been crushed into the sod—but another unshaped, ungainly daughter of Congo—her name on the bills—[Jennie] Jackson. . . . The Scandinavian can range, and the Teuton can write the score; but from Africa must come the voices to realize their conceptions, and impress their harmonies upon the soul."[8]

The Jubilees' music was no less a revelation to some of the African Americans who came to their concerts. A correspondent for the *Christian Recorder* wrote:

> As we sat enraptured, . . . we pondered upon the notable fact, that the chiefest of European composers were Jews: Mendelssohn, Meyerbeer, Halévy, Rossini and Offenbach—and we thought of the seeming possible connection between suffering and song. We, as a race, have had the suffering part; will we have the song part? Judging from the present appearance of the subject, we should not be surprised if the suffering Negro be in the future what the suffering Jew was in the past, a very prince of song. . . .[9]

By early March, the Jubilees had moved into a Brooklyn hotel called the Mansion House, where the proprietor refused to serve them tea until they sang for him. When they returned that evening from a concert, Sheppard reported, there was "trouble between the Northern & Southern boarders" that soon escalated into open warfare.[10]

"This morning there was a combat on our behalf," America Robinson mordantly reported the next day to her fiancé, James Burrus.

> A southern man was enraged because the proprietor took us in. A northerner asserted that if we had been refused admittance, he would have taken *his* departure and told the southerner that he was a half "nigger" himself. The southerner attempted to throw the paper at the northerner so the northerner struck him on the mouth with a chair. Many boarders threatened to leave.

The Jubilees zigzagged up through Connecticut, performing with varying success in New Haven, Middletown, Waterbury, and Hartford. On March 8, they reached Boston, where Mark Twain jotted a note to Theodore Seward asking why he had not included "John Brown's Body" on the program. "I remember an afternoon in London," he said, "when their 'John Brown's Body' took a decorous, aristocratic English audience by surprise and threw them into a volcanic eruption of applause before they knew what they were about. I never saw anything finer than their enthusiasm." If the Jubilees would only agree to sing it again for him that evening, "it would set me down in London again for a minute or two, and at the same time save me the tedious ocean voyage and the expense." Seward, of course, obliged.

Clemens noted that the success of the Jubilees was attested to "by the fact that there are already companies of imitators trying to ride into public view by endeavoring to convey the impression that they are the original Jubilee Singers."[11] He meant it as a compliment, but now White was no longer shrugging off the danger these proliferating troupes posed to his own progenetive enterprise. "Those 'wild cat' companies are a nuisance," he declared, "and their name seems to be legion, and now I see the 'Hamptons' are to take the field again. While the Jubilees do New England, they will devour all that remains of the line of N.Y. Central and West."[12] During the singers' sojourn in Boston, they found themselves following behind phantom troupes that left such "a very unfavorable impression" that they began to tell on the turnout for the Jubilees' own concerts.[13]

The most blatant of them was the Famous Colored Jubilee Singers, organized by the self-styled "Professor" W. F. Phillips for the supposed benefit of a nonexistent Jackson University. Their advertisements lifted entire quotes from the reviews the Fisk Jubilees received, even including accounts of their singing for Queen Victoria and Gladstone. "They ought to have a reception wherever they go as warm as the sheriff can make it," wrote the New York *Independent*. "We earnestly ask for the co-operation of the Pulpit and the Press," read one of the A.M.A.'s cautionary broadsides, "in the exposure of these pretenders, as well as their aid in furthering the noble efforts of the true JUBILEE SINGERS, who are once more in the field, under the auspices of the American Missionary Association, to complete their grand work for Fisk University and the Colored Race."[14]

In Boston, Cravath apparently took America Robinson aside and told her that if the troupe's receipts did not improve he might have to send her back to Nashville. After interrupting her studies to go on tour, Robinson saw this as a breach of her contract, which stipulated a full two years' service if she performed satisfactorily. White backed her up. "The contracts were made in good faith," he scolded his brother-in-law. "*I* shall not break faith with the singers if no money is made." Robinson remained with the troupe, but it was a portent of a struggle between Cravath and the managers on one side and White and the singers on the other that would plague them for the rest of the life of the troupe.[15]

On St. Patrick's Day, the Jubilees were honored by successive visits with William Lloyd Garrison and Wendell Phillips. That these champions of abolitionism did not visit jointly was symptomatic of the chasm that now separated them. The autocratic Garrison was seventy years old and suffering withdrawals from a battle won. He was in some ways an unlikely champion of the Jubilees, for he denounced theaters in general as "deep and powerful sources of evil." But his love of sacred music must have overcome his doubts about the Jubilees' enterprise. Tall, erect, with features softened only by his spectacles, he was humorless and curiously credulous. Hating slavery as "the sum of all criminality," he had devoted his life to its eradication, denouncing the Constitution—he once burned a copy at a rally—as a compromise with tyranny. After the war, Garrison had turned his sights on prohibition, women's suffrage, the eradication of prostitution, and the rights of the American Indian. "Liberty for each, for all, and forever," Garrison now wrote in the Jubilees' autograph book.[16]

Sixty-four-year-old Wendell Phillips was the handsome, cultivated son of Boston's first mayor. He had been converted into a whole-hog Christian by Lyman Beecher, turned into an ardent abolitionist by his wife, and steeled in his opposition to slavery by the sight of Garrison being dragged through the streets and nearly lynched by a pro-slavery mob. Phillips shared Garrison's fearlessness; it was he who had barely escaped a lynching in Cincinnati. He came into prominence denouncing the murderers of the antislavery publisher Elijah Lovejoy and evolved, with Frederick Douglass, into one of the most persuasive of all abolitionists: an antidote to the monotonous dogmatism of his ally Garrison.

With emancipation, Garrison had declared the work of the American Anti-Slavery Society at an end and proposed its dissolution. But Phillips believed the society should stay in business until blacks obtained the vote, and he defeated Garrison in the bitter balloting that followed. Though Phillips had championed many of Garrison's postwar causes, now these two old warriors were hardly on speaking terms. All they could agree upon, for the moment, was the Jubilee Singers.

The Jubilees had "a very pleasant visit" with the courtly Phillips, who entertained them with anecdotes about Douglass, Garrison, and the women's suffragist Elizabeth Cady Stanton. "Speaking of our work," Sheppard wrote, "he remarked that we were 'laying one of the main cornerstones toward removing prejudice.'"

"Peace if possible," Phillips wrote that afternoon in the Jubilees' book, "liberty at any rate."[17]

On April 16, the Jubilees headed west for Detroit and Chicago, where imitators and the depression were beginning to tell on their receipts. "Concert in Park Congregational Church," Sheppard wrote from Chicago. "Attendance did not come up to expectations. Fraud or bogus troupes under the auspices of the Y.M.C.A. hurt prospects."[18] They sang to a "very poor house" in Milwaukee and met with only "fair attendance" on their return to the Windy City.

Gustavus Pike followed their progress from England, where he was now serving as a liaison between the A.M.A. and Shaftesbury's Freedmen's Missions Aid Society. In his opinion, the real blame for the Jubilees' poor receipts lay with Fairchild. "The work in America during the past winter was all done on a wrong basis," he wrote Cravath. "It was almost wholly outside the church and missionary influences. . . . I feel *quite certain* that with Bro. Fairchild at the helm we shall not get our money."[19]

The religious element would have borne Pike's opinion out at Oberlin, where they were still so popular among Congregationalists that "special trains were run from Elyria & other places." But in the end, the concert "was not much enjoyed," wrote Sheppard. The singers were "very uncomfortably seated" in a "poor house for sound. The piano was perched upon the [dais] which brought the pedals about one foot from the chair," and her "chair was low. My position was perfectly grotesque as well as exceedingly uncomfortable. Altogether the concert was given under very embarrassing circumstances. Many said they enjoyed it," but some said they had preferred the "Hamptons."[20]

White paced about, fretting over every report of new rivals and poor gates. "I can't help thinking and planning Jubilee work as long as I have any thing to do with it," he said. At first, White had believed that the proper course was to tour the United States until Jubilee Hall was dedicated. In the meantime, the troupe could look for fresh harvests in "St. Louis and the river towns to St. Paul and back east through Wisconsin, Mich. &c. during June" and perhaps even into Canada. He adamantly maintained that

> it would be *of little use to us to cross water until Jubilee Hall is completed and ready for occupation, and all the world knows of it.* I never would attempt to explain to our English friends why it was not done. *That building* was the center of our work. The people were interested in it, and it will be utterly useless to undertake to get up much enthusiasm over any thing else as far as F.U. is concerned until that is done & dedicated.

In fact, progress on Jubilee Hall was only crawling along. The main structure had just been shingled, and the interior of its vast shell remained to be finished. White was at first "fully convinced that if there is no way of completing Jubilee Hall and furnishing the necessary facilities for opening the university with vigor next September, that we had better close the work at Nashville and sell the property for use elsewhere." But he began to realize that he could not afford to make his tour the captive of a building project. He was between a rock and a hard place: though he felt he could not go overseas until the hall was completed, it looked more and more as though it could not be completed without the kind of funds he could only raise overseas.

White decided not to wait on Jubilee Hall any longer but to rejoin his troupe and proceed with them to Britain on a fund-raising tour for the construction of a second building to be dubbed Livingstone Missionary Hall, after the late Scottish missionary and explorer. It meant breaking White's promise to Robinson that she could read her senior paper at commencement, but, he told her, it could not be helped. White said Dickerson had reported "that there is much enquiry in regard to the return of the Singers. People want to hear them. Moody and Sankey are to be in London April, May & June. If the Singers reach London in time to work somewhat in cooperation with them, we can greatly aid them in their meetings and they can benefit us. . . . I don't mention that as making merchandise out of Revival meetings," White hastened to add, "but in *doing good.*"[21]

George White rejoined his "children," as he still called the Jubilees, and on May 15, 1875, they sang at a crowded farewell concert in New York's Academy of Music, which they "had the honor of opening . . . to the colored people for the first time." General Fisk himself was present and gave "a capital speech," Sheppard wrote, and a delegation of black teachers "presented us with a lovely bouquet."[22]

The next morning, leaving a floundering Gabriel Ousley behind, they set sail for England on the Cunard steamer *Algeria*. Now it was America Robinson's turn to be seasick. "I try to eat but do not get seated before I have to contribute to the sea," she wrote Burrus. "I never was so sick. . . . Finally the doctor came to my rescue. He assists me to my bed. The stewardess undresses me and I am soon in the arms of morpheus. I sing to see if I can sing but oh it is very weak. It sounds like a wee baby's voice." Soon she got her sea legs and delighted in the sight of a passing iceberg and the sheen of the Atlantic at night. "The waters spread out in one silvery sheet," she said. "Everything is beautiful and brilliant 'neath the fairy moonlight."

After ten days' voyage, they landed at Liverpool and rode the train to London, where Robinson was so chilled that she wore all of her "heavy clothing just the same as I wore all winter."[23] On May 27, they made their way to Moody and Sankey's meeting and took seats in the upper gallery, from which they delighted a startled Moody after a silent prayer with a rendition of "Angels Hovering 'Round." At the next day's service, Sankey startled them in turn with his revised version of "Steal Away," to which he had appended his own verse: "Our God is calling / that nation's are awaking." "O I am so thankful," wrote Sheppard, "for the blessed privilege of being present & one of the helpers in so good a work."[24]

On May 31, the Jubilees made their first return appearance before the annual meeting of the earl of Shaftesbury's Freedmen's Missions Aid Society at the City Temple in London. The news of their arrival "drew an audience that not only packed every inch of space in that capacious church, but filled the large lecture hall below with an overflow meeting." Shaftesbury himself had to squeeze into the door to get in and shoulder his way to the platform, where, catching sight of the singers standing in the gallery, he gave them a cordial bow.

Shaftesbury was moved to uncharacteristic eloquence by the Jubilees' return. "When I find these young people, gifted to an extent that does not often fall to the lot of man, coming here in such a spirit, I don't want them to become white, but I have a strong disposition myself to become black. If I thought color was anything—if it brought with it their truth, piety, and talent—I would willingly exchange my complexion tomorrow. In the name of this vast mass of British citizens," he said, gesturing across the enormous crowd, ". . . we receive them with joy again to our shores, and will do all that in us lies to advance their holy cause."[25]

The audience was so vast that after singing in the upper hall of City Temple, Robinson reported, the Jubilees "went down a great number of flights and sang to the lower hall," and still vast numbers could not hear them. On June 1, they held their first benefit concert in Exeter Hall "to quite a full & appreciative house." Robinson was too weak to make it through the entire concert and was almost glad to leave, "for I did not want those English people to shake my hand off. Every one seems to think he must shake hands with us. They encore everything."[26]

The next day, the singers paid a visit to Edmund Havell's studio to check on his progress on their portrait. As a pretty thirteen-year-old protegée of Havell's named Ruby read " 'The Dog's Ambition,' sang 'Andavella' & spoke one or two other pieces for us," the singers scrutinized their life-size likenesses on Havell's vast canvas. Sheppard "was very much pleased with the Jubilees' portrait" but thought "Tom's, Mabel's & Maggie's were not good." Havell agreed and arranged "to have us sit again now that he has an opportunity." Weeks later, Sheppard returned to pose in a jacket she borrowed from Georgia Gordon. The studio was filled with Havell's friends, patrons, and sycophantic hangers-on, who largely ignored Sheppard as she posed. "O such a stiff set are English people!" she exclaimed afterward. "One could hardly be interested in their questions, so stupid or ignorant were they about Americans and the negro."

The singers moved into their old lodgings in Upper Norwood, opposite the Crystal Palace. On June 8, they sang for their old champion Newman Hall and his guests at Swiss Cottage. "Many sat gazing steadily & seemed drinking in every word of the precious songs of trouble," Sheppard recalled. "Others wept & others smiled."[27] After a succession of concerts in London, Stratford-on-Avon, and Kingston, the singers were due for a rest. But White told them of the grumblings he had begun to hear from the troupe's English friends, who, as he feared, "thought we had come back to England too soon. . . . Unless some thing would be done," he told the troupe, he believed they would have to give up the tour and return to America.

"The feeling was very general and outspoken," said Pike, "that we had returned too soon after our former success, with our appeal for help, and outside a few individuals there was little interest and no enthusiasm in the object of our mission."[28] The Jubilees' only hope, White told them, was to hook up at once with Moody and Sankey, who were appearing at a series of meetings at Bow Road Hall.[29] After securing White's promise of an extended vacation to follow, the singers agreed.

"O such a mass of beings," Sheppard exclaimed after the first meeting. "The attendance at the meetings is immense," Robinson reported: some ten to twelve thousand, plus many others who could not get in.[30] "I never witnessed anything similar to it before." She was not as impressed as Lewis had been by Dwight Lyman Moody, whom Robinson deemed "an alarmist" because he prophesied "that such great religious excitements are sure to be followed by some great judgment." Nevertheless, it may have been Moody's influence that accounted for Robinson's new interest in the Bible; rather than continuing to tease Julia Jackson about her immersion in scripture, she now took to reading the Gospel with her regularly.[31] "We are surely being led by a divine hand," wrote Sheppard.

> [At one meeting] it fairly made me tremble to see & know the cause of such a congregation of unconverted souls. No doubt they said to their own hearts that they were going to hear the singing but I earnestly believe it was the Gospel truth their souls really sought. Anyway, thank God, they did hear the Gospel & in a way both by preaching & singing that they shall never forget, whether heeded or not.[32]

For almost a month, the Jubilees sang for Moody and Sankey nearly every day. Their renewed association helped to restore their reputation as selfless evangelists.[33] "The way in which these American (or African?) friends have stuck to their posts at Bow-road Hall is beyond all praise," declared Moody's campaign organ, the *Christian*, "though we feel assured they seek, not the praise of men, but the glory of God, in the redemption of their fellows."[34]

It was no wonder to Loudin that the Jubilees' songs exerted such power. "These songs are the pure waters of our affliction," he explained.

> They gushed forth from us when we were smitten by the hand of man, as the waters gushed from the rock in the wilderness when

smitten by the rod of Moses. These songs came to us, as it were, fresh from the hand of God, as He gave them to us, in order to give utterance sometimes to our woes, and sometimes to our joys.[35]

After one of their last meetings, a fifteen-year-old girl came up to Sheppard and begged to speak with her:

She said that she had been converted since these meetings began and, that every time we sing, the songs just lift her up & that her soul was so full she must speak to me. On leaving me she kissed me. Mr. White came to the meeting for a few moments & heard us sing the first [piece]. He said he had never heard anything so beautiful, that it fairly thrilled him through. O what couldn't the Jubilee Singers do if they were only in the spirit to do it.

Moody was abjectly grateful. When White told Moody "of the anxious throng & multitude" flocking to hear the Jubilees, "he just fell down upon his knees & thanked & praised the Lord." Perhaps in part to compensate the troupe for the bootleg Jubilee books "made up of all sorts of fibs" that enterprising "book boys" had taken to selling outside the Bow Road meetings,[36] Moody's hosts voted the Jubilees five hundred pounds, and Moody presented each singer with a thirty-pound Bagster's Bible with Russian leather covers containing "notes, references, chronological tables."[37] It was a gift that would "ever call up thousands of such glories & beautiful associations," wrote Sheppard, "as lift one up away from Earth, right up to the Master."[38]

To lift the Jubilees before the British public, Moody also provided White with a semiliterate but nonetheless invaluable letter of introduction:

To my friends in Great Britain.

This will introduce to you my personal friend Mr. White of AM who is in this country with the Jubee Singers to raise money to educate the collard people of our land. I know their object to be a most worthy one & any help you can render them will be doing God's service.

Yours truly,
D. L. Moody[39]

Mountains of letters tumbled into the Jubilees' lodgings at Upper Norwood: invitations, engagements, propositions. Sir Bartle Frere asked if the singers might consider performing for Barghash ibn Sa'id, the visiting sultan of the East African kingdom of Zanzibar, "hoping," Sheppard reported, that after "seeing & hearing emancipated slaves of [America] sing" he might be more earnest "in his efforts to suppress the great slave trade in his island." Sheppard thought it "perfectly awful" that anyone implicated in this traffic was allowed into Britain, let alone wined and dined, but judged "that all the missionary societies are making a special effort to interest him so that when he returns . . . he may use his power, for one word from him can stop . . . the African slave trade."

During the 1860s, the British government had accepted its share of the burden for ending the slave trade in West Africa, where its own traders had once played such a prominent part. But for years, it refused to take a leading role in the eradication of the trade in East Africa, which it regarded as an Arab matter. In fact, Britain feared that if it leaned too heavily on the sultan, His Majesty might turn for comfort to Britain's French and German competitors in the nascent "Scramble for Africa" that within less than thirty years would subject almost all of Africa's ten million square miles and 110 million people to European rule. The foreign office argued that closing down the sultan's slave markets would only lead to anarchy in Zanzibar and a proliferation of Arab slave markets along the coast. But when, in 1873, at the urging of Livingstone's former lieutenant Sir John Kirk, Barghash reluctantly shut down his markets, neither came to pass.

The sultan conscientiously enforced his ban not only on the island of Zanzibar but in his possessions along the coast. But by 1875, about twelve thousand slaves were being shuttled up a terrible, pestilential route through the inland bush, along a trail littered with the dead and dying. Sheppard was horrified to learn that "if a woman on any one of the gang of slaves becomes too ill to proceed, . . . the trader or driver chains them to a tree or any other firm object & leaves them there to die. If a baby is too fretful it is thrown aside on the wayside to perish in the way. The result of such cruelty is that thousands . . . perish annually."[40]

Barghash despised the heavy-handed Sir Bartle Frere, who threatened to blockade Zanzibar with gunships if he did not submit to British will. So in the end, the singers never got an opportunity to perform for the sultan, who, by the time of his death in 1888, would see most of his dominions carved up among Great Britain, Germany, and Italy.[41]

America Robinson was astonished by the frenzied enthusiasm of the Jubilees' English fans. "When our concerts are out we have much difficulty in getting through the crowds," she reported.

> The crowd generally opens to let us pass and on either side they offer us their hands to shake. Sometimes they say "Will you please let us shake your hands[?] We think it such an honor." One woman rushed through the crowd and came and stood by me saying that she felt it a great honor to be near me.[42]

"I stayed all night with a young lady last night who wanted to know if we kissed in America," Robinson wrote. "She wished to kiss me goodnight before retiring but was rather timid. English people seem to like kissing." After an appearance at Bow Road Hall, "everyone tried to get a kiss from us. I had rather too many," Robinson teased James Burrus. "Though we kissed no gentlemen."

Burrus wrote back, concerned that her experience in England was turning her against her own country. But Robinson was not contrite. Just as she "could not help liking the North far better than I did the South," she liked "England better than any country I ever was in because there is not an atom of prejudice here." Nevertheless, she assured her fiancé,

> while I should prefer to live where I feel highly respected, I would sacrifice this to be with my friends. I did not realize that I would miss you so much or long to see you so much until I left Fisk. When I was there I did not think that you loved me, but still it pained me to leave you. It is wonderful how we still love people whether they love us or not, isn't it? It is something I can not solve.[43]

For Frederick Loudin, England was a revelation. "It seemed to me as if I had always been walking about blind before," he would recall. "We were astonished to find such freedom, . . . such an entire absence of race prejudice. . . . I gradually realized that I could do what anybody else could do, if I had capacity enough; and I could go where I pleased and do what I pleased, without any prohibitions on the ground of my color."[44]

In their free time, the singers ventured out to explore England a little.

On a visit to Chelmsford Criminal Court, Robinson was more impressed by the wigs and robes and gold chains of the judges and counselors than she was by British jurisprudence. "The poor criminals stood up all day in their working apparel," she reported.

> One was convicted and sentenced to ten years imprisonment; the other to five years. . . . I thought how little those men knew in regard to the real nature of the case. . . . I am not much in favor of lawyers. These men pronounced a verdict on the accused as carelessly as if they were doing some very trivial thing.

On July 20, White took the Jubilees to Wales, itself a wellspring of song. At Builth, they performed at a classic Welsh eisteddfod, an assembly of bards and minstrels once held in ancient times and recently revived. A torrential rain drenched their concert audience that evening as it stood patiently under a temporary shelter, but "still they kept quiet and stayed until the concert was over."

Afterward, the Jubilees were allowed to rest for twelve days. Sheppard spent her time recovering from a succession of visits to a local doctor to have her ear drained. Robinson ventured out into the countryside, visiting the town's salt and sulfur baths and "rusticating to my heart's content." White urged her to collect ferns and "analyze flowers" for Fisk, but she "did not like to do it," she said. "It is too troublesome." The females of the troupe were invited to the lodge of a Mr. Maitland, where they "went rowing on the pond and played croquet on the lawn" and "partook of a splendid luncheon," though Robinson dismissed the ice cream in Builth as "nothing but frozen water."

Stranded one day by a rainstorm while strolling with Maggie Porter, Robinson accepted a ride to her hotel on the back of an elderly farmer's horse. "I had to put my arms around the old man to keep from falling off, he went so swiftly," she said. "The old man hurrahed to every one he met and the people around set up a loud shout. Every one came running to their doors to see what was the excitement. I never laughed so much in all my life."

When the singers departed, almost the entire population came out to see them off. "Your young men left some very sad ladies behind," Robinson reported to Burrus. "Mr. Rutling became enamored with the Belle of

Builth," and "she seemed very sad when he left. . . . The people in Builth declared they could not get along without us.

"My company is select," said Robinson.

> I know that gentlemen over here are not so backward as in America.
> They come up without an introduction and speak and hold conver-
> sation with you. We think nothing of it here whereas we should call
> a man rather fresh in America, who would act as they do here.

In the meantime, Theodore Seward was not up to the peculiar demands of a Jubilee tour. Apparently he had a history of nervous breakdowns and suffered from debilitating headaches. After directing the singers at a few appearances in early August, he temporarily withdrew from the troupe in a state of collapse, leaving White and Sheppard to direct the singers.[45] "Poor man," Sheppard wrote. "I am so sorry for him." They performed in Wey-mouth and Plymouth and rested a few days at the seaside resort of Torquay, where the singers "went rowing upon the smooth sea" with George White. "The Jubilees' boats met upon the water," Sheppard sighed, "and all joined in singing. Singing on the quiet water is always beautiful. Mr. White sat qui-etly & listened. I know his very soul was full of the peace & loveliness around."

The next day on a fishing expedition that brought in thirty-seven mack-erel, Sheppard acted as a kind of chaperon to White and Miss Gilbert, whose affection for each other was apparently deepening. But White's health remained poor, his rheumatism and consumption compounded by a crippling case of piles, and on the following day, he announced that the singers might not see him again until they returned to America. He told them tearfully that he had to "leave the work entirely, that to give the Ju-bilee singing into other hands & leave or separate himself from the work was like rending his soul from the body. I was perfectly dumb with surprise & grief," Sheppard mourned. "To have Mr. W, our own dear first & only leader leave us was such a thing as never entered our mind before. It was not til I bade him good-bye that I fully realized what it all meant. . . . We all wept & had it not been for the blessed fact that our merciful Father was dealing with our loved leader & us the parting would have been all sad-ness."[46]

Meanwhile, the Jubilees' managers sought out every venue they could find. From Swansea to Stockton, the singers performed some twenty-three concerts in a little over a month.[47] Everywhere they went they continued to be plagued by parasitic book boys hawking bootleg copies of their books. They were "very impertinent," Sheppard reported. "They engaged a third boy to assist them who called out, 'Black niggers concert book, one penny,' while they themselves laughed and called, 'Jubilee Singers concert book, six pennies,'" and offered one of the Jubilees' official book boys ten shillings if he would stop warning the crowd not to buy the pirated copies.

Their reception was sometimes mixed. In some places, hundreds mobbed the doors and windows of the Jubilees' hotels and ran alongside their carriages.[48] But the Exeter *Gazette*'s critic thought that the singers' "most cordial welcome" reflected particularly well on the English themselves:

> English people entertain the kindliest feeling towards the African race, and the announcement that ten negro students of an American university, established for the purpose of training negro teachers, will give a concert in aid of the institution, is sufficient in every town of the kingdom to attract a numerous audience.

He deemed the troupe "certainly worth seeing," as "piety and pleasure form a delightful combination." But the singers' performances were "simply the introduction of Christy minstrelcy into the services of the chapel," he maintained.

> Travellers in the Southern States have described the humorous method adopted by the negroes in their religious songs, and the Jubilee Singers give us samples of this. English audiences smile at the oddity, and comicality, and originality of the tunes and words, but what would satisfy the uncultivated negro is hardly likely to prove other than amusing and interesting to the educated European. Some of the melodies are plaintive and touching, and marked by religious fervour; others border on the ridiculous, and seem more calculated to raise a laugh than to inspire a serious thought; but it must be remembered that they are meant for a race that is at once rollicking and tender, influenced by coarse enjoyment as well as tender fancies.[49]

The delicacy of the *Gazette*'s sensibilities notwithstanding, the Jubilees continued to appeal to the "coarse enjoyment as well as tender fancies" of the British public. In Scotland, "Lord Shaftesbury's letters preceded us everywhere," Sheppard recalled, "and led even Edinburgh, Glasgow and other cities officially to invite us to visit them."[50] They sang to standing-room-only audiences under the patronage of provosts and magistrates, earning more per concert than they had taken in during their first tour.

On the nineteenth, they attended a breakfast for "over 2,000 poor of all ages & stages of poverty" in a tent on Glasgow Green. Sheppard was befriended by an earnest young street preacher she identifies only as "Robert," about whom the other singers began to tease her. On one of their walks through Glasgow, "Robert stopped almost every stray, looking for persons to speak to or hand a tract," but most turned away.

The singers visited the elegant home of a family named Dewar that had made its fortune in the Jamaican slave trade. "Their home is beautiful," conceded Sheppard, "but there is a skeleton if even with all that earth can contribute, but such is life. Its happiness outside of Christ amounts to but very little." Mrs. Dewar was especially attentive to Sheppard because she had "a cousin very much like myself. . . . She is colored. Her mother was a negress." The Dewars were by no means exceptional in this regard. There had been ten thousand blacks in Georgian London. By the mid-1870s, their descendants no longer saw themselves as a distinct community. Intermarriage with whites had been common, and many had melded into Britain's gene pool. They were British, though most of them were poor.[51]

In late September at Inverness, Seward arranged for the troupe to hear a lecture by the leading champion of the tonic sol-fa system, the Reverend John Curwen. "To explain how very simple their method is [Curwen] wrote an exercise & melody. The choir took it down as he sang each part," then he asked them to perform it. Though they sang it with "perfect ease," Sheppard was unimpressed. "The lecture," she said, "didn't amount to very much."

In early October, the troupe was invited to visit forty-seven-year-old Francis Alexander Keith-Falconer, the eighth earl of Kintore. His Lordship met the singers at the station with his younger son, Arthur, and led them on a tour of his estate in Aberdeenshire. A Liberal Party man and friend of William Gladstone's, he proved an enthusiastic host. When Sheppard paused to ask the earl if he had named the lake on his estate, he "gave me the privilege of naming it, which I did, with pleasure, calling it 'Jubilee

Loch.'" He agreed to "Jubilee" but not to "Loch," since he was a Low-lander and "Loch" was a Highland term. "Let me drink a toast," he declared after luncheon. "I welcome you . . . to Keith Hall, . . . not only as brothers & sisters in Christ but as brothers & sisters indeed, for we are of one blood, though it may be of different color. Whether we be Scythian, Parthian, English, American or Scotch, we are pining for the same home & serving the same master."

The gentlemanly Frederick Loudin rose to reply:

My Lord, you can but little realize why & how your words have touched our hearts—we of the oppressed race, so unaccustomed to words of kindness & cheer. In the name of the millions of our race who were so long made mute by the chains they wore, and in the name of the cause we have come here to represent and labor for, and in the name of my associates, the Jubilee Singers, I thank you and yours, and the friends who are gathered here, more than I have language to express.

"My soul praised the Lord," wrote Sheppard, "for such a great blessing."

The Scottish damps were wearing out the troupe, however. Georgia Gordon took to her bed, and Sheppard's rheumatic back ached so badly she hardly ventured out. In September, at Pike's urging, Cravath had sailed to England to take charge of the tour, arriving in Glasgow in mid-October.

Sheppard was moved by the poverty she saw around her in Glasgow, where the worldwide depression had thrown thousands out of work. She had apparently sponsored several disabled Glaswegian girls at a school run by a man named Forsythe, who, in turn, sponsored one of Mary Wells's students, a black girl named Rebecca Winckel. "I am not so fortunate as other girls," Winckel had written to Sheppard, "having been burned when an infant which caused the loss of all my fingers of the right hand and scarred my face very much. My tongue is not afflicted, and with that I can work for Jesus"—words that struck Sheppard as "certainly those of a Christian."

In Glasgow, Sheppard visited one of her Scottish adoptees, a consumptive named Roseanne Cameron, who lived in a tenement room down a city close. "We had such a precious meeting singing & praying & talking," Sheppard reported. "She seemed so happy. Her mother said that she had been looking forward to our coming with great eagerness. I felt so glad that I was privileged to visit her." Together they sang "Swing Low, Sweet Chariot" and "In Bright Mansions."

Again and again, Sheppard was overwhelmed by the fellow feeling she and the poor engendered in each other.[52] Performing in Edinburgh, the Jubilees would sing to a "vast sea of unkempt heads and begrimed faces," as the Daily Mail described them. When Seward recounted Sheppard's life history and reached the part where she was taken from her mother, "a young mother just in front of him suddenly strained her baby to her breast as though the thing was to be done to her own self & baby. It was only for a moment, but showed how intensely she loved that baby & how she appreciated what Mr. [Seward] was relating."[53]

On October 18, Julia Jackson received word of the death, after a brief illness, of her mother: the same slave mother who had bought Julia's freedom by hiring herself out. "Julia was not at all prepared for it. I never saw her weep before this morning. . . . Every girl when she knew of Julia's trouble had a frantic presentiment that her own mother was in danger."[54] "Poor dear Julia," wrote Sheppard, whose own mother was ailing. "It seems so hard. So sad that she should be so far away, & then just receive news when her mother has been dead over two weeks."[55]

A week later, the troupe received even more tragic news: Benjamin Holmes had died of tuberculosis two weeks before. "We feel greatly afflicted," Spence wrote, though "still comforted that his faith and resignation was complete." It had been a pestilential autumn at Fisk: still jammed into the old barracks even as Jubilee Hall finally limped to completion, Holmes was one of three students to die that season. "We were all quite prepared for his death on account of his long illness," wrote Robinson, nevertheless "we all felt it deeply. Everybody loved Mr. Holmes."[56] In fact, Sheppard could only hope that his death would put an end to the bitterness she still felt after his machinations at the close of the previous tour. "My heart is heavy," she confessed to her diary, "still I do not weep that Bennie Holmes is gone, for I know that he is gone to live in bright mansions. It is enough that his ear can no more be poisoned against me. He has gone before. I shall soon follow, & there our friendship can no more be severed by evil whispers."[57] Eventually Robinson and Georgia Gordon would become exasperated with the Jubilees' capacity to forget all about Holmes. They asked the troupe to contribute toward a memorial in his honor. "Every one has pretended to think so much of him save us two," Robinson would write in May, "and they have not even written a line in memoriam, so we waited this long and no one has done anything. . . . I imagine already what some will give."[58]

But Holmes had already written his own memorial. He once wrote the readership of Lewis Douglass's *New National Era*:

> I will say to parents, kindle in the bosom of your children a flame of love of God and their race which will radiate as they grow, and which cannot be quenched by ambition. And to the colored youth, strike out boldly and fearlessly to attain those things which will make you look pleasing to both God and man. Have those qualities about you which cannot be separated from you, and seek those attributes against which there is no law, and the nation which is being judged from you as the standard will exalt your name for evermore.[59]

He was twenty-eight years old.[60]

NO BACKSLIDING

SCOTLAND AND IRELAND

NOVEMBER 1875–JUNE 1876

In Scotland, the Jubilees were reunited briefly with another former colleague, Isaac Dickerson, now a student at the University of Edinburgh. "He was as full of fun as ever," Robinson reported. "He is always on the go. I do not see what time he has for study. . . . He is engaged to a millionheir," she said, and "flirts with all the Scottish lassies."[1]

Among Edinburgh's most-beloved residents was the late David Livingstone's oldest daughter, Agnes Livingstone Bruce, the "Nannie" to whom he had written many of his letters from the bush. For Cravath, it was imperative that she endorse the singers' campaign to build a hall in her father's memory, and he endeavored to put his best foot forward, bringing with him only the infinitely decorous and pious Ella Sheppard to represent the troupe. Mrs. Bruce showed them several of her father's books "with presentation notes written in his own writing to her, also many notes &c. belonging to Henry Stanley," and "his card, which was found in Dr. L's trunk, showing that Stanley really did meet him. We were shown L.'s cap, the last he probably wore." Mrs. Bruce presented them with portraits of herself and her father and Livingstone's personal autograph, which Edmund Havell was to include somehow in the singers' portrait. "Our visit was one of the pleasantest I shall ever have in this life, perfectly enjoyable &

one which I consider more of an honor than though if I had been enter-tained by Her Majesty at court."[2]

On November 22, the Jubilees proceeded across the North Channel to Ireland. "The lower classes of the Irish only bear resemblance to our Amer-ican emigrants from this country," Robinson observed. "You would not recognize the real ladies and gentlemen as being allied to this nation."[3] Ma-bel Lewis supposed that their coming had been advertised, for "people were up in trees and anywhere they could hang out. When we got to the hotel, the proprietor had to take the hose to drive the crowd away."[4] At their first concert, Sheppard reported, "fifteen hundred applicants for tick-ets were turned away."[5] Lewis remembered that "there were two long blocks of people who could not get into the Hall, waiting to get in. And then the people would cry when they heard us sing."[6] A lady complained to Georgia, "We cannot get in. What shall we do, dear?" Georgia replied, "Come back tomorrow night."

In Dublin, their audience packed the Round Room of the city's enor-mous Rotunda. Fully half an hour before the concert, there was standing room only, and people stuck in the back rows began to surge forward, "causing much confusion." Loudin stepped up to say how surprised the Ju-bilees were by their reception in Ireland and reckoned that the Irish "on the other side of the water" were not a "true representation or true ideal of the manliness of the Irish heart." To the audience's delighted applause, he suggested that after hearing them sing the audience would see that "with, perhaps, the slight difference of the texture of their hair or the colour of their skin . . . they were just like other people."[7]

Riding a wave of indignation over a British admiralty order not to in-terfere with slave ships, Loudin performed "The Standard of the Free," a poem protesting the order set to music by Seward. "It has had great accep-tance," Robinson reported.[8] Jennie Jackson performed Stephen Foster's "Swanee River," which one critic called "a melody of the truly negro type," and the Jubilees led the audience in a rendition of "Rule, Britannia." "A few hissed," Sheppard recalled, "then the entire building fairly shook . . . with applause & some called out, 'Fenians! Fenians!' "[9] But it was still the spiri-tuals that moved the Irish most. The *Irish Times* said that quite apart from the fact that they were relics of slavery, some of the Jubilees' hymns were "really the finest to be found."[10]

On their return to England in early December, the Jubilees were invited again to visit their old friend Gladstone. Now almost sixty-six years old, he had submitted his resignation to a much-relieved Queen Victoria, handed over the reins to his old nemesis Disraeli, sold his home at 11 Carlton House Terrace, and, to settle his debts, disposed of most of its furnishings. Temporarily disengaged from politics, the old hawk was spending more and more of his time now at his vast Hawarden Castle estate near Lancaster, where, when he was not chopping down trees and addressing a daily tidal wave of correspondence, he spent his time unpacking what remained of his London library and happily arraying it along his shelves.

The Gladstones had intended to meet the Jubilees at the station, but "it snowed & the wind was very chill," wrote Sheppard. "Mrs. [Gladstone] poured out a glass of wine for us soon after our arrival & when told that we were all teetotalers, she exclaimed, 'What, in this cold weather?'" Catherine Glynne Gladstone struck Sheppard as "very sweet, much like a child." But the visit began on an unfortunate note when she handed Loudin one of her son's wedding presents to inspect: an open-faced chatelaine watch that was "a mass of diamonds & emeralds &c. Mr. Loudin unfortunately let the watch fall to the floor & broke the crystal to pieces." Mrs. Gladstone apparently took the accident in stride, but Loudin was shaken. "Poor man," Sheppard wrote. "We deeply felt his embarrassment."

Gladstone himself emerged from his study to join them for luncheon. "Mr. & Mrs. Gladstone at first sat down with me," Sheppard reported, "but afterward they arose & instead of having the servants do the waiting they did it themselves & had the servants stand back except when some waste dish or such needed to be removed. Then when all help was unnecessary they sat down again & took tea with us & the gentlemen . . . did most of the waiting. This was a very special honor indeed, one that we shall long be proud to remember. What hath God wrought?"

After tea, the Jubilees assembled in the drawing room and sang "I've Been Redeemed" and "The Bells," and Loudin performed "The Standard of the Free." "While we sang, [Gladstone] kept time with his whole body sometimes," wrote Sheppard:

When Mr. Loudin sang his solo, the honorable gentleman stood like a statue & when he had finished, Mr. [Gladstone] turned off a moment to collect himself.

. . . When he turned round he said, with tears in his eyes, "That song is *thrilling* & will *stir the heart of England*."

All was silent for a moment, and then came "John [Brown]" after which he replied, "No song can equal that one" & Mrs. [Gladstone] said "I have prayed *God* to *spare me* long enough to *hear that song* again and now my prayer is *answered*. I do so thank you."

The two remarks were worth all the strength & effort spent to accept their invitation.

Afterward, Gladstone boyishly displayed his collection of axes. "Odd sort of pet," thought Sheppard, "these axes." But Gladstone's favorite amusement was cutting down trees. "His estate affords ample scope," she reckoned, ". . . as it cover some nine thousand acres."

As the Jubilees departed, Mrs. Gladstone handed each of them a flower. When one of them thanked Gladstone for his kindness, he said he hoped it would help break down American prejudice. "The Lord sometimes uses very humble means," he said, "for the accomplishment of this grand purpose."

Word of the singers' visit to the Gladstones must have circulated widely by the end of the day, for their concert that evening in the "very small stiff old town" of Chester was "a perfect jam." When they sang "Rule, Britannia," "many gentlemen, even in the gallery, arose & bared their heads just as is customary when 'God Save the Queen' is sung."

On the morning of December 8, the troupe performed near Kendal at the Royal Asylum for the Idiotic, whose young inmates were the "saddest sight" Sheppard ever saw.

> While we sang it was interesting to notice how music affected them. Some began to cry. Others laughed. Some sat gazing at us with rapt attention, evidently taking in every note while others gazed as they did, not taking in anything we were doing. Others cast glances all around as if in search of the sound & [were] quiet only when we were quiet. One little girl jumped down from her seat & ran laughing down the aisle til caught by the nurse. Only two had to be taken from the room.

When their director told them to applaud, "some understood, but others had to be shown how. Once started they were hard to stop." Two of the boys were microcephalic "with heads like a bird, more something like the bill of a bird. . . . My heart was so full as I gazed," wrote Sheppard. "I thanked God that he had not made me so."[11]

The singers improvised a stateside Christmas at Stockton-on-Tees. Sheppard sent a present of five pounds to Mr. White, who was spending "a lonely Christmas in London." Susan Gilbert assembled a yuletide feast of "the choicest meats & pastry & ice cream," and after dinner, Cravath announced that by New Year's he expected the troupe to have raised some twenty thousand dollars and to have cleared sixty thousand dollars by the following July. Sheppard "was astonished we had done so well, for at the beginning of the year we were so far behind." They had "a delightful meeting," though two singers, probably Porter and Jackson, sat out the festivities in their rooms. "It does seem," sighed Sheppard, "that the absence of trouble is *absolutely impossible* with us."[12]

It could hardly have been otherwise. The managers were working the Jubilees like horses. Touring the small towns of nineteenth-century Britain involved riding on rattling trains through whose windows and doors cinders blew. It meant waiting in unheated stations; walking through unpaved, muddy streets; singing without amplification in vast halls and drafty churches; sleeping on damp beds in country hotels whose fare was coarse and meager. It meant keeping up the standard of their reputation in performances that demanded such physical, intellectual, and psychological exertion that they often left the stage drenched in perspiration. To prove the intelligence, dignity, and educability of the American freedman, they were to behave all the while with impeccable decorum.

That White and the rest of their managers shared in their privations and held their mission to be holy only seemed to deepen the singers' dilemma. If they complained, White could accuse them of selfishness, for look what he himself had sacrificed for the good of their race. To protest was to let down a sacred cause. They were constantly reminded that the hardships of touring were trivial compared with the slavery and poverty from which they had emerged or the danger and deprivation in which their people still toiled back home. The engine that dragged them so relentlessly from town to town was monetary: the need to raise enough funds to keep the A.M.A. afloat, not to mention pay, feed, transport, and shelter the Jubilees themselves. It all combined with the paternalism of their managers to make the singers ripe for a peculiarly insidious brand of exploitation.

The strain of singing and conducting before such diverse crowds shattered Sheppard's nerves. Night after night she was unable to sleep. The doctors she consulted at various stops all told her she had no chance of recovery without absolute rest, but their various regimens were "laughable. Dr. H. said, 'Stay on your feet all the time if possible & work off the nervousness.' Dr. [Embleton] said 'Lie down just as much as possible, use the back very little & don't even take much usual exercise.'"[13]

With Ella "feeling wretched" and Georgia and Jennie often too ill to perform, White sent for Maggie Carnes. "I am sorry to have to break into your choir again," he wrote Spence, "but there is a good deal at stake for the University and our work must not be allowed to fail." Sheppard was "not strong," he reported, and "it is thought best for her to stop singing— and as the weather is very trying we think it quite necessary to strengthen the sopranos."[14]

All that fall, as the workmen put the finishing touches on Jubilee Hall, Adam Spence would drive out from his quarters in the barracks and gaze fearfully at the new building's grand roof and vaunting tower. "We feel a good deal of doubt if the fineness of our building pleases the Lord," he wrote his mother. "We all think it a mistake."[15] But back in England, Cravath was fed up with the delays and embarrassed by the British public's continuing inquiries about a building it had every right to believe was already up and running. He commanded Spence to occupy Jubilee Hall by the end of the year and dedicate it on New Year's Day, 1876, less than a week shy of Fisk's tenth anniversary.

When the staff and students moved into the hall in late December, the structure was still not finished, Matson recalled, and "our first supper was in the basement . . . off the workman's bench. The house was full of friends and guests of the North, as well as former teachers and friends of the university, working in other places in the South."[16] On January 1, as the Jubilees performed far away in Newcastle, England, General Clinton Bowen Fisk himself presided with expansive charm over the dedication of the building the singers had literally sung into existence. At one point, after asking all those who wanted to attend the primary school to come forward, Fisk "marched promptly to the place, toed the line like a little child with his arms hanging by his side and his head meekly inclined forward" as if he wanted "to join the primary school, a thing he had not had the privilege of doing when he was a poor, fatherless boy in Michigan."[17]

It was a banner day for Fisk University. The band of the Sixteenth Col-ored Infantry played as one-armed General Oliver Otis Howard of the de-funct Freedmen's Bureau marched to the dais.[18] Letters were read from Dwight Lyman Moody and future president James A. Garfield. Gustavus Pike, whom Clinton Fisk would describe as having grown "more *African* from day to day," returned from England for the occasion and in his re-marks urged Fisk's graduates to go to Africa.[19] "Tropical Africa has been re-served for the black man," he told them. "God made the country for him and him for the country. Its riches are for him. Its future civilization must be developed by him. . . . So let Fisk University be the grand missionary college of the South for the promotion of African evangelism."[20]

Whether or not Pike meant to imply that America had been "reserved" for the white man, his remarks became a feature of the Jubilees' circulars, proof that Fisk was prepared to share Britain's evangelical burden in Africa. Spence had already established a Society for the Evangelization of Africa, and in the students' mail that year would tumble a heap of tracts about African missions, distributed by the A.M.A.[21] The cause of Africa became so pervasive that, back in Nashville, Henrietta Matson thought that even the African mahogany paneling in the front entrance of Jubilee Hall "seemed to speak to us of the mission to which the school was called."[22]

One attendee at the dedication was as impressed with the "gentle ways and pleasing manners" of Fisk's students as with its new building:

[I] saw . . . how the Gospel, and mental culture elevated them—made them ladies and gentlemen. I saw again, as often before, and long ago as well as later—how the Musical faculty was largely be-stowed upon them. I considered the . . . courage of their race, along with their patience and forbearance under injuries, and I sighed to think how the South might rise from depression and decay if its elite would cherish this portion of their people instead of despising and casting them out:—if they would employ better common weal this mighty force close at hand every where like the coal that fills their mounds . . . instead of scorning and rejecting it![23]

Meeting together "amid the noise of . . . carpenters, painters and plumbers," Fisk's faculty and students prayed that "the same sense of His presence that had so graciously and so continually been worshipped in the old barrack buildings" would likewise suffuse Jubilee Hall. It apparently did. Soon after the dedication another revival swept furiously through halls still smelling of sawdust, wet plaster, and shellac. "The students prayed so much in their rooms," one told Matson, "it troubled me." They exulted in the midst of classes and prayer meetings, testifying with such ardor that classes "were practically suspended for two weeks. 'Blessed interruptions!'" Matson exclaimed. "Even the Angels in Heaven could pause in their ministrations to rejoice over one sinner that repenteth." The revival was like a divine consecration. "How beautiful Jubilee Hall was to our eyes!" a once dubious Matson now exulted. "A God-given gift to the university."[24]

In arguing for Jubilee Hall, Cravath had insisted that "the colored people would be glad on account of the uses to which it would be put—the Southern white people would give it more respect than [they] would a mean building; and every cultured person of whatever sort would enjoy it for its symmetrical proportion and harmonious architecture."[25] But the dedication did not quiet those in the African American community who had come to see Fisk as just another of the A.M.A.'s "Southern plantations," an outpost of Northern white arrogance and racism. Suspicions ran so high that a rumor circulated that Fisk's trustees could not possibly intend to devote such a grand building as Jubilee Hall to black education but planned eventually to turn it over to whites.

In part to put such rumors to rest, Spence hired James Burrus, his protégé and America Robinson's fiancé, to teach mathematics. One black paper, the *True Republican*, had attacked Fisk "for being too exclusively white in our corps of teachers and trustees." Spence hoped Burrus's appointment would "please the colored people who have found so much fault because we are white," though he thought "such men will [always] have something to grumble about."[26] They were not the only grumblers. One of his own staff proclaimed the hall and the enormous amount of money it took to build it as "one of the most wicked things I have ever known."[27]

The hall's turret, from which fluttered both American and British flags, was meant to symbolize the educational beacon Fisk intended to become, but it also had a more practical utility. For years, it would serve as a watchtower where Fiskites took turns as armed sentries, scanning the countryside for the white arsonists who would eventually burn down and threaten to burn down scores of other black schools and churches throughout Nashville, Tennessee, and the South: so many that within a year the Continental Insurance Company of New York would cancel all its policies on A.M.A. schools.[28]

At their quarters in Leeds on the other side of the Atlantic, the Jubilees marked the dedication of Jubilee Hall by sending a telegram to Fisk. "British friends & Jubilee Singers send greetings," it said. "Hitherto hath the Lord helped us. May Fisk University be inspiration to struggling humanity in America. Light to Africa's millions. May Great Britain & America ever thus work to extend Christ's kingdom." Within a few hours, Fisk telegraphed back: "All hail, and thanks for the friends in this country & in the land of Wilberforce & Sharpe. We own what God hath wrought. May the two flags floating today over Jubilee Hall ever symbolize the united purpose of both countries to elevate the freedmen of America that they may carry light to Africa."

By now, Sheppard's condition so alarmed Susan Gilbert that she sent her off to London to recuperate. For Sheppard, her departure was like a defeat; in more than four years of touring, it marked her "first rest or departure from the class & it may be my last for my strength seems all going." Over the coming weeks, she would undergo a regimen that included doses of hyposulfite of soda, enemas, and salt baths, as the singers concertized in Huddersfield, Bradford, Duncaster, York, Sheffield, Manchester. On January 26, Maggie Carnes joined the troupe to replace Ella Sheppard's soprano in the ensemble.

The implication of Carnes's arrival was not lost on Frederick Loudin. Rather than allow Sheppard to rest long enough to recover her voice, the managers had simply shipped in a replacement. Sheppard was apparently to be retained because she could continue to function as an assistant choir director. But what, Loudin wondered, would become of less central members of the Jubilee cast when their voices gave out?

Desperate to pack as many appearances into the Jubilees' schedule as he possibly could, Cravath tried to change the terms of their employment. He dismissed the previous summer's tour as "light concert work" and attempted to factor in daily downtime between rehearsals and concerts as part of their vacation time. But Loudin dug in his heels, insisting that if the Jubilees were to be compelled to sing through their vacation time, they should be paid extra.

Cravath called him a mercenary who had lost sight of the Jubilees' missionary purpose. Probably thinking he could isolate Loudin, Cravath demanded that every singer write a letter on the subject. Loudin was the first to oblige, reminding Cravath of the terms of his contract and repeating White's promise of two months' vacation in comfortable summer quarters at the troupe's expense or four months' lightened schedule.

"Would Miss Gilbert, you or any teacher in the employ of the A.M.A.," Loudin asked, "consider they were having vacation if they were compelled to work two or three hours a day? . . . I am sure not. . . . The managers have only thought of how much you could get out of the singers," he told Cravath, "rather than how much we can endure without injury."

Why was it, he asked, that most vocalists could sing ten, twenty, even thirty years without breaking down while within one to five years the Jubilees fell by the wayside? It was true that they were compelled to sing from eighteen to twenty pieces a night, but "the singing is so divided as to compel no one to sing on the outside more than six to ten pieces at the extreme." So why was it that the Jubilees were so feeble?

After a rundown of their breakneck schedule, Loudin said he had not complained at the time, "for it seemed plain to me that success could not be attained in any other way." But now that success had "followed the sacrifice of rest," he believed they should be rewarded for it. "This I think is but fair and right." Carnes's arrival demonstrated to him that, as the singers broke down, they were to be "shelved or turned out to die":

Three years killed Mr Holmes and but for a miracle would have killed Mr White. Three years broke down Dickerson, but *rest* restored his voice. A less time broke down [Mabel] Lewis. Rest has built her up again. Ella is quite gone. Jennie Jackson is failing as all can see. . . . Still you seem determined to drive ahead as if we were all superhuman and in fact as we are killed, you put in a new one, while one of the managers rests while another keeps us a going until another takes his or her place. I know you will say this is a hard saying but I feel that the facts will verify what I have said. No one feels more the . . . *great* need of diligent work than I. I realize most keenly to my own sorrow the . . . great necessity there is for accomplishing the greatest amount of good work in the shortest possible space of time. But I realize that I owe a duty to myself which forbids that I should break myself down in two or three years when with a *reasonable* amount of work I might last much longer. . . .

Respectfully yours for the right,

F. J. Loudin[29]

If Cravath hoped to marginalize Loudin, it did not work. "Miss Gilbert," Georgia Gordon wrote, "I don't know how you and the managers count the days and weeks of our rest. So far as I can remember we had a few days rest in Builth, likewise in Edinburgh, wether this makes one month's rest I have not yet decided but we can decide this when we have our talk." In any case, it only counted as "last year's rest."[30] Maggie Porter also counted only a month's rest over the previous year. "Mrs Gilbert," she wrote, "if I do not understand what *two* months rest means I am willing to be set right, but *29* days is all the actual rest I can account for. . . . When Mrs White & the managers were in darkness, they came to us and we gave up our rest, worked day and night" with Moody and Sankey. Porter believed that if White were alerted to Cravath's attempt to shorten their rest time he would object. "I am sure he will speak," she said. "I am sure I am in need of *rest*. It tells [in] the loss of sleep & I think in my voice."[31]

An ailing Jennie Jackson wrote:

My dear friends, . . . I don't see why you ask this of us, to write out about our rest, [when the managers] all know just what we need. . . . We have had but a month and if you call that just then we dont agree. I am sure Mr White knows what we have had and he will say what is right and I know you will all do what is right. . . . If we had enough rest in the summer . . . we should not have been so [mercenary] and you all know we are not in as good trim as we would be if we had a rest of three months. . . . I dont see why you have not settled this among you when you know as much about it as we do.[32]

"I do not call the work which we did last summer—'light-concert work,' " Rutling declared. "We have sung *every* summer; never did we call for pay before. I think we (the singers) have *given* as much work as *any one*, connected with the work. I think we should have something. I am *not satisfied* and have not been. I will say nothing about the past or present—But— shall trust *you* to do the *right thing*."[33]

In the face of such startling unanimity, and at the urging of White and Gilbert, an exasperated Cravath gave in and arranged for a two-month vacation in Geneva, Switzerland, but not until he had led the troupe on a grueling, breakneck tour of the Manchester and Liverpool area, through dismal rain and hail storms. In April, they were joined by one of Fisk's founders, the good-humored Edward Parmelee Smith, who had moved with Clinton Fisk from the freedmen field to the Indian Commission, where he met "merciless opposition" from "designing men who sought to profit at the expense of the Indians." After a stint as president of Howard University, Smith was now "on his way to Africa," Sheppard was told after her return from London, "to investigate & find a place for another missionary station in West Africa." His lecture to the Jubilees on Africa was "exceedingly interesting. I almost wished I was going as a *Christian Missionary*," Sheppard lamented. "My heart goes out to Africa." But Smith's example would prove less inspirational than cautionary. Upon his arrival three weeks later at the Cape of Good Hope in South Africa, he died of a shipboard fever.[34]

The Miss Gilbert to whom Porter and Jackson had written was not to remain a Miss Gilbert much longer. Over the course of their long tours, Susan Gilbert and the ailing widower George White had arrived at an understanding. In April 1876, they were married at Wolverhampton, where White had been recuperating from his consumptive fits.[35] White's courage, suffering, and muscular faith had endeared him to Gilbert, and he found much to admire in her as well. A tall, gracious New Yorker with a "quiet, loving spirit," she was one of the A.M.A.'s ablest toilers. As a missionary at Beaufort and Wilmington, she had been one of the very few female principals in the association's hierarchy and before joining White on the Jubilees' second tour had served as the venerable George Whipple's secretary in New York.

Susan Gilbert would be "our mother during all the seven years through which we labored for Fisk University," Sheppard later recalled. She "kept the home idea among us and was the embodiment of Christian culture and refinement, an ever-present reminder of and inspiration to high and noble attainments, so necessary to protect and hold us while in public life as we, inexperienced and unprepared, were whirled through such exceptional social recognition."[36] Her greatest challenge was Maggie Porter. The lead soprano in a troupe whose arrangements often featured soprano solos, Porter knew what she was worth to White and the managers and was not above throwing her weight around as prima donna, alienating Gilbert and many of her fellow singers with her boasts and airs and fits of temper.

Ella Sheppard was devoted to Susan Gilbert. It was to "Gibbie's" room that she retreated from the "fuss" of the choir, sitting and sewing and reading histories of the people of Israel and the inspirational novels of Dinah Maria Mulock Craik. Her visits were the source of some jealousy on the part of the other singers, and yet Sheppard believed herself somehow unworthy of Gilbert's friendship and was always startled by Gilbert's displays of affection. Gilbert donned a gown of brown silk and married White at the registrar's office before repeating the ceremony for the benefit of the late-arriving troupe. Before leaving for London the next day with his new bride, Sheppard reported, "White expressed their united appreciation of our endeavor to make their occasion a pleasant one & the gifts, he said, would ever be pleasant reminders of our love & esteem."

On the Jubilees' return to London in late April, they sang again at Willis's Rooms. Lord Shaftesbury presided once more, though apparently in one of his periodic funks, for he seemed to Sheppard "troubled or absent-minded." Twenty-eight-year-old princess Louise attended with her in-laws, the duke and duchess of Argyll, who, as they had after the singers' London debut three years before, invited them to an aristocratic gathering at Argyll Lodge that lacked, this time, the queen of England.

At another "drawing room meeting" on May 8, they encountered Dr. Robert Moffat, Livingstone's father-in-law, who told Sheppard stories of his experiences as a Congregationalist missionary in Africa. Hoping he might inspire the Jubilees to follow him to Africa, Moffat recounted a Sabbath he had spent in a Dutch settlement with a slaveholder. Moffat asked if he could preach to the man's slaves, "but the master in a rage said, 'Did you come to preach to dogs?' " Moffat discarded the text he had chosen for his sermon and selected Mark 7:28 instead: "Yet the dogs [under the table] eat of the [children's] crumbs," whereupon the slaveholder suddenly arose and told his son "to go to the hills & bring every slave to the service at once." At least one of the Jubilees was immune to Moffat's inducements: Maggie Porter, whose father had gone off to Liberia just before the Civil War and was never heard from again.

On May 12, Sheppard was almost as honored to visit the home of one of her favorite authors, Dinah Maria Mulock, now fifty and married to a publisher named Craik. "Mrs. Craik was taller than I am & just such a figure as Georgia Gordon," Sheppard wrote. "Has gray hair, soft blue eyes & pretty features somewhat spoiled," she thought, by "a mustache as heavy as an Englishman of twenty or twenty-two years. . . . She seemed pleased that I had read most of her works," wrote Sheppard.

"And did you really know of me," asked Mrs. Craik, "and wish to see me? I thought I was alone in hoping for that pleasure."

> She said she was one day visiting Crystal Palace & while walking around she noticed one of our posters. She read it & wondered who we were or if we were *real* emancipated slaves. . . . The more she read the more interested she became until finally she made up her mind to attend. . . . When we entered the stage & had sung "Steal Away" & "The Lord's Prayer" she felt such a feeling come over her of inexpressible joy & surprise that the tears rushed to her eyes & she wept like a child. . . . She said the feeling was perfectly divine. . . . She thought she would come to speak to us but the thought struck her that she would be an intruder & that we would not likely wish to see her.

Sheppard was not merely touched but astonished and humbled by Mrs. Craik's praise:

> As I remember that concert, it was one of our poorest. Somehow this fact came over me when she was speaking & a sadness came over me with the pleasure. To think that in our audience was such a noble woman weeping with sympathy & thinking she was inferior to us in some respect so that she felt an intruder. To think of this along with the fact that at that moment we sang carelessly, indifferent to our mission, made me long for such an outpouring of His spirit that we would turn to use the talents & opportunities more worthily.

A few days later, the Jubilees heard Christine Nilsson perform under the baton of Arthur Sullivan and rode in carriages through Hyde Park. "I never saw a more beautiful & grand sight than these crowded avenues five coaches abreast," Sheppard wrote, "and such elegant coaches of every description with their gaudily dressed occupants & liveried servants. We saw no less than ten or twelve royal carriages." But she was "surprised to see so few handsome faces." Several parties recognized them and bowed to them, but here and there passengers laughed at the sight of the Jubilees. "Why, I don't know, for no two carriages of ours were together. Possibly," she surmised, "they were Americans."[37]

Everyone from the managers to the Jubilees' friends back home worried that all the attention was turning their heads. Pike was concerned that the singers could never "come down" from the heights they had attained. Burrus continued to fret that Robinson might be on the verge of renouncing her citizenship and abandoning her stateside friends. "You said I seem to hold the American below par," she replied with her usual angularity. "Not at all, except those who consider me so. You quoted Cicero 'Old Friends Before New.' So think I. But I take special care to see who my old friends are. I am sorry to say I have few among the American whites." In subsequent letters, she continued to needle her earnest intended by signing herself as "Her Majesty's subject."

Back in America, Burrus toured the South in search of students for Fisk, did his best to evade Klan patrols, lived on dried beef and potatoes, forbore the microscopic scrutiny of his white colleagues. It must have seemed as if his fiancée were writing from another planet. But for all her accounts of teas and tours, Robinson's letters contained more and more frequent reports of acrimony among the exhausted troupe. First there was strife among Thomas Rutling, Hinton Alexander, and Edmund Watkins. "The Jubes are talking at a terrible rate," she had reported in February. "They commenced with love and are now talking about school boy fights."[38] Then it seemed to spread to the women. Georgia Gordon demanded she be allowed to go home and complete her education; Julia Jackson announced she would not sing another year; Mabel Lewis's nerves were shot; and then there was the case of Maggie Porter.

"We have never grown haughty," Georgia Gordon would write of the Jubilees long after they had disbanded.[39] She must have smiled a little as she wrote it, or momentarily blocked her memories of Maggie Porter. Porter was perhaps the haughtiest of all the original singers. Vain and sharp-tongued, but also brave, audacious, and with a wicked sense of the ridiculous, she possessed the troupe's strongest and most durable soprano.

By the spring of 1876, the Jubilees' temperamental prima donna had worn out not only White and Cravath but the singers themselves. "They say in the class that she has every year grown worse and worse," wrote Robinson, "till now she has come to think herself the ruling power of the class.

. . . It matters not where we are, . . . she says the most cutting and uncalled for things." One night in London, Porter finally broke with her last friend among the Jubilees, her hitherto loyal "shadow," Jennie Jackson.

"We had come home from the concert, and had all gone to bed when we were aroused—those of us who roomed below them—by a terrible rumbling and noise," Robinson recalled.

> Presently some[thing] went down with a crash, then we heard fierce and angry voices. . . . Oh you do not know how we felt when we knew that it was two of our own number engaged so disgracefully—Mrs White and some of us rushed upstairs—Mrs White was long in quelling the disturbance, [and] slept in the drawing room all night. It was occasioned by Jennie's refusing ventilation while Maggie stood out for it. Mr Cravath had them up and they swore they would never room together another year. Maggie sent in her resignation and behaved in a most haughty and insolent manner. All the Singers were most indignant over her behavior and lack of repentance—we were indeed shocked.[40]

"I never felt such a *disgust* in my heart for anything human as I feel toward those two girls," fumed Sheppard. "To think of their acting so shamefully after all the advantages they have had for the past four years."

The next day, the battle raged on, even onto the backstage of Lewisham Chapel, where Ella Sheppard had to stand in the hallway outside their dressing room trying to drown out the sound of arguing by chatting with their English friends at the top of her voice.

> Good old Dr. Moffatt & family were present. The contrast between that good old man who had given 60 years of his life in toil & sacrifice for the Africans & we who can't sacrifice a *moment's* rest or forbearance for our own people was so great I could have wept my life away for shame.

Desperate to find reinforcements for his wavering Jubilees, White left his new bride in London and set sail for America to spend a month in Nashville training new voices for the troupe. It thus fell to Susan White to contend with the bickering troupe. "Her nerves are all unstrung from anxiety & loss of rest," Sheppard reported. "I begged her to go to bed which she did. She seemed content to do so now that I had come." And yet Sheppard could still not believe that Mrs. White regarded her as her friend. "I sometimes think it strange," she wrote, "that God should crowd so many blessings on worthless & unlovable me."[41]

Georgia Gordon agreed to hold off on her own departure and give White six months to find and drill her replacement. But Mabel Lewis was growing weaker and weaker, and even the robust Robinson, whose voice seemed invulnerable to colds and fevers, was considering leaving the troupe to study in Germany.

Meanwhile, the Jubilees' tour continued. In a week that had them singing at least once every day, they performed at the enormous Dome at Brighton, where the mayor introduced them, commending to the audience's "favourable consideration the self-abnegation displayed by the singers." A local paper thought their spirituals sounded Scottish. Dickerson stood up and pitched *The Jubilee Singers and Their Campaign for Twenty Thousand Dollars*, reminding the audience that the more copies they bought the sooner Livingstone Missionary Hall would be ready for them to visit. (The singers had been obliged to autograph copies of the book: Cravath paid America Robinson a guinea for writing her signature 160 times.)[42]

With only four concerts to go before they were to depart for Geneva and their long-overdue vacation, the strain of touring claimed another Jubilee. Thin, tense, pious, Julia Jackson had never been the hardiest singer in the troupe. But subsisting on her friendship with America Robinson and their daily immersions in scripture, she had managed to carry her own weight through three years of touring. On Saturday, June 17, the troupe traveled to Norwich to complete a series of concerts in the northeast of England and arrived at their hotel just in time for supper. In the middle of their meal, Julia Jackson got up from the table complaining of a headache and staggered off to her room. Four o'clock the next morning, she was found lying across her bed, unable to move.

"We went in and tried to put her in bed, but could not as she was suffering from such severe pains that she could not let us touch her," Robinson reported.

Meanwhile, she kept asking for her other foot. We smiled thinking it was the uncomfortable position in which she lay. I caught hold of her foot and ruffed it, but she said she could not feel my touch at all.

It never entered our minds that such a dreadful thing as paralysis had taken hold upon her, but it was even so. She had a severe and sudden paralytic stroke which has left one whole side of her powerless. . . . The doctor has very faint hope of her entire recovery. He says that she may be paralyzed for life. . . . She is very patient and says she has great comfort in knowing that she rests safely in the love of Jesus.[43]

SWEET CANAAN

SWITZERLAND AND HOLLAND

JUNE 1876–FEBRUARY 1877

In late June, the Jubilees left Julia Jackson under Georgia Gordon's care in England and limped off to Geneva, Switzerland, for a two-month vacation. "We are all longing for a rest," sighed Robinson, "for we are very tired, all."[1] The impetus to choose Geneva instead of some English watering place for their vacation may have come from the singers themselves but more likely from the managers, as it would conveniently separate the Jubilees from their English friends, who might stir up discontent with their advice and inquiries about the singers' education, treatment, and prospects. If so, isolating the singers from their English-speaking public would eventually backfire, for in their isolation they had only themselves to turn to at a time when they were already—most of them—heartily sick of each other's company.[2]

On June 28, they took the steamer *Lord Cardigan* from Grimsby to Rotterdam and proceeded to Cologne and Mainz, where they lingered long enough to catch a glimpse of seventy-nine-year-old Kaiser Wilhelm I of Germany passing to and fro in his carriage. The most powerful autocrat in all of Europe caught a glimpse of them, too, swiveling around in his carriage to leer at Jennie Jackson as she peered at him through her hotel window. Sheppard was moved by the emperor's guardsmen as they lined the streets for his passing. "Some of the officers were most beautifully developed in form," she sighed, "and as their uniforms fitted close they were seen to advantage."[3] Robinson wished Burrus could have seen the German officers. "They are the finest and best looking men in the world."[4] Sheppard seemed especially impressed by German feet. "Every one of the officers had beautiful feet & wore their boots to fit like wax. Most of the soldiers & indeed almost everybody we saw had pretty feet & wore boots. It seemed like being at home. The English or British people have such large feet," she said, "and wear ugly shoes." The hotel's string quartet tried to honor the Jubilees and America's upcoming centennial by playing "Yankee Doodle" and "Hail, Columbia." But Sheppard regretted that they should play such ditties on the Sabbath and "felt as though I was insulting my maker by listening to it."

Three days later, they arrived at last in Geneva to find the Stars and Stripes fluttering from the hotel roofs and windows. A fifteen-minute carriage ride brought them to their summer home, Le Campagne d'Asters, a "clean white house" set on a broad, shady lawn.[5] After the demolition of the city's medieval fortifications in 1849, Geneva grew pell-mell along the southwestern extremity of its namesake lake. For twenty-three years, John Calvin himself had ruled Geneva as a theocracy, burning rival thinkers at the stake, and his influence remained so great that "Genevan" and "Calvinist" had become synonymous. One legacy of the city's Calvinism was the dreariness of even its grandest architecture. But the lake was lovely, and its summer weather cool and dry. For the next few weeks, the singers passed the centennial of the American Republic amid Swiss market gardens, orchards, and vineyards. But it appeared the vacation had come too late not only for Julia Jackson but for Mabel Lewis as well. "Everyone remarks on how bad she looks," Robinson said. "Mr Loudin thinks she will not live long. . . . She may yet live longer than any of us. But one thing I *know* and that is that this work has too much bang-about in it for Mabel."[6]

Back in Nashville, Spence had found White's presence such "a nervous matter: so many schemes and plans," that he was relieved when White departed at the beginning of June.[7] The school was not prospering financially, and Spence had sent his wife out on a fund-raising tour of her own that would soon raise the ire of the A.M.A., whose agents were competing with her for donors. The final push to complete Jubilee Hall had drained the school's finances. At the middle of June, Fisk was overdrawn by six hundred dollars, and the city was pressing Spence to clean out the old privies at the abandoned barracks. In September, Spence would have to turn off the gas in Jubilee Hall and revert to coal fires. When his wife begged for money to sustain her on her tour, Spence had to refuse.

"You must think me heartless," he wrote her. "It seems as if I was unwilling to give you money and leave you a beggar among strangers. It makes me sick at heart." But he reminded her "how much we dislike the spirit of speculation which [has so] pervaded this institution and has brought a fearful debt upon us. Let us avoid a like course."[8]

The A.M.A. itself was facing a deficit of twelve thousand dollars. "Appeals were made," reported the *American Missionary*, "and the responses in July gave hope of relief, but the receipts . . . are falling off. Our only hope of an even balance sheet for the year is that our receipts from all sources for September shall aggregate $20,000."[9]

As the feebler singers recuperated in Geneva, the others hiked and rowed and took French lessons from a Madame LuFund. George White returned to the Jubilees in July, and in late August rehearsals resumed. Loudin took advantage of the eight-week lull to travel to Italy with his able wife, Harriet, who had joined the Jubilees' retinue to help with the troupe's accounts and correspondence. Loudin returned unshaven from his Italian jaunt, "looking rather bearish." Maggie Porter grew ever more hostile and restless, loudly declaring her intention to return to London to launch a solo career. When rehearsals began, Mabel Lewis was still languishing, and Robinson found that the summer heat had drained away her strength.

Cravath returned to the United States to check on conditions at Fisk, while White and Seward worked with the troupe.[10] The Jubilees made a couple of appearances in Geneva, performing one Sabbath at a local church run by Americans. The audience seemed to enjoy their singing though it was hard to tell, for the church forbade applause.[11] Robinson was taken with the family of the minister, a New Englander named L. W. Bacon. They were "not at all like Americans," she said. "They are so sociable and kind to us." The Bacons invited Thomas Rutling and Hinton Alexander to their home to play on an American baseball team against a team of Swiss. One white man from Georgia "refused to play on the American side at first," Robinson reported, "but when the match came off he took his place as pitcher. Alexander was said to be the best player on the ground and knocked the furthiest balls." They beat the Swiss by seventeen points.

Invigorated by his voyages to and from America, liberated by Cravath's absence, and pacified by the calming influence of his new bride, White seemed unusually lighthearted that summer. He paid half the cost of some sketchbooks for Robinson, in which she drew castles and cathedrals. "Mr. White has been joking me today about you again," she wrote Burrus. "I was playing croquet and the Singers were out there so I did not turn my head, but my face felt dreadfully hot." But she did not care if White teased her, she said, for "I can work twice as well for knowing that you love me, James, and that my own heart is in such safe keeping."

By now White had the energy to face up to the Maggie Porter question. "She has treated Mr. White like a heathen," Robinson reported. "Indeed Mr. White says that if a white person had used the same language to him he would have slapped his or her face. . . . She has called the managers liars and fools in public." After conferring with the other singers, White decided at last to accept her resignation and send for a replacement: a junior at Fisk from Warren, Missouri, named Ella M. Hildridge.

His decision apparently called Porter's bluff. "She had no thought that she would ever be sent home," Robinson reported.

> She thought herself of so much consequence she evidently felt her importance more than others. It is very sad to see Maggie go home, but we have all breathed freer since we knew that we were to be rid of our tyrant. I hope that this sudden humbling [of] her pride and hauteur will do her good.

The morning of her departure, "No one was up to tell her good-bye save Mr and Mrs Loudin."

> Mr Loudin says she did not cry when she left although she felt most miserable. It was a great trial to her to leave the class I know. She endeavored to appear happy and careless but every day I saw traces of

tears around her eyes and there was such subduedness about her all the time. I did feel so bad for her, poor girl.

But the Jubilees were not to be rid of Maggie Porter so easily, nor was she about to go home.

Few Swiss had ever laid eyes on black people, and the Jubilee Singers' presence that summer tantalized Geneva society. Small crowds followed them in the streets, and children paused by their windows as they rehearsed. One afternoon, Robinson and Maggie Carnes had ducked out of the rain and into the lobby of the Hôtel des Bergues, where the porters were so excited by their arrival "you might have imagined a show on hand." Still, it was "rather lonely here at times," Robinson sighed. The Swiss were "friendly enough, but the great trouble is that we can not talk with them." Nevertheless, White was intrigued by the sensation his singers seemed to cause wherever they ventured, and moved by Genevans' faltering pleas to have the *esclaves nègres affranchis* perform in public. Cravath and the other managers had long flirted with the idea of taking the singers to Europe. At last White decided, with some trepidation, to test the universality of Negro spirituals before a non-English-speaking audience.

In the 1870s, Geneva was torn between a Radical government and the Roman Catholic Church. A rival denomination calling itself the Christian Catholic Church had absorbed a community of friars founded by Charles Loyson, an eloquent, truculent French ex-Carmelite better known as Père Hyacinthe. Father Hyacinthe had denounced the Napoleons and the popes as despots and rejected the principle of papal infallibility. For his pains, he had to flee France and was excommunicated by Rome in 1869. Hyacinthe believed that a priest should reconcile himself to his own human nature, for it was "only by tearing himself away from the traditions of a blind asceticism, and of a theocracy still more political than religious, that the priest will become once more a man and a citizen." In 1872, he deemed himself man enough to take an American wife.

In the summer of 1876, Père Hyacinthe was forty-nine years old and one of Geneva's most revered figures. He was the perfect luminary to host the Jubilees' experimental concert: though a Catholic, he was not a papist, a type the Jubilees and especially their managers deplored; and though a proponent of religious music, he did not understand a word of English.[12] Seward found Hyacinthe

> very genial and agreeable, and his American wife no less so. Madame acted as interpreter, and there was none of the stiffness or awkwardness that might have been expected under the circumstances. We were all greatly amused by his little boy of about four, who seemed puzzled but not at all frightened by the array of black faces. He was sitting on Mr. Watkins' lap, and when he thought there was no one looking, we saw him slyly rub his fingers against the back of Mr. Watkins' hand, and then look at them to see if the black came off.

Before the singers were allowed to perform, Seward had to submit his program to a board of censors in case it might include "any heresy, privy conspiracy, or otherwise incendiary influence that might . . . undermine the body politic."[13] On the evening of the Jubilees' first European concert, Geneva's large Salle de la Réformation was crowded to overflowing. Speaking in French, Hyacinthe called "the songs that were about to be sung . . . the sole literature of slavery that had survived its bloody extinction. A whole race of human beings," he said, "held in enforced darkness, forbidden to read or to write, shut out by brutal laws even from the joys of domestic affection, had found in these songs, that had been cherished in their unwritten traditions, the only solace of their bondage, the only outlet of the soul."[14]

As the Jubilees performed such *chants d'esclaves* as "Preserve-moi de la perdition" and "O frère vous preparez-vous?" the crowd's "enthusiasm rose to white heat."[15] A local English-language paper ascribed their warm reception more to their cause and story than their music, which it deemed "the crudest, not to say rudest."[16] The singers had also managed to upset the local censors. After they sang an encore that had not been cleared beforehand, they were "seriously threatened with a fine of a hundred francs, . . . and only escaped the penalty on the score of our lamentable ignorance."[17] But the concert earned them about fifteen hundred Swiss francs, and although the Genevans could not understand the language, Ella Sheppard observed to her astonishment that "they applauded, wept, or smiled at the same places as an English audience."[18] When White asked several Genevans through an interpreter how they could so enjoy the songs when they could not understand the words, "the answer was, 'We cannot understand them, but we can feel them.' "

"The success of this concert may have an important bearing on our future plans," Seward declared, for "if 'foreigners' find the same enjoyment in these simple songs that all English-speaking audiences have invariably done, it may mean that there are new worlds to conquer in the Continental countries."[19] Exclaimed Sheppard, "Dear, beautiful Switzerland!!!"[20]

At the beginning of September, the singers returned to England via Paris to resume their British concerts. "It does good to be in a country where our mother tongue is spoken," Sheppard wearily declared. "One feels like weeping for joy even though it greeted us with the inevitable rain which caused many of us to take wretched colds," including White, whose voice was now a whisper.[21]

Before commencing another chilly round of concerts, this time through Kent, the singers received a report on Julia Jackson. "Julia improves slowly," Robinson wrote.

> She can hobble around chairs. Once only has she taken two or three steps alone. She is able to put her lame hand into her pocket and thrust her thumb through her fingers all of which is very encouraging knowing how absolutely helpless she has been all along. Her removal will be by degrees. I think she will be taken to Edinburgh as that is the most cheerful place in Scotland.[22]

Pausing at Newport on the Isle of Wight on September 11, White received a distressing letter from an Englishman named Stone. On her return to London, Maggie Porter had approached Matthew Henry Hodder, the Jubilees' British publisher, and asked the whereabouts of Stone, who had once expressed an interest in helping Porter acquire an education. "Without waiting to be asked," reported Hodder, Stone "generously promised to help her pecuniarily and otherwise . . . to relieve her anxiety & in the belief that her object was a very laudable one." Porter had evidently bent his ear about the unfair treatment she had suffered, and now an indignant Stone lambasted White for "putting his heel into the neck of a 'poor lone girl' " and abandoning her to her fate. Stone demanded that the matter of Porter's banishment be put to the vote of the entire troupe and enclosed a letter from Porter that was "a combination of all that could possibly convey the impression that she had the same defiant spirit of evil & that she did not regret anything," according to Sheppard.

> The p.s. of her letter, expressing a hope that if she "had done anything to cause sorrow & trouble" to the class that we would forgive her, distinctly showed that she had read the letter to Mr. Stone & that he had reminded her that she had not said she was sorry or regretted the trouble she had caused.

When a distraught White asked the troupe to vote on Porter, everybody agreed to keep her away except Rutling, Watkins, and especially Loudin, who "blasted & bellowed so loudly," Sheppard reported, "that I would have left the room in disgust had not Mr. [White] stopped him." In the end, the three men abstained from an otherwise unanimous vote to keep Porter out of the troupe. "But somehow we feel she is going to cause us just as much trouble as possible," Sheppard predicted, and "that she has no intention of letting us forget her."[23]

At the end of the singers' tour of eastern England, Rutling was too sick to continue and retired for a while to the Jubilees' London lodgings in Upper Norwood. Ella Hildridge was proving too feeble to tour and had performed only once or twice since her arrival. But in other respects, the singers were thriving without Porter. One night in Glasgow, they performed "a little play just among the girls," Robinson reported.

> Maggie Carnes and I were the Troubadours—Georgia and Mabel were in white, short dresses and pink ribbons. . . . I cannot describe Jennie's costume. I laughed till I cried when she came in. . . . Her face was powdered. . . . We had jolly fun, we sang solos and acted and danced and did every thing funny we could think of.

They did not miss their derisive prima donna firing potshots from the sidelines. Porter had "become what I should call a professed beggar," sniffed Robinson, "instead of the boastful independent she has always prided herself that she was."[24] But as the British publisher of *The Singing Campaign for Ten Thousand Pounds*, Hodder stood to gain from the Jubilees' continued success and worried that if the Porter affair were noised about, it would turn the public against White and the troupe.[25] He therefore artfully conspired to deprive Porter of Stone's support and force her back into the choir.[26] It was apparently at Hodder's urging that she had offered to return, and now he convinced her that if she did not rejoin the Jubilees, no one in England would come to her assistance and that she needed to approach the managers in a spirit of true or at least more convincing contrition.

At the end of September, Porter traveled with Stone and Hodder to Glasgow and met with the troupe. "We are *at one* again," White exulted afterward. Porter had "made a full and satisfactory acknowledgment of her wrong & asked forgiveness. This was done both to the managers—and to the Company." White saw it as "evidence that God has this work in his keeping, and that He hears & answers prayer."[27]

Porter reported to Cravath that she was "to be again among them." Though she would no longer be lead soprano, she said, "I fancy . . . *that* is of little consequence."[28] The troupe did not, however, welcome her back, exactly. All of the girls except Mabel Lewis refused to room with her, and some threatened to leave the company if they were ordered to. "It was painful," Sheppard wrote, "to see how 'that girl' had made every one of the girls especially despise her. It was decided I should room with her," she groaned. "Lord help me."[29]

"She has seemed quite changed," Robinson conceded. "I believe the girl means to do what is right."[30] With Porter back on board, Georgia Gordon, influenced perhaps by Frederick Loudin, with whom she had grown infatuated, abandoned her plans to return to the United States. So White sent sickly Ella Hildridge home, urging Spence "to save Miss H. from embarrassment & make her return & stay at the school pleasant," as she was going back to Fisk "through no fault of hers," for he had been impressed by her "spirit & general deportment."[31]

By the middle of October, Rutling had recovered enough to rejoin the troupe as well and was "as mischievous as ever." At Edinburgh, the singers were often visited by Rutling's old pal Isaac Dickerson, who had broken his elbow and his wrist performing bicycle stunts for his classmates at the University of Edinburgh. "His bicycle seems very fatal to him, poor fellow."[32]

White was encouraged by the morale of his recuperated troupe. "The Singers are recovering from their colds and are all able to do duty & are singing remarkably well," he reported. "Georgia & Maggie Carnes have improved very much & also the tenors—Miss Lewis is not strong but is doing her work well," and Rutling was thrilling audiences with his solo in a new piece called "The Jubilee Anthem" written by a Glaswegian composer named James Merrylees in honor of Jubilee Hall and dedicated to the singers themselves.

Seward was still shaky, but White had to admit that his own health was pretty good, though he predicted that the upcoming fall weather would tell on his lungs. White asked Spence to make sure that his students wrote letters of thanks to their British donors, reporting on progress at Fisk. This was especially important because the Jubilees now had "to work under the burden of 'hard times.' " The depression that had afflicted America was making itself felt in Britain, and now that Serbia and Montenegro had declared war on the Ottoman Empire, there was a "sudden demand on the sympathy & liberality of the British people caused by the . . . consequent suffering in the East" that was working "much against our success."[33]

Back in Nashville, Erastus Milo Cravath spent only a couple of interrupted weeks at Fisk. At first, Adam Spence found him "exceedingly pleasant" and "so different from White." Enrollment was down to only eighty students, but Cravath was encouraged that a higher proportion of them were paid up than ever before. Cravath released funds to continue landscaping the campus for Jubilee Day, commemorating the day five years before when the troupe first set forth from Fisk to "sing the money out of the hearts and pockets of the people."

Spence deemed Cravath a spendthrift.[34] At Cravath's insistence, Spence printed a handbill announcing that Jubilee Hall's grounds were "now being fenced, graded, and laid out with walks and drives" and asking the university's friends to donate trees in their names at a dollar apiece. At a time when the school could not afford to heat its downstairs and the food was so bad that Spence forbade his visiting mother from partaking of it, the handbill declared that Fisk was "in a very prosperous condition in all respects."[35] Spence dreaded the day Cravath returned to Nashville to take the reins. "He is a good man and a strong man," Spence judged, "but his mind rather turns to business."[36]

In late October, the Jubilees left Glasgow, and Sheppard said goodbye to "Robert," the pious young man who used to stroll with her through the dingy streets handing out tracts to urchins and prostitutes. "I was awfully joked about 'Robert,'" she complained, "all the way . . . to Edinburgh," where they found Julia Jackson still barely able to walk.

Earlier in the year, the British Masons had announced their intention to allow people of color to form their own lodges, whereupon a consortium of Southern lodges sent a Colonel Hickman across the Atlantic to "reconcile the English people in their way of thinking," as Robinson put it.

On the morning of November 3, Jennie Jackson went down to the dining room of the Jubilees' Edinburgh hotel and encountered the colonel and his wife sitting down to breakfast. As Jackson approached, they "didn't conceal" that they were "much disgusted that she sat with them at table d'hôte."

Two days after his encounter with Jennie Jackson, the good colonel was dismayed to find himself sitting with the singers in church. "After worship, there was a second singing, a sort of sociable," wrote Sheppard.

> Colonel [Hickman] remained til after Maggie had sung & Loudin had sung "Flee as a Bird," &c. Then he disappeared. Afterward I saw he & wife standing on the upper landing of the stair near the coffee room. . . . As soon as they saw me [they] "sciddaddled" but soon after were seen behind the adjoining room door listening.

"Poor fools!" exclaimed Sheppard. "Too proud to listen *openly*, publicly, to a *negro* sing, yet would sneak about like thieves."[37]

In November, the Jubilees and their entourage returned to Ireland for another round of concerts. Their reception was tremendous. Performing at a revival meeting in Dublin, they required two halls—one large enough for eight thousand, a second for another four thousand—while thousands more stood outside. The presiding minister ordered the doors locked so that the faithful would not leave after the Jubilees were finished performing. The next day, the troupe sang to raise funds for a London refuge for children.[38] Building on the good feeling they had engendered by their good works, a week later they earned £165.[39]

The segregationist Colonel Hickman did not fare so well. In Scotland, he had been "pelted with paper balls," Robinson reported, and now the Irish "would not suffer Col. H. to come to Dublin." At Dublin's Metropolitan Hall, Loudin delivered an eloquent speech about American Masonry. "But for my color I should blush to say that in my own country *all those whose skin is colored like mine* are excluded from the Templar organization in *their own States*," he said, "and in the name of my race I thank the British Representatives from the bottom of my heart for the noble stand they have taken on this question."

After Loudin had finished speaking, the officers of the local Wesley Lodge held a "hurried consultation" and showed, as Robinson put it, that "they were willing to practice what they preached" by inviting the singers and their directors to form their own lodge "and bring a charter back to Fisk University, enabling them in that institution to carry on the good work so well begun." The Jubilees immediately took their degrees and eventually formed a cell of their own, dubbed "Jubilee Lodge."[40]

While in Dublin, America Robinson entertained a proposal of marriage from a young man, which she carefully reported to James Burrus, from whom she had now been separated for almost two years. "I have known him one year, and without my knowledge he says he has loved me all that time," she said.

> Four years ago he loved a young girl who died and when he saw me he said that I bore such a striking resemblance to her that he loved me unconsciously at first sight. I told him that my love was engaged and therefore I could not return his. He told me that he resolved when he asked me that if I refused him he would never ask another woman to be his wife and now has written to London to engage himself as a missionary and is expecting to be sent out to who knows now where, any day.[41]

Contrary to White's prediction, his health seemed to improve that fall, until he felt hardy enough to relieve the nervous Theodore Seward and return to directing the troupe himself. Seward agreed to go back to Fisk to head up the music department and train more Jubilees as needed. In return, White informed Adam Spence, Seward was to be allowed "to introduce the Tonic Sol-fa system of notation" into the curriculum "on account of its cheapness and simplicity and for other reasons which Prof. Seward will explain when he arrives."[42] Cravath insisted that he "must have a class of Jubilee Singers trained so that we can have recruits. . . . There is no man in the country who can give better vocal culture than Prof. Seward & all the students will have special advantages. Let this be considered & see if it cannot be used to bring in some durable students."[43]

Though large audiences greeted them everywhere in Northern Ireland, some local priests forbade their flocks from attending their concerts. The Jubilees' tours of Catholic cathedrals held some unexpected perils for Mabel Lewis, who despite her conversion at Moody's hand never managed to shake her Catholic upbringing. "People always seem to know that I have been a Catholic," she told an interviewer. While the Jubilees were visiting a cathedral and examining the holy water in a font, an indignant man singled her out as a lapsed Catholic and struck her. "Many times people have asked me if I had not been a Catholic," she later wrote. "I suppose it is because I have the habit of looking down. We are taught that and I cannot help it."[44]

Until now, Cravath had managed to discourage other A.M.A. singing troupes from coming to Britain. But ever since April, a troupe calling itself the Wilmington Jubilee Singers had been dogging their footsteps and exhausting their welcome under the apparently false pretext of raising funds for a teaching institute in Wilmington, North Carolina. The Wilmingtons were "imitating us in everything—our posters, programs, etc.," Robinson reported. "I am truly sorry that they are here. They are not far from us. They are deceiving the people too."[45]

It was like a repeat of the singers' experience in America: hard times compounded by competing troupes. As before, White and Cravath began searching elsewhere for a fresh venue. After the Jubilees' success in Geneva and their struggles in Britain, Cravath had urged White to take them back to the Continent. But White was dubious. Such a venture would be expensive and conspicuous, and the Jubilees' entire reputation would hang in the balance. There was no room for failure.

Then, one evening in Surrey, White was approached by a Dutch businessman named G. P. Ittman, Jr., who begged the Jubilees to perform in Holland, promising he would do everything in his power to ensure their success. Cravath and his fellow A.M.A. secretaries urged White to accept Ittman's invitation, set aside his Livingstone Missionary Hall campaign, and raise funds in Holland for an endowment.

White dug in his heels. "The very name 'Endowment' and the idea of 'money invested for the support, etc.' is repulsive to a large majority of Dissenters in this country. I learned that, during our first visit." Pleas for endowments had not only fallen on deaf ears; White believed they had been "a dead weight to us, and that we have won what success we have had rather in spite of it than because of it. . . . Our English and Scotch friends—without exception, as well as our own co-workers hold the same opinion."

It outraged White to be advised on how to raise money by a board that had given him no support when he started off and had mismanaged the Jubilees' funds ever since. "A small portion of the results of two years' work has been used legitimately under the head of 'support & Enlargement,'" he sneered, "but the rest so far as fulfilling any expectation raised in the minds of those who have aided us goes, has 'gone where the woodbine twineth,' and whither we get much or little it will be found at the end of the year to have been all 'borrowed' to the same end." He worried that unless the Jubilees raised money fast and rescued Fisk from its financial embarrassment,

> we shall be called on to explain that which will be difficult to do satisfactorily—except to the very few with whom we can have personal interviews & who have confidence in the integrity of our purposes—as well as sympathy for our mission. If a full and complete statement of the true condition of our finances should be published (in connection with a circular) I believe it would *ruin* us. . . . Knowing what I do, and feeling as I do, I would not subscribe a dollar to Fisk University—or labor to further its interests with others—in the present condition of its affairs—were I an *outsider* and not mixed up in it. . . . The trouble began during our first campaign when we announced—supposing it to be true—that . . . £18,000 (the wildest estimate that anybody ever made) would pay for the site & *complete* the building. . . . The fact is, explain it as you may—we have been working for two years to pay debts belonging to the new site & Jubilee Hall, which we did not anticipate. . . . You need in Holland just what we need here—a definite thing to be done, something which will carry the sympathies of people, which will *take hold* without requiring much thought.[46]

By the time of the singers' departure for Holland in late January 1877, White and his wife had both come down with chronic bronchitis and had to retreat to the relative warmth of Torquay. Maggie Porter was so ill that even after her reconciliation with the troupe she nonetheless had to remain with her hosts, the Stones, to recuperate. The others "felt a little nervous as to the result," wrote White, "for they were wearied by their severe Winter's work in England, and throats and voices were suffering from the effects of a climate, which, to say the least, is quite in contrast with that of Tennessee."[47]

The Jubilees' Dutch patron, G. P. Ittman, had worked hard to pave their way. He enlisted a minister named Adama van Scheltema to translate Pike's book into Dutch and A. van Oosterzee of Amsterdam to publish it as *De geschiedenis van de Jubilee-Zangers met hunne liederen.*

"Our arrival created a greater sensation than a circus in the United States," Sheppard recalled. "We could not go walking or shopping on foot, because crowds of children in wooden shoes surrounded us so closely that we could not get on. . . . Where there were no halls of suitable dimensions the churches were tendered to the Singers, and even the great cathedrals."[48]

They performed under Theodore Seward's direction at a private concert in the drawing room of the baron van Wassenaer de Catwijck's home in The Hague. It turned into an even more dazzling replay of their performance for Queen Victoria at the duke of Argyll's lodge almost four years earlier. Queen Sophia Fredericka Mathilde of the Netherlands had only a few months left to live. Intelligent, well educated, a patroness of the arts, Sophia was the daughter of the king of Württemberg and, according to White, could speak ten languages. But the House of Orange was not a happy one. Estranged from her sixty-year-old husband, the notoriously promiscuous William III, Sophia had borne him three sons over the course of forty-six years of marriage, none of whom would survive their father.

The troupe's hotel was directly across the street from the baron's palace, "but court etiquette required that we drive across to their door," Sheppard remembered.[49] "A red carpet showing that royalty was expected was stretched from the hall to the carriage."[50] Though the women of the troupe wore their "usual simple dresses," Sheppard was relieved to find that their "reception was most cordial and enthusiastic."[51]

A servant with a hot ladle of perfume walked through the baron's rooms, scenting the air, until the clocks clanged nine o'clock and in swept Queen Sophia, cutting a far more regal figure than Victoria had.

The display of diamonds was extraordinary. Every one had on diamonds, even down to the Baron's butler who wore diamond studs.

The Queen wore the largest diamonds I ever saw; her crown was studded with diamonds. Her necklace was diamonds. Her brooch was a large diamond with enormous pearl pendants attached.[52]

The Dutch had played a central role in the African slave trade, warring with their English, French, and Iberian competitors in the West Indies and along the western coast of Africa. Like their rivals' royal families, the House of Orange had invested heavily in the trade. The Dutch shut it down in 1814, but the profits the royal family had derived from slavery over two centuries accounted for at least a few of the diamonds and pearls that dripped from the ensembles of Her Majesty and her retinue.[53]

Sophia was accompanied by her family in court dress and a hundred courtiers and diplomats in all their splendor.[54] As the queen took her place on a brown satin sofa, the American consul presented the Jubilees. Unlike Victoria, Sophia came forward and cordially "spoke to each one of us," wrote Robinson.[55]

"When she got to me," Mabel Lewis remembered, "she said, 'And where did they get you? What makes you so much lighter than the rest?'

"I just smiled, and she turned to the man next to me and said, 'Why are you so dark?'

"He said, 'Ugh!'

"I guess she thought we were ignorant creatures, for all she got was a grin and a grunt."[56]

"There was not the least stiffness during the whole evening," Robinson declared. "The Queen was very much pleased with the singing" but less moved by their spirituals than by a gimmicky composition of Seward's called "The Bells," in which the singers imitated the tolling and echoing of church bells. She called for it twice, and "when we finished singing it, she exclaimed, 'It is *very* beautiful!' "[57]

In fact, Her Majesty found their singing so beautiful that a few days later she attended one of their subscription concerts: a glittering figure in a gilded royal box, hovering over the lamp-lit stage. A week later, the Jubilees sang for William III himself at Loo, his country retreat. "He is said to be cross and crabbed and all the people are greatly surprised that we have got an audience before him," Robinson reported. "He never calls meetings, only certain times in the year. He does everything as by clock work."[58] But for all his crotchets, William III could be generous with his money, and some years contributed half his private income to help balance his kingdom's budget. Moved by the Jubilees' songs, His Majesty donated a "generous subscription" to Livingstone Missionary Hall.[59]

The Jubilees' Dutch benefactors came in many guises. "Last night in Kampen, a lady was in the waiting room to speak with us," Robinson reported.

> She looked very rusty and commonplace and the singers being tired paid no attention to her when she came up to them to speak. Finally she came up to me where I was standing near the stove and engaged in a conversation with me. I suppose I must have pleased her for she gave me 60 florins for the Institution and some books—about $25.00 in money. . . . It is not, we find, always the well dressed people who have the most sympathy for our work and give the most.[60]

Coming from a school where an entire faculty panel was once appointed to deal with a report that a single student named Toby Frizes had been caught smoking, Robinson was shocked by the Dutchmen who puffed in church.[61] "It seemed so irreverent," she said. "At the stations there are no suitable waiting rooms for ladies. Men smoke everywhere."[62] Loudin observed that Dutch audiences were "slower" than English audiences but caught on eventually. "They do not take hold as quickly," he said, "but when they do they hold on."[63]

The Wilmington Jubilees followed them to Holland, still claiming "to have built a Normal School at Wilmington, N.C., and to be now singing for its maintenance. . . . They are meeting with poor encouragement," and White "noticed in one of their late advertisements they appealed for money with which to get home to America." White claimed he had "no objection to people's singing, and heartily bid God-speed to such companies as [Central Tennessee College's] Tennesseans and the Hampton students, who work under their own name, and on their own merits; but, for the good name of the colored people, we most heartily rejoice that this fraudulent business, which has become as cheap as it is mean, is dying out."[64]

The Wilmingtons did not seem to harm the singers' astonishing reception. At a little town called Zutphen, the singers "could not go out on account of the mob that would follow us around the streets. Hundreds met us at the station, some climbed upon the busses and carriages to get a glimpse of us," and the troupe had to slip out the back of their hotel to avoid the crowds that waited to accompany them to their concert at a local church. Robinson found all the attention oppressive:

> I always feel drowsy when I can not walk out because such immense crowds follow us from the Hotel door to the end of the walk, hur-rahing and shouting. You are not allowed to slap any one on the street but you can pinch as much as you like. I felt strongly inclined to resort to the latter, but knew I could not hurt them through their thick homespun.

Nearing another town, the Jubilees found "the roads lined on either side with the common people who were awaiting our arrival. The crowds were dense as we got into the town, all the policemen . . . besides many of the citizens, were engaged in keeping the crowd from being run over." After only two months of performing in Holland, the Jubilee Singers had raised another ten thousand dollars for Fisk.

For all their success, the Jubilees were being driven to the point of exhaus-tion. They were "growing very weak every day," Robinson reported. "We should not be surprised to see them terminate like the 'One horse shay' any day."

Robinson was scornful of Jennie Jackson, who seemed at sea after her estrangement from Porter. "I do not see for my part how one woman can ever drag with as many clothes as Jennie wears," Robinson said.

> Every one speaks of it—she takes no one's advice in anything. She has been working so long, and it is a great wonder to me she has lasted this long. She is very imprudent in her diet as well as dress. She eats great plates of meats at night after the concert. She never goes to bed any night without taking a plate of oranges to her room to eat before retiring. She never masticates her food well. She says she has the consumption of blood but Mr White says it is the con-sumption of food.

Having "exhausted all her strength," Jennie Jackson had to be left in Am-sterdam under the care of some "Protestant charity sisters" to recuperate from what a doctor had diagnosed as "a bilious attack and inflammation of the bowels."

An even greater threat to the survival of the Jubilees was the blossoming love affair between Georgia Gordon and the married Frederick Loudin. "Mr White and Mr Seward have tried to stop Mr Loudin's going with Georgia, and at one time they thought they had succeeded, but of late they are together more than ever," Robinson reported.

> Mr [Seward] would get Mr Loudin out of the class if he could, for he believes him to be almost a demon. He worked his meshes around her until he has her just where he wishes. Every one can see that she loves him. . . . He lavishes his smiles and soft words on Georgia and cuts his wife up at every turn. . . . Whenever his wife comes around—you know she does not stay with us—it is pitiable to see how cool he treats her. He gets furious. He does not like to have her come. She writes and tells him she is coming, and he does not even get a room for her. Every one pities her. She is a perfect lady and very intelligent. If you only knew the half, it would astonish you to know that such things took place among the Singers.

Robinson also blamed Gordon for the affair. "I can not see," she said, "how a young girl can suffer a married man to play the lover when she knows he is not free" and "knows too that it is breaking his poor wife's heart." The affair further frayed Seward's feeble nerves and had entirely isolated Gordon from the rest of the troupe. "There is not a person connected with the Singers that she even likes save Mr. Loudin," Robinson reported. "She does not like me as I know, she acts deceitful with me as with the rest." Gordon told her that she despised everyone in the troupe.[65] "We are still . . . simple, unassuming children," Georgia Gordon would write decades later. But after the mellifluous Loudin was done with her, Gordon was no longer "the same girl she used to be."[66]

25

AIN'T GOIN' LAY
MY MISSION DOWN

ENGLAND AND GERMANY

MARCH–NOVEMBER 1877

Writing from Torquay, where "it rarely freezes in winter—the fields and lawns are always green—and flowers bloom in the open air the winter through," White urged Adam Spence to get Livingstone Missionary Hall under way.

> It will be worth a great deal to us to have the building actually commenced—indeed, I don't suppose we can ever raise the money without its help. I wish that we might lay the cornerstone in connection with your commencement exercises. I hope that you will like the plan of the building.

White conceded that the plan for Livingstone, like Jubilee Hall, was grandiose, but anything less could never capture the imaginations of potential donors.

> We had to plan a building *that we could raise money for* as well as one that it would be strict economy to build. The missionary character of our work is the only hope of Fisk University—and especially in its outlook towards Africa. Fisk University cannot exist for long as a

mere educational institution, or even as an institution for the "Christian education of the Freedmen" if its support is to come in any great degree from England, but let it *appear* [emphasis added] that *its students actually go to Africa as Missionaries*—and its future support will be easy.

As always, White followed his coldest calculations with a convulsion of piousness. "O," he prayed, "that the presence of the Spirit of God may baptize & consecrate the very spot on which our new building shall stand. . . . I wouldn't ask these things that Fisk University may live, but let Fisk University *live* that these things may be done."[1]

Spence reluctantly arranged for a groundbreaking ceremony in March.[2]

As for the Jubilees themselves, the future seemed cloudy. "If we go on there must, I think, be some changes in the company," White warned Spence. "There is no certainty about Jennie's being able to sing more," Robinson reported. Porter was still sick in England, Mabel Lewis was so weak that White had decided to send her home, and in May a compromised Georgia Gordon was due to sail home in disgrace. Now Cravath was in danger of losing two more of his singers: Maggie Carnes and America Robinson. The issue was pay.

Cravath was an imposing presence: "a cool headed man," Spence had called him, "shrewd in his business, politic, unspiritual in methods."[3] But he did not frighten Robinson. Angry that Cravath wanted her and the other newcomers to work for less money than the veterans, Robinson threatened to return home. Cravath was contemplating a tour of Belgium, France, Germany, and Austria and asked how many Jubilees would agree to remain in the troupe on his terms. "All said they would go home save Mr Loudin, Tom, Alexander, and Maggie Porter. Of course this would be too few to think of going on another year." Robinson and Carnes believed they had Cravath over a barrel. "They would be obliged to bring in too many new members. This would be very expensive, and, besides, they could not produce the same harmony and effect."

There were barely enough Jubilees left to perform. In April, Maggie Carnes fell ill, and the Whites had set sail for America with an invalid Julia Jackson. Jennie Jackson was still under the care of the good sisters in Amsterdam. "So there were not any save Ella and Georgia to sing soprano and their voices are so weak. We had but faint sounds. I think Jubilee work will not last much longer." Since the singers had to pay their own medical expenses, Robinson demanded that Cravath cease making engagements and give her time to rest. "It is a very discouraging time just now," she said. "It is bad to stop in our busiest time, but I think we should not allow our strength to ebb away without taking some pains to stop it," for she "felt that I could not sacrifice my health and strength," because if she "should get ill there would be no further notice taken of me."

On May 19, the singers returned to England and settled in for a rest at Arundel in West Sussex to find Cravath had called in a vacationing Clinton Bowen Fisk to back him up in his negotiations with the formidable America Robinson. But she was not to be intimidated. So "General Fisk is going to join our band," Robinson declared sardonically. "We need a few more white people still. I do not see what we will do with them all."

After tea, Fisk and Cravath solemnly summoned Robinson and Carnes and asked if they really intended to quit if they did not receive parity. Robinson replied that they did. Cravath professed to be "astonished that I would let such noble work hinge for the sake of a few hundred dollars and base my decision on money, etc." But Robinson pointed out that Cravath seemed equally willing to sacrifice the troupe "for the sake of a few hundred dollars. . . . He did a lot of talking showing the Christian and not the money side," Robinson reported, "but was unable to convince me that I was wrong in the course I had taken."[4]

She saved her doubts for herself and Burrus. "Last night as I sat thinking over the past and the future my heart grew sick," she said. Burrus had written her, announcing that he had been admitted to Dartmouth.[5] "The time for us to meet again—if our present intentions are carried out—seemed far, far away. If I remain another year with the singers, and you go to school two years more, it will be 1880 before we see each other." Could they wait so long?

As Robinson considered her prospects in Britain, she was not inspired by the example of Isaac Dickerson, who had become "the most arrogant and haughty *darkie* of the age" in her opinion.

He will not be found associating with any but the wealthiest. He does not mingle with tradesmen. He has a bicycle, which thing is all the go at Lemmington. He failed in his examinations again. He was trying for M.A. Think of studying two years in the university of Edinburgh for M.A. beginning where Dick did! It is absurd and too he never studies. He is not exactly a gay debauchee but approaches it. He fools more girls than a little. He makes love to rich gentlemen's daughters—gets their attention riveted on him and then tires of them; gives no cause for abrupt departures.

While Cravath deliberated, General Fisk did his best to divert the troupe by taking them out in his carriage on tours of Kenilworth, Harwich Castle, and Stoneleigh Abbey, with Robinson seated between him and the driver. After a jaunt to Stratford-on-Avon, Robinson deemed General Fisk "one of the pleasantest gentlemen I have ever met . . . especially as he could tell us so much about you all at the school."[6]

With Seward out of commission, Cravath turned to White for support, but his rheumatic brother-in-law was appalled by the damage Cravath had done to the troupe.

> Your understanding of affairs, your method of work, and the con-
> clusions which you draw, are so totally different from mine that I
> have no hope of being understood or of influencing your decisions.
> . . . I have been perplexed ever since the Singers went to Holland,
> about the condition of the Company. You had one opinion,—Profes-
> sor Seward, Mr Ryder, and all the Singers had quite another. Who-
> ever was right, disaster after disaster has come to you, until the
> company was about broken up. You were compelled to take the two
> weeks rest and now poor Mr. Seward, as the result of his [tenacity]
> and struggle to save the Singers, is broken down and lost to the
> work. Miss Sheppard will go next and then the Jubilee Singers
> work, at least such work as has been done, will be at an end.[7]

Cravath desperately tried to lure a singer away from the Wilmingtons, begged White to send him two new female singers from Fisk, and proposed hiring a Professor Palmer to replace Seward.[8] But White maintained that the orthodox Palmer had "just the talents and training that we do not want in Jubilee Singers work. If I was ever to have to do with the Company again I would not want a musician of his school to touch it. . . . There is nobody else that I know anything about who can do the work." He blamed himself and the other managers for Seward's breakdown, since "we knew his weakness, and he should have been helped instead of crushed." White's wife was still too weak to join the company, and even if she could she would never agree to join the troupe in the fall without her husband accompanying her. Cravath had asked him to prepare new vocalists for the troupe, but White could find few candidates. Minnie Tate refused to join, and Lucinda Vance knew "nothing whatever of music" and had to be taught every note "parrot-like. . . . The fact is," wrote White, "the conditions of life in continuous contact with the Company have been such that it is impossible for any one to stand it very long who has nervous sensibility enough to appreciate the work & successfully *do it*, and by the time you have made [arrangements] with the lowest grade of singers in the company, you perpetuate one difficulty & beget others which are quite enough to break any one down within the year."[9]

Cravath turned to one of those who had himself broken down from his labors with the Jubilees: Gustavus Pike. Pike proposed disbanding the current troupe and reorganizing it on more favorable terms as a missionary, rather than professional, enterprise.

> With nine singers as there would be if Miss Sheppard managed the concerts as I suppose she does now, the public demand would be met for the most part. You could afford to go to Germany and even Australia, returning by California and having a magnificent campaign. . . . If Mr Loudin wants his wife, he must take her at his own expense, letting the enterprise employ her when it would have to employ any one, to do such work as she is able to do. If his services cannot be secured in that way some other man might be had.[10]

Which was easy enough for him to say. But Cravath knew that if he disbanded the current troupe there might never be another.

As Susan Gilbert White convalesced in her father's house in Fredonia, New York, White remained at Fisk, trying to make himself useful. But he had little role to play. He spent most of his time working on the plans for Livingstone Missionary Hall and scouting for limestone. In his spare time, he rushed around the campus, taking stock of Spence's shortcomings as a manager. White discovered that the reason none of Fisk's students had written letters of thanks to British donors was that they had not received any of the money. He reported that the heat in the laundry room sometimes exceeded one hundred degrees and had claimed the lives of two laundry women, so he ordered the ironing stove moved into a well-ventilated room he was having built. He told Cravath that he intended to dig a better root cellar outside Jubilee Hall to store sweet potatoes, since the school's previous crop had spoiled. At commencement that spring, he had enjoyed a speech by a Tennessee missionary named Kelley until his seat-mate, Maggie Porter's sharp-tongued mother, wondered aloud if the good reverend "had repented of having sold his slaves to her owner when he started away as Missionary to carry the gospel to China."[11]

In July, White was alarmed by an article in the New York *Observer* that depicted the singers living high on the hog in Europe. "The contrast be-tween the situation of these people here and in America is something almost incredible," it said.

> Here they "put up" at the most fashionable, expensive and aristo-cratic hotels, from which many tourists turn away on account of the great expense. . . . To-day I saw them in front of one of the most el-egant and luxurious hotels in England. . . . They were in fine car-riages, with elegant equipage and horses; and the colored young women were escorted from the door of the hotel to their carriages by the white servants, with the same obsequiousness that would be shown to her Royal Highness the Princess of Abyssinia. . . . They were having a thoroughly "good time," raising money for the Uni-versity.[12]

White condemned this characterization as a dangerous slander, "which, if true, would justly condemn the enterprise in the minds of all." He in-formed the readers of the *Observer* that appearances were deceiving. The Ju-bilees " 'put up,' when possible, at Temperance hotels," he insisted, "where they get good comfortable board at a reasonable price," though in fact the travel agent and prohibitionist Thomas Cook had once taken the singers to task for passing up temperance hotels for more elegant alternatives. "If this is not possible," White continued, "accommodations are secured in the best hotels that will entertain them at a price they are able to pay, which is usu-ally from $1.50 to $2.00 per day, rarely more. Occasionally," he conceded, "through the generosity of friends, as on the occasion mentioned by your correspondent, they are treated to a ride in a turnout which they could not themselves afford. They never appear in fine carriages with elegant equipage and horses, for a ride among the people of wealth and fashion, *at the expense of the enterprise*." He pointed out that over the past year "six members of the company and management have been seriously ill from the effects of the fatigue and exposure incident to their concert work. . . . Statements conveying an idea of a life of ease, luxury and extravagance on the part of the Jubilee Singers and their management, are giving us untold embarrassment in our work."[13]

In early July, General Fisk escorted a lovesick Georgia Gordon and a feeble Mabel Lewis back to the United States.[14] Cravath went to Geneva to pursue his European plans and considered a trip to Italy to see the pope, before whom one of his Dutch Protestant friends had advised him to bend at the knee, "not in worship but customary etiquette."[15] But Cravath was not proving a gifted travel agent. When the singers went off to Scarborough for their vacation, they found that he had neglected to reserve rooms. "There we were tired with no place to go," complained Robinson.

> We are all furious at Mr Cravath. It was well he was in Geneva at the time or he should have had a volley of maledictions fired at him. As it is we shall not see him before winter when the wintry winds shall have somewhat blown away our intense anger.[16]

Writing from Geneva, Cravath had sadly concluded that Fisk could not expect "the raising of the funds for current expenses by the Jubilee Singers." The troupe had not raised as much money after its return from Holland as he had predicted, so Fisk could not "venture on more than the stone foundation & the securing of the coarse lumber for [Livingstone Missionary Hall] this fall. . . . There seems to be no lifting of the hard times either in Great Britain or the U.S. Our burdens do not lighten. . . . We have as the result of this year the improvements at the University & the reduction of Bank indebtedness of some $12,000," he said, but that was not nearly as much as they "had hoped to accomplish."[17]

In the meantime, White had trained two new singers for the troupe: Lucinda Vance and Minnie Butler. Convinced by now that there was no dissuading Cravath from taking the singers to Germany, he agreed to lead the troupe once more. In late August, as the Jubilees cavorted through a six-week vacation in Scarborough, White left Nashville for Fredonia, New

York, to collect his wife, and in early September, he arrived in Manhattan with Vance and Butler.

Lucinda Vance was a contralto from Washington, D.C., but little else is known about her, except that White had found training her voice "a sore tax on my strength." Vance "will be a trial," White warned Cravath, "but she *can* sing & is strong & healthy." Minnie Butler was "not so robust" as Vance, White reported, but had "a good voice, is something of a musician & a very pleasant ladylike girl."[18]

In case Ella Sheppard collapsed, White hired a white woman from Auburn, New York, named Mrs. Swart to act as assistant music director and arrived in New York City to meet with General Fisk.[19] He was outraged to discover that the Livingstone Missionary Hall funds had been spent "for other purposes" and remained to be "accounted for." He told Fisk that it was "absolutely necessary" that construction proceed so he could face his English audiences, even if only at the glacial rate of two hundred dollars in costs per week. White got Fisk to agree to pay for "the quarrying & hauling stone," but the A.M.A. would relay only five thousand dollars to Fisk University and expected the Jubilees to make up the difference, something White "squarely refused" to do.

On September 8, White sailed for England with his wife, Susan, Mrs. Swart, Butler, and Vance. They arrived eleven days later after a "pleasant steamer voyage," though Vance had lost her trunk in New York and had to wait a week on the other end to get it, so that White had to order a dress for her in Glasgow. By the twenty-second, Vance was reunited with her luggage and White with his fractious troupe to find the tour a shambles. A man Cravath had hired had scared up a few far-flung small-town engagements that kept the singers zigzagging great distances for little return. "Our railway fares yesterday & today have been over £15," White reported on the twenty-seventh. "I don't wish to be always finding fault," he said, "but it does seem a *crime* for us to wear out so much strength needlessly. The Company *cannot be kept in condition to give good concerts with such management*. These two days will unfit the Singers for good singing, or any profitable practice for half next week." Jennie Jackson and Thomas Rutling came down with sore throats, Robinson had to go back to London to recuperate from bronchitis, and Vance was proving so incapable of performing that Mrs. Swart had to crouch behind the singers during their performances and sing the contralto part while Vance mouthed the words.

It all made the prospect of performing in Germany even more dreadful. "We shall have to work the educational idea rather than the religious in Germany," White believed, and depend on German curiosity. "I have had a talk with the Singers about the needs of the work in Germany," he reported a week later. "They all seem heartily interested to fit up in the best possible way, and I feel sure if we had half a chance I could bring back some of the old *power & fire* to the company." But not if their strength was expended on profitless concerts in the North of England.

Though Cravath blamed the troupe's current lack of success on financial conditions, White blamed poor management. "There was no plan of work to begin with," he complained, "and when the singers began their concerts after vacation there were not more than five or six appointments definitely fixed." His London concerts had too little lead time to advertise adequately. No one had scouted their upcoming venues since the summer, and now Harriet Loudin had to go down to make arrangements. He complained that an advance man named Jones had returned from Bath and Bristol to report that "the people there did not want the Jubilee Singers to come," but when Charles J. Ryder and a Dr. White of the Freedmen's Missions Aid Society went there, they received a "hearty reception." Jones had also reported that the Southwestern Railway refused to provide them with a discount, but when White and Loudin applied, they were able to get second-class tickets at a third-class fare. A false advertisement J. Hamilton Halley had placed in the area in the spring had "muddled up" their prospects for success.

"Now all this looseness," White scolded, "comes from the want of a disciplined mind right in contact with the work." He coyly refused to criticize Cravath for going to the Continent to rest, "but I do think that ten days spent in England and three or four in Holland would have put everything in a very different shape, would not have hindered you materially in Germany, & would have saved up life & strength to a good many of us." White complained that too much was falling to him, leaving him little time to train Mrs. Swart to direct the concerts. Harriet Loudin was a great help and "worth more" than Cravath's agents "to do the detail work of a concert— if she is told what to do."

"As you well know, continued success in Germany depends on the Singing," he told Cravath.

But good singing depends on certain conditions, as much as the growth of wheat or rose. I can do something but I can't work impossibilities with the singers, neither can I give my head & strength to other things & have anything left of the musical perception & thought which are essential to putting the fine touches on the chorus.

In the first week of October, the troupe was scheduled to travel several hundred miles to give three or four "doubtful" concerts "at most." White deplored the money and wear and tear the past weeks in the London area had cost the troupe, when they could have made at least as much money in Yorkshire and Wales, away from London's polluted air. "I fear we shall have nothing tonight but Loudin's solo," he wrote. "We are doing our best to patch up the weak places & cure up the sore chests & throats." White could not even promise to observe Jubilee Day on October 6 if the troupe was too "[knocked] up" by a "220-mile ride." Nevertheless, at their morning meeting, Hinton Alexander prayed for Cravath, who was "engaged in so difficult a work in a strange land for us."[20]

On the nineteenth, White and the Jubilees left England for Holland, where they performed for the friends they had made on their first visit more than nine months earlier. White was too ill with bronchitis to attend their concerts, and now the usually hardy Edmund Watkins was also out of commission. But on Friday, October 26, they all pressed on into Germany, pausing at Hanover, whose king had been chased out by the Prussians eleven years earlier during the Seven Weeks' War. Sheppard was told that "the Hanoverians don't want them there ever."

The Hohenzollerns were now the rulers of a united German Empire. After the Napoleonic wars had shattered the old Holy Roman Empire, the Congress of Vienna redrew the map of Europe to encompass thirty-nine German states in a rather flimsy confederation. At first, Austria dominated it, but in the Seven Weeks' War of 1866, Prussia defeated Austria and annexed seventeen smaller German states into something called the North German Confederation. Prussia solidified its position as the foremost German power by leading them to victory in the Franco-Prussian War, after which, leaving Austria out of the mix, the southern German states combined with the North German Confederation to form the German Empire.

Greater Germany was, in a sense, Greater Prussia: the kaiser was Prussian, Chancellor Bismarck was Prussian, and so was most of the army. The empire had gradually melded the absolute monarchism of the Holy Roman Empire with an increasingly bureaucratic state. Though Wilhelm I and his

Iron Chancellor were reactionary conservatives, in the 1870s Germany was passing through perhaps its most liberal decade, for the empire provided a lot of what German liberals had been working toward: an end to the old feudal order in the countryside, a measure of official accountability, and parliaments with real powers, albeit subject at any time to declarations of imperial—martial—law.

Wilhelm had accepted the German crown with some reluctance, for Bismarck's empire seemed at first a fiction. Most of his subjects spoke German, but then there were the Poles, the Danes of Schleswig-Holstein, and the French-speaking denizens of Alsace-Lorraine, all of whom Wilhelm and his chancellor viewed as enemies of the state. Gladstone once remarked that Bismarck had made Germany great but Germans small. The chancellor's support among the German public depended in large part on his ingenious but ultimately fatal cultivation of the worship of the strongman and his manipulation of German fears and hatreds.

The Jubilee Singers were met in Berlin by Erastus Cravath, who dampened their hopes of a triumph in Germany with the news that everyone to whom he had letters of introduction was on vacation and the imperial family itself was about to depart from Potsdam. On Sunday, October 28, the Jubilees listened to the king's choir perform Mendelssohn in Berlin's magnificent Dom Cathedral. The music only whetted the singers' appetites for more, but, anxious to make the best possible impression on the German public, White forbade the troupe from attending the opera or the theater. When some of the Jubilees appealed to Cravath, he told them that White's word "was law & any feeling they could not comply to this must withdraw from the company." No one did. "At last," Sheppard wrote approvingly, "Mr [Cravath] maintains his nice position in supporting Mr. & Mrs. White."

Their first performance in Germany was at a private reception hosted by a local British minister named Davis. Among the guests was Kögel, the emperor's court preacher who was known in Germany as the "Soldier's Preacher" for his pastoring to the army during the Franco-Prussian War. "We were delighted with our first impressions of a German gathering," Sheppard wrote, although the Jubilees were a little mystified that no one applauded. But Kögel was "highly demonstrative." Opting to use "good German" instead of "bad English," he explained through Davis "that we must consider their silence as keener appreciation than clapping—that the songs sank too deeply into the heart to be expressed with the hands."

The next day, those Jubilees who had been lobbying for the right to attend the opera were somewhat mollified when Davis gave them tickets to a performance of the *Messiah* at the Dom, in a pew usually reserved for ministers of state. But they had to leave after the first portion to perform at the home of a "pleasant" local American dentist named Abbott. "Dr. Abbott had quite a company of friends to meet us," Sheppard reported, "but I did not enjoy it so much." Perhaps the interruption of the *Messiah* had dampened her spirits, for though "most of the singers thought it a more enjoyable because a jollier party," she found "there didn't seem to be that culture and intelligence which marked last evening."

Not every German they encountered was cultured and intelligent. At a reception the next day, a professor, "who was inquiring much regarding the songs," wrote Sheppard, "was greatly surprised that I could write & told Mrs. [White] that I spoke 'such good English.' "[21] At another reception, Sheppard reported:

[I] felt so keenly that a certain Countess' eyes were constantly fixed upon me that I could not help asking her in broken German, "What is the matter?"

She, in equally broken English, replied: "Oh, I so astonished, you speak English—beautifully, and oh, you *dress*, like we."

I replied, "Why, what did you expect me to have on?"

She replied, "Oh, Africani, Africani."

I suppose she expected us to have on only five yards of calico wrapped about us *à l'Africaine*.[22]

At yet another reception, given by a German banker, the Jubilees "were disappointed in some respects and wished ourselves at home once or twice, particularly when he so rudely invited all the guests out to tea & then told us to follow. Most of the singers resented it then & there & rather rudely." Sheppard explained the German's bigotry by observing that he had "been in the U.S.A. & lived a while there."

The next day, the singers had the strange experience of first touring the grand Royal Palace (where the men were required to wear cloth slippers over their boots) and then returning to their hotel to learn that the royal family had invited them to sing for them the following afternoon. The news "greatly surprised and pained us," Sheppard wrote. "Surprised us, because it came so early & when we had almost given up hope of appearing before [Their Imperial Highnesses]." Pained them because they would have to perform on a Sunday.

The Jubilees solemnly deliberated about violating the Sabbath, concluding at last that "our mission of sacred song before a christian family may accomplish some *spiritual* good to all parties." In any case, wrote Sheppard, they would "go *expecting* such results. Special prayer is offered for it."[23]

At two o'clock on Sunday, November 4, 1877, the Fisk Jubilee Singers set off from their hotel suites in Berlin. Their departure had been dispiriting. Several of their German hosts had apparently complained that they had not expected the singers' entire entourage to accompany them everywhere, and on several occasions a new place had to be set to accommodate their assistant director, the unprepossessing Mrs. Swart. "Often," wrote Sheppard, "our host felt the intrusion of any who had not some duty which admitted of a tangible explanation." It now fell to Mrs. White to inform Mrs. Swart that she could not come to the palace. "Mrs [Swart] resented it by a martyr-like expression," Sheppard uncharitably observed, "her habitual manner," and Mrs. White felt so badly for her that she volunteered to remain behind as well. But Cravath "insisted on her doing her duty as Preceptress."[24]

And so they set off by train for Potsdam, where they were met by a fleet of the emperor's carriages. "Now, *this* is comfort," Hinton Alexander remarked, adjusting his top hat and settling into a seat upholstered in white satin as corps of soldiers of the emperor's *Lehrbataillon* presented arms along their route eastward through the vast *Lustpark*.

Here and there, Ella Sheppard noticed groups of Germans standing along the lane, "on the look out for a glimpse of our dark faces."

At Frederick the Great's massive brick edifice, the "New Palace," they awaited their imperial summons in an anteroom draped in floral satin and warmed by a generous fire. At last a footman escorted them down a "lofty hall lined with massive pillars of marble" and onto the dazzling polished floor of a banquet hall shimmering with mirrors and frescoes, where servants were still clearing away the dishes after an imperial luncheon.

As they stationed themselves before a row of empty gilded sofas and chairs, two enormous doors opened and in strode Crown Prince Friedrich Wilhelm Nikolaus Karl and his consort, Victoria. Born in 1840, Crown Princess Victoria was the first of Queen Victoria's nine children. It sometimes seemed that she had used up her generation's allotment of brains; certainly she left very little for her brother Prince Albert. For better or worse, she was her mother's favorite, and over the course of their lives, they would exchange literally thousands of letters. Vicky was artistic and inquiring, liberal in her politics, and she read widely if sometimes cautiously for fear her selections of English philosophers and French novelists might offend her Prussian in-laws.

Alone among all her brothers and sisters, she was not in the least afraid of her father. In 1858, at the age of seventeen, she had married "Fritz," the twenty-seven-year-old prince Friedrich Wilhelm, son of the then heir to the Prussian throne. Her parents had worried she was too young to marry but consoled themselves that at least she had not married earlier; after all, she and Fritz had fallen in love when she was just fourteen. Despite her mother's constant cautions about the "sufferings and miseries and plagues" that were "the yoke of the married woman," Vicky and Fritz immediately began begetting children. Victoria smothered her with advice about maintaining her Englishness in her husband's court. She obeyed at her peril, for she was suspected of Anglophiliac disloyalty and a kind of alien English liberalism that did not sit well with her husband's Hohenzollern relatives and courtiers. Nevertheless, she influenced her beloved husband much as her father had influenced her mother, appealing to Fritz's better nature, though it put her at perilous odds with not only Chancellor Bismarck but her eldest son, Willy.

Fritz and Vicky approached the singers rapidly, eagerly greeting each member. Vicky was tiny, quick: a pretty version of her mother in black silk and white frill and "a tiny French cap of white & black fastened with a diamond & a diamond brooch." Fritz was kindly, gallant, and tall—though not as tall, he noticed good-naturedly, as George White. The crown prince's erect military bearing and officer's uniform festooned with medals from his service in the Danish, Seven Weeks', and Franco-Prussian wars were somewhat temporized by a benign expression, a slender frame, and a long, drooping mustache.

The first Prussian prince to attend a university, Fritz carried a copy of one of the singers' illustrated souvenir books tucked under one arm. Having studied the group portrait in the frontispiece, he immediately recognized various Jubilees as he shook hands all around. To Frederick Loudin, he said, "I remember you. You stand leaning on a book in the photograph."

He turned to Thomas Rutling. "And you I know from the mischievous expression," he said.

"And you are one of the *old* members," he teased Maggie Porter.

The forty-six-year-old crown prince and his consort worked their way along the line of astonished Jubilees, recognizing Jennie Jackson, Edmund Watkins, and thin, frail Ella Sheppard.

They were joined by Fritz and Vicky's children, including their haughty, disappointing, crippled oldest son, Willy, the future kaiser Wilhelm II, who, on the death of his father a decade later, would turn on his liberal English mother and eventually take a manic part in precipitating World War I. Vicky and assorted ladies of the court sat in chairs and sofas while the men of the imperial family stood and small children looked in from the doorway.

The Jubilees opened with "Steal Away," followed by the Lord's Prayer. No sooner had they chanted "Amen" than the octogenarian kaiser Wilhelm I himself arrived to inquire, through an interpreter, if the Jubilees were Christians. He was delighted to learn that they were and asked a number of questions about freedmen's schools, glancing at Jennie Jackson, at whom he had leered in Mainz a year and a half before.

The elderly emperor insisted on standing as the Jubilees continued their performance with "O Brother, Are You Getting Ready?" and "Nobody Knows the Trouble I See."

"During the latter piece," Ella Sheppard would confide to her diary that night, "the Princess Victoria wept. Afterward she remarked she hoped we did not think her silly, but she could not help weeping. She is in mourning, I think, for a child"—her favorite son, Sigmund—"and the song probably reminded her of the lost one." Between each rendition, the family pressed around Ella Sheppard, talking "as finely and socially as could possibly have been expected between equals." "These songs, as you sing them," sighed the crown prince, "go to the heart. They go through and through one."[25]

White came in for his share of praise. "One of the ladies present—a princess, I think—asked me who our teacher was," Sheppard wrote, "and remarked that we must have studied many years to be able to sing as beautifully together. Such perfect intonation she had never heard before—& she seemed surprised to find our Mr. director was not a *German* but an *American*."

In the imperial family's faces, Sheppard could see "that our labor had . . .

accomplished all our prayers had asked. I shall never forget that one insight—without ceremony—into the home circle of the grandest royal house in the world." Back at the hotel that night, "we had devotions when all united in one common prayer of thanksgiving & praise to our heavenly & loving Father for His wonderful kindness & loving guidance through paths of which we know nothing. The song or hymn selected was 'Praise God from Whom All Blessings Flow'—which ended this day of the greatest & most peculiar honor to the Jubilee Singers."[26]

26

ALMOST HOME

GERMANY

NOVEMBER 1877–JULY 1878

The day the singers received their invitation to Potsdam, Sheppard had caught herself darkly wondering, "What will follow?"

What would follow at first was sweetness and light. The next morning, the Jubilees received word directly from the palace that "the Princess Victoria was so impressed with the singing that she could not rest all night—& could think nor talk of anything else. Thank God," wrote Sheppard, "for another evidence of the good results of our dear old sacred slave songs." But the Jubilees would not bask for long in their triumph at Potsdam. Mrs. Swart was still sulking over her exclusion from the grand event, and Watkins announced a day later that he was fed up with Jubileeing and had "decided to leave at once": a day before the Jubilees were to perform in their first full-fledged concert at Berlin's Sing Academie.[1] With Benjamin Thomas ailing, this left Loudin the sole bass, but Sheppard cryptically told her diary that she could not feel sorry for him since "he is the original source of the present mischief." Instead of gently persuading him of the "great wrong" Watkins was doing "not only to his people but himself," Cravath had exacerbated the strife with long delays followed by "bitter reproaches. . . . It seem[s] to all of us," wrote Sheppard, "that we must not expect *justice* in the class."

Watkins was not alone in his anger and restlessness. Jennie Jackson had words with White and began furiously to pack her bags, intending, she said, to leave that night. Sheppard was unable to persuade Watkins to perform, and though Jackson agreed to sing that night, Sheppard could not snap her out of her funk. The troupe's collective mood sometimes seemed manic-depressive. "I never knew it to fail," she groaned, "that just as soon as we have a day of unusual success or honor & special rejoicing it is followed [by] almost unparallel[ed] trouble & perplexity."

Under the circumstances, their Berlin concert debut was a kind of miracle. Sheppard fretted when she peeked out at the audience at the grand Sing Academie and saw that Berlin's music critics, supposed to be the most discerning in the world, were all seated in an acoustic dead zone in the very front row.[2] They were not necessarily kindly disposed. The *Protestanten-Zeitung* correspondent objected from the first to the singers' performing their sacred songs before strangers. But, as soon as they began to sing, his objections vanished, "for I felt that at once they were not public singers but missionaries, using with holy zeal their gifts for the kingdom of God, not only among the colored race of America and Africa but also among us civilized Europeans."[3]

The *Vossiche (Privilegirte) Zeitung*'s critic had expected, "at the most, to find that satisfaction which the first timid 'but well meant' effort of a child could afford. . . . We found ourselves mistaken." "They are so marvelously accurate," wrote someone in the *Berlinische Zeitung*, "well-trained and efficient, and can produce such magic effects of beauty," that he hoped they would teach something to German culture, whose foundations "are beginning to decay."[4] The critic for the *Berlinische Musikzeitung* agreed. "What wealth of shading!" he exclaimed. "What accuracy of declamation! . . . The performances of these singers are the result of high artistic talent, finely trained taste, and extraordinary diligence. . . . Something may be learned of these Negro singers if only we will consent to break through the fetters of custom."[5] And this from "*the* authority for Germany musically," Sheppard was told, before whom "all the finest teachers must pass an examination."[6]

On November 8, the Jubilees sang in the ancient city of Magdeburg, the capital of Saxony. Rather than give the singers a share of the gate, the managers paid them nine hundred marks outright plus expenses. But due perhaps to short notice, the hall was not filled, and Sheppard feared that the Odeon's managers had lost money. More concerts followed at the Sing

Academie. "Every night our concerts are full," Robinson reported, and studded with military officers who "make the house look well." Even "the Americans over here are very friendly," she said. "They see that we go where they can not" and "are rather proud of us."[7]

Sheppard's inner ears were plaguing her again, causing headaches and dizziness. Porter and Alexander were complaining of headaches and sore throats, and a severe attack of colitis prevented Jennie Jackson from going home. It was not until the fourteenth that the entire troupe appeared together again, and, despite performances Sheppard deemed inadequate, they packed houses and delighted critics, even in the enormous Dom Cathedral.

On December 3, the Jubilees left Berlin for Brandenburg and bid farewell to Jennie Jackson as she set off in a doctor's care for her voyage home. "Another of the *originals* gone," grieved Sheppard. "There are now only three of us left. Tom. Maggie Porter. And myself." Jackson would return to Nashville to find that no one would honor the note she had been given to cover her wages: Fisk's treasurer had no funds to give her, and Gustavus Pike, writing on behalf of the A.M.A., informed her that "they had no funds available for her note, nor for that of Mabel Lewis," which was due to mature in February. In a rage, Jackson went into town and bought herself a piano and parlor furniture and told the store to charge it to Fisk. But Jackson would not be paid until the rest of the troupe came home.[8]

At Brandenburg, the Jubilees learned that the kaiser had donated three hundred marks to the Jubilee fund, and they performed for Empress Augusta, who "came late & remained only through the sixth piece," Sheppard wrote. "We were somewhat disappointed in her."

At their final Berlin concert, the "audience was the finest, choicest we've yet had, as almost every leading branch of German society & culture were gathered there," including Crown Princess Victoria. "There was much good bying & congratulating from our friends & it seemed real hard to say good bye & be able to express our gratitude to those from whom we have received such abundant assistance, kindness & honor."[9] Some German aristocrats remarked that they "could not take even our German peasantry and reach such results in art, and conduct, and character, in generations of culture, as appear in these freed slaves."[10]

An artist named Döning presented Sheppard with a portrait that gave her eyes an "Evangeline expression." Susan White told Sheppard that it looked just like her "when I am at my best" and hoped that she would "learn to live *out* of myself more & more each day."[11]

On December 8, they began to tour Germany in earnest, traveling from Berlin to Yutebog and from Yutebog to Wittenberg, where they spent a "strange Sabbath" inspecting Martin Luther's artifacts at the Augustus Convent and "stood in the center of Luther's room & sang 'Praise God from whom all blessing flow' by Mr White's request as a fitting tribute to Luther and the sacred day & spot."[12]

The German Empire was two-thirds Protestant and one-third Catholic. Anti-Catholicism, exacerbated by the same papal declaration of infallibility that had chased Père Hyacinthe out of the church, had resulted in the expulsion of Jesuits from the German Empire in 1872, the arrest and imprisonment of clergy, and the brutal repression of the Catholic working-class crowds that tried to come to the rescue of their priests. Most Germans, whether or not they attended church or even believed with much conviction in Jesus Christ, regarded themselves as Protestants: anything else seemed un-German, somehow.

In Germany as elsewhere, Protestantism had many faces. On the conservative side, there were the Lutherans, Calvinists, and Pietists. The latter group centered its faith on the Bible and personal belief and was largely responsible for the wave of revivalism that occasionally agitated a generally indifferent middle class. The great majority of churchgoing Protestants were women, and, perhaps not coincidentally, philanthropy was regarded by Germans as a feminine virtue. It was the conservative, not the liberal, Protestants who served the empire's missions to the poor and would welcome the Jubilees with the greatest enthusiasm.

Unlike America, Britain, and Holland, Germany had taken almost no role in the African slave trade except to provide, at considerable profit, some of the textiles and brassware with which traders bartered for slaves.[13] But it would soon enter the "Scramble for Africa" and eventually commit, of course, its own abomination, whose portents were surfacing in the worldwide depression of the mid-1870s. Though most Germans had delighted in their burgeoning prosperity, they liked to think of themselves as nonmaterialistic. After the crash of 1873 exposed the same degree of reckless, hollow speculation in Germany that had precipitated the crash in America, many Germans chose to blame the Jews.

Until the crash, the status of German Jews had been rising. In 1869, the North German Confederation had put its imprimatur on the emancipation of German Jews, providing in most of its states for their ostensible civil equality, albeit at the cost of some of their more "oriental" observances. But many German hotels and eateries restricted their clientele to Christians, and anti-Semitism (a German would invent the term a year after the Jubilees' departure) was rife in churches and schools; any Jew who wanted to step up the academic or civil service ladder was well advised first to obtain a baptismal certificate. The increasing assimilation of German Jews made them all the more suspect as enemies within. Although it is unlikely that the Jubilees were aware of it, some of their lyrics—"The Jews killed poor Jesus," "The Jews crucified Him, and nailed Him to the tree," "Some say John the Baptist was nothing but a Jew"[14]—may have struck a dismal chord with some of their German fans.[15]

After Wittenberg, the Jubilees performed for "the Grand Duke of Sax Weimar, the Duchess, the prince & wife and others of the family & many ladies & gentlemen of the court." During the first part of their concert, the Jubilees had "kept our eyes fixed on the elegant box just opposite the stage thinking that must be *the* royal box," where Ella thought she had spotted the duke. But "behold our astonishment & amusement to learn that the Duke & the family occupied the box on the left of the stage just above the piano," where they "had not even glanced." Nevertheless, the duke was delighted, invited White to tell him about Fisk University, and even offered to send his court physician to minister to an ailing America Robinson.

In Eisenach, Bach's birthplace, they saw the first snow of the year and performed at a small but well-filled hall. On December 15, they proceeded through the deep, majestic Wüningian forest to Wiesbaden, where Mrs. Swart fell down the stairs and tore a tendon in her ankle, condemning her to weeks in bed and Ella to almost the entire responsibility of rehearsing the Jubilees. This did not sit well with Frederick Loudin, who, though a relative newcomer to the troupe, regarded himself as Ella's superior. As the sole bass, he had single-handedly held up the bottom of the singers' sound, but Sheppard was unimpressed; some of her concert notes tended to single out Loudin for singing too loudly, unclearly, or off pitch.[16] "I wish I had more confidence in [Loudin]," Sheppard wrote a few days before:

> I seem to lose more & more each day instead of being charitably inclined toward his weaknesses. In the rehearsal today in reply to our joking him about his not coming in in time on his verse on "Gospel train" he began to brag by saying it didn't matter it was *his* singing & person which took up most, . . . which so disgusted me that I rebuked him.

Running the rehearsals was "extremely fatiguing," and she feared "its result as I had begun to mend." Exhausted, her health failing again, her infected ears stopped up with fluid, Sheppard became more fretful onstage, missing cues and misplacing sheet music.

The homesick troupe spent Christmas at Wiesbaden, assembling at Susan White's room and exhibiting their presents. "I had too many to enumerate," gushed Sheppard. "I gave Mrs [White] sleeve buttons & Mr [White] a paper weight & [Maggie Porter] a silver thimble." She gave cards to the others, but it was "so unlike the Xmas at home," she sighed, where Tennesseans celebrated the Savior's birth by shooting off guns and firecrackers.

As his Christmas present to the troupe, White announced that he had sent for Georgia Gordon and Patti Malone. There was "much surprise at [Malone's] coming," Sheppard said, "but all glad of Georgia's return."[17]

The Jubilees were amused by a caricature of the males of the troupe that appeared in a German humor magazine. "It is not a burlesque on them," Robinson insisted, "but a slur on some religious members of Parliament. But it [is] too comical to see the gents in evening dress. I know you will enjoy it. The paper they are taken from is called the *Punch* of Germany."[18]

New Year's Eve found them in the Hesse-Nassau capital of Cassel, whose inhabitants charged through the streets, banging so heartily on bells and iron pipes that it sent shivers down Sheppard's back. For their part, the Jubilees passed the midnight hour on their knees in prayer. They were often at odds with their surroundings. In Cassel's museums, they found the paintings "too voluptuous to be enjoyed."[19] Robinson supposed that the paintings "would disgust the majority, as they are mostly women in a nude state.

There are some very coarse and vulgar paintings of men with goats' legs," she added.[20]

From Cassel, the Jubilees proceeded to the university town of Götting-en and from Göttingen to Hanover, where they sang to a poor house, ow-ing to an opera that was being performed on an adjacent stage.[21] On January 5, they returned to Hamburg to find Georgia Gordon and Patti Malone healthy and happy to see them, though looking "awfully fat." Within two days, Gordon was up to speed again, performing with the singers just "like old times," as Patti Malone sat in the audience with the limping Mrs. Swart.

Patti Malone was a bright, striking young woman from Athens, Alabama, a favorite of the Spence children and a disciple of Mary F. Wells.[22] Though her family's owner, a prosperous landowner named Malone, had beaten Patti's mother so severely that he left scars on her head, Patti had helped him hide from the Yankees during the Civil War. After emancipation, she was among the first students to apply to Wells's Trinity School, but local whites did everything they could to prevent her and other black students from at-tending. They stole books and supplies, threatened students with beatings, refused to hire students or their parents. Patti nevertheless persevered, at-tending even when she was so sick that she could not sit up. Impressed by her tenacity, Wells sent her in 1873 to Fisk, where White had discovered the richness of her mezzo-soprano. He would have included her in the third Ju-bilee tour from the start had she not proved too sickly to travel.[23]

With Gordon and Malone on board, White announced he was sending Minnie Butler home. Loudin noisily protested, blaming her failure on the managers' relentless scheduling. But none of the other singers appeared to agree with him, and in his frustration, Loudin ended up "bellowing" at Sheppard.[24]

From their base in Hamburg, they concertized in Kiel, Lübeck, and Al-tona, overlooking the Elbe. Patti Malone was proving a feeble replacement for the departed Jennie Jackson and had to remain in Hamburg to have a tooth pulled. Her debut was unpromising. White asked her to sing a song she had taught him called "Chilly Waters," but she "began in a squeak & nearly scared the life" out of Sheppard, who saved the day by precipitously changing the key to a lower register. "It was laughable," said Sheppard.

Nevertheless, a despondent Minnie Butler was sent home the next day. At Bremerhaven, Sheppard encountered "the coolest audience I ever saw," and a local artist apparently insulted Carnes and Vance by posting their caricatures in the hotel dining room. But Vance was unfazed. "I am having a very nice time traveling over the country," she reported to Spence's daughters back in Nashville, "singing for people and seeing fine palaces and nice pictures galeries and museums and churches and ever so many nice things. . . . I have been quite well since I have been over hear." She asked the Spence children to tell Sheppard's half sister Rosa that "she laughs like Ella. Rosa has a nice sister," she said. "I like her very much."[25]

They celebrated America Robinson's twenty-third birthday in Osnabrück, where Porter had to retire to her bed with a cold and stomach pains. In Essen, there were not enough beds at the hotel, leaving Sheppard and Malone to sleep on sofas, and the hall was so cold that the chill seemed to seep into the singers' bones. Some of the German audiences who crammed into small town halls were so ripe as to render the air almost unbreathable. Cravath's advance work was unimpressive; he had apparently paid two hundred marks for a hall he could have obtained for seventy-five. On February 1, they fared somewhat better at the iron and coal capital of Barmen, but Sheppard was being pecked to death by the other singers and deemed her twenty-seventh birthday, on February 4, "one of the saddest I ever knew."

It was symptomatic of the troupe's distrust and exhaustion that the issue was the pitch. As their voices wore out, the other Jubilees began to accuse Sheppard of giving the wrong pitches before each song. The next day, White took them to task for making her life so miserable. As usual, "quite an excited discussion followed from Rutling, Loudin & [Maggie Porter], . . . [Alexander] & others spoke less unkindly. One result was that Mr [White] made them choose their own pitch for 'Gospel train' & 'Bright Sparkles' (bones of contention) & at the concert those very pitches proved to be far worse than any I had given. . . . They won't believe in even the *tuning* fork."[26]

In a concert at Cologne, "the singing was the worst I ever heard," Sheppard complained, "owing to the ill feeling in the company." As a somewhat mended Mrs. Swart fumbled through her accompaniment, Loudin and Porter showed not "the slightest regard [for] her feeling & no patience [with the] difficulties she is under."[27] Their concert was not a success, owing, they thought, to the city's Catholic majority.[28] At Aachen on February 27, Sheppard reported that the "resistance" was still apparent; Porter ignored Sheppard's pitches, launching into pieces at her leisure and in her own improvised key. "I am fretted awfully by this unkindness," Sheppard groaned, "cannot get hold of any fairness from them." She tried to ignore the strife by immersing herself in local lore: visiting, her Baedeker's at the ready, the relics in the old cathedral at Aachen, Charlemagne's tomb and *Königsstuhl*, the bones of St. Stephen, "some manna from the wilderness," a nail of the cross, the arm of Simeon "on which he bore the infant Jesus," a lock of the Virgin Mary's hair.

Soon Rutling had replaced Patti Malone as the troupe's invalid. Malone did well on her first solo effort at Gladbach: a rendition of "What Are the Wild Waves Saying?" But Loudin's contingent made fun of Lucinda Vance when she tried, in her small voice, to sing Jennie Jackson's solo piece, "Old Folks at Home." Porter was returning to her old form, breaking up re-hearsals and even openly ridiculing White's earnest, prayerful sermon on charity in the Gladbach railroad station. At Düsseldorf, there was yet an-other "fuss" as they set off for a concert in what must have been a beer gar-den, where, to the Jubilees' initial dismay, the audience sat at long tables eating, smoking, and drinking. Yet the Jubilees "enjoyed it greatly," for there was "the most perfect order . . . during the performance" and "everyone listened attentively."

It took over a week for everyone to settle on the pitches for their per-formances, "but peace does not come," Sheppard groaned. "Lord have mercy upon us miserable sinners!" She was now "utterly exhausted from these troubles," she said, and had to let Mrs. Swart take over all the ac-companying. Porter contrived to exclude Sheppard from an invitation that was intended for the whole troupe, and then lied about it when Sheppard confronted her. At last, fed up and dangerously weak, Sheppard bid the singers good riddance and accepted an invitation from a Dutch family named Van Hermstra to recuperate in Rotterdam in a hospital "reserved for the nobility." For six happy weeks, she would be free of the singers, the managers, and their strife and crotchets and "treated like a sister beloved" by deaconesses Fanna, Sophia, and Christine.[29]

The rest of the Jubilees proceeded to the Hesse capital of Darmstadt to perform for an audience that included Queen Victoria's second daughter, Alice, now the grand duchess of Hesse-Darmstadt, and two future kings of England: her brother Bertie, the duke of Wales, who had heard the singers four years earlier at Gladstone's luncheon; and his twelve-year-old son, George Frederick Ernest Albert, the future George V. "After the concert," wrote Hinton Alexander, "we were summoned to the royal box and Princess Alice received each with a pleasant greeting. The Prince of Wales told us how much he had enjoyed our singing."[30] and asked the singers who had performed for him at Gladstone's to identify themselves.[31] "They all talked very freely with us and wished us much success."[32]

As they traveled by train through rain and snow, the sight of the broad brown Rhine put Robinson in mind of Patti Malone's lyrics: "I know that water am chilly and cold." In early March, she reported from Leipzig that "for four days the wind has not ceased to spend its force and the swaggering trees send forth a dismal wail, equal almost to the miserere of the pines." Though they were given the use of the city's famous Gewednhaus for their concert, "everyone," Robinson said, "has complained of a depression of the spirit." On the eighth, they sang at the beautiful city of Dresden, "the Florence on the Elbe," for a "brilliant and large company" that included "the King and Queen of Saxony," who were "highly pleased," she said.[33]

In Germany, the Jubilees would perform in an astonishing sixty-eight concerts in forty-one towns in ninety-eight days, not counting impromptu performances in churches, hotels, and private homes. Some of the concerts were lucrative, but admission prices had to be kept low in a country still in financial crisis. For all the glittering luminaries who flocked to their concerts, it was as if they were reliving the dark old days in Ohio more than six years before. By late March, White was nearing the end of his rope. At Halle, Robinson's and Vance's tardiness kept the grand duke waiting, and when Susan White scolded them, Vance indignantly took to her bed. "The fact that we are making so little money and the difficulty of keeping the company in a condition so that we can reasonably hope to escape disgrace is so great that I get very much cast down about the future," White wrote Cravath, who was resting in Breslau.[34] They could still move audiences. At Halle, the birthplace of George Frideric Handel, "one lady came up after the concert and presented us with a beautiful bouquet of flowers" and was "so touched by the sings that she could not speak for the emotion."

But the tour was no longer paying off: not for the singers, not for Fisk, not for the A.M.A.

At the beginning of April, Sheppard disobeyed her doctor's orders and returned to the troupe. "I might fill this book," she told her diary, "with the record of the many happy days of these six weeks & then not tell all. Who would have thought that Madam—the Dr & sisters wd refuse to accept a penny for *any* thing, saying I had been a blessing in their house! What I've done to merit such praise no one can find out. Tis *His love* in their hearts. By His grace" she was now determined "to live nearer & nearer, deserving it each day hence forth." Leaving the tender care of the deaconesses of Rotterdam for the strife of the Jubilees was "like leaving a happy home, but I feel that *He* calls me—so I go against the Drs' and Sisters' will."

She was saddened by the tepid reception the singers gave her. "Some seemed glad to see me," she said, but "[Maggie Porter], Mrs [Loudin], Rutling, received me most coolly, even haughtily to my great surprise. Why, God only knows. It seemed to chill my heart. I could have wept." No sooner had she returned to the tour than she began to suffer from severe headaches and a palsy so severe she could hardly write. And yet outwardly, at least, the tour seemed to be going well. She was astonished by the crowds that continued to greet the Jubilees. At Eisleben, the birthplace of Martin Luther, "the peasant girls and boys in their tattered garments stood awaiting our arrival with the most eager expectancy. I suppose nothing has so stirred up that old town since the days of Luther as our coming."[35] As elsewhere, part of the attraction was the singers' color. Later, Robinson would complain that on her walks with the darker-skinned Lucinda Vance, they "collected a vast array of children, men and women," whereas the light-skinned Robinson rarely had "any trouble when I am alone."

Sheppard continued to distract herself with local history, never tiring of visits to Lutheran sites. They sang at St. Andreas cathedral in Eisleben, where Luther preached his last sermon. "It all seemed so strange that I could scarcely realize that we, emancipated slaves, were privileged to sing the songs of our bondage where three hundred years before that great religious hero had fought the battle for the religious liberty of his people," wrote Robinson.

> When our concert ended darkness was just gathering over the town and in the gloaming we visited the scene of his death. Everything was so quiet and still within that we seemed almost in the presence of the illustrious dead. As we stood in the corner where he breathed his last we sang "Praise God from whom all blessings flow."[36]

On April 5, they returned to Berlin to appear again at the Sing Academie before many of their old admirers, including the empress Augusta.

Their performance was ragged and embarrassing. Though the supporting singers did their best, Loudin and Porter were too hoarse to sing their solos, and Rutling's voice broke on the high note of "Tempest." "The enthusiasm was not great," White said, "two pieces only being rather feebly recalled." Augusta sent for White and inquired about their tour of her husband's empire: "where we had been and how we had been received, where we were going, how the Singers were in health, about the University &c. &c." White was so weak that he could hardly talk but hoped at least that his emaciated condition gave the empress some idea of the *"need of the Company in some respects."*[37]

Cravath wrote the A.M.A., proposing to extend the singers' tour through the rest of Europe, but in mid-April received a discouraging reply. "The Trustees will probably take no risk or responsibility in regard to any future movements of the Jubilee Singers," it said, "that will be likely to increase the present indebtedness. This may imply the same want of faith as was shown in the beginning of the enterprise, but with our view of the experiences of the past twelve months, and with the threatened aspect of Europe and the continued financial depression here, we are brought to this decision quite inflexibly."[38]

The trustees also tried to squirm out of the contracts White had negotiated with the Jubilees. But he refused to "argue questions & policies which were discussed at the time." He wrote Cravath:

> The question now with me is what can be done. . . . I cannot go on as we are any longer. The sacrifice is too great. I simply cannot endure the life we now live—and the daily burdens that come with it. I have hoped against hope and struggled against the constantly increasing tide of evil until the mental suffering I have must be relieved or I must be sacrificed to a vain effort to accomplish an impossibility. I cannot go away from the company and leave Mrs. White and Miss [Ella] Sheppard to battle with the difficulties. Miss Sheppard is brighter and perhaps a little stronger than when she went away, but when she comes in contact with the difficulties of the work she wilts—like a broken reed. . . . I am willing to sacrifice every dollar of my salary except just enough to get me through the summer. Neither Mrs. White nor I have been able to do one thing towards straightening up our own accounts, nor are we able to do much towards attending to things which ought to be done here in

Berlin. . . . The response of the people to our appeal for sympathy &
help has been & is simply grand—and yet *the stench* of the *dead corpse*
that we carry with us is horrible beyond description.[39]

He was finding less "sympathy for the race" in Germany than he could
count on in England and Holland, which meant that the Jubilees' success
depended almost entirely on the quality of their singing: the very thing
White could no longer guarantee. Ever since Berlin, he had been struggling
"in an almost hopeless effort to cover up our weakness & keep faith with
the public," he said, but "matters have grown steadily worse with the exception of the few times when for a moment we could get hold of the
Singers." Unless he was allowed to "put the knife right into the Company &
cut out three or four & send them *squarely home*, and throw the burden of
making a success onto the others, with the alternative of financial loss to
themselves, the University & their people," he was going to resign.[40]

Sheppard was now so afflicted with palsy that by the middle of April
her usually thorough diary simply listed the towns where they performed.
The troupe's morale had reached the breaking point, and at Liegnitz on
April 22, a desperate George White "put the knife right into the Company"
and decided to cut out not the obstreperous Maggie Porter or the vaunting
Frederick Loudin but the unpopular Mrs. Swart, the composed and re-
silient America Robinson, and Robinson's devoted roommate, Maggie
Carnes.
    "I am not surprised," wrote Sheppard in the first full entry she could
bring herself to write. "Such troubles as have gone on for the past few
weeks could not go on without some one's leaving." The bruised Mrs.
Swart may have asked to be allowed to go home; her rehearsals had been a
disaster. But why White chose to banish Robinson and Carnes instead of
the nearly mutinous Loudin and Porter may have stemmed from several
factors. Since Robinson's defiance about her remuneration had already
alienated Cravath, White might have figured that Cravath would welcome
her departure more than any of the others'. Also Loudin and Porter were
his star performers at a time when he could not afford to lose his strongest voices. Besides, Porter despised Robinson and Carnes; perhaps White
hoped that removing them might pacify his prima donna.

At first Cravath seemed to go along with White, but when Robinson and Carnes refused to travel with Mrs. Swart, and then Hinton Alexander and Thomas Rutling gallantly announced they would resign from the troupe if Robinson and Carnes were sent away, Cravath capitulated and announced he would "keep them all."

Humiliated, countermanded, White had no choice but to offer his resignation. He had done this countless times before, but on this occasion, to Sheppard's horror, it was accepted.

"Mr [Cravath] has asked me to stay," she wrote.

> My very soul recoils from it. I can scarcely conceal the utter & indelable contempt I feel for today's proceedings. I *cannot* feel it right for me to remain, yet to go would make matters worse. If I stay I must face probably *fatal* results! If I go I have hope of regaining strength. O, Lord, show me my duty! I can only fall *mute* before Thee. My burden seems *too hard!*

Sheppard prayed on the matter through a long, sleepless night and the next morning met with Cravath and her old mentor. She mildly told Cravath that she would accept leadership of the troupe on the sole condition that everyone be allowed to return home when they had met their current engagements. But White's resignation had given Cravath new hope that he could convince the troupe to continue their tour into Europe, even Australia and the American Far West. Now "he flew into a passion" and "said he would make no such agreement," nor, he said, would he "beg me to stay" if she "chose to desert." Storming out of the room, Cravath ignored White's protest at his accusing the most stalwart and loyal Jubilee of desertion.

"Tho' I live to be an old woman," Sheppard raged, "the scar of that word '*Desert*' will remain upon my heart. As hard as I worked for *seven* years—late & early doing *extra* work—to at last be called a deserter!!!" And yet now she felt she was "compelled to stay." She "could not go after being told I would be marked as a *deserter* by the *President of Fisk*." And yet the moment she said "I'll stay," she felt as if she had given up "all hope of life or health." She experienced an "intense thirst to lay aside my wrongs" and pledged "to give love and kindness in return," but she "seemed to have no heart left. 'Tis like a stone." She did not "seem to care whether any love is given in return. I would lay me down & die—but since He says work! I wish for strength to finish it & no more." Distraught, despairing, she wrote home to bid her mother and sister farewell.[41]

In his letters to Spence, Cravath put as handsome a face on these proceedings as he could. "Mr. and Mrs. White have found their strength failing," he reported, "and have had to stop work." Cravath hoped "rest & relief from the share of this work" would soon give the Whites back "their health and strength," if not their prosperity;[42] the Whites had to beg the A.M.A. for money to get home.[43] Cravath blamed the troupe's travails not on the singers' exhaustion or his own mismanagement but on "the times of great depression & anxiety as now prevails all over Europe." Nevertheless, he claimed the singers' success in Germany had been "the most remarkable in Jubilee history" and assured the A.M.A. that everyone was "well and in good spirits."[44]

Separated now from her mentor and his wife, her closest friend, Sheppard was neither well nor in good spirits and became an even more vulnerable target of the others' jealousy and resentment. The Jubilees proceeded from Germany to Switzerland, performing in Basel, Winterthur, Zürich, Bern, Neuchâtel, and back to their old resting ground in Geneva before returning to Germany. In late May, they performed in the ancient Black Forest spa of Baden-Baden for the grand duchess of Baden-Württemberg and the empress Augusta. "The Empress purchased 42 reserved tickets" but arrived late, and Rutling had to interrupt his solo of "Tempest" until she was seated. Following Cravath's itinerary, they performed in Strasbourg, which the Prussians had pried away from France six years before in the Franco-Prussian War, and then in the industrial city of Stuttgart in early June. Cravath booked them to play mostly in spas and cultural centers that June, but over the course of traveling some five hundred miles by train and carriage, the southern German towns and cities in which they performed became a dismal blur: Stuttgart, Heilbronn, Würzburg, Nürnburg, Mannheim, Neustadt, Speyer, Heidelberg, Wiesbaden, Bonn, Siegburg, Barmen, Hagen, Dortmund, Duisburg, Hamm, Minden.

At last, even Cravath could see that they had had enough. On June 28, Ella Sheppard and the exhausted Jubilees finally collapsed in Hamburg and prepared for the journey home. Cravath reported:

> The strain of the year has been constant, and much of the time severe. [I am] glad . . . to report myself in good general health & con-

dition, [but] if the Jubilee Singers are reorganized considerable time must be given to rest the old members & train new ones. I am not clear on the question of future plans for them. One thing is certain, the University must not rely on the Singers as the only or the chief agency. The Trustees have not met their responsibilities in properly supplementing the work of the Singers. In fact they have taken no action on my repeated & earnest recommendations. Too much has been expected of the Singers & too little effort made in other ways.[45]

By now, however, the trustees had acted, however ineffectively, by sending Professor and Mrs. Adam Knight Spence on their long-contemplated fund-raising tour of Scotland. The British Freedmen's Missions Aid Society would have preferred to receive the Jubilees. Hearing that the troupe was on the brink of collapse, an F.M.A.S. functionary wrote to ask if Cravath would consider letting selected members of the troupe tour England for a few months. "I know that some of them would be glad not to go back," he said, "and if we had Loudin, Rutling, Maggie Porter, Vance and Jenny, say, till Christmas to try, and in the Spring if you do not need them before [they] could have drawing room [dwellings] that I am sure would answer, and it would not in the least interfere with another visit of the whole company at some future time."[46] Arriving from Germany on board the *Alsatia*, White was in no position to promise that the singers could return to work in England, at least not until he had determined "what available material there may be among the fragments" of the troupe. Though the German campaign had revived interest in the singers, considering the worldwide depression, another tour could support only a much smaller troupe. Nevertheless, White urged that the Jubilees return to America via England so they might at least appear before the annual meeting of the Freedmen's Missions Aid Society.[47] "If this can be carried out," wrote the F.M.A.S., they could have "a large meeting" at which the Jubilees could "let every body know what is being done for Africa."[48]

What Fisk had done for Africa was to convince four of its most promising students to sail for the Mendi Mission near the Cape of Good Hope. Their leader was Albert P. Miller, a former Mississippi slave of pure African extraction whose master had taken him from place to place to avoid emancipation, until at last he set him free on the outskirts of Nashville, where, at the age of fourteen, Miller learned his letters.

In 1869, he attended a country school taught by one of Fisk's student teachers, but a year later, his father ordered him out of school and into the fields. Spence bought off the senior Miller for ten dollars and took Albert in as a student. Almost destitute, dressed in cast-off clothing from missionary barrels, Miller earned his tuition looking after the drunken scion of a wealthy Nashville family named Petway, studying his Greek and Latin in the saloons and whorehouses of Smoky Row. The senior Petway wrote that though Miller had been "exposed to the vice & temptations of the day," he had "steered clear of the corrupting influences that have wrecked hundreds & thousands of young men," like Petway's son. In fact, it was "not too much to say, that he is the best boy I have ever known—*true, faithful, honest.*"[49]

Miller became one of the most beloved and respected students at Fisk. He wanted to become a minister, but Spence and Matson saw him as the perfect emblematic emissary of Fisk's newfound African mission and persuaded Miller to forget graduation, abandon his brothers and sister, marry his fiancée, and go to Africa. As the *Christian World* posed the proposition:

> If the African negro sees a few men and women of his own race, well educated, industrious and thrifty, able to stand on the same level with white men, there will be opened a new field of thought to him, and a new and quickening force introduced among his people. The well-educated American negroes will start in this work on a much higher plane of civilisation, and with immense advantages over natives taken from the ranks of heathenism and educated amid all the surroundings of a stolid and savage life.[50]

"Africa must be redeemed," Miller agreed, convinced at last that "the coloured people of the United States must do it." "I firmly believe," wrote Miller's fellow missionary, Andrew E. Jackson, apparently a grandson of Andrew Jackson's slave liveryman and a cousin of Jennie Jackson, "that I have thus far been made an instrument, through the name of Jesus, of bringing . . . souls from the error of their ways into the light of the gospel."[51] But he agreed to go only on condition someone else go with him, for "the disciples he said were sent forth two by two."

Jackson and Miller "talked with the young ladies to whom they were engaged to be married." In Jackson's case, this was none other than Ella Hildridge, the decorous Missouri soprano White had sent home with such regret. "The girls wanted time to think of it, but a few days later they both consented to go." Spence fretted about their poor health, but another faculty member insisted, "*they are just as likely to live as anyone*, and I hope you will not let that be an obstacle," for they were "splendid material" and "their decisions have stirred the school deeply."[52] Though they were "liable to fall at any time, in any clime," Miller bravely rhymed, "we are not to busy ourselves so much about the *falling*, but we are to see about the *standing*, at the post of duty, only waiting till He calls."[53] So far, God had called quite a number of white missionaries: of the forty-nine the A.M.A. sent to Africa, sixteen had died in the field and another thirteen had been invalided home within a year of their arrival—a dismal record that the A.M.A. blamed on its toilers' excessive zeal.[54]

By October 1878, Miller and the heavily bearded Jackson and their brides would find themselves on a coffee farm forty miles from the Cape of Good Hope, sawing lumber. Despite no knowledge whatsoever of the local language, they did their best to spread the Gospel, though little children fled "to the bushes" when they saw Jackson coming. "They seemed to be afraid of me," he explained: a legacy of the slave trade that had taught them to fear "all men with long beards."[55]

On July 1, 1878, the Fisk Jubilee Singers performed their last concert in Lüneburg, on the Ilmenau River, a brief train ride from Hamburg. Rutling claimed he was too ill to sing, and the two male quartets had to be altered to make up for his absence. "Trouble to the last," groaned Sheppard. The next evening, "our last together," the Jubilees "met, had worship & confided each other to the love and mercy of our Father in Heaven." They went to the landing pier the following morning and rode out to the steamer *Lessing* to begin their voyage home. They paused at Le Havre, where they ran into a Boston bandmaster who was touring the Continent with a brass ensemble. After months in Germany, Sheppard was pleased by the sight of black men at work on the gunboats docked in the fortified harbor. " 'Tis so nice to see them," she sighed, "even as servants. A few colored *gentlemen* we have seen, both in the streets & at the theater."[56]

Cravath had hoped to encounter Spence on the journey home and discuss with him finally taking up the reins of Fisk's presidency.[57] But they would miss each other by a matter of hours. Leaving Robinson to study singing in Strasbourg and Rutling to recuperate in Switzerland, they set sail for the United States on July 6. The voyage home was monotonous but "pleasant & rather smooth," Sheppard wrote, punctuated by the occasional whale and flying fish.

On Tuesday, July 16, while almost within sight of New York harbor, the remnants of the Jubilee Singers sang one last time for an audience of passengers in a performance that would prove a microcosm of all they had passed through in the last seven years.

"Cabin full," Sheppard reported. "After much singing we sang 'Star Spangled Banner' and answered the encore with 'John Brown.' The 2nd verse we [emphasized] particularly as there were southerners and especially a 'Virginian' present."

> *He captured Harpers Ferry*
> *With his nineteen men so true,*
> *And he frightened old Virginia*
> *Till she trembled through and through.*
> *They hung him for a traitor,*
> *Themselves the traitor crew,*
> *But his soul is marching on.*

"The ['Virginian'] said 'Dam John Brown' when we sang out the words with such vim & enjoyment," but "all the rest were delighted. Many wept during the evening," Sheppard reported, "and one lady followed me to my room, weeping."

At Sheppard's cabin door, the woman suddenly threw her arms around Sheppard's neck and kissed her.

"I never thought I would or *could* kiss a negro before!" she cried. "I do thank you. I never *felt* such music before!"

"How much good we might do not only for others but for our own people & hearts!" Sheppard exclaimed in the very last entry of her diary. "May our Father forgive us!"[58]

WANT TO CROSS OVER

THE LAST TOURS

JULY 1878–1903

The rest of the world would have been astonished by Sheppard's despair. In its eyes, the Fisk Jubilee Singers had accomplished more than anyone could ever have imagined who had stood on the platform of the Nashville Chattanooga Depot six years and nine months before and waved goodbye as they set off on their raggedy foray into the North. And though they were never to sing for Fisk again, some were soon to resume their work and battle with even greater vigor "for the good of our people & hearts."

Five of the Jubilees remained abroad. Maggie Porter stayed a few months in Germany.[1] America Robinson broke off her engagement to Burrus after receiving a letter that seemed to confirm her suspicion that after years of waiting he no longer loved her but had remained engaged only out of duty to his vow. "When I think of the past and all these recent troubles and transactions," Robinson wrote him from Valentigney, just across the Swiss border in France, "I feel as if I have really had the heavy burdens of life rolled on to my shoulders, and I almost feel as if I would sink beneath their weight." After a month in France, she intended to return to Strasbourg, to study German, French, and music.

Oh you can never know how my heart is born with pain when I think that never more can we meet as of yore. We may never meet here again. I [seem] doomed to be a wanderer on the face of the earth, while you have no settle[d] home. Perhaps you may find soon a peaceful home. God grant that you may and bless you with the blessings of heaven.[2]

But eventually America Robinson would cease her wandering and return to the nation whose name she bore but whose society she had come to despise. She married one Ed Lucas and moved to Noxubee County, Mississippi, where, in the tradition of Fisk's first students, she eventually opened a teacher's institute in Macon and dedicated the rest of her life to the education of black children. In a later composite portrait of the four alumni of Fisk's first graduating class, it does seem as though the "heavy burdens of life" were bearing down on her, and it is hard to reconcile the wide, scowling visage of the middle-aged Robinson with the slender, amused young woman who first set off with the Jubilees.[3]

Robinson was apparently mistaken about the depth of Burrus's love. He never married, and despite Robinson's request that he burn her love letters, he kept them among his most cherished effects. After a career in academia, he made a small fortune in real estate and pharmaceuticals. On December 5, 1928, this pallid, blue-eyed black man died of a heart attack in the colored section of a Nashville streetcar, leaving his entire estate to Fisk, including eighty-five houses and more than $120,000 in stocks and bonds.[4] "We believe," wrote one of Fisk's officers, that "this is the largest donation ever given by a Negro to education."[5]

Edmund Watkins also remained abroad for a while, still "fearing he might become a slave" if he went back to the South. The former field hand eventually returned to the United States, however, and lived in New York, where as an old man he was looked after by Paul Cravath, Erastus Milo Cravath's son, a Fisk trustee, and one of the most powerful lawyers in America.[6] Watkins died in 1929.[7]

Two of the Jubilees never returned to the United States. After fleeing to Switzerland, Thomas Rutling undertook a walking tour of the Jura Mountains. A minister persuaded him to perform a recital of songs and stories, and he was surprised to find that, despite his halting French, picked up from Madame LuFund, he was well received. Deeming himself too old and unlettered to pursue a B.A. at Fisk, he decided to stay in Europe and learn as many of its languages as he could. "My sojourn in Switzerland," he wrote, "where I learned French," and apparently fathered an illegitimate son,[8] "was the happiest of my life; Germany was polite, and Italy was charming," but though he studied singing with some of the best voice teachers they had to offer, "none of these countries seemed to be the right place for me to dwell in." So he finally moved to England and, under the sponsorship of Sir Augustus Manns, performed a solo recital at the vast Crystal Palace.

"Herr Manns being a well known musical director, I imagined myself singing at Grand concerts, getting grand pay, and sending donations to Fisk University." But engagements did not follow, and after a bout of pulmonary influenza, Rutling decided to become a voice teacher. Several schools offered him teaching positions, "but the Britons have not been used to being taught by black men," he noted, "and after working during fifteen years with the determination of a man trying to make the dominant race truly believe that God is the Father of all races of men, in 1907 [at the age of about fifty-three] I took to the 'boards' again." His engagements were "solely with Nonconformist churches, which are usually poor. I have sung and spoken in a good number of these, and have often rejoiced to find that some of the older members are still very much interested in Fisk University." But, he added, as if with a sad sigh, "Great Britain has changed in many ways since 1873."[9] Rutling was haunted by the notion that he had made a mistake in not returning home. "If there was a reason he returned to England," Rutling supposed it was to "try to help the Britons to realize more and more that the negroes have a right—after much suffering under Christian civilization—to be admitted, too, as sons of God, among the nations of the earth."[10]

In 1915, Rutling suffered a stroke while seated on the beach at Morecambe on the Irish Sea. After a partial recovery, he was brought to Harrogate by some longtime English friends and placed in a nursing home. Before his death on April 26, Rutling told an English friend of his named Dobson that he was "trusting in the atoning blood of the saviour about whom he had often sung."

"I asked him during his illness," wrote Dobson, "which of all the Jubilee songs he used to sing appealed to him most.

"He replied, 'Steal Away to Jesus.' "

Rutling was buried in the cemetery plot of a family named Birkenshaw, who paid for his funeral. "We are all sincerely grateful," wrote Dobson, "that we have been able to do anything to show our affection for one who so well rose above the disabilities of his race and early life, and was able, by his gift of song, to give much pleasure (and profit) to all who heard him sing."[11]

Rutling's best friend, the eloquent Isaac Dickerson, also remained abroad. After leaving Edinburgh University and completing his theological studies at Nottingham, he went to France to evangelize. "When I had gained sufficient knowledge of the language to preach and sing," he wrote home in 1880, "I found open doors in all parts of the country. . . . For six months I went from town to town carrying the good news on my bicycle. I have now visited all the towns in the south of France. My only difficulty, in all these small towns, has been to find halls large enough to hold the people who flock to hear the gospel. . . . The great cry in France, is more light, and I feel that the cry of his workers should be *more light*." Bicycling through Italy and Palestine, Dickerson collected lantern slides of holy places with which he would illustrate his "well-known and popular" lectures.

He spent his last years throwing light on St. Paul's Mission in Plumstead, one of London's poorest sections, where "his burly figure and genial smile were well known and cordially welcomed everywhere." He died suddenly in 1900 of an aortic aneurysm at the age of forty-eight.[12] At his funeral, his congregation testified "to the spiritual benefit derived by them from Mr. Dickerson's powerful addresses" while the Stratford Grove Baptist choir sang jubilee songs.[13]

The rest of the Jubilees returned to an America that had changed since their first tour through New England, and not for the better. White America was weary of the freedmen's cause. Northern white resentment of black migration and Southern white fears of black advancement had begun to mutate into a bigotry that was becoming formalized by legislators, judges, and the pseudoscientists of racialism. In the South, Reconstruction had given way to an era of lynchings and Jim Crow.

Soon after the first Jubilees trickled back into Nashville, a yellow-fever epidemic spread throughout the city, carried by refugees from the rest of Tennessee who crammed into the Broad Street Bottoms and Smoky Row. So many died and so many fled that for a time the neighborhood was nearly depopulated.[14] By early November, the fever had just about run its course, but it told on the students who dared to enroll at Fisk that fall.[15] The fever had devastated "large areas from which our students come," wrote Catherine Spence. "Some of them fell a prey to the disease, and many others suffered by the general derangement of society, and also by sickness and death of friends."

In January 1879, the depression was still being felt in America, especially among the blacks of the South. "Thousands of people must be fed, or starve. The winter, thus far, has been one of unusual severity. Many have died of cold and hunger. The benevolent are taxed to the utmost to meet home wants. We can get little now except prayers and good wishes."[16]

The fever and depression spurred on the Exoduster movement. Hundreds of Nashville's twenty-seven thousand freedmen rode out of Chattanooga Depot for Kansas, "where we can grow lawyers, doctors, teachers and other things," wrote an emigrant named Randall Brown, "where we can be Representatives, Congressmen, Judges and anything else. Let us behave ourselves so the world will respect us."[17] Conditions in Tennessee were so grave that even some white missionaries encouraged the exodus. "Let these colored folks," said one, "leave off waiting tables in hotels, blacking boots, and shaving folks, and running little errands, and doing little jobs about our cities, branch out and in colonies go out West, get homes in fee simple, enjoy the full fruits of their own labor, educate their children, and become a prosperous people."[18]

With its manicured grounds and flags fluttering from the watchtower of its grand Jubilee Hall, Fisk may have looked like an island of prosperity, but it struggled with the same old problems. Almost every advanced student had to teach part of the year to try to earn his or her tuition, but often even a full summer's stint did not pay enough to meet expenses. Unless more money was raised for operating expenses, Fisk faced the prospect of having to dismiss some of its most promising students or fall into irretrievable debt.[19]

Led by Frederick Loudin, some of the Jubilees wanted to resume their touring on Fisk's behalf. But with the Spences in the field in Scotland and the A.M.A. already juggling the campaigns of a number of school choirs, neither Cravath nor the A.M.A. would consider sending out a fourth Fisk troupe. So Loudin turned to George White to reorganize the company as a private enterprise. It seemed an unlikely proposition, considering all White had suffered and lost. But he was bankrupt and fed up with Fisk, and touring with the Jubilees was the only life he knew. Having somewhat recovered his health, in the summer of 1879, White assembled yet another troupe that would consist, with comings and goings, of Jennie Jackson,

Maggie Porter, Georgia Gordon, Mabel Lewis, Patti Malone, Frederick Loudin, Hinton Alexander, Benjamin W. Thomas, and newcomers like R. A. Hall, Mattie Lawrence, and George E. Barrett.[20] An agent named A. Cushing took charge of their bookings.

The last tour had nearly killed Ella Sheppard, and she had already taken much of her earnings and begun to build a house for herself and her mother near Fisk's campus. But she considered herself too old to resume her studies at Fisk, and she was too disillusioned by President Cravath to resume her instructorship. She was devoted to her mother and half sister, but her heart was with the Whites. During the past seven years, they had been the closest thing to a family she had known. Having invested her earnings in the house for her mother and tuition for her sister, Sheppard had little left to live on aside from what she made giving music lessons.

After her return to Nashville, she was courted by a promising young Fisk student and lay minister named George Washington Moore, who had taken over Fisk's old Howard Chapel, a small Gothic Congregational church that the school had left behind at the old barracks when Jubilee Hall was completed. But his congregation and income were minuscule, he would not graduate from Fisk until 1881, and his immediate prospects were muddled by his ambition to study theology at Oberlin. Believing that the Jubilees' mission was ordained by God, on September 26, 1879, Sheppard set out with White's troupe for a fourth Jubilee tour.

Cravath issued a statement "saying that this was the genuine company of Jubilee Singers though not singing for the university."[21] But Loudin, for his part, would try to reassure him that their going forth without sanction did not mean they intended to break with the school they had saved from extinction. "Some children go forth from the family and marry into other families, and yet they are children still," he would gently explain.

> Their love does not cease to grow in other lands. Although we have ceased to work for Fisk University, we are one with you and you are one with us. We must stand or fall together. . . . As we go forth singing the songs of our fathers, we shall endeavor to fight against prejudice, which rises up against us.[22]

And fight they did. Representing neither Fisk nor the A.M.A. but themselves, and emboldened by their extraordinary reception overseas, the

Jubilees were now at greater liberty to stand up for their rights. Their clippings file became filled not with reviews and profiles but with accounts of their clashes with hotel proprietors, ticket agents, railway lines in an increasingly segregated North.

Their dispute with Boston's New Marlborough Hotel made front-page news after the proprietor ordered them to sit at a separate table from his white patrons.[23] They began to wield their European fame like a sword. "This treatment is in striking contrast with the marked hospitality they received in Great Britain and Germany," wrote the *Daily Evening Traveller*.

> They breakfasted with Mr. Gladstone, took supper in the new palace of Frederick the Great, at Potsdam, had every attention from the Emperor of Germany, Queen Victoria, the Prince of Wales, members of both Houses of Parliament, etc., etc. . . . It is a little too late in the day to eject a company of respectable colored people from a hotel. The members of the Fisk company are refined and educated persons, and if they could be the guests of kings, queens, emperors and lords, they certainly would not disgrace the proprietor or guests of a hotel. Much of the work of the Jubilee Singers hitherto has been in removing prejudice. From the foregoing it will be seen that their work in this respect is not completed yet—even in Massachusetts.[24]

It was a point that would be made again and again as White's Jubilees toured the American North. "During the years that they spent abroad," wrote the Washington gossip columnist Fannie B. Ward, "in countries more civilized than ours, where the vulgarism of color-prejudice is unknown— they were received and entertained in high places where neither you nor I, dear reader, can ever hope to go. 'You will find things different now that slavery is no more,' said our charitable cousins across the sea to the Jubilees on the eve of their return; but, having been born here, they knew us better, and came back to the 'land of the free' without special enthusiasm."[25]

On returning to America, "what did I find?" Loudin asked a Pittsburgh audience.

> We could not be accommodated at [Pittsburgh's] Monongahela House or the Central Hotel because we were colored people. And this, too, in what I call my own old home. . . . Naturally, I expected

better treatment; but we were treated in the same way at Harrisburg, where we were actually turned out in the rain, because we were black. . . . Now, when such things occur, isn't it hard for us to believe that the new era has dawned? In Europe we were welcomed in the houses of royalty, and in Germany we had the pleasure of stopping in the palace of the Crown Prince. So it was elsewhere until we came to our own land.

"I could not help speaking of this," he concluded.[26]

"They are negroes, but not *niggers*. I am proud to say," wrote their erstwhile music teacher B. C. Unseld, from Orange, New Jersey. "No one need be ashamed to invite them to his house."[27] When a reporter for the Cincinnati *Post* tried to dismiss the Jubilees' European patrons as "ignorant foreigners," the *Commercial* wished "more of them should come here and teach this 'Superior' reporter of the 'nigger-be-dam' sentiment he represents something about justice, humanity, and the principles of American liberty."[28]

The fight went on. In Lancaster, Pennsylvania, White confronted a proprietor who said he had not realized the Jubilees were black when he booked them. "When he found we were better looking than that," Loudin reported, "he wanted to turn us out."[29] White tried to convince the landlord "that the color of his guests' eyes might perhaps form as proper a subject for inquiry as that of their skins," wrote a local reporter, "but I fear the reluctant host did not view the matter in quite the same aspect. . . . Only upon Mr. White's threatening to carry the matter into the courts did the other, after much pitiable shuffling, consent to receive the singers."[30]

Even after they were admitted, however, the trouble did not stop. A guest entering a hotel dining room in Utica "happened to see Miss Sheppard sitting at table," the Warren *Mail* reported. "He instantly turned and went out grumbling and blustering to complain to the clerk because a 'nigger' was permitted to eat in the same room with a 'white man.' "[31]

They were again refused accommodations in Lincoln's hometown of Springfield, Illinois. Governor John M. Palmer himself handsomely protested, and Lincoln's brother-in-law, Clark Moulton Smith, declared the Jubilees' treatment "a burning shame and a disgrace to the people."[32] But Loudin would not let his audience off the hook. "It was deeply humiliating that this should have happened beside the grave where sleeps the sacred dust of the great emancipator who struck the shackles from the limbs of most of those whose voices you are here to listen to," he told them.

> It was the privilege of the great State of Illinois to give to the world the man who should fulfill the prophecy that the Nation should be born in a day. It may be their privilege yet to define what is the meaning of American citizenship and what are the rights and privileges of those thus endowed, and to lead the Nation to a higher plane of justice and right. . . . May God hasten the day when throughout this broad land there shall not be left a rood of territory over which floats the flag we have helped to defend . . . where we shall be excluded from the full enjoyment of the rights of American citizenship, and where we shall not be permitted to enjoy its fullest privileges; and may the day soon dawn when manhood shall be measured by its worth, regardless of race, color, or previous condition.[33]

A year later, when they were again shut out of Springfield's hotels, one hotel keeper was far from contrite. "Yes, sir, by God, I did refuse 'em," boasted Horace Leland to a reporter for the *Chicago Tribune*. "I am not going, by God, to buy cheap beefsteaks for niggers and expect my guests and my friends to sit down by their sides and eat them too. No, sir, not by a God damned sight. . . . They're all well enough in their place, but God damn me if I want to eat with them, or sleep with them, or have any of my relatives marry 'em, by God, sir."[34]

In Leland's bluster, the *Inter Ocean* newspaper heard the tread of the "heavy foot of human slavery" and an "insult to those who fought and died for the equality of men."[35]

For the first time, the Jubilees ventured to concertize in at least the upper South. At Wheeling, West Virginia, they were surprised to be admitted into the "first hotel of the place, and receive splendid treatment," wrote one of the company. In fact, there was nothing, "so far as our treatment is concerned, to remind us that we are in a Southern State."[36]

The Jubilees were just as vocal about injustice in the South as they had been in the North. At a concert in Louisville, Kentucky, they announced from the stage that though they had paid for first-class tickets to Nashville to sing for free at Tennessee's centennial exhibition, they had been told they would not be allowed in a first-class car. "We determined before we would go in the smoking-car home we would go back North," wrote one singer, "and Mr. Loudin told the people so at the concert. I wish you could have heard the shout that went up as he did so."[37] There was not a man or woman in the audience "who did not feel angry and ashamed at the injustice," wrote the Louisville *Commercial*.

> We are certainly a very superior people—much superior to the effete nations of Europe. . . . The fact that shows our superiority is that these people whom Kings and Emperors and Prime Ministers welcomed and fêted are so inferior to us that we do not allow them to travel in a first class railway carriage even when we have taken their money for the privilege.[38]

At a second Louisville concert, "when we sang the last verse of the 'Gospel Train,' the house nearly came down," wrote one of the female singers.

> *The fare is cheap and all can go,*
> *The rich and poor are there,*
> *No second-class on board the train,*
> *No difference in the fare . . .*
>
> *Get on board, children*
> *Get on board, children.*
> *Get on board, children,*
> *For there's room for many a more.*

Men stood up and clapped their hands sore, and screamed their throats dry, then quieted down and burst out again. Some of the strongest rebels in Louisville were there, and they, too, caught the spirit.

They sang to the first integrated audience in the history of Louisville's Library Hall, where all the attendees behaved as if "they were of the same color, save a smile now and then from a more 'fortunate white' when he saw a black . . . sit next to some other white. . . . We have done some good we hope for our people."

The singers would make sure the whole country knew about their treatment by the Southern railroads, and as far away as New Hampshire, editorialists would take up their cause. "If, after once being charmed with the music of the Jubilee Singers," asked the Warren *Mail*, "you were to see them rudely thrust out of their seats in a railroad car, on account of their color, and jostled into a smoking car, how would you feel about it?"[39]

At Cravath's urging, George Pullman himself arranged to provide a Pullman car for the Jubilees' journey home and pledged to integrate all Pullman cars thereafter: a policy his company adhered to—officially, at least—for the next twenty-five years.[40] In the end, however, the troupe refused to sing at Tennessee's centennial because the managers couched their invitation as though they were reluctantly giving the Jubilees permission to appear. "The whole matter has been clothed with a sort of feeling," wrote the *Daily Herald*, "which is the result of race prejudice."[41]

The Jubilee Singers did appear at Fisk's commencement, however, to present the university with a bell. White told Fisk's students and faculty that his new troupe had "met with many difficulties, and for the first few months our way was cloudy, but at last it pleased God to give us financial success. . . . We have been permitted to do as much to lift the burden for your people, to touch Christian hearts and to lead men to Christ as ever before," he said.

> As we have been permitted to go on in the old way it occurred to us, as a company, to make a thank offering to God for His goodness. It came to us that we might give Fisk University a bell, and it would have a meaning which no other gift would have. . . . We give it as, in some sense, the cap-stone of what we have accomplished.[42]

Perhaps the last thing in the world Fisk needed at that point was a bell. Nevertheless, the gift inspired Adam Knight Spence, now dean of the faculty and newly returned from his woefully unsuccessful fund-raising tour of Scotland, to versify. "Well, well, dost thou swing and swell," he recited in his small voice, "Oh, welcome and well-beloved bell!"[43]

In Washington, the Jubilees sang for one of the icons of the Old South, the diminutive former vice president of the Confederacy, Alexander Hamilton Stephens, now a wheelchair-bound U.S. congressman. Always more

of a states' rights than a pro-slavery man, Stephens had nonetheless declared slavery the foundation stone of the Confederate cause. He was "a
practical Confederate, even to the enjoyment of a residence as a prisoner
of state in Fort Warren, until released by Andy Johnson." White's troupe
sang "Steal Away" for Stephens and chanted the Lord's Prayer.

> When they struck the words "Our Father," he covered his face with
> his hands and ceased to beat the time. As they breathed this prayer in
> soft and almost whispered notes, it seemed as though they were
> bearing the old man on their hearts to the throne of the Grace.
> There was not a sound, not even the stirring of a hand lest the soft
> melodious notes should be lost.

When they were done, Stephens echoed Gladstone. "O, it is wonderful!"
he exclaimed. "I never heard anything like it."

Loudin stepped forward to thank the little Georgian, "whose sympathy
and kindness have always sustained and encouraged our people."

"I have never ceased to feel the deepest interest in your race," Stephens
replied. "It commenced long before emancipation. I have done what I could
in the cause of humanity and education, and I shall continue to feel and to
act in your behalf as long as I live.

"Now," Stephens said, brightening, "I would like to hear you sing a good
old revival song to a rousing old camp meeting tune."[44]

For all that, the Jubilees had few illusions about the South. When a
Southern white denounced their depictions of Southern racism, proclaimed himself and his fellow whites the true friends of the Negro, and
asked why, if this was not so, the Jubilees continued to live in the South,
the singers issued a joint reply:

> Bitter experience teaches us that, while there are some humane and
> Christian people in the South, the masses are not our "best friends."
> . . . Our condition at present in the South—in the majority of the
> cases—especially in the country districts, is but very little, if any,
> better than before emancipation; with the single exception of not
> being bought and sold. . . . Further, among those who have emi-
> grated from the South, in what is known as the exodus, there are
> personal acquaintances, and in every instance the case of their leav-
> ing was oppression in the South. . . . Our homes continue in the

South simply because we believe that the unexceptional advantages we have enjoyed can be better employed for the elevation of our less fortunate people in the South by living among them.[45]

"They are fighting the battle of their race," cheered one paper, "—and gaining it, too—in hotels and halls and social circles, and in some places in rail cars, as they everywhere command respect for themselves as cultured ladies and gentlemen."[46] But Cushing, the troupe's agent, was tired of fighting "the battles of the colored race in the railroad cars and hotels." It was a "burning shame," he said, that "men and women of unblemished character, who have given their best years for the advancement and education of the race . . . should be refused entertainment simply on account of color, when gambler, thief, prostitute or anything bad in human form that has a white skin can find accommodation in any hotel in any state."[47]

Early in the tour, the Jubilees were delighted to visit the poet and abolitionist John Greenleaf Whittier at his home in Hampton Falls, New Hampshire. Whittier was seventy-two years old and the most beloved American poet of his day. He invited the Jubilees into his "workshop," where they sang "Steal Away," "Go Down, Moses," "John Brown," and "Swing Low, Sweet Chariot." Moved, Whittier showed them the Declaration of Emancipation, to which he had been the youngest signatory back in 1833. Like Douglass, Whittier had broken with William Lloyd Garrison over the latter's rejection of the Constitution and believed—perhaps mistakenly—that emancipation could be accomplished by political means.[48] He signed the singers' autograph books with the following lines:

> *Voice of a ransomed race: sing on,*
> *'Till Freedom's every right is won,*
> *And slavery's every wrong undone.*
> *John G. Whittier*[49]

By now, Loudin had moved well beyond Holmes's and Dickerson's old role of troupe spokesman to champion his people with a boldness and a sonorous eloquence worthy at times of Frederick Douglass. In his speeches, he began to question the craze for African missions and wondered why he no longer heard much "about the elevation of our own race in our own native land. Here, my dear friends, are four millions of our race that you and

I, and I emphasize the word *you*, must educate; or the result—who can tell?" After years of touring abroad, he had come to "believe firmly, as I believe in my own existence, that we are not so unlike other people. We want an equal chance, and we ask for nothing more; and we shall be able to work out for ourselves as glorious and noble a future as that which marks the onward march of any other race upon the earth."[50]

His words stirred editorialists to their own heights of eloquence. An editor in Elmira, New York, asked how it was that whites "resign ourselves unquestioningly to the hands of our colored barber, . . . but when we are compelled to sit opposite him at the hotel table, our Anglo Saxon blood asserts itself, and we at once feel wronged and insulted!"

> A colored man will answer splendidly as a porter, a coachman, or a waiter, but what merchant thinks of employing one as a clerk, a salesman, or a book-keeper? What school finds use for a colored teacher? What white man likes to engage the services of a colored lawyer? What white congregation would afford the living salary of a colored pastor to baptize their children, bury their dead, solemnize marriage, administer the sacrament, visit their sick, teach them the Scriptures, and guide them on the road to the Heavenly Jerusalem?[51]

In August, the Jubilees appeared at the amphitheater at Chautauqua in New York at a reunion of the United States Christian Commission, which had provided relief during the war to the Union army. The Jubilees shared the stage with their grizzled old friend George Hay Stuart of the Young Men's Christian Association and a chastened Schuyler Colfax, who had enjoyed their singing on their first visit to Washington when he was still Grant's vice president. But the guest of honor was General and now Senator James A. Garfield of Ohio, who had just edged out his old commander for the Republican presidential nomination.

During the proceedings at Chautauqua, a reporter noticed that R. A. Hall, one of the new Jubilee tenors, "was the only one who was thoughtful enough to offer the general a hymn book." The future president deemed their music "one of the great triumphs of our republic. I have some belief," he said, "in the effects of forces that come down away from the ages behind us, and I wondered if the tropical sun had not distilled its sweetness, and if the sorrows of centuries of slavery had not distilled its sadness" into the Jubilees' voices. "I thank that choir for the lesson they have taught me."[52]

Free of the constraints of the A.M.A., Loudin replied with what amounted to a political endorsement. "You cannot realize," he said, "with what hope and expectation we look to your elevation to the lofty seat that is within the gift of this country."[53] Whatever his intentions toward black Americans, Garfield would serve only four months before he was assassinated by a disappointed office seeker named Charles J. Guiteau.

The Jubilee Singers' little triumph at Chautauqua came at a terrible cost. George White's health had been relatively good. Without Cravath and the A.M.A. in the equation, he had been able to work at his own speed, directing Cushing to make bookings commensurate with the troupe's health and morale. But while rehearsing the Jubilees two days before Garfield's speech, White "accidentally stepped from the high platform to the floor, breaking my right thigh bone, dislocating my right knee, severely injuring my right foot and ankle and straining my left knee." He was transported back to his in-laws' house in Fredonia and confined to his bed for the next four months.[54]

The Jubilees almost disbanded, but Loudin and Cushing persuaded them to continue under their temporary management until White was fit to return. Loudin's emergence was inevitable. He was demonstrating not just outsize charisma as singer and orator but an expansive entrepreneurial and promotional streak. The Jubilees performed at a series of successful concerts under his and Cushing's management, and it must have been with some ambivalence that Loudin returned the reins to a crippled George White in July 1881.[55]

In September, the Jubilees proceeded into Canada, expecting perhaps to find a respite from their struggle with discrimination. After all, it had been in Canada that fugitive slaves had found freedom before the Civil War. But to their dismay, they were refused accommodations by four of Toronto's best hotels and charged prohibitively high prices by a fifth.[56] The mayor and various other leading citizens put the Jubilees up in their homes until at last another proprietor, tantalized by his competitors' bad press, telegraphed from America that they could stay at his hotel. In fact, as one paper observed, the furor made the Jubilees even "better known and more fully appreciated than they might otherwise have been. Had this been an ordinary troupe of 'Christy Minstrels' we should have been sure that it was a 'put up job' between the singers and the taverns."[57]

Canadian critics praised them highly. "Any language, however commendatory, would seem to fall short of the merits of the entertainment," wrote the *Daily Expositor*. "Miss Jennie Jackson is the life and soul of the choruses, and her voice rang out as clear as crystal above her companions. Her solos were gems of song. . . . Miss Sheppard is more than a mere accompanist. Her support is so judicious that the instrumental and vocal chord perfectly."[58]

Returning to Boston, the Jubilees continued to draw raves. "What is the secret of their success?" asked the *Evening Traveller*.

> The reply is, they give true music. . . . They do not deal in noise and clap-trap. . . . It seems to well up from the soul. . . . Men who are never moved by what has been denominated, "artistic music," of the Italian or German school, listen, with tears, to the music of the Fisk Jubilee Singers.[59]

But not everyone agreed. Musically they sometimes met with resistance, and from unexpected quarters. Though Mattie Lawrence was the daughter of a former student at the Oberlin Conservatory, Professor Rice of the conservatory advised his students not to attend the Jubilees' concert because the music "would not be of a high order."[60]

George White was in no condition to continue touring. For almost two years, he would have to walk on crutches and for the rest of his life could only shuffle short distances and then solely "by the support of a heavy cane."[61] White had so bound himself up with the Jubilees that in his pain and exhaustion he could not accept that the troupe might have a future without him. Claiming that he saw no prospect of the Jubilees continuing to make money, in May 1882 he abruptly declared the troupe disbanded and returned with Susan to Fredonia.

But the outsize Frederick Loudin and his ally Cushing were convinced that the Jubilees' best days lay ahead. Over White's strenuous objections, they began to recruit singers for their own troupe, including Maggie Porter and her new husband, Daniel Cole, plus Maggie Carnes, Georgia Gordon, Jennie Jackson, and even the elusive young songbird Minnie Tate, who had declined to sing for White after the Jubilees' first tour.[62]

Mabel Lewis refused to join, as did the Jubilees' longest serving and most prominent veteran, Ella Sheppard, who was never an admirer of Loudin. At a "heavy pecuniary sacrifice," she decided instead to follow the Whites to Fredonia, where her "pleasant manners" and "Christian conduct . . . won the friendship and respect of all who . . . made her acquaintance."[63]

"In September, 1882, a Negro steps to the helm and henceforth directs the now famous Jubilee Craft." So begins Loudin's account of the final chapter in the story of the Jubilee Singers. Loudin had "fully realized" not only that it would be "no easy task to come out of the ranks, where he had been on equal terms with the rest of the company, and take command" but that "it would greatly damage the cause of the Negro, if, under the management of one of the race, there should be in any respect a failure." He knew that thousands of people, white and black, "who have no confidence in the leadership of the Black Man, would say significantly, 'I told you so,' or 'I knew it.' "[64]

The troupe got off to a rocky start. It took Loudin months to complete the troupe. After an initial tour of Canada and the United States proved less profitable than they had hoped, Loudin and Cushing went their separate ways. Perhaps inevitably, Maggie Porter and her husband abandoned the troupe and formed their own company under Cushing's management, calling themselves the Original Fisk Jubilee Singers, a name to which Porter, as one of the founding Jubilees, felt she had more right than Loudin.

As far as Cravath was concerned, however, neither of them had a right to the name. "There is no company of singers now in existence," he declared in October 1884, "that is properly entitled to the name made famous by the colored students sent out by Fisk University."[65]

Regrouping, Loudin engaged a new agent and decided "to circumnavigate the globe," singing their spirituals "in lands where they had not yet been heard, and where we were entire strangers." In April 1884, they arrived in Britain, where they were greeted, as before, by the earl of Shaftesbury. Though His Lordship understood they were no longer singing on behalf of the great cause of black education that had first brought them to England, he saw their new mission as educational: advancing "the temporal and eternal interests of the white population."

Loudin's new advance man made the "sad mistake" of booking the Jubilees in the south of England during the hottest season, when "it was so warm that all indoor entertainments were failures." By July, their losses had amounted to several thousand dollars. Meanwhile, Porter and Cushing tried to lure some of Loudin's singers away with promises of higher fees. One of Loudin's singers—possibly Gordon—abandoned the troupe, but Loudin managed to keep the rest together.

In the late summer, the old magic seemed to return. They sang for audiences numbering in the thousands and stayed three nights in the castle of the earl of Tankerville, whose courtyard and ramparts the Jubilees filled to overflowing with an audience that seemed to pour in "like a river." At Hengler's Cirque in Liverpool, they sang before seven thousand, "the largest audience where an admission fee was charged to which the Jubilee Singers had ever sung." They sang in Ireland again, and then set off in April 1886 for the Antipodes.

During their forty-four-day voyage to Melbourne, Australia, they endeared themselves to passengers and crew by raising $150 for Liverpool's Aged Seamen's Home with a concert on deck. "There was none of that insolent color prejudice to confront us," Loudin reported, "as we were the only Americans on board." Though their advance man had been detained by a quarantine, so many invitations came in from prominent Australians that "wherever we went . . . flowers were strewn along our pathway." For twenty-five nights, they filled Melbourne's thirty-two-hundred-seat Town Hall, breaking every box-office record. They sang sixty nights in Sydney, forty in Adelaide, thirty in Brisbane, and tested the universality of their music to the utmost by performing for aborigines at a mission station.

At first, the aborigines were "far from cordial," Loudin recalled, "in fact they gave us to understand by their actions that they did not wish to have anything to do with us" and "seemed like unwilling children forced to go to Sabbath school." But as soon as the Jubilees began to sing "Steal Away,"

what a change of expression the tones of the old slave song awoke! First, wonder . . . then joy, as the full volume of the melody filled the humble little church. . . . When we had finished they gathered about us, and, with tears still flowing, they clasped our hands and in broken accents exclaimed, "Oh! God bless you! we have never heard anything like that before!" As we drove away, they climbed upon the fences and up in the trees, and until our carriages were lost to view, they waved us good-bye.

In New Zealand, the Maori "seemed to take to us at once, and though their songs have a limited scale of only three tones, still they were charmed with our music." One Maori woman began to follow them from concert to concert. "It seems as if your singing makes me crazy," she explained.

After fully three and a half years of performing in Australasia, Loudin's troupe sailed to India, where the viceroy, the marquess of Lansdowne, gave them his patronage. They sang almost exclusively to European and Eurasian audiences, though in Bombay they noticed that large numbers of Parsis came to hear them. At Agra, the Jubilees were overpowered by the "indescribable beauty" of the Taj Mahal, where they "were destined to have an experience of which we had not dreamed."

After obtaining the caretaker's consent, the enterprising Loudin "told a few friends, including the proprietor of one of the leading papers, who engaged a special reporter to write up the event." Loudin recounted the scene:

> As we entered the arched door-way, we met Mohammedans coming out; they had been within to bedeck the tombs of Shah Jehan and his wife with the fresh flowers of the morning, and with shoeless feet had repeated in the (to them) sacred presence their morning prayers. We looked with friendly glances into one another's dark faces as we met and passed; they inquiringly, while our faces must have been aglow with expectant delight. . . . We gather around the sarcophagi and soon the great lofty dome echoes the first Christian song it has ever caught up, and that song the cry of a race akin to those whose dust sleeps in the crypt beneath. As the tones of that beautiful slave song, "Steal Away to Jesus," which we had sung before emperors, presidents, kings, and queens, awoke the stillness of that most wonderful of temples, we were so much overcome by the unique circumstances that it was with the utmost difficulty we could sing at all.

They performed in Lucknow, and at All Souls Church in Cawnpore, in honor of the British who had died in the mutiny of 1857. From Calcutta, they sailed to Rangoon, where they were greeted by their homely old friend, teacher, and evangelist Henrietta Matson, who, perhaps in protest over Cravath's "business-like" regime, had left Fisk after seventeen years and come to Burma as a missionary.[66] The Jubilees sang for the Karen, hill people whom Baptist missionaries were busily converting in large numbers and who now reciprocated the Jubilees' performance by singing a number of Sankey's hymns.

The Jubilees proceeded to Hong Kong and Japan, where Loudin observed that "a much larger percentage of the Japanese attended our concerts than any of the other Oriental races." At a performance at a Congregational girls' school, Loudin never saw "a more interested and enthusiastic audience; they gave expression to their delight by clapping their hands and deep-drawn sighs, which . . . was their mode of expressing the highest degree of delight, and when we left, the girls ran down to the hedge which surrounds the school-house grounds and waved us good-bye as we were drawn away in our Rickshaws."

After a rough, cyclonic voyage to San Francisco, the troupe headed eastward and were "not long in finding out that we are no longer free from that prejudice which confronts a Negro at every turn in life, and which we had not met with in any other quarter of the globe." More than six years after it had set out, Loudin's troupe disbanded, but "as an answer to the predictions of our failure, I would say that at no period in the history of the company was its success more marked," he wrote.

> Some of the singers were enabled to buy for themselves comfortable homes; while I may refer, with, I trust, pardonable pride, in view of the discussion now being waged on the "Negro Problem," to the fact that I was able to become the largest stockholder in a shoe manufactory at my home, Ravenna, Ohio; that the stockholders did me the honor to name the company the F. J. Loudin Shoe Manufacturing Company, and . . . the shoes we manufactured the "F. J. Loudin Shoe."[67]

The "first man to make a successful six-years' tour around the world . . . with a company of colored singers, singing chiefly music composed by the Negro," Frederick Loudin built his own home from rare wood he had shipped back from all over the globe. He patented a window fastener and employed both blacks and whites in his shoe factory. He and his wife, Harriet, were childless, but they adopted a young man named Alec Turner and paid for his education. Turner became a distinguished Chicago physician and married Loudin's niece and accompanist.

Loudin toured repeatedly with various troupes, long enough to observe one unfortunate legacy of the Jubilees' success. In 1897, he reported from England that in "just two months . . . he had seen more Afro Americans than during all the years he was over there before and that they do not 'help matters one bit.' They seem to be 'left overs' from Uncle Tom's Cabin, minstrel, octoroon and snide jubilee companies and you know what sort of people as a rule they are and just about how they would 'represent' us."[68]

In 1903, Loudin was "stricken with a complete nervous collapse." Confined to a wheelchair with severe rheumatism, he died a year later at his home in Ravenna, surrounded by the "objets d'art, tapestries, brocades, furnishings," glass canes, and other mementos of a great and sui generis career.[69] He left his library to Fisk University.[70]

STEAL AWAY

EPILOGUE

In the end, the Jubilee Singers raised more than $150,000 for Fisk University in their first three tours. Calculated purely on the basis of inflation, that amounts to a little over two and a half million in today's dollars. But considering that it was enough to sustain the American Missionary Association and also build Jubilee Hall and at least a portion of Livingstone Missionary Hall as well—buildings that today would cost many more millions of dollars to construct—the true dollar value of what they raised was much higher.

Trapped by the sheer worthiness of their work, driven to the limits of endurance by their white managers, the first troupe's experience presaged the exploitation that would characterize the treatment accorded thousands of black performers who would follow in their footsteps. But such was the courage and resourcefulness of the singers themselves that Loudin, Porter, and Jackson and their troupes would also help to pioneer the antidote to such exploitation with their own autonomous enterprises.

No troupe of singers could hold back the deluge of racism that swept through the country after the Civil War. But no troupe of singers ever did more to try to evoke the better angels of America's nature. What the Jubilees accomplished for themselves and the nation was to demonstrate the dignity, intelligence, and educability of black Americans. In the circles of the wealthy, a man might once have gotten away with casually remarking that higher education was wasted on blacks. But without abandoning their own culture and traditions, the Jubilees provided vivid and convincing proof to the contrary. Their music demonstrated to the world that there was something of lasting value in African American culture.

In their encounters with American racism, they resolutely turned their own humiliation against those who discriminated against them, shaming hoteliers, railway magnates, school boards, politicians, impresarios, churches, theater managers, travel agents into changing their ways. That their victories were sometimes temporary and selective, that they did not always translate into permanent gains for their people, was not their fault but the nation's. By accepting the burden of personifying their people's aspirations, they made the cause of the freedmen, once the exclusive province of radicals and missionaries, plausible and respectable among vast numbers of American whites who would otherwise have turned away.

"It is said," Hinton Alexander once wrote, "that the story of the Jubilee Singers seems almost as little like a chapter from real life as the legend of the Argonauts who sailed with Jason on that famous voyage after the Golden Fleece." Hinton's voyage eventually landed him back in Tennessee, where he worked in Chattanooga as a postman. On the fiftieth anniversary of the troupe's departure from Nashville, Alexander appeared at Fisk with Mabel Lewis and Eliza Walker to sing "We'll Anchor By 'n' By" and "My Lord, What a Mourning."[1] He died four years later in 1925.[2]

After leaving the troupe in 1872, Greene Evans became a protégé of Ed Shaw, the black Memphis saloon keeper and political boss. Evans was elected to Confederate general Nathan Bedford Forrest's old seat on the Memphis City Council. In 1885, he was elected to the General Assembly, one of the "free men of high class" who fought against the depredations of Jim Crow. Though he served in the state legislature for only two years, Evans would be pivotal in winning, however briefly, the right of blacks to vote and hold office in Tennessee.

Georgia Gordon continued to have bad luck with men. She eventually returned to Tennessee, where she married Nashville's leading black entrepreneur, Preston Taylor. A former Union army drummer and railroad contractor for Collis P. Huntington, he was the founder of the Lea Avenue

Christian Church, Greenwood Park, and the city's chief black burial ground, Greenwood Cemetery, in which Gordon would become the first of several Jubilees to be interred. After their only child died in infancy in 1891, Preston Taylor fell in love with a younger woman. Gordon died in 1913 at the age of fifty-eight—of a broken heart, her family said.[3]

After the charismatic Jennie Jackson had returned to Tennessee, her fellow Jubilees were amused to hear that she had become president of a music club at Fisk "when she scarcely knows one note from another." But, teased Robinson, "Jennie is old and likes young folks' company, consequently she must provide a way to be with her 'dear boys.'"[4] Be that as it may, Jackson toured again, first with White's new troupe, then with Loudin's, and finally with Maggie Porter's. She eventually married the Reverend A. J. DeHart of Cincinnati and toured with her own troupe, the Jennie Jackson DeHart Jubilee Club. She died in 1910.[5]

Julia Jackson never fully recovered from her stroke and died in St. Louis in 1890.[6] Patti Malone moved to Limestone County, Alabama, but died on tour with Loudin in Omaha, Nebraska, in 1897.[7] Mabel Lewis remained devoted to the Whites and spent a winter at their house in Fredonia in 1884. She married a man named Imes and eventually formed her own troupe. As an old lady, she performed frequently at Fisk, astonishing audiences with the volume of her voice. On one of her later visits south, her nephew told her, "Auntie, when you get to Cincinnati, you'll have to go into the Jim Crow car." After living in the North, she "wasn't used to that sort of thing," and as her train left Cincinnati, "I expected every minute to get put off," she recalled.

> Finally I asked the brakeman—I wanted to put it in a nice way, so I said—"Do I have to change here?"
>
> He said, "No."
>
> But the conductor kept looking at me and at my ticket. At last he said, "You get off at Nashville?"
>
> "Oui, monsieur," I said, and he let me stay on that car.[8]

Still amused by life and revered by her family, Mabel Lewis died in Cleveland in 1935.[9]

Maggie Porter continued performing with her troupe, but after years of trouble on trains and in hotels, she eventually vowed never to set foot in the South again. She kept that vow until 1931, when Fisk finally induced her to return to Nashville for the sixtieth anniversary of the day she and the Jubilees first set off from Fisk. As an old lady, she was a much-revered figure in Detroit. Like many another difficult prima donna, she lived a long time—longer than any of the other original Jubilees—dying in 1942 at the age of eighty-nine.[10]

For George White, the disbanding of his troupe marked the end of his life's work among the freedmen. That some of his most gifted and devoted singers should defy him and go on without him seemed base ingratitude for all he had done for "his children," as he still called them. In October 1882, White would write the equable Henry Bennett of Fisk, asking that his connection with the Congregational church there be severed so he could join the Presbyterians of Fredonia.

"If I am granted this request," he wrote with great sadness, "it will separate me from any immediate connection with the mission work for the region, after twenty four years of more or less continuous service. I have hesitated to break this last tie which binds me to the work," he said.

> It will be the only step which I have taken voluntarily in the direction of leaving it, and it is not without sadness and regret that I make the change. The best years and strength of my life have been given to Fisk University, and around it and its work cluster the most tender and sacred memories of the past. To its service was consecrated every power of soul, mind and body, and my separation from it is the severing of these. . . . Permit me also to assure you of my deep and abiding affection for you all, as brethren and sisters in Christ, and of my continued love for and faith in the work in which you are engaged, and in which we were permitted to serve together, during so many eventful years.[11]

White's health continued its steady decline until, according to his doctor, his constitution was entirely "broken" and the only work he could do was clerical, which he accomplished only "through sheer determination or [when] forced to by pecuniary circumstances."[12] Poverty compelled him "to break my home in Fredonia" and move to Ithaca, where his brother-in-law was business manager of Sage College at Cornell. His children by his first wife, Laura, would survive him, but his only child by Susan Gilbert died in

1890.[13] A year later, he deemed himself "an old man at 53—broken in health, and so seriously crippled that I find it very difficult to earn a support." In the end, the erudite Susan Gilbert White was reduced to accepting "the position of housekeeper," the sort of job from which she and her husband had devoted their lives to rescuing black women. On Saturday, November 9, 1895, George White suffered a massive stroke and died at the age of fifty-eight.[14]

At his memorial service at Fisk, Ella Sheppard read some remarks, and Loudin's Jubilee Singers returned to sing "Steal Away" and "We Shall Walk through the Valley."[15] White believed not only that the jubilee songs "expressed the highest possible spiritual fervor," wrote Mary E. Spence, "but that they were capable of receiving the highest possible culture."[16] On all occasions, wrote Georgia Gordon, White "was the true and tried friend of the singers, and a staunch friend of the Negro race."[17]

Erastus Milo Cravath spent the rest of his life building on the Jubilee Singers' accomplishment, raising more funds from private donors, and holding firm to his conviction that black Americans could achieve the highest academic standards. Booker T. Washington, with whom he had clashed over the ideal of black education, attributed Fisk's austerely classical "character and atmosphere" to Cravath.[18] (For all his differences with Fisk's approach, Washington married an alumnus, sent all his children to Fisk, and served on the board of trustees.) During his reign, Cravath led Rutherford B. Hayes, Frederick Douglass, Admiral George Dewey, and Theodore Roosevelt on walking tours of his thirty-five-acre campus and told them the story of Jubilee Hall.

Through its portals would pass such distinguished Americans as W.E.B. Du Bois; James Weldon Johnson; John Wesley Work, Sr., Jr., and III; Margaret Murray Washington; Arna Bontemps; Elmo Brady; Roland Hayes; John Hope Franklin; John Lewis; Hazel Reid O'Leary; Julius Lester; Nikki Giovanni; David Levering Lewis. By the turn of the century, five hundred students were enrolled. Of the 400 Fisk departmental graduates the university could trace, 1 was a college president, 8 were professors, 46 were principals, 165 were teachers, 20 were ministers, 9 were lawyers, 2 were editors, 13 were in business, and 9 worked for the federal government; at least 700 Fiskites who never graduated were teachers.[19] From the beginning, Fisk had to fight to survive, and it struggles still. But it outlasted its competitors in Nashville. Both Roger Williams and Central Tennessee College fell prey to arsonists and strife. Roger Williams closed and merged with Memphis's LeMoyne, and Meharry Medical School is all that remains of John Braden's enterprise.

Cravath ruled Fisk with an iron hand, but students like W.E.B. Du Bois respected him as "honest and sincere." Once he grew into his presidency, racial bigotry was about the only thing that could discompose him. When asked by a reporter about the discrimination the Jubilee Singers had encountered, Cravath "spoke with an increase of warmth over his usually quiet manner." Here he was training Negro girls "to reach a stage of refinement and self respect" only to have them relegated to "the company of brutes in a smoking car." Segregation should be eliminated, he said, out of "common justice."[20]

As an old man, he used to greet every male student with a salute, every female with a tip of his hat. "I saw him meet a colored washer-woman coming out of Jubilee Hall one day," an alumnus recalled, "and he lifted his hat as politely as if she were the queen of England." Cravath was always quoting Moses to his students and in old age looked "like one of the prophets of old."[21] He died in 1900.

Adam Knight Spence preceded Cravath to the grave by a couple of months. All his life, he remained, in his own odd and sometimes morbid fashion, a fearless and tireless champion of the African American.

"Dear white Christians of Nashville," he bravely piped up from a pulpit in 1890. "What are you doing for the colored people of our city? . . . For twenty years I have been amongst you with an aching heart on this matter. . . . What are you doing for the people whom by adoption I call mine? Do you seek them out in your [shacks] and cellars, in your alleys and hovels? Do you bring them the love of your Master?"[22]

Spence stood up to his students as well. Over time at Fisk, "there was a belief on the part of many that there could not possibly be anything good connected with or brought over from the former condition of servitude," wrote a faculty member.

> It was their desire to stop singing their religious songs, so many of which reminded them forcibly of their physical distresses and expressed their helplessness except as the Lord himself might reach

down and bring to them freedom from bondage. They would sing only "white" songs.[23]

Once, when Fisk students refused to sing spirituals to some visitors, an aging Spence faced his pupils and sang the old songs alone in his sharp, wavering tenor. During a ride through Washington, D.C., in 1891, Spence's carriage overturned, throwing him down a twenty-foot embankment and blinding him in his right eye. The injury affected his left eye eventually, and by the time of his death nine years later, he had become nearly blind.[24]

After studying at Fisk and Harvard and in Germany, W.E.B. Du Bois deemed Spence "a great Greek scholar by any comparison."[25] Henry Hugh Proctor respected Cravath but loved Spence. Once, when a local theater refused to seat his black students anywhere but in the gallery, Spence sat with them instead of with his colleagues in the loge. "It made us love him," wrote Proctor, "in a way we could not love them," for he had "shared our estate."[26] Spence allowed "no difference because of race . . . in the treatment of his students," his daughter wrote. "They could be all that any people are."[27]

In December 1882, Ella Sheppard and George Washington Moore were wed. As far as George White was concerned, no one was good enough for his most accomplished and devoted disciple. But Moore came close. He was a pious, brilliant, cheerful, and abundantly confident young man. His ancestry was predominantly white. His father, Rice Moore, was a slave descendant of Winfield Scott of Virginia, a hero of the Mexican War and Lincoln's venerable general in chief of the army at the outbreak of the Civil War. A pale and lanky man with the hooded eyes of a prize fighter, Rice Moore tried several times to escape from slavery, but he was so valuable as a craftsman, and his features so "strongly marked . . . and easily recognized," that he was always caught. His wife, Elizabeth Corry, was a white woman who had been abducted as a child and sold into slavery. Indeed, she and her son George were sold repeatedly, the last time to a man who took them to Augusta, Georgia, at the beginning of the Civil War.

By then, Rice Moore was the property of William Moore of Nashville, who taught him the tinner's trade. After emancipation, the upright and tenacious Rice Moore gathered up his far-flung family and established a tin shop in a ramshackle stable in an alley, from which he supplied buckets and

ladles, gutters and dustbins to George White and the Fisk Free Colored
School. He legally married Elizabeth Corry and tried to urge an education
on his ten-year-old son, George. But for six years, George was content to
spend his time on the streets smoking cigarettes, selling tinware and sulfur
water, and carrying market baskets for the prostitutes of Smoky Row.

"Father remonstrated both with voice and rod," George would recall,
"but in vain." Finally, on an August morning in 1871, a desperate Rice
Moore took his dissolute son with him on a walk that eventually covered
thousands of miles. Leaving his business in his wife's hands and leading
George away "with only his tinker tools and thirty cents in money," Rice
Moore took his son over the ground he had traveled "when a fugitive from
bondage." Living off whatever they could earn repairing tin buckets, roofs,
and gutters, George and his father "walked the same paths through the
woods of the hill country, drank from the same springs, saw the thickets"
where his father had "hid by day and stopped at the cabins where he had received food and shelter." They walked from Tennessee to Kentucky and on
into Indiana, Illinois, Missouri, Arkansas, Louisiana, and Mississippi. In the
North, Rice Moore impressed upon his son "the thrift, intelligence and
wealth of a free people"; in the South, he pointed out "the results of slavery, the then unhealed scars of the war, and the ignorance and wretched-
ness of the emancipated slaves."

"By the wisdom and energy of this unlettered freedman," George
would recall with awe and gratitude, "his son had been given an object-
lesson which changed his whole character and purpose in life." On his return, George jumped at the chance to attend Fisk School.[28] Nevertheless,
when he arrived at Fisk, he seemed to Henrietta Matson "hard and heedless
and unpromising." But he began to change while teaching a country school
and, after returning to Fisk in the fall, struggled "alone for hours" with the
Holy Spirit. Finally, "it was good old professor Spence," he wrote, "who
knelt by my side and pointed me to the Lamb of God" until "shouts of
praise burst" from George's lips.[29]

Soon afterward, he passed some of his old cronies playing ball "and using profane language." Though he was afraid they would "revile him for his
newfound religion," he was overwhelmed with pity for them. "Some of
them threatened to punish him for his interference," but soon "they all
gathered around him, as he told them how changed he was, and what the
dear Lord had done for him." He decided then and there to become a
preacher and was appointed co-pastor of Howard Chapel in 1876.[30]

Moore held "that vital Christianity is the work of Christ Church, no denomination will save a person, nothing but the blood of Christ can do this. I find that the great need of our people is a greater knowledge of the *Scriptures*," but he could not "recount all their needs for they need so much. If they are industrious, economical, and prudent and trust in the Lord, He will supply all their wants."[31]

Henry Bennett regarded Moore as his most promising student and urged the A.M.A. not to let him slip through its fingers. By 1882, Moore had entered the Oberlin seminary and was a year away from earning his bachelor of divinity. That summer, he had been put in charge of three white churches in southern Ohio, "where he worked so acceptably as to receive a unanimous call to return," but he had decided to work for the freedmen through the A.M.A.[32]

On the windy evening of December 22, 1882, Ella Sheppard married George Washington Moore among the pine wreaths and vines of George and Susan White's parlor in Fredonia. "The instruments of home remain strong in your people," intoned the minister, "despite their sorrowful history while in the house of bondage."[33]

During the celebration that followed, Sheppard handed slices of cake to all the guests and "with excellent good taste"—more taste, incidentally, than either Mrs. Gladstone or Agnes Livingstone Bruce had shown—made "no display of the wedding gifts," though, as White added, they were "by no means meager."[34]

Ella Sheppard Moore moved with her new husband to Oberlin and, precisely nine months after the wedding, gave birth to a son they named George Sheppard Moore. Ella proceeded with her husband and her elderly mother, Sarah Hannah Sheppard, to Washington, D.C., where Ella gave birth to a daughter she named Sarah.[35] In 1884, she paused from her feedings and changings to report to Fisk alumni that she and her husband found their work "interesting and in good condition."[36] During the nine years George was pastor of Lincoln Memorial Church, the Moores were the scourge of the local saloon keepers. They eventually shut down thirteen drinking establishments and turned the neighborhood known as Hell's Bottom into "one of the best resident sections in the District of Columbia."[37] For five years, George Moore taught biblical history and literature in the theology department of Howard University and, at the time of his appointment in 1885, was Fisk University's only black trustee.[38] It was during this period that he and Ella became friends of Frederick Douglass's, just

as he rose from the doldrums of a dispiriting old age to battle with his former eloquence and fearlessness against the abomination of lynchings.

In 1892, Moore accepted the religious version of Erastus Milo Cravath's old post, moving to Nashville as field superintendent of Southern
church work for the American Missionary Association, in which position he
would serve until his death. Shortly after moving to Nashville, Ella gave
birth, at the age of forty-one, to another son and lived with her mother in
the house she had built for her within view of Jubilee Hall.

Sarah Hannah Sheppard lived with Ella until her death in 1912, watching as the little baby she had nearly drowned continued to fulfill Mammy
Viney's prophecy. In her last hours, Sarah rose from her deathbed to join in
her daughter's mournful singing of "Swing Low, Sweet Chariot," the secret
lullaby Sarah had sung to her in the days of their bondage.

Ella Sheppard Moore became the president of Tennessee's Women's
Missionary Union and published articles about the early days of the Ju-
bilees and the plight of women in slavery. She became a mentor to the
Work family at Fisk in their labors on behalf of the "Negro folk song" and
continued to train and inspire Fisk's student choirs.[39] After her mother's
death, she toured the country, visiting old friends she had made during her
Jubilee days and dropping in on the schools and universities of the A.M.A.
During one of these visits, the young missionary Lura Beam observed how
Ella's "indefinable air of leisure and perfection and the lack of self-
consciousness set her apart. . . . She looked to be out of this world," Beam
thought, "and was certainly of another century."[40] Adam Knight Spence's
daughter Mary, who would remain at Fisk until her death in the 1960s, was
devoted to her and believed that "in intellect, in spirit, and in musical at-
tainment" Ella Sheppard Moore "was one of the gifted women of the
world."[41]

In 1913, Ella appeared at the close of a Jubilee concert at Nashville's
Ryman Auditorium to sing again, in her small, true voice, "Swing Low,
Sweet Chariot." On June 3, 1914, she gave the commencement address at
Mary Wells's Trinity School in Athens, Alabama. On her way home, she had
an attack of appendicitis, and a few days later, this skinny, frail, and infinitely courageous woman who had survived a childhood of slavery, grief,
and deprivation and eleven years of grueling tours across America, Canada,
Britain, and Europe died of sepsis on the operating table at the age of sixty-
three,[42] still "hopeful," as she once wrote in an account of her life, "of the
ultimate triumph of righteousness and the redemption of her people."[43]

———

Though Thomas Alva Edison invented the phonograph in 1876, two years before the end of the singers' third tour, apparently no recordings exist of any of the original Jubilee troupes that sang on behalf of Fisk University. The earliest recordings of the Jubilees' descendants are of a male quartet that set out in 1899 under the direction of first tenor John Wesley Work, Jr. The recordings they made during a northern tour in 1908 have been reissued on two CDs by Austria's Document Records.

By the early twentieth century, minstrel troupes had adapted some of the original Jubilees' repertoire in their parodies of black religious observances. Performing in concert halls in full regalia, Work and his singers set out to restore the Jubilee canon to respectability. During World War I, they performed for American troops in bases and hospitals, and their recordings for Victor and, later, for Columbia under Work's successor, James Myers, were widely disseminated. From 1916 to 1925, Fisk sometimes fielded two fund-raising Jubilee groups: a professional quartet and a student choir.[44] In 1924, the Jubilees and their music helped persuade Nashville's white community to raise the undreamed-of sum of fifty thousand dollars to assist Fisk in meeting a matching grant of a million dollars.

White school songbooks routinely featured such Jubilee classics as "Swing Low, Sweet Chariot" and "Deep River," and white choirs closed their own concerts with "Ezekiel Saw the Wheel" and "Deep River." But in much of black America, the Jubilee repertoire fell out of favor. In the early twentieth century, some African American churches—including George Washington Moore's Congregationalists—refused to admit spirituals into their canon, dismissing them as shamefully primitive throwbacks. Determined to demonstrate that American black churches could free themselves from Africanisms, some black Baptists, Methodists, and Episcopalians tried to adhere to the European canon.

By the 1920s, however, both European and slave hymns had been displaced in African American worship by the spiritual's immediate descendant, gospel music, which combined its antecedents with the fervor of black street Pentecostalism and the influences of blues and ragtime. To the champions of gospel, like Thomas Andrew Dorsey, the Jubilee repertoire was simultaneously an anachronism and a jumping-off place for their own exuberant invention.

The Jubilee quartets nonetheless exerted an enormous influence over the gospel quartets that followed. Work and Myers saw themselves as protecting the spiritual from the unholy influences of jazz, but their renditions of "Little David, Play on Your Harp" and "Poor Mourner Got a Home at Last" presaged the improvisations of such great gospel performers as the Soul Stirrers, the Dixie Hummingbirds, the Original Five Blind Boys of Alabama, and the Swan Silvertones.

The spiritual survived as a bridge between black and white America. Even as the last of the original Jubilees passed away, the tradition was being carried forward by jubilee choruses and quartets from not only Fisk but other black schools like Hampton, Tuskegee, and Howard, as well as in the concerts and recordings of Paul Robeson, Marian Anderson, and the great baritone Roland Hayes, who could not perform them without the tears rolling down his cheeks. Choruses like the Robert Shaw Chorale, Fred Waring and the Pennsylvanians, and the Oberlin College Choir routinely featured spirituals in their repertoire, saving them for the end of their concerts as if serving up dessert.

In the folk music revival of the 1950s and 1960s, such artists as Odetta, Harry Belafonte, Leon Bibb, and the Phoenix Singers reintroduced them to white audiences. But the spiritual saw its most dramatic revival during the civil rights movement, when demonstrators sang "No more auction block for me," "This little light of mine," and "Before I'd be a slave, I'd be buried in my grave," the very lyrics Sarah Hannah Sheppard had sung for her daughter Ella and Ella, in her turn, had taught the Jubilees.

The popularity of spirituals seems to rise when, in the anguished history of American race relations, new generations of blacks and whites revive the same hope for justice and reconciliation that animated the original Jubilees. And it recedes when the gulf between black and white Americans widens, for singing these ancient outpourings from the heart of bondage demands a level of trust from black performers, and of understanding from white audiences, that sometimes proves elusive. Among some African Americans, the spiritual's enduring appeal to white audiences has made it suspect, tainted as its reception has often been by racist misinterpretations. Today, it is sometimes dismissed as a relic not just of slavery but of nineteenth-century black accommodationism.

Even as the jubilee tradition ebbs and flows, however, the singers' contribution to American music is as permanent as it is incalculable. The Jubilees helped to rescue American music from its obsequious bondage to the often insipid, secondhand trappings of the English and European tradition. They contributed to the creation of a music so all-embracing as to accommodate not only African American strains but Latin, Asian, Jewish, and Native American influences as well. (Nashville's own international reputation as the "Music City" began not with Grand Ole Opry but with the Jubilee Singers.) In 1895, the Czech composer Antonín Dvořák, then head of the National Conservatory of Music in New York, declared that if America ever intended to develop its own music, it need look no further than the African American songs to which the Jubilee Singers had provided the gateway.

You can hear an echo of the Jubilees in the works of Gershwin, Copland, and Ellington. It infuses the chords and cadences of jazz, even down to the disposition of instruments and the improvisational matrix of the classic jazz quartet. The Jubilees haunt the arrangements of Fletcher Henderson and Benny Goodman; the muted lyricism of the early Miles Davis; Charles Mingus's "Wednesday Night Prayer Meeting"; the riffs of Thelonious Monk, Mose Allison, and Jimmy Smith; the call and response of Little Richard, Ray Charles, Aretha Franklin, Whitney Houston.

The Fisk Jubilee Singers were the fountainhead of a continuing stream of musicians who trace their source back to the praise and sorrow songs that Ella Sheppard and her schoolmates first shyly performed for their white mentor 130 years ago, in the curtained dark of Fisk's decaying barracks.

In August 1897, Maggie Porter performed with five other members of her troupe in a beer garden in Lucerne, Switzerland. In the audience was Mark Twain, now a nearly impoverished old man of sixty-one, grieving on the first anniversary of the death of his beloved daughter Susy. Ever since her death, he had been almost inconsolable, convinced that the world was "horrible" and "odious": the one "true hell."[45] Nothing, it seemed, could lift his spirits until he walked into a beer hall and encountered Porter's Jubilees.

"How charming they were," he exclaimed, "in spirit, manner, language, pronunciation, enunciation, grammar, phrasing, matter, carriage, clothes, —in every detail that goes to make the real lady and gentleman, and welcome guest." The Swiss audience sat "at round tables with their beer mugs in front of them—self-contained and unimpressionable looking people, an indifferent and unposted and disheartened audience."

> Then rose and swelled out above those common earthly sounds one
> of those rich chords the secret of whose make only the Jubilees pos-

sess, and a spell fell upon that house. It was fine to see the faces light up with the pleased wonder and surprise of it. No one was indifferent any more. . . .

Arduous and painstaking cultivation has not diminished or artificialized their music, but on the contrary—to my surprise—has mightily reinforced its eloquence and beauty. Away back in the beginning—to my mind—their music made all other vocal music cheap; and that early notion is emphasized now. It is utterly beautiful, to me; and it moves me infinitely more than any other music can.

Wishing that the spiritual "were a foreign product," so that his countrymen "would worship it and lavish money on it and go properly crazy over it," Twain concluded "that in the Jubilees and their songs, America has produced the perfectest flower of the ages."[46]

NOTES

SOURCES

ACKNOWLEDGMENTS

INDEX

NOTES

Key to Abbreviations

AKS   Adam Knight Spence Collection
AMA   American Missionary Association
FB   Freedmen's Bureau
FU   Fisk University
JSS   Jubilee Singers Scrapbooks
MES   Mary Elizabeth Spence Collection
OC   Oberlin College Archives
TSLA Tennessee State Library and Archives

1: GOD'S OWN TIME

1. Sheppard, "Negro Womanhood: Its Past," undated clipping (FU).
2. The name of the fellow Donelson slave was Jimmie Sheppard.
3. Pike, *Jubilee Singers* (1873), pp. 49–50; Marsh, *Story of the Jubilee Singers* (1881), pp. 103–5; Moore, "Bondage and Freedom: The Story of a Life," unidentified journal article courtesy of Beth Howse; United States, Census records, Nashville, 1860; Moore (Sheppard), "Historical Sketch of the Jubilee Singers," *Fisk University News*, Oct. 1911; Sheppard, "Negro Womanhood: Its Past"; additional genealogical information courtesy of Martha Mullin, curator of the Hermitage.
4. Ella Maples told several stories about the parrots her master used to at least ap-

pear to spy on his slaves. She said her master kept some in the trees to keep watch while the slaves were working. "If a nigger stop to rest a little while the parrot he holler out, 'Marse, the nigger ain't working.' " According to Maples, the master had a parrot that would cry, "Marse, nigger stealing, nigger stealing." "Them parrots, they was hateful things." Eventually one of the master's parrots lied to him, "and he get up and get his gun and shoot that old parrot dead 'cause the parrot lie and Master say he ain't going to have no lying parrot round him." "Our boss didn't keep no parrot to tell on the niggers but some did. And you ought to hear them parrots call and sic the dog if a nigger was doing something wrong." One old lady kept a parrot in her kitchen so it might repeat what the slaves were saying out of her earshot. Ella Maples in Rawick, ed., *American Slave*, supplement, series 2, 7 (Texas): 2574–75; Horatio Williams in Rawick, ed., *American Slave*, supplement, series 2, 10 (Texas): 4088; Lucy Gillum(?) in Egypt, ed., *Unwritten History of Slavery*, p. 20.

5. Work, *Folk Song of the American Negro*, p. 80.

6. Though Jackson could be cruel to his slaves, he and Uncle Alfred apparently adored each other, and Alfred claimed to have been present at the old man's deathbed to hear his last words: "Weep not for me; weep for yourselves." In his old age, he claimed to be Jackson's body servant, but that distinction really went to George Jackson, the grandfather of Jennie Jackson of the Jubilee Singers (see chapter 3). Though General Jackson provided in his will for Uncle Alfred's manumission, he never left the Hermitage. He was the only one of the president's old servants to remain during the federal occupation of Nashville and conducted tours of the property for curious Yankee officers. Courtly, a gifted orator, Uncle Alfred Jackson remained a fixture at the Hermitage until his death in 1901. When he was introduced to Rutherford B. Hayes, who did more to unravel Reconstruction than any other president, Uncle Alfred barely deigned to shake his hand. "If you had been as great a man as General Jackson," he explained to Hayes, "I could have most shook your hand right off." He became an icon of the proverbial "loyal slave" and a ward of the Ladies' Hermitage Association. On his death, the association allowed him to be buried, as he requested, just to the north of General Jackson's tomb. James Hay, "And Ten Dollars Extra, for Every Hundred Lashes Any Person Will Give Him, to the Amount of Three Hundred," *Tennessee Historical Quarterly* 36:468; Goodstein, *Nashville*, p. 74; Bancroft, *Slave Trading in the Old South*, p. 300; Goodstein, *Nashville*, p. 83; obituary in Nashville *Daily News*, Sept. 5, 1901, courtesy of David Steele Ewing.

7. There are many contradictions in the various versions of Ella Sheppard's early life. In Pike's *Jubilee Singers* (1873), there is an ostensibly firsthand account in which she says she was taken to Mississippi and became sick at the age of fifteen months; when her father found out, he came to her and purchased her for $350. He then came back to Mississippi, as this story goes, and arranged to buy his wife. He returned to Nashville with his wife and his former master's overseer, and they were about to close the deal when Sarah's master reneged on the agreement, "and so she was obliged to leave her husband and child at once, and go back again into

slavery" (pp. 49–50). But in an account written later in life, and published under her name in the American Missionary Association's journal, she tells the story about Mammy Viney, which does not jibe with the previous account. Ella could not have spied on her mother at fifteen or sixteen months, and in this later version, she and her father never went to Mississippi but remained in Nashville. Sheppard's mother lived with her in later life, and it may be that at the time Pike's book was published, Sheppard did not recall the full story. In any case, Pike may have scrambled some facts in transcription. Sheppard no doubt owned a copy of the Pike version and, had she believed it accurate, would have predicated her later account upon it. Though the Mammy Viney story smacks of folklore, I tend to give Sheppard's later version greater credence.

8. The case was not unique. Nobody knows how many slave children were killed by their parents to prevent them from becoming slaves. One former slave recalled that an owner sold one of his slave's three children when they got to be a year or two old. When she gave birth to a fourth child, she poisoned it rather than let him sell it. "Course didn't nobody tell on her, or he'd have beat her nearly to death." Unidentified in Botkin, *Lay My Burden Down*, p. 154.

9. *Republican Banner*, undated clipping (1858).

10. One of the most dramatic prewar efforts to educate blacks was initiated by a wealthy St. Louis freedman named John Berry Meachum, who first taught black children to read and write in Sunday schools and then, when whites objected, anchored a steamboat on the federally controlled Mississippi, equipping it with classrooms and a library and rowing black students out on a skiff for daily classes. One of his students was James Milton Turner, a future American consul to Liberia. Greene et al., *Missouri's Black Heritage*, pp. 67–68.

11. Moore (Sheppard), "Before Emancipation," *American Missionary*, n.d., pp. 7–8.

12. Napier sent his own sons to Wilberforce Academy and Oberlin College. Goodstein, *Nashville*, p. 144.

13. Ibid., pp. 144, 152.

14. The census record for 1860 shows Simon Sheppard owning no property.

15. Roustabout song and Charles Dickens (1842) in Federal Writers' Project, *Cincinnati*, pp. 38, 62.

16. With a curse on both their houses, he left Cincinnati in 1851.

17. In July 1863, Confederate colonel John Hunt Morgan considered attacking Cincinnati but veered instead with 2,400 cavalry into Indiana and southeastern Ohio, where, by the time of his surrender, he would lose all but 335 men. Federal Writers' Project, *Cincinnati*, pp. 64–65.

18. Diary of Ella Sheppard, Dec. 6, 1877.

2: FROM EVERY GRAVEYARD

1. Civil War pension file of George Leonard White.

2. Ibid.; Seventy-third Ohio Infantry Volunteers Web page.

3. A slave named Jack Maddox watched in horror as a party of rebel Home Guards punished a deserter named Bob Anderson. "They tied him with a rope and tied the other end to the saddle of one of the men. They went off with him trotting behind the horse." Maddox followed after them and thirteen miles down the road saw "where he fell down and drag signs on the ground. Then when I come to Hornage Creek I seen they had gone through the water. I went across and after a while I found him. But you couldn't tell any of the front side of him. They had drug the face off him." But slaves had witnessed such atrocities against their own kind and were not so shocked by them as by mass warfare. Jack Maddox in Rawick, *American Slave*, supplement, series 2, 7 (Texas): 2536.

4. Cato Carter in Rawick, ed., *American Slave*, supplement, series 2, 3 (Texas): 648.

5. Jack Harrison in ibid., 5 (Texas): 1655.

6. William M. Thomas in ibid., 5 (Texas 4): 97, 1655.

7. Lucy Thomas in ibid., supplement, series 2, 9 (Texas): 3803.

8. Anderson Brown in Wiley, *Southern Negroes*, pp. 15–16.

9. Charles Davenport in Rawick, ed., *American Slave*, 7 (Mississippi): 40.

10. Chattanooga *Confederate* and Hague in Wiley, *Southern Negroes*, pp. 15, 17–19, and nn. 106, 107, 109.

11. Pike, *Jubilee Singers* (1873), p. 56.

12. Anderson Brown in Wiley, *Southern Negroes*, p. 19.

13. Love, *Life and Adventures of Nat Love*, p. 14.

14. Escott, *Slavery Remembered*, p. 121.

15. Grigsby, *Smoked Yank*, p. 160.

16. Greene et al., *Missouri's Black Heritage*, p. 83.

17. Some months later, his one surviving son returned to the farm, shut himself in the shed, and cut his throat. "There a piece of paper say he not care for to live," Annie Row recalled, " 'cause the nigger free, and they's all broke up." In Botkin, ed., *Lay My Burden Down*, pp. 235–36.

18. Katie Rowe in ibid., pp. 103–4.

19. *Anti-Slavery Advocate* in Blassingame, ed., *Slave Testimony*, p. 360.

20. Egypt, ed., *Unwritten History of Slavery*, p. 81.

21. Hughes, *Thirty Years a Slave*, pp. 154–55.

22. Berlin et al., eds., *Free at Last*, pp. 112–13.

23. Sarah Debro in Hurmence, ed., *My Folks Don't Want Me to Talk about Slavery*, p. 57.

24. Goodrich, *Black Flag*, p. 50.

25. Maslowski, *Treason Must Be Made Odious*, p. 98.

26. Mrs. James Abernethy and Mrs. W. H. Neblett in Wiley, *Southern Negroes*, pp. 52nn and 76.

27. Cimprich, *Slavery's End in Tennessee*, p. 24.

28. Anonymous in C. H. Johnson, ed., *God Struck Me Dead*, p. 102.

29. Harriet Robinson in Baker and Baker, eds., *WPA Oklahoma Slave Narratives*, pp. 359, 361.

30. Egypt, ed., *Unwritten History of Slavery*, p. 253.

31. Wiley, *Southern Negroes*, p. 70.

32. Fitzgerald, *Visit to the Cities and Camps*, p. 124.

33. Magnolia Plantation Records in Wiley, *Southern Negroes*, p. 78.

34. Ibid., p. 68.

35. Hannah Crasson in Hurmence, ed., *My Folks Don't Want Me to Talk about Slavery*, p. 20.

36. Rachel Cruze in Mellon, ed., *Bullwhip Days*, p. 215.

37. Lee Guidon, John G. Hawkens, Charley Williams, and Liza Jones in Botkin, ed., *Lay My Burden Down*, pp. 65, 114, 193, 205.

38. James Thomas in Schweninger, ed., *From Tennessee Slave to St. Louis Entrepreneur*, p. 172.

39. Wiley, *Southern Negroes*, p. 71.

40. Cimprich, *Slavery's End in Tennessee*, p. 30.

41. Pike, *Jubilee Singers* (1873), pp. 57–60.

42. Robinson was born in 1855, and the Battle of Murfreesboro she witnessed was in January 1863.

43. Orland Kay Armstrong in Wiley, *Southern Negroes*, pp. 13–14 and nn.

44. Rutling, *Tom*, pp. 14–15.

3: BY THE THUNDER

1. Rawick, ed., *American Slave*, 16 (Tennessee): 2.

2. Alexander Winchell and anonymous soldiers in Hoobler, *Cities under the Gun*, p. 71.

3. Ibid., pp. 17–19, 29, 41.

4. *Republican Banner*, undated clipping (1858).

5. Fitch, *Annals of the Army of the Cumberland*, pp. 628–29.

6. Ibid., p. 631.

7. Louisa Brown Pearl in Hoobler, *Cities under the Gun*, pp. 18–19.

8. Lorenza Ezell in Rawick, ed., *American Slave*, supplement, series 2, 4 (Texas): 1324.

9. Interview with T. Vance Little.

10. Goodstein, *Nashville*, p. 141.

11. Though Uncle Alfred Jackson (see chapter 1) claimed to be Jackson's body servant, Hermitage records suggest he was his coachman.

12. McPherson, *Negro's Civil War*, appendix B; Taylor, *Negro in Tennessee*, p. 27.

13. Fourth Ward. Goodstein, *Nashville*, pp. 86–87, 124, 134, 137, 141.

14. Marsh, *Story of the Jubilee Singers* (1881), pp. 107–9.

15. Whetstone, "History of Knoxville College," p. 5.

16. Hoobler, *Cities under the Gun*, pp. 22, 65.

17. Fitch, *Annals of the Army of the Cumberland*, pp. 632–33; Cimprich, *Slavery's End in Tennessee*, p. 65.

18. Charles in C. H. Johnson, ed., *God Struck Me Dead*, p. 33.

19. Ayer to Lyman, 1863, in Civil War (Federal) Collection, box F25, folder 6 (TSLA).

20. J. Eaton in Wharton, *Negro in Mississippi*, p. 29.

21. Cimprich, *Slavery's End in Tennessee*, p. 48.

22. Knox, *Slave and Freeman*, pp. 56–57.

23. Estimates ranged from seven to ten thousand. Simpson, "Sketch of the Early Days of the Mission"; Nashville *Dispatch* in Taylor, *Negro in Tennessee*, p. 125.

24. J. G. McKee in Hubbard, *History of the Colored Schools*, pp. 31–32.

25. "The moment the Union army moved into slave territory," wrote W.E.B. Du Bois, "the Negro joined it. . . . It made no difference what the obstacles were, or the attitudes of the commanders. It was 'like thrusting a walking stick into an ant hill,' says one writer. And yet the army chiefs tried to regard it as an exceptional and temporary matter, a thing which they could control, when as a matter of fact it was the meat and kernel of the war." J. Eaton and W.E.B. Du Bois in Wharton, *Negro in Mississippi*, pp. 26, 29.

26. Cimprich, *Slavery's End in Tennessee*, p. 54.

27. Knox, *Slave and Freeman*, p. 57.

28. Cimprich, *Slavery's End in Tennessee*, p. 57.

4: CAN'T YOU READ?

1. Scouller, *Manual*, pp. 628–29.

2. Before the war, Harriet Jacobs condemned churches for sending missionaries abroad and neglecting "the heathen at home. Talk to American slaveholders as you talk to savages in Africa," she implored them. "Tell *them* it was wrong to traffic in men." In Gates, ed., *Classic Slave Narratives*, p. 402.

3. Scouller, *Manual*, p. 415.

4. Pettijohn to Toulin, April 23, 1864 (AMA).

5. Frederick Douglass to Rev. J. Miller McKim, May 2, 1865, in McFeely, *Frederick Douglass*, p. 241.

6. Hoobler, *Cities under the Gun*, p. 35 (illus.); J. G. McKee in Hubbard, *History of the Colored Schools*, pp. 31–32; Whetstone, "History of Knoxville College," p. 5.

7. Simpson, "Sketch of the Early Days of the Mission."

8. Scouller, *Manual*, p. 415.

9. Cimprich, *Slavery's End in Tennessee*, p. 48.

10. Nat Black in ibid., p. 54.

11. Charles in C. H. Johnson, ed., *God Struck Me Dead*, p. 34.

12. Lovett, *African-American History of Nashville, Tennessee*, p. 23.

13. Whetstone, "History of Knoxville College," p. 6; Simpson, "Sketch of the Early Days of the Mission."

14. J. G. McKee in Hubbard, *History of the Colored Schools*, pp. 31–32.

15. Goodstein, *Nashville*, pp. 143, 150–52; Hubbard, *History of the Colored Schools*, pp. 4–6; Simpson, "Sketch of the Early Days of the Mission."

16. Levi Pollard in Hurmence, ed., *We Lived in a Little Cabin in the Yard*, p. 63.

17. John Sella Martin in Blassingame, ed., *Slave Testimony*, p. 709. The enterprising

William Wells Brown learned a lesson in the value of literacy. One day his master sent him off with a note to give the local jailer. Suspicious of what it might say, Brown persuaded a sailor to read it to him. It turned out to instruct the jailer to give Brown a whipping for spilling wine on a visiting slave buyer. Brown thereupon found another slave who looked like him and, deceiving him into believing that the note was a request for a trunk he was supposed to pick up, paid his unwitting stand-in a dollar to deliver the note for him. The slave accepted Brown's offer and took the letter to the jailer, who promptly took away his dollar, whipped him badly, and gave him a note to return to his master. Brown bought the note from the indignant slave for fifty cents and found a stranger to read it to him. "Dear Sir," it began, "By your direction, I have given your boy twenty lashes. He is a very saucy boy, and tried to make me believe that he did not belong to you, and I put it on to him well for lying to me." Brown went home, returned the note to his master, and, affecting a limp, declared, "I had never had such a whipping in my life." Brown always regretted the incident but blamed it on slavery. "Slavery makes its victims lying and mean," he explained, "for which vices it afterwards reproaches them, and uses them as arguments to prove that they deserve no better fate." Brown in Andrews, ed., *From Fugitive Slave to Free Man*, pp. 49–51.

18. Charlie Davenport in Mellon, ed., *Bullwhip Days*, p. 375.
19. Anonymous in Egypt, ed., *Unwritten History of Slavery*, p. 173.
20. Rose Maddox in Rawick, ed., *American Slave*, supplement, series 2, 7 (Texas): 2526.
21. Caldwell, "Brief History of Slavery in Boone County, Kentucky," p. 3; Clarke and Clarke, *Narratives*, pp. 104–5.
22. Ellen Butts in Botkin, ed., *Lay My Burden Down*, p. 126.
23. Maggie Whitehead Matthews in Rawick, ed., *American Slave*, supplement, series 2, 7 (Texas): 2624.
24. Millie Simpkins in Rawick, ed., *American Slave*, 16 (Tennessee): 67.
25. Edward Walker in Blassingame, ed., *Slave Testimony*, p. 517.
26. Maggie Whitehead Matthews in Rawick, ed., *American Slave*, supplement, series 2, 7 (Texas): 2624.
27. Emma Knight in Howard, *Ralls County, Missouri*, p. 63.
28. Cimprich, *Slavery's End in Tennessee*, p. 79.
29. John Sella Martin in Blassingame, ed., *Slave Testimony*, p. 709.
30. John Crawford in Rawick, ed., *American Slave*, supplement, series 2, 4 (Texas): 967.
31. Levi Pollard in Hurmence, ed., *We Lived in a Little Cabin in the Yard*, p. 63.
32. Frazier, *Negro Family in the United States*, p. 28.
33. Joseph Farley and anonymous in Egypt, ed., *Unwritten History of Slavery*, pp. 122, 171.
34. Mattie Hardman in Baker and Baker, eds., *WPA Oklahoma Slave Narratives*, p. 184.
35. John McAdams (Nashville) in Rawick, ed., *American Slave*, supplement, series 2, 7 (Texas): 2465.
36. J. W. Stinnett in Baker and Baker, eds., *WPA Oklahoma Slave Narratives*, p. 412.

37. Sarah L. Johnson Berliner in Rawick, ed., *American Slave*, supplement, series 2, 10 (Texas): 4333.

38. Lewis Clarke in Blassingame, ed., *Slave Testimony*, p. 154.

39. Osofsky, ed., *Puttin' On Ole Massa*, pp. 25–26.

40. Rev. William Washington Brown in Frazier, *Negro Family in the United States*, p. 27.

41. James Thomas in Schweninger, ed., *From Tennessee Slave to St. Louis Entrepreneur*, p. 81.

42. John Sella Martin in Blassingame, ed., *Slave Testimony*, p. 712.

43. Stephen Jordan in Albert, *House of Bondage*, p. 108.

44. Marrs, *Life and History*, pp. 12, 17.

45. "When I was in Virginia I used to study some. I learned my A,B,C, and begun to spell some in my blue-back spelling book. I could spell 'ba-ker' and 'sha'dy,' and all along there in the spelling book; but after I came to Louisiana I forgot every thing." Charlotte Brooks in Albert, *House of Bondage*, p. 18.

46. Anonymous in Egypt, ed., *Unwritten History of Slavery*, pp. 46, 143.

47. Louvinia Young Pleasant in Rawick, ed., *American Slave*, supplement, series 2, 8 (Texas): 3102.

48. Marsh, *Story of the Jubilee Singers* (1881), pp. 109–10.

49. Cimprich, *Slavery's End in Tennessee*, pp. 77, 111–12.

50. Simpson, "Sketch of the Early Days of the Mission"; Whetstone, "History of Knoxville College," p. 6.

51. Hubbard, *History of the Colored Schools*, pp. 30–33.

52. Simpson, "Sketch of the Early Days of the Mission."

53. Maslowski, *Treason Must Be Made Odious*, p. 116.

5: WE'LL OVERTAKE THE ARMY

1. "C.V.S." in *New York Times* quoted in Maslowski, *Treason Must Be Made Odious*, p. 142.

2. Andrew Johnson in Maslowski, *Treason Must Be Made Odious*, p. 36.

3. E. P. Smith in Fisk *Expositor*, Dedication of Jubilee Hall (FU).

4. Anonymous in C. H. Johnson, ed., *God Struck Me Dead*, p. 154.

5. J. P. Bardwell to M. E. Strieby, Dec. 13, 1864 (AMA).

6. Ten black regiments were recruited from the environs of Nashville alone. Maslowski, *Treason Must Be Made Odious*, p. 109.

7. John Finnely in Rawick, ed., *American Slave*, 4 (2/Texas): 39–40.

8. Charles in C. H. Johnson, ed., *God Struck Me Dead*, p. 36.

9. Ballard, *Long Shadow*, p. 3.

10. Maslowski, *Treason Must Be Made Odious*, p. 109.

11. E. P. Smith in Fisk *Expositor*, Dedication of Jubilee Hall (FU).

12. Simpson, "Sketch of the Early Days of the Mission."

13. Cimprich, *Slavery's End in Tennessee*, p. 52.

14. Simpson, "Sketch of the Early Days of the Mission."

15. Ibid.; C. B. Fisk to J. G. McKee, July 7, 1865 (AMA).

16. McFeely, *Grant*, pp. 62–63, 69, 71.

17. Taylor, *Negro in Tennessee*, p. 231.

18. Anonymous, "A Tennessee Planter and a Negro School," *American Missionary*, Jan. 1866; Henry Watkins to Clinton Fisk in "Speech of Gen. Clinton B. Fisk," *American Missionary*, July 1867 (FU).

19. During the Civil War, Harding's slaves had stood by him: all except Henry Watkins. "In the year 1864, Gen. Harding had me sent off with the rebels just because I told him that I wanted to be free. He told Gen. Hood to take me as far as wind and water. . . . Now," he wrote Clinton Fisk in 1867, "he wants to lock arms with me and go into the saloon, but I can't see it. . . . Not long ago at the State house, a rebel said a negro had as much right with the ballot box as a monkey had with a razor; but thanks be to God and to our earthly friends we have got the ballot box and the razor too from the rebels, and we will give all the rebels a nice shave as soon as the water is warm." Clinton B. Fisk in "Speech of Gen. Clinton B. Fisk."

20. Among the other religious societies that sponsored missions in Nashville were the American Baptist Home Missionary Society, the Association of Friends for the Aid and Elevation of the Freedmen, and the Indiana Yearly Meeting of Friends Executive Committee for the Relief of Colored Freedmen. Secular sponsors included the Indiana Freedmen's Aid Commission of Indianapolis, Chicago's Northwestern Freedmen's Aid Commission, Philadelphia's Pennsylvania Freedmen's Relief Association, and Cincinnati's Western Freedmen's Aid Commission. Black sponsors included the Black Odd Fellows and the Order of Sons of Relief. Cimprich, *Slavery's End in Tennessee*, pp. 54–55.

21. Simpson, "Sketch of the Early Days of the Mission."

22. Spence to Catherine Spence, May 11, 1866, AKS (FU).

23. J. M. Richardson, *Christian Reconstruction*, pp. 6–7, 88.

24. "Obituaries: Rev. E. P. Smith," *American Missionary*, Oct. 1876 (FU).

25. McKee to Clark, Jan. 15, 1866 (AMA).

26. Smith to M. E. Strieby, Oct. 11, 1865 (AMA); see also Nellie M. Horton to Spence, May 2, 1871 (AMA).

27. Ogden, "Fisk University," n.d. (AMA).

28. Maslowski, *Treason Must Be Made Odious*, p. 129.

29. Spence, "History of Old Barrack Buildings," n.d.

30. Ogden to A.M.A., n.d. (AMA).

31. Washington, *Up from Slavery*, pp. 29–30.

32. Henrietta Matson to George Whipple, Oct. 6, 1868 (AMA).

33. An A.M.A. missionary named Lura Beam, who taught in the South during the Jim Crow era, recalled how everyone in black communities was still "mad for education." One old lady on her deathbed entrusted Beam with an envelope that she feared "no one will care about" after she was gone. "Will you promise to keep it," she asked, "so I will know I am not gone all too soon?" The envelope contained her university credits, "accumulated after attending night school and working all

day." Robbins, "World-within-a-World," p. 2; Beam, *He Called Them by the Lightning*, p. 96.

34. *Colored Tennessean*, July 18, 1866.

35. Anderson to Whiting, July 2, 1865 (AMA).

36. William F. Mitchell to C. B. Fisk, Jan. 18, 1866 (FB).

37. Some Northerners would assume that the school was named after the voracious financier James Fisk, Jr., and wonder why he could not keep it afloat. "This is a remarkable mistake," huffed the *American Missionary*. "If the benevolence of Mr. Fisk ever took the direction of patronizing colored schools we never heard of it." "Fisk University, Its Name and Connection," *American Missionary*, March 1872 (FU).

38. Interview with Lula Crosthwaite by Mary E. Spence, undated, 1911. MES, Notebooks (FU).

39. William Gannaway Brownlow in Joe M. Richardson, "Fisk University: The First Critical Years," *Tennessee Historical Quarterly* 29, no. 1, p. 27.

40. "Opening Exercises of the Fisk Freedmen's School in Nashville, Tennessee," *American Missionary*, March 1866 (FU).

41. E. M. Cravath to George Whipple, Feb. 13, 1866 (AMA).

42. In her biography in Pike (1873), Porter said she attended Wadkins's school, then McKee's, then Fisk. In the interview from which this quote comes, she says she was at Wadkins's school, but the interview was conducted when she was a very old lady and she probably confused the two. There was no play yard at Wadkins's school, which was held in an outbuilding behind his house on High Street. Cole (Porter), "Maggie Porter-Cole," *Fisk News*, Dec. 1939.

6: THE ANGELS CHANGED MY NAME

Epigraph: Spence, undated transcription, MES, Notes (FU).

1. Thomas Rutling in Marsh, *Story of the Jubilee Singers* (1881), p. 57; Rutling, *Tom*, p. 16.

2. JSS (FU).

3. Rutling, *Tom*, p. 17.

4. Ogden to Fisk, Dec. 31, 1865 (AMA).

5. Asa Severance Fisk to John Eaton, March 13, 1863 (AMA).

6. E. P. Smith to M. E. Strieby, Oct. 11, 1865 (AMA).

7. S. F. Porter, July 1, 1865 (AMA); Memorandum of Expenditures for the Fisk School Nashville Tenn. prior to Feb. 1, 1866 (AMA); Elizabeth A. Easter, Teachers' Monthly Report, April 1866 (AMA).

8. Nellie M. Horton to Pike, Oct. 23, 1870 (AMA).

9. J. M. Richardson, *Christian Reconstruction*, p. 172.

10. E. M. Cravath to M. E. Strieby, Jan. 10, 1866 (AMA).

11. Hubbard, *History of the Colored Schools*, p. 1.

12. Journal of the Tennessee Annual Conference, Oct. 11, 1866, Methodist Church, Northern Branch, Records, 1866–1888 (TSLA microfilm 647).

13. L. Humphrey to A.M.A., June 11, 1863 (AMA).

14. Robbins, "World-within-a-World," p. 45.

15. Beam, *He Called Them by the Lightning*, p. 14.

16. Simpson, "Sketch of the Early Days of the Mission."

17. Beam, *He Called Them by the Lightning*, p. 12.

18. Proctor, *Between Black and White*, p. 20.

19. Escott, *Slavery Remembered*, p. 99.

20. Wayman Williams in Rawick, ed., *American Slave*, supplement, series 2, 10 (Texas): 4146.

21. After emancipation, Ishe Webb wearied of a steamboat captain who "never called any man by his name. . . . He was a rough man who always carried a gun in his pocket and a gun in his shirt." Against his fellow dockworkers' advice, Webb walked up to him and said, "Captain, I don't know what your name is, but I know you is a white man. I'm a nigger, but I got a name just like you have. My name's Webb. If you call me 'Webb,' I'll come just as quick as I will for any other name and a lot more willing." The captain peered at Webb a moment, asked where he was from, and then put his arm around Webb's shoulder and told him he was right. "You have a name," he said, "and you have a right to be called by it." In Botkin, ed., *Lay My Burden Down*, p. 245.

22. Washington, *Up from Slavery*, pp. 34–35.

23. Martin Jackson in Rawick, ed., *American Slave*, 4 (2/Texas): 192.

24. Redford and D'Orso, *Somerset Homecoming*, p. 89.

25. Elizabeth Botume in McPherson, *Negro's Civil War*, p. 119.

26. James Thomas in Schweninger, ed., *From Tennessee Slave to St. Louis Entrepreneur*, p. 171.

27. Simeon S. Jocelyn in J. M. Richardson, *Christian Reconstruction*, pp. 94, 52.

28. A.M.A. records contain receipts for shipments of McGuffey's *Readers*. Gates and Gamble to Fisk Academy, Jan. 18, 1866 (AMA).

29. Easter continued: "Her husband was sold from her in /50 and sent to New Orleans but when freedom was given them he came back and by one of the mysterious providences of God they were brought together again and are now living happily and thankfully fearing none but God who has brought them into the promised land." E. A. Easter to A.M.A., Feb. 12, 1866 (AMA).

30. Teachers' Monthly Report, Jan. 1866 (AMA).

31. Simpson, "Sketch of the Early Days of the Mission."

32. C.A.J. Crosby to A.M.A., Jan. 31, 1868 (AMA).

33. Rev. Edward Anderson in *Congregationalist and Recorder*, in *American Missionary*, Aug. 1867.

34. Joe M. Richardson, "Fisk University: The First Critical Years," *Tennessee Historical Quarterly* 29, no. 1, p. 28; Cravath to Ogden, April 21, 1866 (AMA). By late February 1866, there were 2,350 students enrolled and 38 teachers employed in Nashville schools. In Tennessee, 8,808 students, 137 employed. Fisk School, "Abstract of School Report," Feb. 26, 1866 (AMA).

35. Benny Bilboe in Fisk, "Speech of Gen. Clinton B. Fisk," *American Missionary*, July 1867.

36. Ogden to C. B. Fisk, March 8, 1866 (AMA).

37. Memphis *Avalanche* in B. P. Runkle to C. B. Fisk, May 23, 1866 (FB).

38. On Saturday, Tade went out "among the hills, where my flock was scattered, [and] called them by their names. They knew the voice & followed." "Colored people killed, 46; whites, 2; rapes on colored women, 5; maltreated, 10; robberies, 100; houses and cabins burned, 91; churches, 9; schoolhouses, 12. Value of property destroyed, $130,991." E. O. Tade to M. E. Strieby, May 21, 1866 (AMA); Taylor, *Negro in Tennessee*, pp. 85–87; J. F. Chalfant, "Persecution in the South," *American Missionary*, Oct. 1866.

39. B. P. Runkle to C. B. Fisk, May 23, 1866 (FB).

40. M. Walsh to J. R. Lewis, Oct. 3, 1866 (FB); Robbins, "World-within-a-World," p. 12. "I desire to know what steps have been taken by the Civil Authorities in Memphis to bring to Justice the Murderers, House-burners, Robbers, Rapers and Rioters generally of the Memphis, May massacre." Fisk to Col. F. S. Palmer, Aug. 7, 1866 (AMA). No action had been taken by the civil authorities against the rioters: "the *Riders* are boldly asserting their intentions to repeat the villainies of May . . . arrests have not been made." Palmer to Fisk, Aug. 15, 1866 (AMA).

41. In February 1866, Fisk expressed his egalitarian view of law enforcement in the answers he gave to a series of questions posed by his field agents.

> When a white man is fined for beating a freedman, and he refuses to pay the fine, how shall I enforce the payment?—Hold him in arrest until he pays it; and if he still refuses, put him in jail.
>
> When I order a white man to appear to answer a claim for debt due a freedman, and he refuses to appear, what am I to do?—You will arrest and fine him for contempt.
>
> What about carrying firearms?—You cannot disarm the negroes when white men of every class are allowed to carry arms.
>
> What about whipping as a punishment for crime?—No! Let the lash be laid aside forever. . . . Should any one attempt to use it on any of his laborers, you will punish him severely." Clinton B. Fisk, "Taking the Bull by the Horns," *American Missionary*, Feb. 1866.

42. Taylor, *Negro in Tennessee*, pp. 31–32.

43. E. A. Easter, Feb. 12, 1866 (AMA).

44. M. A. Parker, April 8 and 9, 1867 (AMA).

45. E. A. Easter to A.M.A., Feb. 12, 1866 (AMA).

46. Ogden to Smith, May 8, 1867 (AMA).

47. Joel Grant to Prof. Henry Cowles of Oberlin College, April 10, 1863 (AMA).

48. C.A.J. Crosby to A.M.A., May 1, 1866 (AMA). Archives H9119.

49. Later her husband returned, "apparently humble and very earnest in his confessions and promises for the future," and took her away, "whither we cannot tell." M. A. Parker, April 9, 1867 (AMA).

50. C.A.J. Crosby to A.M.A., Jan. 31, 1868 (AMA).

51. C.A.J. Crosby, Oct. 1867 (AMA).

52. Eliza Elsey in Baker and Baker, eds., *WPA Oklahoma Slave Narratives*, p. 140.

53. Anonymous in Egypt, ed., *Unwritten History of Slavery,* p. 1.

54. William B. Trotter in Sydnor, *Slavery in Mississippi,* p. 137. "Some niggers dies, but more was born," recalled James Green, " 'cause Old Pinchback sees to that. He breeds niggers as quick as he can, 'cause that money for him. No one had no say who he have for wife. But the nigger husbands wasn't the only ones that keeps up having children, 'cause the masters and the drivers takes all the nigger gals they wants. Then the children is brown, and I seed one clear white one, but they slaves just the same." In Botkin, ed., *Lay My Burden Down,* p. 160.

55. Martha Buford Harrison recalled how whites used to bring their slaves to camp meetings to show them off. " 'I'll show you my niggers,' they'd say to each other, and they would come 'round and look at each other's niggers. . . . White folks was crazy about their nigger babies," she explained, "because that's where they get their profit." In Egypt, ed., *Unwritten History of Slavery,* p. 116.

56. Rawick, *American Slave,* 16 (Tennessee): 78.

57. Lulu Wilson and Primous Magee in Mellon, ed., *Bullwhip Days,* pp. 322, 352.

58. Mollie Dawson in Rawick, ed., *American Slave,* supplement, series 2, 4 (Texas): 1122.

59. Cimprich, *Slavery's End in Tennessee,* p. 74.

60. L. Humphrey, "Thanksgiving in Camp," Aug. 20, 1863 (AMA).

61. Albert Todd in Rawick, ed., *American Slave,* supplement, series 2, 9 (Texas): 3884.

62. Jordan, *Black Confederates and Afro-Yankees,* p. 125.

63. Lulu Wilson in Rawick, ed., *American Slave,* 5 (4/Texas): 192. Some mothers did not experience separation from their children until after emancipation, when their remarried slave husbands from whom they had been separated by sales now returned to claim their children. "My father was sold away from us," Mollie Watson recalled, but after the war he returned to retrieve Mollie and took her to his new family. She tried to run back to her mother "every chance I got, till finally he took me so far away that I couldn't come back." In Baker and Baker, eds., *WPA Oklahoma Slave Narratives,* p. 454.

64. *Colored Tennessean,* Oct. 7, 1865, and March 31, 1866.

65. Tines Kendricks and Lee Guidon in Botkin, ed., *Lay My Burden Down,* pp. 66, 74.

66. Marsh, *Story of the Jubilee Singers* (1881), pp. 105–6.

67. Adelaide J. Vaughan in Botkin, ed., *Lay My Burden Down,* p. 155.

68. Hughes, *Thirty Years a Slave,* p. 204.

7: GIDEON'S BAND

1. "My mother, a victim of slavery's occurrences, on January 28, 1863, gave me, a little unwanted babe, the blessed privilege of sharing a long and happy life with her." Caldwell, untitled MS, MEK, Burrus (FU).

2. Sheppard, "Negro Womanhood: Its Past," undated clipping (FU).

3. Daniel Payne, "The History of the Origin and Development of Wilberforce University," Wilberforce University Web page.

4. Sheppard calls her "Madame Rivi." Information courtesy of Barbara Dawson of the Cincinnati History Museum.

5. Ogden to J. M. Walden, Aug. 26, 1865 (AMA).

6. Ogden to Fisk, Feb. 24, 1866 (AMA).

7. J. M. Tracy to S. W. Groesbeck, Sept. 17, 1867 (FB).

8. Isaac M. Newton to Ogden, May 16, 1868 (AMA).

9. F. Ayer, Oct. 2, 1865 (FB).

10. E. H. Truman to Samuel Hunt, June 28, 1866 (AMA).

11. J. M. Richardson, *History of Fisk University*, p. 6.

12. White to Smith, Sept. 1869 (AMA).

13. Civil War pension file of George Leonard White.

14. Oberlin alumni directory and files (OC).

15. Tennessee extract from Report of 1867 (AMA).

16. Ogden to Smith, April 11, 1868 (AMA).

17. JSS (FU).

18. Ogden to Whipple, Feb. 29, 1868 (AMA).

19. On a memo dated January 29, 1866, it is called Fisk Academy (AMA).

20. Cravath to Ogden, April 21, 1866 (AMA).

21. J. M. Richardson, *History of Fisk University*, p. 59.

22. Ogden in Pike, *Jubilee Singers* (1873), p. 33.

23. President Theodore Roosevelt once remarked to a visitor that he thought a primary education was all a black person needed.

What about black teachers? asked his visitor.

"I suppose they ought to have a high school education," conceded Roosevelt.

Then what about the ones who taught the high school teachers? his visitor persisted.

"Well," said the president, "I suppose they ought to go to college."

"Really," Roosevelt said after a pause, "there's no end to the thing, is there?"

"A Milestone at Fisk," *New York Times,* Nov. 9, 1947.

24. Thomas Jefferson in James, *Real McCoy,* p. 28.

25. Robbins, "World-within-a-World," p. 26.

26. Charles Grandison Finney in Jeal, *Livingstone,* p. 13.

27. Rev. David Peck in *Gazette and Courier* (Ohio), quoted in *Lorain County News,* Dec. 21, 1871.

28. Sherlock Bristol in Brandt, *Town That Started the Civil War,* p. 39.

29. Anonymous, "Erastus Milo Cravath," TS (FU).

30. Fisk University obituary notice, n.d., MES, Fisk List (FU).

31. Anonymous teacher in J. M. Richardson, *History of Fisk University,* p. 20.

32. Photograph (caption), "First Teachers in Fisk University, Nashville, Tenn. June 1866" (FU).

33. Fisk Board of Trustees to Peabody Fund, June 25, 1869 (AMA).

34. Joe M. Richardson, "Fisk University: The First Critical Years," *Tennessee Historical Quarterly,* 29, no. 1; Ogden to To whom, July 9, 1868, MES, Burrus (FU); Memorandum of Incorporation, 1867 (AMA).

35. Richardson, "Fisk University: The First Critical Years."

36. Moore (Sheppard), "Historical Sketch of the Jubilee Singers," *Fisk University News,* Oct. 1911 (FU).

37. Marsh, *Story of the Jubilee Singers* (1881), p. 10.

38. Anonymous ex-slave in Adam Knight Spence, "Interesting Personal Experiences," *American Missionary,* April 1873.

39. James Thomas in Schweninger, ed., *From Tennessee Slave to St. Louis Entrepreneur,* p. 158.

40. Cimprich, *Slavery's End in Tennessee,* p. 22.

41. Ogden in J. M. Richardson, *Christian Reconstruction,* p. 227.

42. Pike, *Jubilee Singers* (1873), pp. 60, 67–70.

43. Porter says it was in Mount View, which I am unable to locate on a map.

44. Pike, *Jubilee Singers* (1873), p. 66.

8: HARD TRIALS

1. See Tennessee extract from Report of 1867 (AMA).

2. A Fisk alumnus from the 1930s was once asked what she meant when she said she and her sister went to Fisk but "weren't *able* to go to Fisk." She laughed. "My father paid, but he paid time by time by time. He would go up and talk to the treasurer and make an arrangement." She laughed again. "My sister and I say, 'We *know* how to graduate on making arrangements.' " Interview with Novella Bass.

3. C.A.J. Crosby to A.M.A., Jan. 31, 1868 (AMA).

4. A. J. Barker to White, April 18, 1870 (AMA).

5. Malnida Stone to John Ogden, June 27, 1868 (AMA).

6. Rachel Ferguson to White, April 10, 1870 (AMA).

7. Alfred E. Anderson to Ogden, Feb. 12, 1868 (AMA).

8. White to Anderson, Aug. 26, 1871 (AMA).

9. G. L. White to E. P. Smith, Nov. 7, 1868 (AMA). "For our own use," he asked for "something *fresh.*" G. L. White to E. P. Smith, Nov. 21, 1868 (AMA).

10. JSS (FU).

11. Moore (Sheppard), "Historical Sketch of the Jubilee Singers," *Fisk University News,* Oct. 1911 (FU).

12. Samuel B. Williams to Spence, Jan. 1, 1866, MES (FU).

13. Spence to Elizabeth Spence, Jan. 15, 1866, Spence, AKS, box 7 (FU).

14. "Testimony of Professor Spence," *American Missionary,* Aug. 1866.

15. Spence to Catherine Spence, May 10, 1866, AKS (FU).

16. Ibid., May 11, 1866.

17. J. M. Richardson, *Christian Reconstruction,* p. 163.

18. Mary Spence, family notes, MES (FU).

19. Julia Spence Chase to Spence, Aug. 17, 1870, AKS (FU).

20. James Spence to Spence, Aug. 13 and 19, 1870, AKS (FU).

21. F. A. Chase to Spence, Aug. 13, 1870, AKS (FU).

22. Anonymous Freedmen's Bureau agent to Spence, Aug. 17, 1870, AKS (FU).

23. Spence to Catherine Spence, Sept. 6, 1870, AKS (FU).

24. Cravath to White, Sept. 7, 1870, AKS (FU).

25. The Harpeth Hills "are too distant to visit on an ordinary ramble." The country-side was once wooded, "but the forests gave place to fortifications and these to ruins & barren fields where no plow can go for the outcropping rocks. War, war!" Spence to Catherine Spence, Sept. 12, 1870, AKS (FU).

26. Spence to Elizabeth Spence, Oct. 31 and Nov. 30, 1870, AKS (FU).

27. Spence to Catherine Spence, Sept. 22, 1870, AKS (FU).

28. Unidentified clipping, JSS (FU).

29. Spence to Catherine Spence, Oct. 23, 1870, AKS (FU).

30. King James Bible, Isa. 55:12.

31. McLain to White, May 25, 1870 (FU).

32. M. L. P. Porter to White, Dec. 20, 1870 (FU).

33. Cole (Porter), "Maggie Porter-Cole," *Fisk News,* Dec. 1939.

34. A. E. Anderson to Ogden, Feb. 29, 1868 (AMA).

35. Sheppard to Spence, March 5, 1872, MES (FU). "Alfred E. Anderson is a free col-ored man, and a Teacher, as well as a Preacher of the Methodist denomination. . . . I have known him for many years. He is a trust-worthy man, and I commend him to the favorable notice of all loyal men, North and South." William G. Brownlow, governor of Tennessee, Certificate of Emancipation, April 26, 1865 (AMA). "Rev. Alfred E. Anderson (is) a most worthy Christian laborer and brother of a kind no-ble and patriotic heart. Devoted to the interest and elevation of his race and countrymen. I visited the city of Knoxville last winter and found him the only remaining Loyal Methodist Preacher, instructing a school of Freed children." Rev. Samuel Lowrey to Rev. M. E. Strieby, Testimonial for Rev. A. E. Anderson, May 18, 1865 (AMA).

36. A. E. Anderson to Ogden, Nov. 10, 1868 (AMA); Anderson to White, Nov. 14, 1870 (AMA).

37. Boston *Herald,* JSS (FU).

38. Marsh, *Story of the Jubilee Singers* (1881), p. 116; 1860 and 1870 census records for Nashville.

39. Bragg, *Georgia Gordon Taylor,* pp. 1–3, 14.

40. J. W. Stinnett in Baker and Baker, eds., *WPA Oklahoma Slave Narratives,* p. 415.

41. Daniel Chapman to Whipple, Nov. 18, 1863, A.M.A. (TSLA) MS.

42. Northern soldiers were appalled by the number of obviously mixed-race children they found in Tennessee and the number of masters who had kept their own chil-dren as slaves. An infantry colonel recalled helping a slave evacuate his master's plantation. His wife was "a good-looking mulatto (the old fellow himself was blacker than ink). . . . A pretty quadroon woman of about thirty, who passed as his daughter—though she couldn't have been of his blood—was helping on to the seat one of the most beautiful white children I ever saw. She was well dressed, and had a fair, clear, rosy skin, and an eye as blue as indigo. Supposing she was the master's child, I asked her where she was going. 'Way up North, massa, 'long with

granddad,' she answered. I was thunderstruck. She was the old woman's grand-child, the planter's own child, and a *slave!* I never until then realized what an ac-cursed thing slavery is." Kirke, *Down in Tennessee,* pp. 16–17.

43. L. R. Ferebee, a black schoolteacher at Roanoke Island, North Carolina, recalled that of the thirty-five boys he prepared to attend Howard University "only three could get any assistance from Northern friends, as Prof. Cardozo, only appeared to look out for those of light hue, or mulatto—none of the dark ones could get assistance." Cardozo, himself a mulatto, explained that it merely broke this way because they had been free before the war and received more education than darker former slaves. Ferebee, *Brief History,* pp. 11–12; J. M. Richardson, *Christian Reconstruction,* pp. 52–53.

44. "There are some few slaveholders who thinks a good deal of their children by their slaves, & some have sent their children north. Some of them have been to Oberlin. There are some slaveholders who have got pretty refined feelings about them, though they are great men to go into these depredations." J. W. Lindsay in Blassingame, ed., *Slave Testimony,* pp. 400–1.

45. "Master John was mad after his slave women," Salomon Oliver recalled. In Baker and Baker, eds., *WPA Oklahoma Slave Narratives,* p. 305. "A yellow child show up every once in a while. Those kind always got special privileges because the Master said he didn't want his children whipped like the rest of them slaves." Frazier, *Negro Family in the United States,* p. 55.

46. "Them yeller women was highfalutin . . . ; they thought they was better than the black ones. Have you ever wondered why the yeller women these days are meaner than black ones about the men? Well, that's the reason for it, their mammies raised them to think about the white men." Mattie Curtis in Hurmence, ed., *My Folks Don't Want Me to Talk about Slavery,* p. 37.

47. J. W. Terril's father was an elderly white saloon keeper. He eventually let Terril's white daughter care for him, but "before my father gave me to my sister, I was tied and strapped to a tree all night in the cold and rainy weather" and released only on the condition that "I must wear a bell till I was twenty-one year old, strapped around my shoulders with the bell about three feet from my head in a steel frame. That was for punishment for being born into the world a son of a white man and my Mammy, a Negro slave. I wear this frame with the bell where I couldn't reach the clapper, day and night. I never knowed what it was to lay down in bed and get a good night's sleep till I was about seventeen years old," when his father died. "When Missy took that bell offen me, I think I in Heaven because I could lie down and go to sleep. When I did I couldn't wake up for a long time, and when I did wake up I'd be scared to death I'd see my father with his whip and that old bell. I'd jump out of bed and run till I give out, for fear he'd come back and get me." In Botkin, ed., *Lay My Burden Down,* p. 166.

48. President Madison's sister once remarked that "we southern ladies are compli-mented with the name of wives; but we are only mistresses of the seraglios" (Fra-zier, *Negro Family in the United States,* p. 64). "Southern wives," fumed a Southern wife, "know that their husbands come to them reeking with pollution from the

arms of their tawny mistresses. Father and son seek the same source of excitement and alike gratify their inhuman propensities. . . . The whole practice is plainly, unequivocally, shamelessly *beastly*" (Margaret Douglass in Jordan, *Black Confederates and Afro-Yankees*, p. 129). "There are no slaves," wrote Lewis Clarke, himself of mixed race, "that are so badly abused, as those that are related to some of the women, or the children of their own husband; it seems they never could hate these quite bad enough" (*Narratives*, p. 12). "Such slaves invariably suffer greater hardships, and have more to contend with, than others. They are, in the first place, a constant offence to their mistress. She is ever disposed to find fault with them; they can seldom do any thing to please her; she is never better pleased than when she sees them under the lash, especially when she suspects her husband of showing to his mulatto children favors which he withholds from his black slaves. The master is frequently compelled to sell this class of his slaves, out of deference to the feelings of his white wife; and, cruel as the deed may strike any one to be, for a man to sell his own children to human flesh-mongers, it is often the dictate of humanity for him to do so; for, unless he does this, he must not only whip them himself, but must stand by and see one white son tie up his brother, of but a few shades darker complexion than himself, and ply the gory lash to his naked back; and if he lisp one word of disapproval, it is set down to his parental partiality, and only makes a bad matter worse, both for himself and the slave whom he would protect and defend" (Frederick Douglass in Foster, *Witnessing Slavery*, p. 79). Sometimes a master's slave grandchild would catch hell for its mother's privileges. Salomon Oliver's "own Mammy, Mary, was the Master's own daughter." Her father ordered his overseers "to leave her alone and not whip her," so the overseer visited his jealousy on her children, their master's grandchildren, to whom he had not extended his protection. "He would whip me just for the fun of it," Oliver recalled (in Baker and Baker, eds., *WPA Oklahoma Slave Narratives*, p. 306).

49. James Thomas in Schweninger, ed., *From Tennessee Slave to St. Louis Entrepreneur*, p. 70.
50. Robert J. Cheatham in Rawick, ed., *American Slave*, 5 (Indiana): 49.
51. Sarah Fitzpatrick in Blassingame, ed., *Slave Testimony*, p. 649.
52. Lewis Clarke in ibid., p. 154.
53. Harding conceded that there may have been "some good white folks," "mighty few, though." In Egypt, ed., *Unwritten History of Slavery*, p. 84.
54. Redford and D'Orso, *Somerset Homecoming*, p. 29.
55. Beam, *He Called Them by the Lightning*, pp. 40, 79.
56. When whites criticized blacks for not presenting a united front, James Thomas explained their dissension along racial lines. "They came from different part[s] of Africa originaly," he wrote, "which means there is some difference among the mixed bloods. Some," like Thomas himself, "are the children of the most exclusive set, men in high places in government. Some are the children of Irish, German, Jew and Negro. So it is not to be wondered that they should have different ideas." In Schweninger, ed., *From Tennessee Slave to St. Louis Entrepreneur*, p. 98.

9: GETTING READY TO DIE

1. Catherine Spence to Elizabeth Spence, Dec. 6 and 21, 1870, and n.d., 1871, AKS, Catherine Macky (FU).
2. Louisa MacDonald to Elizabeth Spence, Jan. 13, 1873, AKS (FU).
3. Catherine Spence to Elizabeth Spence, n.d., 1871, AKS, Catherine Macky (FU).
4. Moore (Sheppard), "Historical Sketch of the Jubilee Singers," *Fisk University News*, Oct. 1911 (FU).
5. Anonymous, "Early Days of Fisk University," AKS, Burrus (FU).
6. Catherine Spence to Elizabeth Spence, n.d., 1871, AKS (FU).
7. Spence to Catherine Spence, June 28, 1870, AKS (FU).
8. White to Cravath, Feb. 13, 1871 (AMA).
9. "Reminiscences of Fisk University," MS, n.d., MES, Matson (FU); Correspondence, Oberlin College Treasurer's Office (OC).
10. Matson, "Reminiscences of Fisk University," MS, n.d., MES, Matson (FU).
11. Matson to Spence, June 20, 1872, MES, Matson (FU).
12. J. M. Richardson, *Christian Reconstruction*, p. 170.
13. Spence to Catherine Spence, Sept. 12, 1870, AKS (FU).
14. Rules and Regulations of Fisk University, 1868 (AMA).
15. Bennett to Board of Trustees of the Peabody Fund, June 24, 1869 (AMA).
16. Proctor, *Between Black and White*, pp. 25–34.
17. Hayes was thrown out of Fisk, apparently on suspicion of violating these rules, though he would never know for sure. Helm, *Angel Mo' and Her Son, Roland Hayes*, pp. 88–90.
18. Oberlin College alumni file for Paul Cravath and Erastus Milo Cravath (OC).
19. Rutling to White, July 7, 1870 (AMA).
20. Rutling to Fisk, March 5, 1870 (AMA).
21. Dickerson to White, March 14, 1870 (AMA).
22. Spence to Mr. & Mrs. Dickinson, Jan. 3, 1871, Spence, AKS, box 11.
23. The school reported that in 1871 it had converted thirty-two out of ninety-nine pupils, forty-one of whom were already professed Christians, and explained that the remaining unconverted twenty-six had not been students for long. American Missionary Association, "Religious Work," in *Twenty-fifth Annual Report*.
24. Mary Spence, "Dear Matson," MES (FU).
25. J. M. Richardson, *History of Fisk University*, p. 21.
26. Among the converts that night was a future Jubilee Singer named Maggie Carnes. Matson, untitled MS, 1878, Spence, AKS, box 9.
27. William Wells Brown in Andrews, ed., *From Fugitive Slave to Free Man*, p. 66; Wiley, *Southern Negroes*, p. 99.
28. Isa. 1:19–20 in Genovese, *Roll, Jordan, Roll*, p. 1.
29. Lev. 25:44–46.
30. Solomon Northrup in Osofsky, ed., *Puttin' On Ole Massa*, p. 292.
31. C. H. Hall in Blassingame, ed., *Slave Testimony*, p. 420.
32. Robert H. Burns in Baker and Baker, eds., *WPA Oklahoma Slave Narratives*, p. 70.

Jenny Proctor recalled how the white preacher her master imported would tell them that what they got from their owners was "all you ever going to get because you just like the hogs and other animals—when you dies you ain't no more, after you been throwed in that hole." In Botkin, ed., *Lay My Burden Down*, p. 91.

33. Frederick Douglass in Osofsky, ed., *Puttin' On Ole Massa*, p. 33.
34. Dickey left the state. Tines Kendricks in Botkin, ed., *Lay My Burden Down*, p. 72.
35. Peter Randolph in Osofsky, ed., *Puttin' On Ole Massa*, p. 34.
36. Clarke, *Narratives*, p. 105.
37. James Curry in Blassingame, ed., *Slave Testimony*, p. 131. A pious master could be a mixed blessing. For most slaves, the Sabbath was the only day they could call their own, but if a master got religion they had to give up "the privilege of hunting, fishing, making splint brooms, baskets, &c., on Sunday" and go to meeting instead. William Wells Brown in Andrews, ed., *From Fugitive Slave to Free Man*, pp. 38–39.
38. H. V. Richardson, *Dark Salvation*, pp. 47–48.
39. Anonymous clergyman in Taylor, *Negro in Tennessee*, pp. 221–22.
40. J. M. Richardson, *Christian Reconstruction*, pp. 143–44.
41. Anonymous clergyman in Taylor, *Negro in Tennessee*, pp. 221–22.
42. W. W. Mallery to S. S. Jocelyn, Nov. 26, 1866 (AMA).
43. J. M. Richardson, *Christian Reconstruction*, pp. 150–51.
44. Joel Grant to Prof. Henry Cowles, April 10, 1863 (AMA).
45. C.A.J. Crosby to A.M.A., May 1, 1866 (AMA).
46. *American Missionary* in J. M. Richardson, *Christian Reconstruction*, p. 154.
47. E. P. Smith to Strieby, July 21, 1865 (AMA).
48. Ogden, "The Bible as an Educator," undated address to teachers (AMA).
49. Rev. H. S. Bennett, address to a convention of American Missionary Association workers, reprinted in the *New York Independent*, July 15, 1875 (FU).
50. Matson to Whipple, Feb. 1, 1869 (AMA).
51. C.A.J. Crosby to A.M.A., Jan. 31, 1868 (AMA).
52. C.A.J. Crosby, Oct. 1867 (AMA).

10: LISTEN TO THE ANGELS

1. Matson to Whipple, Oct. 6, 1868 (AMA).
2. Moore (Sheppard), "Historical Sketch of the Jubilee Singers," *Fisk University News*, Oct. 1911 (FU).
3. Spence, undated lecture, MES, Notebooks.
4. Moore (Sheppard), "Historical Sketch of the Jubilee Singers."
5. Mary Spence, note, Jan. 12, 1940; Work, *Folk Song of the American Negro*, pp. 79–80.
6. Newark *Evening Courier*, JSS (FU).
7. Rutling, *Tom*, p. 20; Fisk *Herald*, Dec. 1884 (FU); caption by Laura White in Fisk photo file (FU). In 1931, Mrs. Ida B. Wright wrote an appeal to Fisk's board of

trustees on behalf of Georgia Hampton, the great-granddaughter of old Uncle Wallace Burton of Atoka County, Choctaw Nation Indian Territory, now long since dead. Mrs. Wright claimed that her ancestor's songs were sung by the Jubilee Singers, for which "Prof. White of Fredonia" and a Miss Ballantyne of Nashville promised "any member of the family descended of old Uncle Wallace would always have a home, living, and schooling" at Fisk. Uncle Wallace's granddaughter, Lizzie Hampton, was clothed and cared for by the school and became an "honored student" under Miss Ballantyne's care, and now Georgia Hampton, her daughter, asked to be admitted. Jones (Thomas E., president of Fisk University), summary of Ida B. Wright to Board of Trustees, Jan. 29, 1931, MES, Notes (FU).

8. Marsh, *Story of the Jubilee Singers* (1881), pp. 125–243.
9. C. P. in Waterbury *Daily American*, JSS (FU).
10. Thomas Wentworth Higginson, "Negro Spirituals," *Atlantic Monthly*, June 1867.
11. Horace Clarence Boyer, interview by Llewelyn Smith.
12. Higginson, "Negro Spirituals."
13. Douglass, *Life and Times of Frederick Douglass*, pp. 141–42.
14. Washington, *Up from Slavery*, p. 20.
15. Theodore Seward in Marsh, *Story of the Jubilee Singers* (1881), p. 122.
16. Anonymous former slave in Raboteau, *Slave Religion*, p. 244.
17. Proctor, *Between Black and White*, p. 59.
18. Taylor (Gordon), "Reminiscences of Jubilee Singers," *Fisk University News*, Oct. 1911 (FU).
19. Mary Spence, "Character Sketch of George L. White," *Fisk University News*, Oct. 1911 (FU).
20. Mary Spence, "Jubilee S.," note, Nov. 24, 1951, MES, Notes (FU).
21. Mabel Lewis in ibid.
22. Mary Spence, note, n.d., MES, Notes (FU).
23. Mary Spence, "Jubilee S."
24. Mary Spence, "Character Sketch of George L. White."
25. Mary Spence, "Jubilee S."
26. Mary Spence, "Character Sketch of George L. White."
27. Mabel Lewis in Mary Spence, "Jubilee S."
28. Cole (Porter), "Maggie Porter-Cole," *Fisk News*, Dec. 1939 (FU).
29. J. M. Richardson, *Christian Reconstruction*, pp. 102, 114.
30. A minister in Athens, Tennessee, asked if Spence had someone who could teach a country school: "Do you know of any colored person that has had the necessary training that could be procured for the place. . . . They would prefer a young man but a lady teacher would answer. . . . In 1868 there were 158 colored children of scholastic age enrolled. A teacher succeeding well for three months might probably after that at his own risk start a subscription school and find support." David M. Wilson to Spence, May 9, 1871 (FU).
31. Spence to Elizabeth Spence, April 24 and May 2, 1871 (FU).
32. White to Cravath, April 7, 1871 (AMA). There is evidence, however, that it was

White and not Spence who tended to overspend. While away during the summer of 1871, Spence had to remind White to buy "plain shelves, not cases." Spence to White, July 6, 1871 (FU).

33. Catherine Spence to Elizabeth Spence, April 26, 1871 (FU).
34. Spence to Elizabeth Spence, March 21 and 28, 1871 (FU).
35. Cravath to Spence, April 19, 1871, Spence, AKS, box 10 (FU).
36. Spence to Elizabeth Spence, March 28, 1871 (FU).
37. White to Cravath, Feb. 13, 1871 (AMA).
38. Broadside for the cantata of *Esther, the Beautiful Queen*, JSS (FU).
39. Catherine Spence to Spence, Feb. 28, 1871 (FU).
40. Spence to Elizabeth Spence, March 13, 1871 (FU).
41. Fisk to White, April 25, 1871 (AMA).
42. A Reverend William B. Brown of Newark, New Jersey, claimed that he had heard the singers perform in Nashville in 1871 and suggested to White that they tour the North to raise money, which, according to the Newark *Evening Courier*, they immediately did. In JSS (FU); unidentified clipping, JSS (FU).
43. White to Cravath, April 7, 1871 (AMA).
44. Program, JSS (FU).
45. Spence to Catherine Spence, June 26, 1871 (FU).
46. Memphis *Daily Avalanche*, June 28 and 29, 1871, JSS (FU).
47. Gould, "Beyond the Smiling," in Gould, *Songs of Gladness for the Sabbath School*, p. 155, courtesy of the Center for Popular Music.
48. Moore (Sheppard), "Historical Sketch of the Jubilee Singers."
49. "We had a fine concert hear last night and everything past off well, and we will leave tomorrow for Atlanta Ga to be gone a week. The people are to have a fair hear on the 13th of Sep and I will be very glad to have you here. Please come. Yours as ever Greene Evans." Evans to Park, Aug. 28, 1871, Spence, Miscellaneous (FU).
50. Moore (Sheppard), "Historical Sketch of the Jubilee Singers."
51. Spence to Catherine Spence, Sept. 18 and 28, 1871 (FU).
52. Edwin Spence to Spence, n.d., 1871, Spence (FU).
53. Spence to Elizabeth Spence, April 9, 1872, Spence (FU).
54. White to Cravath, Sept. 21, 1871 (AMA).
55. J. M. Richardson, *History of Fisk University*, p. 25.
56. John Lawrence in ibid.
57. J. M. Richardson, *Christian Reconstruction*, p. 96.
58. Cole (Porter), "Maggie Porter-Cole," *Fisk News*, Dec. 1939 (FU).
59. Cravath to Spence, Oct. 14, 1871 (FU).
60. White to Cravath, Sept. 29, 1871 (AMA).
61. Spence to Elizabeth Spence, n.d. [1871], MES (FU).
62. Clinton B. Fisk, "Dedication of the Hall," *American Missionary*, Feb. 1876 (FU).
63. George White in C. Robert Tipton, "The Fisk Jubilee Singers," *Tennessee Historical Quarterly* (Spring–Winter 1970), p. 43.
64. In Sarah M. Wells's transcription, the quote is in the past tense. George White in

Wells, "Character Sketch of Professor Adam Knight Spence," *Fisk News,* Oct. 1911 (FU).

65. The student was John Work. Mary Spence, note, Jan. 26, 1961, MES, Notes (FU).

66. Spence to Elizabeth Spence, Oct. 8, 1871 (FU).

67. Morgan to Cravath, Oct. 29, 1871 (AMA).

68. Anonymous (Charles H. Williams) in Egypt, ed., *Unwritten History of Slavery,* p. 87.

69. According to Mary Spence, the parents of the girls at Fisk were the "city people" in Sheppard's 1911 account who objected to their touring. In MES, Notes (FU).

70. "A pity is it not," wrote Spence. "I have no idea there is any cause for it. We are going to have a good deal of trouble this year, I think." Spence to Elizabeth Spence, n.d. [1871], MES (FU).

71. It is intriguing, however, that her future husband would succeed Bennett as pastor of Howard Chapel. J. M. Richardson, *Christian Reconstruction,* p. 223.

72. Minutes of the Union Literary Society, vol. 1 (FU).

73. J. M. Richardson, *Christian Reconstruction,* p. 115.

74. Mary E. Spence, note, May 4, 1949, MES, Notes (FU); J. M. Richardson, *Christian Reconstruction,* p. 115.

75. Mary F. Wells in J. M. Richardson, *Christian Reconstruction,* p. 219.

76. Bean, Hatch, and McNamara, eds., *Inside the Minstrel Mask,* p. 224.

77. *Daily Beacon* (Akron, Ohio), undated clipping, JSS (FU).

78. Moore (Sheppard), "Historical Sketch of the Jubilee Singers."

79. Spence to Elizabeth Spence, Oct. 8, 1871, 11f4 (FU).

80. Adam Spence in Wells, "Character Sketch of Professor Adam Knight Spence."

81. Moore (Sheppard), "Historical Sketch of the Jubilee Singers."

82. Cole (Porter), "Maggie Porter-Cole," *Fisk News,* Dec. 1939 (FU).

11: INCHING ALONG

1. "Such things never occurred that I saw" in the slave South, Thomas wrote, "which was easy enough to understand. In clubbing and abusing the Negro they would find they had abused a piece of property that had a protector." Most of the Southerners who went North were too poor to own slaves in the first place, he recalled long after the Civil War, "and there are still men living along the border who strenuously pursued the fugitives for reward." In Schweninger, ed., *From Tennessee Slave to St. Louis Entrepreneur,* pp. 89, 124.

2. White to Cravath, Sept. 29, 1871 (AMA).

3. Marsh, *Story of the Jubilee Singers* (1881), p. 17.

4. Clinton B. Fisk, "Dedication of the Hall," *American Missionary,* Feb. 1876 (FU).

5. White to Cravath, Sept. 29, 1871 (AMA).

6. Pike, *Jubilee Singers* (1873), p. 47.

7. Cole (Porter), "Maggie Porter-Cole," *Fisk News,* Dec. 1939 (FU).

8. 1870 broadside (FU).

9. Cincinnati *Gazette* in Pike, *Jubilee Singers* (1873), pp. 76–77.

10. White to Cravath, Sept. 29, 1871 (AMA).

11. Marsh, *Story of the Jubilee Singers* (1881), pp. 16–17.

12. Cole (Porter), "Maggie Porter-Cole." In old age, she said this was at Detroit, but in fact Marsh placed it at Cincinnati, and his dates for the concert (October 8, 9) and the fire (October 8–10) jibe.

13. Citizens of Chillicothe in Pike, *Jubilee Singers* (1873), p. 81.

14. Moore (Sheppard), "Historical Sketch of the Jubilee Singers," *Fisk University News,* Oct. 1911 (FU).

15. Unidentified (Cincinnati *Gazette*) in Marsh, *Story of the Jubilee Singers* (1881), pp. 18–19; JSS (FU); Pike, *Jubilee Singers* (1873), p. 82.

16. Marsh, *Story of the Jubilee Singers* (1881), p. 19; Pike, *Jubilee Singers* (1873), p. 84.

17. Pike, *Jubilee Singers* (1873), p. 85.

18. H. V. Richardson, *Dark Salvation,* pp. 105–7, 111.

19. Cole (Porter), "Maggie Porter-Cole."

20. Moore (Sheppard), "Historical Sketch of the Jubilee Singers."

21. Marsh, *Story of the Jubilee Singers* (1881), p. 20.

22. *Daily Beacon* (Akron, Ohio), undated clipping, JSS (FU).

23. Moore (Sheppard), "Historical Sketch of the Jubilee Singers."

24. Delaware, Ohio, *Gazette* quoted in a broadside, JSS (FU).

25. Spence to Elizabeth Spence, Nov. ?, 1871 (FU); and Nov. 7, 1871, Spence, AKS, box 11.

26. Marsh, *Story of the Jubilee Singers* (1881), pp. 20–22.

27. Cleveland *Herald* in Pike, *Jubilee Singers* (1873), p. 93.

28. Sheppard to Spence, Feb. 12, 1872, MES (FU).

29. Spence, "A Character Sketch of George L. White," *Fisk University News,* Oct. 1911 (FU).

30. Marsh, *Story of the Jubilee Singers* (1881), pp. 20–23.

31. J. M. Richardson, *Christian Reconstruction,* p. 98.

32. The college was taking a precarious perch on the line between radicalism and conservatism, perhaps best exemplified by its new president's commentary on the new arrivals in town. "Many of them," said James Fairchild, "having recently come from slavery, retain, in a great measure, the ignorance and peculiar habits of that institution. A more intelligent, cultivated population would be desirable; but if asked to exchange them for an equal number of foreigners, of which we have none, we should beg to be excused." In Brandt, *Town That Started the Civil War,* p. 262.

33. "Death of Rev. Geo Whipple, D.D.," *American Missionary,* Nov. 1876 (FU).

34. "Thirty years ago, a national Congregational council could not have been gathered. . . . If held, Oberlin could not have been the place. Oberlin was then in the nadir of unpopularity—its doctrines were misapprehended—its mixed education of sexes and colors was feared, and, above all, its abolitionism was hated. But the

world has moved." So had Oberlin. "The Council at Oberlin," *American Missionary,* Jan. 1872 (FU).

35. One tradition has it that they began with standard hymns, which failed to gain the attention of the assembled divines, whereupon one of the singers decided to try a spiritual. But nothing I was able to find in the contemporary accounts seems to confirm it. Horace Clarence Boyer, interview by Llewelyn Smith.

36. *Lorain County News,* Nov. 23, 1871.

37. "The Council at Oberlin."

38. Cravath to Spence, Nov. 21, 1871 (FU).

39. Pope was born in Strongsville, Ohio, in February 1840. His alumni file suggests some serious rifts in his family. By 1908, he was "running a private ministerial relief enterprise on a fruit farm" in Flippin, Arkansas. He died ten years later in Cottage Hill, Florida. His two "natural" sons (apparently he had adopted sons as well) disappeared "one at a time" and at the time of their mother's death in 1938 were presumed dead. Oberlin College alumni file of George Stanley Pope (OC).

40. Marsh, *Story of the Jubilee Singers* (1881), p. 24.

41. Spence to Elizabeth Spence, Dec. 26, 1871 (FU).

42. Spence to Elizabeth Spence, Jan. 2, [1872], 10f1 (FU).

43. Spence to Elizabeth Spence, Nov. 23, 1871, AKS (FU).

44. White to Cravath, Nov. 26, 1871 (AMA).

45. Broadside, JSS (FU).

46. Moore (Sheppard), "Historical Sketch of the Jubilee Singers."

47. White to Cravath, Nov. 26, 1871 (AMA).

48. Moore (Sheppard), "Historical Sketch of the Jubilee Singers."

49. Ibid.

50. Pike, *Jubilee Singers* (1873), p. 98.

51. Holmes to Spence, Nov. 23, 1871, AKS (FU).

52. "But in twelve hours I grew better so there is yet hope of my recovery." Sheppard to Spence, Dec. 5, 1871, AKS (FU).

53. Marsh, *Story of the Jubilee Singers* (1881), p. 27.

54. Pike, *Jubilee Singers* (1873), p. 100.

55. An Akron broadside in George White's scrapbook contains the first mention I have been able to find of a building fund. JSS (FU).

56. White to Cravath, Dec. 6, 1871 (AMA).

12: THE GOLDEN STREET

1. Spence to Elizabeth Spence, Nov. 14, 1871, AKS (FU).

2. Spence to Elizabeth Spence, Oct. 8, 1871, AKS (FU).

3. Barnum to Ogden, Oct. 26, 1869 (AMA).

4. Spence to Elizabeth Spence, Oct. 8, 1871, AKS (FU).

5. Cravath to Spence, Oct. 28, 1871, AKS (FU).

6. Spence to Elizabeth Spence, Oct. 8, 1871, AKS (FU); undated list attached to Cravath to Spence, Jan. 24, 1872, AKS (FU).

7. Contributions continued to trickle in. Spence described the recipient of an old overcoat one of General Fisk's relatives sent to the school. He was "a white man, who had been teaching colored children in Arkansas and had a long sickness [and] sold off his clothes and was penniless He had had nothing to eat for about a day and lodged with a colored man the night before. Had walked nearly a hundred miles and found the people unfriendly. He is a native of Baltimore and has a southern accent. Poor fellow, the tears came to his eyes as he told me his story. He seemed intelligent." Spence to Elizabeth Spence, Nov. 23, 1871, AKS (FU).

8. Linda T. Wynn, "First Colored Baptist Church," Tennessee State University Web site.

9. Spence to Elizabeth Spence, Oct. 26, 1871, AKS (FU).

10. Spence to Elizabeth Spence, Dec. 26, 1871, AKS (FU).

11. Cravath to Spence, Jan. 11, 1872 (AMA).

12. Spence to Elizabeth Spence, n.d., 1871, AKS (FU).

13. Edwin Spence to Spence, n.d., 1871, AKS (FU).

14. Cravath to Spence, Oct. 28, 1871, AKS (FU).

15. Mary F. Wells, "Character Sketch of Professor Adam Knight Spence," *Fisk University News,* Oct. 1911 (FU).

16. Marsh, *Story of the Jubilee Singers* (1881), p. 27.

17. Sheppard to Spence, Dec. 5, 1871, AKS (FU).

18. Marsh, *Story of the Jubilee Singers* (1881), p. 28.

19. Pike, *Jubilee Singers* (1873), p. 102.

20. White to Spence, Dec. 8, 1871 (FU).

21. White to Cravath, Dec. 8, 1871 (AMA).

22. Pike, *Jubilee Singers* (1873), p. 102.

23. Marsh, *Story of the Jubilee Singers* (1881), p. 28.

24. Ibid.

25. White to Spence, Jan. 19, 1872, MES (FU).

26. Spence to Elizabeth Spence, Dec. 13, 1873, AKS (FU).

27. Hibben, *Henry Ward Beecher,* p. 194.

28. Henry Ward Beecher in Harper, ed., *Social Welfare Forum,* p. 120.

29. Hibben, *Henry Ward Beecher,* p. 172.

30. Hibben, *Henry Ward Beecher,* pp. 172, 194, 198–199, 207, 215, 217, 239, 242.

31. P. S. Foner, *Business & Slavery,* pp. 162–63.

32. Wood in E. R. Ellis, *Epic of New York City,* p. 285.

33. Richmond *Dispatch* in P. S. Foner, *Business & Slavery,* p. 317.

34. Strong in E. R. Ellis, *Epic of New York City,* p. 316, also p. 326.

35. J. M. Richardson, *Christian Reconstruction,* p. 88.

36. "Death of Rev. Geo Whipple, D.D.," *American Missionary,* Nov. 1876 (FU).

37. Cole (Porter), "Maggie Porter-Cole," *Fisk News,* Dec. 1939 (FU).

38. Anonymous admirer in Hibben, *Henry Ward Beecher,* p. 215.

39. Rev. Henry Ward Beecher in *American Missionary,* supplement, n.d.

40. Pike reported that it was "O How I Love Jesus," but Porter insisted in two accounts that it was "Steal Away." Cole (Porter), "Maggie Porter-Cole."

41. Cole (Porter), "Maggie Porter-Cole"; "The Jubilee Singers on the Ocean and in Europe," *Fisk University News,* Oct. 1911 (FU).

42. Pike, *Singing Campaign for Ten Thousand Pounds,* p. 109.

43. Mary Spence, "A Character Sketch of George L. White," *Fisk University News,* Oct. 1911 (FU).

44. Rev. Henry Ward Beecher in *American Missionary,* supplement, n.d.

45. Cole (Porter), "Maggie Porter-Cole."

46. Spence to Elizabeth Spence, Dec. 26, 1871; advertisement, JSS (FU).

47. White to Spence, Jan. 13, 1872, MES (FU).

48. Pike, *Jubilee Singers* (1873), p. 111.

49. "Concert at the New England Church," Brooklyn *Times,* in *American Missionary,* supplement, n.d.

50. Goodrich, "Slave Songs," *N.Y. Evangelist,* in *American Missionary,* Jan. 1872.

51. JSS (FU).

52. Ibid.

53. White, Miscellaneous notices.

54. Pike, *Jubilee Singers* (1873), p. 112.

13: GET ON BOARD

1. White to Spence, Jan. 19, 1872, MES (FU).

2. Moore (Sheppard), "Historical Sketch of the Jubilee Singers," *Fisk University News,* Oct. 1911 (FU).

3. "When he was about to publish the 'Story of the Jubilees' with a selection of their songs, he wanted to state therein his indebtedness to me for the aid I had rendered. I was too modest to give my consent My boys have told me often since that I missed the only chance I ever had of getting my name on the roll of fame." Rev. Alexander Reid to Bro. Edwards, Jan. 15, 1884, published in *Presbyterian,* Sept. 10, 1890.

4. T. F. Seward, Chautauqua *Assembly Herald,* Aug. 4, 1881, JSS (FU).

5. Moore (Sheppard), "Historical Sketch of the Jubilee Singers."

6. "The Methodist Festival," Boston *Journal,* in *American Missionary,* supplement, n.d. One A.M.A. contributor, however, suggested that the singers would do well to include more European pieces. After one of their Boston concerts, she "overheard remarks in substance like the following, 'They sing finely, and finely because they are so emphatically at home with the pieces. Were they to attempt *our* style, failure would be the result.' I, of course, questioned the discrimination of persons drawing such conclusions, but perhaps a trifle more of variety might be pleasing." Elizabeth E. Backup to Cravath, Jan. 23, 1872 (AMA).

7. Horace Clarence Boyer, interview by Llewelyn Smith.

8. MES, Notes (FU).

9. Wells to Cravath, Jan. 23, 1872.

10. Agreement dated Jan. 5, 1874 (FU).

11. J. M. Richardson, *Christian Reconstruction,* p. 89.

12. Pike, *Singing Campaign* (1875), p. 1.

13. Wood, *Origins of American Slavery,* pp. 95–96.

14. Ibid., pp. 102–9.

15. Harley, *Timetables of African-American History,* p. 66.

16. Fogel and Engerman, *Time on the Cross,* pp. 35–36.

17. Catterall, ed., *Judicial Cases concerning Slavery,* 4:415.

18. Such was the pro-slavery sentiment of certain prosperous corners of Connecticut that when the son of the minister of the First Congregational Church of Old Greenwich joined the Union army, pro-slavery elders forced his father to resign. Stamford Historical Society.

19. Pike to Cravath, Jan. 27, 1872 (AMA).

20. Pike to Cravath, Jan. 28, 1872 (AMA).

21. Pike to Cravath, Feb. 2, 1872 (AMA).

22. White to Cravath, Feb. 16, 1872 (AMA).

23. Pike to Cravath, Jan. 28, 1872 (AMA).

24. Hartford *Courant* in Salamo and Smith, eds., *Mark Twain's Letters,* p. 316nn.

25. Clemens to Thomas Hood, March 10, 1872, in Pike, *Singing Campaign for Ten Thousand Pounds,* pp. 14–15.

26. Pike to Cravath, Feb. 27, 1872 (AMA).

27. Moore (Sheppard), "Historical Sketch of the Jubilee Singers."

28. White to Cravath, Feb. 14, 1872 (AMA).

29. Pike, *Singing Campaign* (1875), pp. 123–25.

30. Julia A. Johnson to A.M.A., March 29, 1872 (AMA).

31. Sheppard to Spence, Feb. 12, 1872, MES (FU). Spence relayed Sheppard's letter to his mother. "I think it will give you a vivid idea of the experiences they are passing through and have passed through. Miss Sheppard is colored you know. Her lack of a thorough education is somewhat betrayed in her letter but still more the haste in which it must necessarily have been written. I think the letter will cheer you. Mr. White writes in the same way. They are evidently up on the top wave of enthusiasm." Spence to Elizabeth Spence, Feb. 19, 1872, MES (FU).

32. Pike, *Singing Campaign* (1875), pp. 126–27.

33. Moore (Sheppard), "Historical Sketch of the Jubilee Singers."

34. "Jubilee Singers," Newark *Evening Courier,* in *American Missionary,* supplement, n.d.

35. Undated clipping, Orange, New Jersey, *Journal,* JSS (FU).

14: OLD SHIP OF ZION

1. Spence to Elizabeth Spence, Feb. 13, 1872 (FU); Moore (Sheppard), "Historical Sketch of the Jubilee Singers," *Fisk University News,* Oct. 1911 (FU).

2. White to Spence, Jan. 19, 1872, MES (FU).

3. Spence to Elizabeth Spence, Feb. 13, 1872, MES (FU).

4. Unidentified Jubilee Singer to Spence, March 1, 1872 (fragment), MES (FU).

5. Blockson, *Black Genealogy*, p. 60.

6. Sheppard to Spence, March 5, 1872, MES (FU).

7. Harry G. Robinson and H. Patrick Swygert, "The Long Walk," Howard University Web site.

8. Cimprich, *Slavery's End in Tennessee*, pp. 101–2.

9. E. Foner, *Reconstruction*, p. 186.

10. Cimprich, *Slavery's End in Tennessee*, p. 118.

11. Lamon, *Blacks in Tennessee*, p. 35.

12. E. Foner, *Reconstruction*, p. 45; Lamon, *Blacks in Tennessee*, p. 36.

13. E. Foner, *Reconstruction*, p. 271; Lamon, *Blacks in Tennessee*, p. 36.

14. In her contemporaneous account, Sheppard says they sang "Home, Sweet Home," but Marsh mentions only "Keep Me from Sinking Down." I tend to trust Sheppard, but since neither says that they only sang one or the other, I am assuming that they sang both.

15. Thomas in Schweninger, ed., *From Tennessee Slave to St. Louis Entrepreneur*, pp. 175–76 and nn.

16. "Negro Ideas of Finance," *American Missionary*, Feb. 1866.

17. Imes (Lewis), "Reminiscences," TS, n.d. (FU); White to Cravath, Nov. 27, 1874 (AMA).

18. Washington Monument Restoration Project Web page.

19. Photograph of "Mr. Robert Foster & Slaves," collection of Thelma Battle.

20. Mrs. Staines's interviewer guessed that Washington's violations of the Sabbath would "weigh infinitely more" with his fellow slaveholders than his "trying to kidnap this woman." Blassingame, ed., *Slave Testimony*, p. 250.

21. Doc Daniel Dowdy in Baker and Baker, eds., *WPA Oklahoma Slave Narratives*, p. 131.

22. W. H. Smith, *Schuyler Colfax*.

23. Rev. J. E. Rankin, JSS (FU).

24. Sheppard to Spence, March 5, 1872, MES (FU).

25. Goldhurst, *Many Are the Hearts;* McFeely, *Grant*. Grant himself was apparently never guilty of more than naïveté, misplaced loyalty, and a conviction that every reformer was out to get him. But in addition to Colfax's transgression, his private secretary and an old army buddy Grant had appointed to the Internal Revenue Service were knee-deep in a massive liquor-tax fraud known as the Whiskey Ring, and his secretary of war, General W. W. Belknap, pocketed tens of thousands of dollars peddling monopolistic trading franchises on Indian reservations. Grant was especially unfortunate in his brothers-in-law. One of them was caught taking bribes as a customs collector; another, a man of the cloth, sold political favors; and yet another facilitated a gold-speculating scheme by Jim Fisk, Jr., and Jay Gould that nearly destroyed the economy. I cannot judge the general too sternly,

however, since my own great-grandfather Ferdinand Ward was sent to Sing Sing for swindling poor Grant out of all his money.

26. Sheppard to Spence, March 5, 1872, MES (FU).

15: I AIN'T GOT WEARY YET

1. Henrietta Matson to Elizabeth Spence, Jan. 1, 1872, Spence, Macky, box 2.
2. Spence to Elizabeth Spence, Jan. 23, 1872, MES (FU).
3. Counting White and Sheppard, who were still on tour, there were twelve. Undated list attached to Cravath to Spence, Jan. 24, 1872, AKS (FU).
4. Edwin Spence to Spence, Feb. 14, 1871, Spence, AKS, box 10.
5. Cravath to Spence, Jan. 8, 1872, Spence (FU).
6. Robbins, "World-within-a-World," pp. 18–19.
7. FASES, MEC, Records, 1866–1910, TSLA, microfilm 536.
8. Robbins, "World-within-a-World," pp. 76–86.
9. Its medical department, however, has survived to this day as Meharry Medical School, which has graduated 81 percent of the South's black physicians and about half of the black doctors and dentists in the country.
10. Pike, *Singing Campaign* (1875), pp. 15–17.
11. Spence to Elizabeth Spence, March 19, 1872, MES (FU).
12. Cravath to Spence, March 30, 1872, MES (FU); J. M. Richardson, *History of Fisk University,* p. 22.
13. Spence to Elizabeth Spence, April 3, 1872, MES (FU).
14. Adams, "Speech of Rev. Dr. Wm. Adams," *American Missionary,* April 1872.
15. White, Miscellaneous notices (FU).
16. Fisk in *American Missionary,* April 1872.
17. White, Miscellaneous notices; Lovell, *Black Song,* p. 412.
18. Fisk to Cravath, March 13, 1872 (AMA).
19. Mark Twain in Neider, ed., *Selected Letters of Mark Twain,* p. 169.
20. Theodore F. Seward, "Speech of Mr. Seward," *American Missionary,* April 1872.
21. J. M. Richardson, *History of Fisk University,* p. 29; Moore (Sheppard), "Historical Sketch of the Jubilee Singers," *Fisk University News,* Oct. 1911 (FU); White to Spence, March 25, 1872, MES (FU).
22. Theodore Seward in Pike, *Singing Campaign* (1875), p. 164.
23. *Tonic Sol-Fa Reporter,* May 15, 1873 (AMA).
24. Rutling, *Tom,* p. 20.
25. Davidson to Cravath, March 11, 1872 (AMA).
26. Clemens to Thomas Hood, March 10, 1872, in Pike, *Singing Campaign for Ten Thousand Pounds,* pp. 14–15.
27. Rutling, *Tom,* p. 21.
28. White to Spence, March 25, 1872, MES (FU).
29. Pike to Cravath, Feb. 5, 1872 (AMA).
30. Beam, *He Called Them by the Lightning,* p. 72.

31. Moore (Sheppard), "Historical Sketch of the Jubilee Singers"; White to Spence, March 25, 1872, MES (FU).

32. Taylor, *Negro in Tennessee,* p. 227.

33. Pike, *Singing Campaign* (1875), p. 153; Moore (Sheppard), "Historical Sketch of the Jubilee Singers"; White to Spence, March 25, 1872, MES (FU).

34. Henry Ward Beecher to White, n.d., AKS (FU).

16: I'VE JUST COME FROM THE FOUNTAIN

1. Bobby Lovett, "Roger Williams University (1866–1929)," Tennessee State University Web site.

2. Bennett to Spence, July 6, 1872, Spence, AKS, box 12.

3. Elizabeth Spence to Spence, May 22, 1872, MES (FU).

4. Pike to Cravath, July 8, 1872 (AMA).

5. Pike, *Jubilee Singers* (1873), pp. 155–57.

6. J. M. Richardson, *Christian Reconstruction,* p. 128.

7. Pike, *Jubilee Singers* (1873), pp. 157–60.

8. J. M. Richardson, *Christian Reconstruction,* p. 137.

9. Anonymous handwritten note in Pike, *Jubilee Singers* (1874), p. 76 (FU).

10. A Nashville slave whose parents remained as wage earners with their former owners after the war, Moore, at nine years of age, had been among the first students at Fisk. When she was fifteen, the daughter of her former master taught her how to play the piano, and during the months the troupe had been on the road she had helped prepare the new members for the second tour.

11. There is no documentary evidence of what part Morgan sang, but I presume he was a tenor; without Rutling, the main choir would have needed one.

12. Imes (Lewis), "Some Hotel Experiences," *Fisk University News,* Oct. 1911 (FU); Imes (Lewis), autobiographical note, Jan. 1929 (FU).

13. L. Ellis, *History of New Bedford,* p. 269.

14. Imes (Lewis), "Reminiscences" (FU).

15. Imes (Lewis), "Some Hotel Experiences."

16. Little, *Cyclopedia of Classified Dates,* p. 266.

17. Moore (Sheppard), "Historical Sketch of the Jubilee Singers," *Fisk University News,* Oct. 1911 (FU); White to Spence, March 25, 1872, MES (FU).

18. Taylor (Gordon), "Reminiscences of Jubilee Singers," *Fisk University News,* Oct. 1911 (FU).

19. Moore (Sheppard), "Historical Sketch of the Jubilee Singers"; White to Spence, March 25, 1872, MES (FU).

20. Marsh, *Story of the Jubilee Singers* (1881), p. 41.

21. Moore (Sheppard), "Historical Sketch of the Jubilee Singers"; White to Spence, March 25, 1872, MES (FU).

22. Nellie M. Horton to Spence, July 14, 1872, MES (FU).

23. *Daily Palladium,* July 12, 1871.

24. Philadelphia Timeline Web site.
25. Salvatore, *We All Got History,* p. 213.
26. Marsh, *Story of the Jubilee Singers* (1881), pp. 42–43.
27. Jubilee Singers' receipts (FU); certificate dated Oct. 21, 1872 (FU); Pike to Cravath, Feb. 5, 1872 (AMA).
28. Moore (Sheppard), "Historical Sketch of the Jubilee Singers."
29. J. M. Richardson, *Christian Reconstruction,* p. 156.
30. Marsh, *Story of the Jubilee Singers* (1881), p. 46.
31. Imes (Lewis), "Some Hotel Experiences."
32. Ibid.
33. Pike, *Singing Campaign for Ten Thousand Pounds,* p. 4.
34. Moore (Sheppard), "Historical Sketch of the Jubilee Singers"; Scott Mingo in Anderson, "Fisk Jubilee Singers," p. 292.
35. White to Cravath, Oct. 21, 1872 (AMA).
36. White to Cravath, Oct. 10, 1872 (AMA).
37. White to Cravath, Oct. 21, 1872 (AMA).
38. Pike to Cravath, Aug. 16, 1872 (AMA).
39. Lovell, *Black Song,* pp. 402–22; Sawyer, *Jubilee Songs and Plantation Melodies.*
40. Fayette A. McKenzie in J. M. Richardson, *History of Fisk University,* p. 80.
41. MacDonald, *George MacDonald and His Wife,* p. 442.
42. Cravath to E. P. Smith, Oct. 16, 1865 (AMA)
43. C.A.J. Crosby to A.M.A., April 4, 1867 (AMA).
44. *Folkestone Chronicle,* Aug. 1876, JSS (FU).
45. Pike, *Singing Campaign for Ten Thousand Pounds,* p. 12.

17: IN BRIGHT MANSIONS ABOVE

1. George MacDonald in *Times of London,* May 7, 1873.
2. Walvin, *England, Slaves, and Freedom,* p. 28.
3. Thomas, *Slave Trade,* p. 199.
4. Catterall, ed., *Judicial Cases concerning American Slavery,* 1:9; Walvin, *England, Slaves, and Freedom,* pp. 26–34.
5. Fogel and Engerman, *Time on the Cross,* pp. 14, 18.
6. George Howard in Finlayson, *Seventh Earl,* pp. 15–16. Father and son's most intimate interaction was apparently to sit together occasionally after supper and "enjoy a deep and unbroken slumber."
7. It was a good thing, too, his friend Florence Nightingale once said, or he might have himself ended up in an asylum. Finlayson, *Seventh Earl,* p. 600.
8. Earl of Shaftesbury in Hodder, *Shaftesbury,* 3:406–7.
9. Earl of Shaftesbury in Finlayson, *Seventh Earl,* p. 344.
10. Harriet Elizabeth Georgiana Leveson-Gower in *Dictionary of National Biography;* unidentified editorial in Hodder, *Shaftesbury,* 2:438.

11. Jubilee Singers program, Feb. 12, 1874.

12. Pike, *Singing Campaign* (1875), pp. 32–33.

13. Henry Ward Beecher in ibid., p. 34.

14. Benjamin Holmes to Lewis H. Douglass, May 14, 1873, in *New National Era,* June 5, 1873.

15. Pike, *Singing Campaign* (1875), pp. 15–16.

16. Moore (Sheppard), "Historical Sketch of the Jubilee Singers," *Fisk University News,* Oct. 1911 (FU).

17. Cole (Porter), "The Jubilee Singers on the Ocean and in Europe," *Fisk University News,* Oct. 1911 (FU).

18. Ramsay Muir in Gerzina, *Black London,* p. 183.

19. Holmes to Douglass, May 14, 1873, in *New National Era,* June 5, 1873.

20. Cole (Porter), "The Jubilee Singers on the Ocean and in Europe."

21. Holmes to Douglass, May 14, 1873, in *New National Era,* June 5, 1873.

22. Cole (Porter), "The Jubilee Singers on the Ocean and in Europe."

23. Pike, *Singing Campaign for Ten Thousand Pounds,* pp. 21–23.

24. *Tonic Sol-Fa Reporter,* May 15, 1873 (AMA).

25. Holmes to Douglass, May 14, 1873, in *New National Era,* June 5, 1873.

26. *Times of London,* May 7, 1873, p. 5.

27. *Examiner*, May 10, 1873.

28. *Tonic Sol-Fa Reporter,* May 15, 1873 (AMA).

29. Ibid.

30. *Times of London,* May 7, 1873, p. 5.

31. Marsh, *Story of the Jubilee Singers* (1881), p. 49.

32. Cole (Porter), "Maggie Porter-Cole," *Fisk News,* Dec. 1939 (FU).

33. Taylor (Gordon), "Reminiscences of Jubilee Singers," *Fisk University News,* Oct. 1911 (FU).

34. The Jubilees next sang "the wildest song of all, 'Didn't my Lord deliver Daniel?' " The *Tonic Sol-Fa*'s man suggested that Seward's transcription of this song and "Nobody Knows the Trouble I See" did not jibe with the version they performed. *Tonic Sol-Fa Reporter,* May 15, 1873 (AMA).

35. Journal of Queen Victoria.

36. Pike, *Singing Campaign for Ten Thousand Pounds,* pp. 36–39.

37. Thomas, *Slave Trade,* p. 238.

38. Journal of Queen Victoria; Holmes to Douglass, May 14, 1873, in *New National Era*, June 5, 1873.

39. Strachey, *Queen Victoria*, p. 351.

40. Weintraub, *Victoria*, p. 213.

41. Queen Elizabeth II once startled a Commonwealth audience by alluding to her African (and Indian) forebears. Courtesy of Mario de Valdes y Cocom.

42. Cole (Porter), "The Jubilee Singers on the Ocean and in Europe."

43. Cole (Porter), "Maggie Porter-Cole."

44. Ibid.

45. Cole (Porter), "The Jubilee Singers on the Ocean and in Europe."

46. Taylor (Gordon), "Reminiscences of Jubilee Singers."

47. By one account, the queen broke down and wept. "Don't think that I am weak be-cause I weep," she told them. "You have touched my heart." But this was more likely a variation on the story of her daughter Princess and later Empress Victoria of Germany crying at the Jubilees' performance in Postdam in 1877. None of the singers claimed that the queen wept.

48. Cole (Porter), "Maggie Porter-Cole."

49. J. M. Richardson, *History of Fisk University*, p. 33.

50. Journal of Queen Victoria.

51. Proctor, *Between Black and White*, p. 59.

18: AT THE WELCOME TABLE

1. Stanley, *Later Letters*, pp. 18–21, 173.

2. Benjamin Holmes to Lewis H. Douglass, June 18, 1873, in *New National Era*, July 10, 1873.

3. Ibid.

4. Pike, *Singing Campaign* (1875), p. 68.

5. Holmes to Douglass, June 18, 1873, in *New National Era*, July 10, 1873.

6. Pike, *Singing Campaign* (1875), pp. 66–70; Walvin, *Quakers*, pp. 126–28.

7. Wiley, *Life of Billy Yank*, pp. 159–60.

8. Holmes to Douglass, June 18, 1873, in *New National Era*, July 10, 1873.

9. Holmes to Douglass, July 9, 1873, in *New National Era*, July 24, 1873.

10. Holmes to Douglass, July 22, 1873, in *New National Era*, Aug. 14, 1873.

11. Pike, *Singing Campaign* (1875), p. 74.

12. Diary of William Gladstone, July 14, 1873, in M.R.D. Foot and H.C.G. Matthew, eds., *The Gladstone Diaries* (Oxford, 1968–1978).

13. Demarara, site of one of the senior Gladstone's plantations, was the most notori-ously cruel of British West Indian settlements: the scene of slave uprisings and barbarous reprisals. Jenkins, *Gladstone*, p. 354.

14. Walvin, *England, Slaves, and Freedom*, pp. 139–40.

15. One of the best answers to the claim that slaves were better treated than En-gland's poor came from Harriet Jacobs, a former American slave who visited the rural poor of England in the mid–nineteenth century: "The condition of even the meanest and most ignorant among them was vastly superior to the condition of the most favored slaves in America. They labored hard; but they were not ordered to toil while the stars were in the sky, and driven and lashed by an overseer, through heat and cold, till the stars shone out again. Their homes were very hum-ble; but they were protected by law. . . . The father, when he closed the cottage door, felt safe with his family around him. No master or overseer could come and take from him his wife, or his daughter. They must separate to earn a living; but

the parents knew where their children were going, and [could] communicate with them by letters. . . . There was no law forbidding them to read and write; and if they helped each other in spelling out the Bible, they were in no danger of thirty-nine lashes." In Gerzina, *Black London*, pp. 202–3.

16. Robert Banks Jenkinson, the second earl of Liverpool (1770–1828), was prime minister from 1812 to 1827. George Canning in Thomas, *Slave Trade*, p. 804.

17. Walvin, *England, Slaves, and Freedom*, pp. 165–66.

18. Jenkins, *Gladstone*, pp. 103–15.

19. Pike, *Singing Campaign for Ten Thousand Pounds*, p. 21.

20. "Many Thousands Gone" is the title given in the singers' 1873 songbook; it is now better known as "No More Auction Block for Me."

21. Holmes to Douglass, July 22, 1873, in *New National Era*, Aug. 14, 1873.

22. Thomas, *Slave Trade*, p. 538.

23. Imes (Lewis), "Reminiscences" (FU).

24. In the letter, Gladstone proposed the twenty-second, but the engagement had to be postponed a week.

25. Pike, *Singing Campaign* (1875), p. 78.

26. Holmes to Douglass, Aug. 16, 1873, in *New National Era*, Sept. 25, 1873.

27. Newman Hall (July 30, 1873) in Jubilee Singers brochure, n.d. (FU).

28. Newman Hall, "Mr. Gladstone and the Jubilee Singers," *New York Independent*, quoted in Fisk Jubilee Singers program, Feb. 12, 1874.

29. Holmes to Douglass, Aug. 16, 1873, in *New National Era*, Sept. 25, 1873.

30. Diary of William Gladstone, July 29, 1873.

31. Kaplan, *Mr. Clemens and Mark Twain*, p. 171.

32. Samuel C. Thompson in Salamo and Smith, eds., *Mark Twain's Letters*, pp. 316nn–17nn.

33. Kaplan, *Mr. Clemens and Mark Twain*, p. 172.

34. Taylor (Gordon), "Reminiscences of Jubilee Singers," *Fisk University News*, Oct. 1911 (FU).

35. Cole (Porter), "Maggie Porter-Cole," *Fisk News*, Dec. 1939 (FU).

36. McFeely, *Frederick Douglass*, p. 131.

37. Taylor (Gordon), "Reminiscences of Jubilee Singers."

38. Imes (Lewis), "Reminiscences" (FU).

39. Moore (Sheppard), "Historical Sketch of the Jubilee Singers," *Fisk University News*, Oct. 1911 (FU).

40. Imes (Lewis), "Reminiscences" (FU).

41. Hine to Pike, Feb. 25, 1874 (AMA).

42. Imes (Lewis), "Reminiscences" (FU).

43. McFeely, *Frederick Douglass*, p. 132.

44. Harriet Jacobs in Gerzina, *Black London*, p. 202.

19: THERE'S ROOM ENOUGH

1. G. R. Beltis to Halley, Dec. 10, 1873 (AMA).
2. Pike, *Singing Campaign for Ten Thousand Pounds*, pp. 44–45.
3. Diary of Ella Sheppard (FU).
4. Moffat may have seen in George White a kindred spirit; his explorer brother-in-law had come to despise and distrust the London Missionary Society as heartily as White deplored the A.M.A. Jeal, *Livingstone*, p. 181.
5. Benjamin Holmes to Lewis H. Douglass, Aug. 16, 1873, in *New National Era*, Sept. 25, 1873.
6. Pike, *Singing Campaign for Ten Thousand Pounds*, pp. 87–88.
7. Holmes to Douglass, Aug. 16, 1873, in *New National Era*, Sept. 25, 1873.
8. Pike, *Singing Campaign for Ten Thousand Pounds*, pp. 94–95; Jubilee Singers' receipts (FU).
9. Pike to Cravath, Jan. 6, [1874] (AMA).
10. Thomas, *Slave Trade*, pp. 239–41, 475.
11. Pike, *Singing Campaign for Ten Thousand Pounds*, p. 98.
12. Since Pike said a later concert at Scarborough earned, at £90, more money than any English concert to that time, I assume that the £140 cited for Hull was gross rather than net.
13. Holmes to Douglass, Aug. 16, 1873, in *New National Era*, Sept. 25, 1873.
14. Charles Grandison Finney in Jeal, *Livingstone*, p. 13.
15. Brandt, *Town That Started the Civil War*, pp. 34–37.
16. Fisk University obituary notice, n.d., MES, Fisk List (FU); Spence to Elizabeth Spence, April 28, 1873, AKS (FU).
17. Holmes to Douglass, Aug. 16, 1873, in *New National Era*, Sept. 25, 1873.
18. Pike, *Singing Campaign for Ten Thousand Pounds*, pp. 110–11, 115.
19. Ibid., p. 117.
20. Goodstein, *Nashville*, pp. 124, 134.
21. Unidentified Belfast paper in Pike, *Singing Campaign for Ten Thousand Pounds*, pp. 123–24.
22. Pike, *Singing Campaign for Ten Thousand Pounds*, pp. 125–26, 128.
23. Moore (Sheppard), "Historical Sketch of the Jubilee Singers," *Fisk University News*, Oct. 1911 (FU).
24. Pike, *Singing Campaign for Ten Thousand Pounds*, pp. 131–33, 137–38.
25. Thomas Cook to Pike, Dec. 22, 1873 (AMA).
26. Colin Brown in Pike, *Singing Campaign for Ten Thousand Pounds*, pp. 143–44.
27. Spence to Elizabeth Spence, June 26, 1870 (FU).
28. Pike, *Singing Campaign for Ten Thousand Pounds*, p. 151.
29. Moore (Sheppard), "Historical Sketch of the Jubilee Singers."
30. Imes (Lewis), "Reminiscences" (FU).
31. Thomas Hoyle to *English Independent*, Dec. 22, 1873, JSS (FU).
32. Imes (Lewis), "Reminiscences" (FU).

20: LET ME GET UP

1. N. Waterhouse to Pike, Jan. 26, 1874 (AMA).
2. White to Cravath, Oct. 29, 1873 (AMA).
3. White to Cravath, Dec. 15, 1873 (AMA).
4. Pike to Cravath, Jan. 6, 1874 (AMA).
5. Certificate, Nov. 24, 1873 (FU).
6. Pike to Cravath, Dec. 11, 1873 (AMA).
7. White to Cravath, Dec. 15, 1873 (AMA).
8. White to Cravath, Oct. 29, 1873 (AMA).
9. Pike to Cravath, Dec. 1, 1873 (AMA).
10. "I have gone so far as to wish I might visit Mendi Mission so as to be able to put in more of interest, pledging to pay my incidental expenses to that mission if we shall sell about 27,000 of Jubilee Singers." Pike to Cravath, Jan. 6, [1874] (AMA). Pike mistakenly dated this and several other January letters 1873.
11. Pike to Cravath, Dec. 1, 1873 (AMA).
12. "He is a distinguished author," wrote Pike, "a prize writer on Systematic Benevolence, the author of a commentary, a *practical* business man." Pike to Cravath, Dec. 11, 1873 (AMA).
13. Pike to Cravath, Jan. 6, [1874] (AMA).
14. Ibid.
15. Jenkins, *Gladstone*, p. 353.
16. Manchester *Examiner*, Jan. 12, 1874, and *Courier*, Jan. 15, 1874, JSS (FU).
17. Imes (Lewis), "Reminiscences" (FU).
18. Pike to Cravath, Jan. 20, [1874] (AMA).
19. Benjamin Holmes to James Burrus and Lindsay Roberts, Jan. 25, 1874, Spence, Burrus, MES (FU).
20. Pike to Whipple, Jan. 16, 1874 (AMA).
21. Holmes enclosed a less pious missive for his friend Lindsay Roberts. "Write me dear Lindsay and tell me the news and let me know how you are progressing in school, and with the girls, and anything that I can do for you ask it and I will try and comply—I hope that you have been altogether successful in life since we last met and that you still remember me as your friend." He gave his address as c/o Jubilee Singers, 18 Adam St., Strand, London. Holmes to James Burrus and Lindsay Roberts, Jan. 25, 1874, AKS (FU).
22. *New Norwich Argus*, Feb. 21, 1874, JSS (FU).
23. *Town Crier*, March 1874, JSS (FU).
24. Pike, *Singing Campaign for Ten Thousand Pounds*, p. 176.
25. "Let me add how very deeply & tenderly we feel for you. Your loss touches our hearts. May God himself be with you & yours." Blaikie to White, March 18, 1874 (AMA).
26. Moore (Sheppard), "Historical Sketch of the Jubilee Singers," *Fisk University News*, Oct. 1911 (FU).
27. Spence to Elizabeth Spence, May 11, 1874, AKS (FU).

28. Pike to Cravath, April 30, 1874 (AMA).

29. Sheppard to Spence, April 28, 1874, Spence, AKS, box 1 (FU).

30. Pike, *Singing Campaign for Ten Thousand Pounds*, pp. 198–200.

31. Pike to Cravath, May 2, May 4, June 3, 1874 (AMA).

32. Civil War pension file of George Leonard White. "George is improving slowly but enough so that we expect to sail on the 5th. . . . We are hoping for much benefit to him from the voyage . . . also (for) rooms at some other Hotel for our family, George, the three children and nurse and myself. For George at some good Hotel near the station from which we shall start West or near the steamer landing . . . so as to make but little riding about for George . . . between New York & Chicago." Addie Williams to Cravath, April 30, 1874 (AMA). British & North American Royal Mail Steam Packet Company to George White, April 4, 1874 (AMA).

33. Pike to Cravath, May 5 and June 8, 1874 (AMA).

21: NO COWARDS IN OUR BAND

1. Spence to Elizabeth and Edwin Spence, Sept. 27, 1872, AKS (FU); Cravath to Spence, Sept. 13, 1872, AKS (FU).

2. Spence to Elizabeth and Edwin Spence, Sept. 27, 1872, AKS (FU).

3. Spence to Elizabeth Spence, Oct. ?, 1872, Nov. 1, 1872, and Feb. 6, 1873, AKS (FU).

4. Chase to Spence, May 22, 1872, AKS (FU).

5. Spence to Elizabeth Spence, Nov. 23 and April 28, 1873, AKS (FU).

6. Nashville Public Schools, *Nashville*, p. 4.

7. Spence to Elizabeth Spence, June 13, 1873, AKS (FU).

8. Morgan to Spence, n.d. [summer of 1873], AKS (FU).

9. Mary E. Spence, note, Jan. 26, 1961, MES, Notes (FU); Oberlin College alumni file of Helen C. Morgan (OC).

10. Spence to Elizabeth Spence, Jan. 31 and March 31, 1874, AKS (FU).

11. Benjamin H. Bristow and J. M. Tomeny in Gillette, *Retreat from Reconstruction*, pp. 196, 248.

12. J. M. Richardson, *Christian Reconstruction*, p. 137.

13. Spence to Julia Spence Chase, Aug. 29, 1875, AKS (FU).

14. Benjamin Singleton in Painter, *Exodusters*, pp. 111, 115, 117.

15. Spence to Elizabeth Spence, May 25, 1874, AKS (FU).

16. Spence to Catherine Spence, Sept. 7, 1875, AKS (FU).

17. Civil War pension file of George Leonard White.

18. Spence to Elizabeth Spence, Sept. 9, 1874, AKS (FU).

19. Concert program (FU).

20. Pike to Cravath, June 3 and 8, 1874 (AMA).

21. Spence to Elizabeth Spence, June 8, 1874, AKS (FU).

22. White to Cravath, fragment, n.d. (AMA).

23. Pike to Cravath, July 2, 1874 (AMA).

24. White to Cravath, Oct. 13, 1874 (AMA); White to Cravath, fragment, n.d. (AMA); White to Cravath, Nov. 27, 1874 (AMA).
25. Henrietta Matson, untitled MS, 1878, AKS (FU).
26. *Good Templar's Echo*, Nov. 1876, JSS (FU).
27. Contract of Maggie Carnes, Nov. 1, 1874 (FU).
28. White to Cravath, Nov. 27, 1874 (AMA).
29. White to L. J. Loventhal, Oct. 19, 1874, JSS (FU).
30. "The Jubilee Singers," *Republican Banner*, Oct. 1874, JSS (FU).
31. Spence to Elizabeth Spence, Sept. 17, 1874, AKS (FU).
32. Mary Spence, "A Character Sketch of George L. White," *Fisk University News*, Oct. 1911 (FU).
33. Spence to Elizabeth Spence, Sept. 17, 1874, AKS (FU).
34. White to Cravath, March 16, 1875? (AMA).
35. Pike to Cravath, June 25, 1875 (AMA).
36. White to Cravath, Dec. 2 and 14, 1874 (AMA).
37. Lovell, *Black Song*, p. 407.
38. White to Cravath, Nov. 30, 1874 (AMA).
39. Spence to Catherine Spence, June 12, 1876, AKS (FU).
40. The other two classmates were Spence's brother John and Virginia E. Walker. "Fisk's First College Class," photograph (FU); Catherine Spence "Tennessee," *American Missionary*, Jan. 1876 (FU).
41. America W. Robinson in J. M. Richardson, *Christian Reconstruction*, p. 182.
42. Ibid., p. 42.
43. A white Dartmouth alumnus would dismiss his degree as "honorary" and claim he took little part in his class. M. W. Adams, "Reminiscences of James Dallas Burrus," in Letters of America Robinson, transcript (FU).
44. Robinson to Burrus, Aug. 16, 1875 (FU).
45. White to Cravath, Dec. 10, 1874 (AMA).
46. White to Cravath, Dec. 10, 1874 (AMA).
47. Oberlin College alumni file of Benjamin Ousley (OC).
48. Pike, *Singing Campaign for Twenty Thousand Dollars*, pp. 110–15.
49. White to Cravath, Dec. 10, 1874 (AMA); Alexander, "Reminiscences of Jubilee Singers," *Fisk University News*, Oct. 1911 (FU).
50. White to Cravath, Dec. 13, 1874 (AMA).
51. Diary of Ella Sheppard (FU).
52. White to Cravath, Dec. 2 and 7, 1874 (AMA).
53. Spence to Catherine Spence, Sept. 7, 1875, AKS (FU).
54. White to Cravath, Dec. 13, 1874 (AMA); Spence to Elizabeth Spence, Dec. 13, 1874, MES (FU).
55. Pike, *Singing Campaign for Twenty Thousand Dollars*, pp. 106–8.
56. Diary of Ella Sheppard (FU).
57. White to Cravath, Dec. 16, 1874 (AMA).
58. Mary Spence, untitled interview with Rosa Sheppard, MES, Burrus (FU); Sheppard to W. E. Whiting, April 6, 1875 (AMA).

59. "The Jubilee Singers," *American Missionary*, Feb. 1875.

60. Bill from Dr. J. P. Dake of Nashville, Jan. 19, 1875, to May 1, 1875, in Jubilee Singers' receipts (FU).

61. White to Cravath, Dec. 18, 1874 (AMA); White to Cravath, Feb. 27, 1875 (AMA).

62. Diary of Ella Sheppard (FU).

22: SEND THEM ANGELS

1. Spence to Elizabeth Spence, Dec. 13, 1874, MES (FU).

2. Commission of Clinton B. Fisk, July 3, 1874 (FU); White to Cravath, Nov. 27, 1874 (AMA).

3. Diary of Ella Sheppard (FU).

4. "A Remarkable Collection," *Evening Journal*, Jan. 6, 1881, JSS (FU).

5. Frederick Douglass, "The Emancipated Man Wants Knowledge," *American Missionary*, Aug. 1875 (FU).

6. "Hon. Frederick Douglass," *American Missionary*, Sept. 1875.

7. Seward to Cravath, Feb. 24, 1875 (AMA).

8. "The Voice of Ethiopia," *Church Union*, in *American Missionary*, April 1875 (FU).

9. "The Jubilee Singers," *Christian Recorder*, in *American Missionary*, April 1875 (FU).

10. Diary of Ella Sheppard (FU).

11. Clemens to Seward, March 8, 1875, in Salamo and Smith, eds., *Mark Twain's Letters*, p. 317nn.

12. White to Cravath, March 16, 1875? (AMA).

13. Diary of Ella Sheppard (FU).

14. George Whipple and M. E. Strieby, "Caution to the Public," Jan. 30, 1875 (AMA).

15. White to Cravath, March 25, 1875 (AMA).

16. "A Remarkable Collection," *Evening Journal*.

17. Ibid.

18. Diary of Ella Sheppard (FU).

19. Pike to Cravath, June 25, 1875 (AMA).

20. Diary of Ella Sheppard (FU).

21. White to Cravath, March 12, 1875 (AMA).

22. Diary of Ella Sheppard (FU).

23. Robinson to Burrus, May 19 and July 14, 1875 (FU).

24. Diary of Ella Sheppard (FU).

25. Earl of Shaftesbury in Marsh, *Story of the Jubilee Singers* (1881), p. 80.

26. Robinson to Burrus, June 2, 1875 (FU); Diary of Ella Sheppard (FU).

27. Diary of Ella Sheppard (FU).

28. Pike to Cravath, June 25, 1875 (AMA).

29. Robinson to Burrus, June 2, 1875 (FU).

30. Marsh, *Story of the Jubilee Singers* (1881), p. 81.

31. Robinson to Burrus, June 2 and Aug. 16, 1875 (FU).

32. Diary of Ella Sheppard (FU).

33. Marsh, *Story of the Jubilee Singers* (1881), p. 82.

34. "Meetings with Mr. Moody," *Christian*, in *American Missionary*, Sept. 1875 (FU).

35. Loudin in ibid.

36. Diary of Ella Sheppard (FU).

37. Robinson to Burrus, July 14, 1875 (FU).

38. Diary of Ella Sheppard (FU).

39. D. L. Moody, July 1875, AKS, Miscellaneous (FU).

40. Diary of Ella Sheppard (FU).

41. Jeal, *Livingstone*, pp. 267, 305, 374–76; Pakenham, *Scramble for Africa*, pp. 285–89.

42. Robinson to Burrus, July 2, 1875 (FU).

43. Robinson to Burrus, July 2 and 14, 1875 (FU).

44. Frederick Loudin, unidentified clipping, JSS (FU).

45. Robinson to Burrus, July 14 and 26, Aug. 2 and ?, 1875 (FU).

46. Diary of Ella Sheppard (FU).

47. Loudin to Cravath, Feb. 20, 1876 (FU).

48. Diary of Ella Sheppard (FU).

49. Exeter & Plymouth *Gazette*, Aug. 20, 1875, JSS (FU).

50. Moore (Sheppard), "Historical Sketch of the Jubilee Singers," *Fisk University News*, Oct. 1911 (FU).

51. Gerzina, *Black London*, pp. 203–4.

52. Diary of Ella Sheppard (FU).

53. Edinburgh *Daily Mail*, Oct. 18, 1875, JSS (FU); Marsh, *Story of the Jubilee Singers* (1881), p. 83.

54. Robinson to Burrus, Oct. 18, 1875 (FU).

55. Diary of Ella Sheppard (FU).

56. The mortality among promising black students was a heartbreak. Lura Beam, who taught under the auspices of the A.M.A. around the turn of the century, knew of one family in the early twentieth century that had been reduced by tuberculosis from seven to one: "The survivor was listening for the saw-whet owl, and waiting, for 'Before a death, the owl hoots at night.' " Beam especially mourned two young students, the most gifted pupils, white or black, she had ever taught. "The active mind, the good body and the satirical wit" of Ivan Crawley were asphyxiated by a faulty gas heater. The other died of typhoid. "I believe in the future," he once declared in class. "It may not be mine, but our moment is only a pencil mark on the ages." His name was Crawford Wilson. Beam, *He Called Them by the Lightning*, pp. 14, 182.

57. Diary of Ella Sheppard (FU).

58. Robinson to Burrus, May 22, 1876 (FU).

59. Benjamin Holmes to Lewis H. Douglass, Aug. 16, 1873, in *New National Era*, Sept. 25, 1873.

60. Pike, *Jubilee Singers* (1873), p. 57.

23: NO BACKSLIDING

1. Robinson to Burrus, Nov. 22 (serial 23), 1875 (FU).
2. Diary of Ella Sheppard (FU).
3. Robinson to Burrus, Nov. 22 (serial 23), 1875 (FU).
4. Imes (Lewis), "Reminiscences" (FU).
5. Moore (Sheppard), "Historical Sketch of the Jubilee Singers," *Fisk University News*, Oct. 1911 (FU).
6. Imes (Lewis), "Reminiscences" (FU).
7. Dublin *Irish Courier* (quotes from paper's paraphrase), Jan. 31, 1876, JSS (FU).
8. Robinson to Burrus, Nov. 22 (serial 23), 1875; Sunderland *Daily Echo*, Dec. 21, 1875, JSS (FU).
9. Diary of Ella Sheppard (FU).
10. *Irish Times*, Nov. 27, 1875, JSS (FU).
11. Lancaster *Guardian*, Dec. 11, 1875, JSS (FU); Diary of Ella Sheppard (FU).
12. Porter was constantly at odds with the troupe, and later, on January 1, 1876, Sheppard alludes to Jennie's absence from a YMCA performance, explaining that "Christ pains her." Diary of Ella Sheppard (FU).
13. Ibid.
14. White to Spence, Dec. 21, 1875, MES (FU).
15. Spence to Elizabeth Spence, Nov. 25, 1875, AKS (FU).
16. Matson, "Reminiscences of Fisk University," MS, n.d., MES, Matson (FU).
17. "Encouraged by his actions, others came forward, and it was [decided] to continue the primary school in the old place as being the most convenient for the children and the institution." Spence, untitled account of early days of Fisk University in MES, Notebooks (FU).
18. "Jubilee Hall," *American Missionary*, Feb. 1876 (FU).
19. Clinton B. Fisk to Cravath, Dec. 16, 1876 (FU).
20. Pike in "The Jubilee Singers" program (FU).
21. Spence to Elizabeth Spence, Nov. 30, 1875 (FU); George Hubbard to Spence, May 1, 1876 (FU).
22. Matson, "Reminiscences of Fisk University."
23. Edgar Ketchum to Spence, Jan. 17, 1876, AKS (FU).
24. Matson, "Reminiscences of Fisk University."
25. Unidentified manuscript, AKS (FU).
26. Spence to Elizabeth Spence, July 6, 1874, and Sept. 9, 1875, MES (FU).
27. S. A. Stevens to Miss D. E. Emerson, March 8, 1877 (AMA).
28. J. M. Richardson, *Christian Reconstruction*, p. 137.
29. Loudin to Cravath, Feb. 20, 1876 (FU).
30. Gordon to Gilbert, n.d., but contemporaneous with Loudin's and Rutling's letters on the same subject (FU).
31. Porter to Gilbert, n.d., but contemporaneous with Loudin's and Rutling's letters on the same subject (FU).
32. Jackson to Gilbert, n.d., but contemporaneous with Loudin's and Rutling's let-

ters on the same subject (FU). Apparently the women wrote to their preceptress, Susan Gilbert, and the men to Cravath.

33. Rutling to Cravath, Feb. 24, 1876 (FU).

34. *American Missionary*, Sept. and Oct. 1876.

35. Robinson to Burrus, May 22, 1876 (FU); Marsh, *Story of the Jubilee Singers* (1881), p. 120.

36. Moore (Sheppard), "Historical Sketch of the Jubilee Singers."

37. Diary of Ella Sheppard (FU).

38. Robinson to Burrus, Oct. 18, 1875, Jan. 17, Feb. 5, and May 22, 1876 (FU).

39. Taylor (Gordon), "Reminiscences of Jubilee Singers," *Fisk University News*, Oct. 1911 (FU).

40. Robinson to Burrus, Aug. 19, 1876 (FU).

41. Diary of Ella Sheppard (FU).

42. Robinson to Burrus, Nov. 22 (serial 23), 1875, and May 29, 1876 (FU).

43. Robinson to Burrus, June 23, 1876 (FU).

24: SWEET CANAAN

1. Robinson to Burrus, June 23, 1876 (FU).

2. As far back as 1866, the A.M.A.'s journal had published an account of the reception blacks were likely to receive in Switzerland not only from the Swiss but from white American tourists: "Some travelers from our country experienced a severe attack, a week since, on seeing a colored man sitting at the *table d'hôte*, at the well-known Gibbon Hotel, in that beautiful city; and they immediately notified the landlord that either they or the colored man must leave. The landlord was weak enough to yield to their bluster, and the colored traveler was compelled to seek another hotel. As no prejudice against color exists in this country, and as Christian people here find it difficult to understand its existence in our land, it may be conceived how the American character suffers by such displays of meanness . . . it is true that, out of simple curiosity at an unusual sight, I saw a crowd of the common people following a very black negro along the streets of Geneva." Rev. W. W. Patton to *Independent*, in "American Colorphobia Abroad," *American Missionary*, Nov. 1866 (FU).

3. Diary of Ella Sheppard (FU).

4. Robinson to Burrus, Nov. ?, 1877 (FU).

5. Diary of Ella Sheppard (FU).

6. Robinson to Burrus, Aug. ?, 1876 (FU).

7. Spence to Elizabeth Spence, June 1, 1876, AKS (FU).

8. Spence to Catherine Spence, June 16 and Sept. 12, 1876, MES and AKS (FU).

9. "Our Last Appeal for This Fiscal Year," *American Missionary*, Sept. 1876 (FU).

10. Robinson to Burrus, May 29 and Aug. 12 and ?, 1876 (FU).

11. The concert benefited a man named Callas. One hundred fifteen years earlier, his ancestor had been "broken on the wheel" by the tribunals of Toulouse, and he had

recently lost his only relative, a son, in the American Civil War. Geneva *Continent*, Aug. 1876, JSS (FU).

12. Robinson to Burrus, Aug. 12, 19, and (post 22), 1876 (FU); Marsh, *Story of the Jubilee Singers* (1881), p. 86.
13. Seward to *Folio*, Oct. 24, 1876, JSS (FU).
14. Geneva *Continent*, Aug. 31, 1876, JSS (FU).
15. Marsh, *Story of the Jubilee Singers* (1881), p. 86; "Programme du concert donné par the Jubilee Singers," May 18, 1878 (FU).
16. Geneva *Continent*, Aug. 31, 1876, JSS (FU).
17. Seward to *Folio*, Oct. 24, 1876, JSS (FU).
18. Moore (Sheppard), "Historical Sketch of the Jubilee Singers," *Fisk University News*, Oct. 1911 (FU); Marsh, *Story of the Jubilee Singers* (1881), p. 86.
19. Seward to *Folio*, Oct. 24, 1876, JSS (FU).
20. Diary of Ella Sheppard (FU).
21. Ibid.
22. Robinson to Burrus, Sept. 18, 1876 (FU).
23. Diary of Ella Sheppard (FU).
24. Robinson to Burrus, Sept. 18 and 26, 1876 (FU).
25. Hodder had not been satisfied with the engravings of the Jubilees' portraits in Pike's book. "Some of the female likenesses are not happy," he wrote the author, "but on the whole I think we cannot complain—especially as we were obliged to hurry the artist." Hodder to Pike, Dec. 22, 1873 (AMA).
26. Hodder to Cravath, Oct. 3, 1876 (FU).
27. White to Spence, Oct. 14, 1876, MES (FU).
28. Now that Porter had returned to the troupe, she asked Cravath to use some of the money in her account "to get mothers winter coal & wood." Porter to Cravath, Oct. 7, year not given, but contemporaneous with Stone's 1876 letter to White (FU).
29. Diary of Ella Sheppard (FU).
30. Robinson to Burrus, Oct. 12–14, 1876 (FU).
31. White to Spence, Oct. 14, 1876 (FU).
32. Robinson to Burrus, Oct. 12–14, 1876 (FU).
33. White to Spence, Oct. 14, 1876, MES (FU).
34. Spence to Catherine Spence, Sept. 4, 6, 8, 12, and 19 and Oct. 4, 1876, AKS (FU).
35. Handbill, Oct. 27, 1876, MES (FU).
36. Spence to Catherine Spence, Oct. 11, 1876, AKS (FU).
37. Diary of Ella Sheppard (FU). The Kelso *Mail* praised the Jubilees' "overpowering fervour of expression, sometimes taking the form of the melting wail of the sufferer crushed under an intolerable burden of oppression and wrong." Nov. 1876, JSS (FU).
38. Robinson to Burrus, Nov. 29, 1876 (FU).
39. White to Spence, Nov. 28, 1876, MES (FU).

40. *Good Templar's Echo*, Nov. 1876, JSS (FU); Londonderry *Sentinel*, Dec. 7, 1875, JSS (FU); Robinson to Burrus, Nov. 29, 1876 (FU).

41. Robinson to Burrus, Dec. 22, 1876 (FU).

42. White to Spence, Nov. 28, 1876, MES (FU).

43. Cravath to Spence, Dec. 9, 1876, MES (FU).

44. Imes (Lewis), "Reminiscences" (FU).

45. Robinson to Burrus, Nov. 29 and Dec. 22, 1876 (FU).

46. White to Cravath, Jan. 25, 1877 (FU).

47. White to *New York Daily Witness*, April 16, 1877, JSS (FU).

48. Marsh, *Story of the Jubilee Singers* (1881), p. 88.

49. Moore (Sheppard), "Historical Sketch of the Jubilee Singers."

50. Robinson to Burrus, March ?, 1877; George White to *New York Daily Witness*, April 16, 1877, JSS (FU).

51. Moore (Sheppard), "Historical Sketch of the Jubilee Singers."

52. Robinson to Burrus, Feb. ?, 1877 (FU).

53. Thomas, *Slave Trade*, pp. 159, 292, 338.

54. Moore (Sheppard), "Historical Sketch of the Jubilee Singers."

55. Robinson to Burrus, Feb. ?, 1877; George White to *New York Daily Witness*, April 16, 1877, JSS (FU).

56. Imes (Lewis), "Reminiscences" (FU).

57. Robinson to Burrus, February ?, 1877.

58. Ibid.

59. Marsh, *Story of the Jubilee Singers* (1881), p. 88.

60. Robinson to Burrus, March 24, 1877 (FU).

61. J. M. Richardson, *History of Fisk University*, p. 49.

62. Robinson to Burrus, March 24, 1877 (FU).

63. Loudin in "The Jubilee Singers: Interesting Chat with the Basso," unidentified newspaper, 1880.

64. White, unidentified clipping, May (?) 1877, JSS (FU).

65. Robinson to Burrus, March 24, 27, and 30, 1877 (FU).

66. Taylor (Gordon), "Reminiscences of Jubilee Singers," *Fisk University News*, Oct. 1911 (FU).

25: AIN'T GOIN' LAY MY MISSION DOWN

1. White to Spence, March 2, 1877 (FU).

2. L. C. Anderson to John Edward Porter, March 26, 1877 (FU).

3. Spence to Elizabeth Spence, April 9, 1872, AKS (FU).

4. Robinson to Burrus, April 11 and May 20? and 27, 1877 (FU).

5. "James Burrus is going to Dartmouth to carry on his mathematical studies in the hopes of fitting himself for professor." Spence to M. E. Strieby, July 10, 1877 (AMA).

6. Robinson to Burrus, May 20 and June 3 and 4, 1877 (FU).
7. White to Cravath, June 1–5, 1877 (FU).
8. Robinson to Burrus, June 3–4, 1877 (FU).
9. White to Cravath, June 1–5, 1877 (FU).
10. Pike to Cravath, June 26, 1877 (AMA).
11. White to Cravath, June 1–5, 1877 (FU).
12. New York *Observer*, July 12, 1877, JSS (FU).
13. White to New York *Observer*, July 2, 1877, JSS (FU).
14. Robinson to Burrus, June 18, 1877; Spence to Catherine Spence, July 12, 1877, AKS (FU).
15. Van Metter to Cravath, July 17, 1877 (FU).
16. Robinson to Burrus, July 22, 1877 (FU).
17. Cravath to Spence, July 31, 1877, AKS (FU).
18. White to Cravath, June 1–5 and September 20, 1877 (FU).
19. *Daily Advertiser*, Auburn, N.Y., 1881, JSS (FU).
20. White to Cravath, Sept. 20 and 27 and Oct. 3, 1877 (FU).
21. Diary of Ella Sheppard (FU).
22. Moore (Sheppard), "Historical Sketch of the Jubilee Singers," *Fisk University News*, Oct. 1911 (FU).
23. Up to then, "the letters which Mr. [Cravath] had secured from distinguished persons of distinction in Germany" had been "of no use, as all the parties were absent from the country & would not return soon. . . . And yet the one desire of our heart and *the* thing necessary to a brilliant success in Germany has come to us in just the most unexpected way," via the intercessions of the Reverend Kögel and a Dutch friend of Sheppard's, Cornelie de Humstra, daughter of the baron, who had apparently written on the Jubilees' behalf to a niece of the emperor. Diary of Ella Sheppard (FU).
24. Ibid (FU).
25. Marsh, *Story of the Jubilee Singers* (1881), p. 93.
26. Diary of Ella Sheppard (FU).

26: ALMOST HOME

1. Diary of Ella Sheppard (FU).
2. Moore (Sheppard), "Historical Sketch of the Jubilee Singers," *Fisk University News*, Oct. 1911 (FU).
3. *Protestanten-Zeitung*, JSS (FU).
4. *Berlinische Zeitung*, JSS (FU).
5. *Berliner Musikzeitung*, JSS (FU).
6. Diary of Ella Sheppard (FU).
7. Robinson to Burrus, Nov. ?, 1877 (FU).
8. E. Gilbert to Cravath, Jan. 9, 1878 (AMA).
9. Diary of Ella Sheppard (FU).

10. Marsh, *Story of the Jubilee Singers* (1881), p. 100.

11. If she only deserved "such a friend!" Sheppard exclaimed, "I might live up to this standard." Diary of Ella Sheppard (FU).

12. Diary of Ella Sheppard (FU).

13. Thomas, *Slave Trade*, pp. 320–21.

14. Marsh, *Story of the Jubilee Singers* (1881), pp. 144, 160, 208–9.

15. "The Jubilee Singers in Darlington," *Echo*, Nov. 15, 1875, JSS (FU).

16. Sheppard, note, "Granville, Illinois, March 9," MES, Notes (FU).

17. Diary of Ella Sheppard (FU).

18. Robinson to Burrus, Dec. 30, 1877 (FU).

19. Diary of Ella Sheppard (FU).

20. Robinson to Burrus, March 8–9, 1878 (FU).

21. Diary of Ella Sheppard (FU).

22. Malone to Mary and Mabel Spence, June 4, 1877.

23. Marsh, *Story of the Jubilee Singers* (1892), pp. 107–9.

24. Diary of Ella Sheppard (FU).

25. Vance to Mary and Grace Spence, Jan. 20, 1878 (FU).

26. Diary of Ella Sheppard (FU).

27. Many brackets indicate places where a portion of the page—about one word's worth on each line—has broken off.

28. Marsh, *Story of the Jubilee Singers* (1881), p. 97.

29. Moore (Sheppard), "Historical Sketch of the Jubilee Singers"; Diary of Ella Sheppard (FU).

30. Alexander, "Reminiscences of Jubilee Singers," *Fisk University News*, Oct. 1911 (FU).

31. Marsh, *Story of the Jubilee Singers* (1881), p. 99.

32. Alexander, "Reminiscences of Jubilee Singers."

33. Robinson to Burrus, March 8–9, 1878 (FU).

34. White to Cravath, March 26, 1878 (AMA).

35. Diary of Ella Sheppard (FU).

36. Robinson to Burrus, April 14–15, 1878 (FU).

37. White to Cravath, April 6, 1878 (AMA).

38. Clinton B. Fisk, Gustavus D. Pike, and M. E. Strieby to Cravath, April 3, 1878, in unidentified MS, AKS, Fisk List.

39. White to Cravath, April 5, 1878 (FU).

40. White to Cravath, April ?, 1878 (AMA); White to Cravath, April 6, 1878 (AMA).

41. Diary of Ella Sheppard (FU).

42. Cravath to Spence, June 24, 1878, MES (FU).

43. White to Cravath, May 15, 1878 (FU).

44. Cravath to Spence, June 24 and 27, 1878, MES (FU).

45. Cravath to Spence, June 24 and 27, 1878, MES (FU).

46. Jones to Cravath, April 25, 1878 (FU).

47. White to Cravath, May 8, 1878 (FU).

48. Jones to Cravath, April 25, 1878 (FU).

49. G. W. Petway to Spence, Jan. 5, 1876 (FU).

50. "American Negroes and Missions," *Christian World*, Aug. 25, 1881.

51. Miller and Jackson in Catherine Spence, broadside, Jan. 10, 1879, MES (FU).

52. James Matson to Henrietta Matson, Feb. 5, 1878 (AMA).

53. Miller in Catherine Spence, broadside, Jan. 10, 1879, MES (FU).

54. *American Missionary*, Nov. 1876 (FU).

55. Jackson to Rev. H. S. Bennett, printed in a supplement to the *Fisk Explorer*, 1882?, JSS (FU).

56. Diary of Ella Sheppard (FU).

57. Cravath to Spence, June 27, 1878 (FU).

58. Diary of Ella Sheppard (FU).

27: WANT TO CROSS OVER

1. "Maggie Porter-Cole," *Fisk News*, Dec. 1939 (FU).

2. Robinson to Burrus, Aug. 4, 1878 (FU).

3. "Mrs. America W. Lucas, *nee* Robinson, at Macon, Mississippi, is doing good work. We have noticed accounts in the Macon *Beacon*, of her success. In the State Teacher's Institute, she played an important part. In an exhibition given by the colored teachers, in honor of the State Superintendent, Mrs. Lucas read a fine paper, 'A European Tour,' which is spoken of very highly." Fisk *Herald*, Oct. 1884 (FU).

4. *Fisk News*, Dec. 1928; M. W. Adams, "Reminiscences of James Dallas Burrus," in Letters of America Robinson Transcript (FU); J. M. Richardson, *History of Fisk University*, p. 45.

5. Gilbert to [Fisk] Park, Jan. 19, 1929 (FU). Though America Robinson was the only Jubilee from the first three troupes to graduate from Fisk, in the late 1970s President Walter J. Leonard of Fisk University conferred honorary degrees on all of the original Jubilees who had sacrificed their education to save the school from extinction.

6. Oberlin College alumni file of Paul Cravath (FU).

7. Anonymous handwritten note in Pike, *Jubilee Singers* (1874), p. 76 (FU).

8. In 1895, one Hans Petritsch of the Alpine-Mountain Society in Vienna wrote to inquire if Mr. Cravath still lived. "I had a great interest to know that because he was a friend and protector of Mr. Rutling, a Jubilee Singer who has been in the year 1878 and 1879 in Switzerland. We did not hear from him till now, and he could not have intelligence from his son at Vienna in Austria." If his previous letters had not reached Cravath, he wanted it unsealed and the recipient to advise "what could be done for the son of Mr. Rutling. He deserves your full interest Sir, and God may bless you if you help him to find his father." Petritsch to [Fisk], Oct. 25, 1895 (FU).

9. Rutling, "My Life since Leaving the Jubilee Singers," *Fisk University News*, Oct. 1911 (FU).

10. "Death of Thomas Rutling: Harrogate Character Passes Away," *Fisk University News*, 1915 (FU).

11. W. D. Dobson to "Principal of Fisk University," April 16, 1915 (FU).

12. Moore (Sheppard), letter to the editor, Nashville *American*, March 17, 1902 (FU).

13. M. L. Crosthwaite, "A Resume," *Fisk University News*, Oct. 1911 (FU).

14. Geo. W. Moore to M. E. Strieby, Oct. 1, 1878 (AMA); Sarah A. Stevens to M. E. Strieby, Oct. 16, 1878 (AMA).

15. Geo. W. Moore to M. E. Strieby, Nov. 4, 1878 (AMA).

16. Catherine Spence, broadside, Jan. 10, 1879, MES (FU).

17. Randall Brown in Taylor, *Negro in Tennessee*, pp. 109, 27.

18. Unidentified missionary in ibid., p. 107.

19. Catherine Spence, broadside, Jan. 10, 1879, MES (FU).

20. Fisk *Expositor*, Feb. 1880 (FU); Concert program, 1879 (FU).

21. Mary Spence, "Spirituals," note, n.d., MES, Notes (FU).

22. Fisk *Expositor*, June 1880 (FU).

23. The proprietor defended himself in the Boston *Daily Evening Traveller:* "I did not request them to leave the house on their refusal to comply with my request to take their meals a half-hour earlier than the other guests, but simply informed them that many of the guests of the house objected to their presence in the dining room at the regular meal hours, but if they insisted upon it they could do so if every other person in the house left in consequence; but to this Mr. White, their agent, objected, saying, if there was any such feeling among the guests he would not be willing to have them remain, and after taking their dinner *with the rest of the guests*, they voluntarily left, Mr. White at the time remarking that he regretted that such a narrow and foolish prejudice should exist, but that he did not in the least blame me for it. Their leaving was an entirely voluntary act on their part, as they did not seem willing to remain if there was any objection to their being here on the part of any of the guests. At the time I contracted to take them I did not know that they were colored, nor after they had arrived here could I control the prejudices of my guests or prevent their giving utterance to them" (William P. F. Meserve to Boston *Daily Evening Traveller*, Oct. 28, 1879). White fired back a reply. "It is true," he said, "that we were not ordered out, or thrown out of the hotel; but we were distinctly informed (to put it mildly) that we were not 'welcome guests,' and could not remain unless we chose to enforce the contract made the day before—the proprietor offering to pay the cost of removing our baggage to another hotel. After it was decided that we must leave, I asked if the singers could have their dinner, as it was their dinner hour, remarking if they could not they would have to go without, as they had an engagement for the afternoon. I was told that they could have their dinner if all the guests left the house, but not that we could remain in the house if all the guests left—exactly the contrary" (George White to Boston *Evening Transcript*, Oct. 29, 1879, JSS [FU]).

24. "The Color Line in Boston," *Daily Evening Traveller*, Oct. 27, 1879, JSS (FU).

25. Fannie B. Ward in *Forney's Sunday Chronicle*, March 1880, JSS (FU).

26. A hotelier named Crossan replied that had the Jubilees applied to him for lodg-

ings he "would have tried to persuade them to make other arrangements. I don't know as I would have succeeded. But you know a great many people object to the presence of colored people sitting at the same tables or in the same dining room with them." Upon recalling an incident in which Frederick Douglass was informed that some of his fellow boarders objected to his presence in the Hotel dining room, Mr. Crossan said, "He replied by asking what was the objection to him. I answered that I had not the slightest doubt that he was a better man, physically, intellectually, and morally than hundreds of men who were entertained at my hotel that week; I did not doubt but that he was more cleanly. Then he asked me if I did not consider the Parker House, Boston, a first class hotel. I answered that I certainly did, and went on to say that our people were not educated up to the same standard as were the residents of Boston—the inhabitants of Massachusetts. A prejudice existed here that did not exist in the East. Then he wanted to know if I did not consider the Souther Hotel, St. Louis, a first class hotel. I answered that I did, and he said that he had been frequently entertained there, and could it be that in the great Republican city of Pittsburgh, where the Republican party had its birth, its very stronghold, that he was to meet with this treatment. I told him that no one regretted the occurrence more than I did, but I not only proposed to give him and his three friends a private dining-room with a servant to attend on them, but to make no extra charge for these accommodations. . . . Still, in this case, there being, as I understand, a large number of colored people in this troupe, I would have preferred to have given them a separate dining-room. I do not think they have been actually refused. They may have found the figures too high to suit them. I presume Mr. Henderson, who is now absent, was the man they applied to. Mr. Loudin, who you say makes the statement, was a servant in this house several years, living here as the private servant of Mr. Wm. M. Lyon. When he first returned from Europe he called upon me and I had a long and interesting chat with him concerning his experiences abroad. If he had come to me about this business, I certainly would have treated him well, but you know it would have made trouble for me to have distributed thirty or forty colored people, no matter how thoroughly cultured and accomplished they might be, through my dining room." *Commercial Gazette*, May 6, 1880, JSS (FU).

27. B. C. Unseld to editor of the Columbia *Courant*, April 24, 1880, JSS (FU).
28. Cincinnati *Commercial*, May 23, 1880, JSS (FU).
29. Loudin in "The Color Line," *Commercial Gazette*, May 6, 1880, JSS (FU).
30. *Evening Transcript*, April 27, 1880, JSS (FU).
31. Warren *Mail*, April 12, 1881, JSS (FU).
32. Unidentified Chicago newspaper, April 29, 1881, JSS (FU).
33. Loudin in *Chicago Tribune*, May 4, 1879, JSS (FU).
34. *Chicago Tribune*, April 29, 1881, JSS (FU).
35. *Inter Ocean*, April 1881, JSS (FU).
36. Unidentified Jubilee Singer [Ella Sheppard?] in "The Bigotry and Caste of Slavery Contrasted with the Power of the Music of the Former Slaves," unidentified Philadelphia journal, June 5, 1880, JSS (FU).

37. Ibid.
38. Louisville *Commercial*, May 21, 1880, JSS (FU).
39. Warren *Mail*, April 12, 1881, JSS (FU).
40. J. M. Richardson, *History of Fisk University*, p. 49.
41. *Daily Herald*, May 26, 1880, JSS (FU).
42. White, 1880, JSS (FU).
43. Spence, "Ode to the Jubilee Bell," 1880, JSS (FU).
44. *Daily Dispatch* (Columbus, Ohio), March 23, 1880, JSS (FU).
45. "Fisk Jubilee Singers" to unknown publication, Aug. 19, 1880, Chautauqua, N.Y., JSS (FU).
46. *Hamilton (N.Y.) Evening News*, Oct. 25, 1880, JSS (FU).
47. *Daily Courier*, May 23, 1881, JSS (FU).
48. Unidentified clipping, Amesbury, Nov. 4, 1879, JSS (FU).
49. "A Remarkable Collection," *Evening Journal*, Jan. 6, 1881, JSS (FU).
50. Loudin in *Assembly Herald*, Aug. 11, 1880, JSS (FU).
51. "Color Prejudice," Elmira *Advertiser*, quoted in Ithaca *Daily Journal*, March 25, 1881, JSS (FU).
52. James A. Garfield in unidentified newspaper, Aug. ?, 1880, JSS (FU).
53. Unidentified newspaper, 1880, JSS (FU).
54. Civil War pension file of George Leonard White.
55. Unidentified newspaper, July 1881, JSS (FU).
56. Toronto *Globe*, Sept. 24, 1881, JSS (FU); Toronto *Evening News*, Sept. 24, 1881, JSS (FU).
57. Toronto *Presbyterian*, Sept. 30, 1881, JSS (FU).
58. "Concert by the Jubilee Singers," *Daily Expositor*, Oct. 15, 1881, JSS (FU).
59. Boston *Evening Traveller*, Jan. 15, 1882, JSS (FU).
60. Clipping from an unidentified history of Oberlin, p. 62, in the Oberlin archives. The clipping states that the father of one of the female singers had attended the conservatory. I believe, by the process of elimination, that this must have been Mattie Lawrence.
61. Civil War pension file of George Leonard White.
62. Fisk *Herald*, Oct. 1884. The Fisk *Herald*'s announcement of George White's memorial service was on the same page as a letter from the Anti-Lynching Committee of England. Fisk *Herald*, Dec. 1895 (FU).
63. Fredonia *Censor*, Dec. 27, 1882, JSS (FU).
64. Frederick Loudin in Marsh, *Story of the Jubilee Singers* (1892), pp. 123–24.
65. "There are several troupes which have in them some of the many singers who were at some time during the seven years of active concert work by the Jubilee Singers, members of the company. All of these troupes are purely private enterprises and no-one has any connection with Fisk University. No one is either in *personnel* or management, the continuation or the representative of the original company." Cravath in Fisk *Herald*, Oct. 1884.
66. Matson died in Birmingham, Alabama, of apoplexy in 1905. Oberlin College treasurer's office correspondence, file of Henrietta Matson (OC).

67. Loudin in Marsh, *Story of the Jubilee Singers* (1892), pp. 123–54.
68. Cleveland *Gazette*, Nov. 27, 1897, JSS (FU).
69. Ravenna *Record-Courier*, March 10, 1971 (FU).
70. "The Jubilee Singers," *Fisk University News*, Oct. 1911 (FU).

28: STEAL AWAY

1. M. L. Crosthwaite, "A Resume," *Fisk University News*, Oct. 1911 (FU).
2. Anderson, "Fisk Jubilee Singers," p. 272.
3. Bragg, *Georgia Gordon Taylor*, pp. 7–8.
4. Robinson to Burrus, April 14–15, 1878 (FU).
5. Mary Spence, "Spirituals," note, n.d., MES, Notes (FU); Anderson, "Fisk Jubilee Singers," p. 220; Moore (Sheppard), letter to the editor, Nashville *American*, March 17, 1902; Fisk *Herald*, June 1884.
6. Moore (Sheppard), letter to the editor, Nashville *American*, March 17, 1902 (FU).
7. Alabama probate records (FU).
8. Imes (Lewis), "Reminiscences" (FU).
9. Fisk *Herald*, March 1884; anonymous handwritten note in Pike, *Jubilee Singers* (1874), p. 76 (FU); Moore (Sheppard), letter to the editor, Nashville *American*, March 17, 1902 (FU).
10. Mary Spence, card, Jan. 21, 1940, MES, Notes (FU).
11. White to Bennett, Oct. 21, 1882 (AMA).
12. Civil War pension file of George Leonard White.
13. His surviving children were William C. White, a lawyer and graduate of Cornell, and Georgia L. White, who, at the time of her father's death, was studying at Cornell. Nashville *Daily American*, n.d. (FU).
14. Fisk *Herald*, n.d. (1895) (FU).
15. Fisk *Herald*, Dec. 1895.
16. Spence, "George L. White," *Fisk University News*, Oct. 1911 (FU).
17. Taylor (Gordon), "Reminiscences of Jubilee Singers," *Fisk University News*, Oct. 1911.
18. Washington in J. M. Richardson, *History of Fisk University*, p. 48.
19. J. M. Richardson, *History of Fisk University*, pp. 47, 53.
20. Cravath in ibid., p. 49.
21. Proctor, *Between Black and White*, p. 34.
22. Spence, "Account of the Old Fisk Buildings," MS, n.d. (1895), MES, Notebooks (FU).
23. H. H. Wright, "Jubilee Songs at Chapel Exercises," *Fisk University News*, Oct. 1911 (FU).
24. Unidentified note in MES (FU).
25. J. M. Richardson, *History of Fisk University*, p. 50.
26. Proctor, *Between Black and White*, pp. 25–34.
27. Mary Spence, "A.K. Spence," MS, n.d. (1895), MES, Notebooks (FU).

28. Moore, "Bondage and Freedom—The Story of a Life" (FU). Some of this account was taken from George White's account of George and Ella Sheppard Moore's lives in the Fredonia *Censor*, Dec. 27, 1882, JSS (FU).

29. Oberlin College alumni file for Adam Knight Spence (OC).

30. Matson, untitled MS, AKS (FU).

31. Moore to M. E. Strieby, April 6, 1878 (AMA).

32. Moore, "Bondage and Freedom—The Story of a Life" (FU).

33. "If at times you should meet with discouragements, with opposition and with the enmity of the inhuman and diabolical spirit of caste, comport yourselves, I pray you, with true Christian dignity and patience, remembering that He who has made of one blood all nations of men, and who will make the redeemed of all nations one kingdom, one church, one family in Christ, will, in due time, extirpate from among them all narrowness and selfishness, injustice and sin." Rev. M. MacGregor in Fredonia *Censor*, Dec. 27, 1882, JSS (FU).

34. Ibid.

35. Fisk *Herald*, Sept. 1883; Oberlin alumni file of George Washington Moore (OC).

36. Fisk *Herald*, March 1884 (FU).

37. Moore, "Bondage and Freedom—The Story of a Life" (FU).

38. J. M. Richardson, *History of Fisk University*, p. 51.

39. Work, *Folk Song of the American Negro*, pp. 40, 81–82.

40. Beam, *He Called Them by the Lightning*, p. 193.

41. Mary E. Spence in J. M. Richardson, *History of Fisk University*, p. 28. Fisk's archivist, Beth Howse, remembers Mary Spence from the 1960s, when she would take her daily constitutionals in her shawl. Correspondence suggests that she lost her voice to esophageal cancer. Mute, almost completely deaf, she holed up with her father's memorabilia, which was found in a pile in the attic of Jubilee Hall and saved. Interview with Beth Howse.

42. Oberlin alumni file of George Washington Moore (OC).

43. *Nashville Globe*, June 12, 1914 (FU).

44. J. M. Richardson, *History of Fisk University*, p. 81.

45. Kaplan, *Mr. Clemens and Mark Twain*, pp. 339–40.

46. Samuel L. Clemens in Meltzer, *Mark Twain Himself*.

SOURCES

ARCHIVES
American Missionary Association Archives (AMA)

Amistad Research Center, Tulane University, New Orleans
This collection contains correspondence and documents relating to the A.M.A.'s missions and fund-raising throughout the country, much of it concerning Fisk University and the Jubilee Singers. The collection is available on microfilm and organized by state.

Fisk University Special Collections (FU)

Nashville, Tennessee
The collection includes the following material, in addition to other miscellaneous files of photographs, documents, broadsides, receipts, minutes, and letters.

Papers of Erastus Milo Cravath
Papers of Clinton Bowen Fisk
Papers of the Fisk Jubilee Singers
Letters of America W. Robinson, April 21, 1875, to Aug. 4, 1878
Diaries of Ella Sheppard, Nov. 7, 1874, to Nov. 14, 1876, and Oct. 19, 1877, to July 15, 1878
Papers of Adam Knight Spence and Catherine Macky Spence
Papers of Mary E. Spence, including the papers of James Burrus and Henrietta Matson

BOOKS, MANUSCRIPTS, RECORDS, AND DOCUMENTS

Adler, Mortimer J., Charles Van Doren, and George Ducas, eds. *The Negro in American History.* 3 vols. Chicago, 1969.

Albert, Octavia V. Rogers. *The House of Bondage; or, Charlotte Brooks and Other Slaves.* New York, 1890.

American Missionary Association. *History of the American Missionary Association: Its Churches and Educational Institutions among the Freedmen, Indians, and Chinese, with Illustrative Facts and Anecdotes.* New York, 1874.

————. *Twenty-fifth Annual Report of the American Missionary Association.* New York, 1871.

Anderson, Toni Passmore. "The Fisk Jubilee Singers: Performing Ambassadors for the Survival of an American Treasure, 1871–1878." Ph.D. diss., Georgia State University, 1997.

Andrews, William L., ed. *From Fugitive Slave to Free Man: The Autobiographies of William Wells Brown.* New York, 1993.

Anonymous. *Army of the Cumberland.* Philadelphia, 1863.

Appiah, K. Anthony, and Amy Gutmann. *Color Conscious: The Political Morality of Race.* Princeton, N.J., 1996.

Aptheker, Herbert. *To Be Free.* New York, 1991.

Armstrong, William Howard. *A Friend to God's Poor: Edward Parmelee Smith.* Athens, Ga., 1993.

Bailey, Fred Arthur. *Class and Tennessee's Confederate Generation.* Chapel Hill, N.C., 1987.

Baker, T. Lindsay, and Julie P. Baker, eds. *The WPA Oklahoma Slave Narratives.* Norman, Okla., 1996.

Ballard, Michael B. *A Long Shadow: Jefferson Davis and the Final Days of the Confederacy.* Jackson, Miss., 1986.

Bancroft, Frederic. *Slave Trading in the Old South.* 1931. Reprint, New York, 1959.

Beam, Lura. *He Called Them by the Lightning: A Teacher's Odyssey in the Negro South, 1908–1919.* New York, 1967.

Bean, Annemarie, James V. Hatch, and Brooks McNamara, eds. *Inside the Minstrel Mask: Readings in Nineteenth-Century Blackface Minstrelsy.* Hanover, N.H., 1996.

Beard, Augustus Field. *A Crusade of Brotherhood: A History of the American Missionary Association.* Boston, 1909.

Berlin, Ira. *Slaves without Masters: The Free Negro in the Antebellum South.* New York, 1974.

Berlin, Ira, et al., eds. *Free at Last: A Documentary History of Slavery, Freedom, and the Civil War.* New York, 1992.

————. *The Wartime Genesis of Free Labor: The Upper South.* Series 1, vol. 2 of *Freedom: A Documentary History of Emancipation, 1861–1867.* Cambridge, U.K., 1993.

Berwanger, Eugene H. *The Frontier against Slavery: Western Anti-Negro Prejudice and the Slavery Extension Controversy.* Chicago, 1971.

Billings, John D. *Hardtack and Coffee; or, The Unwritten Story of Army Life.* 1887. Reprint, Lincoln, Nebr., 1993.

Bingham, Jennie Maria. *The Life of the Seventh Earl of Shaftesbury, K. G.* New York, 1899.

Blackbourn, David. *The Long Nineteenth Century: A History of Germany, 1780–1918.* New York, 1998.

Blassingame, John W., ed. *Slave Testimony: Two Centuries of Letters, Speeches, Interviews, and Autobiographies.* Baton Rouge, La., 1977.

Blockson, Charles L. *Black Genealogy.* Baltimore, Md., 1991.

Boime, Albert. *The Art of Exclusion: Representing Blacks in the Nineteenth Century.* London, 1990.

Boles, John B. *Masters and Slaves in the House of the Lord: Race and Religion in the American South, 1740–1870.* Lexington, Ky., 1988.

Bontemps, Arna Wendell. *Chariot in the Sky: A Story of the Jubilee Singers.* New York, 1971.

Botkin, B. A., ed. *Lay My Burden Down: A Folk History of Slavery.* Chicago, 1969.

Bragg, Emma W. *Georgia Gordon Taylor: An Original Fisk Jubilee Singer.* Nashville, Tenn., 1997.

Brandt, Nat. *The Town That Started the Civil War.* Syracuse, N.Y., 1990.

Brown, Barbara W., and James M. Rose, eds. *Black Roots in Southeastern Connecticut, 1650–1900.* Detroit, Mich., 1980.

Brownlee, Frederick Leslie. *New Day Ascending.* Boston, 1946.

Butchart, Ronald E. *Northern Schools, Southern Blacks, and Reconstruction: Freedmen's Education, 1862–1875.* Westport, Conn., 1980.

Caldwell, Merrill S. "A Brief History of Slavery in Boone County, Kentucky." Paper delivered to the Boone County Historical Society. Florence, Ky., June 21, 1957.

Catterall, Helen Tunnicliff, ed. *Judicial Cases concerning American Slavery and the Negro.* Vols. 1 and 4. Washington, D.C., 1926–1937.

Cimprich, John. *Slavery's End in Tennessee, 1861–1865.* University, Ala., 1985.

Clark, Clifford E., Jr. *Henry Ward Beecher: Spokesman for a Middle-Class America.* Urbana, Ill., 1978.

Clarke, Lewis, and Milton Clarke. *Narratives of the Sufferings of Lewis and Milton Clarke, sons of a soldier of the Revolution, during a Captivity of more than Twenty Years among the Slaveholders of Kentucky, one of the So Called Christian States of North America.* Boston, 1846.

Clark-Lewis, Elizabeth. *Living In, Living Out: African American Domestics and the Great Migration.* New York, 1996.

Clayton, W. W. *History of Davidson County, Tennessee, with Illustrations and Biographical Sketches of Its Prominent Men and Pioneers.* 1897. Reprint, Nashville, Tenn., 1971.

Cornelius, Janet Duitsman. *"When I Can Read My Title Clear": Literacy, Slavery, and Religion in the Antebellum South.* Columbia, S.C., 1991.

Crutchfield, James A. *Williamson County: A Pictorial History.* Nashville, Tenn., 1980.

Curry, Richard O., ed. *The Abolitionists: Reformers or Fanatics?* New York, 1965.

Davidson, Basil. *The African Slave Trade: Precolonial History, 1450–1850.* Boston, 1961.

Douglass, Frederick. *Life and Times of Frederick Douglass: His Early Life as a Slave, His Escape from Bondage, and His Complete History.* New York, 1993.

———. *Narrative of the Life of Frederick Douglass, an American Slave. Written by Himself.* 1845. Reprint, New York, 1968.

Duberman, Martin, ed. *The Antislavery Vanguard: New Essays on the Abolitionists*. Princeton, N.J., 1965.

Du Bois, W.E.B. *Black Reconstruction in America, 1860–1880*. New York, 1935.

Egypt, Ophelia Settle, ed. *Unwritten History of Slavery: Autobiographical Account of Negro Ex-Slaves*. Nashville, Tenn., 1945.

Eisenschiml, Otto, and Ralph Newman. *Eyewitness: The Civil War as We Lived It: The American Iliad*. New York, 1956.

Elkins, Stanley M. *Slavery: A Problem in American Institutional and Intellectual Life*. Chicago, 1976.

Ellis, Edward Robb. *The Epic of New York City*. New York, 1966.

Ellis, Leonard. *History of New Bedford and Its Vicinity, 1620–1892*. Syracuse, N.Y., 1892.

Escott, Paul D. *Slavery Remembered: A Record of Twentieth-Century Slave Narratives*. Chapel Hill, N.C., 1979.

Faust, Drew Gilpin, ed. *The Ideology of Slavery: Proslavery Thought in the Antebellum South, 1830–1860*. Baton Rouge, La., 1981.

———. *Mothers of Invention: Women of the Slaveholding South in the American Civil War*. New York, 1997.

Federal Writers' Project. *Cincinnati: A Guide to the Queen City and Its Neighbors*. Cincinnati, Ohio, 1943.

Ferebee, L. R. *A Brief History of the Slave Life of Rev. L. R. Ferebee and the Battles of Life, and Four Years of His Ministerial Life: Written from Memory, to 1882*. Raleigh, N.C., 1882.

Filler, Louis. *The Crusade against Slavery, 1830–1860*. New York, 1960.

Finkelman, Paul. *Slavery and the Founders: Race and Liberty in the Age of Jefferson*. London, 1996.

Finlayson, Geoffrey B.A.M. *The Seventh Earl of Shaftesbury, 1801–1885*. London, 1981.

Fitch, John. *Annals of the Army of the Cumberland*. Philadelphia, 1864.

Fitzgerald, Ross. *A Visit to the Cities and Camps of the Confederate States*. London, 1865.

Fletcher, Robert Samuel. *A History of Oberlin College: From Its Foundation through the Civil War*. New York, 1971.

Fogel, Robert William, and Stanley L. Engerman. *Time on the Cross: The Economics of American Negro Slavery*. New York, 1989.

Foner, Eric. *Reconstruction*. New York, 1988.

Foner, Philip Sheldon. *Business & Slavery; the New York Merchants & the Irrepressible Conflict*. Chapel Hill, N.C., 1941.

Foster, Frances Smith. *Witnessing Slavery: The Development of Ante-Bellum Slave Narratives*. Westport, Conn., 1979.

Frazier, Edward Franklin. *The Negro Family in the United States*. New York, 1951.

Fry, Gladys-Marie. *Night Riders in Black Folk History*. Knoxville, Tenn., 1975.

Gamble, Paul. "Prologue to Tomorrow." Unpublished play. 1958.

Garrison, Webb. *Civil War Curiosities: Strange Stories, Oddities, Events, and Coincidences*. Nashville, Tenn., 1994.

Gates, Henry Louis, Jr., ed. *The Classic Slave Narratives*. New York, 1987.

Genovese, Eugene D. *The Political Economy of Slavery: Studies in the Economy and Society of the Slave South*. New York, 1967.

————. *Roll, Jordan, Roll: The World the Slaves Made*. New York, 1976.

Gerzina, Gretchen. *Black London: Life before Emancipation*. New Brunswick, N.J., 1995.

Gillette, William. *Retreat from Reconstruction, 1869–1879*. Baton Rouge, La., 1979.

Gladstone, William A. *United States Colored Troops, 1863–1867*. Gettysburg, Pa., 1990.

Glatthaar, Joseph T. *Forged in Battle: The Civil War Alliance of Black Soldiers and White Officers*. New York, 1990.

Goldhurst, Richard. *Many Are the Hearts: The Agony and the Triumph of Ulysses S. Grant*. New York, 1975.

Goodrich, Th. *Black Flag: Guerrilla Warfare on the Western Border, 1861–1865*. Bloomington, Ind., 1995.

Goodstein, Anita Shafer. *Nashville, 1780–1860: From Frontier to City*. Gainesville, Fla., 1989.

Gould, J. E. *Songs of Gladness for the Sabbath School*. Philadelphia, 1869.

Green, Nathaniel E. *The Silent Believers*. Louisville, Ky., 1972.

Greene, Lorenzo, Gary R. Kremer, and Antonio F. Holland. *Missouri's Black Heritage*. Columbia, Mo., 1993.

Grigsby, Melvin. *The Smoked Yank*. N.p., 1888.

Gutman, Herbert G. *The Black Family in Slavery and Freedom, 1750–1925*. New York, 1977.

Halberstam, David. *The Children*. New York, 1998.

Haley, James T., ed. *Sparkling Gems of Race Knowledge Worth Reading: A Compendium of Valuable Information and Wise Suggestions That Will Inspire Noble Effort at the Hands of Every Race-Loving Man, Woman, and Child*. Nashville, Tenn., 1897.

Harley, Sharon. *The Timetables of African-American History: A Chronology of the Most Important People and Events in African-American History*. New York, 1995.

Harper, Bernice Catherine, ed. *Social Welfare Forum*. New York, 1981.

Haydn, Hiram C., ed. *American Heroes on Mission Fields: Brief Missionary Biographies*. New York, 1894.

Helm, MacKinley. *Angel Mo' and Her Son, Roland Hayes*. Boston, 1945.

Hibben, Paxton. *Henry Ward Beecher: An American Portrait*. New York, 1942.

Hildebrand, Reginald F. *The Times Were Strange and Stirring: Methodist Preachers and the Crisis of Emancipation*. Durham, N.C., 1995.

Hirshson, Stanley P. *Farewell to the Bloody Shirt: Northern Republicans and the Southern Negro, 1877–1893*. Chicago, 1968.

Hobson, Fred. *But Now I See: The White Southern Racial Conversion Narrative*. Baton Rouge, La., 1999.

Hodder, Edwin. *The Life and Work of the Seventh Earl of Shaftesbury, K.G.* 3 vols. London, 1887.

Hoobler, James A. *Cities under the Gun: Images of Occupied Nashville and Chattanooga*. Nashville, Tenn., 1986.

Hopkins, Alphonso Alva. *The Life of Clinton Bowen Fisk*. New York, 1888.

Horton, James Oliver, and Lois E. Horton. *In Hope of Liberty: Culture, Community, and Protest among Northern Free Blacks, 1700–1860*. New York, 1997.

Howard, Goldena Roland. *Ralls County, Missouri*. New London, Mo., 1980.

Hubbard, G. W. *A History of the Colored Schools of Nashville, Tennessee.* Nashville, Tenn., 1874.

Hughes, Louis. *Thirty Years a Slave: From Bondage to Freedom: The Institution of Slavery as Seen on the Plantation and in the Home of the Planter.* 1897. Reprint, Miami, Fla., 1969.

Hurmence, Belinda, ed. *Before Freedom, When I Just Can Remember.* Winston-Salem, N.C., 1989.

————. *My Folks Don't Want Me to Talk about Slavery.* Winston-Salem, N.C., 1993.

————. *We Lived in a Little Cabin in the Yard.* Winston-Salem, N.C., 1994.

Hurst, Jack. *Nathan Bedford Forrest: A Biography.* New York, 1993.

James, Portia P. *The Real McCoy: African-American Invention and Innovation, 1619–1930.* Washington, D.C., 1989.

Jeal, Tim. *Livingstone.* New York, 1973.

Jenkins, Roy. *Gladstone: A Biography.* New York, 1997.

Johnson, Clifton H., ed. *God Struck Me Dead: Voices of Ex-Slaves.* Cleveland, Ohio, 1993.

Johnson, Isaac. *Slavery Days in Old Kentucky.* 1901. Reprint, Canton, N.Y., 1994.

Jones, Jacqueline. *Labor of Love, Labor of Sorrow: Black Women, Work, and the Family from Slavery to the Present.* New York, 1986.

Jordan, Ervin L., Jr. *Black Confederates and Afro-Yankees in Civil War Virginia.* Charlottesville, Va., 1995.

Kane, Joseph Nathan. *The American Counties: Origins of Names, Dates of Creation and Organization, Area, Population, Historical Data, and Published Sources.* 3rd ed. Metuchen, N.J., 1972.

Kaplan, Justin. *Mr. Clemens and Mark Twain.* New York, 1966.

Katz, William Loren, comp. *Flight from the Devil: Six Slave Narratives.* Trenton, N.J., 1996.

Khan, Lurey. *One Day, Levin . . . He Be Free: William Still and the Underground Railroad.* New York, 1972.

Kirke, Edmund. *Down in Tennessee and back by Way of Richmond.* 1864. Reprint, Westport, Conn., 1970.

Knox, George L. *Slave and Freeman: The Autobiography of George L. Knox.* Edited by Willard B. Gatewood, Jr. Lexington, Ky., 1979.

Kraditor, Aileen S. *Means and Ends in American Abolitionism: Garrison and His Critics on Strategy and Tactics, 1834–1850.* Chicago, 1989.

Kunhardt, Dorothy Meserve, and Philip B. Kunhardt. *Mathew Brady and His World.* Alexandria, Va., 1977.

Lamon, Lester C. *Blacks in Tennessee, 1791–1970.* Knoxville, Tenn., 1993.

Lester, Julius. *To Be a Slave.* New York, 1968.

Little, Charles E. *Cyclopedia of Classified Dates with an Exhaustive Index.* New York, 1900.

Litwack, Leon F. *Been in the Storm So Long: The Aftermath of Slavery.* New York, 1980.

————. *North of Slavery: The Negro in the Free States, 1790–1860.* Chicago, 1961.

Love, Nat. *The Life and Adventures of Nat Love, Better Known in the Cattle Country as "Deadwood Dick." A True History of Slavery Days, Life on the Great Cattle Ranges and on the Plains of the "Wild and Woolly" West, Based on Facts, and Personal Experiences of the Author.* 1907. Reprint, Lincoln, Nebr., 1995.

Lovell, John, Jr. *Black Song: The Forge and the Flame: The Story of How the Afro-American Spiritual Was Hammered Out.* New York, 1972.

Lovett, Bobby L. *The African-American History of Nashville, Tennessee, 1780–1930.* Fayetteville, Ark., 1999.

Lovett, Bobby L., and Linda T. Wynn, eds. *Profiles of African Americans in Tennessee.* Nashville, Tenn., 1996.

Lowe, Allen. *American Pop from Minstrel to Mojo: On Record, 1893–1956.* Redwood, N.Y., 1997.

Lowry, Thomas. *The Story the Soldiers Wouldn't Tell: Sex in the Civil War.* Mechanicsburg, Pa., 1994.

MacDonald, Greville. *George MacDonald and His Wife.* London, 1924.

Maclean, Fitzroy. *Scotland: A Concise History.* London, 1993.

Marrs, Elijah P. *Life and History of the Rev. Elijah P. Marrs.* Louisville, Ky., 1885.

Marsh, J.B.T. *The Story of the Jubilee Singers, with Their Songs.* New York, 1881; Cleveland, Ohio, 1892. S.v. Frederick Loudin, "Supplement."

Maslowski, Peter. *Treason Must Be Made Odious: Military Occupation and Wartime Reconstruction in Nashville, Tennessee, 1862–65.* Millwood, N.Y., 1978.

McElroy, John. *Andersonville: A Story of Rebel Military Prisons.* Toledo, Ohio, 1879.

McFeely, William S. *Frederick Douglass.* New York, 1991.

———. *Grant: A Biography.* New York, 1981.

McPherson, James M. *The Abolitionist Legacy: From Reconstruction to the NAACP.* Princeton, N.J., 1975.

———. *Battle Cry of Freedom: The Civil War Era.* New York, 1988.

———. *The Negro's Civil War: How American Negroes Felt and Acted during the War for the Union.* New York, 1965.

Mellon, James, ed. *Bullwhip Days: The Slaves Remember, an Oral History.* New York, 1988.

Meltzer, Milton. *Mark Twain Himself: A Pictorial Biography.* New York, 1960.

Miller, Randall M., ed. *"Dear Master": Letters of a Slave Family.* Ithaca, N.Y., 1978.

Morison, Samuel Eliot. *The Oxford History of the American People.* New York, 1965.

Nashville, City of. Birth records: 1881–1891.

———. Chancery and Circuit Court records.

———. Death register, 1874–1913.

———. Index to birth records, 1881–1913.

———. Marriage records. Nashville Metropolitan Archives.

———. Tennessee Centennial 1897 Exposition.

Nashville city directories for 1867 to 1918. TSLA.

Nashville Public Schools. *Nashville: The History and Culture of a City.* Nashville, Tenn., 1977.

Neider, Charles, ed. *The Selected Letters of Mark Twain.* New York, 1982.

Oates, Stephen B. *The Fires of Jubilee: Nat Turner's Fierce Rebellion.* New York, 1975.

Oberlin College alumni files (OC).

Oberlin College Treasurer's Office correspondence (OC).

Osburn, William. *Biographical Sketch and Memorial of Rev. John Braden, D.D., Late President of Central Tennessee College.* Nashville, Tenn., 1900.

Osofsky, Gilbert, ed. *Puttin' On Ole Massa: The Slave Narratives of Henry Bibb, William Wells Brown, and Solomon Northrup.* New York, 1969.

Painter, Nell Irvin. *Exodusters: Black Migration to Kansas after Reconstruction.* New York, 1992.

Pakenham, Thomas. *The Scramble for Africa, 1876–1912.* New York, 1991.

Perdue, Charles L., Thomas E. Barden, and Robert K. Phillips, eds. *Weevils in the Wheat: Interviews with Virginia Ex-Slaves.* Charlottesville, Va., 1976.

Peters, Harry T. *Currier & Ives: Printmakers to the American People.* New York, 1942.

Pickard, Kate E. R. *The Kidnapped and the Ransomed. Being the Personal Recollections of Peter Still and His wife "Vina," after Forty Years of Slavery.* Syracuse, N.Y., 1856.

Pike, Gustavus Dorman. *The Jubilee Singers and Their Campaign for Twenty Thousand Dollars.* Boston, 1873; New York, 1874.

———. *The Singing Campaign for Ten Thousand Pounds.* New York, 1875.

———. *The Singing Campaign for Twenty Thousand Dollars.* New York, 1877.

Prebble, John. *The Lion in the North: One Thousand Years of Scotland's History.* London, 1981.

Proctor, Henry Hugh. *Between Black and White.* Boston, 1925.

Puckett, Newbell Niles. *Black Names in America.* Boston, 1975.

Raboteau, Albert J. *Slave Religion: The "Invisible Institution" in the Antebellum South.* Oxford, 1978.

Rawick, George P., ed. *The American Slave: A Composite Autobiography.* 41 vols. Westport, Conn., 1972–1979.

Redford, Dorothy Spruill, and Michael D'Orso. *Somerset Homecoming: Recovering a Lost Heritage.* New York, 1988.

Reilly, Wayne E., ed. *Sarah Jane Foster, Teacher of the Freedmen: A Diary and Letters.* Charlottesville, Va., 1990.

Reis, Richard H. *George MacDonald.* New York, 1972.

Richardson, Harry V. *Dark Salvation: The Story of Methodism as It Developed among Blacks in America.* Garden City, N.Y., 1976.

Richardson, Joe M. *Christian Reconstruction: The American Missionary Association and Southern Blacks, 1861–1890.* Athens, Ga., and London, 1986.

———. *A History of Fisk University, 1865–1946.* University, Ala., 1980.

Robbins, Faye Wellborn. "A World-within-a-World: Black Nashville, 1880–1915." Ph.D. diss., University of Arkansas, 1980.

Robert, Charles Edwin. *Negro Civilization in the South; Educational, Social, and Religious Advancement of the Colored People: A Review of Slavery as a Civil and Commercial Question. The "Divine Sanction of Slavery." A Glance at African History. Ethnological Status of the Negro, etc.* Nashville, Tenn., 1880.

Robinson, William. *From Log Cabin to the Pulpit; or, Fifteen Years in Slavery.* Eau Claire, Wis., 1913.

Rollins, Richard, ed. *Black Southerners in Gray: Essays on Afro-Americans in Confederate Armies.* Murfreesboro, Tenn., 1994.

Roman, Charles Victor. *Meharry Medical College: A History.* Nashville, Tenn., 1934.

Rose, James, and Alice Eichholz. *Black Genesis.* Detroit, Mich., 1978.

Ross, Fitzgerald. *A Visit to the Cities and Camps of the Confederate States.* London, 1865.

Rutling, Thomas. *Tom: An Autobiography.* London, 1907.

Salamo, Lin, and Harriet Elinor Smith, eds. *Mark Twain's Letters.* Vol. 5. Berkeley, Calif., 1997.

Salvatore, Nick. *We All Got History: The Memory Books of Amos Webber.* New York, 1996.

Sawyer, J. J. *Jubilee Songs and Plantation Melodies.* Boston, 1884.

Scarborough, Dorothy. *On the Trail of Negro Folk-Songs.* Hatboro, Pa., 1963.

Schweninger, Loren. *James T. Rapier and Reconstruction.* Chicago, 1978.

————, ed. *From Tennessee Slave to St. Louis Entrepreneur: The Autobiography of James Thomas.* Columbia, Mo., 1984.

Scouller, James Brown. *A Manual of the United Presbyterian Church of North America, 1751–1881.* Harrisburg, Pa., 1881.

Simpson, Aggie Walker. "A Sketch of the Early Days of the Mission." *Aurora* (Knoxville College), Dec. 1893 and March 1894.

Smith, Willard H. *Schuyler Colfax: The Changing Fortunes of a Political Idol.* Indianapolis, 1952.

Smith, Z. F. *The History of Louisville.* N.p., 1886.

Stanley, Lady Augusta. *Later Letters of Lady Augusta Stanley, 1864–1876.* London, 1929.

Stearns, Charles. *The Black Man of the South and the Rebels.* 1872. Reprint, New York, 1969.

Strachey, Lytton. *Queen Victoria.* New York, 1921.

Sydnor, Charles S. *Slavery in Mississippi.* New York, 1965.

Tadman, Michael. *Speculators and Slaves: Masters, Traders, and Slaves in the Old South.* Madison, Wis., 1996.

Taylor, Alrutheus Ambush. "Fisk University and the Nashville Community, 1866–1900." *Journal of Negro History* (April 1954).

————. *The Negro in Tennessee.* 1941. Reprint, Spartanburg, S.C., 1974.

Tennessee, State of. Civil War (Federal) Collection (TSLA).

Thomas, Hugh. *The Slave Trade.* New York, 1997.

Toney, Marcus Bearden. Diaries (TSLA).

Twelvetrees, Harper, ed. *The Story of the Life of John Anderson, the Fugitive Slave.* London, 1863.

United States. Census for 1850, 1860, 1870.

————. Census records, Nashville, 1860.

————. Civil War pension files.

————. *Ku Klux Conspiracy: Report of the Joint Select Committee to Inquire into the Condition of Affairs in the Late Insurrectionary States.* Washington, D.C., 1872.

————. Records of the Bureau of Refugees, Freedmen, and Abandoned Lands.

————. Regimental records of the Seventy-third Ohio Volunteer Infantry.

U.S. Congress. *The War of the Rebellion: A Compilation of the Official Records of the Union and Confederate Armies.* Washington, D.C., 1882.

U.S. Library of Congress. *Recording of Slave Narratives and Related Materials in the Archive of Folk Song: Reference Tapes.* Washington, D.C., 1981.

Victoria. Journal of Queen Victoria. Unpublished MS. Quoted by the gracious per-
     mission of Her Majesty Queen Elizabeth II.

Walvin, James. England, Slaves, and Freedom, 1776–1838. Jackson, Miss., 1986.

————. The Quakers: Money and Morals. London, 1997.

————. Questioning Slavery. London, 1996.

Washington, Booker T. Up from Slavery. 1901. Reprint, New York, 1986.

Watson, M. S. "Nashville during the Civil War." Master's thesis, Nashville, 1926.

Weintraub, Stanley. Victoria: An Intimate Biography. New York, 1987.

Wharton, Vernon Lane. The Negro in Mississippi, 1865–1890. New York, 1965.

Whetstone, Rea. "History of Knoxville College." McGill Library, Westminster College
     Archives, n.d.

Wiley, Bell Irvin. The Life of Billy Yank. New York, 1952.

————. The Plain People of the Confederacy. Chicago, 1963.

————. Southern Negroes, 1861–1865. 1938. Reprint, New Haven, Conn., 1965.

Williams, Eric. Capitalism & Slavery. 1944. Reprint, Chapel Hill, N.C., 1994.

Williams, George W. A History of the Negro Troops in the War of the Rebellion, 1861–1865,
     Preceded by a Review of the Military Services of Negroes in Ancient and Modern Times.
     New York, 1888.

Williams, James. Life and Adventures of James Williams, a Fugitive Slave. San Francisco,
     1873.

Williams, Walter, ed. A History of Northeast Missouri. Chicago, 1913.

Wilson, Joseph T. The Black Phalanx. Hartford, Conn., 1888.

Wilson, Peggy Stephenson, ed. Nolensville, 1797–1987: Reflections of a Tennessee Town.
     Nolensville, Tenn., 1989.

Winn, Ralph B., ed. A Concise Lincoln Dictionary: Thoughts and Statements. New York,
     1959.

Wish, Harvey, ed. Slavery in the South. New York, 1964.

Wood, Betty. The Origins of American Slavery: Freedom and Bondage in the English Colonies.
     New York, 1997.

Woodson, Carter G., ed. Free Negro Owners of Slaves in the United States in 1830, Together
     with Absentee Ownership of Slaves in the United States in 1830. 1924. Reprint, New
     York, 1968.

Woodward, C. Vann. The Burden of Southern History. New York, 1969.

Woodworth, Charles Louis. The American Missionary Association, Its Work among the Freed-
     men. N.p., 1866.

Work, John Wesley. Folk Song of the American Negro. Nashville, Tenn., 1915.

Young, Robert, J.C. Colonial Desire: Hybridity in Theory, Culture, and Race. London,
     1995.

Zack, Naomi. Race and Mixed Race. Philadelphia, 1993.

Zarefsky, David. Lincoln, Douglas, and Slavery: In the Crucible of Public Debate. Chicago,
     1990.

ACKNOWLEDGMENTS

This book derives primarily from two sources: the Fisk University Special Collections and the American Missionary Association archives of the Amistad Research Center at Tulane University, which I reviewed on microfilm at Harvard University and the Tennessee State Library and Archives.

At Fisk, I wish to thank Special Collections librarian Beth Howse, a descendant of Ella Sheppard, for her kind and patient assistance. There was not a visit during which she did not bring forth some new treasure relating to the Jubilees, and for her advice and encouragement I will always be grateful. I thank also her predecessor, the archivist Ann Ellen Shockley, for her assistance when I first visited Fisk on another project that led me to the story of the Jubilees. The Fisk University Archive is one of the treasures of African American history and deserves major funding for its maintenance and enrichment. I also wish to thank Robert Poole, vice president for institutional advancement; Associate Professor Reavis Mitchell of the history department; and Paul T. Kwami, director of the current Fisk Jubilee Singers, who gave me the uniquely inspiring experience of hearing his students perform in the costume of the original troupe.

I thank the following American archives and archivists for their assistance: Roland M. Baumann and Tammy L. Martin of the Oberlin College

Archives; the Auburn Avenue Research Library on African-American Culture and History of the Atlanta-Fulton Public Library; Harvard University library; Barbara Dawson of the Cincinnati History Museum; the Seattle Family Research Center of the Church of Jesus Christ of Latter-day Saints; the Founders Library of Howard University; Ann Webster of the Mississippi State Archives; the National Archives and Records Administration; Joan Kiso of the Missouri State Archives; Mattie McHollin of the Meharry Archives; Adrienne Cannon of the Library of Congress; Dr. Jim Goodrich of the University of Missouri; Diana Latchatanere of the Schomburg Library; the genealogical staff of the Seattle Public Library and the University of Washington library; the Wilberforce University Archives; the Yale Divinity School library and the Yale Center for British Art.

In Great Britain, I wish to thank the earl of Shaftesbury and his assistant, Mrs. H. J. Garrick, of the Shaftesbury Estates; Margaret Kirby; Pamela Clark, the deputy registrar of the Royal Archives; Elizabeth L. Pettit of the Clwyd Record Office, Hawarden Branch; L. Donald of the North East of Scotland Library Service; the University of Southampton Library Special Collections; Dr. C. M. Woolgar of the University of Southampton; the University of Edinburgh; and the University of Nottingham.

In Nashville, I want to thank the following people for their help: Dr. Emma W. Bragg; Randy Elder of Elder's Bookstore; David Steele Ewing; Corrine Garrett; Novella Bass; Edith Dowdy; Robert Mosely, Jr., of Greenwood Cemeteries; James Hoobler, the curator of art and architecture at the Tennessee State Museum; the Reverend Charles E. Jenkins; Martha Mullin, the curator of the Hermitage; Dr. Bobby Lovett, the dean of the arts and humanities, Tennessee State University; Steve Rogers of the Nashville Historical Commission; the Nashville Historical Society; T. Vance Little; the Nashville Metropolitan Archives; Carol Kaplan and Mary Glenn Hearn of the Nashville Room of the Nashville Public Library; the Reverend William H. Hardy of St. Peter A.M.E.; Chaddra Moore and Dr. Wayne Moore of the Tennessee State Library and Archives; Sybil Marshall of the University of Tennessee Law Library. I also want to extend my gratitude to Sam McClain for singing the old songs for me, George Bolejack for his reminiscences of former slaves, Thelma Battle for her pictorial and genealogical assistance, and the Center for Popular Music for its assistance in hunting down lyrics and song titles.

My thanks to Professor Horace Clarence Boyer of the University of Massachusetts at Amherst for generously reviewing parts of this book dealing with freedmen, spirituals, and the musical achievement of the Fisk Jubilee Singers. I also wish to thank the leading authority on freedmen's missions and author of the definitive history of Fisk University, Professor Joe M. Richardson of Florida State University, for his encouragement and for kindly reviewing portions of my manuscript relating to the A.M.A. and Fisk. Thanks also to Dr. Walter J. Leonard, former president of Fisk University, for his insights into the Jubilee Legacy.

I thank Toni Passmore Anderson of the LaGrange College music department for her pioneering thesis; I look forward to her own upcoming book on the Jubilees. I am grateful that my brother-in-law, Allen Lowe, happens to be one of the leading authorities on early American music, and I thank him for his advice and help in directing me to pertinent books and his own network of expert friends and colleagues.

I am indebted to Paul Gamble, archivist emeritus of the McGill Library at Westminster College, for material relating to Joseph Gillespie McKee. Thanks also to Geoffrey B. Cooke, a descendant of General Clinton Bowen Fisk, for permission to quote from his ancestor's papers. Thanks also to Desalyn M. Stevenson for sharing material on her ancestors and their claims to the composition of some of the spirituals the Jubilees popularized.

I want to thank the staff of WGBH's *The American Experience* for their support and assistance during this project. As creative consultant and co-writer of a documentary on the Jubilees, I am especially indebted to the producer, Llewelyn Smith, for helping me think this story through and sharing his many leads, finds, insights, and resources with me. Thanks also to the associate producer, Ann Bennett, the production assistant, Caroline Toth, and the picture researcher, Meredith Wood, of the Fisk Jubilee Singers Project for all their generous help and creative problem solving. I am indebted to the staff of *The American Experience*, especially the executive producer, Margaret Drain, and the senior producer, Mark Samels, for teaching me a lot about not only filmmaking but how to tell a story. Thanks also to *The American Experience*'s Joseph Tovares, Susan Mottau, Helen Russell, and Nancy Farrell. My thanks to John Hope Franklin for honoring and enriching our film with his presence.

Though Doug Seroff did not take part in the making of our film or the research for this book, I would be remiss if I did not acknowledge the seminal contributions he has made to the preservation of the legacy of the Jubilees, manifested by the enrichment of the collections I consulted.

I also want to thank Erin Moody, Brendan Kiley, and Elizabeth Hagan for helping me with transcriptions and research. Thanks also to Jacqueline Lawson of Diversitudes for her genealogical research into the Jubilees. My love and gratitude to my parents, Frederick C. and Duira B. Ward, for their careful reading of this manuscript.

I thank Ellen Levine, my vigilant and abiding agent, for helping me through the anguished evolution of this project. I am also grateful to my editor, John A. Glusman, for his faith and encouragement and rigorous work on this manuscript under the pressure of a very tight deadline. Thanks also to Ingrid Sterner for saving me many embarrassments, and Bailey Foster for her patient persistence in guiding my manuscript through production.

Most of all, I want to thank the former Deborah Lathrop Huntington for her wonderful patience with a book that went through many permutations before it finally took shape. Without her faith, encouragement, and love, I could hardly write anything at all, let alone this book.

INDEX

Getting Ready to Die.

Get-ting read-y to die, get-ting read-y to die, Get-ting read-y to die, O Zi-on, Zi-on.

When I set out, I was but young, Zi-on, Zi-on, But now my race is al-most run, Zi-on, Zi-on.

Religion's like a blooming rose, Zion,
    Zion.
And none but those that feel it knows,
    Zion, Zion.
      Getting ready to die, &c.

The Lord is waiting to receive, Zion,
    Zion.
If sinners only would believe, Zion,
    Zion.
      Getting ready to die, &c.

All those who walk in Gospel shoes,
    Zion, Zion.
This faith in Christ they'll never lose,
    Zion, Zion.
      Getting ready to die, &c.